HISTORY OF WOMEN IN THE UNITED STATES

HISTORY OF WOMEN IN THE UNITED STATES
Historical Articles on Women's Lives and Activities

Edited by Nancy F. Cott

Series ISBN 3-598-41454-4

1. Theory and Method in Women's History
   ISBN 3-598-41455-2 Part 1
   ISBN 3-598-41477-3 Part 2

2. Household Constitution and Family Relationships
   ISBN 3-598-41456-0

3. Domestic Relations and Law
   ISBN 3-598-41457-9

4. Domestic Ideology and Domestic Work
   ISBN 3-598-41458-7 Part 1
   ISBN 3-598-41475-7 Part 2

5. The Intersection of Work and Family Life
   ISBN 3-598-41459-5 Part 1
   ISBN 3-598-41476-5 Part 2

6. Working on the Land
   ISBN 3-598-41460-9

7. Industrial Wage Work
   ISBN 3-598-41461-7 Part 1
   ISBN 3-598-41693-8 Part 2

8. Professional and White-Collar Employments
   ISBN 3-598-41462-5 Part 1
   ISBN 3-598-41694-6 Part 2

9. Prostitution
   ISBN 3-598-41463-3

10. Sexuality and Sexual Behavior
    ISBN 3-598-41464-1

11. Women's Bodies: Health and Childbirth
    ISBN 3-598-41465-X

12. Education
    ISBN 3-598-41466-8

13. Religion
    ISBN 3-598-41467-6

14. Intercultural and Interracial Relations
    ISBN 3-598-41468-4

15. Women and War
    ISBN 3-598-41469-2

16. Women Together: Organizational Life
    ISBN 3-598-41470-6

17. Social and Moral Reform
    ISBN 3-598-41471-4 Part 1
    ISBN 3-598-41695-4 Part 2

18. Women and Politics
    ISBN 3-598-41472-2 Part 1
    ISBN 3-598-41697-0 Part 2

19. Woman Suffrage
    ISBN 3-598-41473-0 Part 1
    ISBN 3-598-41696-2 Part 2

20. Feminist Struggles for Sex Equality
    ISBN 3-598-41474-9

HISTORY OF WOMEN IN THE UNITED STATES

Historical Articles on Women's Lives and Activities

6. Working on the Land

Edited with an Introduction by

Nancy F. Cott
Yale University

K · G · Saur
Munich · New Providence · London · Paris · 1993

Publisher's Note

The articles and chapters which comprise this collection originally appeared in a wide variety of publications and are reproduced here in facsimile from the highest quality offprints and photocopies available. The reader will notice some occasional marginal shading and text-curl common to photocopying from tightly bound volumes. Every attempt has been made to either correct or minimize this effect.

Copyright information for articles reproduced in this collection appears at the end of this volume.

Library of Congress Cataloging-in-Publication Data

History of women in the United States : historical articles on women's lives and activities / edited with an introduction by Nancy F. Cott.

p. cm.

Includes bibliographical references and indexes.

Contents: 1. Theory and method in women's history -- 2. Household constitution and family relationships -- 3. Domestic relations and law -- 4. Domestic ideology and domestic work -- 5. The intersection of work and family life -- 6. Working on the land -- 7. Industrial wage work -- 8. Professional and white-collar employments -- 9. Prostitution -- 10. Sexuality and sexual behavior -- 11. Women's bodies -- 12. Education -- 13. Religion -- 14. Intercultural and interracial relations -- 15. Women and war -- 16. Women together -- 17. Social and moral reform -- 18. Women and politics -- 19. Woman suffrage -- 20. Feminist struggles for sex equality.

ISBN 3-598-41454-4 (set)

1. Women--United States--History. 2. Women--United States--Social conditions. I. Cott, Nancy F.

HQ1410.H57 1992

305.4'0973--dc20 92-16765

CIP

Die Deutsche Bibliothek - CIP - Einheitsaufnahme

History of Women in the United States: historical articles on women's lives and activities / ed. with an introd. by Nancy F. Cott.

- Munich ; London ; New York ; Paris : Saur.

ISBN 3-598-41454-4

NE: Cott, Nancy F. (Hrsg.)

Vol. 6. working on the land - (1993)

ISBN 3-598-41460-9

Printed on acid-free paper/Gedruckt auf säurefreiem Papier

A Reed Reference Publishing Company

Printed in the United States of America

Printed/Bound by Edwards Brothers Incorporated, Ann Arbor

ISBN 3-598-41460-9 (vol. 6)

ISBN 3-598-41454-4 (series)

Contents

Series Preface ix
Introduction xi

History from the Inside-out: Writing the History of Women in Rural America
JOHN MACK FARAGHER 3

Native American Women and Agriculture: A Seneca Case Study
JOAN M. JENSEN 24

The Ideal Woman in the Antebellum South: Lady or Farmwife?
D. HARLAND HAGLER 43

The Role and Status of the Female Yeomanry in the Antebellum South: The Literary View
KEITH L. BRYANT, JR. 57

"Not Gainfully Employed": Women on the Iowa Frontier, 1833-1870
GLENDA RILEY 73

Images of the Frontierswoman: Iowa as a Case Study
GLENDA RILEY 101

"You May Depend She Does Not Eat Much Idle Bread", Mid-Atlantic Farm Women and Their Historians
JOAN M. JENSEN 115

Forgotten Persephones: Women Farmers on the Frontier
ANNE B. WEBB 133

Autonomy and Dependency in the Lives of Dakota Women: A Study in Historical Change
PATRICIA C. ALBERS 167

Female Planters and Planters' Wives in Civil War and Reconstruction: Alabama, 1850-1870
JONATHAN M. WIENER 193

CONTENTS

Black Women in American Agriculture
MINNIE MILLER BROWN 208

Women Homesteaders on the Great Plains Frontier
SHERYLL PATTERSON-BLACK..219

Women and Their Families on the Overland Trail to California and Oregon, 1842-1867
JOHNNY FARAGHER and CHRISTINE STANSELL 241

"A Helpmate for Man Indeed": The Image of the Frontier Woman
BEVERLY J. STOELTJE...258

Women in the Agricultural Settlement of the Northern Plains
MARY W.M. HARGREAVES 275

Women and Men in Western History: A Stereoptical Vision
SUSAN ARMITAGE 286

Single Women Homesteaders in Wyoming, 1880-1930
PAULA M. BAUMAN...301

Rural Life among Nineteenth-Century Mormons: The Woman's Experience
LEONARD J. ARRINGTON 333

Farm Women's Roles in the Agricultural Development of South Dakota
GLENDA RILEY 341

"How're You Gonna Keep 'Em Down on the Farm?": Rural Women and the Urban Model in Utah
CYNTHIA STURGIS..380

"I've Worked, I'm Not Afraid of Work": Farm Women in New Mexico, 1920-1940
JOAN M. JENSEN 398

CONTENTS

The Ideal Rural Southern Woman as Seen by *Progressive Farmer* in the 1930s
PAMELA TYLER 424

Copyright Information 443

Index..447

Series Preface

In the space of one generation, women's history has become the fastest-growing area of scholarship in U.S. history. Since the resurgence of feminism in the late 1960s and 1970s, insistent questions about the historical meanings of "woman's place" have sowed and reaped a garden of scholarship. Where scholarly works used to be bare of mention of women, academic enterprise has now produced a vigorous growth of books and articles, bringing to light diverse women of every region, race, class and age. This research is marked by a renovating intent that refuses to accept as "human" history a history of men. Interest is lively and debate is stimulating and sought after: attendance at the Berkshire Conference on the History of Women rivals the size of the annual convention of the American Historical Association.

While books in women's history are daily increasing in numbers and strength, as in any fast-developing field the scholarly literature in the form of articles is most expansive and up-to-the-minute. All the history journals now publish articles on women's work, domestic settings, family relations, household matters, female politics and organizations and so forth, and new journals have sprung into being to concentrate on such topics. Women's historians publish in numerous regional and thematic history journals as well as in feminist outlets and in journals of other social science disciplines. This series brings together a collection of outstanding articles from the field, almost all written in the past twenty years and more than half published during the 1980s. It brings together, in volumes organized by topic, essays otherwise widely dispersed. These volumes reprint only articles that originally appeared in journals, not chapters of books; review articles are not included. Articles have been chosen for overall quality and for range. Each one was chosen for one or more of the following reasons: because it is the standard authority on its subject matter; represents an important statement on a topic by a recognized scholar; presages an important book to come; provides a first look at new evidence or new methods; or opens an untapped area or new controversy. Older articles have been reprinted if their data or interpretation have not been surpassed or if they marked an important stage in the historiography, even if since superseded.

The historical coverage of the series extends from the Revolutionary era to the 1960s. The articles themselves are dated from the 1940s through 1988. Volumes are organized by topic rather than time period. Within each volume, the articles are ordered chronologically (with respect to substance), so that the whole can be read as an historical overview. The only exception to this ordering principle is Volume One, on Theory and Method, in which the contents are arranged in order of publication. Within each volume there is an attempt to include articles on as diverse kinds of women as possible. None of the volume topics is regionally or racially defined; rather, all volumes are topically designed so as to afford views of women's work, family lives, and public activities which cut across races and regions. Any volume in the series stands on its own, supplying as full a treatment of a designated subject matter as the scholarly literature will provide. Several groupings of volumes also make sense; that is, volumes two through five all center around domestic and family matters; volumes five through nine consider other varieties of women's work; volumes nine through eleven concern uses and abuses of women's bodies; volumes twelve through fourteen look at major aspects of socialization; and volumes fifteen through twenty include organizational and political efforts of many sorts.

As a whole, the series displays in all its range the vitality of the field of women's history. Aside from imbuing U.S. history with new vision, scholarship in this area has informed, and should continue to inform, current public debate on issues from parental leave to the nuclear freeze. By bringing historical articles together under topical headings, these volumes both represent accurately the shape of historical controversy (or consensus) on given issues and make historians' findings most conveniently available for current reference.

Introduction

Most women, for most of American history, have lived and worked on the land, although the drift in women's history as in the rest of history has been to focus on the urban and commercial centers of innovation. This volume intends to correct that trend, to an extent, by gathering together articles which bring attention to women's rural location and agricultural employments. Some of the articles examine images of rural women; more examine women's work in farming. They range from coverage of Native American women in several locations, to white and black women in the South and East, pioneers on the overland trail and in the Great Plains and the far West. The indispensable work women perform in agricultural communities is a consistent theme, played in many keys.

In Native American communities, before the development of settled agriculture, men typically were the hunters of game and women the gatherers of edible plants, roots and berries. It is quite plausible, because of this sexual division of labor, to credit women with the innovation of planting and domesticating corn. While the men remained hunters, the women were responsible for planting, tending, harvesting and grinding the corn, which became the staple support of Native Americans for hundreds of years. Native American women's responsibility for corn production, parallel to men's responsibility to provide animal food, gave them prominence and leadership in their communities.

Just as the English and European concept of steadfast property ownership differed essentially from the Native American belief that the earth was for all to use and none to own, the European traditions of agriculture which white settlers of America brought with them differed in virtually every respect including the relative power and status accorded to men and women in it. Although women's work was always involved in agricultural production, men's was considered the primary and definitive part. The neutral word "farmer" evokes a male image, as does the word "pioneer." Yet women have been farmers and pioneers along with men, throughout American history.

While men largely carried on the heavy field work, clearing, plowing, planting and harvesting, women planted, weeded, tended and harvested vegetable gardens, kept the poultry and collected eggs, kept the dairy (milking, making butter and cheese), accomplished all sorts of food preservation (from smoking and salting meat to pickling vegetables and making jams and jellies), prepared three meals a day for family members and hired "hands," sewed and mended the family clothes, scrubbed the laundry, cleaned house, nursed the sick and raised the children. Whereas men's work on the family was seasonal, women's work was constant year-round.

On family farms not only men who produced the staple crop were involved in market transactions; women's "butter and egg money" often formed a crucial portion of the household budget, and so might surplus cloth from the households of women who worked looms. Many women found ways to add to family income by making home-based crafts, such as straw hats, for sale. A Southern journal, the *American Cotton Planter*, enthused in the 1850s, "We know a country woman of ours, a farmer's wife, who takes care of her own domestic matters, with five children to manage too, who has, during the last season, sold above $200 worth of baskets, manufactured during her leisure hours, out of the common swamp willow"![1] And in addition to commonly-defined sorts of "women's work," in urgent situations, during emigration west, in pioneer settlements, or in other exigencies, women took on men's work as well. Harriet Noble, for instance, a recent emigrant from New York to Michigan in the 1820s, found her husband "taken with ague" just after their first harvest, and disconsolate about the fate of their cattle if the hay was not stacked. "I said to him," she later recalled, "'I believe I can load and stack the hay, if my strength permits." So she did. That November, her husband's hand was "blown to pieces" with an accidental gunshot, so, she recounted, "The hay I had stacked during the summer I had to feed out to the cattle with my own hands in the winter, and often cut the wood for three days at a time. The logs which I alone rolled in, would surprise any one who has never been put to the test of necessity, which compels people to do what under other circumstances they would not have thought possible."[2]

Many women crossing the U.S. with their families did what, back East, they would not have thought possible, both on the trip West and once they settled in new terrain. From the "Gold Rush" years of the 1840s through to the 1870s, between a quarter and a half million people took the Overland Trail to Oregon and California, most aiming to find new land for themselves. Gradually, by treaties, by negotiations, by violence and relocation, the U.S. government extinguished Native American claims to their lands and instituted a reservation system. The federal government declared "public domain" the land once occupied by Native Americans, and beginning with the Homestead Act of 1862, there were provisions for heads of households to gain plots of land (usually 160 acres) by paying a modest amount and then "proving" the claim by clearing and working the land for a number of years. Between 1868 and 1917 over 170 million acres of federal land was transferred to private hands.[3]

Although land in the public domain was cheap, moving West to claim it required some resources. White Easterners and immigrants were those able to take advantage of the offer, by and large. Immediately after the Civil War, the Freedman's Bureau (set up by the federal government to deal with emancipated slaves) did little to enable blacks to settle on federal land, and in the succeeding decades relatively few rural blacks were able to gather the resources to move from the South to lands farther West. Black women and their families remained working on Southern land as sharecroppers and tenant farmers. The Act of 1862 did, however, explicitly extend its provisions to women over twenty-one, so long as they were citizens or had filed papers to become naturalized. This was the first large-scale opportunity for women to become landowners, and many white women were able to take advantage of it. In their experience was compounded constant work and the reward of seeing the products of one's own hands, frequent loneliness and the satisfaction of community-building, which also characterized women's rural lives more generally.

Notes

1. Quoted from "Productive Industry," *American Cotton Planter* 1 (December 1853), 379, in D. Harland Hagler, "The Ideal Woman in the Antebellum South: Lady or Farmwife?" *Journal of Southern History* XLVI:3 (August 1980), 415.

2. "Emigration from New York to Michigan by Harriet Noble," in *Root of Bitterness: Documents of the Social History of American Women*, Nancy F. Cott, ed. (N.Y., E. P. Dutton, 1972), 228.

3. Joan M. Jensen, *With These Hands: Women Working on the Land* (Old Westbury, N.Y., Feminist Press, 1981), 102-03.

Working on the Land

HISTORY FROM THE INSIDE-OUT: WRITING THE HISTORY OF WOMEN IN RURAL AMERICA

JOHN MACK FARAGHER
Mount Holyoke College

IN THE PAST DECADE HISTORIANS HAVE GROWN ACCUSTOMED TO CALLS for a new history of the "inarticulate." Certainly American rural farm women, who until well into the twentieth century constituted a majority of the female population, are among the most underrepresented of all Americans in the standard histories. In part this reflects gaps in the documentary record. Some rural women—Native Americans, Afro-Americans, Chicanas, Mexicanas, and Hispanics—have suffered a historical silence in direct relation to the social conditions that kept them nearly totally illiterate. Even among Euro-Americans, only a few country women left written records, for even white female illiteracy was commonplace until at least the second half of the nineteenth century.[1] Combine illiteracy with farm work loads that kept even "scribbling women" too busy to write much, and cultural attitudes that consistently devalued women and their documents, and it is a wonder that we have any historical materials at all. Documents there are, however, and if we consider the factors operating against them, they exist in surprising quantity. There are, first, the basic documents of social history: the census schedules, probate materials, and the tracings of individuals and families in the official record. Used carefully these provide the necessary skeleton for women's, as well as men's, social history. There are reminiscences, autobiographies, and oral testimonies transcribed by family members and antiquarians long before historians seriously considered oral history. Even male accounts of local and personal happenings contain valuable

[1] Kenneth Lockridge, *Literacy in Colonial New England* (New York: W. W. Norton, 1974), 97, suggests that women's literacy in the United States may have reached a national level of fifty percent by 1850; literacy would have been lower in the countryside.

materials for a history of rural women. There are abundant town and county histories, many dating from the mid-nineteenth century, in which women as well as men wrote of their experience. Moreover, there are many subjective records of women's experience; rural women's letters and diaries, while scarcer than men's, exist in a large enough number seriously to effect the writing of a new history with female as well as male subjects. The problem has been blindness, not inarticulateness.[2]

Historians have not heard rural women because they have listened to the powerful, not the powerless. Over the past century of historical scholarship there have been solid contributions to "domestic" history, but such works were dismissed by academic historians as mere "pots and pans" history. Without a theoretical framework for understanding and interpreting the experience of the inarticulate, the impulse to document resulted in a valuable but unsystematic *mélange*. The advantage of academic history was that it selected with a notion of historical process: history was not simply what had happened, but the record of human achievement, embodied largely in the growth and extension of public institutions, a process to which men had disproportionately contributed. We may now wish to reject this interpretation of the past in favor of one that incorporates the sexual dimension, but we must replace it with a vision equally able to discriminate among the available data and allow the writing of a new historical narrative. Our problem is not so much discovering new evidence as knowing what to do with what we have already. We must approach the world of hearths and trammels, piggins and noggins, if not pots and pans, and know what questions to ask.

As farmer, frontiersman, booster, and democrat, the "western" male has been investigated, scrutinized, and otherwise made the subject of literally hundreds of scholarly monographs, but it is fair to say that the basic monographic research into the history of rural women is just beginning. Nonetheless, over the past century general works on rural or western women have appeared with some regularity; in their form and interpretation these works have fallen into common patterns. Elizabeth

[2] In the past few years several new collections of rural women's materials have appeared which must be integrated into the documentary readings of history classes and history texts: Gerda Lerner, ed., *The Female Experience: An American Documentary* (Indianapolis: Bobbs-Merrill, 1977), contains many valuable rural materials; Eve Merriam, ed., *Growing Up Female in America: Ten Lives* (New York: Dell, 1971), includes autobiographical material on several rural women; Christiana Fischer, ed., *Let Them Speak For Themselves: Women in the American West, 1849–1900* (New York: Dutton, 1979), concentrates on the greater Southwest; Norman Juster, ed., *So Sweet to Labor: Rural Women in America, 1865–1895* (New York: Viking, 1979), reprints articles, letters, and miscellany from rural publications which cast new light; Joan M. Jensen, ed., *With These Hands: Women Working the Land* (Old Westbury, N.Y.: Feminist Press, 1980), is a broad, multicultural collection of essential documents.

Fries Ellet's *Pioneer Women of the West* (1852) is an early and typical nineteenth-century example of the genre. Ellet's work set the style for many other works—multiple biographical accounts of Euro-American women presented as moral lessons, as a unique stage for the acting of moral drama.[3]

An equally persistent continuity in theme is the notion of women as a civilizing force on an otherwise rough-and-tumble male frontier. "Those who live within reach of all the advantages of civilization," wrote Mrs. Ellet, "can hardly understand the difficulties in the way of improvement which existed in a pioneer settlement": no schools, no churches, "nor did there seem to be any Sabbaths." It was women's role to set about changing these conditions; "thus was a good foundation laid for the advantages afterwards enjoyed. . . ."[4] Ellet's understanding of the work of women in promoting "civilization" was fully in keeping with the Victorian ideology of "separate spheres" for men and women; women added refinement to a social world carved from the wilderness by men. Dee Brown's *Gentle Tamers* was essentially an elaboration and update of these ideas for a 1950s audience.

Julie Roy Jeffrey's *Frontier Women* (1979) brings the "civilizer" thesis into the 1980s with the gloss of the new women's history. Women not only accepted the division of spheres, Jeffrey suggests, but utilized it as a means toward their own self-activity. Faced with the conflict between their gender roles as guardians of virtue and the harsh masculine conditions of the countryside, women took up a "civilizing mission" through churches, missions, and schools. Yet rather than seeking an explanation of sexual hierarchy, Jeffrey accepts the nineteenth-century formulation of separate spheres as an adequate analytical starting point. Asking Victorian questions—how did women perform in their roles?—Jeffrey, not surprisingly, comes up with answers with which Victorians would feel quite at home. Unfortunately, Jeffrey's interpretation, along with all those of the "civilizer" variety, must of necessity ignore the experiences of any but white ("civilized") women to the history of the countryside.[5]

Another persistent theme concentrates upon the contrast between the essential work of rural women and the leisure of urban ladies. Mary Meek

[3] Elizabeth Fries Ellet, *Pioneer Women of the West* (New York: C. Scribner, 1852); Nancy Wilson Ross, *Westward the Women* (New York: Knopf, 1944); Dee Brown, *The Gentle Tamers* (Lincoln: Univ. of Nebraska Press, 1958); Dorothy Gray, *Women of the West* (Millbrae, Calif.: Les Femmes, 1976). For a complete historiographic essay see Joan M. Jensen and Darlis A. Miller, "The Gentle Tamers Revisited: New Approaches to the History of Women in the American West," *Pacific Historical Review*, 49 (1980), 173–213.

[4] Ellet, *Pioneer Women*, 364.

[5] Julie Roy Jeffrey, *Frontier Women: The Trans-Mississippi West, 1840–1880* (New York: Hill and Wang, 1979).

Atkeson, for example, asserted that "there was no doubt of her equality in those days because she showed herself equally capable in all the tasks of their life together. . . . Her position and dignity and age-old strength was that of the real help-mate in everything that touched the welfare of the family and home." Similarly, Arthur Calhoun wrote, "reciprocity in the marriage relation was the logical consequence where woman bore a man's share in the struggle for existence." Reciprocity resulted from equally shared responsibility in work, inequality from the withdrawal of women into leisure. Industrialization, in other words, should be seen as a backward step for women, because when work left the home, in Dorothy Gray's words, the "man and woman were no longer partners in work and survival." But "the West was different. Here women were scarce, valuable, and valued. They were not valued as decorative objects but for their real skills and their true sexuality. . . . The West was fair. Those who had to pull their own weight became independent, reached for their full rights and got them." This romantic notion of a sexually egalitarian rural environment has strongly influenced the modern feminist imagination. In her useful study, *Women's Work*, Ann Oakley drew a picture of "traditional pre-industrial" society as a place of equal toil for both sexes and considerable independent action for women. Caroline Bird, in an important feminist polemic of the 1960s, rhapsodized that the American West "motivated men and women to similar or androgynous goals."[6]

Without question women's work was essential to successful agriculture. Indeed, abundant evidence demonstrates that from colonial times through the nineteenth century, Euro-American women engaged in from one-third to more than one-half of all the food production on family farms. Moreover, everywhere women were likely to be found helping men with the field work, especially at peak planting times. Aside from food production, women were solely responsible for all food preparation, all household chores, all textile and clothing manufacture, childcare, and all work obviously necessary to the reproduction of the farmstead.[7]

[6] Mary Meek Atkeson, *The Woman on the Farm* (New York: Century, 1924), 4–5; Arthur Calhoun, *A Social History of the American Family*, (1917; rpt. New York: Barnes and Noble, 1945) I:106–07, 109; Gray, *Women of the West*, 3; Ann Oakley, *Woman's Work: The Housewife, Past and Present* (New York: Vintage, 1976): ch. 2; Caroline Bird, *Born Female* (New York: David McKay, 1968), 22.

[7] Among the studies that document rural women's work see Julia Spruill, *Women's Life and Work in the Southern Colonies* (Chapel Hill: Univ. of North Carolina Press, 1938); Minnie Miller Brown, "Black Women in American Agriculture," *Agricultural History*, 50 (1976), 202–12; Sue Armitage, "Household Work and Childrearing on the Frontier: The Oral History Record," *Sociology and Social Research*, 63 (1979); John Mack Faragher, *Women and Men on the Overland Trail* (New Haven: Yale Univ. Press, 1979), 49–65.

Precisely the enormity of rural women's work load, however, has provoked others to question helpmate equality.[8] To be sure, the notion of women as helpmates was a rural ideology that set forth the ideal relations of marriage and family on the farm; but to nineteenth-century folks there was little implication of equality in the relation of helpmate. That women worked hard at essential productive work was hardly surprising, but expected. The question of status is not primarily a question of what people do, but rather of the recognition they are granted for what they do and the authority that recognition confers. Despite the essential work done by Euro-American rural women there is little evidence to suggest that their husbands and sons granted equal power for equal work. In the English tradition the marriage was an economic and social partnership; as Benjamin Wadsworth wrote in New England in the early eighteenth century, husband and wife should "unite their prudent counsels and endeavors, comfortably to maintain themselves and the Family under their joint care . . . ." But nonetheless, Wadsworth continued, "the Husband is ever to be esteem'd the Superior, the Head, and to be reverenc'd and obey'd as such." As Mrs. Ellet wrote about one woman pioneer, "she had the appearance and used the language of independence, haughtiness and authority," yet "it could be said of her without any question that she 'reverenced her husband.'" Writing of highland Kentucky at the turn of the century, John C. Campbell insisted that "from boyhood the boy is the favored lord of all he surveys. There is a dignity, a conscious superiority, in his youthful mein that says more clearly than spoken words that womenkind are not his equals." "The saying that 'a woman's work is never done,'" Campbell wrote, "is much truer generally than that 'man works from sun to sun.'"[9]

The distinction between "civilizer" and "helpmate" interpretations operates within the polarities of opposing stereotypes. The traditional views do not offer ways of seeing that will help to write a new historical narrative in which men and women are equally subject to the flow of events. We are reduced to arguing the pros and cons of certain stereotypes, rarely penetrating beneath surface generalizations to the substance of relations. Indeed, as sexual ideology, the notion of women as "civilizers" or wives as "helpmates" functions precisely to deflect attention from relationships between real men and women on to the well-thought-out defenses of the established cultural order. The ideologies

[8] See, for example, David Potter, "American Women and the American Character," in *History and American Society: Essays of David M. Potter*, ed. Don E. Fehrenbacher (New York: Oxford Univ. Press, 1973).

[9] Wadsworth, *The Well-Ordered Family* (Boston: B. Green, 1712), 29, 35; Ellet, *Pioneer Women*, 35; Campbell, *The Southern Highlander and His Homeland* (Philadelphia: Russell Sage Foundation, 1921), 124, 135–36.

themselves need to be historically analyzed, and for this we need a way of breaking away from their powerful frame of reference.

* * *

Lucinda Casteen, her husband, and five children, moved to west-central Illinois in 1831, one of thousands of families who crossed north over the Ohio River in the 1820s and thirties. Throughout the decade she wrote home regularly to her mother, Mary Peters, in Kentucky, letters that have preserved her story.[10] By 1833 Lucinda, in her early thirties, was caring for a new baby girl, and doing all the work required of a farm wife. "My baby grows and fattens very fast," she wrote home in November.

> She has been troublesome in day but less troublesome of a knight than any of my children. I have but little time for Settled work but less oppertunity to write as i cant have mi mind composed with as many around me. So that you eccuse all my mistakes & Scrabling if you can only make out to read it. I find it difficult to write with my noisy Children around me & my babe in my lap part of the time which must be sufficient apology.

Although the neighborhood was "filling up" (the nearest neighbor only a mile away), there was no nearby village, so all the necessities that could not be grown or otherwise produced on the homestead had to be purchased from peddlers. By 1834 the Casteens had spent their meager savings on essentials such as flour; because there was no mill in the vicinity, they were forced to buy what they had originally hoped to produce. Lucinda found the work load around the single-room cabin difficult to manage, and when the neighbors pooled enough resources to hire a teacher and set up a school she worried that she would not be able to send the children. "I fear we cant go on regular, but I think of sparing them 4 hours a day if possible." She needed them for what she called "our school at home"—the farm work she had to assign to the children. "I have been distressed to think of my children not going to school," she wrote, "especially Louisa," her eldest and dearest.

Yet she counted herself lucky. Her children were healthy and Henry was a good husband. She thought it was essential to marry, "to come or go where you can have a home of your own," she wrote to her unmarried little sister, "but never give your hand or heart to a lasy [sic] man." Her brother, Isham, who had accompanied her to Illinois and lived on an adjoining claim, was a source of constant worry. She never saw him, he

[10] Lucinda Casteen collection of ms. letters, Illinois State Historical Library (ISHL), Springfield, Ill.; spelling and punctuation slightly altered. I want to thank Cheryl Schnering for her assistance and encouragement in working with the the ISHL materials.

worked too hard, was single-mindedly ambitious, and drank too much. How could he manage, Lucinda often asked herself, without a wife? Isham had "come so well provided in cloths" that he was not yet wanting for weaving; Lucinda herself had somehow found the time to make him a suit of jane cloth she'd been able to spare, and had done all his sewing and mending. He'd hired a woman from up the road to do his washing for two bits a month, and "he expects to get his neighbor's wife to milk for him." "He gets it all tolerably well done," she wrote, yet it was worrisome, a kinsman, a brother, living alone like that. Isham needed a wife, and when he married, in 1838, Lucinda rejoiced, in spite of the jealousy she seems to have felt toward her new sister-in-law.

By 1838 she had two more children, quite a large family, and Lucinda opened each letter home with an account of how much work it meant for her, how much her abscessed teeth pained her, and, invariably, how she knew in her heart that she would never see her mother again. Cholera first struck the Mississippi River settlements in 1832 and lingered on over the next few years. Its ravages were frightening and Lucinda felt blessed when they were all spared. But early in 1839 an unnamed infectious disease hit the Casteen family. With several children very ill and her darling Louisa failing, Lucinda doubled her usual pace. In February Louisa died after a long and painful illness, and the same day Lucinda collapsed, exhausted, distraught, and herself infected. Now she and her newest babe, just fifteen months, shared the death bed, but with no doctors, no medicine, and no knowledge of the disease, there was nothing to be done. On February 16, 1839, Lucinda Casteen died, her youngest daughter following the next day. The mother and her two daughters were laid together on the prairie alongside the cabin. We have been left only Lucinda's letters, and a final, awful letter from Henry to Lucinda's mother Mary, recounting her last days.

Lucinda Casteen's story is one of many preserved in such documents. Women's materials like hers, often more so than men's, evoke the quality of everyday life. The richness of the description focuses our attention on the domestic and the intimate; interpretation of a mass of such material requires an orientation that informs us of the meaning of the personal in a social and historical context. If we are to write a history of rural farm women, as well as of farm men, we will need to find ways of linking the worlds of the Lucinda Casteens with the worlds of farmers and frontiersmen. The stereotypes of helpmate, oppressed farm wife, or civilizer do little to provide such linkages. Despite her hard years and useless death it is hard to think of Lucinda as a victim, and certainly not as an advocate of "true womanhood." These images have little relation to the ways she saw herself. There is sadness, pain, sorrow, as well as pride and joy in Lucinda's correspondence, but little evidence of self-pity or self-righteousness. If we are to be guided by her own thoughts as reflected in her letters home, we must seek the interpretation of her life in the mundane arrangements of her family, for it was as wife, mother, sister, and daughter, as well as woman, that she defined herself.

* * *

We must plunge, then, into the depths of family and kin relations and of gender—waters made murky by the muddying effect of sexual ideologies. Sexual ideology—cultural rationalizations for a specific social ordering of the relations between men and women—hinges on the notion of a universal gender character; ideology proclaims the existence of dichotomous essences for males and females (the "masculine" and the "feminine"), then links those natures directly to the work that men and women perform in society. Thus is set up an unbroken loop, continuously connecting "essence" and "behavior," a loop that gives gender a timeless and universal feel and convinces historical individuals that the roles laid out for them are nothing more than cultural reflections of their natural selves. Yet on the contrary, whatever the biological differences between men and women, life in society is so completely shaped by culture as to make innate differences largely irrelevant. Sexual distinctions are but a starting point for gender; societies begin by systematically assigning roles and character by sex—constructing gender—in accordance with their own particular allocation of meanings. Gender makes the difference, and gender contrasts with sex precisely in that it is socially and culturally constructed. It follows, then, that just as cultures differ from one another so too do their orderings of gender. Even childbearing, the nearest thing to a universal force in the lives of women, has varied tremendously from society to society in its frequency, its value and meaning, and in the social controls placed upon it. Far from constant, the shape of gender appears in almost infinite variety.[11]

Moreover, although gender points to an "essential" character for women and men, in fact each sex plays out multiple roles within a specific organization of family and kinship and a specific organization of production and work. As Karen Sacks has persuasively argued, women's relations as sisters on the one hand, wives on the other, may involve important conflicts between power as sibling and dependence as spouse. Not only is the power of sisterhood a factor in matrilineally organized groups,

[11] Perhaps the best short study of gender variability is Ann Oakley, *Sex, Gender and Society* (New York: Harper and Row, 1972), but see the classic statement of the relativist persuasion in Margaret Mead, *Sex and Temperment in Three Primitive Societies* (New York: William Morrow, 1935).

but in any society that uses kinship as a link to the ownership of socially critical property.[12]

The relativity of gender and the importance of kinship roles have important implications for historical study. In the first place, since gender and kinship effect all persons, men as well as women (with all due respect for the recent outstanding contributions of women's history), it seems appropriate to reconceive our object of study, to focus not just on women but on what Joan Kelly-Gadel calls "the social relations of the sexes."[13] Lucinda Casteen's sense of obligation and duty may be understood only when we cast her lot, as she cast her own, with her husband's. As Isham's labor on his homestead was incomplete without the necessary compliment of a woman's service, so Lucinda's work will appear incomplete until we fit it within its place in the social division of labor. On the other hand, we beg important questions if we assume that Lucinda was "essentially" a wife; we ought to investigate her important attachments to her brother, to her mother and family left in Kentucky, and the ways in which affinal relations situated women in the social order. Gender and kinship are fundamental agents of social classification and as such are directly tied to a specific social structure. We need to analyze, then, how gender and kinship derive their meanings from concrete relations to the social and sexual division of labor and the struggles over the distribution of the surplus, to the ownership of productive property, to the forms of sexual reproduction, including the struggle between classes and sexes over controls on fertility and sexuality, and finally, to the nature of institutional stratification, hierarchy, and authority. In a phrase, we require history written from the inside-out.[14]

Reading documents of rural life—account books, diaries, letters, travelers' descriptions, reminiscences—one may conclude that in the estimation of rural antebellum farm people themselves the relationship between men and women was at the heart of rural society. A structural analysis of the productive relations of midwestern society reinforces this

[12] Karen Sacks, *Sisters and Wives: The Past and Future of Sexual Equality* (Westport, Conn.: Greenwood Press, 1979).

[13] Joan Kelley-Gadel, "The Social Relations of the Sexes: Methodological Implications of Women's History," *Signs*, 1 (1976), 809–23, esp. 812–17. See also my discussion of this point in *Women and Men on the Overland Trail*, 1–3.

[14] Gayle Rubin's pioneering piece, "The Traffic in Women: Notes on the 'Political Economy' of Sex," in *Towards an Anthropology of Women*, ed. Rayna Reiter (New York: Monthly Review, 1974), 157–210, was the first to call for the study of "sex/gender systems." Among the most important theoretical statements see Sacks, *Sisters and Wives;* Michele Zimbalist Rosaldo, "The Use and Abuse of Anthropology: Reflections on Feminism and Cross-Cultural Understanding," *Signs*, 5 (1980), 389–417; and the forthcoming study by Elizabeth Fox-Genovese, *Writing Women into History* (New York: Oxford Univ. Press).

contemporary view. Commercial agriculture was stymied by isolation and poor transportation; even enterprising farmers were frustrated by prohibitive farm-to-market costs. The economy of the local countryside faced inward, not outward; a multiplicity of complicated economic exchanges in labor, goods, or credit took place, but little or no accumulation or capitalization occurred. The basic unit of production was the farm family, and the means of production were commonly owned by the head of the household. Hand tool technology, moreover, set limits on production which precluded large trading surpluses. Under these conditions the majority of owner-farmers did not manage their operations as units of capital. Money—notoriously scarce in specie and unreliable as paper—did not function so much as the universal solvent of all exchanges and relations but rather as one of a number of exchangeable items which included products, tools, livestock, or labor.

Moreover, labor power was by no means marked as the most significant, nor even an ascendent commodity in the antebellum economy. Before the 1850s there were few agricultural wage workers—most farmers simply did not have the means to hire them. And since men like Isham Peters could, with relative ease, improve enough acres for self-support, labor was scarce and wages relatively high. So, rather than hiring labor, farmers shared labor and tools in patterns long established in North American rural society. The exponential increase in agricultural wage workers was a phenomenon associated with the "agricultural revolution" of the late 1850s, the sixties, and beyond, when farms were converted, in economic terms, into units of capital. In the meantime, abundant food and fiber for the family, as well as a small trading surplus, were the hopes and goals of family production.[15]

These productive forces and relations did not produce a society of extreme social stratification, but one rather more egalitarian than societies of commercial agriculture, merchant commerce, or industry. True, shopkeepers and merchants were able to accumulate, and land speculation and stock-raising offered investment opportunities for outsiders with capital; nonetheless the distribution of productive property did not reflect great inequities. (In Auburn township, a typical rural area of Sangamon County, Illinois, the richest ten percent of the residents in 1835

[15] On midwestern antebellum economy see James A. Davis, *Frontier America: 1800–1840* (Glendale: Arthur C. Clark, 1977), 20, 138, and ch. 7; as well as Faragher, *Women and Men on the Overland Trail*, ch. 2, and the bibliography for further references. Michael Merrill, "Cash is Good to Eat: Self-Sufficiency and Exchange in the Rural Economy of the United States," *Radical History Review*, 3 (Winter 1977), 42–71, is an essential discussion; see also the exchanges over his conceptualization in the subsequent issues of the *Radical History Review*: no. 18 (Fall 1978), 166–71; no. 22 (Winter 1979–80), 129–46.

held only twenty-six percent of the taxable property, a low figure comparable to other frontier and "subsistence" sections.) The median farm size was one hundred acres—precisely the same as the mean size for the township if the richest and poorest tenths of the residents are disregarded. In other words, property was quite evenly distributed.[16] Specialization was also rare, the local craftsmen and merchants practicing their trades as sidelines to farming. In short, before the 1850s and the market revolution in prairie and Great Lakes agriculture, class relations of production were not the most salient features of rural midwestern society.

The family was the basic unit of production and its success depended upon the full participation of both partners; production was structured upon the sexual division of labor. Certainly the multiplicity and complexity of women's work signals their central position in the family economy. Women were crucial, too, because children were an economic necessity to a growing and successful homestead operation. Indeed, given the many tasks under the wife's responsibility, most mothers agreed with Lucinda that it was difficult to spare children from chores. Although the Casteens, with eight children born before Lucinda's fortieth birthday, were a large family, the typical wife in Auburn township could expect to bear and raise, on average, seven children.[17] Since at least the time of Franklin's remarkable essay on population in the mid-eighteenth century, social observers have noted the high rates of North American colonial fertility. By the nineteenth century, however, the birth rate had begun a decline that has continued, with minor variations, to the present. This "demographic transition" did not begin uniformly in all rural regions; rather, it was associated with the regional triumph of commercialism on the farm, the rising price of land, and the emergence of new priorities in farm management. In those areas where subsistence farming continued into the nineteenth century, fertility levels remained high. One explanation of decline in commercial areas was the desire of parents to keep family size in balance with local supplies of accessible farm land. In areas dominated by

[16] Distribution of property calculated from Marilyn Wright Thomas and Hazelmae Taylor Temple, eds., *1835 Tax List, Sangamon County, Illinois* (Springfield, Ill.: n.p., n.d.). For a comparison see Jackson Turner Main, *The Social Structure of Revolutionary America* (Princeton: Princeton Univ. Press, 1965); Edward Pessen, *Riches, Class, and Power Before the Civil War* (Lexington, Mass.: D. C. Heath, 1973); J. G. Williamson and P. H. Lindert, "Long Term Trends in American Wealth Inequality" (unpublished ms., 1977).

[17] In 1850 the mean number of children for women in Auburn township who had completed their childbearing years (45 years or older) was 6.8. Computed from Family Reconstitution Form completed with the use of the federal manuscript census, county records, and genealogical materials in ISHL. These figures must be considered preliminary, although I do not expect further work to alter them significantly.

household production, on the other hand, there may have been continued viability in seeing children as an essential labor force for the farm.[18]

Women's work in production, in the maintenance of the home, in child care, and in health care were highly valued, and rightly so, for without women the economic order would have collapsed. In short, everywhere on the continent, agricultural society was impossible without the work of women; as demographic studies of what once was considered a "male frontier" have demonstrated, and as Joan Jensen has correctly insisted, women have always been present in nearly equal force to men, working on the land.[19]

The sexual division of labor, however, was a division of authority, prestige, and remuneration as well. From the public world outside the family, rural women were, before the late nineteenth century, usually forbidden entry. The isolation of most wives in their homes was a social fact introduced by the division of labor and often reinforced by settlement patterns. In some parts of New England women could enjoy the relatively close company of female villagers, but in antebellum central Illinois, by contrast, only about eight people lived to the square mile, and homesteads were not clustered but thinly spaced. Men's responsibilities allowed them to lay aside their plows or flails for the day, especially at slack seasons, and ride out to visit a neighbor or frequent the village. But women, with their constant responsibilities a home, especially the care of children, could not be so casual; even in more densely settled districts a walking visit to neighbors could take an entire morning or afternoon, and in the division of labor this could not be counted as productive time but rather time away from domestic duties. In 1869 a farmer of Wisconsin remembered that in the early years

> the country was all open and free to roam over, as one great park. There was excitement in all this—a verge and scope, a freedom, and independence and abandon, suited to our rougher nature and coarser tastes. We could roam and fish, or hunt as we pleased, amid the freshness and beauties of nature. But how

[18] See Nancy Folbe's argument in "Patriarchy and Capitalism in New England, 1620–1900" Diss. Univ. of Massachusetts, Amherst, 1979. The persistence of older patterns in rural areas is discussed by Richard A. Easterlin, "Factors in the Decline of Farm Fertility in the United States: Some Preliminary Research Results," *Journal of American History*, 63 (1976–77), 600–14. For a discussion of the contribution of children to agricultural societies see M. Nag, "The Economic Value of Children in Agricultural Societies: Evaluation of Existing Knowledge and an Anthropological Approach for Studying It," in James T. Fawcett, ed., *The Satisfaction and Costs of Children* (Honolulu: East-West Center, 1972).

[19] Jack D. Eblen, "An Analysis of Nineteenth Century Frontier Populations," *Demography*, 2 (1965), 399–411; David J. Wishart, "Age and Sex Composition of the Population on the Nebraska Frontier, 1860–1880," *Nebraska History*, 54 (1973); Davis, *Frontier America*, 101–18; Jensen, ed., *With These Hands*.

was it with our wives: From all these bright, and to us fascinating scenes and pastimes, they were excluded. They were shut up with the children in log cabins. . . .[20]

The numbers of children shut up in there with the women was itself a "political" and not a "natural" fact. We know that women in simple societies have struggled quite successfully to limit their fertility by numerous means. It is also a historical fact that the transition to sedentary agricultural society was associated not only with population growth but—as the means to such growth—with the establishment of control over women's sexuality and reproductive decision-making as an aspect of social policy; the suppression of the means of fertility limitation made possible the rapid rise in population associated with agriculture. High fertility was frequently viewed as a key to social success in agricultural society. As one New Englander argued in the seventeenth century, he and his countrymen enjoyed a biological edge over native peoples through their capacity "to beget and bring forth more children than any other nation in the world." If, given the available resources of an Indian-free North American countryside, population growth and unlimited fertility were "rational" for male expansionists, they may have simultaneously seemed "irrational" to the women who bore the children. Certainly on the basis of cross-cultural evidence, as well as the historical trends in fertility, we know that women would have enjoyed the opportunity to limit the burden of childbirth.[21]

Of equal importance, most of the work of the public world—establishing connections among the families and homesteads in community institutions, the work of politics of law and order—was the domain of male responsibility. In their local elections Euro-American male heads of household chose male representatives to make policy for, to administer, and to sanction the social and economic order. This was a male state—as have been all the state societies of recorded history—and the legal code that men wrote, perpetuated, and defended granted husbands extraordi-

[20] Charles M. Baker, "Pioneer History of Walworth County," *Report and Collections of the State Historical Society of Wisconsin*, 6 (1869–72), 470.

[21] Philip Vincent, *A True Relation of the Lake Battel Fought in New England* (London, 1638), quoted in Richard Drinnan, *Facing West: The Metaphysics of Indian-Hating and Empire-Building* (Minneapolis: Univ. of Minnesota Press, 1980), 50; Folbe, "Patriarchy and Capitalism," 95, but see her entire argument. For the fertility increases associated with agriculture see Rae Lesser Blumberg, "Fairy Tales and Facts: Economy, Family, Fertility and the Female," in Irene Tinker et al., eds., *Women and World Development* (New York: Praeger, 1976), 11–21. Elizabeth Fisher, *Woman's Creation: Sexual Evolution and the Shaping of Society* (Garden City: Anchor, 1979), Pt. V, discusses the historical establishment of social control over fertility decisions. See also Linda Gordon, *Woman's Body, Woman's Right: A Social History of Birth Control in America* (New York: Grossman/Viking, 1976), chs. 1 and 2.

nary powers over the lives and affairs of their wives. Wives were *femme covert*, as the law said, without civil, political, or property rights apart from those of their husbands.[22] To the extent that women actively and independently participated in church- and school-building in the nineteenth-century West, they carved out an important public arena for women's work which distinguished them from previous generations of women and may help to illuminate the complex process of change taking place in the late nineteenth-century countryside. To be appreciated and understood, however, this activity must be situated within the context of the history of the relations of the sexes. The rule of man in civil society was accompanied by an ancient theory of domestic politics which made the father head of the household: he ruled women, children, and servants alike. Hierarchical relations within the family reflected the hierarchical organization of the society, the family a mirror for the state.[23]

In the Midwest then, under conditions of primarily self-sufficient farming, where not class relations but familial relations were the most significant feature of productive life, the regulation of the sexual division of labor was achieved through the perpetuation of a hierarchical and male-dominant family structure, linked to a public world from which women were excluded. This relationship of the sexes was not only one of male domination but of female exploitation: women labored beyond the time necessary for the provision of their own or even their children's subsistence so that men might be freed from such labor to pursue other, nonproductive activities. Men were free to pursue the work of the public world precisely because the inequitable division of labor at home made them the beneficiaries of women's and children's labor. This was not an exploitation that we can reckon in savings or accumulated capital, but an exploitation that we might count in male time freed from labor. In this household mode of production the exploitation of women as wives was a central dynamic of the system. This argument ought not to be misconstrued as a suggestion that farmers were lazy or slothful; that indeed would be trivial, for to be sure, farming was hard work for all. But farmers have always been palpably freer than farm wives from work around the farm and granted the prerogative of social participation, participation that took place while their women were home working with children, chickens, and cows. Men were freed from labor, in theory, to participate in the work of the larger social process.

[22] For an introductory discussion of the legal status of women see Leo Kanowitz, *Women and the Law: The Unfinished Revolution* (Albuquerque: Univ. of New Mexico Press, 1969).

[23] An excellent introduction to theories of sexual politics is Susan Moller Okin, *Women in Western Political Thought* (Princeton: Princeton Univ. Press, 1979).

Local and special conditions lent to North American rural society a special character. Paramount was the wide availability of relatively cheap land, which lead to the predominance of the freehold farm and the absence of relations of clientage or landlordism outside the South and Southwest. But once we shift our attention to the structure of everyday life and the relation of the sexes, the commonalities with other rural forms deserve emphasis; there is much to be said for the application of *longue durée* to American history. The basic features of this relationship of the sexes are worth summarizing, for they seem to constitute a structure. First, the family and household operated as the basic unit of labor: the production of material necessities and the reproduction of life itself were not separated as distinct forms of activity, but were part of the same process, the self-support of the family. Second, both sexes were involved in important portions of the family division of labor: women, in particular, played central roles in both productive and reproductive work. Third, rates of fertility were higher than those of simpler foraging societies or more complex industrial ones. And fourth, the husband ruled as head of the household, legitimized by a sexually-segregated public world and a male state-structure. These four mutually sustaining and reinforcing features have characterized the sex/gender systems of most state-level agricultural societies. The term "patriarchy" ought not to be extended indiscriminately to all societies in which men dominate, but may be properly used to refer to this structure as a whole.[24]

This analysis may assist us in discarding notions of a preindustrial, rural golden age, and it may offer the outlines of a new approach to the study of men and women in rural societies, but it cannot offer satisfactory explanations of affective life. We know on this social ground—the household mode of production in the antebellum Midwest—women did not mount much sustained criticism, nor much evident resistance to male rule. There were the beginnings of feminist consciousness and movement in the Midwest, but these remained, until the last quarter of the century, largely confined to urban centers or centers of rural industry. Women were powerfully aware of the inequities of their lot and in private and woman-to-woman communication expressed their views on the subject deeply and often bitterly.[25] But most of the energy women expended was not in the

[24] Barbara Ehrenreich and Diedre English, *For Her Own Good: 150 Years of Expert's Advice to Women* (New York: Doubleday, 1978). For another stimulating overview see Margaret Legates, "Anthropological and Historical Perspectives on the Nuclear Family," *Women's Studies*, 6 (1979), 259–76.

[25] For a literature of women's bitterness see Faragher, *Women and Men on the Overland Trail*, ch. 6. Juster, ed., *So Sweet to Labor*, reprints many letters from rural women which movingly document their awareness of oppression.

direction of resisting, but of accommodating to and shaping the family order. If we are to judge women like Lucinda Casteen not by the cultural standards of late twentieth-century feminism, but by standards appropriate to her own time, we will examine and attempt to understand the powers of endurance that permitted her to act out the roles of good wife and faithful mother through those hard years.

We must ask, then, by what means did women transform this male-dominant situation into one that was more satisfying for them than the analysis of patriarchy thus far suggests. The dominating feature of patriarchy is the subordination of women as wives. If we shift our attention, however, to women's roles as sisters and mothers we find within the same social structures opportunities for greater activity. It seems to have been the case, for example, that second and third generation daughters of original central Illinois settlers were much less mobile than the sons. Typically, fathers passed land to one or two sons, while others were forced by circumstance to look for land elsewhere. These migrating men were generally unmarried, so few women left with them. Daughters more frequently married locally and settled on homesteads nearby their parents.

These demographic patterns suggest a form of emergent, practical uxorilocality; that is, a pattern of newly married couples establishing residence near the house of the wife's parents. After 1835 or so, original settlement families typically found themselves with more female than male blood kin in the area. With the passing of another generation the phenomena of strong female kin networks was reinforced. Such a pattern may have been common in rural North America. We know, for example, that single men were present in great numbers on all western trails; they left behind thousands of sisters, women who married and settled near their parents and maternal kin. In this way the male privilege of midwestern life was turned on its head. Men, as public actors, had to face up to leaving kin and settled society. Women, as dependents, more likely stayed and played preeminent roles in the making of the family, kin, and neighborhood order. Recent reexaminations of working-class families and families of other groups where men are required to move or migrate have similarly noted the importance of "matrifocal" kin networks, where mother-daughter and sibling relations provide the webbing.[26] Lucinda Casteen was one of the original settlers. The special pain for her was in

[26] See Carol Stack, *All Our Kin* (New York: Harper and Row, 1972); Ann Cornelisen, *Women of the Shadows* (Boston: Little, Brown, 1976); Nancy Tanner, "Matrifocality in Indonesia and Among Black Americans," in Michele Rosaldo and Louise Lamphere, eds., *Woman, Culture and Society* (Stanford: Stanford Univ. Press, 1974), 129–56; Mina Davis Caulfield, "Imperialism, Family, and Cultures of Resistance," *Socialist Revolution*, 20 (1974), 67–85. Sacks, *Sisters and Wives*, ch. 7, discusses the persistence of sisterly relations in class-based societies.

leaving her mother in Kentucky. But had life taken a different turn for her, she would probably have been able to establish a satisfying relationship with Louisa and her other daughters which might well have sustained her in her later years.

We might think of sustenance here in a variety of ways. First, and most obviously, a network of women united by kinship in the local area would have been a powerful way of overcoming women's social isolation. These kin networks were important vehicles for sharing work, especially the care of children. Movement of children from one household to another, often for extended periods of time, frequently followed the lines established by female kinship. Such sharing was critically important in two instances: when a mother's illness or death left children motherless they were provided with kin care, and when husbands were long absent or died there was kin support available for the woman's children. The kinship connection created emotional and material support for women.

Second, and perhaps more important, these kin networks were a social foundation for a strong and important female cultural tradition. The defining characteristic of the men's world was action; theirs was a cultural world of closely shared identifications, expectations, and assumptions. In the standardized and even ritualized behavior of men in the public world lay an ability to communicate without excessive verbal expression. "The men generally," William Oliver, an English visitor to Illinois in the 1840s, reported, "are not very talkative." For women, however, articulation was at the very core of their world, for verbal expression could achieve an interpersonal closeness that was socially denied by the exclusion of women from the public world and their isolation at home. The typical gathering of women would have been one of female kin and neighbors, to work together spinning, sewing, quilting; and the vehicle of communication was not action but language. Oliver remarked that, in contrast to men, he had frequently overheard women "unfasten the sluces [sic] of their eloquence, and fairly maintain the character of their sex."[27]

Women's roles as oral communicators show up clearly in the vast amounts of collected folklore that we can attribute directly to women. Traditional wisdoms and superstitions about the female life cycle, health, the care of children, courtship and marriage, the domestic economy, all are stamped with the impress of women's culture. From contraceptive remedies to gardening secrets, women's lives were firmly a part of traditional culture. To an extent, men possessed a lore that was theirs alone, but in the world of men such a guiding lore was largely unnecessary, for

[27] Oliver, *Eight Months in Illinois* (1843; rpt. n.p.: Readex, 1966), 185, 195. I work out the interpretation suggested in this paragraph and the one following in detail in *Women and Men on the Overland Trail*, ch. 5.

standards of conduct were actively articulated as part of masculine social relations. The majority of the collected lore belongs to women.

Women's traditional culture tied them firmly to certain structures of the household productive system. Lore about hearthside and garden, family health and reproduction were not simply "women's"; these were in women's keeping, and served a larger process and goal. Both women and men were part of a cultural tradition that declared marriage to be a relationship of reciprocal labor:

> Go tell him to clear me an acre of land,
> Rozy-marrow and time:
> Between the salt sea and the sea sand,
> And then he can be a true lover of mine.
>
> Go tell the young man when he gets his
> work done,
> Rozy-marrow and time:
> To come to my house and his shirt will be done,
> And then he can be a true lover of mine.

Or more plainly:

> Here stands the loving couple,
> Join heart and hands:
> One wants a wife,
> And the other wants a man.
>
> They will get married,
> If they can agree:
> So its march down the river,
> To hog and hominy.[28]

Women's industries, women's lore, women's culture, and women's networks based in the kinship system were all aspects of the social and cultural whole of the household mode of production, as were those that placed men in the dominant position.

In the public world of antebellum Illinois, however, farmers were being encouraged to consider a new way of thinking. The traditional way of farming—based often on interpretations of astrological signs, the effects of the moon, the transmutation of crops, as well as the calculus of self-

[28] "The Cambric Shirt," in Henry M. Belden, *Ballads and Songs Collected by the Missouri Folklore Society* (Columbia: Univ. of Missouri Press, 1955), 23; "Hog and Hominy," in Charles Neely, *Tales and Songs of Southern Illinois* (Menasha, Wis.: George Banta, 1938), 203.

sufficiency—was subjected to the thoroughgoing critique of commercialism and scientism as articulated through the printed media. This fight against backwardness and superstition in the name of progress and capitalism was undertaken as a fight against traditional culture as a whole.[29] The tendency of men to reject traditional culture in their struggle for a more commercial world created a gender dimension to the conflict between traditional and popular culture. "Backward" farming was also the farming culture in which women's work was fully integrated as an essential part; "progressive" farming might eliminate the old notions of "reciprocity" without even a bow in the direction of women's roles in work and life.

Elizabeth McDowell Hill, writing in the 1890s, remembered when her father first successfully began to market commodities in Chicago during the '50s. "Wife and daughters," she remembered him announcing, "store away your loom, wheels, wraping bars, spool rack, winding blades, all your utensils for weaving cloth up in the loft. The boys and I can make enough by increasing our herds and driving them to Chicago for sale." It was no longer necessary to weave either for family cloth or for trading surplus in textiles. "There appeared to be a spirit of progressiveness all over the country," she remembered, but "the old ladies could not give up holding up their end of the 'single tree' as yet, so they continued with the spinning."[30] The "single tree," a crosspiece for connecting harnesses, was a metaphor for the cooperative and reciprocal labor of men and women in the self-sufficient family.

Our understanding of rural antebellum political economy must begin by recognizing women's exploitation and subordination. But within the structures of patriarchy women created a strong place for themselves and demanded that these places be preserved if not acknowledged. From this base, although they were victimized, midwestern women acted as something more than victims. There was a quality of women's relations with men that was strong, assertive. An English traveler recorded a woman calling her husband in from the fields:

> "John! You, John B–u–l–l! Stop that nonsense about old Zach Tailer, and come to your supper. What does Gineril Tailer care for such chaw-bacons as you! The hominey's spillin'. Fetch in the gem'man what drove the sleigh, and tell that 'er young 'un his supper's waiting." Mr. Bull turned his red eyes and

[29] On this fight see, for example, Richard Bardolph, *Agricultural Literature and the Early Illinois Farmer* (Urbana: Univ. of Illinois Press, 1948), 112–17 and passim; and Frank R. Kramer, *Voices in the Valley: Mythmaking and Folk Belief in the Shaping of the Middle West* (Madison: Univ. of Wisconsin Press, 1964).

[30] "Illinois Women," mss. collection, ISHL.

> heavy countenance upon me and pronounced, with a growl, a single, but magic word—"Supper!"[31]

This image of an assertive, even domineering, wife is repeated time and again in the sources. Especially in the male record a picture of women emerges that is not quite that of the victim. "Went to Beardstown to shooting match for beef," John Drury recorded in his diary on August 2, 1830, and continued, "Polly got home and raised hell again by scolding."[32]

It is perhaps worth adding here that it was only after the beginning of the break-up of the older household order that this assertive side to women's character broke free from a culture of accommodation. It was in the postbellum years—after the process of full capitalization of midwestern agriculture had well begun, after the swelling of the ranks of rural wage laborers and tenants, after the destruction of women's domestic industries and the end of household production—that women's self-assertion found cultural vehicles of protest and resistance. The woman suffrage and temperance movements not only spoke directly to the needs of women for inclusion in the public world and for domestic reform, but struck directly at the male social solidarities of the poll and the cup.

* * *

The long-term view of sex and gender change poses a problem for the condition of women's history. Because the structure of patriarchy extends back to such distant beginnings, a structural interpretation of rural women may further encourage the notion that women's experience is essentially unchanging. On the contrary, we ought to see the enduring structures of patriarchy as parameters and limitations within which historical men and women struggled to achieve material rewards and existential dignity. Once we understand rural patriarchy as a structure, we may write the local and temporal histories of women, men, and families in all their distinctive and critical variation. Women's history, in other words, cannot be artifically separated from general history; economic change, as well as changes in politics and ideology are central to understanding women's historical experience. In the North American nineteenth century, economic and institutional revolution shattered the structure of patriarchy in the countryside, and set men and women alike on a new course.

[31] John Lewis Payton, *Over the Alleghanies and Across the Prairies* (London: Sunkin, Marshall, 1870), 318.

[32] John Drury, ms. diary, ISHL.

By setting the object of the study as the social relations of the sexes, we may write of men and women in a common narrative. This subject demands that historians be sensitive to questions of work, of social and sexual divisions of labor, but also to areas that traditionally have been the province of anthropologists, including the study of sexuality and its regulation, of kinship and family relations and structures, and of gender. Not only does this approach help to integrate women into history, but perhaps as important, will help to transform our understanding of what men have done. Although such work has now begun in earnest, it deserves and requires far greater encouragement within the body of historical scholarship. Because this approach stresses analysis of such fundamental areas of human relations, it also offers the best hope for overcoming the stereotypes that continue to burden our interpretations of men and women in the past. By taking a relational approach to women's history we may avoid the error of seeing women in "essentialist" terms.

Finally, and for the study of the North American case, this approach to the social history of rural men and women offers a theoretical framework that is cross-cultural and comparative. Dramatically interesting contrasts could be developed between the lives of prairie women of Euro-American and Native American backgrounds. In such a spirit, Joan Jensen and Darlis Miller have called for a multicultural approach to the study of rural women;[33] I want to second that call, adding that embedding the study of the sexes in the study of economics, reproductive strategies, and the social structures of power and authority provide us with the opportunity to be comparative as well.

[33] Jensen and Miller, "The Gentle Tamers Revisited."

Native American Women and Agriculture: A Seneca Case Study[1]

Joan M. Jensen
New Mexico State University

This study examines the impact of European invasion on the mode of production, household lives, and ideology of one group of Native American women, the Seneca. Seneca women had high public status, a balanced division of labor, ownership of the land, and control over the means of agricultural production. The power derived from their role in production and the social institutions which had developed from this production were difficult to destroy, despite the efforts of missionaries, government, and reformers. The effects of disease, war, and the market economy on the Seneca women are specifically examined. Also described are attempts to impose the ideology of individualism and nuclear household patterns on the Seneca by withdrawing women from production outside the home and establishing male ownership of private property.

At the time Europeans first arrived in North America, and for centuries after, Native American women dominated agricultural production in the tribes of the eastern half of the United States. In many of these tribes, the work of the women provided over half of the subsistence and secured for them not only high status but also public power. Yet this immense contribution to the economy and to the culture of the Native Americans has never been studied systematically by historians. We have no complete history of Indian agriculture.[2] We have no study of how women functioned in these agricultural societies. We do not know what happened to the women and their agricultural production under the impact of the Europeans' invasion (Carrier, 1923; Holder, 1970; Terrell & Terrell,

[1] Criticism by many women helped the development of this article at different stages. Anthropologists Bea Medicine and Peggy Sanday, women historians at Arizona State University, and community women in Phoenix all made valuable contributions to its evolution.

[2] I use the term *agriculture* rather than *horticulture* because horticulture, along with "hoe culture," has so often been used negatively (Kramer, 1967).

1974; Wallace, 1970; Will & Hyde, 1917). Using the Seneca women, I would like to provide a prototype of what we can learn about the history of Native American women and agriculture.

Several theories have recently been presented by anthropologists to describe the status of women. Peggy Sanday (1973, 1974) has suggested that there is a high correlation between female status and a balanced division of labor and that women do not develop public power unless some of their energies are employed in economic production. Judith Brown (1970a, 1970b) has argued that women must not only produce in agricultural societies but must also control the means of production – land, seeds, tools – and the methods of work to achieve public power. The history of the Seneca women seems to confirm both these theories and also to show that this power, once achieved, was difficult to dislodge even by the combined efforts of missionaries, government, and reformers.

Unfortunately, we have no verbatim transcripts from early Native American women about agricultural production. Our only account is by Buffalo Woman, a Hidatsa who provided a lengthy description of the philosophy and techniques of agriculture in 1912. Buffalo Woman spent over a year with an anthropologist in North Dakota demonstrating in minute detail the cultivation, planting, and hoeing process. She described the cooperative work groups of the women and sang their work songs. Her account conveys a feeling of the pride and care with which Native American women performed their work. But to develop a picture of the community power women derived from this agricultural production, and the struggle to maintain that power under the impact of change, we must turn to the records of those who were the agents of change. If used critically, these records provide a starting point for the study of Native American women and agriculture (Wilson, 1917).

When White colonists arrived in the seventeenth century, they found many of the best bottomlands near creeks and rivers cleared, sometimes abandoned, but often filled with the neat and clean corn fields of the Native American women. An early account by Roger Williams told of the "very loving sociable speedy way" in which men and women joined together to clear fields, and how women planted, weeded, hilled, gathered, and stored the corn. In some areas, tribal women had as many as 2,000 acres under cultivation and in most areas they had accumulated surpluses which were traded to hungry settlers (Carrier, 1923). Colonists were often more interested in commerce than in laborious clearing and planting, and even when engaged in agriculture many were not careful farmers. Records mention that Native American women sometimes ridiculed colonists for neglecting to keep their fields well weeded.

At first colonists occupied abandoned fields or purchased cleared fields from the Native Americans. War soon added a third method by which the colonists obtained fields. "Now," said Edward Waterhouse after the Indian attack of 1622 in Virginia, "their cleared grounds in all their villages (which are situated in the fruitfullest places of the land) shall be inhabited by us, whereas heretofore the grubbing of woods was the greatest labour" (quoted by Washburn, 1971). During the next 300 years the Native American agricultural societies underwent a drastic transformation as trade, warfare, and disease disrupted their subsistence economies. The Seneca, like other tribes, felt the impact of these disruptions on their economy.

The foremothers of the Seneca were among the women of the League of the Iroquois whose well-tended fields surrounded their western New York villages, and whose origin myth began with a female deity falling from the sky to give birth to the first woman. Sky Woman brought earth, seeds, and roots from which wild trees, fruits, and flowers grew. The domestic plants – potatoes, beans, squash, corn, and other crops – sprang from the grave of Sky Woman's daughter. Later, according to several corn legends, the Corn Maiden brought corn to the Seneca, taught the women how to plant, how to prepare the corn, how to dance the corn dances, and which songs to sing at the dances. Seneca women believed that a great power pervaded all nature and endowed every element with intelligence. Each clod of soil, each tree, each stalk of corn, had life and consciousness. At a winter ceremony each year the women gave thanks for every object in nature. At springtime they offered thanks to the sap and sugar from the maple trees, which they made into syrup. Later there were planting feasts, a June strawberry feast, then a corn feast, and finally completing the cycle, a harvest feast. The purpose of these feasts was to show that life was desired and that the people were thankful for it (Hewitt, 1918; Parker, 1923, 1926).

Seneca family life centered on the longhouse, a joint tenement shared by families of kin, the entire clan household being composed of as many as 50 or 60 people. The domestic economy of each household was regulated by an older woman who distributed household stores to families and guests. Households were clustered in compact villages of 20 to 30 houses or in larger towns of 100 to 150 houses. The more densely populated towns usually shifted location every ten years; the smaller towns might occupy the same site for twenty years or more. These compact towns proved particularly vulnerable to seventeenth-century disease and warfare. In 1668, for example, almost 250 people in one town died of disease, and, in one month in 1676, 60 small children in another town died from pneumonia. The French destroyed large Seneca towns in 1687 and 1696 (Hawley, 1884; Morgan, 1965).

Communal living, as practiced by the Seneca, provided stable care for all the children of the village. Children inherited their property and place in the clan through their mothers; and women who were childless or had few children adopted any orphan children. Seneca women showed extraordinary affection for their children, as one of the earliest Jesuit visitors observed in 1668, and children had great respect for their parents. Elders in the longhouse shared the responsibility of teaching children necessary physical and social survival skills. After their mothers had arranged their marriage, a young couple traditionally joined one of the mothers' communal households.[3] In no case did the couple set up a separate nuclear family. According to early Jesuit accounts, most marriages were monogamous, but a few Seneca women had two husbands. If husbands were absent too long or failed to provide their share of subsistence for the household, the woman would take another marriage partner (Hawley, 1884; Lafitau, 1724).

Seneca women had possessory rights to all cultivated land within the tribal area. The women's clans distributed the land to households according to their size, and organized farming communally. Each year, the women of the town elected a chief matron who directed the work. Sick and injured members of these mutual aid societies had a right to assistance in planting and harvesting; and after hoeing the owner of each parcel of land would provide a feast for all the women workers. According to Mary Jemison, the Irish capative who spent the second half of the eighteenth century with Seneca women, their work was less onerous than that of White women (Seaver, 1824). They had no drivers or overseers and worked in the fields as leisurely as they wished with their children beside them. The women formed *Tonwisas*, ritual groups to encourage the good favor of the "three sisters" – corn, beans, and squash. The leaders of these groups performed rites, carrying armfuls of corn and loaves of corn bread around a kettle of corn soup. After harvest, women braided or stored the corn in corncribs or shelled and stored it in bark barrels. Women later ground the corn in large oak mortars with four-foot-long maple wood pestles. The rhythmic sound of the women grinding corn was the first sound heard in the villages each morning (Parker, 1968b; Seaver, 1824).

Seneca women also controlled the distribution of surplus food and – by virtue of the right to demand captives as replacement for murdered kinspeople – often influenced warfare. The matrilineal Seneca women retained a powerful position in the community through control of land and agriculture. Women had their own councils and were represented in the council of the civil rulers by a male speaker, the most famous of whom was Red Jacket. Women also had the power to elect the civilian rulers and to depose those guilty of misconduct, incompetence, or disregard of the public welfare (Parker, 1952; Wallace, 1970).

By the 1780s the Senecas had already experienced the most common disruptions of agricultural village life: warfare, disease, and trade. The Seneca were one of the League of Six Nations who supported the British, in part because the American revolutionaries offered them no guarantee of the peaceful possession of their territory. In August 1779, on General Washington's orders, American troops under John Sullivan laid waste to the Seneca lands. By army estimates,

[3] It is not clear from early accounts whether the Seneca couple always joined the household of the woman. Parker (1952) says the couple lived with her women for the first year, then with his women. Other accounts say the Seneca couples joined the husband's household. The Seneca may have changed from living with the wife's clan to living with the husband's clan because of the increasing military demands on the tribe (Martin & Voorhies, 1975).

they uprooted, girdled, or chopped down 1,500 orchard trees; destroyed 60,000 bushels of corn, 2,000 to 3,000 bushels of beans, and cucumbers, watermelons, and pumpkins in such quantities, one major recalled, as to be "almost incredible to a civilized people" (Parker, 1968b). An estimated 500 acres of cultivated crops were destroyed, along with 40 large towns and villages of communal long-houses. The warriors fled to the protection of the British and the women and children hid in the forests. Although Washington had urged the capture of women as well as men, none were taken, and the refugees crowded into Fort Niagara that winter where the British furnished meat and rations. The next spring the Seneca women returned to plant corn, potatoes, and pumpkins along the bottoms of the south side of Buffalo Creek at the eastern tip of Lake Erie and made maple sugar in their old way. Smallpox ravaged the communities the following year, however, and deaths led to demoralization and loss of confidence. The corn supply again was exhausted and the people applied to Fort Niagara for supplies. The officer at Fort Niagara complained that the Seneca had improvident habits but he sent the supplies (Fenton, 1956; G. H. Harris, 1903; Houghton, 1920).

By 1789, trade had also drastically altered the women's way of life. They now had iron and steel hoes, awls, needles, shears, and cloth. Women had substituted cloth for fur garments and beads for porcupine quills in much of their decorated work. The estimated contact population of 10,000 had been reduced to several thousand survivors. There were about 2,000 in western New York along the Buffalo and Cazenovia creeks clustered in three or four villages.

Women retained their political power, however. When Washington sent Colonel Proctor to obtain the support of the Seneca in negotiating with other tribes in May 1791, the women intervened to urge peaceful negotiation. It was a time of crisis for the Seneca. Warriors had just brought in an Indian scalp with the story that White people were making war. The rulers had met in council and refused to negotiate. Next morning the elder women appeared before Colonel Proctor's lodge, where he was talking with a number of chiefs, and announced that they had considered his proposition:

> you ought to hear and listen to what we, women, shall speak, as well as to the sachems; for *we are the owners of this land,* – and it is ours. It is we that plant it for our and their use. Hear us, therefore, for we speak of things that concern us while our men shall say more to you; for we have told them. (quoted by Stone, 1841, p. 56)

Later that day the council reassembled and Red Jacket, the spokesman for the women, announced that the women were "to conclude what ought to be done by both sachems and warriors," and that the women had decided that for the good of them and their children a peace delegation would be sent (Stone, 1841).

Women also spoke during the negotiations of the Treaty of 1794 with the United States government. In 1797 they still had a dominant voice. When Thomas Morris arrived in August of that year to negotiate a land sale for his father, the women again vetoed the decision of the sachems and insisted, "It is we, the women, who own the land" (quoted by Parker, 1952). Morris promised the women that if they agreed to the treaty, they would never again know want. Warriors often went to White settlements to sell furs and buy food while the women and children might go hungry, he reminded them. He said that the $100,000 offered to them for the land could be put in a bank so that "in times of scarcity, the women and children of your nation can be fed." The warriors supported the treaty, because Morris promised that hunting rights would not be impaired. To the women Morris offered special gifts and a string of wampum to remind them – should they turn down the offer and then become impoverished – of the wealth they had rejected.

Certainly, this was economic pressure of the rankest kind, and yet, given the difficult circumstances, it is easy to see why the women decided to sell the land. Morris's tactics were successful. "This had an excellent effect on the women [who] at once declared themselves for selling, and the business began to wear a better aspect," Morris wrote in his journal (quoted by Parker, 1952).

Government and speculators had reduced the land of the women. The way was now open for teachers and missionaries to end women's domination over agriculture. The Quakers had dispatched their first mission to the Seneca in 1789 to teach the men agriculture and the women "useful arts," but the people exhibited little interest. Two years later a Seneca leader appealed to Washington to teach the men how to plow and the women to spin and weave. Washington sent a teacher; and the Secretary of State, Timothy Pickering, urged the Six Nations to fence their lands, raise livestock, and farm "as white people do" (Howland, 1903). Buffalo Creek and other villages refused to admit teachers or missionaries.

The leader who appealed to Washington for technical assistance was Cornplanter, who was not a traditional chief.[4] He spoke only for his own village on the Allegheny River; there he exercised unusual power because he had received personal title to the land for negotiating the sale of Indian lands to Pennsylvania (Parker, 1927). The Quakers were quick to accept Cornplanter's invitation and soon arrived at the Allegheny village ready to retrain both men and women. At this time women were tending the fields and men were trading furs. The women refused to appear, though the Quakers specifically asked to talk to them. To the men, the Quakers proposed an incentive system, promising to pay cash to men who would raise wheat, rye, corn, potatoes, and hay, and to women who would spin thread from flax and wool. Later the Quakers conducted an experiment to prove that plowed fields produced a greater yield than fields hoed by women.

[4] Cornplanter's mother was a hereditary matron of the Wolf clan who passed over him to nominate her younger full-blooded son as sachim. Cornplanter had no official title but became an elder and was given the right to sign treaties because of his military role. His mother later lived in his village.

It was "unreasonable," the Quakers argued, to allow mothers, wives, and sisters to work all day in the fields and woods, and men to "play" with bows and arrows. The men warned the Quakers not to expect too much (Deardorff & Snyderman, 1956).

The Reverend Elkanah Holmes (1903) reported that the Tuscarora tribe of the Iroquois told him in 1800 that among the Senecas and the western tribes women did all the field work. Among the Tuscarora, the men had already begun to substitute agricultural work for hunting and Holmes reported them at work in the fields along side the women planting, hoeing, and harvesting corn. In 1801, however, the Seneca requested oxen to plow with and spinning wheels. By 1804, a Quaker reported a large plow at work in a Seneca village above Buffalo Creek drawn by three yoke of oxen and attended by three Native American men; he reported considerable "progress" in agriculture (Holmes, 1903).

At Allegheny two Quaker women soon began to teach spinning and weaving, and in 1806 Seneca women promised to take up these White women's arts. Gayantgogwus, sister of Cornplanter and one of the most influential persons in the community, brought her granddaughter and another young relative to show visiting Quakers how they could knit and spin. The Quakers urged the men to spread out their farms, arguing that it was better for farming and cattle raising to be separated. The Quakers also introduced wheat and other new crops. Already 100 families had chosen to fence their farms individually and to embrace the nuclear family, while 30 new homes clustered at Cold Springs (Deardorff & Snyderman, 1956; Visit of Gerard T. Hopkins, 1903; Wallace, 1970).

We do not know what prompted women at Allegheny to adopt their new role so quickly. Brazilian women, moving more recently from a women's work group to a shared work situation with men, have explained that they wanted to share the burden of supplying food more equally with men whose ability to hunt had decreased with the decline in game. They also wanted the benefits in consumer goods which a cash income would bring. Among the Seneca women, there was a split. Some of the older women saw the change as a threat to their strong position in the community and reasserted their traditional powers against the divisive new economy and way of life being forced upon them. Old women advised their daughters to use contraceptives and abortion and, if necessary, to leave husbands who took up the new ways. Handsome Lake, who had recently replaced Cornplanter as the new chief of the League of the Iroquois, attacked the older women. "The Creator is sad because of the tendency of old women to breed mischief," he warned. He accused them of witchcraft (Murphy & Murphy, 1974; Parker, 1968a).

Witchcraft accusations occur when social relations are ambiguous and tensions cannot otherwise be resolved. They are often an instrument for breaking off relations or withdrawing community protection from certain individuals (Douglas, 1970). The older Seneca women formed a rival faction to the changes which Cornplanter, Handsome Lake, and the Quakers wished to institute, and a power block which Handsome Lake wished to break. The accusations split the ranks of the women still further and realigned some in support of the new system and its leaders. Handsome Lake made many accusations among the Senecas and, though he opposed them, some executions did occur. In a few cases, accusations were followed with trials by council and swift execution. One old woman was reported cut down while at work in her corn field in 1799. Another was reported executed on the spot after a council decided on her guilt. Four of the "best women in the nation" narrowly escaped execution at Sandusky when the executioners refused to carry out the sentence. Probably not many old women died but the lesson was clear (Houghton, 1920; Smith, 1888; Wallace, 1970).

As Handsome Lake, Cornplanter, and the Quakers asserted their influence more clearly over the village of Allegheny and its agricultural pattern, the witchcraft accusations ceased. Handsome Lake became the prophet of the supremacy of the husband–wife relationship over the mother–daughter relationship. Men were to harvest food for their families, build good houses, keep horses and cattle; women were to be good housewives. By 1813 Seneca women were operating spinning wheels, and two Seneca men, trained by the Quakers as village weavers, turned out 200 yards of linen and wool cloth that year. Well pleased with the transition at Allegheny, the Quakers estimated that the average farm had ten acres, horses or oxen, cows, and pigs. In 1821, a painted box sent from the first school portrayed Seneca girls learning to spin and weave with quotes from the Bible above their busy activity: "She layeth her hands to the spindle, and hands hold the distaff . . . . She looketh well to her household and eateth not the bread of Idleness" (Fenton, 1956; Wallace, 1970).

While Allegheny seemed a model agricultural village and thus – the Quakers hoped – on its way to eventual Christianity, the villages at Buffalo Creek were still in crisis. During 1818 to 1822, there was an outbreak of witchcraft accusations at Buffalo Creek and women were executed there and at Tuscarora. Like the women of Allegheny, the older women of these communities seemed to be opposing the new order. Jabez Backus Hyde, a Presbyterian schoolteacher reported from Buffalo Creek in 1820 that

> Their ancient manner of subsistence is broken up and when they appear willing and desirous to turn their attention to agriculture, their ignorance, the inveteracy of their old habits, and disadvantage under which they labor, soon discourage them; though they struggle hard little is realized to their benefit, besides the continual dread they live in of losing their possessions. If they build they know not who will inhabit. If they make fields they know not who will cultivate them. They know the anxiety of their white neighbors to get possession of their lands. (Hyde, 1903, p. 245)

When the New York Missionary Society requested that a mission be established at Buffalo Creek, the Seneca there called a council to debate the matter. Men and women, converts and traditionalists, agreed to allow a mission to be established, and in 1819 the first evangelical minister arrived to preach and teach. Subsidized by the government to teach agriculture to the boys and instructed by the mission society to teach all the children to work and be industrious, the new school attempted to teach girls to knit and sew. But the little girls proved especially troublesome and, when disciplined, complained to their parents. Complaints brought objections by the chiefs and a request that the children be persuaded and coaxed into obedience and, if disobedient, left to the parent to reprove. If all else failed, the child could be considered heathen and expelled. Such a doctrine of education was unacceptable, the Reverend T. S. Harris (1903) confided to his journal, because "the rod is the plan of God's own appointment."

Despite Harris' severity with the young girls, the school supplied a new community focus to replace the old communal activities being destroyed by fences and isolated farming. A group of older non-Christian women soon appeared before Harris and asked to be taught as well. The minister agreed that the school would do so as soon as a female teacher was procured. Education and new skills learned in a group were attractive alternatives to the isolation of the new farmsteads and compatible with the women's new relationship to the economy. The third wife of Red Jacket – he was now leader of the anti-Christian faction – left him to join the church, and 20 persons, mostly women, asked the minister to instruct them. A number of women adopted Christian names and became members of the mission (T. S. Harris, 1903).

The years between 1837 and 1845 were times of trouble for the Seneca and for other tribes who were all being pressured to move west of the Mississippi. As early as 1818 a delegation of Cherokee women had opposed westward removal and urged missionaries to help them maintain the bounds of the lands they possessed. Cherokee women took up the ways of White women to prove their worthiness to remain on their land. They learned to spin and weave and to wear bonnets and allowed their men to replace them in the fields. Their efforts were ignored by the government. When the army took the Cherokee women out of Georgia in 1839, they left a large number of spinning wheels and looms behind. Other Cherokee women fled to the mountains with a small band who refused to leave. Seminole women, deported that same year from Florida, criticized the men for allowing deportation and for refusing to die on their native soil (Foreman, 1953; Malone, 1956).

The Senecas would have been forcibly removed too, but for the efforts of the Quakers and the missionary Asher Wright, who had moved to Buffalo Creek in 1831. The Quakers mobilized public opinion against a treaty calling for removal of all the Senecas, and Wright helped negotiate a compromise treaty allowing them to keep the Allegheny and Cattaraugus reservations but giving up the valuable Buffalo Creek land (*Case of the Seneca Indians,* 1840; Fenton, 1956).

When the Seneca voted on the compromise treaty, there was still no consensus, which traditionally would have meant rejection. The Quakers charged that bribery and secrecy had been responsible for the majority of the chiefs signing the first treaty and that many opposed the compromise treaty as well. The Buffalo Creek Seneca were especially bitter at the removal, held a meeting, and resolved to have nothing to do with Christian Indians, missionaries, or the gospel. Under protest, they were removed from the Buffalo Creek reservation 35 miles south to the Cattaraugus reservation. Their ancestral lands eventually became part of the city of Buffalo (Caswell, 1892; Fenton, 1956).

At the time of the negotiations in 1838, the women were still working the land, making beadwork, brooms, baskets, and other articles for sale, and picking berries to sell at local markets. The women bathed twice a week and dressed neatly in beaded skirts of brightly colored calico, long tunics and leggings, and wore their hair parted in the middle and tied back loose or in a knot with ribbons. They acted and felt, remarked Henry Dearborn (1904), Adjutant General for Massachusetts, "on a perfect equality" with their husbands, advised and influenced them, and were treated well in turn. "She lives with him from love," noted Dearborn a bit wistfully in his journal, "for she can obtain her own means of support better than he can." Senecas still traced descent through the female and were affectionate, careful, kind, and laborious in the care of their little children. They were "equals and quite as independent in all that is general to both, and each separately forming his or her duties as things proper and indispensable for the interest and happiness of themselves in their several domestic private and common relations" (Dearborn, 1904).

Other Whites assured Dearborn that the condition of the Seneca, despite appearances, was deplorable, the men and women intemperate and dissolute and not able to raise sufficient provisions for their support. Once the flats of Buffalo Creek had been one continuous corn field, said one informant; now the fields were overgrown and the Senecas' chief subsistence was begging. Judge Paine of nearby Aurora advised emigration before the Seneca became extinct. All groups were equally wretched, the judge told the visitor, and they were causing great injury to those around by obstructing agriculture. Land values would be enhanced if the White people owned and settled the land, one trader assured Dearborn (Dearborn, 1904).

Dearborn was skeptical about the "pretended mercies of the villanous white man," and romantic about "the noble race of the Senecas." Yet he concluded they must be forced to work and that all efforts at change must begin with the women, who had traditionally tilled the land, manufactured the clothing, and managed the domestic and economic concerns of the family. First, the land must be divided and owned in severalty to be sold, devised, or inherited as with Whites. Representation must be by landowners only. Cattle and plows should be provided to the men to break up the land, and hoes, rakes, and shovels to the women. Children should be taught to read and write and premiums should be given mothers for each 12-year-old son who regularly worked on the land or at some mechanical trade; and at 16, the sons should be allowed half this premium. In one generation, Dearborn (1904) wrote, in words reformers would echo through the century with each new plan to "civilize the Indians," all the Native Americans would be good farmers skilled in the useful mechanical arts, independent, intelligent, industrious, and on the march to "moral excellence and refinement." The "ridiculous" corn feast and other rites, said Dearborn, must be abandoned.

Dearborn had already witnessed the corn feast where a third of the assembled people were women – teenagers of 14 to old matrons. Five women had distributed the food – corn, beans, squash, vegetables, and deer soup – in baskets and kettles to the other women who then carried the food to their families – husbands and children scattered in groups on the grass – or home. The feast symbolized the fact: women were still in charge of production and distribution of the food (Dearborn, 1904).

Seneca women continued their important economic role in the community. In 1846 they were reported by anxious Quakers as still working in the fields, wearing their traditional tunic and leggings, living in log huts with earth floors, and cooking a pot of venison stew for the family's main meal (Kelsey, 1917). Quakers urged Seneca men to withdraw their women from the fields for the domestic duties of the household and, at a council meeting with the Seneca that year, a female Quaker appealed to the women to change, arguing that "to mothers, properly belongs the care and management of the education of their children." The Seneca woman Guanaea responded that it was the earnest desire of the Seneca women in council to have their children instructed in the manner desired and to do all in their power to cooperate in and promote that goal (Kelsey, 1917). As a result of this meeting, the Quakers opened a Female Manual Labor School at Cattaraugus where young women under 20 were taught to card and spin wool, knit stockings, cut out and make garments, wash and iron clothes, make bread, do plain cooking, and perform "every other branch of good housewifery, pertaining to a country life" (Kelsey, 1917).

Published records do not indicate what role the women had in the establishment of a republican government with laws and a constitution in 1848. The communities had lost 70 people in a typhoid epidemic, and political dissension again divided the people. Presumably, however, the women performed their traditional role in divesting the old chiefs of their horns, the symbol of life tenure, to allow the new constitution to be legally established. Under the new constitution men and women elected 3 judges to the judiciary and 18 legislators to the council. Three-fourths of the voters and three-fourths of all the mothers had to ratify all decisions.[5] While confirming important political power

[5]The Seneca replaced this new government with the older "government by chiefs" in 1854 but people of both sexes over the age of 21 had to consent to the sale or lease of reservation land under this second constitution.

to the women, the new constitution also legitimized the replacement of consensus by majority rule among the women, thereby acknowledging the fragmentation of their power. That same year, 1848, White women were meeting less than a hundred miles away at Seneca Falls to demand the right to vote and be heard in the politics of their nation (Caswell, 1892; *Constitution of the "government by chiefs,"* 1854).

The Seneca women were also able to continue to exert economic control over the annuities paid by the federal government from the interest on a trust fund from the sale of their lands. This was the money that Morris had promised would allow them to live forever without poverty if they gave up their lands. The Seneca annuities were first paid in blankets, calico, and yarn annually at Buffalo Creek. As with other tribes, these annuities were a main source of complaint against government policies. Native Americans often complained because some treaties had set a particular sum in gold to be paid in food and commodities, but financial fluctuations, especially inflation, reduced the quantity of goods received, sometimes by half. In addition, businesses with government contracts were notorious in their willingness to supply poor quality goods, and government officials were known for their willingness to purchase commodities which the Native Americans did not want and could not use. A cash payment was soon substituted for the Senecas, funds allotted to the heads of families, and tribal members encouraged to buy from merchants licensed to sell on the reservation. After 1834, allegedly to end frauds, Congress decided the money would go to the chiefs. Chiefs thereafter represented the tribes and received the money from the government; but among the Seneca the money was then divided by the chiefs among the mothers of the families, usually depending on their need. The women were given credit by the merchants and thus were able to retain some control over the distribution of food and commodities. The annuities were never enough to prevent poverty, however. In 1850, the Seneca received only $18,000. Still the $50 to $80 each woman received annually was an important supplement to her earnings. The women also attempted to make the chiefs accountable not only to the women, but sometimes to White creditors as well (Allen, 1903; Morgan, 1904; Trennert, 1973; U.S. Congress, 1867; E. E. White, 1965).

Nor were Seneca women agreed on the benefits of the White women's culture, which the Christians worked so hard to inculcate. During the 1850s Laura Wright, the missionary wife of Asher Wright, established an orphanage to care for young children and began to instruct the older women in their wifely duties. She believed women should be taught to be Christian housekeepers, needlewomen, and laundresses, and planned to buy material and teach them to make garments for sale. She began by sponsoring dinners at which she gave lessons in making clothing, housekeeping, and child care. But during these dinners, the non-Christians – still at least a third of the women – would gather outside in an opposition meeting to ridicule the converts. They considered sewing a ruse to break down the old religion and insisted on observing the old rites (Caswell, 1892).

Later Ms. Wright borrowed $800 to invest in material and contracted to supply the government with 650 duck coats and red flannel shirts for the western tribes. Several women even purchased sewing machines on credit, hoping to pay for them with the proceeds from the contract. After a long wait, the government finally paid for the garments, but the amount was so small that the women did not consider it worth their time to continue sewing for sale. They did, however, continue to sell their beaded work, baskets, and berries to nearby Whites, and they continued to farm (Caswell, 1892).

By all evidence, the Seneca women still had a strong political, religious, and economic role in the 1850s. It is surprising, therefore, that when the Victorian anthropologist Lewis Henry Morgan began his studies of the Iroquois in 1846, he did not perceive the importance of the economic role of the women.[6] It was not that he believed the Native American women were unproductive. He noted in his journals of 1862 (L. A. White, 1959), while visiting the western tribes: "Among all our Indian nations the industry of the women is proverbial." But he encouraged the women in domestic manufacture, the products of which could be purchased by government agents to reimburse the women for their labor. The women then would support the whole tribe, he suggested, and after a time the men would unite with them in the labor. Such a plan might have been good half a century earlier, but industrialization had already made it unlikely that women would continue domestic manufacturing, as Laura Wright had found out.[7] Among the Native American women only traditional manufactures, such as pottery and blanket weaving in the Southwest, ever provided much of an income and even then it was very low (Fee, 1974; Morgan, 1965; L. A. White, 1959).

Like other American men, Morgan continued to place his main hope for the progress of all women in the "affections" between the sexes, in the perfection of the monogamous family, the education of women, and private ownership of land. After a visit to the Iroquois in 1846, he claimed that the males considered the women to be inferior, dependent, and their servants – and that the women agreed. Later Morgan wrote of the power the Iroquois women exercised through their clans, but he never mentioned the economic functions of the women as he meticulously traced their kinship systems. He certainly did not agree with Frederick Engels, who drew upon Morgan for *The Origin of the*

[6] The reason for Morgan's reluctance to discuss women's production seems to have been his desire to protect Native Americans from criticism by Whites. Since Morgan believed that male industry replacing female industry was a sign of progress, he seldom commented on the widespread women's work, but praised men's labor when he found it.

[7] Many White women sewed at home during the Civil War and into the twentieth century, and later Puerto Rican women stitched nightgowns for wealthy New Yorkers in their island slums, but women resorted to sewing in their homes only when desperate.

Family, Private Property and the State, but who concluded that the only way to liberate women was to bring them back into public industry and abolish the monogamous family as an economic unit (Engels, 1972; Fee, 1974; Morgan, 1904; Sacks, 1974).

By the end of the nineteenth century, Morgan's goals had become those of most reformers in America who were concerned about the "Indian problem." In the 1870s the federal government began encouraging the training of a few Native Americans for "higher spheres," that is, to teach common school. Some Seneca women from the Cattaraugus orphanage, which was now named the Thomas Indian School and now financed by the state of New York, went to Oswego Normal School or Geneseo State Normal School. Most, however, went to Hampton Normal and Agricultural School; there from 1878 Indians were taught in classes separate from the Black students, though both groups were expected to become agriculturalists, mechanics, or teachers. Hundreds of young Native Americans were educated in the East in "rigidly organized society," anthropologist Alice Fletcher wrote, so that they could resist the restless experimenting and energy of the West when sent there as teachers. The Carlisle Indian School in Pennsylvania was founded on the same principles as Hampton, with the difference that its founder did not believe Native Americans should be exposed to Black students and accepted only Indians (Hampton Institute, 1888).

In 1881, Secretary of the Interior Carl Schurz praised the Carlisle School for keeping the girls busy "in the kitchen, dining-room, sewing-room, and with other domestic work" (quoted by Prucha, 1973). The education of Indian girls was particularly important, he wrote, because he felt that the Indian woman had only been a beast of burden, disposed of like an article of trade at maturity, and treated by her husband alternately with "animal fondness" and "the cruel brutality of the slave driver." Attachment to the home would civilize the Indians, he predicted, and it was the woman's duty to make the home attractive. She must become the center of domestic life and thus gain respect and self-respect. "If we educate the girls of to-day," Schurz predicted with the reformer's usual assurance, "we educate the mothers of to-morrow, and in educating those mothers we prepare for the education of generations to come" (quoted by Prucha, 1973).

Reformers quite commonly ignored the agricultural traditions of the women and inisted that Indians had all depended on game for subsistence. The reformers argued that the Indians had no right to the land because they had simply roamed over it like buffalo. Reformers always saw the key to civilization in the family, a family in which the man held the land. Individualism, private ownership, the nuclear family – all were marshalled to defend the breakup of reservation life. Tribal government meant socialism to many and thus had to be destroyed. Daughters, the reformers were fond of saying, must be educated and married under the laws of the land instead of sold "at a tender age for a stipulated price into concubinage to gratify the brutal lusts of ignorance and barbarism" (quoted by Prucha, 1973). Coeducation would lift the Indian woman out of servility and degradation, said Seth Low, later president of Columbia University, so that their husbands and men generally would "treat them with the same gallantry and respect which is accorded their more favored white sisters" (quoted by Prucha, 1973). The plan for education remained the same: cooking, sewing, laundry work, teaching.

During the years while reformers spoke long and piously of breaking up tribal life, the Seneca women struggled with disease and lack of food. Cholera, smallpox, and typhoid fever swept the reservations in the 1880s. A drought caused the loss of the corn and potato crop, and the orchards produced little fruit. The government further reduced the annuities. When Laura Wright died in 1886, after 53 years of missionary work among the Seneca, she was still giving out meat and flour, and trying to devise a plan for a Gospel Industrial Institute where women could learn to cook and sew and clean (Caswell, 1892).

At the Thomas Indian School, the old educational goals of the early nineteenth century were translated into modern terms by the Whites and continued into the twentieth century. In the classes of 1907 the boys were taught agriculture, the girls "household science." The school reported with confidence in 1910 that girls needed instruction in the comfortable, sanitary, and economic arrangement and management of the home. Girls learned to make quilts and buttonholes and nightdresses and to mend socks. They were trained for general laundry work and scientific cooking, for their own homes and for the homes of others. During vacation they might earn as much as $4 per week as domestics in one of the local homes in Silver Creek or Buffalo (Thomas Indian Schools, 1906, 1911, 1914). The most intelligent young women were also channeled into teaching and targeted to teach on other reservations. Many, however, dropped out of Hampton and returned to the reservation. Some were ill, other were needed at home.

White educators expected most Seneca women to marry and settle on the reservation. Many women did marry and continue to live on the reservation. Others taught for a few years or cleaned and washed dishes for Silver Creek families. In 1910, the Census recorded 2,907 Senecas, all but about 200 in the State of New York (U.S. Department of Commerce, 1915). Over 60% of the 1,266 males were gainfully employed, mainly as farmers and farm laborers, although a few worked in the railroad, chemistry, and building industries. Less than 12% of the 1,219 women were gainfully employed, although girls were more likely than boys to attend school and 75% of them could read and speak English. The women's occupations were reflective of their place in the White world: 23 were servants, 6 were dressmakers, and 6 were teachers. Still 31 were listed as farmers and 8 as basket makers, reflecting how tenaciously the older women had maintained their traditional occupations (U.S. Department of Commerce, 1937).

According to the Census of 1910 (U.S. Department of Commerce, 1915), 85% of all Native American men 25 to 44 years of age were gainfully employed while over 80% of the Native American women of the same age were not. Of the 19.6% of Native American women who were gainfully employed, almost one-third were employed in traditional White women's work – as servants, laundresses, and teachers. More than two-thirds were employed in home industry – manufacturing baskets, pottery and textiles – or as farm laborers and farmers. These two-thirds, while engaged in occupations considered traditional for the Native American woman, were actually in new occupations geared to the market economy and reserved for working-class women of certain ethnic groups. Black, German-American, and Swedish-American women, along with Mexican-American and Japanese-American women, were still in the fields. Immigrant women still stitched in their tenement houses. A Cherokee woman in the fields of an Oklahoma farmer, a Navajo woman weaving outside her Arizona hogan, a Seneca woman cleaning the home of a White New Yorker – all were accepted in practice as working women but considered exceptions to the ideal that the Native American woman's place was now in the home.

The policy of the federal government, of missionaries, and of reformers to move the Native American woman from her traditional role as farmer into the accepted White woman's role as housewife and mother and to move the man from his traditional role of hunter and warrior into the accepted White man's role of farmer seemed to have been successful. Native American men had developed a functional relationship to the dominant White man's economy and Native American women had retreated to a dysfunctional relationship with the economy, that is, they expressed their productivity indirectly through the home and husband.

What Carl Sauer (1969) has called the "Neolithic agricultural revolution," the domestication of plants by women, was ending in North America approximately 5,000 years after the revolution of the plow began in Mesopotamia. Whether or not plow culture began as the German geographer Eduard Hahn suggested – with sacred oxen drawing the ceremonial cart and pulling the plow, a phallic symbol for the insemination of the receptive earth – the husbandman had taken over agricultural operations in many areas of the world and the women had retired to the house and to garden work. Male hierarchies prevailed where cattle, plowed fields, and wagons became dominant institutions. Wherever the plow was introduced, women lost their old relationship to the agricultural economy. The process in North American was now almost complete (Sauer, 1969).

In spite of the disappearance of their traditional economic function, Native American women continued to be active in tribal organizations and to display independence and strength in arranging their lives. In addition, they kept alive older traditions which conflicted with the new ideology of private property, profit, and subordination of women to men. Many reservation lands were lost and divided, but some tribes clung to their communal lands, refused to divide land into separate plots permanently, refused to give up their annuities, and continued to believe in the Native American culture as a better way of life than that which the White Americans had offered to them. The U.S. Commissioner of Indian Affairs (1910) reported that he was still trying to get rid of the Seneca annuities but the tribe had refused. They still held lands communally and their tribal organizations were strong. The Seneca tribe had maintained its control over the reservation and its internal government. They refused to recognize the White man's marriage laws. Marriage was often cohabitation and divorce separation at pleasure, complained one government official. Such conditions were "abhorrent to the finer sensibilities of civilized mankind," he told the U.S. Commissioner of Indian Affairs (Lurie, 1972; Randle, 1951; U.S. Commissioner of Indian Affairs, 1910, 1915).

Seneca mothers had not lost their reverence for the land. Though agriculture was now male and plow dominated and some Seneca men participated in the industrial, large-scale, technological, and profit-oriented agriculture, the older attitudes from the matrilineal subsistence agriculture survived. Their relation to the land had made the women strong and enabled them to keep alive the belief that the purpose of land is more than just to bring profits to those willing to exploit it.

REFERENCES

Allen, O. Personal recollections of Captains Jones and Parrish and the payment of Indian annuities in Buffalo. *Buffalo Historical Society Proceedings*, 1903, *6*, 539-542.

Brown, J. K. Economic organization and the position of women among the Iroquois. *Ethnohistory*, 1970, *17*, 151-167. (a)

Brown, J. K. A note on the division of labor by sex. *American Anthropologist*, 1970, *72*, 1073-1078. (b)

Carrier, L. *The beginnings of agriculture in America*. New York: McGraw-Hill, 1923.

Case of the Seneca Indians in the state of New York. Philadelphia: Merrihew & Thompson, 1840.

Casewell, H. S. *Our life among the Iroquois Indians*. Boston: Congregational Sunday School, 1892.

Constitution of the "government by chiefs" of the Seneca nation of Indians. Buffalo, N.Y.: Thomas & Lathrop, 1854.

Dearborn, H. A. S. Journals. *Buffalo Historical Society Proceedings*, 1904, *7*, 60-137.

Deardorff, M. H., & Snyderman, G. S. A nineteenth-century journal of a visit to the Indians of New York. *American Philosophical Society Proceedings*, 1956, *100*, 582-612.

Douglas, M. (Ed.). *Witchcraft: Confessions and accusations*. London: Tavistock, 1970.

Engels, F. *The origin of the family, private property and the state*. New York: International, 1972.

Fee, E. The sexual politics of Victorian social anthropology. In M. Hartman & L. W. Banner (Eds.), *Clio's consciousness raised: New perspectives on the history of women*. New York: Harper & Row, 1974.

Fenton, W. N. Toward the gradual civilization of the Indian natives: The missionary and linguistic work of Asher Wright (1803-1875) among the Senecas of western New York. *American Philosophical Society Proceedings*, 1965, *100*, 567-581.

Foreman, G. *Indian removal: The emigration of the five civilized tribes of Indians*. Norman, Okla.: University of Oklahoma Press, 1953.

Hampton Institute. *Ten years' work for Indians at the Hampton Normal and Agricultural Institute, 1879-1888*. 1888.

Harris, G. H. Life of Horatio Jones. *Buffalo Historical Society Publications*, 1903, *6*, 383-514.

Harris, T. S. Journals. *Buffalo Historical Society Proceedings*, 1903, *6*, 313-379.

Hawley, C. *Early chapters of Seneca history: Jesuit missions in Sonnontouan, 1656-1684.* Auburn, N.Y.: Cayuga County Historical Society Collections, 1884.

Hewitt, J. N. B. (Ed.). Seneca fiction, legends and myths. In U.S. Bureau of American Ethnology, *Annual Report 1910-1911*. Washington, D.C., 1918.

Holder, P. *The hoe and the horse on the plains: A study of cultural development among North American Indians.* Lincoln, Neb.: University of Nebraska Press, 1970.

Holmes, E. Letters from Fort Niagara in 1800. *Buffalo Historical Society Publications*, 1903, *6*, 187-204.

Houghton, F. The history of the Buffalo Creek reservation. *Buffalo Historical Society Publications*, 1920, *24*, 3-181.

Howland, H. P. The Seneca mission at Buffalo Creek. *Buffalo Historical Society Publications*, 1903, *6*, 125-160.

Hyde, J. B. Teacher among the Senecas. *Buffal Historical Society Proceedings*, 1903, *6*, 245-270.

Kelsey, R. W. *Friends and the Indians, 1655-1917.* Philadelpha: Friends on Indian Affairs, 1917.

Kramer, F. L. Eduard Hahn and the end of the "three stages of man." *Geographical Review*, 1967, *57*, 73-89.

Lafitau, J. F. *Moeures des sauvages Ameriquains.* 2 vols. Paris: Hochereau, 1724.

Lurie, N. O. Indian women: A legacy of freedom. In R. L. Iacopi (Ed.), *Look to the mountain top.* San Jose, Calif.: Gousha, 1972.

Malone, H. T. *Cherokees of the old south: A people in transition.* Athens, Ga.: University of Georgia Press, 1956.

Martin, M. K., & Voorhies, B. *Female of the species.* New York & London: Columbia University Press, 1975.

Morgan,, L. H. *Houses and house-life of the American aborigines.* Chicago & London: University of Chicago Press, 1965.

Morgan, L. H. *League of the Ho-De-No-Sau-Nee or Iroquois.* New York: Dodd, Mead, 1904.

Murphy, Y., & Murphy, R. F. *Women of the forest.* New York & London: Columbia University Press, 1974.

Parker, A. C. *Seneca myths and folk tales.* Buffalo, N. Y.: Buffalo Historical Society, 1923.

Parker, A. C. Analytical history of the Seneca Indians. *New York State Archeological Association Researches and Transactions*, 1926, *6*, 1-162.

Parker, A. C. Notes on the ancestry of Cornplanter. *New York State Archeological Association Researches and Transactions*, 1927, *7*, 4-22.

Parker, A. C. *Red Jacket: Last of the Seneca.* New York: McGraw-Hill, 1952.

Parker, A. C. The code of Handsome Lake, the Seneca prophet. In W. N. Fenton (Ed.), *Parker on the Iroquois.* Syracuse, N.Y.: Syracuse University Press, 1968. (a)

Parker, A. C. Iroquois uses of maize and other food plants. In W. N. Fenton (Ed.), *Parker on the Iroquois.* Syracuse, N.Y.: Syracuse University Press, 1968. (b)

Prucha, F. P. (Ed.). *Americanizing the American Indians: Writings by the "Friends of the Indian" 1880-1900.* Cambridge, Mass.: Harvard University Press, 1973.

Randle, M. C. Iroquois women, then and now. In W. N. Fenton (Ed.), *Symposium on local diversity in Iroquois culture* (Bureau of American Ethnology Bulletin No. 149). Washington, D.C., 1951.

Sacks, K. Engels revisited: Women, the organization of production, and private property. In M. Z. Rosaldo & L. Lamphere (Eds.), *Woman, culture and society.* Stanford, Calif.: Stanford University Press, 1974.

Sanday, P. R. Toward a theory of the status of women. *American Anthropologist*, 1973, *75*, 1682-1700.

Sanday, P. R. Female status in the public domain. In M. Z. Rosaldo & L. Lamphere (Eds.), *Woman, culture and society.* Stanford, Calif.: Stanford University Press, 1974.

Sauer, C. O. *Seeds, spades, hearths and herds: The domestication of animals and foodstuffs* (2nd ed.). Cambridge, Mass.: Massachusetts Institute of Technology, 1969.

Seaver, J. E. *Life of Mary Jemison: White woman of the Genesee.* Canandaigua, N.Y.: Beamis, 1824.
Smith, D. Witches and demonism of the modern Iroquois. *Journal of American Folk-Lore,* 1888, *1,* 184-193.
Stone, W. L. *The life and times of Red-Jacket, or Sa-Go-Ye-Wat-Ha.* New York & London: Wiley & Putnam, 1841.
Terrell, J., & Terrell, D. M. *Indian women of the western morning: Their life in early America.* New York: Dial, 1974.
Thomas Indian Schools. *Annual Report for 1906.* Albany, New York State, 1906.
Thomas Indian Schools. *Annual Report for 1910.* Albany, New York State, 1911.
Thomas Indian Schools. *Annual Report for 1913.* Albany, New York State, 1914.
Trennert, R. A. William Medill's war with the Indian traders, 1847. *Ohio History,* 1973, *82,* 46-62.
U.S. Commissioner of Indian Affairs. *Report 1910.* Washington, D.C., 1910.
U.S. Commissioner of Indian Affairs. *Senecas and other Indians.* Washington, D.C., 1915.
U.S. Congress, Joint Special Committee on the Conditions of the Indian Tribes. *Report.* Washington, D.C., 1867.
U.S. Department of Commerce, Bureau of the Census. *Indian population in the United States and Alaska, 1910.* Washington, D.C., 1915.
U.S. Department of Commerce, Bureau of the Census. *Indian population of the United States and Alaska.* Washington, D.C., 1937.
Visit of Gerard T. Hopkins. *Buffalo Historical Society Proceedings,* 1903, *6,* 217-222.
Wallace, A. *The death and rebirth of the Seneca.* New York: Knopf, 1970.
Washburn, W. *Red man's land/white man's law: A study of the past and present status of the American Indian.* New York: Scribner's, 1971.
White, E. E. *Experiences of a special agent.* Norman, Okla.: University of Oklahoma Press, 1965.
White, L. A. (Ed.). *Lewis Henry Morgan: The Indian journals, 1859-1862.* Ann Arbor, Mich.: University of Michigan Press, 1959.
Will, G. F., & Hyde, G. E. *Corn among the Indians of the upper Missouri.* Lincoln, Neb.: University of Nebraska Press, 1917.
Wilson, G. L. *Agriculture of the Hidatsa Indians: An Indian interpretation* (University of Minnesota Studies in the Social Sciences No. 9). Minneapolis: University of Minnesota, Press, 1917.

The Ideal Woman in the Antebellum South: Lady or Farmwife?

By D. HARLAND HAGLER

HISTORIANS OF THE ANTEBELLUM SOUTH HAVE DEPICTED THE southern woman largely in terms of the lady. Works dealing with the plantation tradition, nineteenth-century romanticism, and antebellum literature have placed a natural emphasis on the lady. Furthermore, there can be no doubt that the ideal of the southern lady exerted a strong emotional appeal to the minds of many people in both the antebellum and the postbellum South.[1]

To date, however, historians have failed to note that an important segment of antebellum society specifically rejected many aspects of the lady ideal and set forth a modified ideal which would be most accurately termed the "farmwoman" or "farmwife ideal." The editors and correspondents of the southern agricultural press all but unanimously espoused the farmwoman ideal. In its totality the farmwoman ideal modified most aspects of the lady ideal and launched a widespread attack on the presumed conduct of ladies.[2]

A degree of confusion arose when some advocates of the farmwife ideal attempted to appropriate the term "lady" for their own set of values. However, when advocates of the farmwoman

[1] See especially Francis P. Gaines, *The Southern Plantation: A Study in the Development and the Accuracy of a Tradition* (New York, 1925), 16, 173–81, *passim*; Rollin G. Osterweis, *Romanticism and Nationalism in the Old South* (New Haven and London, 1949), *passim*; William R. Taylor, *Cavalier and Yankee: The Old South and American National Character* (New York, 1961), 162–76, *passim*; Anne F. Scott, *The Southern Lady from Pedestal to Politics, 1830–1930* (Chicago and London, 1970), 4–79, *passim*.

[2] The following antebellum agricultural periodicals were used in the research for this essay: *Agriculturist*, 1840–1845 (Nashville, Tenn.); *American Cotton Planter*, 1853–1861 (Montgomery, Ala.), title varies; *American Farmer*, 1819–1861, 1866–1897 (Baltimore, Md., and Washington, D. C.), subtitle varies; *Farmer and Planter*, 1850–1861 (Pendleton and Columbia, S. C.); *Southern Agriculturist*, 1829–1846 (Charleston, S. C.), title varies; *Southern Cultivator*, 1843–1935 (Augusta, Athens, and Atlanta, Ga.), title varies; *Southern Planter*, 1841– (Richmond, Va.), title varies; *Valley Farmer*, 1848–1864 (Louisville, Ky., and St. Louis, Mo.), title varies.

MR. HAGLER is assistant professor of history at North Texas State University.

ideal used the term lady in a positive sense, they usually referred to decorum and good manners and to little else. For example, an item in the *Southern Cultivator* noted that "A celebrated writer says: 'No woman can be a lady who can wound or mortify another. No matter how beautiful, how refined, how cultivated she may be, she is in reality coarse, and the innate vulgarity of her nature manifests itself here. Uniformly kind, courteous and polite treatment of all persons, is one mark of [a] true woman.'"[3] A contributor to the *Farmer and Planter* elaborated on the same point:

> There is no farm-house where the daughters of a wise, pains-taking mother may not grow up lady-like and pleasing to the eye of the most refined. One, the child of very humble, hard-working parents, rises before me as I write—a fair, sweet vision. . . . She is . . . ignorant of all that boarding schools can teach . . . but she can wash and iron, make bread and butter, and cheese, cook a good farmer's dinner, and set the daintiest of little stitches in all kinds of plain sewing; and she has learned it all of that excellent, kind mother.[4]

Insofar as being a lady meant good manners, demureness, kindness, and gentleness the proponents of the farmwife ideal had no quarrel with the concept of the lady.

Furthermore, the lady and the farmwife ideals shared the belief that southern women should be sensible and practical and should strive to be perfect wives, devoted mothers, and impeccable homemakers. Moreover, both groups agreed that the ideal wife should be her husband's helpmeet and loyal partner through prosperity or adversity. Significant studies of the lives of antebellum southern women indicate that many ladies actually led lives that corresponded to both the lady and the farmwife ideals.[5] However, advocates of the farmwife ideal remained convinced that those women who aspired to be ladies would, as a result, become useless.

The cult of the lady, which emerged in the decade of the 1830s, provided special impetus for the agriculturists' attack. In addition to the ideals of wife, helpmeet, mother, and homemaker, the cult of the lady embodied concepts of fashion, leisure pastimes, and such ornamental attainments as playing the piano and speaking French. The correspondents of the southern agricultural press believed such cultural objectives incompatible with the more domestic accomplishments.[6] In a discussion of the proper education for girls, a

[3] *Southern Cultivator*, XVIII (November 1860), 360.

[4] "Farmers' Daughters," *Farmer and Planter*, XI (June 1860), 189.

[5] See especially Julia C. Spruill, *Women's Life and Work in the Southern Colonies* (Chapel Hill, 1938), *passim*; and Scott, *Southern Lady*, 4–44.

[6] For the development of the cult of the lady in nineteenth-century America see Barbara Welter, "The Cult of True Womanhood: 1820–1860," *American Quarterly*, XVIII (Sum-

letter to the *Farmer and Planter* maintained that "A young lady, with ever so fashionable an education *if she possessed no knowledge of the kitchen, and the different departments of house-keeping,* however well she might show off in the parlor or drawing room, would make a farmer a very unsuitable companion; she would not be worth as much as Lot's wife after she became saltified, because he could procure from her salt for his porridge."[7]

In particular, southern agriculturists inveighed against the education they believed most girls received at boarding schools. A letter in the *Farmer and Planter* put the matter succinctly:

> Many farmers will scrimp themselves to send their daughters to boarding schools to make ladies of them. These ladies return after a year or two, mostly full of genteel notions; they have learned to play the piano, knit edging, and work sky blue dogs in worsted. They have, as I said, become ladies; they not only will let their hard working mothers do all the house work and oversee the diary [*sic*], but they have such great ideas of their own worth they will hardly recognize their former associates because they are farmers and mechanics and work for a living; such occupations they despise, but they are greatly charmed with profes[s]ional men and such, who live by their wits.[8]

An item in the *Southern Cultivator* maintained that "It does not look well for farmers' daughters to be always talking about piano playing and the trillings of Signor Cantanini; while they do not know of what butter is made, and pretend to suppose a cow a rhinoceros."[9]

Advocates of the farmwife ideal added their voices to the widespread attack on novels in nineteenth-century America. They regarded novels, as well as piano playing, as major obstacles to the proper education of women. Moreover, they considered both novel reading and piano playing a waste of time better spent in various "useful" labors. In addition, the popular novels of the day frequently emphasized the cult of the fashionable lady to which southern agriculturists objected so strenuously. Thus, both the piano and the novel wasted valuable time, and novels also repre-

---

mer 1966), 151–74; and Gerda Lerner, "The Lady and the Mill Girl: Changes in the Status of Women in the Age of Jackson," *Midcontinent American Studies Journal,* X (Spring 1969), 5–15.

[7] "The Education of Farmer's Daughters," *Farmer and Planter,* I (August 1850), 94; here and in future citations the italics are in the original unless otherwise noted.

[8] "Agricultural Education," *ibid.,* VII (April 1856), 85; for similar points see also "Domestic Labor Honorable," *ibid.,* XI (July 1860), 218–19.

[9] "Eight Things That Do not Look Well," *Southern Cultivator,* I (November 22, 1843), 191–92; see also "Things That Have Been Seen," *ibid.* (October 11, 1843), 165; 'Monroe,' "Female Education," *Agriculturist,* IV (September 1843), 136–37.

sented an insidious source of false ideas.[10]

A frequent correspondent to southern agricultural periodicals wrote under the pseudonym "Lizzie Linn." She proclaimed "the rage for fashionable and showy accomplishments" to be "the root of the evil which exists in our present system of education . . . ." She then advocated abandoning boarding schools altogether. Lizzie Linn argued that "our schools of every kind, stand in great need of reformation, but even in the present imperfect state, the 'old field mixed school,' is far preferable to a fashionable boarding school. As far as is practical I believe in educating girls at home—*entirely at home* . . . ."[11] In the same vein, the *Farmer and Planter* warned young women that improper education and "*fashionable extravagance*" would frighten "young men away from all intention of matrimony."[12]

[10] 'Lucy,' "Advice to Farmers' Daughters," *Southern Cultivator*, I (December 20, 1843), 204; 'Lucy,' "To Farmers' Daughters," *ibid.*, II (November 27, 1844), 185; 'Shirley,' "The Modern Young Lady," *ibid.*, XVI (September 1858), 274–75; "Influence of Woman," *Farmer and Planter*, VIII (July 1857), 158.

[11] 'Lizzie Linn,' "The Proper Education of Children," *American Cotton Planter and the Soil of the South*, N.S., III (December 1859), 381; for similar attitudes on education of young women see Mrs. L. M. Child, "Hints About Female Education," *Valley Farmer*, V (October 1853), 374–75; "The Home School," *ibid.*, XII (July 1860), 223; "Home Education," *Farmer and Planter*, III (May 1852), 71–72. The sex of "Lizzie Linn" and the other pseudonymous correspondents of the agricultural press is not known. A few women wrote under their own names, thus indicating that women contributed to the agricultural press; for examples see "Report by Mrs. M. A. Lewis," *Southern Cultivator*, VI (January 1848), 16; Mollie Allin Mabry, "We Correspondents," *American Cotton Planter and the Soil of the South*, N.S., III (August 1859), 257; Bessie Ray, "The Country Girl's Response," *ibid.*, (September 1859), 290–91. Internal evidence indicates also that most, if not all, of those who used feminine pseudonyms were women. One editor published a letter from Lizzie Linn in which she requested a "Ladies' Department" and claimed to "represent my sex in general . . . ." The editor responded to Lizzie Linn's request by publishing her letter, along with a letter from "Pra[i]rie Girl," under a section headed "Ladies' Department." He prefaced the two letters with remarks in which he stated that now that he had created a "Ladies' Department," young ladies should "Write or select something valuable or interesting for every month. Stimulate your female friends to assist you in this department." For the above exchange see "Ladies' Department," *ibid.*, N.S., II (October 1858), 322–24. Other editors also urged women to contribute to the agricultural press and occasionally identified their pseudonymous correspondents as women. For examples see "Advice to Farmers' Daughters," *Southern Cultivator*, I (December 20, 1843), 204; and "Letter from Lucy," *Farmer and Planter*, VII (July 1857), 176. Men, writing under their own names and persons using masculine pseudonyms exhibited no reluctance to address women on "proper" female conduct. In short, the southern agricultural press does not appear to have adopted a practice whereby members of one sex wrote under pseudonyms of the opposite sex. However, if it is correct to conclude that most correspondents using feminine pseudonyms were women, it must be recalled that all the editors of the southern agricultural press were men. Only the *Valley Farmer* had a woman in charge of the "Ladies' Department": Mary Abbott, the wife of the editor. Thus, all material submitted by women underwent masculine scrutiny as a matter of editorial routine.

[12] "Young Woman's Part in Life," *Farmer and Planter*, IX (May 1858), 120; for similar attitudes toward the evils of fashion see "Sad News," *Agriculturist*, I (December 1840), 288; "A Wife," *American Farmer*, VIII (August 4, 1826), 157; "What Extravagance Is Doing

Though southern agriculturists maintained that the evils of mis-education and fashion infected both the country and the city, they tended to associate undesirable, ladylike qualities with the city. Lizzie Linn, writing for the *American Cotton Planter and the Soil of the South,* attacked "The pale devotees of fashion, who throng the watering places, and nightly dissipate in [a] . . . crowded ball-room, displaying on their cheeks *roses* which mysteriously vanish just before their heads press the pillow . . . ." Lizzie Linn then offered as a favorable contrast to the sickly, urban lady of fashion the "ruddy-cheeked, mirth-loving country lassie; young, buoyant, healthy, sensible, full of nature's graces."[13] The Jeffersonian view of the evils of urban life deeply influenced the rural view of the proper female role. The *Valley Farmer* proclaimed that "'God made the country—man made the town;' and we might add that God made the country girl, and that the devil made the city lady—or, rather, fashion did, which is just as bad."[14] Still another correspondent noted that he had advised a young man seeking a wife to "go away out in the country, and look for the daughter of some good farmer, who had taught his family that it is honorable to engage in all the useful employments in which the greater part of the duty of woman consists—one who could sit down happily at home, and study household good, without sighing for the excitement of fine dress, fashionable furniture, fashionable visits, and all those fashionable things that disturb the peace of young housekeepers . . . ."[15]

In its efforts to further the farmwoman ideal the *Southern Cultivator* published a poem entitled "She's Nothing but a Country Girl." The editorial comment preceding the poem stated that "A young lady, daughter of an agriculturist, after having been introduced to a company of *professed ladies* in a neighboring city, heard one of them remark to the others in a low tone, accompanied with a scornful smile, 'She's nothing but a country girl.'"[16] The poem then proceeded to contrast country and city girls attributing all desirable, natural qualities to country girls and rural living. Similar themes appeared in other journals, always contrasting the glories and virtues of being a country girl or a farmer's wife with the fash-

---

and What Economy Might Do," *American Cotton Planter and the Soil of the South,* N.S., I (April 1857), 110–11; "What a Man Wants His Wife to Know," *Southern Cultivator,* XV (April 1857), 118; "Young Ladies Should Be Natural," *Farmer and Planter,* VIII (February 1857), 47–48.

[13] 'Lizzie Linn,' "Hints to Country Girls," *American Cotton Planter and the Soil of the South,* N.S., II (November 1858), 352; for similar points see also Metta Victoria Fuller, "Country Girls," *Southern Cultivator,* XIV (September 1856), 270.

[14] "Farmers' Daughters," *Valley Farmer,* VI (April 1854), 155.

[15] 'Lucy,' "To Farmers' Daughters," *Southern Cultivator,* II (August 21, 1844), 133; see also "Country Girls—Errors in Dress, &c.," *ibid.,* XVI (November 1858), 331.

[16] "She's Nothing but a Country Girl," *ibid.,* III (September 1845), 144.

ionable, useless life of the urban lady.[17] If, however, the undesirable lady was associated in rural minds with the city, it is clear that they feared her influence would spread to the country and ruin good farmwomen.

In the debate over the proper character for southern womanhood, the advocates of the farmwoman and lady ideals shared some concepts and values. Each group considered marriage and motherhood the natural and desirable goals for all women; the home was the proper sphere of a woman's influence, and the woman should make the home an ideal habitation for her husband and children. Moreover, as an extension of her roles as wife and mother, it was permissible, indeed desirable, that a woman nurse the sick.[18] The advocates of the farmwife and lady ideals also agreed that women should know how to cook, sew, and garden.[19]

Occasionally, in these areas of fundamental agreement on the role of women, southern agriculturists made concessions to the lady ideal. A number of articles appeared in the agricultural journals concerning the management of servants. Still other articles stressed that the lady, or young girl, who would never have to do her own kitchen and household work, should have a firsthand knowledge of such matters in order to direct servants.[20]

Nevertheless, agriculturists accused the lady of not living up to standards of proper womanhood and motherhood. Supporters of the farmwife ideal charged that in order to lead her useless life of fashion the lady delegated the care and training of her children to nurses. An article in the *American Farmer* summed up the position

[17] "The Farmer's Wife," *Southern Planter*, XX (March 1860), 164; "'He's Nothing but a Farmer,'" *Valley Farmer*, VI (September 1854), 363; Nellie C. Fenn, "Only a Farmer's Wife; or, Gossip on a Rail Car," *ibid.*, XII (February 1860), 63-65.

[18] "Note," *Agriculturist*, IV (May 1843), 69; "The Farmer's Home," *American Cotton Planter*, III (April 1855), 107; "A Whisper to a Newly-Married Pair," *American Farmer*, VIII (April 14, 1826), 31; "Education of the Female Sex," *ibid.*, XI (April 17, 1829), 37; "Female Humanity," *ibid.*, XII (August 27, 1830), 190; "Letter from Lucy," *Farmer and Planter*, VIII (July 1857), 175-76; "The Wife at Home," *Southern Agriculturist*, XII (April 1839), 216-18; "Home Affections," *Southern Cultivator*, II (June 26, 1844), 104; "The Household of Sympathy," *ibid.*, XI (August 1853), 251; "Home and Women," *ibid.*, XVI (December 1858), 377; "Address of Dr. Thomson. To the Intelligent Farmers of the Present Day," *Southern Planter*, X (March 1850), 68-69; "Woman's Mission," *Valley Farmer*, V (March 1853), 112; 'Hettie Hayfield,' "Hints to Housewives," *ibid.*, X (February 1858), 65-67; Scott, *Southern Lady*, 23-44.

[19] Scott, *Southern Lady*, 31.

[20] For examples of farmwife concessions to the lady ideal see the following: "Education of Females," *American Farmer*, X (June 27, 1828), 117-18; 'Monroe,' "Female Education," *Agriculturist*, IV (September 1843), 136-37; "Duties of a Lady in Her Household," *Southern Cultivator*, XVII (August 1859), 233-34; W. W. Gilmer, "Management of Servants," *Southern Planter*, XII (April 1852), 106-107; 'Cecilia,' "Management of Servants," *ibid.*, III (August 1843), 175; 'Nancy,' "Housekeeping," *Farmer and Planter*, VIII (November 1857), 270-71; "The Science of the Kitchen," *Valley Farmer*, X (November 1860), 354.

of those who disparaged the lady: "And woe to the mother who is obliged to abandon her children during the greater part of the day to hirelings—no, not obliged; for there is no duty so imperious, no social convenience or fashionable custom so commanding as to oblige her to such shameful neglect: *for maternal care, let her remember, supersedes all other duties.*"[21] The *Southern Cultivator* published a tirade against the fashionable mother:

It is a sad truth that fashion-pampered women are almost worthless for all the great ends of human life. They have but little force of character; they have still less power of moral will, and quite as little physical energy. They live for no great purpose in life; they accomplish no worthy ends. They are only doll-forms in the hands of milliners and servants, to be dressed and fed to order. They dress nobody, bless nobody, and save nobody. They write no books and set no examples of virtue and womanly life. If they rear children, servants and nurses do all, save to conceive and give them birth. And when reared, what are they? What do they amount to, but weaker scions of the stock? Who ever heard of a fashionable woman's child exhibiting any virtue or power of mind, for which it became eminent? Read the biographies of our great and good men and women. Not one of them had a fashionable mother. They nearly all sprang from strong minded women, who had about as little to do with fashion, as with the changing clouds.[22]

In the areas of homemaking and housekeeping the farmwife advocates considered no sphere more important than the kitchen. Southern women were expected to be good cooks themselves, not merely to hire or own one. Both the *American Cotton Planter* and the *Farmer and Planter* carried identical articles maintaining that "None of our excellent girls are fit to be married until they are thoroughly educated in the deep and profound mysteries of the kitchen."[23] The deep and profound mysteries of the kitchen encompassed much more than preparing tasty meals; they also included the canning and preservation of foods, the butchering and curing of meat, and the making of butter and cheese. The farmwife should achieve expertise in all these activities.[24]

While the advocates of the lady and farmwife shared the belief

[21] "A Whisper to a Newly-Married Pair," *American Farmer*, VIII (April 21, 1826), 37; for similar attitudes see "The Home Mother," *Farmer and Planter*, V (May 1854), 105–106; "Black Nurses for Children," *Valley Farmer*, V (October 1853), 372–73.

[22] "Fashionable Women," *Southern Cultivator*, XVII (August 1859), 252.

[23] "The Kitchen," *American Cotton Planter*, IV (August 1856), 240; "The Kitchen," *Farmer and Planter*, XI (November 1860), 335; for similar attitudes see also "Girls Should Learn to Keep House," *ibid.*, VII (February 1856), 44–45.

[24] "Learn to Cook Well," *Farmer and Planter*, VI (January 1855), 15; "Curing Bacon," *ibid.*, VII (October 1856), 217–18; "Southern Cheese," *ibid.*, 215–16; "What a Man Wants His Wife to Know," *ibid.*, VIII (July 1857), 167; "Pickles," *Southern Planter*, VII (November 1847), 339; "Churning," *ibid.*, X (December 1850), 364–65; "Butter," *ibid.*, XV (April 1855), 116; 'Hettie Hayfield,' "Hints to Housekeepers," *ibid.*, XVII (March 1857), 155–57.

that sewing represented a significant aspect of womanhood, southern agriculturists attacked the lady's contributions. They denigrated her meager output and the decorative pieces she scattered about her home. Supporters of the farmwife ideal emphatically distinguished between what they considered ornamental sewing on the one hand and the practical sewing, carding, weaving, and spinning that they advocated on the other.[25]

The southern agricultural press unanimously recommended gardening to everyone. It by no means opposed ornamental gardening, but it stressed that utility and beauty could be combined. More to the point, gardening was considered the special province of women. The ideal farmwife would thus contribute to the family larder, and perhaps cash receipts as well, from her flourishing garden.[26]

As previously noted, the lady as well as the farmwife was expected to be a wife, mother, homemaker, cook, seamstress, and gardener. Nevertheless, advocates of the farmwife ideal feared that it was precisely these qualities that the lady ideal would stifle. Moreover, proponents of the farmwife concept espoused a work ethic that they believed to be incompatible with the habits of the fashionable lady. An article in the *Farmer and Planter* maintained that "Industry and toil make all the difference between the useless and the useful. Did the world consist of ladies, we should be starved, famished and poisoned; or did it contain none but gentlemen unfit for manual labor, we must all perish for want of the common necessaries of life."[27]

Advocates of the farmwife ideal attacked the custom of making fashionable social calls. One correspondent ridiculed the idle who levied "a very heavy tax upon the industrious, when by frivilous

[25] "The 'Fine Art' of Patching," *American Cotton Planter*, III (October 1855), 303; "The Music of the Wheels," *Southern Cultivator*, XVII (December 1859), 359; Ellie Watson, "The Sewing Machine," *Southern Planter*, XVIII (November 1858), 700; "'Can She Spin?'," *Farmer and Planter*, III (February 1852), 21; "Sewing in Visiting Hours," *ibid.*, VII (September 1856), 209-10; "Women and Machinery," *Valley Farmer*, X (July 1858), 223.

[26] "Work for January," *American Cotton Planter*, III (January 1855), 19-20; "How to Popularize a Taste for Planting," *American Cotton Planter and the Soil of the South*, N.S., I (September 1857), 274; "The Fall Garden" *ibid.*, N.S., II (August 1858), 250; "The Homestead and the Garden," *American Farmer*, III (February 1848), 259; "The Value of a Garden," *Farmer and Planter*, VI (September 1855), 195; "Profits of Fruit," *ibid.*, II (July 1851), 92-93; "Cultivation of Flowers," *Southern Agriculturist*, X (April 1837), 188-89; L, "The Season at the North—Preserving Fruit Fresh, &c.," *Southern Cultivator*, XVI (July 1858), 217; "A Word About Gardening," *Southern Planter*, X (September 1850), 262; "Woman in the Garden," *ibid.*, XIX (September 1859), 580; 'Hettie Hayfield,' "Hints to Housewives," *Valley Farmer*, X (March 1858), 97-98.

[27] "The Pleasures and Advantages of Labor," *Farmer and Planter*, III (April 1852), 60; for similar attitudes see "True Female Nobility," *Southern Cultivator*, I (April 12, 1843), 48; "The History of the Thrifty and Unthrifty," *ibid.*, III (November 1845), 163-64.

[*sic*] visitations they rob them of their time."[28] When accused of being a lady of leisure, the prolific Lizzie Linn protested indignantly: "I do assure you, my young friends, that Lizzie Linn is not an *elegant lady of leisure*. It is all work, work, with her, from morning till night . . . ."[29] An article in the *American Farmer* emphasized the work ethic to the point of arguing that women were "more happily circumstanced" than men because "the important and fatiguing advocations of men necessarily impose seasons of inactivity . . . ." Women, on the other hand, need never cease their labors; while visiting or "resting" they could do their practical sewing.[30] The *American Cotton Planter* advised parents that if they "would render their children happy and wealthy, they should early inculcate in them a desire for and a knowledge of labor, both manual and mental."[31] The *American Farmer* singled out Mrs. Freelove Drury of Florida as an example to be emulated because of her productiveness in the carding and spinning of linen and wool and her sewing accomplishments in general.[32] Clearly the work ethic applied to both sexes.

In addition to their general espousal of the work ethic, the advocates of the farmwife ideal filled the columns of the agricultural press with editorials, letters from subscribers, and general articles urging women to pursue various types of labor and giving detailed instructions for their pursuit. The labors designated as "women's work" covered a wide range, and numerous articles offered practical instructions on bedmaking, laundering, soapmaking, and butchering.[33]

[28] "Idle Visits," *American Cotton Planter and the Soil of the South*, N.S., I (February 1857), 57.

[29] "Lizzie Linn to the Young Folks," *ibid.*, N.S., III (August 1859), 255; for an additional attack on fashionable calls see "A Note from 'Mattie,'" *Farmer and Planter*, VIII (January 1857), 23.

[30] "Female Employments and Duties," *American Farmer*, IX (July 27, 1827), 150.

[31] *American Cotton Planter*, III (July 1855), 208.

[32] "Female Industry," *American Farmer*, IX (August 3, 1827), 157; for additional examples of items praising women for work see "Women of Ancient Days," *Agriculturist*, II (January 1841), 6; "Female Education," *Farmer and Planter*, II (August 1851), 98; "Labor," *Southern Cultivator*, I (July 19, 1843), 120; "Merrimack Agricultural Society. Report on Butter," *Southern Planter*, VIII (March 1848), 91–92; "English Women—Their Good Sense and Practicality," *ibid.*, XX (September 1860), 534–35; "The Peasant and His Wife," *American Farmer*, I (August 13, 1819), 160.

[33] "Ladies' Department," *American Farmer*, VIII (June 16, 1826), 99–100; "Valuable Suggestion," *ibid.*, IX (November 30, 1827), 295; "A Letter from Lucy," *Farmer and Planter*, VII (August 1856), 187–88; "A Short Chapter on Bed Making," *ibid.*, VIII (March 1857), 70; "Soap Making—Information Wanted," *Southern Cultivator*, XIV (January 1856), 19; "House Cleaning," *Southern Planter*, X (May 1850), 158; "To Make Good Starch for Bosoms and Collars," *ibid.*, XIV (May 1854), 140–41; "Labor Saving Soap," *ibid.*, XV (July 1855), 221; "The Housewife," *ibid.*, XVII (February 1857), 120; 'Hettie Hayfield,' "The Laundry," *ibid.*, XVII (November 1857), 701–704.

They considered the dairy, in particular, to be the special province of women and children. Proponents of having women work in the dairy argued that not only would it be good for the health of the family, but the dairy could become a source of profit and cash supplement to the family income. Thus, farmwomen could contribute directly to the family income rather than living on their husbands' incomes, as agriculturists believed the cult of the lady to encourage.[34]

Advocates of the farmwife ideal also regarded the raising and care of poultry as the woman's sphere.[35] The *American Farmer* expanded the list to include not only the dairy and poultry as woman's work but also the care of pigs, sheep, and calves.[36] As in the case of gardening, the woman's labors in the dairy and the poultry yard were expected to add food to the family table and additional money to the family income.

In their eagerness to find work for women, southern writers sometimes went outside the realm of agriculture. An article in the *American Farmer* advocated the establishment of manufacturing in the Southeast in order to stop westward migration. The article specifically pointed out that factories would provide employment for women, children, and infirm and aged men.[37] Still another article recommended that women and children be employed in the making of shoes and suggested that thousands of women "might be profitably and honorably employed in light mechanical occupations, whose services are not required in any vocation usually followed by women, and who have neither natural gifts [n]or pecuniary means to fit them for a profession."[38] However honorable work in a factory, the making of shoes, or other "light mechanical occupations" might be, they were the antithesis of occupations suitable for a lady.

[34] "Secret for a Farmer's Wife," *American Cotton Planter*, I (December 1853), 368; "Letter To A Dairy-Woman," *American Farmer*, XIV (December 1858), 193–94; "Eight Things That Do not Look Well," *Southern Agriculturist*, III (September 1843), 357; "A Wife Worth Having," *Southern Cultivator*, II (February 7, 1844), 21; "A Secret for a Farmer's Wife," *ibid.*, XI (December 1853), 374; "Teaching Boys and Girls to Milk," *Southern Planter*, X (July 1850), 205; "A Fair and Happy Milkmaid," *ibid.*, XIX (January 1859), 48.

[35] "Look to the 'Ladie's [*sic*] Department,'" *Farmer and Planter*, VIII (September 1857), 219; "The Death of My Good Old Hen," *ibid.*, IX (June 1858), 136; "Plan for a Beautiful Hen House," *ibid.*, IX (January 1858), 9–10; *Southern Cultivator*, XI (June 1853), 177; "A Tender Lay," *ibid.*, XVII (January 1859), 15; "Swinging Roost for Fowls," *Southern Planter*, XIV (March 1854), 87–88; Lydia Jane Peirson, "Chickens," *ibid.* (May 1854), 143–44; N. F. S. of Prince Edward, "Gapes in Chickens," *ibid.*, XVI (September 1856), 274; 'Agriculturist,' "Spring Chickens," *ibid.*, XVIII (May 1858), 269–70.

[36] 'Cogitativus,' "Domestic Industry," *American Farmer*, I (November 12, 1819), 264.

[37] 'Opifici Amicus,' "Domestic Manufactures," *ibid.* (June 11, 1819), 85–86.

[38] "Employment for Women," *Valley Farmer*, VI (March 1854). 122–23.

Agricultural editors and their correspondents never tired of suggesting ways in which women and children could contribute to the family income. A correspondent to the *American Cotton Planter* noted enthusiastically:

We know a country woman of ours, a farmer's wife, who takes care of her own domestic matters, with five children to manage too, who has, during the last season, sold above $200 worth of baskets, manufactured during her leisure hours, out of the common swamp willow. Her eldest daughter, (11 years old,) has made over $25 worth, being her first effort. Ten years ago, this ingenious women [*sic*], upon examining a willow basket, conceived the idea that she could make one. . . . The aggregate of the ten years exceeds $1000. All this too, has been done without neglecting household duties, and with no assistance save the cutting of the willows by her husband in the spring.[39]

This woman was indeed a paragon of the farmwife ideal.

A few supporters of the farmwife ideal even praised women for entering aspects of agriculture beyond the confines of the garden, dairy, and poultry yard. The *Agriculturist* claimed that a woman had discovered the cause of wheat disease and held her up as an example to be emulated.[40] The *Southern Planter* advocated that women enter the commercial aspects of agriculture by marketing pickles and other produce from their gardens.[41] The *Southern Cultivator* praised a woman in Texas, "the wife of a thrifty farmer," for earning $60 from her sage crop.[42]

Under the proud title, "A Daughter of South Carolina," the *Southern Cultivator* published the following article. "Miss Peggy Land, a young woman of Pickens District, about twenty-four years of age, after trying weaving, carding, spinning and sewing, last year went to farming, and made cotton which netted her $100. Her corn crop was two hundred and fifty bushels, worth sixty cents per bushel, and she made thirty-five bushels of wheat, worth one dollar and fifty cents a bushel. She accomplished this herself, without any assistance or hiring. She plowed, drove the cart, cut her wheat and cribbed her corn, &c."[43] The *Southern Agriculturist* drove home

[39] "Productive Industry," *American Cotton Planter*, I (December 1853), 379; for additional articles on related topics see 'A Friend to Females,' "Manufacture of Straw," *Southern Planter*, VIII (June 1848), 183–84; 'Broomsedge,' "Why and Because," *Farmer and Planter*, III (June 1852), 92; *ibid.*, XI (June 1860), 180.

[40] "The Hessian," *Agriculturist*, II (March 1841), 69.

[41] 'E. G. Eggling,' "Put up Pickles for Market," *Southern Planter*, XVII (July 1857), 442–44.

[42] "Texas Economy in Domestic Life," *Southern Cultivator*, XI (January 1853), 10.

[43] "A Daughter of South Carolina," *ibid.*, XIV (May 1856), 140; for praise of a woman agriculturist in a managerial capacity see "A Female Agriculturist," *Southern Agriculturist*, IX (October 1836), 558.

the same lessons when, under the title "Beat this who can," it reported that a young girl "not ten years of age, lately planted two acres of land with potatoes in one day. What a wife for a farmer!"[44]

The announcements of impending agricultural fairs and the subsequent reports on exhibits at the fairs make it clear that the achievements of the farmwife were not to be hidden from public gaze; rather, they were to be celebrated, lauded, and emulated. The agricultural press urged southern women to exhibit such items as homespun, bed quilts, domestic carpeting, preserves, and cured hams, and they lauded them when they did so.[45] One item even suggested that fairs give premiums to women for the best specimens of darning and patching.[46]

No attempt is made here to argue that the concept of the lady lacked importance in the antebellum South; the agricultural press itself reveals the importance of the lady ideal. Not only did a number of articles make concessions to the lady, but the intensity of the preoccupation of the agricultural press with the concept of the lady is in itself evidence of the lady's significance. Nevertheless, an important segment of southern society vigorously opposed aspects of the cult of the lady and offered the modified ideal of the farmwife. The *American Farmer* summarized the farmwife ideal in its totality when it described her as "a woman in all the noble attributes which should dignify that name; a wife, a mother, a housekeeper, a farmer, a gardener, a dairy woman, a kind neighbor, a benefactor to the poor, a Christian woman, 'full of good works, and almsdeeds which she did.'"[47] Supporters of the lady ideal concurred in all these "noble attributes"; however, proponents of the farmwife ideal believed the lady ideal included elements inimical to the farmwife ideal as well as to the shared values of the two ideals.

The farmwife ideal of the nineteenth century harked back to a much older tradition. Women in colonial America and in seventeenth-century England had worked the fields, cared for the poultry, and been solely responsible for the dairy, as well as engaging in numerous crafts. Furthermore, this older tradition had

[44] "Beat this who can," *Southern Agriculturist*, IX (September 1836), 502; for additional praise of women in agriculture see "Note," *Agriculturist*, II (September 1841), 203; "Ladies in Agriculture," *Farmer and Planter*, XI (March 1860), 92.

[45] 'Broomsedge,' "Southern Central Agricultural Society," *Farmer and Planter*, VI (January 1855), 16–17; "Agricultural Fairs, &c." *Southern Cultivator*, V (July 1847), 111–12; "Annual Fair at Stone Mountain," *ibid.*, VI (July 1848), 104; "The Atlanta Fair!" *ibid.*, XIV (October 1856), 312; Philip St. George Cocke, "Virginia State Agricultural Society," *Southern Planter*, XIII (June 1853), 178–79; W. C. Rives and B. J. Barbour, "Virginia State Agricultural Society," *ibid.*, XV (December 1855), 363–64.

[46] "New Premiums—A Good Idea," *Valley Farmer*, V (April 1853), 137–38.

[47] "Pencil Sketches," *American Farmer*, I (July 1845), 26.

viewed the wife as a full, though not equal, partner in her husband's enterprises. She was expected to be his helpmeet while he lived and to carry on his business affairs if he preceded her in death.[48] In short, the farmwife ideal of southern agriculturists represented an earlier historical reality.

As a matter of fact, the farmwife ideal approximated the realities of life for thousands of contemporary southern women as well. Not only did the majority of southern women, who belonged to the white yeoman class, labor in the variety of tasks and occupations recommended by southern agriculturists, but many women in the planter class did so as well. Indeed, one scholar has suggested that southern women engaged in such work as dairying to a greater extent than did their northern counterparts.[49]

Thus, nineteenth-century advocates of the farmwife ideal urged the retention of, and where erosion had occurred the return to, an older ideal of woman. The often strident tones of the farmwife advocates apparently represented a fear of change, a change they believed imminent or already under way. The new, fearful element of change in the lives of mid-nineteenth-century American women was the cult of the lady; a cult which, according to its detractors, raised idleness and uselessness to the height of fashion and made women merely ornamental.[50]

Though the farmwife ideal received widespread support in the antebellum South, it does not appear to have been unique to that region. Not only was this ideal rooted in earlier English and colonial American ideals of womanhood, but many contemporary northerners advocated essentially the same role for women. Much additional research will be necessary to determine the extent and details of the farmwife ideal in the North. However, both internal evidence, such as reprints from and references to northern articles and periodicals in the southern agricultural press, and various secondary studies make it clear that the farmwife ideal had widespread advocacy in the North.[51] For some time now historians have noted

[48] Spruill, *Women's Life and Work in the Southern Colonies*, 13-14, 80-84; Alice Clark, *Working Life of Women in the Seventeenth Century* (New York, 1920), 40-92, 145-57, 234-35, 290-308, and *passim*.

[49] David E. Schob, *Hired Hands and Plowboys: Farm Labor in the Midwest, 1815-60* (Chicago, 1975), 199.

[50] For a discussion of the development of the cult of the lady see Lerner, "The Lady and the Mill Girl," 11-12; for an earlier parallel development in England see Clark, *Working Life of Women in the Seventeenth Century*, 41, 92.

[51] Schob, *Hired Hands and Plowboys*, 191-208; see also Rex Burns, *Success in America: The Yeoman Dream and the Industrial Revolution* (Amherst, 1976), 19-20; Howard S.

the popularity of the yeoman ideal in the North; it is only to be expected that the proper spouse for a sturdy yeoman would be a true farmwife.[52] Furthermore, in her study of New England women, Nancy F. Cott's description of the realities of life for eighteenth-century rural women is all but identical with the southern farmwife ideal.[53]

In the South the agricultural press served as the chief vehicle for elaborating and expressing the farmwife ideal. Not merely the editors, but their correspondents and contributors, male and female, expressed general agreement with the concept of the farmwife. Scholarly works on the southern woman have shown that the realities of life for many southern ladies approximated the farmwife ideal; moreover, the lady and the farmwife ideals advocated markedly similar codes of conduct. Nonetheless, the agricultural press of the antebellum South repeatedly attacked the conduct of ladies, and contended that the lady ideal itself contained elements inimical to proper, farmwife conduct.

Russell, *A Long Deep Furrow: Three Centuries of Farming in New England* (Hanover, N. H., 1976), 202, 288-89, 314-16; Daniel T. Rodgers, *The Work Ethic in Industrial America, 1850-1920* (Chicago and London, 1978), 182-209. For a contemporary northern work expressing many aspects of the farmwife ideal see Catharine E. Beecher, *A Treatise on Domestic Economy . . .* (Boston, 1841), *passim*.

[52] For discussions of the yeoman ideal in the North see Henry N. Smith, *Virgin Land: The American West As Symbol and Myth* (New York, 1950), *passim*; and Burns, *Success in America*, 17-87.

[53] Cott, *The Bonds of Womanhood: 'Woman's Sphere' in New England, 1780-1835* (New Haven and London, 1977), 21-22, 40-42.

The Role and Status of the Female Yeomanry in the Antebellum South: *The Literary View*

KEITH L. BRYANT, JR.

No group of antebellum Southerners has received so little attention from historians as middle class white women. The female descendants of those ninety "virtuous maidens" who arrived at Jamestown in 1619 have been ignored not because of their limited number or their lack of importance.[1] Even the House of Burgesses upon the arrival of these women noted that "in a new plantation it is not knowen [sic] whether man or woman be the most necessary."[2] Generally, social and literary historians have justified omitting the female yeomanry from major studies with the argument that little source material existed for such an endeavor.[3] Yet, by the end of the Civil War, the women in the largest white class in the South obviously represented a significant segment of the society. Indeed the female yeoman seems to have played a major role and held high status in her family—that is, as Ellen Glasgow so eloquently writes, among the "good people":

> . . . 'good people,' a comprehensive term which implies, to Virginians, the exact opposite of the phrase, 'a good family.' The good families of the state have preserved among other things, custom, history, tradition, romantic fiction, and the Episcopal Church. The good people, according to the records of clergymen, which are the only surviving records, have preserved nothing except themselves. Ignored alike by history and fiction, they have the inconspicuous place in the social strata midway between the lower gentility and the upper class of 'poor white,' a position which encourages the useful rather than the ornamental public virtues.[4]

The little attention directed toward the "good people," or as Frank Owsley and his students referred to them, the "Plain Folk," has been concentrated on their place in Southern society vis-a-vis the planter class.[5] Antebellum observers, however, noted the similarity in cultures of the Northern and Southern yeomanry in terms of traditions, religion, and political involvement.[6] This point has been repeated by many historians, yet the Southern female yeomanry still has not received the study it deserves.[7]

For too long historians remained deluded by the observations of Frederick Law Olmsted and other abolitionists and the mythology of a two-class South of planters and poor whites.[8] The works of Paul Buck and Shields McIllwaine, and most twentieth-century Southern fiction, reinforced the stereotype of a poor, dirty, depraved, disease-ridden "slum element" counterbalanced by the planters and their slaves.[9] The books, articles and monographs by Owsley and his students restored the yeomanry to its rightful place, but only as a "folk society." They did not explore in depth internal family relationships or the status and roles of family members.

Owsley emphasized the integrity and independence of the yeomanry and its devotion to the land as the richest of God's blessings. He noted the upward mobility of the yeomen, their complex social patterns, and the origins in the British Isles which produced their speech patterns, manners and customs.[10] His employment of technologically crude quantification methods led to conclusions not far removed from those to be found in antebellum literary accounts such as *The Old Pine Farm*.[11] Indeed, in a more recent and splendidly conceived study of the yeomanry, Clement Eaton utilizes the tales of the Southern humorists to reconstruct the middle class white culture.[12] Like Owsley, Eaton described a gregarious, vital, optimistic folk imbued with a sense of equality and democracy. But when Eaton quotes the humorists, such as W. T. Thompson, the references are virtually all masculine.[13]

The evidence concerning the role and status of middle class white women found in most plantation romances and in antebellum essays on political economy is no more substantial. As William R. Taylor has noted, the romances often featured matriarchally dominated planter families, but virtually excluded the middle class from consideration.[14] One of the leading essayists, Thomas R. Dew, proclaimed that women were suitable only for "domestic occupation and sedentary employments." Women were, Dew wrote, passive, dependent and weak, and sought seclusion and meditation.[15] George Fitzhugh echoed this view, noting that "woman naturally shrinks from public gaze."[16] These writers reflected in a coolly detached manner the male chauvinism of Southern society. At a cruder level, an elderly man in

1848 gave this advice to a young yeoman on the selection of a suitable bride:

> "Now young gentlemen," said he, "I will give you some directions how to tell a good wife,—a good wife will be like three things and she will not be like them. She will be like the snail, who stays at home; and will not be like the snail who carries all he has on his back. She will be like the echo, that speaks when spoken to; and she will not be like the echo, always to have the 'last word.' She will be like the town clock, that speaks at the right time; and she will not be like the town clock, heard all over town."[17]

The desirable characteristics of females—as defined by males—differed by class. While planters believed that women were excitable, enthusiastic, capricious and virtuous, though weak of muscle, the frontier maiden or female yeoman should be strong, daring, self-reliant, skillful, industrious and educated in nursing, "book learning," and the agricultural sciences.[18] But, defining the traits that were valued does not reveal the status of women or their roles in the family or in the society at large.

In order to understand the structure of the white middle class in the antebellum South, one must examine the economic status of women and their role in childrearing and family decision making. It is important to view the reality of women's roles rather than society's concept of the "proper place." The result will be a fuller history of the Southern civilization before the Civil War.[19] As Gerda Lerner has noted, however, in the period from 1800 to 1860 it is very difficult to establish even descriptive facts about middle class women. The most successful efforts to define the place of women in pre-Civil War America concentrate on the literate upper-middle or upper class residents of the Northern states.[20] While ground-breaking, these studies ignore the rural, middle class female both in the North and the South.

This essay attempts to define the role and status of the Southern female yeomanry largely through literary sources. I have utilized other materials—memoirs and travel accounts—but most of my sources are novels, short stories, essays, and humorous tales. These are similar to the sources used so effectively by Eaton in his study of the yeoman.[21] This rich body of material is not a substitute for systematically accumulated knowledge, but it adds another dimension to the total view of the society.[22] Virtually all of my literary sources were written in the period from 1820 to 1860 by Southern authors. Many of the writers sought to accurately portray all social classes, while others mention the yeoman only in passing, and often in condescending, or even bitter, language.[23] Together with traditional sources, literary works can provide insight into the status and role of the female yeomanry.

Existing studies of antebellum middle class American women often echo the observations of Tocqueville. Where that sensitive traveler recognized the influence of women in shaping the mores of the society, he contended that marriage terminated the freedom of the woman-child in the United States. The confident, reasoning young maiden traded the freedom of her father's home for the cloister of her husband. Energetic and courageous, the mother and wife submitted herself to her husband.[24] A recent sociological study supports the view that some freedoms were sacrificed by marriage, and that families tended to be patriarchal, although women exercised authority in the home in the area of child-rearing and on moral issues. That marriage was generally based on romantic love seems well documented.[25] A similar study using content analysis of popular magazines stresses the internal changes taking place in the American family between 1794 and 1850. Indeed, one of the major inducements for marriage and mate selection appears to have been upward mobility and higher status. While noting a marked increase in the authority of women in the family, these studies do not detail alterations in status, nor analyze role changes other than in relation to progeny.[26]

A study of antebellum Southern literature, travel accounts, memoirs, essays and magazines suggests that the conclusions of the sociologists that a redefinition of status and role was taking place may be too hesitant. The rural, actually frontier, middle class female yeoman participated in an evolutionary process of defining her place in the family. Clearly the scarcity of females in the frontier South encouraged this evolution as early as the colonial period.[27] But more than scarcity or population imbalance is required to explain the alterations of the female position. While women selected mates for reasons of romantic love, social mobility or upward status, marriage and sex roles generally changed in an atmosphere of competition. On the frontier the attitude of competition became one of cooperation as women participated virtually on an equal basis in all phases of agricultural labor. More importantly, on the subsistence farms of the yeomanry, the females often produced the only cash crops. A fellowship based on work emerged as labor specialization declined. Women gained confidence in their abilities and often initiated new economic activities.[28] As widows, their economic independence often led to enhanced fortunes.

The confidence gained within the economic sector of family life provided the basis for self-assertiveness in the educational and moral realms. Females became the teachers within the schoolless rural South, and as such the sources of parental authority. Similarly, the female yeomanry served as the moral arbiters in the family and community even if they did not serve as church officers. By the time of the Civil War, the female yeomanry occupied a significant place in the social structure of the "plain folk."

In the economic life of the family unit, the female yeomanry played a major role. While it has been argued that rural middle class females and the "hired girls" in the North only rarely worked in the fields, this was not the case in the South.[29] Examples can be found of female yeomen who were financially ambitious and who made the significant economic decisions in their middle class families.

In 1862, early in the Civil War, *The Countryman* of Putnam County, Georgia, noted that women of the rural South had always been resourceful, but now they sought economic independence.[30] The demands of the war years caused more white women to enter the fields to do hand labor, but the female yeomanry had been performing such labor for over two hundred years. From colonial Maryland and Virginia to the frontier outposts of Missouri before the Compromise of 1820, women joined husbands, sons and brothers in the fields where they wielded hoes and scythes and plowed straight furrows.[31] Throughout the period from 1800 to 1860, farm women joined men in planting crops, weeding, and harvesting. They cut the brush on new lands and helped fell trees for the fences. In the tobacco areas they helped worm and cure the crop. One of the most widely circulated magazines for Southern women lauded these endeavors and quoted an English journal to demonstrate that one could "warm the heart" of the most hardened bachelor through such labor.[32]

The products of the field and garden were transformed by the women into food, clothes and other items which enhanced the family's standard of living. They created at home what planters and others bought at the country stores. Thread, cloth and clothes came from their spinning wheels and looms, and they also produced soap, candles, and starch.[33] The farm wife often traded her thread and cloth to males living in the area in exchange for help in plowing and harvesting, but some of her output was for the family. She used butternut, black walnut hulls, indigo and copperas to dye her production before the cutting and sewing began.[34] As one observer noted, "When I see a farmer appear in company genteely dressed in homespun, I think of Solomon's description of a good wife . . . if the farmer's family wants new clothes, the industry of his wife supplies them."[35]

By the 1840s, the indirect economic benefits of the labor and production of the female yeomanry were becoming obvious to the society. There was a sense of pride in these accomplishments, and there was also legal recognition. In describing a Georgia farm family in her novel *The Planter's Northern Bride*, Caroline Lee Hentz has the farmer brag about his wife's economic activities and the fact that she was literate. But more than this, some farmers legally recognized the contributions in their wills by granting all or the bulk of their estates to the widow who had been "an equal partner." Even Olmsted admitted that some of the farm women were more industrious and ambitious than the men.[36]

Indeed, some evidence suggests that the females provided the bulk of the cash income of the Southern yeomanry. Most middle class farmers produced food and fiber for domestic consumption or for bartering. Numerous references are to be found describing the sale of fabrics produced by the female yeomanry to country stores. William Gilmore Simms describes Rachel Bostwick and her daughter Dory in *Woodcraft* as spinners and weavers who earned enough cash to purchase a farm. Some hill country female "plain folk" traveled together to market centers to sell their thread, cloth and other products. The Ramsay family of Mississippi received its cash earnings from the sale of the wife's cloth for $2.50 a yard at the Mobile market. Similar references can be found for families in Virginia and Alabama.[37]

Some of the female yeomanry openly expressed their economic

ambitions. "Eliza," in a letter to the *Republican Banner* of Nashville, Tennessee, urged Southern women to make silk to bring prosperity to their families. Simms disliked the audacious female, but in *As Good as Comedy* admitted that some were quite financially secure. Olmsted describes a Blue Ridge farm family in which the wife wants to move to Texas because a female friend who had gone there was "making good money."[38] W. H. Sparks recalls his Georgian mother who forced her husband to help her regain her rightful inheritance. "He [the father] did as she bid him," wrote Sparks, "everybody about the house did that."[39]

The economic independence, or at least the financial ambitions, of the female yeomanry suggests a family structure which was not patriarchal. If everyone did as Mrs. Sparks said, was the Sparks family unique? It is very important to know how the antebellum Southern yeoman's family functioned in order to establish the role of the women in these units.[40] Some contemporary and secondary accounts have contended that the family structure of the yeomen was patriarchal and that women played minor roles.[41] Indeed, some have argued that upper class Southern men required the subordination of blacks and women, as well as non-slaveholding whites, and that this led to the retention of the patriarchal family structure in the region.[42] This point has been carried further to argue that Southern white families were so conservative, so concerned with preserving old values, that they were less receptive to change than families in the North.[43]

The yeoman families of the seventeenth and early eighteenth centuries may have come close to these stereotyped views. Several studies of such families maintain that, as in the English style, the father dominated the family. The male served as master and had virtually absolute power. Girls married early, and their primary purpose was to increase the population; as a consequence, they suffered an extremely high death rate. The "best" mother was the one who bore the largest number of healthy children. The wife/mother was a domestic laborer, performing the commonplace in a subordinate role.[44]

A more recent study of families in Maryland during the seventeenth century modifies these views. While the death rate for women was high, many survived their husbands and inherited the family property.

Wills provided for the education of daughters, and courts moved to protect widows and orphans. Fathers did exercise great control, but young girls had considerable freedom in selecting mates. Indeed, a sizeable percentage were pregnant at the time of the marriage ceremony. Scarcity of females provided the circumstances which allowed "romantic love" or a desire for mobility to surface as motivations for marriage.[45]

The courting and wooing of the young girls of the nineteenth century appears to have taken place on the terms established by the females. Whether the source be the ribald humorists of Georgia or Mississippi, the male chauvinist Simms, or the most genteel of the literary magazines, the stories of courtship emphasize the role of the women. The girls are described as being teases of young men, of pitting them against each other, and organizing social functions where courting could take place.[46] The girls decided which of the young men could court them and the parameters of the courtship in terms of physical involvement. The girls are described as "thinking" or "feeling" women who could be "lofty" when taken for granted by beaux. Strong willed girls forced suitors to pledge both their love and, occasionally, their property.[47]

The girls demanded attention and respect on their terms, and fiances were kept waiting until the ladies were "ready." Parents were often only consulted about the mate selected. When a young man was pursued by a young lady, it was not proper to chastise her for being "forward." A lady spurned could go to court, and sometimes did, leading to quiet weddings or financial remuneration. Quite often mothers and daughters refused to accept prospective grooms selected by husbands and fathers. While the strong willed women of Simms's novels often are "punished," he admits that they selected mates, and society accepted their right to make the decision. Romantic love serves as the basis for mate selection in many cases, but there are also instances of vertical social and economic mobility as prime factors.[48]

Courtship and marriage often had economic overtones with the female yeoman in the advantageous position. Young women possessing property—land, looms, cattle, furniture—were aware of the importance of their holdings. Several Southern states gave women some property rights before 1860, and common practice often protected them when the law did not.[49] Thus courtship did not always provide the basis upon which to establish a male-dominated family unit.

The new brides discovered that they were expected to bear children soon, and with great regularity. But there are examples of women who forcefully expressed themselves about family size and the rearing of children. Some refused to bear additional children, and others selected names for their babies over the husband's objections. And while some of the husbands considered themselves the dominant figure, others admitted that their wives could, and did, exert themselves. Husbands agreed that their wives made many decisions relating to childrearing, especially on educational and moral questions. While the frontier may have been "a single woman's paradise and a married woman's hell," some wives and mothers occupied roles with authority. Women who were scorned or abused sometimes abandoned their husbands and families, as indicated by newspaper advertisements for runaway wives.[50] Few men went so far, however, as a convicted criminal about to face the gallows in Abbeville, South Carolina, in 1836: "I haven't treated my wife right and she is one of the best women God ever made and has been a mighty good wife to me. I will say on my dying bed this much for her. She will make any of you a mighty good wife and I hope some of you will find it convenient to take her as she is a good woman and handy and no mistake."[51]

The recognition of his wife's qualities by the man nearing execution suggests the importance of the female role on moral questions. In the absence of schools and churches on the frontier and in rural areas, the female yeomanry served as teachers and exhorters. Even the most dedicated of Southern male chauvinists, such as "K.M.P." in *The Southern Field and Fireside*, accepted the moral force of the female in the home. At a time when basic education had substantial religious overtones, women taught not only spinning, weaving and the domestic arts to daughters, but also reading, writing and arithmetic to boys and girls alike. It was argued that not only were mothers obligated to instruct children, but even that educated women made better wives.[52] While a character in Augusta Wilson's bestseller *St. Elmo* declares, "The less book-learning you women have the better," it was the female in the yeoman family who educated the children.[53] William Gilmore Simms and Nathaniel Beverley Tucker railed against the "overeducated" woman, but the absence of rural elementary schools gave the female yeomanry an additional obligation, and also an opportunity to exercise another role in the family.[54]

Religion played a significant part in the lives of Southerners in general, and among the yeomanry in particular, in the three decades before 1860. It solidified social mores and established guidelines for public and private behavior. Numerous accounts of Southern society delineate the impact of religious institutions on the family, and most emphasize the passive participation of women. A few comment on the larger role for females by the 1850s, especially in benevolent societies and in aiding missionaries.[55] But it is also noted that women did not preach, hold church office, or engage in theological debates. Thus they are depicted as passive observers.

In his classic study of the "plain folk" Owsley describes the part played by church services and camp meetings in the lives of the yeomanry. He emphasizes the social context of the religious institutions of the middle class.[56] Only in studies of the evangelical sects of the Southern "plain folk" and in fiction is the role of the female yeomanry revealed, and it was not passive.

In the church services and revival meetings of the yeomanry women did not preach; they exhorted, led the singing, spoke in tongues and gave witness. Men may have dominated ecclesiastical authority, but the women participated at all levels of the services. They acted as functionaries at revivals where they often took control of the conversion experience. Sexual segregation, which was practiced in some evangelical churches, collapsed during the feverish pitch of the revivals. While women assumed practical leadership, they also gained a sense of equality in the baptismal service. Rebecca Felton remembered that at the revivals there was little difference between a praying woman and a shouting woman.[57]

Again and again, in memoirs and works of fiction, women take a leading role in church services. Corra Harris wrote that women courageously "took over" the services in rural Methodist churches in Georgia. They offered prayers and read the scriptures during the meetings, professing their sins and declaring their new faith. Some even performed "holy dances." At the end of the camp meetings, men and women mingled together shouting and clapping their hands.[58]

There is some evidence that considerable "mingling" took place during the course of the revivals. They were described as "mating grounds," and as places for "sparking." One young female in attendance at a Georgia camp meeting in 1846 wrote of her many beaux—too many for her spiritual good. An Alabama girl three years later wrote that all the young women enjoyed camp meetings.[59]

If the girls found beaux and pleasures at revivals, their mothers sought institutional reinforcement for their moral position in the home. Women fought against excessive drinking, card playing and horse racing, and they sought to protect their daughters from untoward advances by males. Within the home they served as moral arbiters in disputes, and this role increased in power as religious institutions came to play a larger part in the lives of the yeomanry.[60]

Literary sources available for the study of the role and status of the female yeomanry suggest that women occupied significant positions among the antebellum "plain folk." They made cash and labor contributions to the economic well being of the family. They selected their mates and gained a sense of equality in a fellowship of labor. The female yeomanry educated the children, established the moral tone of the home, and gradually gained greater prominence in religious institutions. The evolving status of the female yeomanry precluded the recreation of a European-style patriarchal family unit. These women were neither docile nor dour. Neither were they "ladies." They were strong, courageous middle class American women striving to gain a place in a social order undergoing rapid transformation.

NOTES

[1]Clement Eaton, *A History of the Old South* (New York: Macmillan, 1966), p. 8.

[2]Ann D. Gordon and Mari Jo Buhle, "Sex and Class in Colonial and Nineteenth-Century America," in *Liberating Women's History: Theoretical and Critical Essays*, ed. Berenice A. Carroll (Urbana: Univ. of Illinois Press, 1976), p. 278.

[3]John C. Ruoff, "Frivolity to Consumption: Or, Southern Womanhood in Antebellum Literature," *Civil War History*, 18 (September 1972), 213-29; Anne Firor Scott, *The Southern Lady from Pedestal to Politics, 1830-1930* (Chicago: Univ. of Chicago Press, 1970), passim; William R. Taylor, *Cavalier and Yankee: The Old South and American National Character* (New York: George Braziller, 1961), passim; Clement Eaton, "The Southern Yeoman: The Humorists' View and the Reality," in *The Mind of the Old South* (Baton Rouge: Louisiana State Univ. Press, 1967), pp. 130-51; Irving H. Bartlett and C. Glenn Cambor, "The History and Psychodynamics of Southern Womanhood," *Women's Studies*, II (1974), 9-24.

[4]Ellen Glasgow, *Barren Ground* (New York: Harcourt, Brace Co., 1925), pp 4-5.

[5]Frank Lawrence Owsley, *Plain Folk of the Old South* (Baton Rouge: Louisiana State Univ. Press, 1949), passim; Frank L. and Harriet C. Owsley, "Economic Basis of Society in Late Ante-Bellum South," *Journal of Southern History*, 6 (January 1940), 24-45; Herbert Weaver, *Mississippi Farmers 1850-1860* (Nashville: Vanderbilt Univ. Press, 1945), passim; Blanche Henry Clark, *The Tennessee Yeomen 1840-1860* (Nashville: Vanderbilt Univ. Press, 1942), passim; see also Owsley's letter to the editor responding to Fabian Linden's review of Weaver's book, *American Historical Review*, 52 (July 1947), 845-49.

[6]D. R. Hundley, *Social Relations in Our Southern States* (New York: Henry B. Price, 1860), pp. 191-222.

[7]Eugene D. Genovese, "Yeoman Farmers in a Slaveholders' Democracy," *Agricultural History*, 49 (April 1975), 341. For a recent review of the female on the northern frontier see Glenda Riley, "Images of the Frontierswoman: Iowa as a Case Study," *Western Historical Quarterly*, 8 (April 1977), 189-202.

[8]Fredrick Law Olmsted, *A Journey in the Seaboard Slave States in the Years 1853-1854* (New York: G. P. Putnam's Sons, 1904), and *A Journey in the Back Country in the Winter of 1853-4* (New York: G. P. Putnam's Sons, 1907).

[9]Paul H. Buck, "The Poor Whites of the Old South," *American Historical Review*, 31 (October 1925), 41-54; Shields McIlwaine, *The Southern Poor-White from Lubberland to Tobacco Road* (Norman: Univ. of Oklahoma Press, 1939), pp. xiii-xxv.

[10]Owsley, *Plain Folk of the Old South*, pp. v, vi-viii, 6-8, 91.

[11]A Southern Country Minister, *The Old Pine Farm: or, The Southern Side* (Nashville: Southwestern Publishing House, 1859), p. 20.

[12]Eaton, "The Southern Yeoman," pp. 137, 139-140.

[13]William Tappan Thompson, *Chronicles of Pineville* (Philadelphia: Carey and Hart, 1845), preface.

[14]Taylor, *Cavalier and Yankee*, pp. 141-44.

[15]Thomas R. Dew, "On the Characteristic Differences Between the Sexes, and the Position and Influence of Woman in Society," *Southern Literary Messenger*, April, June, and August, 1835, passim.

[16]George Fitzhugh, *Sociology for the South* (Richmond: Morris, 1854), pp. 214-215.

[17]"A Good Wife," *The Southern Lady's Companion*, November, 1848, p. 192.

[18]Taylor, *Cavalier and Yankee*, p. 61; Julia Cherry Spruill, *Women's Life and Work in the Southern Colonies* (Chapel Hill: Univ. of North Carolina Press, 1938), p. 83; William W. Fowler, *Woman on the American Frontier* (Hartford: S. S. Scranton, 1878), passim.

[19]Gerda Lerner, "New Approaches to the Study of Women in American History," *Journal of Social History*, 3 (Fall 1969), passim; Lois Green Carr and Lorena S. Walsh, "The Planter's Wife: The Experience of White Women in Seventeenth-Century Maryland," unpublished paper presented at the Newberry Library Colloquia on the Family and Local History, 18 September 1975.

[20]Barbara Welter, "The Cult of True Womanhood, 1820-1860," *American Quarterly*, 18 (Summer 1966), 151-74; Ronald W. Hogeland, " 'The Female Appendage': Feminine Life-Styles in America, 1820-1860," *Civil War History*, 17 (June 1971), 101-114; Ernest Earnest, *The American Eve in Fact and Fiction, 1775-1914* (Urbana: Univ. of Illinois Press, 1974), passim; Gerda Lerner, "The Lady and the Mill Girl: Changes in the Status of Women in the Age of Jackson," *Midcontinent American Studies Journal*, 10 (Spring 1969), 5-14. Nancy F. Cott, in *The Bonds of Womanhood: "Woman's Sphere" in New England 1780-1835* (New Haven: Yale Univ. Press, 1977), studies urban or small town residents in New England who left diaries and letters.

[21]Eaton, "The Southern Yeoman," pp. 130-31.

[22]Lewis Coser, ed., *Sociology through Literature* (Englewood Cliffs, N.J.: Prentice Hall, 1972), pp. 2-3.

[23]Eaton, "The Southern Yeoman," pp. 131-32, 140-41.

[24]Alexis de Tocqueville, *Democracy in America* (1835; rpt. New York: Harper and Row, 1966), pp. 560-67.

[25]Frank F. Furstenberg, Jr., "Industrialization and the American Family: A Look Backward," *American Sociological Review*, 31 (June 1966), 326-37.

[26]Herman R. Lantz, Jane Keys and Martin Schultz, "American Family in the Pre-Industrial Period," *American Sociological Review*, 40 (February 1975), 21-36; Herman R. Lantz, Raymond L. Schmitt and Richard Herman, "The Pre-Industrial Family in America: A Further Examination of Early Magazines," *American Journal of Sociology*, 79 (November 1973), 566-88.

[27]Gordon and Buhle, "Sex and Class in Colonial and Nineteenth Century America," p. 279.

[28]Three anthropological studies argue that a balanced division of labor leads to higher female status, and that when the family is the basic unit of agricultural production there is greater emphasis on male-female economic cooperation. See Peggy R. Sanday, "Female Status in the Public Domain," pp. 189-206; Karen Sacks, "Engels Revisited: Women, the Organization of Production and Private Property," pp. 207-222; and Bette S. Denich, "Sex and Power in the Balkans," pp. 243-62, all in Michelle Zimbalist Rosaldo and Louise Lamphere, eds., *Woman, Culture and Society* (Palo Alto: Stanford Univ. Press, 1974).

[29]W. Elliot Brownlee and Mary M. Brownlee, eds., *Women in the American Economy: A Documentary History, 1675-1929* (New Haven: Yale Univ. Press, 1977), pp. 91-92; David E. Schob, *Hired Hands and Plowboys: Farm Labor in the Midwest, 1815-60* (Urbana: Univ. of Illinois Press, 1975), pp. 191-208; Mary Sterrett Moses, "The Pioneer Woman: Community Life," *The Historian*, 2 (1939), 5-16. For similar conclusions about English countrywomen see G. E. Fussell, "Countrywomen in Old England," *Agricultural History*, 50 (January 1976), 175-78. Glenda Riley argues that Iowa frontierswomen labored in the fields "occasionally." See Riley, "Images of the Frontierswoman," p. 198.

[30]*The Countryman* [Turnwold, Putnam County, Georgia], 6 October 1862. For the economic role of the female yeomanry in the Confederacy see Bell Irvin Wiley, *Confederate Women* (Westport, Conn.: Greenwood Press, 1975), pp. xii, 147-76.

[31]Carr and Walsh, "The Planter's Wife," passim; Edmund S. Morgan, *Virginians at Home: Family Life in the Eighteenth Century* (Charlottesville: Univ. of Virginia Press, 1952), pp. 40-42; Spruill, *Women's Life and Work*, pp. 242-43; Jerena East Giffen, " 'Add a Pinch and a Lump': Missouri Women in the 1820's," *Missouri Historical Review*, 65 (July 1971), 478-504; F. D. Srygley, *Seventy Years in Dixie* (Nashville: Gospel Advocate Publishing, 1893), pp. 90-92.

[32]Emily Burke, *Reminiscences of Georgia* (Oberlin: James M. Fitch, 1850), pp. 21-22; Henry Ashworth, *A Tour in the United States, Cuba and Canada* (London: A. W. Bennett, 1861), p. 108; Robert R. Russel, "The Effects of Slavery upon Nonslaveholders in the Antebellum South," *Agricultural History*, 15 (April 1941), 115; Olmsted, *A Journey in the Back Country*, I, 219-27; John Hebron Moore, *Agriculture in Ante-Bellum Mississippi* (New York: Bookman Associates, 1958), p. 132; Guion Griffis Johnson, *Ante-Bellum North Carolina: A Social History* (Chapel Hill: Univ. of North Carolina Press, 1937), p. 231; *The Southern Lady's Companion*, February, 1853, pp. 321-25.

[33]Everett Dick, *The Dixie Frontier: A Social History* (New York: Alfred A. Knopf, 1948), pp. 283-86; Owsley, *The Plain Folk*, pp. 34-35; F. Garvin Davenport, *Ante-Bellum Kentucky: A Social History* (Oxford, Ohio: Mississippi Valley Press, 1943), pp. 3-8; Mary J. Welsh, "Recollections of Pioneer Life in Mississippi," *Publications of*

the Mississippi Historical Society, 4 (1901), 345-48; Olmsted, *A Journey in the Back Country*, I, 153-73.

[34]Bell Irvin Wiley, *The Plain People of the Confederacy* (Chicago: Quadrangle Books, 1963), p. 39; Arthur K. Moore, *The Frontier Mind: A Cultural Analysis of the Kentucky Frontiersman* (Lexington: Univ. of Kentucky Press, 1957), p. 60; Walter F. Peterson, ed., "Rural Life in Antebellum Alabama," *Alabama Review*, 19 (April 1966), 137-46.

[35]*Miner's and Farmer's Journal* [Charlotte], 11 October 1830.

[36]John F. H. Claiborne, "A Trip Through the Piney Woods," *Publications of the Mississippi Historical Society*, 9 (1906), 525-26; Eaton, "The Southern Yeomen," pp. 146-50; Scott, *The Southern Lady*, pp. 28-29; See Caroline Lee Hentz, *The Planter's Northern Bride* (Philadelphia: A. Hart, 1854), for a description of a rural Georgia family; Owsley, *The Plain Folk*, pp. 18-22; Olmsted, *A Journey Through the Back Country*, I, 258-61. See also Henry Clay Lewis (Madison Tensas, M.D.), "A Tight Race Considering," in *Old Leaves from the Life of a Louisiana Swamp Doctor* (Philadelphia: Carey and Hart, 1843).

[37]Weaver, *Mississippi Farmers*, pp. 56-61; T. W. Lane, "The Thimble Game," in Franklin J. Meine, ed., *Tall Tales of the Southwest* (New York: Alfred A. Knopf, 1930), pp. 373-82; William Gilmore Simms, *Woodcraft* (Philadelphia: Lippincott, Grainco & Co., 1853); Burke, *Reminiscences of Georgia*, pp. 21-27; Owsley, *The Plain Folk*, pp. 67-68; James Kirke Paulding, *Letters from the South by a Northern Man* (New York: Harper and Bros., 1835), I, 111-13; Olmsted, *A Journey in the Seaboard Slave States*, II, 40-42; Lewis Atherton, *The Southern Country Store 1800-1860* (Baton Rouge: Louisiana State Univ. Press, 1949), pp. 73-75, 82-83; Johnson, *Ante-Bellum North Carolina*, pp. 245-50. It has been argued that an increased demand for goods produced by women results in the development of economic rights which can lead to a change in status. See Sanday, "Female Status in the Public Domain," p. 206.

[38]Lewis Cecil Gray, *History of Agriculture in the Southern United States to 1860* (Gloucester, Mass.: Peter Smith, 1958), I, 439; Clark, *Tennessee Yeomen*, p. 136; "Mrs. Foster" in William Gilmore Simms, *As Good As Comedy* (Philadelphia: A. Hart, 1852), is an example of the ambitious female; Olmsted, *A Journey Through the Backcountry*, II, 30-34.

[39]W. H. Sparks, "Mother's Nap Was Up," in *The Memories of Fifty Years* (Philadelphia: Claxton, Remsen and Haffelfinger, 1870).

[40]William E. Bridges, "Family Patterns and Social Values in America, 1825-1875," *American Quarterly*, 17 (Spring 1965), 3-11.

[41]See for example, Rosser H. Taylor, *Ante-Bellum South Carolina: A Social and Cultural History* (Chapel Hill: Univ. of North Carolina Press, 1942), pp. 59, 60-61; and Owsley, *The Plain Folk*, pp. 94-95.

[42]Taylor, *Cavalier and Yankee*, p. 279; Scott, *The Southern Lady*, pp. 16-17.

[43]Arthur W. Calhoun, *A Social History of the American Family* (New York: Barnes and Noble, 1960), II, 148.

[44]Ibid., I, 245, 247-8, 273, and II, 107-108; Spruill, *Women's Life and Work*, pp. 3, 43-44, 59, 136.

[45]Carr and Walsh, "The Planter's Wife," passim.

[46]J. B. Cobb, "The Bride of Lick-the-Skillet," in *Mississippi Scenes* (Philadelphia: A. Hart, 1851); Harden E. Taliaferro, "Courtship" in *Fisher's River (North Carolina) Scenes and Characters* (New York: Harper and Brothers, 1859), pp. 112-121; Srygley, *Seventy Years in Dixie*, pp. 97-105, 152-153.

[47]See "Margaret Cole" in William Gilmore Simms, "Sergeant Barnacle," in *The Wigwam and the Cabin* (Chicago: Belford, Clark, 1888); and "Bess Matthews" in William Gilmore Simms, *The Yemassee* (New York: Harper Brothers, 1835); A. B. Longstreet, "The Dance" in *Georgia Scenes* (New York: Harper Brothers, 1840),

pp. 6-21; Dick, *Dixie Frontier*, pp. 133-37; Johnson, *Ante-Bellum North Carolina*, pp. 191-223.

[48]See "Jane Mathews" in "The Cottage Girls," by the author of "The Elopement," *Southern Literary Messenger*, May, 1843, pp. 275-280; in Richard Johnston, "Miss Pea, Miss Spouter and the Yankee," in *Georgia Sketches* (n.p.: Stockton & Co., 1864), "Georgiana Pea" chases and marries a Yankee visitor; "Miss See" in the "Disappointed Bridegroom," *Southern Literary Messenger*, July, 1856, pp. 47-50; in Joseph Glover Baldwin, "Cave Burton, Esq., of Kentucky," in *The Flush Times of Alabama and Mississippi* (San Francisco: Sumner Whitney & Co., 1876), pp. 113-129, "Susan" brought a breach of promise suit; See "Brown Bess" in William Gilmore Simms, *Border Beagles* (Chicago: Bedford, Clarke and Co., 1888); "Margaret Cooper" in William Gilmore Simms, *Charlemont* (Chicago: Belford, Clarke, 1888); and "Sally Myers" in John Esten Cooke, *Leatherstocking and Silk* (New York: Harper and Brothers, 1854).

[49]George W. Paschal, *Ninety-four Years: Agnes Paschal*. (Washington: M'Gill and Witherow, 1871), pp. 36-43; Suzanne D. Lebsock, "Radical Reconstruction and the Property Rights of Southern Women," *Journal of Southern History*, 43 (May 1977), 196-97.

[50]Calhoun, *A Social History of the American Family*, I, 285-96 and II, 11-21; Taylor, *Ante-Bellum South Carolina*, pp. 66-67; Johnson, *Ante-Bellum North Carolina*, pp. 739-41; See "Peggy Adair" in John Pendleton Kennedy, *Horse-Shoe Robinson* (New York: G. P. Putnam and Sons, 1872); Daniel K. Whitaker, "Reminiscences of a Tour to the South West," *The Southern Literary Journal*, II (June 1836), 297; See "Mrs. McCulloch" in George Tucker, *The Valley of Shenandoah* (New York: Charles Wiley, 1824), pp. 166-67; see "Emmeline Walker" in William Gilmore Simms, *Richard Hurdis* (Chicago: Belford, Clarke and Co., 1888); "A Cottage Home," by Cottager of Macon County, Alabama, in *The Southern Ladies Companion*, November, 1851, pp. 291-92; Thomas D. Clark, *The Rampaging Frontier* (Indianapolis: Bobbs-Merrill Co., 1939), pp. 281, 284-85.

[51]*Abbeville* [South Carolina] *Press and Banner*, 26 July 1836, quoted in Taylor, *Ante-Bellum South Carolina*, p. 79.

[52]"A Word to Mothers" by "a Mother in Arkansas," in *The Southern Ladies Companion*, September, 1848, p. 142; K.M.P., "Woman—Her True Destiny and Proper Training," *The Southern Field and Fireside*, 29 October 1859, p. 179; Whitaker, "Reminiscences of a Tour to the South West," *Southern Literary Journal*, 3 (September 1836), 26-28; Paschal, *Ninety-four Years*, p. 23; John R. Thompson, "The Free Schools and the University of Virginia," *Southern Literary Messenger*, February, 1854, p. 66; "E. T.," "Female Education," *Southern Literary Messenger*, September, 1858, pp. 218-221.

[53]Augusta Jane Evans Wilson, *St. Elmo* (New York: Carleton, Publisher, 1867), p. 25.

[54]Simms attacks the "overeducated" woman most vigorously in *Charlemont* and in *Beauchampe* (Chicago: Belford, Clarke and Co., 1888); Tucker's *George Balcombe* (New York: Harper and Brothers, 1836) echoes Simms's views. An anti-feminist article, "The Progress of the Republic", *DeBow's Review*, 17 (August 1854), 129, is typical of the opposition to education for women.

[55]Scott, *The Southern Lady*, pp. 8-14; Taylor, *Ante-Bellum South Carolina*, p. 76; Johnson, *Ante-Bellum North Carolina*, pp. 424-26.

[56]Owsley, *The Plain Folk*, pp. 97, 100.

[57]Dickson D. Bruce, *And They All Sang Hallelujah* (Knoxville: Univ. of Tennessee Press, 1974), pp. 64, 76, 79, 86-87; Rebecca Latimer Felton, *Country Life in Georgia* (Atlanta: Index Printing Co., 1919), pp. 64-67.

[58]Corra Harris, *A Circuit Rider's Wife* (Philadelphia: Henry Altemus Co., 1910);

Marion Harland, "Camp Meeting Scene," in Mary Forrest, *Women of the South Distinguished in Literature* (New York: Derby and Jackson, 1861), pp. 199-208; Fredrika Bremer, *The Homes of the New World* (London: Arthur Hall, Virtue and Co., 1853), I, 315-18; Srygley, *Seventy Years in Dixie*, pp. 209-235; Taliaferro, "Johnson Snow," in *Fisher's River*, p. 35. New England women also found religious services a place to assert themselves. See Cott, *The Bonds of Womanhood*, pp. 140-41 and 159.

[59]Diary of Clara Frederick of Georgia, 11 October 1846, and letter of Elvira Frederick, 29 September 1849, both quoted in Charles A. Johnson, *The Frontier Camp Meeting: Religion's Harvest Time* (Dallas: Southern Methodist Univ. Press, 1955), pp. 209-210.

[60]Bruce, *And They All Sang Hallelujah*, p. 64; See for example "Betsy Pickett" in Simms's *Richard Hurdis*. This conclusion is supported by the findings of Riley that the Iowa frontierswoman "enforced morality and religious values," in "Images of the Frontier woman," p. 200.

"Not Gainfully Employed": Women on the Iowa Frontier, 1833–1870

Glenda Riley

The author is a member of the history department in the University of Northern Iowa.

To STUDY PIONEER WOMEN through census data alone can be a frustrating and often deceptive effort. Certainly this is true for Iowa between 1833, when the area was opened for settlement by the Black Hawk Purchase Treaty, and 1870, when the United States Bureau of the Census declared the Iowa frontier "closed." Admittedly, the rich census data available for Iowa reveal a great deal about the population in general. The typical migrant, according to Allan Bogue's reading of the data, was "a married man between the ages of twenty-five and forty-five who had started his family before he moved to the . . . Iowa frontier."[1] The Iowa territorial census of 1838 allows scholars to expand on Bogue's analysis in significant ways. It shows that most of the new arrivals lived in households which averaged 5 to 6 members and with a ratio of 4 men to 3 women. This census also indicates that most people were attached to some type of family and that few people lived alone.[2] The next territorial census in 1840 demonstrates that the preponderance of pioneers were engaged in agricultural pursuits. There were,

The author wishes to thank the Newberry Library for research support.

[1] Allan G. Bogue, *From Prairie to Corn Belt: Farming on the Illinois and Iowa Prairies in the Nineteenth Century* (Chicago, 1968), 22–24.

[2] Iowa Census of 1838 (Microfiche, University of Northern Iowa Library), 190–191.

for example, 10,728 people listed as engaged in agriculture as opposed to 1,594 in manufacturing and trade, while only 348 were grouped in the "learned professions."[3] Summary statistics given in the state census of 1880 confirm that the agrarian-oriented migration persisted throughout Iowa's frontier period with the gross number of farms in Iowa rising from 14,805 in 1850, to 61,163 in 1860, and 116,292 in 1870.[4]

This statistical picture is revealing, and perhaps even predictable, but it leaves many questions unanswered, especially regarding women. The census did count white men and women separately (blacks and those born in other countries were frequently lumped together with no differentiation by gender), so it is clear that the white males outnumbered the white females throughout the frontier period.[5]

	1838	1850	1856	1860	1865	1870
Male population	24,355	101,052	278,584	354,493	383,272	625,917
Female population	18,757	91,162	239,291	320,420	346,086	568,103

Anecdotal evidence supports the contention that women were constantly in demand as wives in this family-farm economy, but other jobs they might have held are lost in generalized census categories such as clerks, teachers, editors, hotelkeepers, boardinghouse keepers, and even loafers. Only occasionally did the gender of the census category—such as seamstress, dressmaker, tailoress, or milliner—make it obvious that women were employed outside the home.[6] Even then, however, the marital status of women employed outside the home were unknown. The census

[3]Iowa Census of 1840, p. 3.

[4]Iowa Census of 1880, p. 57.

[5]*Ibid.*, 168–170.

[6]Iowa Census of 1856, pp. 12, 19, 25, 31, 35. Another possible source of women's occupations outside the home for the later part of the frontier period is city directories. The 1870 Mt. Pleasant city directory, for example, lists some women's names (with the titles of Miss or Mrs.) along with the occupation of milliner, seamstress, dressmaker, tailoress, dry-goods dealer, teacher, assistant principal, and professor of English literature. There were, however, many women's names listed with the title Mrs., but no occupational category or source of support is given for these women. E. H. Annewalt, comp., *Mount Pleasant City Directory: Containing a Catalogue of Inhabitants* (Burlington, Iowa, 1870), 27–58.

did not count single people at all. Only the married and widowed were identified, but even they were not counted by gender.

Clearly, to study Iowa pioneer women through census data requires asking some very modern questions of statistics whose limitations mirror the perspectives and philosophies of another era. This problem is demonstrated, in particular, by the various census reports which summarily group Iowa women under the heading "Not Gainfully Employed." This categorization raises some surprising and, in a sense, shocking questions regarding frontierswomen. Was their labor worth so little that they were not considered workers? Was their contribution to the westward movement so inconsequential that it could be easily dismissed?

These questions cannot be answered in the affirmative since abundant frontier lore pictures pioneer women as hard workers. They were economic producers who manufactured all manner of domestic goods, gave birth to and trained future laborers, helped with "men's" work, and generated small amounts of cash income. Why, then, did census takers label them "not gainfully employed"? The answer is simple. The census did not reflect the actual work of frontier women; rather, it reflected a moneyed society which tended to equate useful work with paid work. During the very early years of American settlement, factors such as barter, trade, subsistence farming, and emergent capitalist structures made it necessary to judge people's labor by standards other than the cash income it earned. But as America became more settled and moved with headlong speed towards its own version of the Industrial Revolution, money and the ability to earn it took on new meaning.

By the 1830s, when the settlement of Iowa was beginning, the eastern United States was already immersed in a system which separated the "paid" worker from the unpaid. Mill girls were employed, farm wives were not. Nursemaids were employed, mothers were not. Businessmen were employed, but the wives who ran their homes and served as their status symbols were not. The idea that the mark of a gainfully employed person was the ability to earn money rapidly became characteristic of American society. Translated into twentieth-century terms, it compels full-time wives and mothers to apologetically proclaim, "I'm *just* a housewife."

Since the idea that domestic work is not gainful work was so pervasive in nineteenth-century America, it is not surprising that census officials sometimes cavalierly extended it to women on the Iowa frontier. In the nineteenth-century East, factories were rapidly taking over women's customary functions of producing foodstuffs, soap, lighting facilities, clothing, and other domestic goods. In the nineteenth-century West, women still produced these goods in their own homes. Frontier women manufactured many items and purchased little, especially in the early years of settlement, because neither the goods nor the cash to obtain them were readily available. By the 1870s, as railroads and cities spilled over the Iowa prairie, this situation had altered radically. But it was too late for the pioneer woman. She went down in history as one who was not gainfully employed.

Revision of this view is long overdue. The frontier woman was not just a domestic drudge whose life was automatically unhappy. Women's diaries, memoirs, and correspondence indicate that she was a full economic producer in her own right within the home. As such, her life could include the same kind of satisfactions that her male counterpart derived from his labor. In fact, the skills she needed in her life's work were of such great consequence that she spent a good portion of her girlhood in apprenticeship to her mother or to another woman to learn them thoroughly.

By the time a frontier woman was of marriageable age, her greatest assets centered around her abilities as a domestic manufacturer. She was rated by her local reputation as a worker in the same way that men were graded as "providers." According to one study on frontier marriage,

> . . . The choosing of a mate on the frontier was a matter of economic necessity far and above individual whim. Good health and perserverance were premium assets while the charm and ability to entertain that one values so highly in a society of mechanization and leisure time was only of tangential significance. . . . [T]he woman who could not sew nor cook had no place on the frontier.[7]

---

[7]Edeen Martin, "Frontier Marriage and the Status Quo," *Westport Historical Quarterly*, X (1975), 100.

Mates, then, were chosen primarily as economic partners. It was considered a bonus if they were also compatible. For the typical frontier couple, their wedding day marked not only the beginning of a shared life but the beginning of a shared business venture as well.

If a pioneer woman opted to remain unmarried or was pushed into living alone by circumstances, such as divorce or the death of a mate, her skills were still crucial. Census figures tentatively indicate that most single women on the Iowa frontier were absorbed by other households: parents, children, relatives, or neighbors. In their adoptive family, women had to pull their own economic weight by continuing to render their share of household services. As in other parts of the country, these unattached females were often assigned the task of spinning flax, wool, and other fibers into thread. This phenomenon left its mark upon the American language in the word spinster (spin-ster) meaning an unmarried woman.

Regardless of their marital status, women were absolutely necessary to the frontier economy. Since domestic labor was so diverse in orientation, it is difficult to know where to begin a discussion of its nature. The picture given by one Iowa man regarding his mother's labors gives some idea of their vast scope.

> Mother bore and cared for the babies, saw that the floor was white and clean, that the beds were made and cared for, the garden tended, the turkeys dressed, the deer flesh cured and the fat prepared for candles or culinary use, that the wild fruits were garnered and preserved or dried, that the spinning and knitting was done and the clothing made. She did her part in all these tasks, made nearly all the clothing and did the thousand things for us a mother only finds to do.[8]

His description clearly indicates that his mother was the chief laborer within the home. It was her responsibility to process the raw materials generated in the fields outside of the home. The woman and her home, or in other words, the worker and her workplace, were the key link in turning unusable raw materials

---

[8] George C. Duffield, "An Iowa Settler's Homestead," *Annals of Iowa*, VI (1903), 210.

into consumable finished goods. She was therefore to her family what the factory was to an industrialized society.

Of all the products that she manufactured, food required the most continuous attention. In an age when people worked long, physically taxing hours and consumed thousands of calories per day to sustain themselves, food preparation was at the hub of domestic activity. Unlike the women of later eras, a pioneer woman had to rely on her own talents and resources for every step from processing through storing to actual preparation.

The first step, processing, began with the gathering of raw foodstuffs. Many of these, such as corn and wheat, were produced by the men of the family. However, the women were often responsible for obtaining vegetables, fruits, herbs, eggs, and milk. Although the men usually did the heavier jobs, such as harrowing and planting the vegetable patch, women did the weeding, picking, and "digging taters." Women also gathered wild and domestic fruits, beginning with currants and cherries in June and ending with strawberries later in the summer. Furthermore, planting herb gardens, gathering wild herbs, collecting eggs, and sometimes even milking the cows fell to the lot of the women. Their labor, combined with the produce of the fields, of farm stock, and of hunting, provided a myriad of raw materials which could be processed into many varieties of usable, and often appetizing, foodstuffs.

Naturally, corn was a staple of the Iowa pioneer's diet. It was eaten fresh, but was also stored for use during the long winter months when fresh foods were unavailable. Drying sweet corn took place during the hottest days of late August when the ears were husked, scalded, and then stripped of the kernels which were spread on pans, covered by a mosquito net, and placed on the roof in the sun. If rain threatened, the pans were rushed back into the house and placed in the oven for drying. This dried corn would later reappear in many forms—cornbread, mush, corncakes, and corn pone.[9] Corn was also commonly processed into hominy, a favorite food served with milk and

[9]Janette Stevenson Murray, "Women of North Tama," *Iowa Journal of History and Politics*, XLI (1943), 296.

some sort of sweetner. The following description of hominy-making was passed on by May Ramsay:

They had a hopper made out of wood up on a stand where they put the wood ashes and made lye. Grandmother would take corn and boil it in lye water until the shell would come off. (That was in a big kettle out doors). Then take the corn to the well and wash it until she had all the lye off. I remember how I watched her and wondered about it. It sure made good hominy when it was washed enough.[10]

Eggs and milk constituted two other standards of the pioneer menu. Milk, of course, was frequently churned into butter. Matilda Peitzke Paul remembered that it was a tedious and time-consuming process.

. . . the milk was put in pans to cool and left long enough for the cream to come to the top which was about 24 hours, then the cream was skimmed off with this kind of skimmer and kept in a cool place if there was one, until there was enough cream to make several pounds of butter in a dash churn . . . . I remember how I used to dread to have mother call me and tell me to help with the churning. It seemed as if the butter never would come [since] sometimes it did take for hours to churn.[11]

Another woman lived near a creek with a shelving rock under the bank where she kept her milk and butter cold even on the hottest summer days. She was an expert butter maker and in 1857, when she sent her "roll of butter, daintily marked and as smooth as marble" to the local fair she easily captured first place.[12]

By the end of the fall, the family's cellar had been transformed into a storehouse which would gradually surrender its precious treasure throughout the long winter. Amelia Murdock Wing always retained fond memories of her family's well-stocked cellar:

A barrel of kraut was made in the fall; chunks of pork were salted down; fruit was canned and kept in long, heavy wooden boxes, many

[10]Edith H. Hurlbutt, "Pioneer Experiences in Keokuk County, 1858–1874," *Iowa Journal of History*, LII (1954), 335.

[11]Matilda Peitzke Paul, memoirs, Iowa State Historical Society, Iowa City, Iowa.

[12]Bessie L. Lyon, "Grandmother's Story," *Palimpsest*, V (1924), 7.

kinds of vegetables could be kept there throughout the winter . . . . In our cellar there was a floor of rock, always cleanly scrubbed. There was a long table for use in handling the milk and butter, and a wooden dash-churn stood beside it. There was a large cupboard whose tin doors had holes for ventilation, and this was where the milk, cream and butter was kept. No one had ice in those days, but our cellar was cool.[13]

Processing of foodstuffs was primarily a summertime chore, but converting food supplies into edible meals was a continual task to be faced day after day, year after year, often with only the most rudimentary kitchen equipment as an aid. During the early years of settlement, the most common cooking utensil on the Iowa frontier was a black iron kettle suspended on an iron crane which swung in and out of the open fireplace. This was complemented by a Dutch oven which consisted of a rather flat-bottomed pot with an iron lid. This oven was set directly in the hot coals and often covered over with coals. Another common implement was a long-handled frying pan, used for both meat and flapjacks which were fried over the open fire. Large meat strips, such as turkey, venison, or pork, might be cooked by suspending it over the fire on a tightly twisted piece of string. As the string unwound it acted as a kind of spit which turned the meat slowly and allowed it to brown evenly. Bread was also baked by the open fire by spreading the dough over a "johnny-cake" board, propping the board up to face the fire, and then turning it until the heat of the fire produced a nicely browned loaf. Sarah Nossaman's directions for this bread gives a good idea of the talent and experience required.

Take a board eighteen inches long and eight inches wide, round the corners off and make the edges thinner than the middle, spread it with well-made corn dough, set it on edge before a hot fire in a fireplace, and it will bake nice and brown, then turn and bake the other side the same way, then you have corn bread that no one will refuse.[14]

---

[13]Amelia Murdock Wing, "Early Days in Clayton County," *Annals of Iowa*, XXVII (1946), 280.

[14]Sarah Welch Nossaman, "Pioneering at Bonaparte and Near Pella," *ibid.*, XIII (1922), 450.

Despite the limitations, many pioneer women gained reputations as competent cooks, an achievement which was particularly difficult when the few receipt (recipe) books that did exist gave directions in terms of a pinch and a handful. Kitturah Belknap was especially pleased after a fleece-sorting party because her women friends were impressed with her chicken dinner and old-fashioned pound cake. "Now my name is out as a good cook," she rejoiced, "so am alright for good cooking makes good friends."[15] Another Iowa woman discovered that she could earn money to purchase her first store-bought clothes by hiring out as a cook. Working with one other woman over an open fireplace in Bonaparte around 1840, she prepared all the meals for forty-five men building a mill. For this feat she was paid the grand sum of seventy-five cents per week which, according to her, "was the best wages that had ever been paid in the country at that time."[16]

Regardless of the rude conditions, the diversity of pioneer menus seemed almost unlimited. On one occasion, Belknap treated her guests to stewed chicken, fried cakes, sausage, and mashed potatoes. Another time she prepared a Christmas dinner for twelve people that would tax the dexterity of a modern cook equipped with all the latest appliances. Her bill of fare, as she called it, was rather extensive:

> Firstly; for bread, nice light rolls; cake, doughnuts: for pie, pumpkin; preserves, crab apples and wild plums; sauce, dried apples; meat first round: roast spare ribs with sausage and mashed potatoes and plain gravy; second round: chicken stewed with the best of gravy; chicken stuffed and roasted in the Dutch oven by the fire.[17]

When confronted by a shortage of some kind, which was frequently the case, many pioneer cooks made up the difference with their own creativity. Harriet Bonebright-Closz recalled that her family lacked a rolling pin which was essential to biscuit making. Instead, they used a wooden stick, peeled fresh

[15]Kitturah Penton Belknap, reminiscences, Iowa State Historical Society, Iowa City, Iowa.

[16]Nossaman, "Pioneering at Bonaparte and Near Pella," 446.

[17]Belknap, reminiscences.

daily. "When it could not be found," she said, "the biscuit dough was rolled with a fresh ear of corn - or mayhap, the cob."[18] Belknap often found herself without the kind of fruit that she needed for preserves so she devised a clever imitation. She squeezed the juice from watermelon, boiled it down to syrup, added some muskmelons and crabapples, cooked them with a little sugar, and produced a substance which at least tasted like preserves. According to her, "You have nice preserves to last all winter (and they are fine when you have nothing better and sugar 12-1/2 c. a lb. and go 40 miles after it)."[19]

Belknap's comment regarding sugar points up the problem that most frontier cooks faced in obtaining sugar, salt, and other spices. Often herbs from their own gardens sufficed for seasonings, but salt had to be purchased, as did sugar, and both were usually very expensive by pioneer standards. In 1856 Sarah Kenyon complained to her mother that sugar was $1.00 for eight to nine pounds and molasses was 85¢ per gallon.[20] Another source listed sugar as wholesaling for 9-8/10 cents per pound in 1856, 9 cents per pound in 1861, and jumping to 23½ cents per pound by 1864 due to the inflationary effects of the Civil War.[21] It is little wonder that frontierswomen did what they could to find substitutes. Sweetners, of course, were more easily replaced than salt. Women kept their eye out for a bee tree which they might rob of its highly prized honey. They tapped maple trees for sap which was boiled down into maple molasses[22] or converted into maple sugar at a "sugaring-off" in the fall.[23] And they stripped cane to produce molasses, a commodity considered so important that children were often kept home from school to help with the "stripping."

As settlements thickened and frontier towns increased in size and number, the problems of the pioneer cook were somewhat

[18] Harriet Bonebright-Closz, *Reminiscences of Newcastle, Iowa, 1848* (Des Moines, 1921), 172.

[19] Belknap, reminiscences.

[20] Sarah Kenyon to her mother, Aug. 29, 1856, Kenyon Family Papers, Iowa State Historical Society, Iowa City, Iowa.

[21] U.S. Bureau of the Census, *Historical Statistics of the United States* (Washington, D.C., 1975), 209.

[22] Lida L. Greene, ed., "Diary of a Young Girl," *Annals of Iowa*, XXXVI (1962), 454.

[23] Wing, "Early Days in Clayton County," 280.

alleviated. Her sparse utensils were augmented by tinware, pewter ware, and various types of pots and pans. Her open fireplace with its pot and crane was replaced by a stove, often with "newfangled gadgets" such as warming ovens. And her stock of foodstuffs was enhanced by the goods offered in the rapidly spreading stores and emporiums.

Those people who could afford the new cooking utensils, stoves, and other food items found them very convenient. The articles of food offered by the new grocers included staples such as flour and salt, but shopkeepers also catered to the appetites of migrants hungry for delicacies that they had enjoyed in their former homes. In 1855 the *Iowa Sentinel* of Fairfield advertised a shipment of raisins and figs as well as fresh Baltimore peaches and strawberries.[24] Oysters were particularly esteemed by Iowans, many of whom were former New Englanders. In 1857 the *Iowa Sentinel* announced the opening of the "Young America Oyster and Lunch Saloon," which claimed that "its patrons, at all hours, will be served with Oysters in every style, also with Welch Rabbits, Hot Cakes and Coffee, Venison, Steaks, Game, etc."[25] Inland merchants also reacted to the demand for oysters, and in 1861 the *Waterloo Courier* heralded a shipment of "Celebrated Baltimore Fresh Oysters."[26]

Of course, the less settled regions of the Iowa frontier did not enjoy such luxuries until the coming of the railroads, primarily after the Civil War. In 1856 Sarah Kenyon's sister Mary mentioned making a meal of "punkin flap jacks" and a few slices of venison, then grumbled that "we don't have anything but 'taters' and punkin here."[27] Even as late as 1869, a newly arrived family of migrants in Clay County subsisted for an entire winter on little more than "sod house soup" made of chunks cut off a "half-of-beef" and mixed with the meager vegetable supply they had brought along.[28]

But as complex and demanding as food processing and preparation were, they only accounted for one segment of the

[24] *Iowa Sentinel*, Jan. 11, 1855.
[25] *Ibid.*, Feb. 26, 1857.
[26] *Waterloo Courier*, April 9, 1861.
[27] Mary Ellis to her mother, Nov. 7, 1856, Kenyon Family Papers.
[28] Abbie Mott Benedict, "My Early Days in Iowa," *Annals of Iowa*, XVII (1930), 341.

frontierswoman's workday. She was also responsible for domestic commodities manufactured from food byproducts, such as soap and lighting facilities. Both required constant attention on her part in order to stockpile the food wastes which in turn would become her raw materials.

Soap-making involved three separate processes: collecting grease, fat, and tallow from meat; saving wood ashes for lye; and boiling the two together in the correct proportion to create a substance known as soft soap. Collection of grease was a year-long procedure. Drip pans were carefuly positioned under spitted meat to catch the drippings and all leftover grease from frying was put aside. Any nonedible scraps of fat from cuts of meat were also diligently hoarded. By spring, there was usually a sizable accumulation of waste grease and fat. This was enlarged upon by the addition of scraps of fat saved from the spring butchering of hogs and beeves.

Wood ashes were also collected throughout the year, but these had to be transformed into lye before they were ready to be combined with the grease. Janette Stevenson Murray described this procedure in detail:

> One neighbor leached lye from wood ashes kept in a barrel. This was perforated in the bottom and set on an inclined board. A circle was chiseled out on the board outside the bottom of the barrel with a groove at the lower edge to let the seeping water run into a wooden pail. This yellow water was the lye. The barrel was kept full of ashes and every once in awhile more water was poured over them.[29]

Soap-making was done out-of-doors in the spring with the children joining in. The lye and grease were carefuly measured into a large iron kettle, a fire was stoked under the kettle, and the concoction was boiled until the women judged it to be of the proper consistency. Matilda Peitzke Paul stated that "This had to be watched most of the time to be kept from boiling over. In the mean time the water was being poured into the leach several times a day until the lye was too weak to hold up an egg, for then it was too weak to make soap."[30]

Once the mixture foamed up and had been carefully stirred together, it was poured into crocks or wooden boxes lined with

[29]Murray, "Women of North Tama," 299.
[30]Paul, memoirs.

cloth. When it hardened, usually in a day or two, it was cut into "bars" and stored away in kegs, wrapped in hay, or just piled lattice-fashion on cellar shelves for use during the coming year. Some women refined the method even further by using pure tallow, rendered from beef fat and molded in pans, to make a whiter soap for clothes, dishes, and hands while they used cracklings and scraps to make a darker laundry soap.[31]

Attitudes toward soap-making seemed to vary widely. Amelia Murdock Wing remembered it as a "process we enjoyed."[32] Paul, however, rather sourly commented that "it took plenty of work to make it."[33] At any rate, soap-making apparently continued to be a home function for a good many years, for there is little evidence, either in manuscript form or in the advertisements of the time, that it was marketed very widely during the pioneer years.

Providing light for pioneer homes called for another skill on the part of domestic women artisans during the early period when kerosene was unavailable. Many families simply relied on the fireplace to light their homes. As soon as possible this scanty light was supplemented by the easiest type of lighting fixture known on the frontier—the saucer lamp. This was merely a saucer, usually of wood, filled with some kind of grease with a piece of twisted rag inserted in it as a wick. The grease might be excess cooking fat, lard tallow, goose grease, or melted lard. Margaret Archer Murray said that their first lights were "grease lamps we had a shallow dish first took a soft rad [rag] twisted it then dipped one end in melted lard layed that end up on side of dish pored the melted lard over that then it was ready to light."[34] Similarly, Sarah Kenyon wrote that "Our light consists of a saucer filled with coons oil with a rag in it."[35]

By modern standards, it is amazing that pioneers managed to complete all their tasks adequately or efficiently with such defective lighting. Since evening and long winter afternoons were crucial work periods for pioneers, it meant that they often mended harness, made nails, carved furniture, processed food,

[31] Murray, "Women of North Tama," 298.
[32] Wing, "Early Days in Clayton County," 280.
[33] Paul, memoirs.
[34] Margaret E. Archer Murray, "Memoir of the William Archer Family," *Annals of Iowa*, XXXIX (1968), 360.
[35] Sarah Kenyon to her mother, Dec. 1, 1856, Kenyon Family Papers.

and sewed the family's clothing by the flickering light of fireplaces and saucer lamps. Bonebright-Closz mentioned in passing that her mother "did much of the family sewing beside the feeble ray of this type of light,"[36] while Margaret Murray went into a little more detail:

> Mother did all her sewing and knitting by that [saucer light] and the light from the fireplace and she sure had a lot of it to do . . . . Mother made all our cloths by hand knit all our stockings and mittens by lamp light.[37]

As soon as they could afford it, most frontierswomen began to produce candles to light their homes. These were of two basic types, the tallow dip and the molded candle, both of which involved some capital investment in supplies. In the case of tallow dips, the tallow itself could be rendered at home from meat fats, but the wicking had to be purchased. Labor was supplied by women who went through the following procedure once every year.

> She filled the wash boiler with tallow; then, she put wicks over some little round sticks and dipped them in the hot tallow and hung them in a row above the boiler. By the time the last stick was hung up, the first sticks were cool enough to dip again. Thus the work proceeded until the candles were of the right size.[38]

Molded candles required not only the purchase of wicking, but an initial investment in an iron candle mold. Paul recalled that her family had a mold that held one dozen candles. "The wick," she explained, "had to be bought at a store and run through the center of each one after that the tallow was melted and poured into the mold and left till perfectly cold and hard."[39] Janette Murray gave a similar account of the process:

> Pieces of candlewick, cut in proper length, were laid over the sticks across the top of the mold, shaken down, pulled through the small holes at the bottom and tied tightly. The molds were then filled with

[36] Bonebright-Closz, *Reminiscences of Newcastle*, 39.
[37] Murray, "Memoir of the William Archer Family," 361.
[38] Wing, "Early Days in Clayton County," 279.
[39] Paul, memoirs.

melted tallow and set outdoors to cool. After heating a moment in the morning, the cream-colored candles could be lifted out.[40]

Most frontierswomen were justifiably proud of their skills and their results. Certainly, no frontier homestead could have survived without them. Furthermore, no frontier family would have been clothed if frontier women had not fit the manufacture of garments into their already crowded schedules. During the first years of frontier settlement, the manufacture of apparel was both difficult and time-consuming. Since commercially produced yardgoods were not generally marketed as yet, early frontierswomen had to begin literally with plants, such as flax, and with animals, such as sheep, to obtain the fibers that would eventually become thread, then cloth, and finally clothing.

Flax and wool, both ubiquitous on the Iowa frontier, required hours of monotonous work before they could be spun into thread. Raw flax was "combed" by throwing the fibers over a hackle and pulling them through its teeth. This hackle was usually made of a wooden base with close-set iron prongs projecting upwards from it. A hackle resembled a medieval instrument of torture, or perhaps a bed of nails, and was just as dangerous if a woman was not alert and agile while using it. Wool was not hackled but was carded with a crude curry-comb type of instrument. Although not as dangerous as a flax hackle, the carding comb also called for patience and endurance on the part of the woman operating it. Once the fibers were combed into smooth strands they were spun into thread on a treadle-powered spinning wheel. The spinning wheel occupied a place of honor in many cabins and consumed untold hours of the pioneer woman's time. It was, however, only the second step in an extensive process. Next the thread had to be woven into cloth: flax into linen cloth; wool into woolen cloth; and flax and wool into linsey-woolsey cloth. This cloth was then colored with dyes that women produced themselves from plants such as indigo, red oak bark, and sumac berries. Finally, the cloth was ready to be laboriously hand-stitched into a finished garment.

---

[40]Murray, "Women of North Tama," 299.

Naturally, women got help with these jobs whenever they possibly could, both by inviting in friends to help and by sending the fibers out to a carding machine or the thread to a weaving mill. In 1853, for instance, the *Wapello Intelligencer* advertised a commercial wool carding service in the town of Wapello.[41] But Margaret Murray's description indicates that while her mother did get some help, she alone was responsible for many tiresome tasks.

After the shearing was done she washed the fleeces then hand picked the wool to get out the burs and the like often had wool picking invite a few women for the day. After that the wool was sent to the carding machine and made into rolls then mother had to spin it into yarn then have that woven into cloth some for jeans for mens cloths and flannel for us children and apart of the yarn for kniting then she did all the coloring.[42]

Belknap's recollections were very much the same. "All this winter I have been spinning flax and tow [coarse, broken fibers of flax] to make some summer clothes," she wrote. "Now the wool must be taken from the sheep's back, washed and picked and sent to the carding machine and made into rolls, then spun, colored and wove ready for next winter." Another year she gave a fuller account:

I'm the first one to get at the wool (25 fleeces). Will sort it over, take off the poor short wool and put it by to card by hand for comforts. Then sort out the finest for flannels, and the courser for jeans for the men's wear. I find the wool very nice and white but I do hate to sit down alone to pick wool so I will invite about a dozen old ladies in an in a day they will do it all up.[43]

When her wool came home from the carding machine, she was pleased with the nice rolls that were all ready to spin. She first planned to spin her stocking yarn, estimating that she could spin two skeins a day and double and twist it during the evening while her husband read the history of the United States.[44]

[41] *Wapello Intelligencer*, May 31, 1853.
[42] Murray, "Memoir of the William Archer Family," 361.
[43] Belknap, reminiscences.
[44] *Ibid.*

Later, Belknap spun thread for the simple dresses which satisfied most women in those years. In 1840, she was elated to get a new calico dress for Sunday and one new homemade dress for everyday. She recalled: "It was cotton warp colored blue and copper and filled with pale blue tow filling so it was striped one way and was almost as nice as gingham." The following year she added a new blue and red flannel dress to her wardrobe. "I am going to try and make me one dress every year," she commented, "then I can have one for nice and with a clean check apron I would be alright."[45]

Besides their own dresses, women also sewed dresses for the young girls of the family and jeans and cotton shirts for the men and boys. All buttonholes had to be painstakingly worked in by hand to accommodate the hooks, eyes, and buttons that were used for fastening. In addition, warm stockings, mittens, mufflers, and wristlets for all were knitted from wool. Hats were plaited from straw or wild grass gathered in the fields. And sunbonnets were made to extend out over the face approximately four inches using pasteboard slats, a design which Bonebright-Closz described as such "an obstruction to sight and an impediment to hearing" that most young women let them hang loosely down their backs rather than using them as a protection from the prairie sun as intended.[46]

As merchants and dry goods stores began to appear, women looked to them to supply them with yardgoods and other sewing materials. In 1862, Sarah Kenyon said she could buy thin cotton cloth for 20 cents, calico for 20 cents, sheeting for 30 cents, thread for 10 cents a spool, but "needles its almost impossible to get." Although she did not give quantities with her prices, her list does signify that these goods were being sold in her area of Plum Creek, Kossuth County, in the north central portion of Iowa by the time of the Civil War.[47]

A survey of some frontier newspapers shows that these goods were widely sold much sooner in areas located along well-traveled routes of settlement and trade. As early as 1836, the *DuBuque Visitor* advertised ready-made clothing and "Calicoes,

[45] *Ibid.*
[46] Bonebright-Closz, *Reminiscences of Newcastle*, 121.
[47] Sarah Kenyon to her mother, Oct. 9, 1862, Kenyon Family Papers.

Ginghams, Muslins, Cambricks, Laces, Ribbands."[48] That fall they featured ads for dry goods, including "Sattinettes, Cassimeres and brodd Cloths."[49] In 1837, the *Iowa News*, also in Dubuque, announced "Ready Made Clothing from New York."[50] And by 1844, Dubuque's *Iowa Territorial Gazette and Advertiser* carried ads for "Hats, Hats," a "Fashionable Milliner and Dress Maker," "Hats and Bonnets," and "Rich Fancy Goods."[51]

Burlington, also located on the Mississippi River, became another supply center. The *Burlington Daily Hawk-Eye and Telegraph* of the 1850s was filled with commercial notices appealing "to the Ladies." One offered "30 pieces fine linen thread edging," assorted black silk lace edging, lisle and silk gloves, black silk mitts, and kid gloves.[52] A few years later the People's Store advertised calicoes, ginghams, silk goods, linens, fancy goods, boots and shoes, with the claim that "The stock is not, and cannot be surpassed in the West."[53] The new Philadelphia Dry Goods and Milliners insisted that "the best, handsomest and cheapest goods, and the greatest bargains" were to be found in their establishment.[54]

Nearby inland towns did their best to compete for the expanding market. In 1854, Mt. Pleasant's *Weekly Observer* called for "Ladies! Ladies!! Ladies!!!" to notice new stocks of "Lawn Satin, Silk and Crepe Bonnets of the latest styles," and "Ribbons, Flowers, caps, and every variety in the millinery lines." They also offered "Fowler's system of cutting dresses taught in 3 lessons for $3, with model patterns cut to fit the figure for 25 cts."[55] Gradually, such goods were marketed in the more interior portions of Iowa, but it was not a smooth east to west movement. Business development gravitated first around the Mississippi River and secondly around the Missouri River. This was due in part to the early steamboats that plied both rivers, bringing settlers and trade goods. Though the Missouri

[48] *Dubuque Visitor*, July 6, 1836.
[49] *Ibid.*, Sept. 14, 1836.
[50] *Iowa News*, July 1, 1837.
[51] *Iowa Territorial Gazette and Advertiser*, June 1, 1844.
[52] *Burlington Daily Hawk-Eye and Telegraph*, July 23, 1855.
[53] *Ibid.*, April 5, 1859.
[54] *Ibid.*
[55] *Weekly Observer*, April 20, 1854.

River was more difficult for steamboats to navigate, towns along its banks, particularly Kanesville (Council Bluffs), benefitted because of the many migrants passing through in their journey to the Far West.

These business developments do not fit well with the popular stereotype of frontierspeople in their rough homespun and animal skin clothing. Moreover, they do not support the image of grinding poverty throughout the prairieland of frontier days. At least in pioneer Iowa, those kinds of conditions were brief and transitory for most frontierspeople. Relative prosperity allowed many Iowans not only to purchase dry goods, ready-made clothes, and accessories, but also to acquire the sewing machine. By the 1850s, the spinning wheel no longer held the place of honor in most Iowa pioneer homes nor was all sewing any longer done by hand. The treadle sewing machine was making its presence felt on many parts of the Iowa frontier. With its many variations in design and price, its ability to lighten work, and its increasing accessibility, it was to the frontier woman what the McCormick reaper was to the frontier farmer. In 1855, a *Davenport Gazette* advertisement for a Wheeler, Wilson and Company's Superior Sewing Machine slightly overstated the effects of the revolution in the domestic manufacture of clothing: "by the use of these machines very much of that which has been a drudgery become but a pleasant task."[56]

That people were purchasing and using sewing machines was substantiated by frequent mention of them in women's diaries and memoirs. Although the machines were foot-powered and rudimentary by today's standards, many women discovered that they relieved them of hundreds of wearying hours of hand-stitching. The new machines also made more complicated fashions possible and allowed the young women of the family to take over a good share of the family sewing at an earlier age than had been possible when they had to be carefully taught various types of stitches. A case in point was Alice Money, a young girl who did all the sewing for her family in the 1860s, including muslin undergarments with yards of ruffles and tucks, calico dresses lined and trimmed with more ruffles,

[56] *Davenport Gazette*, June 14, 1855.

tucks, and bias bindings, and shirts and suits for the boys and men. She must have treadled hundreds of miles on her family's early model of a Wheeler and Wilson machine which was said to have "made a noise like a threshing machine and ran almost as hard."[57]

In addition to the production of clothing, women were also saddled with its complex and tiring care. In an era which predated commercial laundries, dry cleaners, or even washing machines, all apparel had to be handled with the utmost care. Brocades and silks were wrapped in sheets and hung away in spare closets. Most women had at least one "good" dress. This was made of black silk and saw her through weddings, funerals, and other special occasions. She would remake it in the latest fashion every four or five years so that it would last most of her lifetime. According to Janette Murray, these and other fancy dresses were made at home or by a local seamstress. "The silk," she explained, "was heavy and rich and the dresses were made with so much lining, crinoline, and boning that they almost stood alone."[58]

Everyday clothing, along with bedding and other linens, had to be washed by hand. On washing day, large wooden washtubs were first laboriously filled with water hauled in from the well and heated by the fireplace or stove. A washboard and some soft soap completed the list of necessary equipment. Women then proceeded to rub the clothing back and forth over a convoluted scrub board. When this step was concluded, the garment was hand wrung and hung outside to dry. In inclement weather the wash was hung and draped about the kitchen to drip on the heads of those working below.

Almost everything, including sheeting, required ironing. This was done with heavy, solid iron flatirons. Several of these were heated in the fireplace or stove while an ironing table was placed near by. As one iron cooled during use, it was carried to the source of heat and exchanged for a hot iron. All ruffles, tucks, fluting, and other frills were ironed in some small flatirons made with various types of ridging especially for this

---

[57]Floy Lawrence Emhoff, "A Pioneer School Teacher in Central Iowa—Alice Money Lawrence," *Iowa Journal of History and Politics*, XXXIII (1935), 378–379.

[58]Murray, "Women of North Tama," 307.

purpose. Many garments had to be starched, and it took a particularly skillful woman to know just when to remove the iron so that the telltale marks of scorched starch would not be left behind.

As Paul mentioned at several points in her memoirs, all of the frontierswomen's duties, from feeding a family through clothing them, "made plenty of work."[59] But on another level, the outcome of her labors also plainly indicated her degree of skill as an artisan in a society which judged a person by immediate results rather than by wealth, family name, or social class. Her ability and industry in the manufacture of suitable domestic wares could determine the "comfort level" of her family's existence in frontier Iowa. Furthermore, her family depended on her as a kind of paraprofessional in a society which quite often lacked pharmacists, doctors, and morticians. Frontierswomen, in addition to all their other capabilities, became accomplished herbalists. After women picked the herbs in the woods or from their own gardens, they dried them and then brewed them into medicinal teas, tonics, bitters, or prepared them as poultices.

As apothecaries, women were guided not only by the family knowledge that had been passed on to them, but by the recipes for medicine, which often outnumbered the recipes for food in the early receipt books, or by a "doctor book" if the family was fortunate enough to own one. Many herbs, which are now ignored by most medical practitioners in the age of antibiotics, were pressed into service as medicine. Crowder listed a few of the most popular used by her mother in treating her own family as well as the many neighbors who depended on her competence in time of illness.

> Many wild plants were used as medicines, most of them steeped and drunk as tea. Among these were "Culver's root" taken "for the liver." The dandelion, both as extract and as wine, was used for the same purpose. Tonics were made from the butterfly weed, sweet flag root, sassafras bark, and boneset . . . . For colds, pennyroyal, prairie balm, and horse mint were popular remedies. Mullen was used externally

[59]Paul, memoirs.

for pleurisy. . . . Smartweed was used externally for boils. Cubeb berries were smoked for catarrh.[60]

Bonebright-Closz added some others to Crowder's list: "skunk-oil and goose-grease, sulphur and sorghum, rhubarb and butternut pills, boneset and burdock bitters, sassafras and smartwood tea, slippery-elm salve and plaintain poultices."[61]

These home remedies were augmented, when possible, by prepared medicines such as quinine, morphine, and particularly whisky. When Paul was struck by a poisonous rattlesnake, the affected foot was kept in fresh mud for six hours and she was dosed with whisky. "This one poison," she dryly remarked, "offset another."[62] Bonebright-Closz was especially graphic in her description of the medicinal use of whisky.

Whisky was the base for all bitters and the vehicle for internal and external application. It was, in fact, an all around remedial rejuvenator . . . . It was taken as an eye-opener before breakfast and a victual settler after meals, an exhilarator between them, and as a nightcap at bedtime . . . . [W]hiskey served in sociability as it did in sickness.[63]

By the 1860s there were also hundreds of patent medicines on the market in Iowa, all offering instant relief for any ailment. Although commercially prepared medications were available, whether they were truly efficacious is an unanswerable question. If, as Bonebright-Closz believed, whisky was actually the base for many of them, they probably did bring a measure of relief to the sufferer, if not a measure of cure. Doctors, on the other hand, were too few or too far away to be prevailed upon for medical care in most cases. So if common preventive medicine, such as the spring doses of sulphur and molasses or the little bag of asafetida (gum resin with a garlic-like odor) tied around a person's neck, did not successfully ward off illness, then it was often up to the women of the family to become both doctor and nurse.

[60] E. May Lacey Crowder, "Pioneer Life in Palo Alto County," *Iowa Journal of History and Politics*, XLV (1948), 183.

[61] Bonebright-Closz, *Reminiscences of Newcastle*, 227.

[62] Paul, memoirs.

[63] Bonebright-Closz, *Reminiscences of Newcastle*, 229.

When Sarah Kenyon's husband fell victim to a serious cold, she insisted that "John would have roared if I had not quelled him with morphene." She treated his symptoms by putting "the physic and hoar hound tea to him nice and kept him on water porridge the next day."[64] Mary Ann Ferrin had a much more difficult time curing her husband of what she called "that terrible Foe, chills and fever." After two weeks of treatment, he was finally attacked by a "sinking chill" which alarmed her because she had no "doctor's medicine" in the house. She prepared hot teas for him to drink, rubbed his limbs vigorously, and "applied hot flannels wrung out of strong mint tea to his stomach and bowels." She continued to give him ginger tea, and in a few days his chills were broken and, to her great relief, he gradually regained his strength.[65]

Ellen Strang's diary gives a particularly good account of her own determined yet unsuccessful treatment of her younger sister for an "Ague chill." Ellen first put mustard poultices on her sister's feet, wrists, and neck and gave her Jamaica Ginger tea once every hour. The next day she tried mustard poultices, and by the end of the week called a doctor who brought her some "medicine." Ellen continued the Jamaica Ginger tea and various poultices through the next week with only occasional success. By the third week the patient felt better, then had a sudden relapse. Ellen responded by rubbing the child's limbs with whisky, giving her more Jamaica Ginger tea, using mustard water to soak her hands and feet, binding sulphur on the joints of her hands and feet, and feeding her meals of corn meal gruel and flour porridge. She finally gave her quinine measured out on the point of a pen knife every two hours and some "powders" brought by the doctor, but after these long weeks of suffering, the little girl died.[66]

Strang's diary temporarily stopped here so there is no record of her feelings regarding the death of her sister nor any description of the funeral. From other sources, it is clear that "laying out the dead" was also assigned to the women, who

---

[64]Sarah Kenyon to her mother, March 18, 1860, Kenyon Family Papers.

[65]Mary Ann Ferrin Davidson, "An Autobiography and a Reminiscence," *Annals of Iowa*, XXXVII 1964), 249–251.

[66]Greene, "Diary of a Young Girl," 448–455.

again used herbs to prepare the body. The explanation behind such tasks being assigned to the women is partly practical and partially ideological. Women were in the house most of the hours of the day so they were present to provide constant service. On the ideological level, women were seen as "natural" caretakers of the sick and dead due to the "greater sensibilities" imputed to them by nineteenth-century cultural norms. Because they were female, they were thought to have an inherent wisdom and softness that men lacked. This also at least partially explains why men were normally excluded from childbirth, a mysterious business which was usually handled by the mother-to-be, a female midwife, and perhaps a few female friends or relatives.

Procreation was encouraged on the frontier both to aid population growth and to provide future laborers for the family farm or other business. Therefore, besides all her other duties, a frontierswoman was also expected to produce and rear future laborers. Once she completed the pregnancy and the birth, a woman was charged with the primary, if not sole, responsibility of supervising her child, assuming that the child survived infancy. It might be added that since women were in the home more than men it was again only "natural" that they should be charged with the task of child care. Actually this was probably more of an eastern perception than a western reality, for in Iowa at least, many women did leave the home to do farm work, carrying their children with them in ingenious ways. Paul hauled up water from the well with her baby tied to her in her apron "to keep her from being trampled on by the thirsty cattle." When she helped her husband with the field work, she took her baby with her and "put her in a large box where she could play" while Paul worked. Even when at home she combined child care with work: "I done all my washing by hand rubbing every garment, and often stood on one foot while rubbing, and rocking the baby's cradle with the other foot, to keep her from waking up."[67]

If the children were indeed to become laborers on the family farm, the assignment of early child care to the mother meant in practice that she become the trainer, organizer, and overseer of

[67] Paul, memoirs.

the family labor force. Therefore, besides her own functions as a worker/producer, she was also thrust into a supervisory position. As manager of the home, she quickly initiated the young children into the tasks of food processing, soap making, candle making, spinning and weaving, knitting, and the like. In their early years, both boys and girls were expected to share in these tasks; there are even cases of Iowa boys taking part in stocking knitting and quilt piecing. As the children advanced in age, a division of labor of sorts began to appear with the boys assuming more of the outdoor chores and the girls more of the indoor work. It was common for boys to be sent for fuel and water, to help with the planting, to help with the stock, and to work in the fields, while the girls continued with the production of food, soap, candles, and with the care of the younger children.

Yet these role divisions were not absolute; the nature of the tasks and the available labor supply quite often determined who would undertake what job. Herding of stock was often assigned to boys and girls alike. Children as young as six and seven were sent out to follow the sound of the bell strapped around the lead cow's neck and to persuade the herd to stop grazing and return home for milking.[68] In addition to this chore, Matilda Paul remembered that as a child she carried in wood for the cook stove, hauled water, and fed the calves in the morning and evening, as well as assisting with the more traditional female-oriented household duties. Along with the other younger children, she also worked in the fields, dropping corn and potatoes into the rows at planting time while older children followed along behind with hoes and covered the holes. Other jobs followed:

> When the corn first came up we had to stay out in the field and chase the black-birds to keep them from digging and eating the corn as fast as it came up. It was our work in spring to pull weeds for the hogs for feed. About the middle of June we used to pick wild strawberries. . . . We often had to watch our cattle to keep them out of other peoples as well as out of our own fields. . . . Before I was old enough to bind grain I helped carry bundles in piles, ready to be shocked up . . . . I often had to get water from a spring and carry it out to the field for

[68]Crowder, "Pioneer Life in Palo Alto County," 160.

drinking for the workers, before I was old enough to do other field work. Later on I helped bind the grain .... We children had to go over the whole field and gather up the roots in piles and when they got dry we used them for fuel. ... After harvest and haying was done we had to dig the potatoes and husk the corn ready for winter.[69]

The complexities of the frontierswoman's task as superintendent are apparent, but she was also frequently called upon to aid with tasks normally considered "men's work." Because Iowa land was cheap and plentiful, "hiring out" one's labor was usually less attractive than taking up land for oneself. As a result of the scarcity of hired hands, many women were called upon to "fill in" until another source of labor became available. Women drove teams of plow animals, dropped seed, harvested crops, and did many of the other heavy field work that nineteenth-century cultural values said women should not and could not do. Caroline Phelps, for example, helped her trader husband "to pack the skins, as we had no man to help."[70] Paul drove the horses on a reaper during one harvest and the next year she drove a harvester.[71] Sarah Kenyon, along with her children, did a variety of field jobs, including reaping wheat. One year when her husband hired a field hand, she told her mother that things were looking up. "John has hired a man to work for him this Summer," she wrote, and "hope I shall not have to dig quite as much out of doors." But when the hired man quit just before the fall corn harvest she took it philosophically:

Our hired man left just as corn plucking commenced so I shouldered my hoe and have worked out ever since and I guess my services are just as acceptable as his or will be in time to come to the country .... I wore a dress with my sunbonnet wrung out in water every few minutes and my dress also wet [and] this was all the clothing ... I wore.[72]

The argument could be made that women doing men's work was a "gainful" employment in that it helped produce a cash crop and/or preserved cash which would have been paid out to

---

[69] Paul, memoirs.
[70] Caroline Phelps, diary, Iowa State Historical Society, Iowa City, Iowa.
[71] Paul, memoirs.
[72] Sarah Kenyon to her mother, Oct. 11, 1861, Kenyon Family Papers.

a hired laborer. Yet since no actual cash passed into *her* hands and because she was laboring within the family unit, she was still not considered to be gainfully employed. This logic was also applied to her production of surplus domestic goods, such as butter and eggs, which were sold outside the home for cash. Historian Gilbert Fite maintains that butter was a primary cash product on the farmer's frontier, its income often keeping farms financially afloat during the rocky years.[73] Since women produced butter and other cash products, they were bringing in money for the operation of the homestead.

Murray remembered that "mother sold Butter Eggs & Bees-wax & anything we could spare off the farm, [and] in the summer and fall we gathered Black Berries wild grapes & anything we raised on the farm that would bring money or exchange for groceries." When her uncle and aunt worked together to build a brick drying kiln, her aunt realized that she could also use the kiln to dry fruit; during the first winter she earned a dollar selling dried peaches.[74] In another case, Belknap discovered that she could add a few coins to the savings box intended for their new home by making a few extra pieces of linen for sale while doing her own spinning and weaving.[75] Crowder recalled her mother being rather successful at producing and selling butter. She took $230 of inheritance money, invested it in milch cows, and from that time on made butter for the market. She packed it away in one hundred pound tubs and stored it in the celler until fall, when it was hauled to Algona, the nearest market, thirty miles and three days away. The money raised was used for winter clothing and supplies. Hogs were also purchased to consume the surplus milk, and hog-raising became the family's principal industry. Crowder states that many frontier women not only produced income by selling their produce, but were aware of their economic importance to the family in doing so.

Frequently enough, while the men were learning to farm, the women and children actually supported the families. They raised chicken and eggs for the table, raised the vegetables and fruit, and made butter to

---

[73]Gilbert C. Fite, *The Farmers' Frontier, 1865–1900* (New York, 1966), 47.
[74]Murray, "Memoir of the William Archer Family," 362, 370.
[75]Belknap, reminiscences.

sell in exchange for things not produced at home. The women were not unaware of this fact and were quite capable of scoring a point on occasion when masculine attitudes became too bumptious.[76]

Another resource that many women used to generate cash income were their own homes. By taking boarders into their already crowded quarters, they created more work for themselves but brought in some much-needed money. Paul, for instance, took care of her husband, two baby girls, and a hired man, yet she opted to board the local teacher for two dollars a week which, she said, "helped out a little."[77] When a branch of the Rock Island Railroad cut through the Newton farm, the family took in some of the laborers as boarders who, with the family's own five children, created a rather large household to care for.[78] And Emery Bartlett later told his children that "for two or three years, with my utmost exertion and strictist economy, I could scarcely tell whether I was gaining or losing and had it not been for the little money my dear wife saved by taking a few boarders, I must certainly have gone under."[79]

In summarizing these economic functions of frontierswomen, it seems almost incredible to realize that their economic significance in the settlement of the frontier has been largely unrecognized for so many years. Food processing and cooking; soap and candlemaking; spinning, weaving, and sewing; washing and ironing; acting as apothecaries, nurses, doctors, and morticians; producing children, caring for them, and training them as laborers; helping with men's work; and generating cash income was no mean list of accomplishments. Since factories and trained professionals have taken over most of these functions in our own world, it is doubly difficult for us to realize just how much skill and labor were involved. Whether nineteenth-century society or the U. S. Bureau of the Census accepted it or not, these frontierswomen were indeed "gainfully employed."

[76] Crowder, "Pioneer Life in Palo Alto County," 178, 181.

[77] Paul, memoirs.

[78] Edith H. Hurlbutt, "Pioneer Experiences in Keokuk County, 1858–1874," *Iowa Journal of History*, LII (1954), 331.

[79] Emery S. Bartlett, "The Bartlett Family of Poweshiek County," Iowa Historical Museum and Archives, Des Moines, Iowa.

Images of the Frontierswoman: Iowa as a Case Study

GLENDA RILEY

The frontiers*woman* is a frustrating subject to tackle because the history of the American West has been derived primarily from the experience of the frontiers*man*. In his famous address to the American Historical Association in 1893, Frederick Jackson Turner stated: "The wilderness masters the colonist. . . . It takes him from the railroad car and puts him in the birch canoe. It strips off the garments of civilization and arrays him in the hunting shirt and the moccasin. . . .he shouts the war cry and takes the scalp in orthodox Indian fashion." [1] To Turner, the frontier was conquered by the "fur-trader, miner, cattle-raiser, and farmer" while women were an invisible or perhaps a nonexistent force.[2]

This attitude was not peculiar to Turner or his era. In a 1922 address to the Mississippi Valley Historical Association, George F. Parker, also a historian of the American West, declared: "I define the American Pioneer as the man who . . . crossed the mountains from the thin line of Atlantic settlement. . . . I mean the man who . . . swept on through the passes. . . . This man steadily solidified his settlement. . . . To me, this man reflects the character of the most effective single human movement in history." [3]

In recent decades a few writers have raised questions regarding the frontier women who crossed the mountains and swept through the passes along with the frontier men. In 1944 a diminutive volume by Nancy Wilson Ross argued that because women "made possible the conquest and civilizing of the frontier they deserved a place in its history." [4] Similarly,

Glenda Riley is associate professor of history at the University of Northern Iowa, Cedar Falls.

[1] Frederick Jackson Turner, *The Frontier in American History* (New York, 1962), 4.

[2] Turner, *Frontier*, 12.

[3] George F. Parker, *The American Pioneer and His Story* (Iowa City, 1922), 3.

[4] Nancy Wilson Ross, *Westward the Women* (New York, 1944), 5.

in 1961 Elizabeth Cochran pointed out that in reading through the history of Kansas, "one is struck by the scarcity of accounts of Kansas women." [5] Yet in 1974, T. A. Larson noted that such laments were still largely unheeded. In a review of western history textbooks he discovered little or no mention of pioneer women, although the authors were reputedly experts on the history of the frontier. "In short," Larson concluded, "standard textbooks used in college and university courses in Western history come close to ignoring women entirely." [6]

That women have been relatively invisible in western history is now widely understood, but why they have been invisible is not. Larson touched upon causality briefly by observing that women on the frontier "did not lead expeditions, command troops, build railroads, drive cattle, ride Pony Express, find gold, amass great wealth, get elected to high public office, rob stages, or lead lynch mobs." [7] Clearly, most pioneer women did not fill dramatic, highly visible roles but worked quietly behind the scenes within the confines of their own cabins or sod huts in customary and often unnoticed female roles.

These women were virtually ignored because, until the emergence of the feminist movement in the 1960s, women's lives were usually regarded as unworthy of study. This attitude was complicated by the fact that the fourteen-to-sixteen-hour day demanded of pioneer women did not leave them much leisure time to record their thoughts and activities in the diaries and journals which serve as source materials for later historians. Folklorist Claire R. Farrer has advised scholars to "no longer base . . . theories, hypothetical constructs, and models on half of the available data." To her, neither the attitude that the dominant (meaning male) areas of activity are the only ones deserving study nor the difficulty of collecting "the other half of the data" should deter scholarly investigation into women's lives.[8]

Although a sensible recommendation, it is a particularly difficult one to implement in relation to western history because in the popular mind the frontier was a male society. The settlement of the West traditionally has been interpreted as a male process replete with male images. Beverly

[5] Elizabeth Cochran, "Hatchets and Hoopskirts: Women in Kansas History," *Midwest Quarterly,* 2 (April 1961), 229.

[6] T. A. Larson, "Women's Role in the American West," *Montana, the magazine of Western History,* 24 (Summer 1974), 4.

[7] Larson, "Women's Role," 4.

[8] Claire R. Farrer, "Women and Folklore: Images and Genres," *Journal of American Folklore,* 88 (January–March 1975), ix.

J. Stoeltje identified three of these male images: the cowboy, the settler, and the outlaw.[9] Other investigators have discussed the mountain man, the gunfighter, the rancher, and the soldier. One has only to examine the modern media to determine that the American West is still viewed as a male undertaking.

The emergence of the male image regarding the frontier was due partly to the fact that physical strength was essential to success in most endeavors and partly to the fact that male easterners, who were the principal writers about the West, saw what they or their readers wanted to see. In *The Western Hero*. Kent L. Steckmesser maintained that "these writers . . . gave Eastern readers narratives that were based upon Eastern preconceptions and expectations. . . . They romanticized frontier characters in response to literary conventions and commercial requirements." [10] Since the resulting mythology of the West remains a profound force in American thought, it is impossible even for historians for the West to avoid its male-oriented influence.

This means that the historian of the frontier has faced essentially two alternatives in studying pioneer women: to cast them in "masculine" terms (tough, sexual, political) or to cast them in "feminine" terms (domestic, submissive yet sturdy, moral). One result of the "masculine" approach has been the Calamity Jane syndrome based upon stories of famous women who acted more like men than women. A second development has been the glorification of the "light ladies" of the West—the prostitutes who both served and embodied male sexuality in the frontier setting.

A third and more significant result has been the proliferation of accounts regarding female suffrage on the frontier. History in general has long been enamored of men acting as political beings contending for power. It follows then that women would be most noticeable and important as suffragists, that is as political beings contending for their share of power.[11] According to one group of commentators, "the general lack of attention accorded to women outside the women's rights movement reflects the implicit assumptions that it is only when women are behaving in ways usually

[9] Beverly J. Stoeltje, "'A Helpmate for Man Indeed': The Image of the Frontier Woman," *Journal of American Folklore*, 88 (January–March 1975), 27.

[10] Kent L. Steckmesser, *The Western Hero in History and Legend* (Norman, 1965), 246.

[11] Glenda Riley, "Is Clio Still Sexist? Women's History in Recent American History Texts," *Teaching History: A Journal of Methods*, 1 (Spring 1976), 16–17.

attributed to men—that is, politically—that they deserve mention." [12] Since woman suffrage first became a reality on the frontier, it is reasonable to expect western history to interpret women in a male, political context.

On the other hand, the "feminine" approach is also inappropriate and inaccurate. The problem revolves around the definition of categories. As psychologist Rae Carlson states, "polarities (of masculinity and femininity) identify dichotomous qualities linked by a relationship of oppositeness." [13] A woman must be defined as having different traits than a man; once enumerated, these diametrically opposed qualities tend to form a category.

The definition of the category of the western woman was greatly influenced, as was the definition of the category of the western man, by eastern standards, or by what Richard Slotkin described as "the images and symbols that are the outer emblems of . . . collective mythology." [14] For the nineteenth century, the ideal woman was domestic, destined to be a wife and mother, passive and submissive yet strong and enduring. Moreover, she was the moral guardian of a society being tested by the demands of industrialization.[15] Transplant this characterization to the frontier, establish it as a category, and the image of the pioneer woman is born. Variously called the Madonna of the Prairies, the Pioneer Mother, or the Sunbonnet Myth, the mystique of the pioneer woman has come to encompass certain related attributes.

The western historians who have devoted some space to the "feminine" frontierswoman have fallen prey to the legacy of the mystique. In 1921 Emerson Hough wrote: [16]

> The chief figure of the American West . . . is not the long-haired fringed-legging man riding a raw-bored pony, but the gaunt and sad-faced woman sitting on the front seat of the wagon, following her lord where he might lead, her face hidden in the same ragged sunbonnet which had crossed the

[12] Ann D. Gordan, Mari Jo Buhle, Nancy E. Schrom, "Women in American Society: An Historical Contribution," *Radical American*, V (July–August 1971), 12.

[13] Rae Carlson, "Understanding Women: Implications for Personality Theory and Research," *Journal of Social Issues*, 28 (No. 2, 1972), 23.

[14] Richard Slotkin, *Regeneration through Violence: The Mythology of the American Frontier, 1600–1860* (Middletown, Connecticut, 1973), 550.

[15] Glenda Riley, "The Subtle Subversion: Changes in the Traditionalist Image of the American Woman," *Historian*, 32 (February 1970), 210–27. For a discussion of the relationship of frontier women to "civilization" see Anne Falk, "The Art of Convention: Images of Women in the Modern Western Novels of Henry Wilson Allen," *North Dakota Quarterly*, 42 (Spring 1974), 18–19.

[16] Emerson Hough, *The Passing of the Frontier* (New Haven, 1921), 93.

Appalachians and the Missouri long before. . . . That was the great romance of all America—the woman in the sunbonnet.

In 1937, Everett Dick included a chapter titled "Women and Children" in his *Sod-House Frontier.* In his view, women led trying lives. They were saddled with "utter loneliness and drab realities," but although becoming leathery and stooped, many bore it without complaint and persevered alongside their husbands.[17] And in 1970, Page Smith claimed that women were:[18]

the shock-troops of Western migration. Clinging to a few treasured heirlooms as reminders of a kinder life, they accompanied their husbands across the continent, suffering the most desperate physical hardships as well as a desolating sense of loneliness. More place-bound than men, more dependent on the company of other women, on the forms of settled social life, they grew old and died before their time, on the trail, in a sod hut or in a rude cabin pierced by icy winds.

Several authors have recognized and decried this mystique, but at the same time they have been unable to escape it. In 1958 Dee Brown described the pioneer woman as "the most conservative of creatures, hating with a passion those three concomitants of the western frontier—poverty, physical hardship, and danger." The "Wild West," he concluded, "was tamed by its petticoated pioneers."[19] In 1974 Richard A. Bartlett generalized:[20]

The new country woman held her head high, and her bright eyes searched the horizon for what lay ahead. She shared with her husband a faith in their future. Beneath her linsey-woolsey or calico frock was a sturdy body. She could walk to Kentucky, or Missouri, or the Pike's Peak country, or to Zion at Salt Lake or to Oregon. She was a builder, along with her husband; she knew her value.

At another point, Bartlett emphasized that "she wrapped a shawl around her shoulders, tied on her sunbonnet, cradled the youngest babe in her arms, and pointed her face West."[21]

[17] Everett Dick, *The Sod-House Frontier, 1854–1890* (New York, 1937), 233–35.

[18] Page Smith, *Daughters of the Promised Land* (Boston, 1970), 223.

[19] Dee Brown, *The Gentle Tamers: Women of the Old Wild West* (New York, 1974), 269.

[20] Richard A. Bartlett, *The New Country: A Social History of the American Frontier, 1776–1890* (London, 1974), 350.

[21] Bartlett, *New Country,* 149.

The addition of this "feminine" interpretation to the "masculine" interpretations of the frontierswoman constitutes four possible typologies of western women: (1) the Calamity Jane, (2) the sex object, (3) the frontier suffragist, and (4) the saint in the sunbonnet. All four types are larger than life—superwomen to match the supermen of the frontier legend. All four are highly stereotypical, with little allowance for individuality or racial and ethnic variations. And all four are highly suspect in terms of their workability and accuracy.

To test these factors, it is necessary to apply the four typologies to an actual frontier situation. Since the Appalachian frontier and the far western frontier have been overresearched to the point of distortion, a segment of the midwestern frontier seems to be a more valid source. Also, the Midwest was typical in that it was family-farm, as was the majority of the West, rather than specialized, as were the cattle, lumber, or mineral frontiers.

Iowa has been selected from the midwestern frontier for several reasons: Primary research materials are extant, the soil was rich enough to prevent it from being the most poverty-stricken of frontier areas, its soil and location provided for relatively rapid settlement so that Iowa was not the loneliest of frontier areas, and Iowa was representative chronologically in that it was not the earliest nor the latest frontier. Frontier Iowa was legally opened in 1833 with the Black Hawk Purchase Treaty, achieved statehood in 1846, and was declared closed by the United States Bureau of the Census in 1870.

Using Iowa as a sample frontier then, the first type—the Calamity Jane—can be easily reviewed, since this particular phenomenon does not seem to have appeared in Iowa. Dee Brown has suggested that the development of the gunslinging female outlaw was associated with the Civil War and its related "guerilla strife" throughout the border states.[22] Since Iowa was not a border state but antislavery in its sentiments and legal structure, raiding parties were largely peripheral to it during the Civil War.

Brown also remarked that many female outlaws were drawn into a life of crime because "they lost their heart to some romantic reprobate." [23] If Iowa did produce its share of notable male outlaws, they must have

[22] Brown, *Gentle Tamers*, 236.

[23] Brown, *Gentle Tamers*, 238.

left their home area to make their reputations and fortunes elsewhere in the West; presumably they found their female companions there as well. It might be hypothesized that frontier Iowa was not very rich pickings for either male or female gunslingers. There were few railroads carrying mine or other payrolls, there were few cattle barons with well-stocked safes, and there were few banks holding large deposits, while the average prairie homestead was hardly attractive to a group like the Hole-in-the-Wall gang.

Futhermore, Iowa's image did not support the idea of outlaws, gunslingers, or other heroic figures riding through its gently rippling corn and wheat. The eastern audiences which so voraciously consumed dime novels about the West and thronged to Wild West shows found it more plausible that such people should be spawned by the wilder Far West. It seems somewhat incongruous, for example, that the colorful Buffalo Bill Cody was born and spent his early boyhood years in a small Iowa town.

So it is possible that Iowa produced other heroes and heroines which she has not yet claimed. It is more likely, however, that most Iowan frontierspeople considered a woman's ability to handle a firearm a necessary part of frontier living rather than a glamorous accomplishment or an introduction to a life of crime. Many women became adept with firearms in order to help protect their homes and children or to help in hunting food for their families. The gun-toting prairie woman is probably best typified by the plucky Iowa wife who after being knocked down once by a treacherous gun and again by a wounded deer "re-loaded her gun and put an end to her adventure by shooting the deer through the head."[24]

The second type, the sexual woman, was almost as ephemeral during Iowa's frontier period as were the Calamity Janes. If scarlet women existed, which they surely did, scant mention is made of them in the letters, diaries, memoirs, and histories of the time. There was a great concern to bring more women into the territory, but they were usually desired as permanent mates rather than as temporary diversion. This was due to the nature of the agrarian economy in Iowa which made it impractical for a man to homestead successfully without a female partner who would manufacture domestic goods, process foodstuffs, and produce a labor supply in the form of many children.

[24] William M. Donnell, *Pioneers of Marion County* (Des Moines, 1872), 307.

The following table gives an indication of the potential number of men interested in finding women to become their marital and economic associates.[25]

	1838	*1850*	*1856*	*1860*	*1865*	*1870*
Male population	24,355	101,052	278,584	354,493	383,272	625,917
Female population	18,757	91,162	239,291	320,420	346,086	568,103

In 1855 the *Davenport Courier* issued a plea to eastern women. "At Fort Des Moines, Iowa, there is a dreadful scarcity of women. . . . It isn't much better in Davenport than at Fort Des Moines, and we are sure it would be an act of humanity if scores of the young maidens who are pining away in the eastern villages for somebody to love would set their faces at once toward Iowa." [26] In 1860, when an eastern woman placed an advertisement for a husband in the *Waterloo Courier*, the editor commented that this presented a "rare chance" for a young man "to obtain that useful and essential article of household furniture—a Wife." [27] He was, of course, expressing exactly what most Iowa pioneers had already learned—a wife *was* invaluable. This was confirmed by John B. Newall, who in his *A Glimpse of Iowa in 1846* unequivocally stated, "Married persons are generally more comfortable, and succeed better, in a frontier country, than single men; for a wife and family . . . may always prove a source of pecuniary advantage." [28]

Unlike the first two types, the third—the frontier suffragist—was very much in evidence. Frontier Iowa was the home base for the activities of Amelia Bloomer (suffragist and editor), Mary Newbury Adams (suffragist and public speaker), Narcissa T. Bemis (suffragist and lobbyist), Martha Coonley Callanan (suffragist and editor), and Adeline Morrison Swain (suffragist and editor), among others. Of these, Amelia Bloomer was the most well known. Much of her notoriety derived from her advo-

[25] Iowa, *Census of Iowa for 1880* . . . (Des Moines, 1883) [binder's title: Iowa, Historical and Comparative Census, 1836–1880], 168–70.

[26] "Pioneering Handicap," *Annals of Iowa,* 26 (October 1944), 89.

[27] Quoted in William J. Petersen, "Boys, Keep Away from Muslin," *Palimpsest,* 50 (November 1969), 643.

[28] John B. Newhall, *A Glimpse of Iowa in 1846; or, the Emigrant's Guide* (Iowa City, 1957), 62.

cacy of the Bloomer costume she wore throughout the 1850s.[29] In addition, she edited *The Lily* for many years, organized the Council Bluffs Soldier's Aid Society, publicly lectured on women's rights, helped organize the Iowa Woman Suffrage Association in 1870, and served as its second president in 1871.[30] She thus became a symbol of sorts for early western suffragism.

Closer examination, however, reveals that neither Bloomer nor her above-named contemporaries were western products. Bloomer was born in Homer, New York, in 1818; after teaching and editing *The Lily* in New York state she migrated to Iowa in 1855 with her husband.[31] Mary Newbury Adams was born in Peru, Indiana, in 1837, was educated at the Emma Willard Seminary in Troy, New York, and in 1856 settled with her husband in Dubuque. Narcissa T. Bemis was born in Alabama, New York, in 1829, was educated in the East, and came to Independence, Iowa, in 1855 to marry. Martha Coonley Callanan was born in Albany County, New York, in 1826, was educated in Albany schools and moved to Des Moines when she married in 1846. Adeline Morrison Swain was born at Bath, New Hampshire, in 1820, became a language teacher in eastern seminaries, then located in Fort Dodge in 1858 with her husband.[32]

All of these frontier suffragists were eastern born and bred, were drawn to the West by husbands instead of by the social and political climate, arrived relatively late in the pioneer period, and lived as city dwellers once in Iowa. This raises the question as to whether the frontier suffragists were inspired by the frontier environment or by conditions more universal to women. Adams's early letters neglect comment on the larger world but do record that "it is the easyest thing in the world for a mother to feel she is a mere drudge (at least it is for me)." [33]

Debates on woman suffrage in the Iowa General Assembly also failed to reflect much concern with the idea that a frontier state was, or should

[29] Philip D. Jordan, "Amelia Jenks Bloomer," *Palimpsest,* 38 (April 1957), 139, 145.

[30] Louise R. Noun, *Strong-Minded Women: The Emergence of the Woman-Suffrage Movement in Iowa* (Ames, 1969), 12–20, 133–40.

[31] Ruth S. Beitz, "Amelia Bloomer's Own Emancipation Proclamation," *Iowan,* 14 (Winter 1965–66), 40.

[32] Benjamin F. Gue, *History of Iowa* (New York, 1903), volume 4, *Iowa Biography,* 2–3, 18, 38–39, 256–57.

[33] Austin Adams Family Papers, Special Collections, Iowa State University Library.

be, more liberal towards women than eastern states. Rather, the supporters of woman suffrage in Iowa were usually advocates of the justice argument. One claimed that "women should have some voice in the making of the laws by which they are governed . . . it is the elementary principle on which we start out our Declaration of Independence," [34] while another introduced a resolution urging that women should be allowed "the right of franchise, for the proper use of which, her quick perception, strong intellect, and above all, her high sense of right and justice, have proven her so well qualified." [35]

Despite the pressure of suffragists as well as that of speakers, petitions, and referendums, Iowa did not extend suffrage to its women until the Nineteenth Amendment made woman suffrage national law in 1920. Whatever the peculiar combination of factors that led to seventeen western states adopting woman suffrage prior to 1920, they did not come to fruition in Iowa.[36] So, although the Iowa frontier did have some embodiments of the frontier suffragist, neither their composition nor their effect fit the accepted expectations.

By logical fiat then, the bulk of Iowa's pioneer women must have fit into type four—the saint in the sunbonnet. But, like most stereotypes, the group of exemplary cases which uphold its claims are offset by individual cases that disprove them. When examined in detail, the image of the sunbonneted saint ruptures into disconnected fragments.

Was the pioneer woman a wife and mother? Despite the need for women to serve in these capacities on the frontier, there were cases of women migrating westward on their own, homesteading alone, or choosing a career without marriage as an accompaniment. The memoirs of Amelia Murdock Wing mentioned both a female friend who filed on a homestead in Dakota and a sister who became an ordained Unitarian minister.[37] Blaine T. Williams's study of the pioneer family in Texas has indicated that if the demographic data for Iowa were closely studied, many cases

[34] "Proceedings of the House, March 29, 1870," *Des Moines Bulletin, Legislative Supplement* (1870), No. 61, p. 2.

[35] Iowa, General Assembly, House of Representatives, *Journal*, March 31, 1870, 530.

[36] See Alan P. Grimes, *The Puritan Ethic and Woman Suffrage* (New York, 1967) and T. A. Larson, "Dolls, Vassals, and Drudges—Pioneer Women in the West," *Western Historical Quarterly*, III (January 1972), 5–16.

[37] Amelia Murdock Wing, "Early Days in Clayton County," *Annals of Iowa*, 27 (April 1946), 257–96.

of single women or of widows opting not to remarry would become evident.[38] Moreover, the fact that a few women rejected marriage in a society which so ardently sanctioned it speaks strongly for the possibility of there being other unrecorded cases of like-minded women.

Was the pioneer woman passive, submitting to her husband's will when circumstances demanded it? For every woman who viewed the frontier experience as a "male enterprise," [39] there was another who said, "I was fond of adventure and preferred to go with my husband." [40] One Iowa woman remembered that her "father always said that whenever he wanted to move he had only to tell mother of his plans and she was ready and willing to go." [41] And if by chance a woman did not favor her husband's plans, passivity was not the only solution. Rather than being left home alone, Clara Ann Dodge demanded and eventually won the right to accompany her husband Augustus during his political sojourns in Washington, D.C., and elsewhere.[42] If passivity and submissiveness were requisites for the nineteenth century's "true woman," the news must not have effectively reached the frontier.

Was the pioneer woman robustly energetic? Most were so by necessity whether their health or inclinations supported it or not. Because workers were generally unavailable for hire in the house or fields even when the cash to pay them was available, the pioneer woman had to produce most of the domestic goods needed by her family, as well as occasionally laboring in the fields. One woman wrote her mother that "our hired man left just as corn plucking commenced so I shouldered my hoe and have worked out ever since and I guess my services are just as acceptable as his or will be in time to come to the country." [43] The son

[38] Blaine T. Williams, "The Frontier Family: Demographic Fact and Historical Myth," in Harold M. Hollingsworth, ed., *Essays on the American West* (Austin, 1969), 55–59.

[39] See Johnny Faragher and Christine Stansell, "Women and Their Families on the Overland Trail to California and Oregon, 1842–1867," *Feminist Studies,* 2 (No. 2/3, 1975), 151.

[40] Mary Ann Ferrin, "An Autobiography and a Reminiscence," *Annals of Iowa,* 37 (Spring 1964), 243.

[41] Katharine Horack, "In Quest of a Prairie Home," *Palimpsest,* 5 (July 1924), 250.

[42] Letters of Clara Ann Dodge, 1841–49, Manuscript Collection, Iowa State Historical Society.

[43] Letters of John and Mary Kenyon, 1856–65, Manuscript Collection, Iowa State Historical Society.

of another Iowa woman described her life as one of constant toil:[44]

She bore and cared for the babies, saw that the floor was white and clean, that the beds were made and cared for, the garden tended, the turkeys dressed, the deer flesh cured and the fat prepared for candles or culinary use, that the wild fruits were garnered and preserved or dried, that the spinning and knitting was done and the clothing made. She did her part in all these tasks, made nearly all the clothing and did the thousand things for us a mother only finds to do.

The memoirs of yet another included accounts of her rocking a cradle with her foot while doing chores with her hands, as well as taking her infants into the field while she plowed, raked hay, picked up potatoes, and husked corn.[45] Although heavy work was a reality in the life of most frontierswomen, it was a reality in the life of most eastern women of the times as well. Thus, it was not peculiar to the lot of those wearing sunbonnets.

Did the pioneer woman civilize the frontier? As Mary W. M. Hargreaves noted, pioneer women tended to carry with them to the frontier the trappings of civilization, such as "pianos, organs, Haviland china, silver candelabra, and similar symbols." [46] Iowa women were no different. When her cabin flooded, one Iowa woman got her family to "bore holes through the upper floor and swing the piano up to the joists" to save it.[47] Another disparaged the "rustic manners" of the pioneers and could not understand the lack of "a spittoon, and a mat for wiping the feet." [48]

In addition, women enforced morality and religious values. One recalled that when "four young men and two girls" accompanied her and her husband on a trip, she "made them promise there should be no sparking and they should all be in their proper places in time of service . . .

[44] George C. Duffield, "An Iowa Settler's Homestead," *Annals of Iowa,* 6 (October 1903), 210.

[45] Recollections of Matilda Pietzke Paul, Manuscript Collection, Iowa State Historical Society.

[46] Mary W. M. Hargreaves, "Women in the Agricultural Settlement of the Northern Plains," *Agricultural History,* 50 (January 1976), 186–87.

[47] Sarah Welch Nossaman, "Pioneering at Bonaparte and Near Pella," *Annals of Iowa,* 8 (October 1922), 452–53.

[48] David T. Nelson, tr. and ed., *The Diary of Elisabeth Koren, 1853–1855* (Minnesota: Norwegian-American Historical Association, 1955), 122, 130.

and if they did not set a good example before the world and show which side they were on they could not go with me and they behaved to the letter." [49]

But frontier men also enforced societal norms. The travel diary of an Iowa family recorded that emigrant families formally observed the Sabbath in one trail camp because the local (male) storekeeper came to the camp every Sunday morning to perform a short service for them.[50] If women were more associated with morality and civilization, it was probably because it was their job rather than an innate talent. As Robert Dykstra argued in his study of Kansas cattle towns, "the gradual domestication of cattle town society" succeeded only "as family groups gradually infiltrated the demographic structure." [51] A similar pattern occurred in Iowa—with women came homes and families and with them came civilization and morality.

The final blow to the mystique of the pioneer woman comes with the query, did she really wear calico and a sunbonnet? Many did, at least for work, but most of Iowa's frontierswomen were very fashion conscious. In the mid-1850s a young Iowa woman's record of her clothing expenses included calico and gingham among more numerous entries for velvet ribbon, a silk apron, a lawn dress, a fan, a pair of kid gloves, a hair comb, a mantle, a parasol, and yards of lace.[52] By the 1870s another remarked that "hoops and great bustles are all the rage" and "almost every girl wears curls or frizzes." [53] Although such elaborate fashions, particularly hoops, caused skirts to singe in open fireplaces, or prevented women from riding horseback, or trapped them when crossing stiles, many of Iowa's pioneer women, like their eastern counterparts, emulated the latest fashion plates as faithfully as possible.[54]

[49] Reminiscences of Kitturah Penton Belknap, Manuscript Collection, Iowa State Historical Society.

[50] Diary of Mary Alice Shutes, 1862, Manuscript Collection, Iowa Historical Museum and Archives.

[51] Robert R. Dykstra, *The Cattle Towns* (New York, 1970), 246–48.

[52] Alice L. Longley Papers, Manuscript Collection, Iowa Historical Museum and Archives.

[53] Janette Stevenson Murray, "Women of North Tama," *Iowa Journal of History and Politics*, 41 (July 1943), 289.

[54] Alice Money Lawrence, "A Pioneer School Teacher in Central Iowa," *Iowa Journal of History and Politics*, 33 (October 1935), 378–79, 383, 387–88.

Apparently, the mystique of the sunbonnet is like the sunbonnet itself: "an obstruction to sight and an impediment to hearing." [55] But if it is, along with the other three typologies, so unrealistic, why do historians continue to rely upon it? Donald W. Gawronski observed that if "the 'common man' has been neglected in historical writing until the modern era, what must be the case of the 'common woman'," [56] while Ray and Victoria Ginger explained that it is easier "to work with published polemics than to begin the enormous task of ferreting out the everyday lives of the anonymous." [57] In the case of western history, this means that historians must shelve inaccurate models and paradigms in favor of digging out the data on pioneer women, for it is only when knowledge about frontierswomen is added to that about frontiersmen that an understanding of frontierspeople will emerge.[58]

[55] Harriet Bonebright-Closz, *Reminiscence of Newcastle, Iowa, 1848* (Des Moines, 1921), 121.

[56] Donald V. Gawronski, *History: Meaning and Method* (Glenview, Illinois, 1975), 94–95.

[57] Ray and Victoria Ginger, "Feminist and Family History: Some Pitfalls," *Labor History*, 12 (Fall 1971), 617.

[58] Glenda Riley, "Women Pioneers in Iowa," *Palimpsest*, 57 (March/April 1976), 53.

"You May Depend She Does Not Eat Much Idle Bread": Mid-Atlantic Farm Women and Their Historians

JOAN M. JENSEN

The words above were written by farmer Esther Lewis, in a letter to her daughter and son-in-law in 1837 about the work of her hired woman. As a widow, Lewis had many responsibilities managing both farm and household. But her words, in many ways, seem to sum up the industriousness of Mid-Atlantic farm women in the antebellum period.

In the past fifteen years, scholars in many fields have vastly increased our understanding of the importance of work performed by women along the eastern coast before 1850. Because women's work has not been the explicit focus of much of this research, however, the implications of this growing body of scholarship are not yet clear. Consequently, the research has not been incorporated by historians in their broader interpretations of the economy. Edward Pessen, for example, has offered a major reinterpretation of the predominantly rural antebellum economy without mentioning women's work. This article provides an analysis of recent historical literature relating to the work of rural women in the Mid-Atlantic from 1750–1850 that should be considered in any overall evaluation of the rural economy.

Some historians say that the Mid-Atlantic is everything left when you take away New England and the South. There is some truth to it. Enough, at least, to have to begin a review of the historiography of rural women in the Mid-Atlantic by enumerating what states are included. I have used the states defined as the Middle States by the United States agricultural cen-

JOAN M. JENSEN is Professor and Head of the Department of History, New Mexico State University.

sus in 1850: New York, Pennsylvania, New Jersey, Delaware, and Maryland. In many ways parts of Delaware and Maryland seem distinctly southern in their heavy reliance on tobacco as a field crop and enslaved black workers as a labor force. Yet for all their many economic and social divisions, these states formed an entity so strong that all remained in the Union even though some still sanctioned slavery in 1860. The Mid-Atlantic states were known for their diversity, and in some ways that diversity defied boundaries. The new research on this area, taken as a whole, points to an emerging historiography of rural women's lives there.[1]

No overall guide exists for the historical literature of women in the Mid-Atlantic region. Douglas Greenberg's 1979 review article, "The Middle Colonies in Recent American Historiography," reflected the then current lack of interest in women as a separate group with a separate history and the neglect by historians of rural history in general. The omission of women in his article helped mask what was even then available on their history. A more recent bibliography by Elizabeth Steiner-Scott and Elizabeth Pearce Wagle on New Jersey women and Trina Vaux's *Guide to Women's Resources in the Delaware Valley Area,* are focused primarily on urban women, and provide only general references to women's history for the Mid-Atlantic region. The few available bibliographies of rural women's history are seldom detailed enough to include specific studies on the Mid-Atlantic. There is, on the subject of rural women, little old ground to clear away.[2]

Culture is a fundamental category for analyzing women's work in the Mid-Atlantic area. As an ethnically heterogeneous area, the Mid-Atlantic cannot be discussed without a basic understanding of cultural differences. The gap is especially evident in ethnic immigration studies. Kathleen Neils Conzen has pointed out for another region what is also true of the Mid-Atlantic, that rural immigrants have just not received as much attention as their urban counterparts. Nor has agricultural history or rural sociology

1. Robert Gough, "The Myth of the Middle Colonies," *Pennsylvania Magazine of History and Biography* 107 (1983): 393–419. Hereafter cited as PMHB.

2. Douglas Greenberg, "The Middle Colonies in Recent American Historiography," *William and Mary Quarterly,* third series, 36 (1979): 396–427. Hereafter cited as *WMQ.* Trina Vaux, *Guide to Women's Resources in the Delaware Valley Area* (Philadelphia: University of Pennsylvania Press, 1983); and Elizabeth Steiner-Scott and Elizabeth Pearce Wagle, *New Jersey Women, 1770–1970: A Bibliography* (Rutherford: Fairleigh Dickinson University Press, 1978). Older guides like Robert V. Remini and Edwin A. Miles, *The Era of Good Feelings and the Age of Jackson, 1816–1841* (Arlington Heights, Illinois: AHM Publishing, 1979) provide some references to useful published sources. Cynthia Horsburgh Requardt, "Women's Deeds in Women's Words: Manuscripts in the Maryland Historical Society," *Maryland Historical Magazine* 73 (1978): 186–204 has a listing of one collection. The best general bibliography is Susan Bentley and Carolyn Sachs, *Farm Women in the United States: An Updated Literature Review and Annotated Bibliography* (A.E. & R.S.I., Department of Agricultural Economics and Rural Sociology, Pennsylvania State University, College Park, PA., May 1984).

paid much attention to immigrants. Most early immigrants borrowed and contributed to the cultures of those already in America in rural or small-town settings. They also maintained distinctive ethnic traits in direct relationship to the presence or absence of an ethnic community. Ethnic churches often provided rallying points, followed by schools, voluntary associations, and a press. Since women gradually became curators of community as well as family culture, their history is central to that rural ethnic history.[3]

The Mid-Atlantic has a rich ethnic history. The history of its Native American population alone is extremely complex. Besides the much-studied Seneca, many tribes of Indians inhabited the area, all gradually displaced by Europeans during the seventeenth and eighteenth centuries. Their cultures varied immensely and the women fared variously in different areas of settlement. Several anthropologists and historians have provided preliminary studies of Seneca women. Nevertheless, much remains to be done using archaeological and historical sources to document the lives of Indian women in the cultures that survived after 1750, particularly on the western frontier.[4]

The Swedes and Dutch also left a visible historical imprint as separate cultures in most of the Mid-Atlantic, at least until the early eighteenth century. Susan Klepp has traced the disappearance of Swedish culture in Pennsylvania in the late eighteenth century and the role of intermarriage by Swedish men with English women in that disappearing culture. Such studies of intermarriage are essential in tracing the fortunes of the cultures that disappeared from the area.[5]

The Swedes and Dutch, of course, were replaced by a complex mix of Northern Europeans and Africans. Irish, Welsh, Scots, and English from Great Britain and Germans from the continent, along with a few French and a large population of Africans in the southern tier, settled in the Mid-Atlantic during the eighteenth century. Thus by the beginning of the nineteenth century, the Mid-Atlantic had substituted a diverse European and

3. Kathleen Neils Conzen, "Historical Approaches to the Study of Rural Ethnic Communities," in Frederick Luebke, ed., *Ethnicity on the Great Plains* (Lincoln: University of Nebraska Press, 1981), 1–18.

4. Bruce C. Trigger, "American Archaeology as Native History: A Review Essay," *WMQ* 40 (1983): 413–52 is an excellent model. See also Anthony F. C. Wallace, "Women, Land, and Society: Three Aspects of Aboriginal Delaware Life," *Pennsylvania Archaeologist* 17 (Spring 1947): 1–35; his *The Death and Rebirth of the Seneca* (New York: Knopf, 1969); Joan M. Jensen, "Native American Women and Agriculture: A Seneca Case Study," *Sex Roles: A Journal of Research* 3 (1977): 423–41; and Diane Rothenbert, "The Mothers of the Nation: Seneca Resistance to Quaker Intervention," in Mona Etienne and Eleanor Leacock, *Women and Colonization: Anthropological Perspectives* (New York: Praeger, 1980), 63–87.

5. Susan Klepp, "Five Early Pennsylvania Censuses," *PMHB* 106 (1982): 483–514.

African immigrant population for the diverse Native American population that had once inhabited the region.[6]

Several recent studies have begun to analyze the emerging black culture and to look at the important work of black women in rural areas. Jean Soderlund has clearly pointed out the early excess of men over women in rural black communities in Pennsylvania and showed that information is adequate to begin assessing women's experiences in black families. Merle G. Brouwer has reminded us of the way in which slavery interfered with family ties among black Pennsylvanians. Black women, it should be remembered, were a large minority of the female population in parts of southeastern rural Pennsylvania by 1850—13 percent in Kennett township in Chester County. Kent and Sussex counties, in the slave state of Delaware, both had large rural free black populations. Hundreds of community-based black churches developed in rural Pennsylvania and Delaware in the early nineteenth century. In late eighteenth-century Maryland, black families took form and increased but remained fragile and subject to disruption by white owners. Demographic studies of these communities are establishing the basis for further study of black rural women.[7]

Much has been written about the predominantly English Quakers. They are one of the most visible Euro-American cultural groups in eighteenth-century Pennsylvania. Because Quaker meetings were at the center of community networks, new studies that describe gender and class patterns within these meetings provide an important context for women's lives.

6. Berry Levy, "The Light in the Valley: the Chester and Welsh Tract of Quaker Communities and the Delaware Valley, 1681–1750," (Ph.D. diss., University of Pennsylvania, 1976) contains some important material on the disappearing Welsh. Older studies of the Welsh, such as Charles H. Browning, *Welsh Settlement of Pennsylvania* (Philadelphia: Campbell, 1912), and Alan Conway, *Welsh in America: Letters from the Immigrants* (Minneapolis: University of Minnesota Press, 1961), contain almost nothing on women. Anne Catherine Bieri Herbert, "The Pennsylvania French in the 1790's: The Story of Their Survival," (Ph.D. diss., University of Texas, Austin, 1981), documents the French presence though it says little about French women.

7. Jean R. Soderlund, "Black Women in Colonial Pennsylvania," *PMHB* 107 (1983): 5; Carl D. Oblinger, "Alms for Oblivion: the Making of a Black Underclass in Southeastern Pennsylvania, 1780–1860," in John E. Bodnar, ed., *The Ethnic Experience in Pennsylvania* (Lewisburg, 1973), 94–119 and "Freedom Foundations: Black Communities in Southeastern Pennsylvania Towns: 1780–1860," *Northwest Missouri State University Studies* 33 (November 1972): 3–23; Lewis V. Baldwin, " 'Invisible' Strands in African Methodism: A History of African Union Methodist Protestant and Union American Methodist Episcopal Churches, 1805–1980," (Ph.D. diss., Northwestern University, 1980); Charles L. Coleman, "The Emergence of Black Religion in Pennsylvania, 1776–1850," *Pennsylvania Heritage* 4 (1977): 24–28; Merle Gerald Brouwer, "The Negro as a Slave and as a Free Black in Colonial Pennsylvania," (Ph.D. diss., Wayne State University, 1973) and "Marriage and Family Life Among Blacks in Colonial Pennsylvania," *PMBH* 99 (1975): 368–72. For Maryland see Russell R. Menard, "The Maryland Slave Population, 1658 to 1730: A Demographic Profile of Blacks in Four Counties," *WMQ* 32 (1975): 29–54; Allan Kulikoff, "The Beginnings of the Afro-American Family in Maryland," in Michael Gordon, ed., *The American Family in Social-Historical Perspective* (New York: St. Martin's Press, 1978); and Jean Butenhoff Lee, "The Problem of Slave Community in the Eighteenth Century Chesapeake," *WMQ* 43 (1986): 333–61.

Research describing the survival strategies of Quaker families—how many held slaves and for how long, and how they decreased fertility to cope with problems of increasing land costs—also help define cultural concerns. The ways in which women participated in these changes and their work lives have yet to be explored by historians. As ministers, doctors, teachers, and reformers, rural Quaker women were among the first to participate in public life and were key actors in the first women's rights movement in New York and Pennsylvania. We need to know more about the communities and families out of which these rural Quaker women emerged, how they created their new public lives, as well as what ideology made it acceptable for them to act as leaders in carving out these new spaces for themselves in American life.[8]

Historians now believe Germans numbered at least a third of the population of Pennsylvania by 1790 as well as a sizeable part of other Mid-Atlantic states. For all the attention given to Pennsylvania German material culture by historians they have yet to explain the ways in which German women created, used, and passed on that culture. Older out-dated studies of German communities tell us little about women but fine new studies, such as those by Marianne Wokeck of Pennsylvania Germans and Elizabeth Kessel of Maryland Germans, are no different. Three hundred years after the first German women settlers arrived to help found Germantown, we still know almost nothing about them despite numerous celebrations to mark the tricentennial in 1983. The research provoked by those celebrations began to ask new, more relevant general questions about the cultures of these people but not specific questions about women.[9]

8. Susan M. Forbes, " 'As Many Candles Lighted': The New Garden Monthly Meeting, 1718–1774," (Ph.D. diss., University of Pennsylvania, 1972); Jean R. Soderlund, "Conscience, Interest, and Power: the Development of Quaker Opposition to Slavery in the Delaware Valley, 1688–1780," (Ph.D. diss., Temple University, 1981) and *Quakers & Slavery: A Divided Spirit* (Princeton: Princeton University Press, 1985); and Joan M. Jensen, *Loosening the Bonds: Mid-Atlantic Farm Women, 1750–1850* (New Haven and London: Yale University Press, 1986). See also Levy, "The Light in the Valley."

9. Forrest McDonald and Ellen Shapiro McDonald, "The Ethnic Origins of the American People, 1790," *WMQ* 37 (1980): 180, document the numbers of Germans but not by gender. Among older studies, F. J. F. Schantz, *The Domestic Life and Character of the Pennsylvania German Frontier* (Lancaster: Pennsylvania German Society, 1900) and Amos Long, Jr., *The Pennsylvania German Farm Family: A Regional Architectural and Folk Cultural Study of an American Agricultural Community* (Breinigsville, Pa: Pennsylvania German Society, 1972) are examples of works on the household that say almost nothing about women. For newer, more carefully documented studies that, unfortunately, add nothing about German women, Elizabeth Augusta Kessel, "Germans on the Maryland Frontier: A Social History of Frederick County, Maryland, 1730–1800," (Ph.D. diss., Rice University, 1981) and " 'A Mighty Fortress is Our God': Germans on the Maryland Frontier, 1734–1800," *Maryland History Magazine* 77(1982):370–387; and Marianne Wokeck, "A Tide of Alien Tongues: The Flow and Ebb of the German Immigration to Pennsylvania, 1683–1776 (Ph.D. diss., Temple University, 1983) and "The Flow and the Composition of German Immigration to Philadelphia, 1727–1775," *PMHB* 105 (1981): 249–78.

These omissions do not occur because the material is lacking. In addition to quantitative sources, there are many literary sources. In Pennsylvania, German opposition to common schools was based on the fact that an effective German language school system was already in place. Literacy was widespread, apparently among women as well as men. Regardless of who read the German publications of the late eighteenth and early nineteenth centuries, they reveal much about women's work lives. Unless the 588 German almanacs published in Pennsylvania between 1750 and 1850 are vastly different from the roughly 2400 almanacs published in English, they contain anecdotal material that helps explain popular attitudes toward gender relations. Pamphlets, such as *Die Berg-Maria,* describe individual German women whose lives gave rise to popular legends. Instructional booklets, such as those for midwives, also exist. One *Weiber-Buchlein* published in 1808 at Euphrata, Pennsylvania contained instructions for midwifery and for dying cloth. When used by historians who have studied the new methodological techniques developed by historians of women, sources such as these can yield important insights about German women.[10]

Information on family and work for the non-Quaker immigrant—for the Scots, Scotch-Irish, Irish, and Welsh, as well as the Yankees, is so scanty that we can still say little about women's work in large areas of the Mid-Atlantic. Some students of Irish immigration are now calling into question earlier generalizations that principally Irish men immigrated during the early nineteenth century. As revised estimates of female immigrants and migrants appear, the task of recreating women's work roles can go forward.[11]

Even without the necessary cultural studies, elements of a new framework are emerging from the studies of rural women and the family in the Mid-Atlantic. Two subjects seem particularly important, the physical reproduction of the family and the cultural reproduction of the life-patterns for the family. Both are central to the management strategies of farm families.

10. Frank Trommler and Joseph McVeigh, eds., *America and the Germans: An Assessment of a Three-Hundred-Year History* (2 vols., Philadelphia: University of Pennsylvania Press, 1985), I, 41–130. Milton Drake, *Almanacs of the United States* (New York: Scarecrow, 1962), lists each of the German almanacs by title and date. The number is just about one-fourth of the English almanacs. Less than a dozen were in French. For "Mountain Mary," see Frank Brown, "New Light on 'Mountain Mary'," *Pennsylvania Folklife* 15 (Spring 1966): 10–15. The *Weiber-Buchlein* (Euphrata, 1806) is in the Pennsylvania Farm Museum Library, Lancaster, Pennsylvania. The Goschenhopper Museum in Green Lane, Pennsylvania contains a wealth of German store accounts that document household purchases.

11. Charlotte Erickson, *Invisible Immigrants: The Adaptation of English and Scottish Immigrants in Nineteenth-Century America* (Coral Gables, Florida: University of Miami Press, 1972), on p. 160 does mention one woman taking in boarders in 1835 and contains general background information on how immigrants coped with economic problems. Karie Diethorn, "Nineteenth Century Immigration and the Family: The Irish of Christiana Hundred, Delaware," (Unpublished paper, 1983) made a preliminary study that indicated large numbers of Irish there.

Fertility studies are one way historians have begun to look at women's reproductive work in various cultures. Historians now estimate that land ownership patterns affected fertility rates in Pennsylvania until 1850. Several historians have built on the ground-breaking studies of Robert V. Wells that document declining Quaker fertility. The links between fertility, land ownership, and culture are also explored in a recent cross-cultural study on York County, Pennsylvania. Daniel Snydacker compared wills from Ulster Scottish Presbyterians, German Lutherans, and English Quakers in York County for the period from 1749 to 1820. He concluded that among those families that kept their land, a large number (76 percent) excluded one child from an equal share. Quakers families were able to avoid excluding children as their holdings shrank by decreasing their family size. Snydacker also found that Presbyterians and Lutherans not only sold their land far more frequently than Quakers but also reduced their fertility much less. Germans who kept their land imposed contractual obligations to avoid excluding children. Presbyterians depended on the maintenance of skills and passing on of tools to achieve the same goal. Those without land excluded far fewer children (22 percent). Snydacker concluded that only Quaker families used family limitation as a strategy to avoid excluding children. Quakers also divided their land into smaller parcels to keep their children from leaving the community and families loaned money to others in their meetings. Such family strategies demanded different roles for mothers and daughters in these families that need more careful analysis.[12]

New York appears to share this relation between fertility, availability of land, and culture. Mark Stern's work on rural Erie County, New York, for example, is an important new study that begins to provide a comparative base from which to build a picture of women's household work. Stern argues that rural New York native-born Anglo-American women, particularly owners as opposed to tenants, restricted fertility to a much greater extent than German women. He maintains this was done not only because of the lack of land but also because of a cultural expectation that they would have fewer children.[13]

12. Robert V. Wells, "Quaker Marriage Patterns in a Colonial Perspective," *WMQ* 29 (1972): 415–42; and "Demographic Change and the Life Cycle of American Families," *Journal of Interdisciplinary History* 2 (1971): 273–82; Daniel Snydacker, "Kinship and Community in Rural Pennsylvania," *Journal of Interdisciplinary History* 13 (Summer 1982): 41–61; and Gary L. Laidia, Wayne A. Schutijer, and C. Shannon Stokes, "Agricultural Variation and Human Fertility in Antebellum Pennsylvania," *Journal of Family History* 6 (Summer 1981): 195–205.

13. Mark J. Stern, "The Demography of Capitalism: Industry, Class, and Fertility in Erie County, New York, 1855–1915," (Ph.D. diss., York University, 1979) and "Differential Fertility in Rural Erie County, New York 1855," *Journal of Social History* 16 (Summer 1983): 49–61. See also Rodger Craige Henderson, "Community Development and Revolutionary Transition in Eighteenth Century Lancaster County, Pennsylvania (Ph.D. diss., State University of New York at Binghamton, 1983.)

These studies merely point to the importance of women's reproductive work as a factor in understanding broader social changes. Closely related to the question of reproduction are ways in which women birthed and reared children. Seasonality of conception, for example, still remains largely unstudied for this region. And scholars have only begun the task of documenting childbirth and childcare practices that can help historians analyze the process of physical reproduction as well as its rate.[14]

The cultural reproduction of the family has been studied primarily through colonial and state family laws that set the boundaries on women's participation in America's developing economy. At one time, scholars believed colonial and early nineteenth-century American women had relatively greater access to property than English women. The research by Peggy Rabkin and Norma Basch on New York, and by Marylynn Salmon on Pennsylvania law, has shown that women were severely limited in control over property in these states. So far there are few studies, such as those of Suzanne Lebsock or Linda Speth on Virginia, Toby L. Ditz on Connecticut or Susan Admussen on English villages, that analyze inheritance patterns of Mid-Atlantic women in the eighteenth century. New research by Gail S. Terry, Jean B. Lee, and Lois Carr for Maryland; David Narrett for New York; and Carole Shammas, Lisa Waciega, and Marilyn Salmon for Pennsylvania, will provide a much more secure base for historians who wish to discuss the extent to which women had access to both real and personal property.[15]

Studies based on the extensive probate records of the Middle-Atlantic

14. Claire Elizabeth Fox, "Pregnancy, Childbirth and Early Infancy in Anglo-American Culture, 1675–1830," (Ph.D. diss., University of Pennsylvania, 1966); Janet McClintock Robison, "Country Doctors in the Changing World of the Nineteenth Century: An Historical Ethnolography of Medical Practice in Chester County, Pennsylvania 1790–1861," (Ph.D. diss., University of Pennsylvania, 1975); Jane Bauer Donegan, "Midwifery in America, 1760–1860: A Study in Medicine and Morality," (Ph.D. diss., Syracuse University, 1972); and Catherine M. Scholten, "Changing Customs of Childbirth in America, 1760 to 1825," *WMQ* 34 (1977): 426–45. For seasonality of conception in England see Ann Kussmaul, "Time and Space, Hoofs and Grain: The Seasonality of Marriage in England," *Journal of Interdisciplinary History* 15 (1985): 755–99 and "Agrarian Change in Seventeenth-Century England: The Economic Historian as Paleontologist, *Journal of Economic History* 45 (1985):1–31.

15. Peggy A. Rabkin, *Fathers to Daughters: the Legal Foundations of Female Emancipation* (Westport, Ct.: Greenwood, 1980); Norma Basch, *In the Eyes of the Law: Women, Marriage, and Property in Nineteenth Century New York* (Ithaca: Cornell University Press, 1982); Marylynn Salmon, "The Property Rights of Women in Early America: A Comparative Study," (Ph.D. diss., Bryn Mawr College, 1980) and *Women and the Law of Property in Early America* (Chapel Hill and London: University of North Carolina Press, 1986). Suzanne Dee Lebsock, "Women and Economics in Virginia: Petersburg, 1784–1820," (Ph.D. diss., University of Virginia, 1977) and her *The Free Women of Petersburg: Status and Culture in a Southern Town, 1784–1860* (New York: Norton, 1984); Linda E. Speth, "More than Her 'Thirds': Wives and Widows in Colonial Virginia," *Women & History* 4 (1982): 5–42; Toby L. Ditz, *Property and Kinship: Inheritance in Early Connecticut, 1750–1820* (Princeton: Princeton University Press, 1986) and Susan Dwyer Amussen, "Governors and Governed: Class and Gender Relations in English Villages, 1590–1725," (Ph.D. diss., Brown University, 1982). Gail S. Terry, "Wives and Widows, Sons and

states, especially wills, can enable us to analyze the role of kinship in women's lives, and women's role in preserving property for male members of the family. These studies will hopefully lead to more precise ways of measuring women's roles in family survival strategies. Once into the nineteenth century, there are sufficient literary sources for scholars to begin to analyze the development of rural middle-class family life as Mary Ryan has done so brilliantly for urban Oneida County, New York.[16]

The wide range of work performed by women is evident through studies of slavery, indenture, and wage work. The decline of slavery in New York and Pennsylvania has been well documented but the conditions of the black women still enslaved has not. There is strong evidence that work conditions for bondswomen declined where slavery continued in Delaware and Maryland, even though in important material ways the lives of all black workers improved in the late eighteenth century. Indentured labor, a form of labor that coexisted with slavery, also decreased in the late eighteenth century, as Sharon Salinger has pointed out. Rural areas north of the Mason-Dixon line may have had difficulty keeping women indentured as well as enslaved. Farley Grubb argues that by the 1770s immigrant servitude in the Mid-Atlantic had shifted from rural agriculture to the urban service sector. Just as surely, the number of native-born servants hired by the year for wages, as seasonal workers, and as migratory workers increased. Lucy Simler and Mark Stern have both argued that ownership of land was not as widespread in the Mid-Atlantic in the late eighteenth and early nineteenth centuries as historians have believed. Greater attention to women's labor, including their wage labor and tenant labor, should help correct the idea that this area was one of land-owning, self-employed farm families.[17]

Daughters: Testation Patterns in Baltimore County, Maryland, 1660–1759," Jean B. Lee, "Land and Featherbeds: Parents Bequests Practices in Charles County, Maryland, 1733–1783," will appear in *The Colonial Experience: The Eighteenth-Century Chesapeake* (University of North Carolina Press, in press). Lois Carr, "Inheritance in the Colonial Chesapeake," David E. Narrett, "Patterns of Inheritance, the Status of Women, and Family Life in Colonial New York," Carole Shammas, "Early American Women and Control Over Capital," and Marylynn Salmon, "Republican Sentiment, Economic Change, and the Property Rights of Women in American Law" will appear in Ronald Hoffman and Peter J. Albert, *Women in the Age of the American Revolution* (University Press of Virginia, in press). Lisa Wilson Waciega, "A 'Man of Business': The Widow of Means in Southeastern Pennsylvania, 1750–1850," *WMQ* (forthcoming) and her "Widowhood and Womanhood in Early America: The Experience of Women in Philadelphia and Chester County, 1750–1850," (Ph.D. diss., Temple University, 1986). Lois Green Carr and Lorena S. Walsh, "The Planters Wife: The Experience of White Women in Seventeenth-Century Maryland," *WMQ* 34 (1977): 542–71, raised many issues about fertility and marriage patterns in the Chesapeake.

16. Mary Ryan, *Cradle of the Middle Class: The Family in Oneida County, New York, 1790–1865* (Cambridge: Cambridge University Press, 1981).

17. For slavery see Soderlund, "Conscience, Interest, and Power" and *Quakers and Slavery*. For labor see Farley Grubb, "Immigrant Servant Labor: Their Occupational and Geographic Distribution in the Late Eighteenth-Century Mid-Atlantic Economy," *Social Science History* 9

Changes in technology and material culture indicate that not only did women's wage labor increase but also that women's labor changed dramatically. British historians have carefully documented the revolution in labor from 1750 to 1850 as women moved out of fields during the transition from sickle to scythe and cradle harvesting. Although we know that transition also occurred in America, we do not know when or how it occurred in the Mid-Atlantic. Travelers' accounts of the presence or absence of women laboring in the fields can only be accepted for the limited areas they actually visited and then must be used cautiously. Account books are more precise guides although they have not been used extensively as yet. Accounts for the Philadelphia hinterland place some women in the field, particularly at harvest time, even after the increase in the use of scythes and cradles at the end of the eighteenth century. Inventories are providing another rich source for studying those women who provided family labor in the eighteenth century. Analysis of inventories of household tools, made at the time of death of the males and widows, is allowing historians to glimpse the scope of women's work in processing food and fiber as well as providing service within households. Historians have already documented the important transition to textile production on Maryland plantations in the late seventeenth century. My own study of dairying tools also indicates women increased household production in the late eighteenth century. Clearly, studying process and change in tools will be increasingly useful in the analysis of women's work.[18]

(Summer 1985): 249–75; Sharon V. Salinger, " 'Send No More Women': Female Servants in Eighteenth-Century Philadelphia," *PMHB* 57 (1983): 29–48 "Colonial Labor in Transition: The Decline of Indentured Servitude in Late Eighteenth Century Philadelphia," *Labor History* 22 (1981): 165–91 and "Labor and Indentured Servants in Colonial Pennsylvania," (Ph.D. diss., University of California, Los Angeles, 1980). On property, see Lucy Simler, "The Township: The Community of the Rural Pennsylvanian," *PMHB* 106 (1982): 41–68; and Stern, "Differential Fertility in Rural Erie County."

18. For Britain see Ann Kussmaul, *Servants in Husbandry in Early Modern England* (Cambridge: Cambridge University Press, 1982); K. D. M. Snell, "Agricultural Seasonal Unemployment, the Standard of Living, and Women's Work in the South and East, 1690–1860," *Economic History Review* 34 (August 1981): 407–33; J. A. Perkins, "Harvest Technology and Labour Supply in Lincolnshire and the East Riding of Yorkshire 1750–1850," *Tools & Tillage* 3:1 (1976): 47–58 and 3:2 (1977): 125–35; and M. Roberts, "Sickles and Scythes: Women's Work and Men's Work at Harvest Time," *History Workshop* 7 (1979): 3–28. The best description of American women's field work is Alexander Marshall, " 'The Days of Auld Lang Syne': Recollections of How Chester Countians Farmed and Lived Three-Score Years Ago," Don Yoder, ed., *Pennsylvania Folklore* 13 (July 1964): 13–19. For dairy tools see Joan M. Jensen, "Churns and Butter Making in the Mid-Atlantic Farm Economy, 1750–1850," *Working Papers from the Regional Economic History Research Center*, 5, nos. 2&3 (1982):60–100 and *Loosening the Bonds*, 92–113. See also Lois Carr and Lorena Walsh, "The Transformation of Household Production in the Chesapeake, 1650–1850." An excellent model for the account books that focuses on late nineteenth century New York is Nancy Grey Osterud, "Strategies of Mutuality: Relations Among Women and Men in an Agricultural Community" (Ph.D. diss., Brown University, 1984.)

Material culture studies also indicate an increase of women's work because of increased household consumption. The work of Jack Michel for the early Delaware Valley and Lorena Walsh for the Chesapeake area, point to a drastic increase in consumption in the second half of the eighteenth century that was probably colony-wide. Material culture, as anthropologist Mary Douglas cautions, should not be read too literally as resulting from rational, practical needs, or as merely frivolous expenditures, but as the language of culture and group values. Regardless of the cause, the increase in material culture signaled a great increase in the work of women. Whether relating to textiles, food processing, or service, creation and maintenance of the material objects all required time, attention, and skill. The growing number of looking glasses and clocks indicate an increasing consciousness of appearances and the time used to maintain them.[19]

For women unable to labor in their own households or those of others, the poorhouses remained a last refuge. The aged, the physically disabled, the mentally ill, and the unemployed all sought refuge in rural poorhouses during the early nineteenth century. Rural poorhouse records are particularly rich for the early nineteenth century, and the few that have been studied, show an increased number of women without families to care for them and deteriorating conditions. Employment patterns seem to have determined both use and conditions in poorhouses. Counties that offered jobs for males, such as Seneca County through which the Erie Canal passed, filled with males. But elsewhere, for much of the early nineteenth century, women and their children accounted for the majority of inmates. Communities provided for these inmates with mounting reluctance. Joan Underhill Hannon calls the period from the 1820s through the 1850s in New York State "a period of perhaps unique stinginess in the public relief system." In New York, Hannon argues, expenditures per resident on poor relief sank to 11 percent of the earnings for common labor in 1835 to 1839. She concludes that poorhouses may have consciously decreased the level of care to avoid serving the unemployed. While the cause of this stinginess is still being debated, a pattern of neglect of poorhouse inmates is emerging from studies of rural Pennsylvania and New York. These conditions probably instilled a great aversion in poor women to entering the poorhouse unless all hope of independent work vanished. When it did,

19. Jack Michel, " 'In a Manner and Fashion Suitable to Their Degree': A Preliminary Investigation of the Material Culture of Early Rural Pennsylvania," *Working Papers from the Regional Economic History Research Center* 5, no.1(1981): 1–83; Lorena S. Walsh, "Urban Amenities and Rural Sufficiency: Living Standards and Consumer Behavior in the Colonial Chesapeake, 1643–1777," *Journal of Economic History* 43 (1983): 109–17; and Jensen, *Loosening the Bonds,* 36–56. Mary Douglas and Baron Usherwood, *The World of Goods: Towards an Anthropology of Consumption* (New York: Basic Books, 1982).

dependent rural women often spent time in rural poor houses under brutalizing conditions within a public support system that declined in effectiveness as commercialization and industrialization dislocated workers and their families.[20]

Despite deteriorating conditions, studies of rural Pennsylvania, Delaware, and New York indicate a rise in the number of dependent poor women. Poorhouse stewards also increasingly labeled many of these women "deranged," "idiot," or "simple." Seventeenth-century English doctors had already noted the disproportionate number of women with mental problems. Were women more prone to mental illness than men? Or, was society simply labeling women's social deviance as mental illness? Nancy Tomes and Ellen Dwyer have provided models of the study of urban asylum inmates. We need more study of the "madwoman" who was not in the urban asylum or in the attic of the middle class, but in the basement of the county poor house.[21]

Rural women also may have been subject to an increasing assortment of urban-based prescriptive literature in the early nineteenth century that advised them to emulate a "true womanhood" inconsistent with the realities of their rural labor. The study of prescriptive literature is an important part of women's history yet there are few regional studies of how this urban-based literature made its way into the back country and was transferred regionally. Leonore Davidoff has done a superb study for the English countryside of East Anglia. Many areas of the Mid-Atlantic could be studied similarly. This literature also needs to be examined for what it says about women of ethnic groups other than Anglo-American. Where foreign language presses existed, particularly the German language

20. Glenn C. Altschuler and Jan M. Saltzgaber, "Clearinghouse for Paupers: The Poorfarm of Seneca County, New York, 1830–1860," *Journal of Social History* 17 (1984): 573–600. Joan Underhill Hannon, "The Generosity of Antebellum Poor Relief," *Journal of Economic History* 44 (Sept. 1984): 810–21, her "Poverty in the Antebellum Northeast: the View from New York State's Poor Relief Rolls," *Journal of Economic History* 44 (1984): 1014; and Jensen, *Loosening the Bonds,* 57–78.

21. Michael MacDonald, *Mystical Bedlam: Madness, Anxiety, and Healing in Seventeenth Century England* (Cambridge: Cambridge University Press, 1981) discusses England. For America see Nancy Tomes, "The Domesticated Madman: Changing Concepts of Insanity at the Pennsylvania Hospital, 1780–1830," *PMHB* 106 (1982): 271–82; Ellen Dwyer, "Sex Roles and Psychopathology: A Historical Perspective," in Cathy S. Widom, ed., *Sex Roles and Psychopathology* (New York: Plenum, 1984) and "The Weaker Vessel: Legal Versus Social Reality in Mental Commitments in Nineteenth-Century New York," in Kelly Weisberg, ed., *Women and the Law: Social Historical Perspectives* (Cambridge, Mass.: Schenkman, 1983). Sharon Ann Burnston, "Babies in the Well: An Underground Insight into Deviant Behavior in Eighteenth Century Philadelphia," *PMHB* 106 (1982): 151–186, points out how anthropology might be used to trace infanticide. In Pennsylvania, women were hanged for infanticide in public executions well into the nineteenth century, before public outrage put an end to them.

press, the output needs to be examined for prescriptive statements about women.[22]

Studies of literature, however, must be grounded on an understanding of agricultural development. Historians cannot assume that urban economic models apply in rural areas. What commodities a farm produced, what work women performed in their production, and how these products fared in the market place are major questions that must be answered. In hard times, farm families reorganized their work and developed different attitudes toward women's traditional work. These changes were in response to commodity production for regional, national, and international trade. Careful studies of regional agricultural production are absolutely essential. Ellinor Oakes' work on dairying provides one such study. The work by Fred Bateman on income from dairy products, central to many Mid-Atlantic farm incomes, points to the importance of women's work in the survival of the farm. Much work considered "traditional" women's work—in dairy, market garden, orchard, hop field, and poultry yard—has not yet been studied. After 1808, for example, when upstate New York farm families discovered the profitability of growing hops, women became a majority of the hop pickers as well as providers of important household services for the entire seasonal work force. Each major city in the Mid-Atlantic—New York, Philadelphia, and Baltimore—had a butter belt surrounding it where the work of women was crucial in milking, processing, and marketing butter. Knowledge of general agricultural conditions and an understanding of the economics of specific commodities is necessary for describing rural women's importance to agricultural development.[23]

Beyond these general studies of economic change, we must have studies of how these changes affected individual women. Biographies of individual rural women are difficult to find because biography seems most appropriate for "notable women" whose lives are well documented and women tend to become "notable" through their work in urban areas. Yet many "notable" women, such as Susan B. Anthony and Mary Shadd, grew up on farms or in rural areas. Short biographies and collective bio-

22. Leonore Davidoff, "The Role of Gender in the 'First Industrial Nation': The Case of East Anglican Agriculture, 1780–1850," (Paper presented at the Women and Industrialization Conference, Bellagio, Italy, August 8–12, 1983). Donald McPherson, "The Fight Against Free Schools in Pennsylvania: Popular Opposition to the Common School System, 1834–1874," (Ph.D. diss., University of Pittsburgh, 1977).

23. Ellinor Oakes, "A Ticklish Business: Dairying in New England and Pennsylvania, 1750–1812," *Pennsylvania History* 47 (July 1980): 195–211; Fred Bateman, "The 'Marketable Surplus' in Northern Dairy Farming: New Evidence by Size of Farm in 1860," *Agricultural History* 52 (July 1978): 345–63; and Joan M. Jensen and Susan Armitage, "Women in the Hop Harvest: From New York to Washington," in *Labor in the West* (in press).

graphies can bring together scattered and brief information on farm women who did not leave for cities or become famous. Unless we know more about the majority of women who stayed down on the farm, who did not go public and become famous, we cannot understand the small minority who did.[24]

When rural women moved into the public sphere, it was most frequently through religious activities. Religion is one of the topics for which new studies have opened up major questions about rural women. Recent studies of Quakers and of evangelical women point to the importance of religion in the lives of women. English studies have shown that women were attracted in large numbers in the seventeenth century to new sects, such as the Puritans and Quakers. When Puritans refused them the right to preach, a number of women turned to Quakerism, and when Quakers controlled their lives too tightly, from Quakerism to utopian communities. Quaker women were among the first women to emerge into public life as ministers, and then beyond the meeting house as active leaders in rural communities. By the early nineteenth century, an evangelical brand of religion was also burning through the Mid-Atlantic, leaving abundant church and private records that make it possible to document leadership, membership, female bonding, education, and missionary work.[25]

Most widespread of women's religious groups were the evangelical maternal associations that spread through the New York hinterland between 1815 and 1860. Richard A. Meckel calls these Protestant voluntary associations a type of "shadow ministry" in which women could preach and evangelize without formal recognition. Revivalists now abandoned Paul's dictum that women must be silent and encouraged them to speak out at prayer meetings. Maternal associationalism swept rapidly through the Presbyterian and Baptist churches, receiving much of its support from the lower middle-class. Mary Ryan has provided a rich case study of how these women's groups functioned in Utica, New York. There must have

24. Elsie M. Lewis, "Mary Ann Shadd Cary," in Edward T. James, ed., *Notable American Women, 1607–1950: A Biographical Dictionary* (Cambridge: Harvard University Press, 1971), 3: 300–01. For methodology see Burton W. Folsom II, "The Collective Biography as a Research Tool," *Mid-America: An Historical Review* 54 (April 1972): 108–22; Richard Jensen, "Family, Career, and Reform: Women Leaders of the Progressive Era," in *The American Family in Social-Historical Perspective,* Michael Gordon, ed., (New York: St. Martin's Press, 1973), 267–80; and Barbara Campbell, *The "Liberated" Women of 1914: Prominent Women of the Progressive Era,* Studies in American History and Culture, No. 6 (Ann Arbor: University Microfilms, 1979).

25. Mary Maples Dunn, "Saints and Sisters: Congregational and Quaker Women in the Early Colonial Period," *American Quarterly* 30 (Winter 1978): 582–601 and "Women of Light," in Carol Ruth Berkin and Mary Beth Norton, eds., *Women of America: A History* (Boston: Houghton Mifflin, 1979), 114–36; Janis Calvo, "Quaker Women Ministers in Nineteenth Century America," *Quaker History* 63 (1974): 75–93; and Jensen, *Loosening the Bonds,* 146–66.

been many others, for all major towns and most outlying villages and settlements along the Erie Canal had these associations by the early 1830s. The movement traveled eastward from frontier to city.[26]

Another outlet for women's religious fervor was the pious memoir. This act of "self-reading" marked not only a new level of literacy but also a consciousness of spiritual autonomy and self-improvement. In the evangelical culture of early-nineteenth-century America, rural as well as urban women expressed themselves in pious memoirs. They too, as Joanna Gillespie has noted, had "full permission to bloom within their station, if not to transgress its boundaries." Women still had a restricted ministry in these evangelical churches but they spoke at Sunday school rallies, stood up to speak in church meetings, and exorted congregations before and after the sermons. Such activities moved rural women to claim a new spiritual equality with men.[27]

Sunday schools were a natural transition for many evangelical women. A public yet restricted space, the Sunday school seemed an acceptable place for women who were unready to claim full freedom in public. Conversion was central to Protestantism and women in Sunday schools assumed major responsibilities for that crucial event in the lives of young people who now provided most converts for evangelical churches. Mid-Atlantic rural women staffed thousands of these Sunday schools gladly, often receiving no pay but an enhanced status in the community.[28]

Secular school teaching provided an even more public role than religion for women. Anne Firor Scott has documented the influence of the feminism of New York's Troy Female Seminary. Rural Quaker seminaries were important training centers in Pennsylvania. Keith Melder has emphasized the oppression of seminary training, but the potential for liberating literacy was certainly there as well, and recognized by the early women who had access to this new higher education. The ideologies of Republican mothers and teaching daughters both flourished in the Mid-Atlantic. Why they flourished and who benefited needs to be documented more precisely. After all, if a rural mother could not write (and Alan Tully

26. Richard A. Meckel, "Educating a Ministry of Mothers: Evangelical Maternal Associations, 1815–1860," *Journal of the Early Republic* 2 (Winter 1982): 403–23; and Mary P. Ryan, "A Women's Awakening: Evangelical Religion and the Families of Utica, New York 1800–1840," *American Quarterly* 30 (1978): 602–23.

27. Joanna Bowen Gillespie, " 'The Clear Leadings of Providence': Pious Memoirs and the Problems of Self-Realization for Women in the Early Nineteenth Century," *Journal of the Early Republic* 5 (Summer 1985): 197–221.

28. Anne M. Boylan, "The Role of Conversion in Nineteenth-Century Sunday Schools," *American Studies* 20 (1979): 35–48; and Ruth C. Linton, "The Brandywine Manufacturers' Sunday School: An Adventure in Education in the Early Nineteenth Century," *Delaware History* 20 (1983): 168–84.

has shown that most women in rural Pennsylvania could not at the time of the Revolution), they could not educate their children as citizens. The move to both functional and liberating literacy of rural-nineteenth-century women was an incredible accomplishment. The consequence of the transition from an oral to a written tradition for women was of enormous significance and cannot easily be dismissed as a leap into oppression.[29]

Last, but certainly not least, women participated in secular volunteer reform. The importance of black people in moving white reformers from abolition to anti-slavery is now quite clear, but beyond sketchy biographies of Sojourner Truth, Harriet Tubman, and Mary Shadd, little is known about the work of black Mid-Atlantic rural women in this first black liberation movement.[30]

On the other hand, studies of white reformers have progressed far enough to pose intriguing questions. Abolition, temperance, and women's rights continue to hold major research interest, but charity and asylum reform are receiving some attention. Gerda Lerner, Ellen Du Bois, Nancy Hewitt, and Judith Wellman have expanded our understanding of the early relationship between abolition and women's rights. The gap in the 1830s, when the abolition activities of white women declined, has still to be explained. What were the reforming women doing? The development of prohibition reform into militant activities by white women is one possible explanation. Temperance began to be politicized in the 1840s. Several studies have concluded that women fused the more popular prohibition crusade to the emerging women's rights movement. The confluence of militant temperance and women's rights in the late 1840s and early 1850s may prove to be more significant than historians have thought. The women's rights movement, like the temperance movement, was extremely popular with nineteenth-century white rural women. Abolition—even more anti-slavery—was not, except with a small group of radical church women.[31]

29. Anne Firor Scott, "The Ever Widening Circle: the Diffusion of Feminist Values from the Troy Female Seminary, 1822–1872," *History of Education Quarterly* 19 (1979): 3–23; Jensen, *Loosening the Bonds,* 167–83; Keith Melder, "Woman's High Calling: the Teaching Profession in America, 1830–1860" *American Studies* 13 (1972): 19–32 and "Masks of Oppression: The Female Seminary Movement in the United States," *New York History* 55 (1974): 261–79. The best study of rural literacy is Alan Tully, "Literacy Levels and Educational Development in Rural Pennsylvania, 1729–1775," *Pennsylvania History* 39 (1972): 301–12.

30. The role of blacks in the Mid-Atlantic early abolitionist movement remains relatively unstudied. Larry Gara, *The Liberty Line: The Legend of the Underground Railroad* (Lexington: University of Kentucky, 1961) rightly emphasizes the influence of the blacks but probably underemphasizes the role of Quaker Hicksites.

31. Gerda Lerner, *The Majority Finds Its Past: Placing Women in History* (New York: Oxford University Press, 1979), 112–201; Judith Wellman, "Women and Radical Reform in Antebellum Upstate New York: A Profile of Grassroots Female Abolitionists," in Mabel E. Deutrich and Virginia C. Purdy, eds. *Clio Was A Woman: Studies in the History of American Women* (Wash-

The question of constitutional rights concerned some early-nineteenth-century reformers. Clearly, during these years a few rural women took their first tentative steps along the road of legal reforms that would lead in later years to demands for full equality. Rural women and their male allies demanded the right of petition. Despite efforts of the United States Congress to convince women that they did not have this right, some women at the state level continued to exercise it. Temperance petitions from women in Pennsylvania testify to the persistence with which women there claimed this right. Demands for married women's property laws that breeched the wall of the doctrine of marital unity opened the way, as legal historian Norma Basch has reminded us, to create a new class of disfranchised property owners—rural as well as urban. In early 1848, 44 women from Genessee and Wyoming counties in New York petitioned their state legislature for equality as women citizens rather than as wives. These petitions from the New York hinterland indicate a major change in the way some rural women were beginning to look at themselves. They saw themselves as citizens with political rights equal to those of men.[32]

Historians need to grapple more fully with this question of the reform activities of rural women, for it may provide an important key to understanding the emergence of the women's rights movement. The Seneca Falls and West Chester women's conferences of 1848 and 1853 took place in rural areas and attracted rural women. The breeding grounds for early feminism may well have been the back country during rapid agricultural development. Early-nineteenth-century feminists demanded legal, political, and occupational rights but still had qualms about dealing with relations in the family. The fact that their movement was rural and family-based may help explain those qualms.[33]

The new research on rural Mid-Atlantic women points to the need for a drastic revision of traditional history that excluded them from discussion of antebellum economy. Rural women were central to that history rather

ington: Howard University Press, 1980): 113–27; Nancy A. Hewitt, *Women's Activism and Social Change: Rochester, New York, 1822–1872* (Ithaca and London: Cornell University Press, 1984), pp. 97–138; Jensen, *Loosening the Bonds*, 184–204; and Ellen DuBois, "Women's Rights and Abolition: the Nature of the Connection," in Lewis Perry and Michael Fellman, eds., *Antislavery Reconsidered: New Perspectives on the Abolitionists* (Baton Rouge and London: Louisiana State University, 1979), 239–51. For temperance see Jed Dannenbaum, "The Origins of Temperance Activism and Militancy Among American Women," *Journal of Social History* 15 (1981): 235–52; and Ian R. Tyrrell, "Women and Temperance in Antebellum America, 1830–1860," *Civil War History* 28 (1982): 128–52.

32. Norma Basch, "Equity vs. Equality: Emerging Concepts of Women's Political Status in the Age of Jackson," *Journal of the Early Republic* 3 (Fall 1985): 297–318.

33. Hewett, *Women's Activism and Social Change*, 130–32; and Jensen, *Loosening the Bonds*, 199–204.

than marginal to it. Indoors and out, upstairs and down, their labor was essential for the survival of the farm economy. As Esther Lewis wrote of her servant woman, they ate no idle bread. Their industriousness must be recognized in any analysis of the development of agriculture in the Mid-Atlantic Historians who continue to treat women's work as irrelevant to agricultural history risk weakening, distorting, and undermining their analysis of rural development.

Forgotten Persephones

Women Farmers on the Frontier

Anne B. Webb

OCCUPATION: farmer. This appellation, usually reserved to men, also describes single women—whether unmarried or widowed—who were present on the Midwest frontier since it opened. In Minnesota, women homesteaded in all regions of the state right from the start. In 1863, when the land offices opened for homesteading, a Minnesota sample shows that one unmarried woman homesteaded for every four unmarried men—a ratio of one out of five, or 20 percent. In another sample, homestead records show that about 2,400 women without husbands homesteaded in Minnesota from 1863 to 1889 for at least a year and gained title to their land. Sixty-six percent made the homestead application in their own name, either as widows or single women. These records, which cover a minimum of five years between settlement and proving up, show that women actively sought and farmed the land by themselves. Many more women bought farms either from the state or federal governments, from the railroads, or from other farmers, who may themselves have pre-empted or homesteaded the land.[1]

These pioneering women in Minnesota were not alone. As early as 1843 women claimed rights to land in Iowa under the 1841 Pre-emption Act. Susan B. Anthony claimed that by the mid-1880s one-third of the land in Dakota Territory was owned by women. And contemporary historian Sheryll Patterson-Black found that in the latter part of the 19th century and early 20th century 11.9 percent of a sample of homestead applicants in Colorado and Wyoming were women. Of them, 42 percent proved up on their claim, more than the 37 percent of the men who proved up.[2]

This is the story of some of these frontier women farmers. It starts with the story of Harriet T. Griswold who was widowed on a pre-emption claim in Isanti County when Minnesota was still a territory. It tells the story of Emeline Guernsey, a widow with five children who sold her farm in Pennsylvania to come "west" to

---

[1] Minnesota Homestead Final Certificates, Land Entry Files, Records of the Bureau of Land Management, National Archives Record Group (NARG) 49, National Records Center, Suitland, Md. From a sample of 200 final certificates in the Winona County land office files, the exact ratio was 25 to 6, and this included men when there was any doubt of their marital status. The data base for this article was a sample of 259 Minnesota women; the 2,400 women constitute about 4 percent of all homesteaders who got title to their land in the state during the same time period; Minnesota Final Homestead Certificates, NARG 49.

More than a third of those applying for Minnesota homesteads between 1863 and 1880 had not filed for final proof by 1885. (Cancelled homestead certificates on file in the National Archives have not been examined.) Paul W. Gates, *History of Public Land Law Development* (Washington, D.C.: Public Land Law Review Commission, 1968), 411; on railroad and state lands, see Gates, 385, 806.

Portions of this article were included in a paper given at the Berdahl-Rolvaag Lectures, Augustana College, Sioux Falls, So. Dak., June, 1985.

[2] Declaratory Statement no. 7, Box 531, Fairfield, Iowa, NARG 49; Susan B. Anthony and Ida Husted Harper, eds., *The History of Woman Suffrage* 4 (Rochester, N.Y.: Fowler & Wells, 1902): 544; Sheryll Patterson-Black, "Women Homesteaders on the Great Plains Frontier," *Frontiers: A Journal of Women Studies* 1 (Spring, 1976): 68.

Mitchell County, Iowa, in the early days of statehood. And, finally, it tells of Pauline Auzjon and Emma Setterlund, both single, immigrant women who separately homesteaded in western Minnesota. Because she is earliest in time and because the letters her family kept describing her first years in Minnesota make her story the richest in detail, we start with Harriet Griswold.

ON AN EARLY October morning in 1856, Harriet Griswold left her New England home in Somers, Connecticut, to travel to the wilds of Minnesota. Carrying her baby in her arms, and with her three older children around her, she set forth with her husband, Allen. They went north by stage or carriage to Springfield, Massachusetts, and then by train past places familiar to the generations who followed after her—Albany, Buffalo, Cleveland, Toledo, Chicago, west to the Mississippi River, to the end of the railroad where the steamboat "Golden Era" took them up the river to St. Paul. It was indeed a golden era they were in search of as they reached for the American dream of riches from speculation in the unclaimed lands of the West. And they were not the first.[3]

Never mind that all their worldly possessions, having been sent the cheaper way by water, were probably lost in a gale on the Great Lakes. Forget that Harriet and two of her children were sick. The important thing was that land was selling well and, as speculators, they could expect some of the riches to come to them. They were not dreaming an idle dream. Minnesota was in the midst of a land boom. True tales of 300 percent profits were commonplace. In her first letter home, Harriet relayed the good news in staccato language, echoing the bulletins from Western Union: "Allen . . . is quite pleased with the investment in lots at Cambridge says they are selling rapidly it is thought the land office will be removed there next spring." The land

[3] H[arriet] T. Griswold to Brother Henry, Oct. 17, [1856?], Griswold Papers, Minnesota Historical Society (MHS), St. Paul. All Griswold letters cited in this article are in these papers; spelling and punctuation throughout this study follow the originals.

office would bring more settlers in its wake, raising prices still further.[4]

The family survived the first Minnesota winter in the relative comfort of St. Paul, and the spring of 1857 found Allen writing, not of orchards and corn, but of town lots and land prices. Speculative expectations looked very good. "[W]hat was stated by me as to the price six months from that time, has been more than realised, My brother R[alph] B has recently sold at the City of Holyoke Mass, four Lots in Cambridge for $500. G[ilbert] G [*another brother*] has sold in Boston some twenty Lots [for] something less, said he was offered $100 a Lot for one Block of twelve, a part of which had been previously sold I have now nineteen Lots in all, and Paid for, these I hold now at $100 per Lot, about fifty five acres of my claim, lies very finely to plot as an addition, should I conclude to do so after a while, this would make about 300 Lots, however my claim is considered to be the most valuable of any there, it lies very finely on the west bank, of a fine Lake [*Paul's, now Florence*] covering more than 200 acres of land, and joining the town, was offered 12 1/2 Dollars an acre last winter for my farm at Sunrise but hold the same at 20 Dollars, it is only one mile from the flourishing Town of Washington."[5]

[4] Rodney C. Loehr, ed., *Minnesota Farmers' Diaries: William R. Brown, 1845-46, Mitchell Y. Jackson, 1852-63* (St. Paul: MHS, 1939), 22-23; H. T. Griswold to Brother Henry, Oct. 17, [1856?]. The author has chosen to use first names throughout the text, partly because this clearly distinguishes individuals from other family members, but chiefly because this is an article about women and use of first names clarifies and emphasizes the gender of the person discussed.

[5] A[llen] H. Griswold to Brother Henry, April 18, 1857. Sunrise and Washington are in Chisago County directly east of Isanti. The land dealings of Allen and Gilbert Griswold, whose brother Ralph apparently did not move west, may be found in Deed Records Book A, p. 5-11, 20-21, 51-52, 54, Land Records, Isanti County Courthouse, Cambridge. On early Cambridge, see Vernon E. Bergstrom and Marilyn McGriff, *Isanti County, Minnesota: An Illustrated History* (Braham: the authors, 1985), 49-51.

The Griswold brothers sold Cambridge lots back East, although Allen bought his Minnesota land from his brother Gilbert only after reaching St. Paul. They sold to people who, in the main, did not intend to come west and live on the land but who, like Allen and his brother, expected to profit as others settled there, forcing prices up. Allen paid $1,980 for his town lots and realized only $870, for a loss of $1,110. However, Allen paid very little for his claim. Under the 1841 Preemption Act, settled farmers had the right to buy the land from the government at $1.25 an acre before it was put up for public auction. Until the land office opened, a family could live on the land free. Better yet, as we learn later, Allen bought a military land warrant, which he could use as if it were currency to pay for the land. These warrants, discounted on the open market, sold for less than the $1.25 an acre that they were worth with the federal government, and Allen probably availed himself of these cheaper prices.[6]

From colonial times, land had been offered as an inducement and a reward to men serving in war. As early as 1776 the Continental Congress offered land (although it did not own any) to soldiers as well as to deserters from the British forces. The British had already done the same to colonists who fought for the Crown. Depending on rank and length of service, veterans were entitled to a certain amount of land. Despite occasional efforts to restrict the sale of these rights, traffic in military land warrants boomed, making rich men out of the likes of Jason C. Easton in Minneapolis who bought and sold them as a business. In 1856 such warrants were issued for almost 17 million acres of land (16,891,890); the next year warrants were

[6] Gilbert Griswold concluded many more land transactions than did Allen; between February and May, 1857, Gilbert realized over $2,300 on his Cambridge land. Neither brother sold land for cash in Cambridge after May, 1857. Deed Records Book A, p. 5-6, 9-11, 14, 20-21, 25-30, 36-37, 50-51, 91-92 and Mortgage Records Book A, p. 9—both in Isanti County Courthouse. On land warrants, see Gates, *Public Land*, 251-283; on pre-emption, see United States, *Statutes at Large*, 5:435-458.

used to enter over six million acres (6,283,920). Both of these figures are the largest for any of the years between 1855 and 1876 and consequently show that the Griswolds entered the market at the height of the land warrant business.[7]

In addition to military land laws, before 1841 Congress from time to time enacted pre-emption laws that gave squatters in specified areas the right to buy the property they were already farming before it was put up for public auction. The Pre-emption Act of 1841 extended this right to squatters on surveyed land everywhere, thereby marking a definite shift in policy away from using the public lands to raise money for the federal treasury and toward a policy of using such laws to settle the country. More than simply accepting the reality of squatters with good grace, the Pre-emption Act of 1841 signaled an attempt by the national government to give reality to the Jeffersonian ideal of a republic of independent farmers. The 1841 act was the first to look into the future, to say all those yet to come, including widows, can have 160 acres for $200 if they cultivate the land. Ironically, Jefferson's own administration saw the passage of harsh legislation aimed at driving squatters off the land, laws which were seldom enforced because there was not the manpower to patrol the vast areas of the west and seldom the heart.[8]

AS they had in the past, the settlers themselves often looked to make big money fast through land speculation. So it was with the Griswolds. They dreamt both dreams. They dreamt of owning their own farm in the new land and of the day when the expansion of the

---

[7] Gates, *Public Land*, 251, 275, 276, 280. Almost 7 million acres (6,959,379) in Minnesota alone were entered under military land warrants through 1871. See also Rodney C. Loehr, "Jason C. Easton, Territorial Banker," *Minnesota History* 29 (Sept., 1948): 223-230.

[8] Gates, *Public Land*, 219-220, 222-240, 431. The sale of public lands accounted for 48 percent of federal revenue in 1836, but only 2 percent in 1861; revenue continued, however, to be a motive for selling public lands.

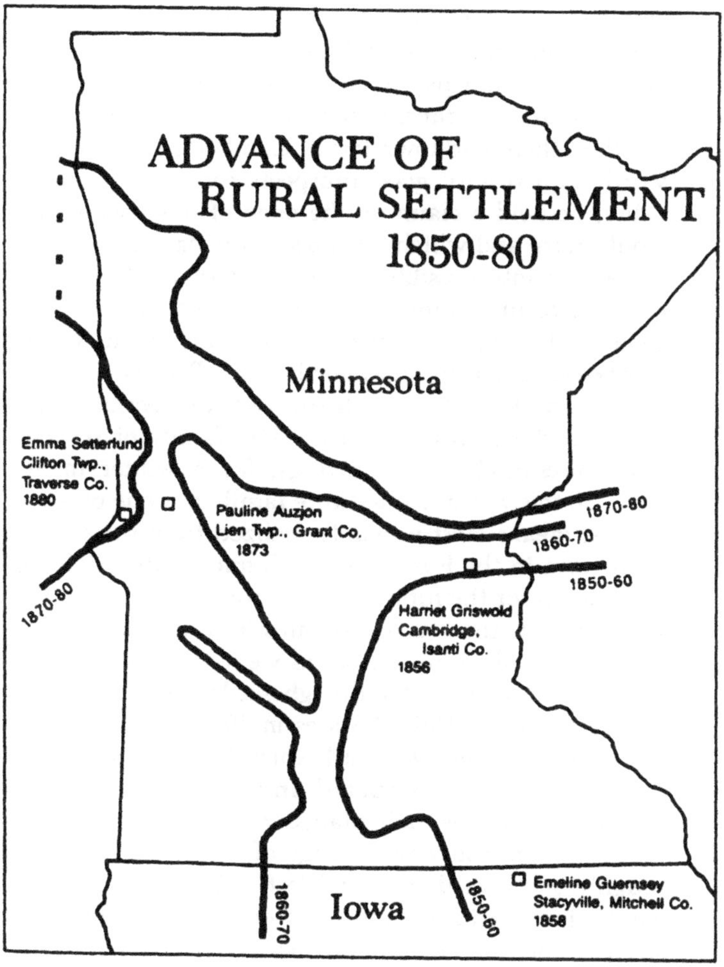

towns of Cambridge and Washington would enrich them. Allen wrote that "the prospect for business the present season is now very fine, I think there never has been a time, in our day when a brighter prospect for successful speculation, in Real Estate lay before us, than the present, here in the present Territory and future State of Minnesota." Already Allen had sold 15 of his 36 lots for a total of $770. The benefits to be reaped from combining the pre-emption and military bounty land laws can be gauged by comparing what the Griswolds would pay to what Emeline Guernsey realized on her Pennsylvania farm. She received $4,000 for her working farm in 1858. Under pre-emption, the Griswolds would pay $200 for 160 acres; with a discounted land warrant, they would pay even less.[9]

Allen, then, had town lots in Cambridge he believed worth $1,900 with good prospects for an increase in value; he held a claim on the edge of town which he would farm and which he hoped some day to turn into more town lots, possibly as many as 300; and finally, he owned a farm at Sunrise he thought worth $20 an acre because it, too, was close to a growing town. Cambridge was some 40 miles north of St. Paul and nearly 30 miles north of Anoka, the nearest substantial settlement on the Mississippi River. The family of six had lived, presumably from savings, for a winter in St. Paul. So this was not a destitute family but one of some means, means most probably realized from the sale of their farm in the East. It was a family with a right to have hopes for the future. But for the Griswolds, as for many others, time turned dreams into nightmares.

It is difficult to remember as we look back over our country's history that although settlers first came to what is now the United States in 1607, two centuries later most of them were still stuck behind the mountains on the Eastern Seaboard. In the next 50 years they flooded across the rich plains, reaching St. Paul by 1860, then on the western edge of a frontier that ran roughly southward to Fort Worth, Texas. Settlement was fairly solid in southeastern Minnesota and stretched beyond St. Paul, down the Minnesota River to New Ulm, and up both the Mississippi and St. Croix rivers. Isanti County was north of the line of settlement, part of the Big Woods, a region of broadleaf woodlands, coniferous forest, and wooded prairie. The

---

[9] A. H. Griswold to Brother Henry, April 18, 1857. There is a discrepancy between Allen's figures and the land records; the latter indicate that he was not selling at a profit, at least when his buying and selling prices are averaged; Deed Records Book A, p. 5-9, 20-21, 52, 54. For the comparison, see Emeline Guernsey to William Guernsey, Sept. 2, 1858, in the private collection of Marygray Orcutt Brown, Bloomington. All Guernsey letters cited in this article are from these papers.

frontier—commonly defined as two people per square mile—had not reached the southern part of the county by the end of the 1850s, but substantial lumbering in the nearby St. Croix Valley created a market for agricultural products. The county itself lay on the edge of profitable farming.[10]

This was the land to which Harriet and Allen Griswold moved in the spring of 1857 with their four children, Arnold, 13, Florence, 9, Frances, 7, and little Albert, 2. Harriet, herself, was 35. The family went to the claim outside of Cambridge, beside the lake. Allen put up a shanty that was 12 feet square as required by the law, and there the six of them lived throughout the summer as they began to farm. In the fall the nightmare began; by mid-September Allen was dead at the age of 44 and the baby very sick.[11]

There appeared to be no thought at the time of Harriet returning to her family in the East. She described the immediate help she received from neighbors and relatives: "Brother Gilbert stopped with us a week and kindly assisted in putting up our cabin which Allen had not commenced when he was taken sick, the neighbours also were very kind both during our sickness and assisting about the cabin which we are sadly in need of for our old one is quite open and cold weather is upon us." Imagine the prospect of a Minnesota winter on a claim first farmed a scant five months before in a county which three years later boasted only 28 farmers substantial enough to be counted in the federal

---

[10] Gilbert C. Fite, *The Farmers' Frontier, 1865-1900* (New York: Holt, Rinehart and Winston, 1966), 2; John G. Rice, *Patterns of Ethnicity in a Minnesota County, 1880-1905. Geographical Reports* (Umeå, Sweden: University of Umeå, 1973), 17; Loehr, *Farmers' Diaries*, 12. It was not until 1930 that 30 percent of Isanti County was under cultivation; with the retreat of the agricultural frontier in Minnesota in recent years, that is no longer true. John R. Borchert and Donald P. Yaeger, *Atlas of Minnesota Resources and Settlement* (St. Paul: State Planning Agency, 1968), 23, 35.

[11] United States Census, 1860, Minnesota manuscript schedules, Isanti County (township not listed), 60, 61, microfilm copy in MHS. This census erroneously lists the third child as Harriet, but the letters are written by Frances to her grandmother in Connecticut.

agricultural census. Her letter continued forlornly: "During the week Gilbert was here I had 4 and 5 men to cook for beside our own family and taking care of Albert which I found wore upon me some I am getting quite nervous but I hope I shall not be sick as I was last fall I think if we are prospered we may move into our new cabin the last of this week we have a good crop of beans, but little corn, as the gophers and birds took a good share of it, and I should think we had about a hundred bushels of potatoes. I think I have been remarkably sustained during my affliction but I trust I have the presence of the Saviour and the guidance of his holy spirit but I tremble when I think of the care now resting on me and I fear it will be a burden which I shall not long be able to bear. . . . I very much dread the long dreary winter before us but I hope we shall suffer for none of the necessaries of life so long as Arnold is well he will be able to keep us in wood though we must depend on others to haul it as we have no team."[12]

The only thing we know she asked from her family was their sympathy and "an interest in your prayers." Because she thanked them, we also know they sent a dollar or even five dollars occasionally in their letters to her. With the help of these sporadic gifts, Harriet kept the family fed and clothed and managed the farm. To supplement her income she took in boarders, mirroring the frequent pattern of colonial days when farmers added a trade or craft to their farm income, a pattern repeated on the frontier by male as well as female farmers. "[W]e had ten men to stop over night with us besides our family and Mr. Shepard [*her regular boarder at the time*], they were lumbermen going into the woods, to drive logs down the river I got supper and breakfast and a lunch for their dinner to day. . . . I have 2 bedsteds up stairs and then I make up a camp bed on the floor up stairs where the men all sleep we have had very few callers this winter Mr Odell who lives about 2 1/2 miles above here keeps all he can and to induce people to stop with him offers to keep them cheaper than I do."[13]

[12] Harriet to Father and Mother, Oct. 24, [1857].

[13] Harriet to Father and Mother, Oct. 24, [1857], Mar. 30, [1858 or 1859]. Shepard was a land surveyor.

Lumbermen, immigrants, fur buyers, new settlers all stayed with her. In the bitter cold of January that year she reported "6 teams loaded with provision passed here one day bound for Superior 3 of them stopped with me over night." At one point she briefly kept the post office, but it was boarders who were the mainstay of her second income after farming.[14]

Having no team, Harriet hired men to plow the land, paying between $1.50 and $2.00 an acre, helping in turn other struggling farmers to add to their meager incomes. Later when she did have a team she still hired men to do the heavy plowing and other difficult labor such as building a split-rail fence around the cultivated land. Fencing was necessary to protect crops from both wild and domestic animals who were generally not penned at this time. Arnold, barely a teenager at his father's death, supplemented this labor with the help of his sisters, all under the supervision of Harriet.[15]

As there were no schools, Harriet had few options. We know she sent her daughter Florence to school in Anoka, where she might have helped in a home in return for part of her board. The other choices were to teach the children at home or move the whole family to Oak Grove, a town some miles to the south in Anoka County, for the winter so that they could attend school. Providing education was a problem on the farming frontier.[16]

But mostly Harriet farmed and made decisions about the land. The second spring of her widowhood she

---

[14] Harriet to Brother Henry, Jan. [no day given, 1858 or 1859].

[15] Harriet to Brother Henry, Jan. [no day given, 1858 or 1859]; to Father and Mother, Mar. 30, [1858 or 1859]; to Father, June 27, [1858 or 1859]; Arnold to Grand Father, May 8, 1859. See also Loehr, *Farmers' Diaries*, 15.

[16] Harriet to Brother Henry, April 29, [1858 or 1859]; Florence to Grandma, Dec. 19, 1859; Arnold to Uncle Henry, Jan. 20, 1860; Frances to Grandpa, enclosed with Harriet to Father and Mother, Dec. 19, [18??]. There are two letters from Frances, one spelled with an "i," the other with an "e." In the sample of 259 Minnesota women homesteaders between 1863 and 1889, 85 percent of all women who had been married are known to have had children; 5 percent of the women said their children were grown; of those who gave the number, 59 percent had one, two, or three children, although a few (6 percent) had eight, nine, or ten. Minnesota Homestead Final Certificates, NARG 49.

A LOG CABIN *such as this may have housed Harriet Griswold and her children near Cambridge, Isanti County.*

wondered "will it be best to let the land warrant go for a team if homestead bill passes [?]" She could sell her land warrant, which she was planning to use to pay for her pre-emption claim, to buy a team—an important capital improvement for any farm; this she would do in the hope that the homestead bill, under which she could claim the land free, would pass. Later that spring, Harriet "came to the conclusion that we could not get along without a team and as I had an opportunity to get a horse here, I thought best to do so, for the Land warrant and $25 I bought the horse, harness, and Sleigh or the Sleigh was thrown in." Without the means to buy a wagon, however, like many other farmers she still had to pay hauling and freight for everything that came in and went out of the farm.[17]

UNFORTUNATELY Harriet was widowed just as the depression of 1857 hit, destroying most expectations. By 1859 she wrote in a vein very different from her husband's early letter: "Could I sell the improvement on the place for any amount I should be tempted to do so and go where we could have the advantages of a school . . . but we can sell nothing now for no one has any money Mr Carlton sold his house and all his improvements for a yoke of Oxen valued at 60 dollars and he moved up here the spring we did." As land prices did not recover from the depression, gone were the early dreams of turning part of their claim into 300 town lots. Indeed, none of Allen's Cambridge lots were sold after May, 1857. Eventually the town of Cambridge was replatted slightly to the north of the original site. Harriet could no longer look forward to a more prosperous future based on land profits. Now it was a question of just hanging on.[18]

Harriet and her neighbors did not own the land. What they sold, or thought of selling, were the improvements to the land—the clearing and plowing, and

---

[17] Harriet to Father and Mother, Mar. 30, [1858 or 1859] and to Brother Henry, April 29, [1858 or 1859]. See also note 38, below.

[18] Harriet to Brother Henry, April 29, [1858 or 1859]; Loehr, *Farmers' Diaries*, 23; Bergstrom and McGriff, *Isanti County*, 51. The Panic of 1857 began in late August.

the buildings that had been put on it. Until the land office opened, their claims were safe, as Harriet described: "[I]t is still said the lands are coming into market and those who wish to hold their Claims must pay for them before the 16th of May." The land sales were repeatedly put off, but so were her early dreams of quick profits from speculation. By the fall of 1861, five years after she came to Minnesota, Harriet was still worrying. "[I]f I could sell the horse could very easily get a land warrant but I see no chance of selling him at present the land sale comes off next week and I must run the risk of loosing [*sic*] my claim." In fact, the wheel had come full circle when in 1860 Harriet questioned whether the land was worth investing in at all. "[H]ave not paid for our claim yet. have been hesitating whether it would be best to invest any more in Cambridge property as it does not seem to pay." Later she confessed, "have sometimes thought it hardly worthwhile to enter it as we must then pay taxes on it." This dilemma was not an unusual one for frontier farmers. Property taxes were the main source of income for local government. For farmers struggling to create new farms with little cash income, taxes were high and they had to be paid in hard cash. On the other hand, if title were not gained, someone else could buy it at public auction, and all the improvements and the investment in time and money would be lost.[19]

Harriet continued to farm the land at least through the early 1860s; she never owned it, although probably she or Allen had filed a pre-emption claim. Most of the heavy work was hired out, but Harriet likely worked in the fields with the children at harvest. It would be easier to harvest her own fields than the wild cranberries she described, probably one of her cash crops.

[19] Harriet to Brother Henry, Mar. 12, [probably late 1850s]; to Father, Oct. 17, [probably 1861]; to Father and Mother, with Arnold's letter to Uncle Henry, Jan. 20, 1860, and Feb. 24, [186?]. There is a reference in Harriet's letter to Henry, Oct. 16, [1861?] to "the man who took my place," but this letter is from Cambridge and concerns farming. On farmers' methods of borrowing against taxes to raise capital, see Robert P. Swierenga, *Acres for Cents: Delinquent Tax Auctions in Frontier Iowa* (Westport, Conn.: Greenwood Press, 1976).

"[T]he marshes where we pick are about 4 miles from here and are very wet the water being about a foot deep all over them, we start soon after breakfast and get home about dark Florence can ride horse back but I do not dare."[20]

From the start they farmed commercially, growing corn, oats, rye, and potatoes. Wheat, oats, and potatoes were exported from the state before the Civil War, but Harriet's soil was too sandy for wheat. She kept track of the market. In 1858 or 1859 she wrote, "I hear wheat has risen from 50 and 55 cts per bushel to 70 and 75 and 80. . . . been told potatoes sell for 15 cts per bushel corn about 30." And later, "have sold our corn." Produce was shipped by river, at least from Anoka. Perhaps Harriet used the Rum River, a mile to the west of her claim, to freight small loads. Besides cash crops, some of which were for her family's own use, Harriet had a garden of "Musk melons, cabbages, Tomatoes, squashes, onions, turnips, carrots, etc." In the spring of 1859, Arnold wrote "our Cow has got a nice calf . . . and Mother thinks she will buy 1 or 2 pigs." Later they had hens as well and Frances described the outbuildings: "our cows stable is covered with coarse hay on top and turfed up the sides and the barn where we sometimes keep horses is built of logs and covered with hay."[21]

As the children got older, more of the farm work fell to Harriet. She wrote, "Florence was gone till the last of Sept so I have a good deal of work to do out of doors. . . . Arnold is gone a good deal which brings all the care on me."[22] Arnold left to harvest cranberries or husk corn, and Florence, too, may have been out working as a hired girl or she may have been visiting. Later,

[20] U.S. Agricultural Manuscript Census, 1860, Isanti County, 13, microfilm copy (frame 274) in MHS. Preemption entry books for Cambridge for this date are lost. Harriet to Father and Mother, Sept. 14, [1858 or 1859].

[21] Loehr, *Farmers' Diaries*, 21; Harriet to Father and Mother, Sept. 14, [1858 or 1859] and Dec. 19, [18??], including Frances to Grandpa; Arnold to Uncle Henry, Jan. 20, 1860, and to Grandfather, May 8, 1859.

[22] Harriet to Brother Henry, Oct. 16, [1861 or later].

Arnold thought of enlisting in the Civil War. This pattern of children leaving in their mid- or late teens was not an unusual one. Often it was the youngest son who stayed to take over the farm.

Harriet complained a lot, but then she may have had something to complain about. As we have seen, a neighbor undercut her price for boarders; other boarders left for parts unknown before paying their bills; she was passed bad money; and the man Florence boarded with in Anoka sold a watch for Harriet and went off to Pikes Peak taking the proceeds with him. And she never did get the sleigh which was "thrown in" with the team. "Mr Abbott seems to be serving me a mean trick as well as some others, I had paid him all up except $7, on the note he held against me when he left, the cutter which was included in the bargain was at Anoka and as he went down to St. Paul he sold that to another man so that he means to cheat me out of that entirely."[23] Here it is clear that Harriet not only sold her farm products commercially but she bought large items partly on credit, giving her personal note for them.

Harriet had more to bear than the work and worry about money. After the first or second harvest on her own, she wrote in very Victorian tones, "It is a question in my mind whether it is my duty to stay here a great while longer. sometimes it seems rather hard that we must live so entirely shut out from the world as we do." In the same letter she brought up the matter of going back East: "have been advised to go back east but whether it would be best even if it were possible I do not know, hope our duty will be made plain to us and that we shall perform it faithfully." Possibly the same year she wrote: "and the thought again comes up must we always stay here?" An obvious choice, besides keeping a boardinghouse in town or returning to her parents, was marriage. She broached the subject, but without much enthusiasm, again putting the ultimate decision on an external force called "duty." Like many women once married who have some semblance of economic independence, the risks as well as the benefits of

[23] Harriet to Father, June 27, [1858 or 1859].

marriage were all too apparent. "What would you say were I to tell you I have some thoughts of changing my name I am sure I do not know what is for the best and fear were I to do so it might be for the worse, hope I shall be guided in the path of duty."[24]

We do not know whether Harriet Griswold remarried or not. In the sample of 259 of the women homesteaders, who were widowed after they came to the land as Harriet was, one in ten remarried before she made her final homestead proof, normally in five years or more. But we do know that Harriet stayed unmarried at least until the early 1860s. In 1860 she was one of 28 farmers in the entire county on the United States Agricultural Census where her farm of about 135 acres with 10 under cultivation was valued at $1,000—a very large amount for that time and place.

Twenty-three of the 28 farms were 160 acres, the maximum size allowed under the pre-emption laws. Eleven farms (almost 40 percent) equaled the value of Harriet's farm, the census taker thought. Of these, two were valued at $2,000 and nine at $1,000, with no valuations in between. One farmer had no livestock, and the farmer with the most livestock did not grow corn,

Table 1. Isanti County Farms at the Beginning of its Frontier Period, 1860[25]

	Number	High	Low	Average	Harriet Griswold
Improved acres	28	60	4	20	10
Total acres	28	165	33	153	133
Value of farm	28	$2,000	$330	$837	$1,000
Horses	9	2	1	1.33	1
Cows	26	8	1	2.3	1
Oxen	15	5	2	3	0
Pigs	27	13	1	5.9	2
Value of livestock	27	$515	$12	$202	$105
Potatoes—bushels	28	400	25	153	125
Corn—bushels	27	500	20	128	40
Butter—lbs.	23	500	25	200	125

[24] Harriet to Father and Mother, Sept. 14, [1858 or 1859]; to Brother Henry, April 29, [1858 or 1859]; to Father, Oct. 17, [probably 1861]. See also Suzanne Lebsock, *The Free Women of Petersburg: Status and Culture in a Southern Town, 1784-1860* (New York: Norton, 1984), 26.

[25] Statistics are from U.S. Agricultural Manuscript Census, 1860, Isanti County, 13.

the second major crop in the county after potatoes. Butter was a big cash crop, usually produced by the women; single male farmers without women probably bought butter from their neighbors.[26] Harriet produced four bushels of peas and beans and six bushels of buckwheat, besides harvesting 20 tons of hay. Although her farm was valued at $1,000, which was more than the average, Harriet's production fell below the average. Perhaps cash crops such as the wild cranberries that the family gathered were included in the total value of the farm; perhaps the buildings were more valuable than most, although from their descriptions that seems unlikely; perhaps the farm was more accessible to travelers who brought cash income as lodgers.

The acres cultivated are a basic measure of the extent of farming. Harriet's fell below the average in comparison to women homesteaders who came after her in the central region of the state.

Time may be the crucial factor here. Data on Harriet's farm comes from 1860, and the census, taken in the late spring, is based on her farming from 1859, when only three seasons of crops had been raised. Data on the

Table 2. Comparison of Harriet Griswold and Women Homesteaders in Central Minnesota[27]

	Harriet Griswold	Sample Women Homesteaders	
		Average	Number in Sample
Size of farm	133	131.1	67
Acres cultivated	10	14.4	66
Age	38	49	22

later women homesteaders gives the number of acres cultivated at proving-up time, at least five years after settlement—1868 at the earliest.

After the early 1860s when the letters from Harriet which have come down to us stop, we lose track of her.

[26] Glenda Riley, *Frontierswomen: The Iowa Experience* (Ames: Iowa State University Press, 1981), 86; Joan M. Jensen, *With These Hands: Working Women on the Land* (Old Westbury, N.Y.: Feminist Press, 1981), 108.

[27] Data shown is from Minnesota Homestead Final Certificates, NARG 49. Out of the sample of 259 women, 68 homesteaded in the central region; complete information for each woman in this sample was not provided.

Mobility was very high on the frontier, and it was not unusual for settlers to move on after a few years.[28]

EMELINE GUERNSEY had a very different story, although she migrated west only two years after Harriet Griswold did. The latter inherited a pre-emption claim and worthless town lots; Emeline Guernsey moved to Iowa as a widow of almost six years with the financial resources to buy a farm. Not only did she have such assets; she had technical experience and competence in running a farm as well. She had a working farm in Pennsylvania which she had operated since her husband Peter's death in 1852. But she had done a good deal of the managing before that as Peter, a superintendent on the railroad, had been necessarily absent from the farm. She settled in Stacyville, Mitchell County, Iowa, near her sister and brother-in-law and where other siblings farmed from time to time. Although she arrived at about the same time Harriet did in Isanti County, conditions were less rugged for her; Iowa was settled earlier than Minnesota, and she had more capital. Mitchell County, however, was still frontier in 1858. The land records only begin in 1854, and land was still being bought from the federal government in the 1860s. Emeline was 39 when she arrived, only four years older than Harriet, with five children ranging in age from William (called Willie) who was 18 years old to Emma, born after her father's death, who was five.[29]

Stacyville, only about five miles south of the Minnesota border, was part of the prairie woodland, making it more profitable farming than the more heavily wooded Isanti County. Emeline, who traveled west to Iowa to farm as a widow, typifies almost half (48.3 percent) of the women homesteaders in the Minnesota

---

[28] A study of an Iowa county shows two-thirds of the pioneers listed in the 1850 census did not appear in the 1860 census; in another Iowa county only 27 percent of pioneer families remained between those years; Julie Roy Jeffrey, *Frontier Women: The Trans-Mississippi West, 1840-1880* (New York: Hill and Wang, 1979), 81-82.

[29] Guernsey family genealogy, Guernsey Papers.

EMELINE GUERNSEY, about 1875

sample of 259. This is by far the largest category. A third of the women were, like Harriet Griswold, widowed after they were on the land but managed to stay and carry on the farming themselves.

Despite the fact that she had two older sons—Henry was 14, one year older than Arnold Griswold—Emeline, like Harriet, not only made the farming decisions but found that as her children grew older, they left the land and the farming to her. In 1858 before she left Pennsylvania, she wrote to her son Willie, already out in Philadelphia where he apparently worked on the railroad as many of the males in his family did: "Well Willie, I have sold out at last, to a man by the name of Swan. . . . He bought last tuesday, is to pay $4000, $2000, down, and the remainder . . . next March. Although this is less than I was to receive . . . I consider it a much better bargain, as I have it all in money, and get more down. I am to give possession immediately. . . . Uncle John says I may go into the house where Aunt Ann lived until the crops are all gathered, and I can dispose of them. another reason, I forgot to mention, why I think this a better bargain than the other is, because I now have my share of the crops." And although she asked Willie's advice, she intended to make all the preparations herself. "I should be glad if you were here to assist in disposing of things but think it will be better for you to remain there, if you keep well, until a week or two previous to our starting."[30] And so she sold the furniture and the livestock and prepared to go to Iowa late in the fall of 1858.

Emeline speculated in land as well as farmed. But she was more successful than Allen and Harriet Griswold, partly because she had more farmland than town lots, partly because it was rich soil unlike the more marginal land of Isanti County, and perhaps partly because she could hold the property longer and so was less affected by the Panic of 1857. Almost immediately on arrival in Iowa, in December, 1858, she bought 480 acres with those land warrants Harriet Griswold so often worried about. All this land had already seen two owners, although no deeds are recorded in Mitchell County before 1854. She bought 320 acres from a group of speculators from Decorah, Iowa, for $600 and an additional 160 acres for $333 from an individual who in turn had bought the land from a single seller less than two years before for $200.[31]

Like the Griswolds she also bought town lots, nine lots for a total of $200. By 1861 she had sold 160 acres to one of her younger sisters, Amelia, and in a separate deed, 80 acres to Amelia's husband, Homer Stacy. The total price Emeline realized from the Stacys was $850,

---

[30] Emeline to Willie Guernsey, Sept. 2, 1858.

[31] Here and below, see Village Deeds, Book B, p. 371, 372, and Book C, p. 472; Deed Record Book C, p. 630, 698, Book G, p. 122, Book H, p. 281, Book I, p. 413—all in Land Records, Mitchell County Courthouse, Osage, Iowa. Stacyville was named for Homer's brother Fitch.

a profit of $400. She sold another 80 acres in 1866 back to its former owner, one of her younger brothers, Erasmus, for $440, a hefty profit of $290. Although research did not uncover more than one sale of a town lot, in general, investment in Mitchell County land was profitable for Emeline. Like Allen Griswold, she clearly was not afraid to put her capital into land, one of the commonest and probably also one of the safest investments before extensive industrialization.

With two sons, 14 and 18 years of age, Emeline might have expected an easier time on her farm in Iowa than Harriet, widowed with younger children in Minnesota, but the Civil War came and Willie enlisted in 1861 and Henry followed not long after. Not only was she left again with all the management but, as the war went on, few men were left to hire to do the heavy farm work and many wives were alone to compete for their services. Early in the spring of 1862 Emeline wrote, "I have engaged some barley . . . for seed, and I think it would be well to have considerable corn planted, and potatoes enough for our own use." In February, 1864, after storing her wheat over the winter she wrote, "Mr. Fuller is going to Mitchell tomorrow with a load of wheat for me. . . . He has been once with a load today. There are some men there buying wheat, and paying 60 cents per bushel, (Greenbacks). . . . The load I sent today will a little more than pay my taxes, after paying for the hauling."[32]

At the war's end Willie, who spent almost four years telling his mother that he could not wait to be home with her and his three young sisters and that he would be contented there forever, returned to Iowa but did not stay long. By 1866 he was back East, working for the railroad, trying to pay back some of the money his mother had loaned him, and putting the responsibility for the farm on his brother, Henry. "Does Henry have any trouble in keeping along. I sometimes fear he cannot keep all things going. then think he can do better than I for I cannot take the interest one should in such things. he seems to like farming and I hope will prove master of it."[33]

[32] Emeline to Willie, April 9, 1863, Feb. 10, 1864.
[33] Willie to Emeline, Oct. 24, 1866.

Henry may or may not have proved master of farming, but he too did not like it. He married and went to Oregon where he worked as a sawyer and manager in a sawmill. In 1872 he wrote from Eugene City, "if they can get a Sawyer they will give me the Overseeing of the whole and not have me do any work in particular I consider my place [job] worth more to me than any farm I ever saw."[34]

The girls, too, began to marry and leave and there was talk of Emeline selling the farm. Although both sons would have liked to use her money, it is clear the decisions were hers and that she had substantial property to make decisions about. In 1872 Henry offered suggestions to his mother: "I wrote you a few days ago about selling out and may be sayed to mutch you know I am very apt to you must not be influanced by me against your own wishes for if you had rather keep the Place I would rather you would but I thought you mite be glad to get rid of the care but if you wish I will see that you have all the debts paid and you can keep the place if you like. I can pay the debts in a few months more I guess so you had [better] not sell on that account I only thought I could make your money do you more good with less care but I guess if you did not owe anyone your care would be some what alayed so you must do as you like and pay no attention to me for I am old enough to take care of my self." We know that at least some, if not all, of the debts were Henry's as there are references in the letters to Emeline paying his notes for him. It is unlikely that he ever found the money to pay most of them back.

In a similar vein, Willie wrote, "I do not know what to say . . . in regard to your going to Osage. I would advise you to come here, before doing anything with a view to locating again. . . . In regard to location—I do not know of any more desirable place. . . . But I do not wish to influence—Come and see for yourself. . . . What do you think of my proposition for your money? If you come here to live you can put in all your money & we will divide the spoil if you wish."[35] Henry wanted her to invest in lumber and Willie in his yet-to-be-established coal and wood business.

[34] Here and below, see Henry Guernsey to Emeline, June 30, 1872.

[35] Willie to Emeline, Dec. 10, 1872.

She did sell her farm in the fall of 1872 to a John Holbach for $3,600. She may then have been living in town as she stayed in Stacyville for some years, then went briefly to Illinois with her daughters, but was back in Stacyville in the 1880s.[36]

EMELINE GUERNSEY and Harriet Griswold were both old-stock Americans, who had been married. But single and immigrant women also settled on the midwestern frontier, and their numbers increased with time. In the 1860s only five percent of the sample of 259 women homesteaders in Minnesota were single; by the 1880s almost 29 percent were. This increase reflected the growing independence of single women as the century progressed and perhaps also the increasing numbers of women who remained single throughout their lifetimes. Through the 1880s, 45 percent of the single women in the Minnesota sample were immigrants.[37]

The Homestead Bill, which gave impetus to this western settlement, had passed in 1860 but was vetoed by President James Buchanan. Under Abraham Lincoln, who ran on a homestead platform in 1860, the bill finally became law in 1862. Anyone could apply for a homestead who was over 21, was a citizen of the United States or who had declared his or her intention to become a citizen, and who was the head of a household. Consequently, from the beginning, homesteading was open to single and widowed women as well as to single, married, and widowed men. To gain title to the land, an applicant had to prove that he or she had lived on

---

[36] Deed Record Book R, p. 63, Mitchell County Courthouse. Other data on Emeline's life was gleaned from reading through the Guernsey Papers.

[37] Minnesota Homestead Final Certificates, NARG 49; Lee Virginia Chambers-Schiller, *Liberty, a Better Husband: Single Women in America: The Generations of 1780-1840* (New Haven: Yale University Press, 1984), 190-191.

A WOMAN FARMER and her children, near Jasper, Pipestone County, 1889

the land and cultivated it for five years.[36]

Minnesota was the first big homestead state; only 8 percent of the state land had been offered for sale before the legislation. For the next six years, formative years for the state, Minnesota led the nation in homestead entries—44 percent in 1865. Thereafter land sales and later still railway sales (railroads held one-fifth of the land in Minnesota) widened the gap, but still it is estimated that about two-thirds of Minnesota farms originated as homesteads.

Pauline Auzjon was one of the single, immigrant homesteaders. She emigrated from Norway in June, 1869, and four years later in November, 1873, the 53-year-old woman filed a homestead application in Grant County on the frontier of west-central Minnesota. It is possible that she abandoned an earlier claim,

[36] Here and below, see U.S., *Statutes at Large*, 12:392; unlike the 1841 Pre-emption Act, the 1862 legislation made it clear that single women as well as widows could claim land. During the 1860s most new farms in Minnesota, unlike those in the rest of the nation, were homesteaded; Gates, *Public Land*, 401, 411; Fite, *Farmers' Frontier*, 16, 20, 23.

for when asked her previous occupation, she replied farming. On her final proof she said, "I lived there as a single woman together with my widowed sister." Perhaps some cultivation had already occurred on the land as she said, "I waited on cancelation for former Homestead." In any case, she had settled on the land a year before making her homestead application. Pauline may have emigrated with her sister and brother-in-law and he may have died in this country; it is more likely, however, that her sister left Norway after she was widowed, since she inherited no claim from her deceased husband.[39]

By 1880, at the time of final proof, Pauline had 18 acres under cultivation and a log house 14-by-15 feet with a lumber addition. The farm was valuable enough to appear on the 1880 agricultural census where she was listed as the owner of 20 acres tilled (including rotation), five acres in permanent pasture, three in woodland, and 135 unimproved acres. The agricultural census gave the value of the farm as $1,200 for the land, fences, and buildings; $40 for farm implements; and $100 for livestock for a total value of $1,340. The value of farm implements varied considerably among farmers who were her neighbors and was not directly correlated to the number of acres cultivated. Clearly some farmers invested in expensive new farming machinery, and probably hired themselves out to work on their neighbors' fields.[40]

The need for hired labor was not directly correlated to size or value of the farm. Pauline, like six of her nine neighbors, used hired labor during the previous year. Pauline paid helpers for 14 weeks; the range was from 5 to 25, so she ranked somewhere about the median. She

---

[39] Rice, *Patterns of Ethnicity*, 17. All quotations of Pauline Auzjon's final proof are from Final Certificate No. 2962, Minnesota Final Homestead Certificates, NARC 49. The 1880 census does not list the sister, but the homestead record, given in full sentences, would seem more accurate. U.S. Census, 1880, Minnesota manuscript schedules, Grant County, Lien Township, 24, microfilm copy in MHS.

[40] On qualifications for inclusion in the agricultural census, see *Senate Documents*, 56th Cong., 1st sess., no. 194, p. 173 (Serial 3856). On farm machinery, see Allan G. Bogue, *From Prairie to Corn Belt: Farming on the Illinois and Iowa Prairies in the Nineteenth Century* (Chicago: University of Chicago Press, 1963), 148-168.

sowed one acre to oats and harvested 24 bushels; 20 acres to wheat for 400 bushels; and one quarter of an acre to potatoes for 30 bushels, probably for her own use. Clearly wheat was the primary cash crop as it was for most of her neighbors. This was typical for farmers in Minnesota. She harvested 20 tons of hay, about average, and had two working oxen, two cows, two calves, and four other cattle; she also had one pig and seven chickens that laid 25 dozen eggs. Pauline made 150 pounds of butter, another of her cash crops, though most farms had made more.[41]

Once the final proof was made, Pauline started paying property taxes on her farm, valued for tax purposes in 1881 at $653. Her land steadily increased in value for five years, reaching $893 in 1887 when she sold her homestead to Robert Beach for $1,280. (Actually the sale did not take place until June 21, 1887, although 1886 taxes had already been transferred to Beach.) By then the taxes had dropped a little from the high of $23 yearly to under $17, not insignificant sums in those times. From census and tax records, it is clear that this was very much a working farm; in fact, in 1883 Pauline bought an adjoining 40 acres of railroad land, but by 1888 that also had been transferred to Robert Beach.[42]

When she sold, Pauline carried the mortgage of $1,112, almost the total purchase price. This debt was probably due in three years, when a new mortgage for $1,200 was written for both the original homestead and the railroad land. Short-term mortgages were common

[41] Fite, *Farmers' Frontier*, 49. The figures are somewhat inconsistent; the breakdown of Pauline's crops on the agricultural census adds up to more than the total tilled listed there, and this in turn was greater than the total claimed for the same year on the homestead final proof.

[42] Here and below, see Real Estate Tax Books, Lien Township, 1881-1886, Treasurer's office; Deed Record Book C, p. 309, Book F, p. 136, Book G, p. 52, 240, Book J, p. 136, Book R, p. 394, Book Z, p. 283, Land Records, Probate Records—all in Grant County Courthouse, Elbow Lake.

Twenty-or thirty-year mortgages as we know them did not exist at this time; the extremely short term of the mortgage was more a guarantee that the lender could sell the land if the buyer defaulted than an expectation of full payment by the stated date.

at this time. In the spring of 1898 a third mortgage was taken out for both pieces of land, this time for $1,500. Beach paid this off in 1903 after Pauline's death. More than the original sum was still owing, $1,567.50, although the interest payments over the years would have been an important source of income to Pauline. It is an indication of the lack of capital on the agricultural frontier that for the 16 years Robert Beach owned Pauline's land, he had paid off virtually none of the purchase price. Pauline still lived in Lien, Grant County, when she died at about 82 years of age, in a small house attached to the house of a friend, Hansine Bartness. Her estate was divided among her scattered, extended family: the bulk went to her two married nieces, one in Minneapolis and the other in Fergus Falls, and large bequests went to her infant grandniece, Pauline Auzjon Torgerson, and her grandnephew, Martin Solensten, both in Terente, South Dakota.

Although she did not continue to farm her homestead—Pauline was, after all, 66 years old when she sold—it was a valuable asset for her, providing an income that, in turn, meant independence in her retirement years. There was nothing unusual for both men and women, particularly toward the end of the 19th century, to use homesteading as a means of creating capital for other uses.[43]

EMMA SETTERLUND, like Pauline, was also an immigrant from Scandinavia. She emigrated with her family from Sweden when she was about 12 years old. Nine years later, in 1880, the same year Pauline was proving up on her land, the 21-year-old Emma made a pre-emption application for 160 acres of prairie land in Traverse County. Because ownership came sooner under the pre-emption law and because requirements were less stringent, settlers continued to make preemption claims under which they paid $1.25 an acre, even though homestead land, except for small filing

[43] Fite, *Farmers' Frontier*, 19-20, 46.

fees, was free. Emma applied for the same type of claim Harriet Griswold had made more than two decades earlier in Isanti County. As the line of settlement moved west from Grant to Traverse County in the 1880s, Emma became a frontierswoman.[44]

In July, 1883, perhaps when payment was due, Emma filed a homestead claim that superseded her pre-emption application. Homesteaders had six months before they had to live on their land, and Emma delayed committing herself: but by October she hired carpenters to build a 12-by-14-foot house, and on December 1, 1883, she moved in. Times were difficult for her. She had not put a crop in that summer nor did she put one in the next summer. Perhaps she simply lacked the capital for further investment after paying to have her house built, or perhaps homesteading was a means to gain capital rather than to have an ongoing farming operation. She explained on the homestead proof that she was away the following winter from the last of November, 1884, until the first of April, 1885, "for the purpose of earning money to purchase the necessaries of life and to improve my land." The next winter she was away for two weeks "just before Christmas" again working. Emma "worked at house work and sewing in Morris, Minn. in the family of a man by the name of George Munroe, and in Minneapolis, sewing for different people, boarding with a family by the name of Johnson." Emma had not worked away from home before homesteading; she lived with her parents in the same county, though in a different township on land which very likely they either pre-empted or homesteaded. When asked her earlier occupation, she had replied, "I assisted my parents on their farm."[45] By the late 19th century many homesteaders, both men and women, worked off the farm for a livelihood.

Homesteading was financially attractive to Emma as an alternative to living with her parents and working for them on their farm, or being live-in domestic help, or finding enough sewing in the city of Minneapolis to make a living. She may have done less of the actual

---

[44] Rice, *Patterns of Ethnicity*, 17.

[45] Information on Emma Setterlund and all quotations about her are from Final Certificate No. 5926, Minnesota Final Homestead Certificates, NARC 49.

farm work herself than Harriet Griswold because we know that she hired the grain farming work done although she kept a couple of chickens and one or two cows. Probably the land had never been cultivated before, although it is difficult to be certain. In any case, Emma cultivated four acres in 1885, five acres in 1886, six acres in 1887, and ten acres in 1888. Her wheat crop increased through the same years to 39 bushels. By 1887 she was also growing garden vegetables. In 1886 and 1887 wheat prices were "between 50 and 60 cents" a bushel, rising steeply to "around 90 cents" in 1889.[46] Still, even if she sold all her wheat, in 1888 Emma would have made only $35. No doubt she used some of the wheat for her own flour. With milk, butter, cheese, eggs, chicken, and vegetables to eat, she should have been able to keep herself in food. Salt, sugar, and tea would have to be bought but very little else. Her profit was small, but domestic servants were paid little beyond their keep and it is unlikely that she could have earned more from sewing after paying board and room.

Emma may have bartered services and goods with her neighbors, exchanging her butter and sewing or domestic help for plowing or harvesting. Further, Emma could expect the land to appreciate in value, especially with her improvements. She described her house as "Built of fine lumber as follows: Studding 16 inches apart. Weather-boarded paper over that and sidded. Papered and oiled inside. shingle roof. Matched floors . . . one window. The house is painted outside. House sits on stone foundation. House is worth at least $200.00. Barn 10 × 12 built of fine lumber worth about $25.00. A few trees around the house in good growing condition, set out by myself. worth at least $15.00. About 10 acres of land broke and under cultivation, worth at least $5.00 per acre. a good well of water worth $10.00 at least." All this, she thought, made a total improvement of $300 beyond the value of the land. Inside the house she had "one bed and bedding. one cook stove, one table, three chairs, dishes, cooking utensils and all other necessary household articles." It was important to report these items as proof that the necessities of life were present on the homestead. De-

[46] On wheat prices at this time, see Fite, *Farmers' Frontier*, 88.

spite the fact that she hired much of the work done, Emma, when asked her occupation at final proof, replied "farmer."

Emma proved up her claim in November, 1888, and although she did not receive the patent from the United States government until March, 1891, the land was now hers, ready to be taxed, mortgaged, or sold. In 1889 Emma began to pay real estate taxes; the county assessments over the next few years indicate the fluctuation of land values in western Minnesota at that time. Emma's land never reached the value of Pauline's land. The valuations were: $400, 1889; $640, 1890; $672, 1892; and $588, 1894. In 1892 when her land had its highest valuation, the southwest quarter of her section (Emma had the northwest quarter) was sold for taxes. The other parts of the section were not taxed, presumably because they were either not owned or they were being homesteaded or pre-empted and title had not yet been gained to them. Emma's taxes that year were $18.68, a general tax of $10.62 and a school tax of $8.06. The county was the taxing agent, passing collected funds up to the state and down to smaller units of government. Relatively, school taxes were very high. Usually land sold for taxes could be redeemed within a three-or five-year period, and often the sale was simply a means for farmers to divert for a few years the little cash they had from taxes to capital improvements.[47]

Throughout this period, Emma was not assessed on the personal property of her farm so that it appears that either her farm operation was very small, or that she continued to work out of town for the major part of her living, and/or that she kept the farm only as a capital investment. But we know that she did keep it until she died. She kept the land free and clear for five years when she took out a mortgage from Thomas A. Morse for $300—about half the land's assessed valuation—at 6 percent payable in three years.

Five years later and ten years after making her homestead proof, Emma, now 39, married Peter Peter-

---

[47] Real Estate Tax Books, Treasurer's office, Traverse County Courthouse, Wheaton; Bogue, *From Prairie to Corn Belt*, 187; Swierenga, *Acres for Cents*, especially chapter 7.

[4—369a.]

HOMESTEAD, PRE-EMPTION, AND COMMUTATION PROOF.

TESTIMONY OF CLAIMANT.

Full and Specific Answers must be given to each Question. Evasive Answers will be Fatal to the Proof.

Emma Setterlund, claimant, being first duly sworn, testifies as follows:

Question 1.—What is your correct name, age, and occupation? If employed by any person, state by whom.

Answer. Emma Setterlund. Age 29 years. Occupation farmer.

Ques. 2.—What is your post-office address?

Ans. Post office address is Wheaton, Traverse County, Minn

Ques. 3.—Are you the identical person who made ~~pre-emption filing No.~~ ______ (or homestead entry No. 7971) at the Fergus Falls Minn land office on the 25th day of July, 1883, and what is the true description of the land now claimed by you?

Ans. I am. It is the N.E. 1/4, section 12, Township 127, Range 46

Ques. 4.—Where did you live before settling upon this land, and what was your occupation?

Ans. In town of Clifton, Traverse County Minn
I assisted my parents on their farm in that town.

Ques. 5.—Are you a citizen of the United States, or have you declared your intention to become such?

Ans. I am a naturalized citizen of the United States.

(In case the party is of foreign birth, a copy of his declaration of intention to become a citizen or full naturalization certificate, officially certified, must be filed with the case. The latter is only required in final homestead entries.)

Ques. 6.—Are you interested in any other entry or filing than the one upon which you now seek to make proof?

Ans. I am not

Ques. 7.—Have you ever made a pre-emption filing for any other tract of land, or made any other homestead entry or filing or entry of any other kind? (Answer each question separately, describe the land, and state what disposition you made of your claim.)

Ans. I have never made any other filing or entry of any kind, except a pre-emption filing on this same land in 1880.

Ques. 8.—Is your present claim within the limits of an incorporated town or selected site of a city or town, or used in any way for trade and business?

Ans. No

Ques. 9.—What is the character of the land? Is it timber, mountainous, prairie, grazing, or ordinary agricultural land? State its kind and quality, and for what purpose it is most valuable.

Ans. It is quite level prairie land. Black loam soil, with Clay sub=soil. It is most valuable for agricultural purposes

Ques. 10.—Is the land valuable for coal, iron, stone, or minerals of any kind? Has any coal or other minerals been discovered thereon, or is any coal or mineral known to be contained therein? Are there any indications of coal, salines, or minerals of any kind on the land? If so, describe what they are.

Ans. None to my knowledge

son of Anoka County on March 26, 1889. The Reverend E. Schold performed the ceremony in Traverse County where Emma still had many relatives, but the couple lived in Anoka until Emma died five months later on August 6. Her husband was her only heir. The next winter her mortgage was paid off, over four years after it was taken out, either by Emma's widower or by her estate. Her husband remarried, and he and his new wife sold Emma's homestead in 1903.[46]

WHAT, then, is the profile we can draw of women farming on the upper midwest frontier from the late

MARY CONROY, who built and occupied this Clay County claim shanty about 1910, is an example of the women farmers who moved west with the shifting settlement frontier.

[46] Mortgage Record Book 7, p. 286, Book 10, p. 575, and Marriage Records, both in Traverse County Courthouse.

1850s through the 1880s? We know that they were there at all times and in all regions. Although the amount of heavy labor they did varied, letters and testimony on homestead records tell us that most women made the day-to-day decisions on their farms and did much of the work.

The four women in this study approached the dream of owning land by the various routes available in 19th-century America. In Minnesota Territory and the states of Iowa and Minnesota—in woodlands and on open prairies from the 1850s to the 1870s and 1880s—they pre-empted land, bought land, and homesteaded. Young and old, both financially secure and precarious, widowed or single, from the eastern United States with Anglo-Saxon names and from Scandinavia, these women sought a life for themselves and for a time, at least, they found it.

Harriet, Emeline, Pauline, and Emma were not alone. All about them women were out farming on the frontier. Even more women were to follow them, taking up land in the Dakotas. In American legend, sturdy, young men conquered the West. But women were beside them, some as wives, others farming on their own. This is the tale of some of those who farmed alone—forgotten Persephones, lost too often from our memories, buried, it would seem, beneath the very ground they farmed.

THE PHOTOGRAPH on p.152 is used through courtesy of Marygray Orcutt Brown; the map on p.139 drawn by Alan Ominsky, is adapted from John Rice, *Patterns of Ethnicity*, 17; the photograph on page 165 is from the collections of the Clay County Historical Society, used with permission. All other illustrations are from the MHS audio-visual library.

Autonomy and Dependency in the Lives of Dakota Women: A Study in Historical Change

PATRICIA C. ALBERS

ABSTRACT: This paper examines certain theoretical issues bearing upon the relationship between race, class and household as these impact the role and status of women. In doing so, it presents a case study of historical contradictions that have influenced the experiences of Dakota women during the past century.

INTRODUCTION

There can be no doubt that sexism is a pervasive feature of the modern division of labor, or that the dimensions of sexism differ across class and racial lines. In the United States women of color are disadvantaged not only because they are women but because they are members of a specific racial group. Racial status serves as an institutionalized marker for segregation in an economy where women of color are concentrated in the lowest paying jobs, have high levels of unemployment and constitute a disproportionate number of the females living in poverty (Lewis 1977; Mora and del Castillo 1980; Puryear 1980; Albers 1983a; Davis 1983; Stallard, Ehrenreich and Sklar 1983).

The poverty under which many women of color live has a significant impact on their household life (Stack 1974; Aschenbrenner 1975; McAdoo 1981; Albers 1982; Ybarra 1982). Class and its dynamics explain many aspects of domestic poverty and its consequences for women's lives. However, it does not always explain why poor American Indian, black, Asian, hispanic, and white women experience the impact of domestic poverty in different ways. Such variation raises important questions about the role of race and ethnicity in women's lives.

This paper examines relationships between race and class as these bear upon the changing position of American Indian women within the developing capitalist United States political economy. Using data drawn primarily from my own research,[1] it focuses on a group of Dakota women whose collective experiences over the past century reveal a great deal about the dynamics of gender, race, and class in the organization of domestic groupings.

HOUSEHOLDS, CLASS, AND RACE: SOME THEORETICAL QUESTIONS

There is a general consensus among feminist scholars that gender is a social construct informed by the historical settings in which women experience their

---

Department of Anthropology, University of Utah, Salt Lake City, Utah 84112.
I wish to acknowledge the National Institute of Mental Health and the Wenner-Gren Foundation for their financial support in carrying out part of the field research upon which this study is based. I would also like to acknowledge my gratitude to William James, Gary Dymski, and Laurie Nisonoff for their editorial and theoretical assistance. Most importantly, I wish to thank the Dakota women at Devil's Lake for their support and hospitality during the years I lived with them and conducted my research.

lives. There is also general agreement that women have been subordinated throughout much of human history. However, there is little agreement on the forms this oppression takes or on the forces that have determined it.

Among the many forces that contribute to the status of women three stand out: household, class, and race. Of the three, the dimension of race is the least understood. While much has been written about the lives and experiences of women from racial minority groups and about the impact of racial status on labor force segmentation, class-standing, and household composition, race has not been a central subject in feminist literature.[2] In part, this has stemmed from the fact that the terms of discourse have largely derived from and related to the conditions of feminists who are also white.[3] Yet, the condition of race and its relation to household and class formations is fundamental to an understanding of all women's oppression (Lewis 1977). By failing to include race, feminist theory runs the danger of becoming myopic — applicable only to the forms of subordination experienced by white women (Simmons 1979). The following discussion is intended to raise some questions regarding the significance of race as a variable in the analysis of women's status in domestic settings.

One major tendency within recent feminist scholarship has been to account for women's oppression in terms of a unified set of forces included under the conceptual umbrella of "patriarchy" (Hartmann 1976, 1981a, 1981b; Delphy 1977; Ferguson and Folbre 1981; Brown 1981). In partial reaction to the inability of Marxist class analysis to account for the existence of female subordination across class lines, some feminists began to focus on those areas of experience which women shared irrespective of their class standing. Increasingly, their attention has focused on the character and dynamics of social relationships within families and households. Drawing largely on the experiences of women in the United States, Canada, and western Europe, some feminists relate women's oppression to the dominance and persistence of a patriarchal ideology and family structure which pre-dates capitalism. Although patriarchal approaches can be criticized on a number of different grounds, which include obvious restrictions on their universal application, they have raised a number of important issues in the development of feminist theory (Edholm, Harris and Young 1977; Beechey 1979; Barrett 1980; Sokoloff 1981; Power 1984).

One of the major contributions of the patriarchal perspective is the focus it has given to the importance of reproduction in the determination of gender experience.[4] Most feminist scholars now accept the fact that women's roles in reproduction are an essential component of their status; but there is considerable disagreement over how these roles are envisioned, how they are determined, and how they act as "causal" forces (Mackintosh 1977; McDonough and Harrison 1978; Benería 1979; Barrett 1980; Sokoloff 1981; Harris and Young 1981; Folbre 1982; Power 1984; Bryceson and Vuorela 1984; Himmelweit 1984). Current understandings of reproduction and its articulation with the forces and relations of production are directly related to conventional understandings of the notion of "household."

Households

In its most basic sense, a household is a group of people who share a common place of residence. Those who form a household usually establish their joint residence through some form of intimate relationship. Households do not equal families, however. Although there is often overlap between the two, the form of household membership is not universally given. At best what can be said is that the household is made up of people (often related by kinship) who share in the responsibility of producing some set of use-values on a generational and/or daily basis.[5]

The fact that all households minimally engage in some form of reproduction has led many scholars to envision them as a discrete sphere of activity and relationship, which is opposed to a "public" or "productive" sector (Rosaldo 1974; Hartmann 1976, 1981a, 1981b; Delphy 1977; Brown 1981). For some scholars, the reproductive activity of households constitutes a separate mode of production with its own internal logic and laws (Sahlins 1972; Harrison 1973; Seccombe 1974; Delphy 1977). In this type of approach households are associated with special economic interests and also distinctive forms of social relationship (e.g., the family). One view which has currency in some social scientific circles holds that the household has an elementary form which persists and remains despite changes in the wider social formations in which households are embedded. Not surprisingly, this view is often associated with the idea that patriarchy is a "natural" feature of household economy. Here reproduction takes on a completely independent analytical status which is largely divorced from the forces and relations of social production.[6] Most scholars who envision households and their relation to society in dualistic terms, however, do not see the reproductive activity of households as totally independent (e.g., Sahlins 1972; Harrison 1973; Seccombe 1974; Hartmann 1976). While the household is associated with a distinct type of relationship, it is nonetheless responsive to a wider set of political economic forces.

No matter how the relationship between households and society is envisioned in dualistic approaches, these perspectives are problematic because, in one degree or another, they project the historically specific character of the separation between production and reproduction under capitalism to all social formations (Roseberry 1985). While this kind of dualism does have some heuristic value for interpreting household formations under advanced capitalism, it is totally inappropriate if we are to understand what happens in other social formations where the relationships of production and reproduction are not divided (Harris and Young 1981).

In many types of societies, production and reproduction have overlapped and have been embedded in a single relational structure defined primarily by kinship (Meillassoux 1969, 1972; Godelier 1975; Kahn and Llobera 1981; Wolf 1982). In most band-type, foraging societies, for example, where the production of use-value was paramount and socially productive, there was no separation between the two in the character of work, who it was organized by, and for what purposes it was performed (Lee 1976; Keenan 1981). In this context, women's work and her role in reproduction was also production, and it did not constitute a significantly different interest or order within the community. Comparatively speaking, under these circumstances women had greater autonomy and power in controlling their reproductive activities (Leacock and Etienne 1980; Sanday 1981; Sacks 1982; Bell 1983; Bryceson and Vuorela 1984).[7]

Even under capitalism it is problematic to separate reproduction from production as if reproduction is a household affair and production an affair of capital. The household is not in all instances solely a unit of reproduction. Households, while often not productive in one class, certainly must be viewed as productive in others (e.g., small family run businesses in the competitive sectors of capitalism, e.g. see Cook 1984). Furthermore, reproduction is not restricted to households and families. Many dualistic approaches fail to adequately address institutions outside the household that deal with reproduction. Today, the state plays a critical role in reproduction through education, public health services, and welfare assistance (Folbre 1981). As reproductive activities become increasingly socialized and capitalized (as evidenced by the growth of the service sector), their separation spatially, conceptually, and relationally from production becomes less and less clear (Young and Harris 1981).

Dualistic approaches do identify many concrete aspects of household formations, but these cannot be adequately comprehended when seen in oppositional or fragmented terms (Power 1984; Himmelweit 1984). Households, while distinguishable and individuated, are not autonomous. They do not exist self-sufficiently, uninfluenced by the larger social formations of which they are a part. While household activities and relationships may be distinguishable from other institutional arrangements, the household does not constitute a separate mode of production (Himmelweit 1984; Roseberry 1985). Households are always connected to others in varying degrees and through different kinds of institutional relationships, and they are always linked to social formations which exist outside the confines of households *per se* (Roseberry 1985). To say that household activity is performed independently is different from saying that it exists independently.

Just as households should not be visualized as separate entities, so the larger social formations in which they are embedded do not represent totally autonomous sectors. What occurs under capitalism, feudalism, or any other mode of production is influenced by the actions of constituent households. Capital clearly requires a "free" labor force that is reproduced in a sector which is not only partially independent but which itself creates use-values necessary for the existence of that "free" labor force (Himmelweit 1984). Thus, while the realization of surplus value may not be based directly on "unpaid" household work, for example, it is certainly dependent on this work for the daily and generational reproduction of the labor force that creates surplus-value (Harris and Young 1981; Folbre 1982; Power 1984). It is, therefore, "socially necessary labor" (Himmelweit 1984).

One could probably argue that, universally, no social formation exists independently of its constituent households, and that no household exists aside from the formation in which it is embedded. If this is the case, then questions regarding the position of reproductive and productive forces are not polemical but relational ones. One major question is: how is the relationship between a given social formation and its households organized, and how does this influence the particular character of articulations between production and reproduction?

Class

An understanding of households under advanced capitalism takes us directly to the centers of debate on the relationship between class, family, and gender. Much of this debate has taken place within very narrow terms. The idea that the household and capital form a dialectical antagonism in which the household (female) is concerned with reproduction and capital (male) with production, is based largely on the historically specific character of proletarian households under advanced capitalism. Under this circumstance, the activity of these households is not considered to be socially productive (Himmelweit 1984). It is confined largely to the realization of use-values, most of which are not produced directly (Folbre 1982). As Susan Himmelweit (1984) correctly argues, households occupy a "client" status. They are spatially and conceptually separate in so far as much activity of daily and generational reproduction takes place within their bounds. Yet, among the proletarian classes of advanced capitalist societies, this activity itself is dependent on the work of wage-laborers who provide the basic means for households to sustain and reproduce themselves.

Households of entrepreneurs in the competitive sectors of advanced capitalist countries, or petty commodity producers in Third World areas, also occupy a client status, but it is noticeably different from that of proletarian households. Here, households do much more than reproduce their members on a daily and generational basis. They are socially productive units. They are places of production, where household members simultaneously produce use-value and exchange-value. These households not only have a different relation to capital, but are also another way of organizing relationships between production and reproduction (Cook 1984).

Households of semi-proletarianized, peasant labor found in many developing areas constitute another case. Here daily reproduction is much more attenuated because the wages workers receive are insufficient to provision themselves and their households. A larger portion of household labor involves the direct creation of use-values, especially in the area of food production (James 1973, 1975; Deere 1976, 1979). Again, the household's relationship to capital and its role in reproduction is of a different order than one totally dependent on wages for its survival (Bryceson and Vuorela 1984).

Then there are households of the lumpenproletariat within the centers of capitalism that are subsidized by the state. Whether or not the state's intention in welfare is to maintain a reserve army of labor for capital, it certainly is the principal agent in the reproduction of large numbers of households with marginalized workers (Folbre 1984). Unable to reproduce themselves because they lack access to steady wage-labor or a means (e.g. land) to create their own use-values, lumpen-class households are largely dependent on the support of the state for their survival.

In the United States, this dependence is organized primarily around women and their children, who represent the largest group of welfare recipients (Stallard, Ehrenreich and Sklar 1983; Kamerman 1984; Folbre 1984). The distribution of assistance under AFDC (Aid to Families with Dependent Children) and other programs has contributed to the growth of female-headed households among all segments of the lumpen-class (Kamerman 1984; Folbre 1984). The manner in which female-headed households are reproduced, however, is not simply a consequence of the structure of state welfare programs, or the result of sex segregation in wages. It is also a product of the "congealed" labor of women (and men) and the organization of domestic provisioning within and between households in poverty. In the United States, at least, the characteristics of both of these may be influenced by race.

Race and Ethnicity

Race and ethnicity are concepts that must be understood dialectically (Albers and James 1986). Both are informed by an objective set of experiences which set one group off from another as well as by a subjective awareness of the significance of that experience for purposes of social differentiation. Groups become distinct in ethnic terms when their members experience a common history and articulate that experience through a unique ideology or culture that has unfolded and established itself over time. In this sense, race designates a particular kind of ethnic grouping in which people are united by their "color." However, the significance of color as a basis for social differentiation and ethnic uniqueness is by no means uniform. It has historically specific dimensions.

In the history of the United States, color or race has played a paramount role in social differentiation. Indeed, there are some who argue that it has been more important than class in organizing and segregating labor. Whether or not this is true, race has acted as a major factor in labor force segmentation, funneling a large percentage of America's racial minorities into the status of a reserve army of labor (Reich 1981). Consequently, a large portion of the households dependent on federal entitlement programs for their survival come from the ranks of minority groups (Stallard, Ehrenreich and Sklar 1983).

With the concentration of large segments of minority populations, such as American Indians, blacks, and hispanics, in the lumpen-class, it is not surprising to find certain gross parallels in the composition of their domestic groupings. Aside from the obvious fact that a large number are headed by females, many follow extended rather than nuclear family structures (Stack 1974; Aschenbrenner 1975; Lamphere 1977; Knack 1980; McAdoo 1981; Albers 1982; Zinn 1982; Lewis 1984). The fact that most minority women are not isolated in their poverty in the same way that many white women appear to be is not without significance in understanding their domestic arrangements (Zinn 1982; Lewis 1984).

In contrast to American Indians, blacks, and hispanics, where large segments of the female and male population are impoverished, poverty is predominately a female experience among whites (Stallard, Ehrenreich and Sklar 1983). Whereas unemployment and underemployment is a permanent condition in the lives of many minority men, it is usually a temporary experience for most white males (Albers 1974; Lewis 1977; Mora and del Castillo 1980). As Diane Lewis (1977) notes, when both men and women are denied access to power and resources, by virtue of their race, they share common interests that take precedence over their gender-based differences.

Whereas many white women are impoverished by divorce and have been able, at least historically, to escape poverty through marriage, this has not been the case for large segments of minority women (Stallard, Ehrenreich and Sklar 1983; Lewis 1984; Folbre 1984). Among some groups of minority women, marriage does not improve the economic well-being of their households. On the contrary, it is often detrimental (Albers 1983b; Lewis 1984). Since large numbers of minority men are chronically unemployed or underemployed, they cannot provide either adequate or reliable means of support. Under these circumstances, marriage is not viewed as an economic arrangement, nor do women expect men to support them (Lewis 1984). Thus, while white women often exchange their dependency on a single, male "breadwinner" for a reliance on the patriarchal welfare programs of the state, this does not characterize the situation of many poverty-stricken, minority women.

There are fundamental differences in the experiences of white and minority women in poverty. These differences can be attributed not only to the marginalized relation of large numbers of minority men to the economy but also to the fact that a larger percentage of minority people live in poverty. Such distinctions have important implications for the strategies that women follow in dealing with their poverty, for the kinds of domestic groupings they form in the process, and for the relationships they maintain with the men of their group.

Whether minority women are American Indians, blacks, or hispanics, their lives and those of their families are profoundly affected by structural barriers based on race. Since these women tend to experience poverty *collectively* rather than *individually*, it is not surprising to find that there are noticeable parallels in the composition of their domestic groupings (Stack 1974; Lamphere 1977; Knack 1980; McAdoo 1981; Albers 1982; Zinn 1982). Yet, despite apparent similarities, there are still subtle as well as obvious differences between these various minority groups. Some of the variations are linked to the historical patterns of each group's entry into, and current position in, the capitalist social formation of the United States (e.g., migrant labor [Mora and del Castillo 1980] and slavery [Lewis 1984]). Yet, they may also be related to unique ethnically-based ideologies which have developed around a group's collective experiences (Zinn 1982; Lewis 1984).

Within modern societies, much of what is identified as ethnic culture is realized and reproduced within an arena of community and domestic relationships that exist on the margins of the market and the state. This has been especially true for the cultures of racial minorities. While aspects of these cultures are sometimes used and co-opted by the mass media, they rarely become an ideological standard bearer (except in national forms of protest and resistence.) For example, in many black and American Indian communities, the ideology of the patriarchal family is not a dominant influence in the day-to-day workings of their households (Albers 1983b; Lewis 1984) as it is in the lives of many chicanas and white women (Zinn 1982). Although this ideology certainly affects all impoverished females through the welfare policies of the state, and through the sex segregated structure of the labor force (Hartmann 1976; Eisenstein 1984a, 1984b; Folbre 1984; Smith 1984), it does not totally permeate their domestic experience. Thus, the particular characteristics of ethnic ideologies and the historical experiences under which they have been created are not irrelevant to understanding either the character of domestic life or the status of women, as the following case study attempts to demonstrate.

THE CASE OF DAKOTA WOMEN

In the case of the Dakota[8] and other American Indian women, an understanding of their lives and experiences cannot be reduced simply to the dimensions of class and race as defined in aggregate terms. While many Indian people are members of the lumpen-class and consequently receive some of the same forms of state assistance as other minority groups in poverty, their class status and dependence on welfare has been created by a distinctive set of circumstances. The place of American Indians, and the history of their relationship with capitalism, has been different from blacks and hispanics. In many respects, their history of incorporation shares much more in common with indigenous peoples in other areas of the world (e.g., Australia and Oceania) than it does with other minority groups in the United States. Some of the unique properties of the relationship of the American Indian to the state and capital need to be highlighted here.

Prior to the emergence of capitalism in the nineteenth century, the Dakota and many other American Indian populations were embedded in mercantilist economies. Throughout the northern regions of the United States and adjoining areas in Canada, there was a long history of native involvement in the Euro-American fur-trade. In this trade, Indian people produced exchange-values by bartering products of native manufacture (i.e., furs and hides) for European goods. Notwithstanding the fact that involvement in the fur-trade brought about many changes in native society, most American Indian populations remained oriented to use-value production and controlled their basic means of production as well.[9]

The late nineteenth century was the period in which the Dakota, along with many other American Indian populations, became incorporated into the state.[10] In the western regions of the United States, this incorporation (which coincided with the expansion of industrial and agrarian capital) was associated with the expropriation of large tracts of Indian land and the resultant alienation of most Indians from their means of production. In the process of expropriating this land, the United States government entered into treaty relationships with various Indian populations. Under the provisions of many treaties, the state agreed to set aside an area of land for Indian occupancy (what is called a "reservation") and to assume trust responsibility over the people and property under a tribe's jurisdiction. The creation of reservation-based, tribal entities with unique sovereign powers and a specialized trust relationship with the United States government has placed American Indians in a distinctive position in the nation's political economy.[11]

The Indian's links to the economy have been monitored almost entirely by the machinery of the federal government. Over the past century, the conditions of Indian participation in the economy, either as land-owners, wage-laborers, or entrepreneurs have been governed by federally-initiated Indian policies. When these and other avenues to the economy are closed, as they have been most of the time, the federal government has also stipulated the grounds under which American Indians receive welfare assistance. In reservation settings, Indians are not only eligible for welfare assistance through general entitlement programs (e.g., AFDC, WIC, Food Stamps), but they also have rights (often guaranteed in treaties) to specialized federal funds for education, health, law enforcement, and resource management. Although the various policies that govern federal trust responsibilities over native lands and peoples were developed ostensibly to work on behalf of American Indian interests, these policies have not done so. Instead, they have benefited the interests of capital owned by white entrepreneurs and corporations. Overall, the net effect of these policies has been the impoverishment of Indian people (Jorgenson 1971, 1972, 1978; Ruffing 1979; Wyler 1984).

In adapting to life on reservations, American Indians have engaged in a persistent struggle against the forces of the state and capital to control their lives. The struggle has been waged most directly over the control of their land and resources (Jorgenson 1979, 1984; Tahkofper 1982). Yet, it has also involved a resistence to federal actions aimed at the destruction of native cultures (Jorgenson 1972; Wyler 1984). The federal government has employed a variety of economic, political, and ideological mechanisms to make Indians dependent on the state and capital, and in the process, to erode the very means and relationships that would support Indian self-determination.

To a large extent, the history of the relationship between Indian people and the state has been a contradictory one. As I wish to demonstrate in the following section, the contradictions that have characterized modern, post-reservation history have contributed, in part, to the persistence of highly attenuated domestic-community formations which stand opposed to many of the institutions created by the state. The lives of American Indian women have been directly impacted by these contradictions in subtle as well as obvious ways. In the case of Dakota women, their post-reservation history has been filled with paradoxes. It is a history in which these women have been able to retain, and in some cases gain, autonomy and power in their own communities while facing a wider oppression and subordination under capital and the state. The evidence presented here reveals important elements in the relationship between ethnicity and class as these bear upon an understanding of the changing and contradictory positions of women.

Early Reservation Era: 1867–1910

When the Dakota were settled on reservations at the end of the nineteenth century, they brought with them an historically developed system of social relationship based on centuries of past experience. In adapting themselves to reservation life, they continued to follow many of the social practices with which they were familiar. In the pre-reservation era, much of their social life was organized by kinship and oriented to the production of use-value. What went on in households was not independently constituted and divorced from what went on in band and village communities. The social relations which organized production and reproduction were most often one and the same (Landes 1968; Albers n.d.). Within this context, women as well as men had rights that guaranteed them control over their own production and the fruits of their labor. Relationships between the sexes were complementary and consistent with a wider Dakota ethos which idealized both individual integrity and collective responsibility. In their essential character, the moral precepts which characterized social relationships among the Dakota were egalitarian and not compatible with European notions of dominance and subordination (Pond 1908; Landes 1968; Albers 1982, 1983b).[12]

It was in this kind of social and ideological setting that the United States government attempted to incorporate the Dakota into American society as self-sufficient, Christian farmers who lived in nuclear family households. Like the whites who would settle on the prairies next to their reservations, the Dakota were to become part of a larger class of petty commodity, agricultural producers. In its efforts to "acculturate" the Dakota, the government imposed a patriarchal division of labor which not only alienated women from production but from some of their traditional controls over reproduction as well. And in so doing, it attempted to isolate Dakota women, their families and households from the wider, kin-based networks in which they were embedded.

The agrarian, patriarchal plan that the federal government implemented on reservations, like Devil's Lake in North Dakota, excluded Dakota women from a viable role in agricultural production and ultimately in the reservation economy at large. First of all, unlike men, Dakota women were not taught how to farm in government or mission-run schools. Instead, they were trained to perform the "domestic" skills of white farm women including canning, quilting, crocheting, and "housework" (Albers 1983b).[13] Secondly, the federal government provided men, not women, with the tools and seeds necessary for agricultural production, and it hired men to work on government-run farms and in other forms of wage-labor. Later, when the Dakota were encouraged to take up agriculture on their own, men were the ones assigned tracts of land on which to farm (Meyer 1967).

In conjunction with its plan to transform Dakota men into agricultural producers, the government also embarked on a plan to "familialize" the Dakota — that is, to transfer economic and political power from the extended kin group to the nuclear family. This transfer was accomplished, in part, by a practice whereby access to farming lands and equipment, as well as the payments for agrarian work, were distributed to the heads of nuclear family households which by the government's definition were always male (Wilcox 1942). And when reservation lands at Devil's Lake were divided under the Dawes Act, male household heads received not only a larger allotment but were often given the prerogative to decide where the land-holdings of other family members would be located (Albers 1983b).[14]

Through its policies and programs, the government systematically denied Dakota women access to those areas of the reservation economy which were linked to a state-run, capitalist production process.[15] Not only were they excluded from production directly, either as wage-laborers or small-scale entrepreneurs, they were even denied direct access to the cash generated from production on lands under their ownership. The net impact of this, at least until the 1920s, was to give Dakota men an economic advantage over women through their prior claims on provisions coming from the state sector of the reservation economy.

The federally-based organization of production and distribution within the reservation had a number of different influences on Dakota household and family arrangements at Devil's Lake. One of the most important was the emergence of an agnatic bias in residence and in the structure of extended-family task groups,[16] a bias which was reinforced by the indoctrinations of missionaries and other agents of acculturation.

Dakota women, however, did not become totally dependent or passive in the process. They continued to play a vital role in the daily and generational reproduction of their households and to exercise important rights and controls in their productive activity. Although Dakota women assisted men in cash-crop production on family-owned allotments, they devoted most of their time to subsistence gardening and foraging activities. The subsistence work of women contributed a wide range of foods which supplemented commodities distributed by the government. Even more importantly, their foods were critical to survival in times when the more vulnerable cash-crops (e.g., wheat) failed as a result of drought or a depressed market (Meyer 1967). Women also engaged in a wide range of manufacturing activities (e.g., beadwork, quilting). Although much of this work was geared towards home consumption, many women created goods to sell or trade in neighboring white communities. The earnings from this work were meager, but they did provide Dakota women and their families with sources of income partially independent of federal control (Wilcox 1942; Albers 1983b).

All of these activities were critical to the survival of Dakota households at Devil's Lake in the early reservation period. Federal subsidies in return for wage-work or petty commodity production were not sufficient to live on. Indeed, it might be argued that the intensification of domestic production through women's work (and men's as well) contributed, albeit indirectly, to promoting grossly unequal exchanges in the selling of cash-crops, and to low wages (in cash or kind) for male employment in the federal sector and in seasonal agricultural work on neighboring white farms.[17]

As in pre-reservation times, Dakota men and women scheduled much of their labor activity separately. Neither sex controlled or directed the pace, intensity, or direction of the other's work patterns. Among both sexes, work activity was carried on alone or in small work groups which pooled their labor. Not only did each sex manage their own work, but they also controlled the distribution of the products that resulted from this labor. Importantly, men did not exert any control over the products of female subsistence and manufacturing activity. Women had the right to determine how the products of their labor would be used, and they had prior rights on monies coming from the sale of their goods in neighboring white towns (Albers 1983b).

The control that Dakota women exercised over their production was consistent with a wider ethos, which honored the integrity and dignity of every Dakota person. Here no one, regardless of sex or age, had the right to forcefully impose their will on another. No person had the right to command or appropriate the possessions of another without that person's permission, nor did a person have the right to engage others in labor through verbal or physical coercion. And while the integrity of every person was to be respected, an equally powerful moral precept exorted all Dakota to be responsible for each other's welfare. Not only should they be generous with their food and other possessions, but they should also willingly cooperate and help others in their day-to-day activities (Albers 1974, 1982, 1983b).

In the Dakota households of the early reservation era, the development and institutionalization of an ideology based on the notion of male providers and female dependents never took hold. Instead, Dakota expected each sex to be proficient and self-sufficient in their respective labor activities. Work autonomy and prior claims on the products of that labor, however, did not preclude voluntary sharing between the sexes. For just as each sex was accorded a certain degree of autonomy, men and women were expected to cooperate and share the products of their respective labors (Albers 1983b).

Autonomy was also extended to Dakota women in marriage. Although a woman's first marriage was arranged by her family, she was not compelled to remain in that union. To the dismay of many early missionaries, Dakota marriages were notoriously brittle. They were dissolved easily by either spouse and there was no stigma attached to those who were divorced. Although the family laws enacted by the federal government attempted to curb the high rate of divorce, these were never very successful. The Dakota simply practiced common law marriages and, therefore, avoided some of the legal sanctions imposed by the government (Albers 1983b).

In the early reservation period, as reported by Dakota women themselves, females continued the practice of spacing children at four-five year intervals. This was done through a culturally-prescribed pattern of abstinence during the period in which a mother was nursing and probably also through various methods of contraception and abortion.[18] Not only did women raise fewer children in this era, but they also did so in a setting where care-taking responsibilities were shared among a wide circle of kin, including older children, unmarried siblings, and grandparents.

The situation that Dakota women faced during early reservation times offered them fewer opportunities to exercise their autonomy. Denied direct access to provisions coming from a state-controlled sector, they had no means to assert their independence except within the confines of their own self-generated subsistence and manufacturing activities. Yet, they did not become totally powerless under these circumstances. They managed their own labor activity and controlled the distribution of products that resulted from this labor. Through their own work, they continued to exercise influence over the distribution of goods within their households, and they played an important role in monitoring distribution taking place between households within their own extended family networks. Thus even though Dakota women had become dependent on men for commodities obtained through federal sources, they were able to maintain some semblance of autonomy through their own productive efforts and the influence of a traditional ideology which guaranteed such independence.

Where Dakota women lost ground was in those areas of the reservation where their households and local communities intersected directly with the state. Women were conspicuously absent in treaty negotiations and other formalized transactions with the state, and they were excluded from tribal leadership positions created by the federal government (Bysiewicz and Van de Mark 1977; Albers 1983b). However, the participation of Indian men in early reservation political institutions was largely "tokenism," which carried little real influence (Wilcox 1942; Meyer 1967). Although men may have gained entry into the federal sector and received some benefit economically, they had no control or power over their new positions. Whatever influence men were able to exercise was ultimately granted or denied by federal officials. Clearly, Dakota men were dependent and exploited in this situation, but Dakota women were doubly oppressed.

Transition: 1910–1945

Although farming continued at Devil's Lake and other Dakota reservations, its relative importance in reservation economies began to decline steadily in the early decades of the twentieth century. What led to the decline was not a lack of initiative on the part of Indian people, but an absence of capital. In running and supporting farming operations, the government stood in competition with private agricultural interests in the region. Ultimately, it withdrew whatever capital it had provided to nurture Dakota farming and advocated a policy of selling and leasing Indian lands to neighboring white farmers with private capital for development (Meyer 1967).

The growing practice of leasing land had an unanticipated advantage for some Dakota women. Those who were divorced and widowed could accrue direct cash benefits from lands in their name. And notwithstanding the federal practice of crediting monies from the sale and/or leasing of lands to the agency books of each male household head, Dakota men often respected their wives' prior claims on these funds (Wilcox 1942). As the size of female land-holdings increased through inheritance, there was less inequality between women and men in land-ownership. However, the overall value and size of land-holdings had declined.

By the 1920s, land no longer supported most Dakota at Devil's Lake, either on a cash or productive basis. Increasingly, Dakota families were forced to survive on wage-labor and federal relief. Jobs, however, were few in number, low in pay, and often temporary in duration. Except for the era of the Works Project Administration during the 1930s, there were few employment opportunities on the reservation. Most of the work that Dakota performed was seasonal farm labor. In nearly all instances, men were given preferential treatment in employment (Wilcox 1942; Meyer 1967; Albers 1983b). In the absence of adequate lease-income and/or wages, the Dakota were in constant need of federal assistance. But not until the 1930s, when the Child Welfare and Social Security Acts were passed, was a major welfare program made available to the Dakota. Before that time, federal aid consisted of food commodities and emergency relief funds for families in dire straits.

Once the agrarian program of the federal government collapsed, a number of important changes took place in reservation social formations. One of the most significant was the gradual decline of the land-based and agnatically-oriented *tiošpaye*, or extended families. While a few of these families were able to hold and/or work large tracts of land, the vast majority were breaking down and becoming reorganized along other lines. Increasingly, *tiošpaye* were landless and residentially dispersed groups which were organized around the kinship bonds of either women or men. In contrast to the previous era, when extended families functioned as productive units, they were now loosely organized units of distribution (Wilcox 1942; Albers 1974).

The process by which this occurred has been described in detail elsewhere (Albers 1974, 1983b). Basically, what had happened was that land-ownership became increasingly associated with the older generation. Young adults were becoming landless. For a short time, family elders were able to support their landless descendants by combining lease incomes with subsistence and petty commodity production. However, as the land-holdings declined, the elders were less able to support their adult offspring. Increasingly, young adults, particularly men, moved away from the rural homesteads of their parents in search of part-time employment. Their movements took them to the reservation's agency, commercial, and mission settlements where they became increasingly dependent on the cash economy.

Since wage-labor was uncertain and federal aid meager, many young couples were unable to support themselves and their dependents alone. One of the ways their households remained viable in the face of economic collapse was to become embedded in wider support networks where kin pooled and shared their incomes as well as labor. There was no set pattern in these networks. Young couples depended on either spouse's kin.

In the years after 1910, the foundations of male economic influence were being gradually eroded. Growing numbers of Dakota men had neither sufficient amounts of unearned income nor adequate jobs and wages to support themselves, much less contribute to the livelihood of a family. In this vacuum, Dakota women began to emerge as an increasingly important source of support in the provisioning of their households and wider kin groups. This was especially true when they began to receive welfare subsidies under AFDC. Yet, it was also the result of the continuing importance of their own unpaid, domestic work — including traditional subsistence and manufacturing activities.

In effect what had happened was that federal policy governing Indian land and its use had undermined the influence of men in domestic settings. By denying men livelihoods either through family farming, wage-labor, or unearned incomes (leasing and welfare), the federal government increasingly shifted the responsibility for household reproduction into the hands of women and their extended families.

The economic uncertainties that the Dakota were facing made the already brittle character of their marriages more fragile. There were more tensions because the traditional Dakota ideals of male-female complementarity were becoming much more difficult to uphold. This was true not only because of the economic conditions they lived under but also because of the ideologies to which they were being increasingly exposed. The younger generation was becoming less familiar with traditional morals and much more influenced by the teachings of white educators. Most of the young people who reached adulthood in this era had been removed from their homes at a young age and sent away to government or church-run boarding schools. Consequently, they had less opportunity to observe culturally accepted female and male behavior. In the Catholic schools, at least, Dakota females were taught to be obedient and dutiful to their spouses, while males were encouraged to assert their rightful place as "breadwinners." Yet, the reality of the lives they encountered in adulthood precluded the formation of the patriarchal families idealized in missionary teachings. Nonetheless, many Dakota were influenced by these teachings, such that attitudes of male supremacy began to emerge in a situation where they had not previously existed.[19]

Although the relative contribution of female incomes to household survival was growing, and even though female influence in household and family affairs was becoming more important as a consequence, women still did not have a major role in reservation government. Legally, they continued to be hampered by anachronistic policies established in early reservation times (Bysiewicz and Van de Mark 1977). Politically, they were excluded from leadership roles where decisions were made about the welfare and future of their communities. However, as in an earlier era, these did not completely disadvantage women because the legal rights and offices that men held still did not confer any real form of power or influence.

The Modern Reservation Period: 1945–1978[20]

In the years after World War II, the Dakota at Devil's Lake and on other reservations in the region fell deeper into poverty; more reliant on temporary jobs, paltry forms of federal relief, and their own ingenious survival strategies. Statistics gathered by various federal agencies from the 1950s to 1970s ranked the Devil's Lake Reservation as one of the most depressed in the United States in terms of family/per capita incomes, tribal revenue, and rates of unemployment and underemployment (House Committee on Interior and Insular Affairs 1953, 1962; Economic Development Administration 1971).

With few exceptions, land-ownership no longer provided a significant source of revenue for Dakota men and women: most Dakota were dependent entirely on wage-labor and welfare. Until the 1970s, most of the employment available in the area continued to be seasonal farm work and temporary government jobs. Overall, the job situation was dismal; nearly 75 percent of the adult population was unemployed or underemployed (Economic Development Administration 1971).

Addressing the chronic unemployment on reservations like Devil's Lake, the federal government launched programs for job training and urban relocation in the 1950s and 1960s. As in the past, the programs and employment opportunities initiated by the government were discriminatory and aimed almost exclusively at Dakota men. The opportunities to learn skills appropriate to participation in the larger economy continued to be a male prerogative, at least until the 1970s. As the federal government tried to funnel men into jobs, it awarded women subsidies under AFDC. Instead of giving women a chance to become occupationally skilled and potentially self-sufficient, the state continued its practice of making them dependent on welfare. Yet when women did find work, the jobs they were able to enter were sex-typed and their wages were lower than the earnings of men in comparable occupations. Furthermore, when employment training programs were finally created for women in the 1970s, they were taught skills that would channel them into low-paying "female jobs" (e.g., typing, nurses' aides, etc.).

Employment statistics on Dakota men and women during this period indicate that a higher proportion of men than women worked, and that when men were employed their earnings were greater.[21] Such evidence, however, obscures the facts that most of the occupations men entered entailed temporary employment, and that most males were not eligible for unearned incomes in the form of welfare and unemployment compensation. Indeed, if incomes of Dakota men and women from earned and unearned sources could have been compared, the pattern would have likely indicated that: (1) the spread in male incomes was much wider than that of females; (2) the averaged annual incomes of women were on par with men's; and (3) female incomes were more stable than men's.

No matter what type of income disparities existed between men and women, the livelihood of Dakota was substandard. Not only were earnings well below poverty limits, they were also erratic due to the transient character of employment. This situation changed for a short period during the mid-1970s at which time employment for both sexes was steadier and more available because of federal programs on the reservation, the building of a factory by the Brunswick Corporation, and the temporary enrichment of the tribe through a large land-claims settlement.[22]

Until the early 1970s, when the amount and distribution of household earnings was in a continual state of flux, men were the ones who experienced the greatest income fluctuations. The welfare incomes of women, though meager, were at least steady. In the face of substandard and erratic livelihoods, Dakota continued to intensify their work in domestic, extended family settings. Although there was a progressive decline in their involvement in direct use-value production, the "stretching" of cash incomes and the products these bought continued as a dominant strategy of household and community survival.

In this period, Dakota households did not exist as isolated and independent entities. They were embedded in extended-family networks which functioned as important reproductive units. Food and other basic necessities were shared widely in these networks and people regularly pooled their labor, or "helped out" as the Dakota would say. Women played a central role in this provisioning through their own incomes as well as unpaid labor. Not only did women make substantial contributions to the livelihoods of their own households but to others as well. As in the past, they controlled how these contributions were going to be used and who would benefit from them (Albers 1974, 1982, 1983b).

The importance of women in monitoring distribution became reflected in shifts in residency and in the organization of extended-family support groups. There were a larger number of female-headed households, and many more extended-family networks with uterine orientations. And even where agnatic principles of residence and organization prevailed among some extended families, women continued to actively support or depend upon their own consanguineal kin (Albers 1974).

A second area where women's influence had grown was in the social networks that organized and supported ceremonial activity on the reservation. Women were primarily responsible for building what the Dakota called "collections," that is, an accumulation of gifts to be distributed in give-aways. Interestingly, most of the goods distributed at these give-aways were domestic goods, including cloth, towels, blankets, quilts, and dishes. Most of these items were either produced directly by female labor, as in star quilts — one of the most prestigious goods in ceremonial exchanges (Albers and Medicine 1983) — or purchased through female incomes. Since women made most of the contributions to give-aways, it was their prerogative to decide to whom gifts would be given in social networks that linked the Dakota at Devil's Lake to Indian people from neighboring communities in Canada and the United States. Through this activity a number of women gained considerable prestige and renown not only at Devil's Lake but on other reservations as well (Albers 1974).

By understanding the influence and control that Dakota women were exercising in family and community networks, it is possible to explain why many of them began to achieve a greater role within the arena of reservation politics and economy most directly connected to the state and capital. Beginning in the 1960s, women played an increasingly important part in directing the course of reservation politics and economy. Their influence in mobilizing and monitoring support for tribal government and administration was inseparable from their position of strength in interhousehold provisioning and ceremonial networks.

To a large extent, reservation and domestic politics on the Devil's Lake reservation were the same in the 1960s and early 1970s. While tribal government was organized around formal offices linked to the state and capital through contractual forms of relationship, what happened at this level was directly influenced by the support or challenges from kin-based networks. These networks had a profound impact on the various machinations of tribal government, including the elective process, council decision-making, and the dispensation of "favors" in the form of housing, jobs, and loans.

The social formations which dominated everyday life at Devil's Lake were defined by kinship and organized around the interests of separate but related domestic groups. Similarly, the issues the tribal governments and their administrators faced were dominated by domestic concerns. One of the primary reasons the tribe faced bankruptcy in the late 1970s was that most of the funds it had received from land-claims settlements were expended in meeting the domestic needs of the people. In essence, involvement in the government and business of the tribe was *ipso facto* domestic in nature. There was not a clear-cut line between so-called "public" and "private" sectors. Indeed, at all levels — that of the household, extended family, local community, and reservation — much of what the Dakota did with their lives was reproductive in character. Indeed, most of the jobs on the reservation were service-oriented, not productive. The one noticeable exception was employment at the newly-built factory on the reservation.[23]

The ascendency of female influence in households, extended-family networks, and in the reservation community at large has not led to a pattern of female dominance in sexual politics. While their increasing economic autonomy vis-a-vis their male kin has given them more influence over their households and communities, it has not given them any real freedom. They remain oppressed by the state's patriarchal welfare policies, by a segregated, off-reservation job market which funnels them into the lowest paying jobs as domestics and nurses' aids, by the racist and sexist abuses of their white neighbors, and by the endemic poverty that they and their families have experienced over the past century.

The poverty that Dakota women have lived under has exacted a high price, especially in the area of health. Like other American Indians, they live in a community with high rates of mortality and morbidity. Alcoholism has become a major health problem, and it has been directly associated with physical abuse against women and in a few cases with child-neglect. (Neither of these practices was, or is, condoned among the Dakota.)

One of the primary consequences of poverty, alcoholism, and high mortality rates, especially among young adults is that much of the responsibility for raising children has shifted to an older generation of women and men. Grandparents have always played a significant role in rearing Dakota children, so that parents could work. Since grandparents lived in the same house, or residential complex, as one or more of their children, they have always shared in child-care responsibilities. Over the past fifty years these responsibilities have increased; in many instances grandparents have become full-time caretakers, because of their children's death, absence from the reservation for temporary employment, or inability to parent (Medicine 1982).

Ironically, the very policies the federal government instituted to make the Dakota dependent on the state and capital have created, simultaneously, a means of autonomy. Unable to live independently of the incomes made available to them, they have maintained a wide range of domestic strategies that insure their survival. These strategies, including the intensification of use-value production and the "stretching" of provisions through distributive mechanisms based on sharing, had always been areas where women had some control. And as the pattern of income distribution changed in modern times, women assumed an increasingly important role in monitoring the provisions essential to their households and wider kin groups.

Nor is it fortuitous that Dakota women, when given the opportunity, used their mutual support networks to censure and exert pressure on the direction of tribal government decisions and actions. The opportunity that allowed this was a change in federal policies which gave tribes greater latitude and support in running their own affairs. As tribes increasingly took over responsibilites for the business and governance of their own reservations, indigenous social formations took on a more important role in defining the character of the institutional structure that had been imposed by the federal government. Since women occupy an important place in kin-based social formations, it is not surprising that they use this position to influence the distribution of jobs and other economic benefits over which the tribe has some control. While women may not have gained parity with men in terms of the number of elected and administrative offices they held in tribal government, the proportion of women who acquired positions at this level increased dramatically in the years after 1968.

The ascendency of female influence, however, has also been a consequence of an historically-based pattern of relationship among Dakota. This pattern emphasizes egalitarian relationships based on sharing and cooperation among a wide range of kin. It is a pattern which, at least ideally, accords to all people a degree of autonomy and the right to exert influence through their own work and example. Whether or not independence is realized has been a matter of circumstance, especially regarding the wider forces and relations of the state that have dominated Dakota life in post-reservation times. The persistence of an egalitarian ethos which applies to women as well as men is not the result of some ideological time lag. It continues in modern times precisely because it works (Albers 1982).

CONCLUSIONS

The contradictory position of Dakota women in modern times has resulted, in part, from the fact that daily and generational reproduction is a central focus of life in contemporary reservation communities. It dominates the affairs of single households and extended family support networks, and assumes a prevalent place in the actions of tribal governments. Much of the emphasis on reproduction in Indian communities is clearly a consequence of the particular ways in which reservations have been linked to the state and the wider capitalist production process. This special linkage, combined with the Dakota's own distinct patterns of social relationship, has given Dakota women a base of influence in their own communities, while denying them power in American society at large.[24] This contradiction will continue as long as Dakota people remain in a marginal political economic position and as long as they continue to survive through state subsidization and through an attenuated, collectively-organized pattern of reproduction.

One of the major lessons to be learned from this particular case is that poverty under capitalism does not bring about a uniform pattern in women's lives. While the welfare policies of the state may be organized in the interest of male domination in the home and workplace (Eisenstein 1984b), the recipients of welfare do not necessarily reproduce themselves in terms of a patriarchal model (Lewis 1984). What is different in the case of many American Indian populations is that women and their households are not isolated; they are embedded in extended, collectively-constituted support networks. In a number of American Indian groups these support networks are not male dominated, nor are they organized by patriarchal interests (Lamphere 1977; Knack 1980; Albers 1982; Conte 1982).

The fact that Dakota women are rarely isolated in their proverty is clearly related to the continuation of an ideology and patterns of kinship which advocate cooperation and sharing.[25] Yet, the very persistence of this ideology is related to the fact that Dakota live in communities which are not divided by class distinctions. Just about everyone is poor, and therefore no one is set apart by their economic status and social standing.

What is important here is that women's role in reproduction, daily as well as generational, is not conceptualized as a source of their oppression. In this situation, women do derive benefits from having larger numbers of children because, as they grow older, it places them in the center of distribution networks from which they can derive and/or give support. For many Dakota, the worst possible situation is to be a member of an "orphan" family where the number of kin are too small to effectively share and cooperate.[26] The Dakota situation appears to contradict some of the feminist arguments (Folbre 1982;

Bryceson and Vuorela 1984), which suggest that child-bearing is a major source of women's subordination. There is no question that these arguments are correct in situations where children's labor benefits men's interests to the exclusion of women's. Yet, in a case like that of the Dakota, who live in a classless community where reproduction is everyone's concern and where there are no significant inequalities between women and men in access to income, women can and do derive tangible benefits from their children.[27]

When there is not a structural separation between reproduction and production within their own communities,[28] the strategic position and interests of women do not represent an order that is substantially different from men's. Under these circumstances, female-male relationships are often more egalitarian in character and women generally have more influence and autonomy within their households, families, and local communities. Yet, the very existence of this situation is predicated on an economy which excludes large segments of the population from its productive sectors in order to maintain a "free" labor force. One consistent way this exclusion has manifested itself, especially in the United States, is along racial lines.

When the condition of race excludes large segments of a population from a viable place in the productive process and makes them dependent on the state, it establishes a set of material, as well as structural conditions, which put women and men in a very different kind of relationship to each other. It is not a relationship built on interests that are divided between the reproductive functions of women and the productive work of men. Everyone is involved in reproductive strategies that allow people to survive in the absence of work which can provide a living-wage. In this situation, the dualism historically associated with capitalism does not divide itself along female-male lines in the same way that it does among the proletarianized classes. Instead, it disenfrachizes entire groups of people, female and male, whose dependency on capital is often secondary to their dependence on the state.

In the end, we must inquire about the implications of a capitalist social formation that segregates reproduction from production, and in the process, places more interest on the realization of capital than on the lives of those who contribute to its creation. By exacerbating the division between production and reproduction, capitalism intensifies the alienation and loss of human dignity for all those who lack control over the productive process. Yet, it doubly alienates those in the lumpen-class who exist on the margins of capitalism because it denies them even the means to make a livelihood free of poverty. While women may have more autonomy under these circumstances, they pay an incredibly high price for this. But their experiences do suggest that one possible road to sexual equality is the removal of material conditions which separate reproduction from production and which create social formations where the productive labor of one class is exploited for the reproduction of another class who control the means of production. It will only be when people work to reproduce people socially undifferentiated by class, race, or sex that production will be a means to equality and human freedom.

NOTES

1. The research on which this paper is based was carried out on the Devil's Lake Sioux Reservation in North Dakota continuously during the years 1968–1972 and also during the summers of 1974 and 1976. Many of the empirical data referred to in this paper are found in more extensive presentations (see Albers 1974, 1982, 1983b).

2. This does not mean that women of color have been absent from the feminist movement or its scholarship. There are several important works by minority feminists (Apodaca 1977; Lewis 1977; Mora and del Castillo 1980; Green 1980; Moraga and Anzaldua 1981; Hooks 1981; Medicine 1982; Ybarra 1982; Zinn 1982; Davis 1983; Lewis 1984). Nevertheless, much of their work and its insights have remained marginal to the major theoretical debates in feminism. This situation has not changed since Margaret A. Simmons first raised the issue in her classic article (1979) on racism and feminism.

3. A survey of two major feminist journals, *Signs* and *Feminist Studies*, over the past decade reveals that less than 10 percent of the articles are devoted to minority women in the United States and/or to the issue of race.

4. One of the most helpful and important discussions of the different meanings of reproduction in Marxist analysis for capitalist, as well as pre-capitalist societies, is an article by Olivia Harris and Kate Young (1981).

5. For good conceptual discussions of households, families, and domestic groups see, Bender (1967), Yanagisako (1979), Harris (1981), and Netting, Wilk and Arnould (1984).

6. For an excellent discussion and critique of this position see, Roseberry (1985).

7. It is important to emphasize that this is not true for all kin-based social formations. Sex inequality is an institutionalized feature of many lineage-type systems. See, Ciancanelli (1980) and Robertson (1984) for excellent case studies of these systems in Africa.

8. The Dakota that are dealt with in this case study originally lived in southern Minnesota and in the eastern prairies of the Dakotas. After a rebellion in 1862, most of them were expelled from their homelands and were settled on over twenty-five different reservations in the United States and Canada. These Dakota include the Yanktonnai and groups who are sometimes referred to in the ethnographic literature as the Santee. Since pre-reservation times much of their history and culture has been different from the more widely-known and reported Teton Dakota who lived on the high plains west of the Missouri River. Not surprisingly, there have been significant differences in the role and status of women among various Dakota populations. Most of the information presented here refers specifically to the conditions of Dakota at Devil's Lake and their Yanktonnai, as well as Santee, forebearers (Albers 1974, n.d.).

9. There is a large literature on the role of the Indian in the fur-trade and the impact this had on indigenous societies. For a review of the better sources on this subject see, Peterson and Anfinson (1984).

10. See, Jorgenson (1978) for an excellent overview and interpretation of the political economic history of American Indians during the past century.

11. See Deloria and Lytle (1984) for a detailed discussion of federal Indian policies as these bear upon an understanding of the sovereignty and trust status of modern tribes.

12. For good discussions of other American Indian women see, Brown (1970), Grumet (1980), Klein (1980), Conte (1982), Albers and Medicine (1983), Buffalohead (1983).

13. Ironically, in pre-reservation times women did the farming. The federal government's effort to reverse this division of labor was accomplished, in part, by the fact that agriculture involved a production process that was different from native horticulture (Albers 1983b).

14. The Dawes Act, also known as the General Allotment Act, was passed by Congress in 1882. Its primary purpose was to make Indians private property owners, and it did so by subdividing reservation lands. All reservation members were assigned individual allotments, whose sizes varied according to the age, sex, and marital status of the principal recipient.

15. Although Indian reservations have always received federal aid, this assistance has not always been in the form of welfare. At various points during the past century, various amounts of federal money have funded Indian economic development within the wider capitalist economy. Early reservation farming is one example of this. Yet, simultaneously and more frequently, federal policy has also actively supported the use of reservation lands, resources, and labor on behalf of white capitalists.

16. Agnatic refers to an organizing principle dominated by relationships between men, whereas in uterine structures the linkages are formed around women. In pre-reservation times, residence involved both types of principles (Pond 1908; Landes 1968; Albers n.d.).
17. John Moore (1985) has recently presented important evidence on the Cheyenne which indicates that federal officials encouraged Indian people to lease their lands in order to provide neighboring white farmers with a seasonal labor force. One ironic consequence of this, which also took place among Dakota at Devil's Lake, was that Indians often ended up working for a wage on lands that they owned.
18. Older women knew of plants used for both of these, but they were often reluctant to talk about them. In part, this reflected the prevalence of "pro-life" attitudes in the late 1960s and early 1970s. Such attitudes not only appear to have been related to the dominance of Catholicism in missionary activity on the reservation but also to values placed on large families for support and survival (Albers 1974, 1982).
19. Beatrice Medicine (1982) describes this problem in greater detail. Mary Lewis (1984) also reports this phenomenon among blacks.
20. This date marks the end of in-depth field research at Devil's Lake. Although I have returned to the community since that time, I do not have adequate data to comment on more recent happenings there.
21. Bysiewicz and Van de Mark (1977) provide general information on this subject for the Dakota as a whole. Material referring specifically to Devil's Lake comes from an unpublished report entitled "Provisional Overall Economic Development Plan, Fort Totten Redevelopment Area" issued in the early 1960s.
22. With cutbacks in federal spending by the Reagan Administration, unemployment has once again soared. The situation at Devil's Lake and on other reservations has returned, in many respects, to a pre-1970 pattern.
23. This factory was built as a joint capital venture between the Devil's Lake Sioux Tribe and the Brunswick Corporation.
24. Similar contradictions appear to confront Oglala (a division of the Teton Dakota) women on the Pine Ridge Reservation in South Dakota (Bysiewicz and Van de Mark 1977; Maynard 1979).
25. This situation is not dissimilar to what has been described for some black communities, where egalitarianism prevails (Stack 1974; Aschenbrenner 1975). Mary Lewis (1984) points out as well that many aspects of female-male relationships in black communities have a long cultural history, which can be traced back to African origins. These values include, among other things, an emphasis on consanguineal (descent) rather than conjugal (marital) relationships.
26. As I argue in much greater detail elsewhere (Albers 1974, 1982), there are real advantages economically, politically, and socially for people embedded in large-sized kinship networks.
27. There are situations, of course, where this is not the case and children may become a burden rather than assets. This happens most often, however, when adult offspring have chronic problems with alcohol.
28. Diane Lewis (1977) makes a similar point for blacks and Maxine Zinn (1982) suggests that this may be applicable to some chicano situations as well.

REFERENCES

Albers, Patricia C. 1974. *The Regional System of the Devil's Lake Sioux*. Unpublished Ph.D. Dissertation. University of Wisconsin-Madison.

______. 1982. Sioux Kinship in a Colonial Setting. *Dialectical Anthropology* 6:253–269.

______. 1983a. Introduction. In, *The Hidden Half: Studies of Plains Indian Women*, P. Albers and Beatrice Medicine (eds.). pp. 1–29. Lathan, MD: University Press of America.

______. 1983b. Sioux Women in Transition: A Study of Their Changing Status in Domestic and Capitalist Sectors of Production. In, *The Hidden Half: Studies of Plains Indian Women*, P. Albers and Beatrice Medicine (eds.). pp. 175-236. Lathan, MD: University Press of America.

______. n.d. Santee (Eastern Dakota). *Handbook of North American Indians: Vol. 14, The Plains* (forthcoming).

Albers, Patricia C. and Beatrice Medicine. 1983. The Role of Sioux Women in the Production of Ceremonial Art Objects: The Case of the Star Quilt. In, *The Hidden Half: Studies of Plains Indian Women*, P. Albers and Beatrice Medicine (eds.). pp. 123–142. Lathan, MD: University Press of America.

Albers, Patricia C. and William R. James. 1986. On the Dialectics of Ethnicity: To Be or Not To Be Santee (Sioux). *Journal of Ethnic Studies* (forthcoming).

Apodaca, Maria Linda. 1977. The Chicana Woman: An Historical Materialist Perspective. *Latin American Perspectives* 4:70–89.

Aschenbrenner, Joyce. 1975. *Lifelines: Black Families in Chicago*. New York: Holt, Rinehart and Winston.

Barrett, Michele. 1980. *Women's Oppression Today*. London: Verso Editions.

Beechey, Veronica. 1979. On Patriarchy. *Feminist Review* 3:66–82.

Bell, Dianne. 1983. *Daughters of the Dreaming*. London: George Allen and Unwin.

Bender, D. R. 1967. A Refinement of the Concept of Household: Families, Co-Residency and Domestic Functions. *American Anthropologist* 69:493–504.

Benería, Lourdes. 1979. Reproduction, Production and the Sexual Division of Labor. *Cambridge Journal of Economics* 3:203–225.

Brown, Carol. 1981. Mothers, Fathers, and Children: From Private to Public Patriarchy. In, *Women and Revolution*, Lydia Sargent (ed.). pp. 239–267, New York: Monthly Review Press.

Brown, Judith. 1970. Economic Organization and the Position of Women Among the Iroquois. *Ethnohistory* 7:151–167.

Buffalohead, Priscella. 1983. Ojibway Women. *Minnesota Historical Quarterly* 48:236–244.

Bryceson, Deborah and Ulla Vuorela. 1984. Outside the Domestic Labor Debate: Towards a Theory of Modes of Human Reproduction. *Review of Radical Political Economics* 16:137–166.

Bysiewicz, Shirley and Ruth Van de Mark. 1977. The Legal Status of Dakota Indian Women. *American Indian Law Review* 3:255–312.

Ciancanelli, P. 1980. Exchange, Reproduction, and Sex Subordination Among the Kikuyu of East Africa. *Review of Radical Political Economics* 12:25–36.

Conte, Christine. 1982. Ladies, Livestock, Land and Lucre: Women's Networks and Social Status on the Western Navajo Reservation. *American Indian Quarterly* 6:105–124.

Cook, Scott. 1984. *Peasant Capitalist Industry*. Lathan, MD: University Press of America.

Davis, Angela. 1983. *Women, Race, and Class*. New York: Vintage Books/Random House.

Deere, Carmen Diana. 1976. Rural Women's Subsistence Production in the Capitalist Periphery. In, *Women and the Economy*. Special Issue, *Review of Radical Political Economics* 8:9–17.

——— 1979. Changing Social Relations of Production and Peruvian Peasant Woman's Work. In, *Women in Latin America*. pp. 26–46. Riverside, CA: Latin American Perspectives.

Deloria, Vine and J. Lytle. 1984. *The Nations Within*. New York: Pantheon.

Delphy, Christine. 1977. *The Main Enemy*. London: Women's Research and Resources Centre Publications.

Economic Development Administration. 1971. *Federal and State Indian Reservations: An Economic Development Administration Handbook*. Washington, D.C.: U.S. Government Printing Office.

Edholm, Felicity, Olivia Harris and Kate Young. 1977. Conceptualising Women. *Critique of Anthropology* 9/10:101–130.

Eisenstein, Zillah. 1984a. The Patriarchal Relations of the Reagan State. *Signs* 10:329–337.

———. 1984b. *Feminism and Sexual Equality: Crisis in Liberal America*. New York: Monthly Review Press.

Ferguson, Ann and Nancy Folbre. 1981. The Unhappy Marriage of Patriarchy and Capitalism. In, *Women and Revolution*, Lydia Sargent (ed.). pp. 313–338. New York: Monthly Review Press.

Folbre, Nancy. 1982. Exploitation Comes Home: A Critique of the Marxian Theory of Family Labor. *Cambridge Journal of Economics* 6:317–329.

———. 1984. The Pauperization of Motherhood: Patriarchy and Public Policy in the United States. *Review of Radical Political Economics* 16:72–88.

Godelier, Maurice. 1975. Modes of Production, Kinship, and Demographic Structures. In, *Marxist Analysis and Social Anthropology*, M. Bloch (ed.). pp. 3–25. London: Malaby Press.

Green, Rayna. 1980. Native American Women. *Signs* 2:248–267.

Grumet, Robert. 1980. Sunksquaws, Shamans, and Tradeswomen: Middle Atlantic Coastal Algonkian Women During the 17th and 18th Centuries. In, *Women and Colonization*, E. Leacock and M. Etienne (eds.). pp. 43–62. New York: Praeger.

Harris, Olivia. 1981. Households as Natural Units, In, *Of Marriage and the Market*, Kate Young, Carol Wolkowitz and Roslyn McCullagh (eds.). pp. 49–68. London: CSE Books.

Harris, Olivia and Kate Young. 1981. Engendered Structures: Some Problems in the Analysis of Reproduction. In, *The Anthropology of Pre-Capitalist Societies*, Joel S. Kahn and Josep R. Llobera (eds.). pp. 109–147. Atlantic Highlands, NJ: Humanities Press.

Harrison, John. 1973. The Political Economy of Housework. *Bulletin of the Conference of Socialist Economists* 3(1):35–52.

Hartmann, Heidi. 1976. Capitalism, Patriarchy, and Job Segregation by Sex. *Signs* 1:137–169.

______. 1981a. The Family as a Locus of Gender, Class and Political Struggle: The Example of Housework. *Signs* 6:366–394.

______. 1981b. The Unhappy Marriage of Marxism and Feminism: Towards a More Progressive Union. In, *Women and Revolution*, Lydia Sargent (ed.). pp. 1–42. New York: Monthly Review Press.

Himmelweit, Susan. 1984. The Real Dualism of Sex and Class. *Review of Radical Political Economics* 16:167–184.

Hooks, Bell. 1981. *Ain't I a Woman: Black Women and Feminism*. Boston: South End Press.

House Committee on Interior and Insular Affairs. 1953. Investigation of the Bureau of Indian Affairs. U.S. Congress House Report No. 2503, 82nd Congress, 2nd Session.

______. 1962. Indian Unemployment Survey. Committee Print 3, 88th Congress, 1st Session.

James, Williams R. 1973. Domestic Group Organization and Processes in a Rural Colombian Town. Research Report No. 55. University of Wisconsin-Madison: Land Tenure Center.

______. 1975. Subsistence, Survival and Capitalist Agriculture: Aspects of the Mode of Production among a Colombian Proletariat. *Latin American Perspectives* 3:84–95.

Jorgenson, Joseph. 1971. Indians and the Metropolis. In, *The American Indian in Urban Society*, J. O. Waddell and O. M. Watson (eds.). Boston: Little, Brown and Company.

______. 1972. *The Sun Dance Religion: Power for the Powerless*. Chicago: University of Chicago Press.

______. 1978. A Century of Political Economic Effects on American Indian Society, 1880–1980. *Journal of Ethnic Studies* 6:1–82.

______ (ed.). 1979. *Native Americans and Energy Development*. Boston: Anthropology Resource Center.

______ (ed.). 1984. *Native Americans and Energy Development II*. Boston: Anthropology Resource Center.

Kahn, Joel and Josep Llobera (eds.). 1981. *The Anthropology of Pre-Capitalist Societies*. New York: Humanities Press.

Kamerman, Sheila. 1984. Women, Children and Poverty: Public Policies and Female-headed Families in Industrialized Countries. *Signs* 10:249–271.

Keenan, Jeremy. 1981. The Concept of the Mode of Production in Hunter-Gatherer Societies. In, *The Anthropology of Pre-Capitalist Societies*, J. Kahn and J. Llobera (eds.). pp. 2–21. New York: Humanities Press.

Klein, Laura F. 1980. Contending with Colonization: Tlingit Men and Women in Change. In, *Women and Colonization*, E. Leacock and M. Etienne (eds.). pp. 88–109. New York: Praeger.

Knack, Martha C. 1980. *Life Is With People: Household Organization of the Contemporary Southern Paiute Indians*. Socorro, NM: Ballena Press.

Lamphere, Louise. 1977. *To Run After Them: Cultural and Social Bases of Cooperation in a Navajo Community*. Tucson: University of Arizona Press.

Landes, Ruth. 1968. *The Mystic Lake Sioux: Sociology of the Mdewakantonwan Santee*. Madison: University of Wisconsin Press.

Leacock, Eleanor and Mona Etienne. 1980. Introduction. In *Women and Colonization: Anthropological Perspectives*, E. Leacock and M. Etienne, (eds.). pp. 1–24. New York: Praeger.

Lee, Richard. 1976. *Kalahari Hunter-Gatherers*. Cambridge: Harvard University Press.

Lewis, Diane. 1977. A Response to Inequality: Black Women, Racism, and Sexism. *Signs* 3:339–361.

Lewis, Mary. 1984. The Black Matriarchy: Exercises in Culture and Ideology. *Economic Forum* 15:17–38.

McAdoo, Harriette (ed.). 1981. *Black Families*. Beverly Hills: Sage Press.

McDonough, Roison and Rachel Harrison. 1978. Patriarchy and Relations of Production. In, *Feminism and Materialism: Women and Modes of Production*. Annette Kuhn and Ann Marie Wolpe (eds.). pp. 11–41. London: Routledge and Kegan Paul.

Mackintosh, Maureen. 1977. Reproduction and Patriarchy: A Critique of Meillassoux, 'Femmes, Greniers et Capitaux.' *Capital and Class* 2:119-127.

Maynard, Eileen. 1979. Changing Sex Roles and Family Structure among the Oglala Sioux. In, *Sex Roles in Changing Cultures*, A. McElroy and C. Mathiasson (eds.). pp. 11–20. State University of New York at Buffalo: Occasional Papers in Anthropology Vol. 1.

Medicine, Beatrice. 1982. The American Indian Family: Culture Change and Adaptive Strategies. *Journal of Ethnic Studies* 8:13–23.

Meillassoux, Claude. 1969. On the Mode of Production of the Hunting Band. In, *French Perspectives in African Studies*, P. Alexandre (ed.). London: Oxford University Press.

______. 1972. From Production to Reproduction. *Economy and Society* 1:93–105.

Meyer, Roy W. 1967. *A History of the Santee Sioux: United States Indian Policy on Trial*. Lincoln: University of Nebraska Press.

Moore, John. 1985. Marx on Horseback: The Significance of Cheyenne Work in the History of American Capitalism. Paper presented at the Political Economic Research Association Conference, University of Utah.

Mora, Magdelina and Adelaida R. del Castillo (eds.). 1980. *Mexican American Women in the United States: Struggles Past and Present*. Los Angeles: University of California, Chicano Studies Center Publications.

Moraga, Cherrie and Gloria Anzaldua (eds.). 1981. *The Bridge Called My Back: Writings by Radical Women of Color*. Watertown, MA: Persephone Press.

Netting, Robert, Richard Wilk and Eric J. Arnould (eds.). 1984. *Households: Comparative and Historical Studies of the Domestic Group*. Berkeley, CA: University of California Press.

Peterson, Jacqueline and John Anfinson. 1984. The Indian and the Fur Trade. In, *Scholars and the Indian Experience*, W. R. Swagerty (ed.). pp. 223–257. Bloomington: Indiana University Press.

Pond, Samuel. 1908. The Dakota as They Were in 1834. *Minnesota Historical Society Collections* 12:319–501.

Power, Marilyn. 1984. Unity and Division Among Women: Feminist Theories of Gender and Class in Capitalist Society. *Economic Forum* 15:39–62.

Puryear, Gwendolyn. 1980. The Black Woman: Liberated or Oppressed? In, *Comparative Perspectives of Third World Women: The Impact of Race, Sex, and Class*, B. Lindsey (ed.). pp. 251–275. New York: Praeger.

Reich, Michael. 1981. *Racial Inequality: A Political-Economic Analysis*. Princeton: Princeton University Press.

Robertson, Claire. 1984. *Sharing the Same Bowl: A Socioeconomic History of Women and Class in Accra, 'hana*. Bloomington, Ind.: University of Indiana Press.

Rosaldo, Michelle. 1974. Women, Culture, and Society: A Theoretical Overview. In, *Women, Society, and Culture*, M. Rosaldo and L. Lamphere, (eds.). pp. 17–42. Stanford: Stanford University Press.

Roseberry, William. 1985. The Ideology of Domestic Production. Paper presented at the Political Economic Research Association Conference, University of Utah.

Ruffing, Lorraine. 1979. The Navajo Nation: A History of Dependence and Underdevelopment. *Review of Radical Political Economics* 2:25–37.

Sacks, Karen. 1982. *Sisters and Wives*. Urbana, IL: University of Illinois Press.

Sahlins, Marshall. 1972. *Stone Age Economics*. Chicago: Aldine.

Sanday, Peggy. 1981. *Female Power and Male Dominance*. New York: Cambridge University Press.

Seccombe, Wally. 1974. The Housewife and Her Labour Under Capitalism. *New Left Review* 83:3–24.

Simmons, Margaret A. 1979. Racism and Feminism: A Schism in Sisterhood. *Feminist Studies* 2:384–401.

Smith, Joan. 1984. The Paradox of Women's Poverty: Wage-earning Women and Economic Transformation. *Signs* 10:291–310.

Sokoloff, Natalie. 1981. *Between Money and Love: The Dialectics of Women's Home and Market Work*. New York: Praeger.

Stack, Carol. 1974. *All Our Kin*. New York: Harper & Row.

Stallard, Karin, Barbara Ehrenreich and Holly Sklar. 1983. *Poverty in the American Dream: Women & Children First*. Boston: South End Press.

Tahkofper, Carl. 1982. Political Pressures Affecting Natural Resource Development on Indian Reservations. *Ethnicity and Public Policy*, Winston Van Horne (ed.). pp. 105–120. Milwaukee: University of Wisconsin System American Ethnic Studies, Coordinating Committee/Urban Corridor Consortium, Vol. 1.

Wilcox, Lloyd. 1942. Group Structure and Personality Types Among Sioux Indians of North Dakota. Ph.D. Dissertation, University of Wisconsin-Madison.

Wolf, Eric R. 1982. *Europe and the People Without History*. Berkeley, CA: University of California Press.

Wyler, Rex. 1984. *Blood of the Land: The Government and Corporate War Against the American Indian Movement*. New York: Vintage Books.

Yanigasako, Sylvia. 1979. Family and Household: The Analysis of Domestic Groups. *Annual Review of Anthropology* 8:161–205.

Ybarra, Lea. 1982. When Wives Work: The Impact on the Chicano Family. *Journal of Marriage and the Family* 44:169–178.

Zinn, Maxine Baca. 1982. Mexican-American Women in the Social Sciences. *Signs* 8:259–272.

Accepted 1 October 1985

Female Planters and Planters' Wives in Civil War and Reconstruction: Alabama, 1850-1870

JONATHAN M. WIENER

STUDIES BASED ON LITERARY SOURCES suggest that the Civil War brought about a transformation in the position of white plantation women in the South. During the war many women operated plantations while planter-husbands fought on the battlefields; war deaths created a "generation of women without men," it has been argued, and defeat of the planter regime undermined the patriarchal ideology that had defined the role of the "lady" in plantation society. As a result, a "significant social change" occurred: women became planters on their own account after the war.[1]

Evidence from the manuscript census does not support this view. On the contrary, it suggests that in many respects the continuities of antebellum patterns were more important than the changes. No increase in the proportion of female planters followed war and Reconstruction; in spite of wartime deaths, females were less likely than males to persist as planters through the war decade. The manuscript census also reveals much about how the war affected the composition of planter families. While there is little evidence of a "generation of women without men" among the elite, certain generaliza-

1 Anne Firor Scott, *The Southern Lady: From Pedestal to Politics, 1830-1930* (Chicago, 1970), 81, 96, 106-07. Scott's argument has been noted recently in George B. Tindall, "Beyond the Mainstream: The Ethnic Southerners," *Journal of Southern History*, XL (February 1974), 15, and W. R. Krauss, "Political Implications of Gender Roles: A Review of the Literature," *American Political Science Review*, LXVIII (December 1974), 1706. See also Susan E. Bloomberg et al., "A Census Probe into 19th Century Family History: Southern Michigan, 1850-1880," *Journal of Social History*, V (January 1971), 26-45.

tions may be drawn. More young women were in households headed by older men, and there is a missing generation of children in planter families after the war. These conditions reflect the extent of wartime deprivation.

The manuscript schedules of the U.S. census of population are an invaluable source, both for identifying the South's planter elite and for studying its sexual composition and transformation through the Civil War decade. In 1850, 1860, and 1870, the census asked each individual for the "value of real estate" he or she owned.[2] The responses can be used to identify the wealthiest landholders in each census year by sex and to study persistence and change in the composition of this planter elite, in order to compare antebellum patterns with the developments that accompanied war and Reconstruction.

Five adjacent Alabama counties were selected as the focus for this study. The five made up the western half of the Alabama Black Belt; in 1860 they had a population of 114,000, of which 74 percent were slaves.[3] Landholding was extremely unequal in the region. In the Black Belts of Alabama and central Mississippi in 1860 the top 5 percent of landowners held 24 percent of the improved acreage, 26 percent of the slaves, 26 percent of the cotton output, and 30 percent of the farm value.[4] Politically, the five counties were a bedrock of planter support; their vote in favor of secession in December 1860 was overwhelming, as was their opposition

2 For the instructions to census enumerators, see Carroll D. Wright and William C. Hunt, *The History and Growth of the U.S. Census,* Senate Doc. No. 194, 56th Cong., 1st Sess. (Washington, 1900), 152.

3 The five are Greene, Hale, Marengo, Perry, and Sumter. Hale was created in 1866 out of parts of Greene, Marengo, Perry, and Tuscaloosa.

4 Gavin Wright, "'Economic Democracy' and the Concentration of Agricultural Wealth in the Cotton South, 1850-1860," *Agricultural History,* XLIV (January 1970), 63-93.

to Republican, Greenback, and Populist candidates for state office in the last quarter of the century.[5]

This study analyzes the 236 planters with the greatest wealth in real estate in each of the three censuses. The number 236 provided the most straightforward wealth cutoffs: the group included all planters with at least $10,000 in real estate in 1850, $32,000 in 1860, and $10,000 in 1870. These 236, who will be referred to hereafter as the "planter elite," constituted approximately the top 8 percent of the landholders in the western Alabama Black Belt and 3 percent of white adult males. Their mean real estate holding in 1860 was roughly 1,600 acres; the smallest holding was around 800 acres, and the largest close to 9,000 acres.[6]

Evidence from the Alabama Black Belt indicates no increase in the proportion of females in the planter elite between 1860 and 1870, the decade of war and Reconstruction. Ten percent of the planter elite was female in 1870, the same proportion as in 1860. Planter war deaths did not increase the proportion of women operating plantations in 1870; a generation of Southern women without men after 1865 may have existed, but elite plantation women do not seem to have been part of it.[7]

The women who were planters in 1870 appear to have been the elderly widows of elderly men who died of natural causes, rather than young widows of young male war victims, since female planters in 1870 were considerably older than

[5] William L. Barney, *The Secessionist Impulse: Alabama and Mississippi in 1860* (Princeton, 1974), 317-18; Allen Johnston Going, *Bourbon Democracy in Alabama, 1874-1890* (University, Ala., 1951), 220-31; William Warren Rogers, *The One-Gallused Rebellion: Agrarianism in Alabama, 1865-1896* (Baton Rouge, 1970), 223, 284, 315.

[6] The figure of $40 an acre for good plantation land in the Alabama Black Belt is suggested by Lewis C. Gray, *History of Agriculture in the Southern United States to 1860* (2 vols., Washington, 1933), II, 642-44.

[7] See also Jonathan M. Wiener, "Planter Persistence and Social Change: Alabama, 1850-1870," *Journal of Interdisciplinary History*, VII (Autumn 1976), 235-60.

male planters as a group (see Table I). Though evidence is not conclusive, it suggests that the females who became planters tended to do so relatively late in life as a result of inheriting the plantations of their elderly husbands.

Of course, females had held plantations in their own names before the war. As Anne Firor Scott points out, some Southern women had been planters in their own right since the

Table I

Female and Male Planters in 1870

	Planters	
	Male	Female
Real Estate		
Top ⅓	35%	17%
Middle ⅓	34	26
Bottom ⅓	31	57
Number of sons:		
None	75	65
At least 1	25	35
Four or more	2	4
Age:		
Youngest ⅓	32	26
Middle ⅓	31	30
Oldest ⅓	29	44
Birthplace:		
South	92	91
Non-South	8	9
Persist from 1860	43%	30%
Do not persist	57	70
Number	213	23

earliest settlement of the South.[8] In the Black Belt of western Alabama, however, no females were among the planter elite in 1850; not until 1860 did females appear in the census lists as elite property owners. This relatively late appearance of women as property owners may have been a consequence of the recent settlement of western Alabama in 1850; that the frontier was settled by men, single or married, rather than by single women might account for the absence of women from the 1850 planter elite.

From this perspective, females became planters in their own right primarily through inheritance—as the widows of male property owners or as daughters of planters without male heirs. Scott discusses a widow who ran an antebellum plantation "from the time her husband died until her son was old enough to assume responsibility."[9] This pattern may well have been typical: females were landowners in their own right primarily as widows without adult sons. Scott cites one case of a daughter inheriting a plantation from her planter-father and another of a daughter following in the footsteps of her planter-mother. Single men regarded such unmarried female landowners as highly desirable spouses, and, given the stigma attached to spinsterhood, it is extremely unlikely that daughters who inherited plantations remained single for very long.[10]

The persistence rate of female planters during the war decade was considerably lower than that for males. Thirty percent of the female planters of 1860 were still members of the elite in 1870, in comparison to 43 percent of the males.[11] Such a percentage would be the expected finding if women

[8] Scott, *Southern Lady*, 34.

[9] *Ibid.*

[10] *Ibid.*, 23-25.

[11] To compare these persistence rates to the national pattern, see Stephan Thernstrom, *The Other Bostonians: Poverty and Progress in the American Metropolis, 1880-1970* (Cambridge, 1973), "The Boston Case and the National Pattern," 220-61.

became planters relatively late in life and only until their sons were old enough to become planters themselves. Many sons would be able to take over the plantation between the beginning and end of a decade; elderly female planters would be more likely to die during the decade than the younger male planter group. Any female heirs would be likely to marry and change their names during the decade. Thus the lower persistence rate of females appears to have been a consequence of the circumstances under which females became planters. Female planters in 1870 were also considerably less wealthy than males. The biggest plantations were almost exclusively operated by males rather than females; women were in the elite, but they tended to be at the bottom rather than the top in 1870.

Scott makes a telling point when she observes that, after the war, the census enumeration of occupations did not indicate the full extent to which women were effectively operating plantations by themselves; she points out that, in many planter families with male household heads, the wives were left in charge of the plantation because husbands were engaged in politics, law, or medicine.[12] While the census did not indicate whether wives were in fact operating plantations listed as the property of their husbands, the occupations of household heads were recorded, and some big landowners gave occupations other than "planter." The elite of Marengo County (one of the five Black Belt counties) was studied in greater detail than that of the other four counties, and the number of such "non-planter" occupations among elite landowners in 1870 was found to have increased considerably over 1860. Twenty-one percent of the 1870 planters listed an occupation other than, or in addition to, "planter," in comparison to only 4 percent of the 1860 elite. If Scott is correct

[12] Scott, *Southern Lady,* 108.

in arguing that wives often operated the plantations of landowning males who had other occupations, the number of females effectively operating plantations after the war may have increased.

Some idea of how the war affected female planters can be gained by comparing the female planters of 1870 with their counterparts of 1860. The postwar female planters were considerably poorer (see Table II). Before the war there was little difference in the landholdings of male and female planters; after the war females were considerably less wealthy. Apparently, the decade of war and Reconstruction had a more deleterious effect on female planters than on males, but without more detailed evidence it would be incorrect to conclude that female planters were less able to "cope" with war and Reconstruction than males. The postwar female planters were considerably older than their antebellum counterparts. If females became planters primarily as heirs of husbands or fathers, perhaps postwar females tended to be widows while the antebellum females were more likely to be daughters who had inherited land.

The postwar female planters had families with fewer sons than their antebellum counterparts, perhaps as a consequence of a lower wartime birth rate, a higher wartime infant mortality rate, and also the greater age of the postwar female planters in comparison to the age of the female planters of 1860.[13] The census did not list any planter families in which both mother and son were elite landholders (though there were a few in which father and son were elite landholders). Probably older female planters had inherited the land from their husbands because they had no sons.

[13] Daughters of planters were not coded for this persistence study because marriage makes it impossible to trace them from one census list to the next. See Jonathan M. Wiener, "Planter-Merchant Conflict in Reconstruction Alabama," *Past and Present*, No. 68 (August 1975), 73-94.

Table II

Female Planters, 1860 and 1870

	Female Planters 1860	Female Planters 1870
Real Estate		
Top ⅓	35%	17%
Middle ⅓	35	26
Bottom ⅓	30	57
Number of sons:		
None	50	69
At least 1	50	35
Four or more	15	4
Age:		
Youngest ⅓	50	26
Middle ⅓	30	30
Oldest ⅓	20	44
Birthplace:		
South	90	91
Non-South	10	9
Number	20	23

In a society in which social life was an intensely local and kinship-based experience, women born outside the region found themselves in a difficult situation, at least at first. As Scott describes life for plantation wives, "the domestic circle was the world," and "visiting was the essence of life." The extended family was usually the basic social unit; the health of relatives was a constant subject of concern, and the courtship and marriage of members of the extended family were social events that received the greatest attention.[14] Women from outside the region were not part of this lifetime web of family ties; more likely than not they had no neighboring blood relatives of their own who could be visited, cared for when sick, or greeted in church. However, since the census listed only the state of birth, rather than the year of migration to the South, it is not possible to determine when non-Southern women came to the region—whether they did so just before marriage, or long before, as children, perhaps with their entire families. Nor is it possible to ascertain whether siblings, parents, or other relatives also migrated into the South. This discussion, then, is in part necessarily speculative.

Women born outside the South made up a small proportion of planter wives, and the proportion did not change over the decade of war and Reconstruction. Six percent of planter wives had been born outside the South, in both the 1860 and 1870 elite groups. Some of these non-Southern women had husbands who also had been born outside the South. In the antebellum period 20 percent of non-Southern planter wives had non-Southern-born planter husbands (see Table III). These were couples in which both members had migrated to the South rather than being native to the region—although the census does not indicate whether this migration took place when they were children or adults. The great majority of wives born outside the region—80 percent—had married planters born within the South.

The decade of war may have brought dramatic change to this antebellum pattern of non-Southern-born women marrying Southern-born planter men. Fully half of the non-Southern-born wives in 1870 were married to husbands who had also been born outside the South. This fact suggests that the

[14] Scott, *Southern Lady*, 42-43. The family "was the core of Southern society; within its bounds everything worth while took place." Francis Butler Simkins, *A History of the South* (3rd ed., New York, 1963), 388.

Table III

Planters' Wives: Husbands' Birthplace and Age

	1850	1860	1870
Southern-born wives:			
Southern-born husband	95%	97%	96%
Non-Southern-born husband	5	3	4
Non-Southern-born wives:			
Southern-born husbands	82%	78%	50%
Non-Southern-born husbands	18	22	50
Age difference from husband:			
Wife older	3%	3%	3%
Same ± 1	18	5	5
Wife 2-5 yrs. younger	24	43	29
" 6-10 " "	37	16	24
" 11-20 " "	16	30	26
" 21+ " "	3	3	13
Husband's age minus wife's age:			
Mean difference	12.0	8.2	8.6 yrs.
Median	7	6	6

pattern of marital choice may have changed over the war decade: before the war, more than three out of four non-Southern wives were married to Southern-born planters; after the war, only 50 percent were. But it is not clear that these marriages actually took place after the war, or that these were cases of carpetbag couples. The non-Southern-born planter couples of 1870 might very well have come to the South and married before the war, and simply not have moved to the Alabama Black Belt until the sixties; or they may have been Alabama Black Belt residents in 1860 but not yet members of the planter elite. And the actual number of such couples in 1870 is not large enough to permit solid generalizations.[15]

The census also makes it possible to ascertain how many Southern-born women had planter husbands who had been born outside the South. Very few such cases existed, and the war did not change the proportion. Three percent of Southern-born wives had non-Southern-born planter husbands in 1860, as compared with 6 percent in 1870. When Northern men came South to become plantation owners, they seldom took Southern-born women as their wives.

One might hypothesize that, if young men died in the war, women who got married after the war would marry older men more often than before. Actually, there was little difference between the 1860 and 1870 patterns of age differences of husbands and wives, further corroboration of the view that the postwar planters had remained unscathed by the war in many aspects of their lives. The differences between 1850 and 1860 were greater than those between 1860 and 1870.

Wives tended to be younger than husbands by several years in both antebellum and postwar periods. The median wife was six years younger than her husband in 1860, as well as 1870, while the mean age of wives was 8.2 years less than husbands in 1860 and 8.6 years less in 1870. Only 5 percent of couples were within one year of each other's age in both 1860 and 1870, and only 3 percent of the wives were more than one year older than their husbands. Virtually none of the wives were considerably older; the Southern elite was not a society in which young men married older women. On the other hand, many wives were considerably younger than their husbands; this pattern was shared by the elite of contemporary Victorian England.[16] A third of all wives were more than ten

[15] On landholding by carpetbaggers, see Wiener, "Planter Persistence and Social Change."

[16] J. A. and Olive Banks, *Feminism and Family Planning in Victorian England* (New York, 1964).

years younger than their husbands, both in 1860 and 1870. Thus the pattern of age differences between spouses is another area that was changed little over the decade of war and Reconstruction.

The war seems to have brought about an increase either in the number of young women married to older men, or in the number of unmarried young women living at home with their widower fathers. If indeed the war had reduced the number of marriageable men in the planter elite, then the effect of the war on planter women was to create not a "generation of women without men," but rather an increase in the proportion of women living with elderly men. Since the census did not indicate the relationship of household members to each other, these men could have been either husbands or fathers. Thirteen percent of females in planter elite families in 1870 lived in households in which the male household head was at least twenty years older than the oldest female; this increase was 10 percent over the 1860 figure.

The Civil War, like most major wars, left a permanent mark on the composition of planter families, particularly in the number and ages of children. Planter families in 1870 had few sons aged five through seven, sons born in the depth of war who survived it. The sons in planter families in 1870 were primarily eight years old or older, or else infants, one and two years old. And, to the extent that the number of surviving sons measures the wartime deprivations experienced even by the South's planter elite, it reveals two noteworthy facts: little deprivation existed in the first two years of the war, and the deprivation during the two years after the war appears to have been considerable.

The census gave the ages of all members of planter households in 1870, and a study of the ages of sons reveals that in 1870 few planters had sons between the ages of two and seven, sons born between 1861 and 1867 who had survived until 1870. The relative absence of this birth cohort from planter families is a consequence of a low birth rate in those years, and a high rate of infant and childhood mortality. However, the census gives no way of determining the relative importance of each factor. Before the war between seven and eight sons were born per year who survived until 1870 in the 236 planter families. In 1870 nine planter families had ten-year-old sons, who had been born on the eve of secession (January 1861); eight families had sons born in the first year of the war, who had been conceived in peacetime but born after the war reduced the number of doctors and the amount of food and medicine available. The same number of surviving sons was born in 1862 as in 1861, indicating that the second year of the war did not bring noticeable change in the number of planter sons who survived birth and infancy.

The change came in 1863. Only two out of 236 planter families had sons born in 1863 who survived until 1870. The census gives no way of measuring the relative importance of fewer conceptions, fewer live births, and more cases of infant mortality. The same small number of sons was born in 1864 and 1865 who survived until 1870 in planter families—three in 1864, and two in 1865, the final year of the war, when hunger was pervasive and starvation a threat to many poorer Southern families.[17] It is remarkable that the number of sons surviving from 1865 births was as high as the preceding two years, given the greater deprivation they and their mothers experienced in the year of their birth.

One might think that the end of the war, the return of men to their wives, doctors to their communities, and laborers to the task of raising food crops, would have brought a re-

[17] Paul W. Gates, *Agriculture and the Civil War* (New York, 1965), ch. 5. On the effect of wartime deprivation on fertility and childbirth in World War I, see Peter Loewenberg, "The Psychohistorical Origins of the Nazi Youth Cohort," *American Historical Review*, LXXVI (December 1971), especially 1473-80.

turn of the birth pattern to its antebellum levels, but the birth rate does not seem to have increased for two more years. Six families in 1870 had sons born in 1866, and five had sons born in 1867. While more surviving sons were born in the two years after the war's end than in its final three years, still significantly fewer sons survived from 1866 and 1867 than from 1861 and 1862. If the number of surviving sons is a measure of deprivation, such deprivation was greater in the two years after the war than in the first two years of the war itself.

If deprivation reduced the number of surviving sons, that deprivation came to an end in 1868, when eleven sons were born who survived until 1870. The following year, 1869, twelve sons were born who survived at least until the census-taker arrived the next year. Some qualifications of this argument are necessary. First, the number of surviving sons in 1870 is not a birth rate, although it is undoubtedly related to the birth rate. Secondly, census enumerators did not record ages very precisely. This list of children's ages depended on the month the census enumerator visited planter homes in 1870 and on the way planters calculated and reported their children's ages. The census gave ages in years, but not months. If the census taker arrived on schedule in June of 1870, children born between May 1868 and June 1869 could have been recorded as being one year old. The dates in the above discussion could be off as much as a year, but no other way seems obvious to calculate birth years. The deprivation that resulted in a smaller number of surviving sons might have set in several months before the close of 1862 and stopped several months before the end of 1867.

In conclusion, evidence from the manuscript census for 1850, 1860, and 1870 indicates that, while the Civil War had a profound effect on the composition of planter families, it did not transform the social position of female planters and planters' wives to the extent that literary sources suggest. The image of white plantation women may have undergone a significant change in the wake of the war, but this change does not seem to have been accompanied by a corresponding change in the social position of planter women, at least to the extent that such developments are revealed in the manuscript census. This gap between the changing ideological representation of elite Southern women and the social reality of persistent antebellum patterns deserves further study.

MINNIE MILLER BROWN

BLACK WOMEN IN AMERICAN AGRICULTURE

This paper attempts to identify some of the major contributions and experiences of Black women in the development of American agriculture. Selected periods of history will be examined because each apparently has distinctive characteristics. In writing of the historical past, one is dependent on the availability of sources. Therefore, an in-depth review and screening of the literature was necessary. Due to the scarcity of literature focusing directly on the subject of this paper, frequent reference will be made to Blacks as a class in the development of agriculture in our nation. This approach seems reasonable since the experiences of Black men, women, and children in American agriculture have been inextricably linked. Furthermore, the role of Blacks in agriculture must be considered in the context of agricultural policies, changes in the occupational patterns of the entire nation under the impact of technological development, and the social and economic environments in which Blacks found themselves.

It is hoped that this paper will provide some deeper insights and lead to a greater appreciation of the valuable role Black women have played in the evolution of American agriculture during the last two centuries.

When the Declaration of Independence was signed in 1776, most Blacks were still in slavery. During this period, Black women, along with their "brothers," labored on plantations, without pay, in the production of tobacco, sugarcane, cotton, rice, and hemp. They also served as cooks, nurses, maids, gardeners, and seamstresses in the homes of the plantation owners. To some extent, Black female slave labor was used in a few textile and cotton mills. The exploitation of Black labor was sanctioned and regulated, and the slaves were held in paternalistic economic dependence by plantation owners.

MINNIE MILLER BROWN is State Agent, Home Economics, and Extension Associate Professor, Adult and Community College Education, North Carolina State University. This paper was presented at the Bicentennial Symposium, "Two Centuries of American Agriculture," in Washington, D.C., 22 April 1975.

Black women in agriculture were valuable property, not only because their labor was capital, but also because they were used as breeders of slaves who were later sold by slaveholders for profitable sums of money. Such is evidenced in a slave dealer's sale receipt:

> Place and date: Richmond, Va., October 1, 1851
> Received of E. H. Stokes $2325 . . . for the purchase of one Negro slave named Margaret. The right and title of said Slave I warrant and defend against the claims of all persons whatsoever, and likewise warrant her sound and healthy. As witness by hand and seal.
> —Benja A. Blankenship[1]

During this period of history, Black women in agriculture were more often than not separated from their families. Some contemporary writers argue that this had a negative impact on the Black family as a physical, psychological, social, and economic unit, and hence on the society of Black people.[2] Despite the conditions imposed by the slave system, the slave mother exhibited fierce devotion to her own offspring. The bonds of affection between mother and children were generally developed in the slave cabin where the Black mother nurtured her brood after laboring from sunup to sundown. Moreover, when the Black father was sold or separated from his family, the slave mother became the authority in the household. Thus, historically, the matriarchal Black family had its origin during the period of slavery when the mother was the most dependable element of the family.

Since Black women and men dominated the plantation system as unskilled laborers, it seems appropriate to look at some of the social effects frequently cited by noted writers. Perhaps the social effects listed in the section which follows will give greater meaning to the dilemma of Black plantation laborers in agriculture, both *then* and *now*.[3]

(1) The plantation system is distinguished by the regimentation of its large gangs of unskilled laborers. It is utterly impossible for the individual to acquire any experience and facility in decision making and all the other mental activities that lead to successful self-direction and self-reliance in an independent way of life. Thus, the fixed routine of the plantation system prevents the laborers from acquiring the skills and aptitudes that must be developed by the worker on a general farm

[1] Lucy Chase Manuscript, *Black Women in White America: A Documentary History*, ed. Gerda Lerner (New York: Vintage Books, 1973), 9.

[2] Andrew Billingsley, *Black Families in White America* (Englewood Cliffs, N.J.: Prentice-Hall, 1968).

[3] T. Lynn Smith, *Studies of the Great Rural Tap Roots of Urban Poverty in the United States* (New York: Carlton Press, 1974).

where *in one man* are combined the functions of entrepreneur, manager, and laborer.

(2) It is almost impossible for the agricultural ladder to operate in the plantation area, because to do so would destroy the plantation system itself in a single generation.

(3) The economic efficiency of the plantation system is not translated into better living for the unskilled agricultural laborers. Studies show that the levels of living are much lower for Black plantation workers than for Blacks on family-owned farms.

(4) One of the major shortcomings of the plantation system is that it does not equip the oncoming generation of Black laborers with the proper habits, skills, and aptitudes to fit into any other scheme of operations.

Thus, the plantation system has not only had debilitating effects on the individual laborer, but it may also be the prime source of social ills affecting masses of people who have left the South.

In short, during the period of slavery, Black women in agriculture worked largely as manual laborers and house servants. They were a major component of the plantation system which has been found to have had many negative effects on the lives of the Black slaves. Despite the hardships and suffering which pregnancy and childbirth often involved, Black women also served as slavebreeders whose children were frequently sold at the discretion of the slaveowner. Thus both their labor and their offspring served as capital. Notwithstanding these adversities, Black women made substantial contributions to the development of American agriculture during this period of history.

In 1863, over four million Negroes were emancipated from almost two hundred and fifty years of slavery. Some two million of these were women. About nine-tenths of the Black population was in the South.

Emancipation did not destroy the old plantation system. The first working arrangement attempted by owners with the freed Black men and women was the payment of cash wages for labor. This proved unsatisfactory. Wages fixed by the Federal Freedmen's Bureau were thought to be relatively high, money was scarce, and the planter could not demand steady work from his hands. Later, when labor was extremely scarce and the planters were forced to make terms with the Negroes, the sharecropping system was adopted.

Under the share system, the landlord supplied everything except labor to make the crop, and the cropper received a share of the harvest at the end of the year, less the advances he had secured. Sharecropping required all possible hands, so the Black woman, and her children, worked alongside her husband as a field laborer just as she did during slavery. It should be noted here that it was only after Emancipation that the Black husband and father laid the foundation for patriarchal authority in his family. His interest in his wife and children rested on an economic tie. Even among sharecroppers, it was customary for the father and husband to make contracts with the landowner, and assume responsibility for his own family.

Some writers describe the sharecropping system as the most pernicious of all systems under which the laborer has been employed. Their argument is that this system leads to idleness on the part of the laborer for most of the year, and to indolence and indifference on the part of the farmowner. On the other hand, a positive factor often cited is that this system does not subject the farmer to loss from crop failure or a decline in value.

In spite of lack of reform, there was a slow rise in Negro small-scale landownership in the South until the turn of the century. A small amount of abandoned and confiscated land was turned over to Negroes by the Union Army and later by the Freedmen's Bureau, but the Bureau had to use most of its small appropriations (less than $18,000,000) for general relief or for educational purposes. Furthermore, the Bureau was allowed to operate for only seven years (1865–1872). So, with few exceptions, the freed Black men and women did not possess land. Some scholars argue that the story of Blacks in American agriculture and their lives in general would have been vastly different had they, at the time of Emancipation, been given greater opportunity to establish themselves as independent farmers, whereby they could have become more firmly attached to the land. They needed the facilities and encouragement to become landowners.

Josephus Daniels, a liberal Southerner, asked an old Confederate, "What was so bad about the promise to give every Negro head of a family forty acres and a mule?" The old man responded:

> . . . it would have made the Negro "uppity," and besides, they don't know enough to farm without direction. . . . we are having a hard time now keeping the nigger in his place, and if he were a landowner he'd think he was a bigger man than old Grant. . . . Who'd work the land if the niggers had farms of their own?[4]

The old man's response represented the prevailing attitude of "keeping

[4] Quoted in Gunnar Myrdal, *An American Dilemma: The Negro Problem and Modern Democracy* (New York: Harper and Row, 1962), 1:227.

the Negro in his place," and the maintenance of traditional dependency and powerlessness.

There are other conditions or reasons why Blacks were unable to make a better showing as independent farm owners:[5]

(1) His background of slavery encouraged dependency, he was seldom encouraged to show much initiative or taught to look after himself.

(3) Until recent years, the educational opportunities for Blacks in the South have been extremely poor.

(4) Blacks were concentrated in plantation areas where comparatively few small holdings were for sale. There was no general land reform, and Blacks did not participate to any extent in the development of the West. There were, however, small holdings for sale largely in run-down unfertile areas where there was a heavy concentration of Blacks, and where plantations began to disintegrate.

(5) Discriminating attitudes of rural whites, such as these:

> Negro landownership . . . can be achieved only by means of a most exacting and highly selective procedure; the would-be owner must be acceptable to the white community . . . be content with the purchase of acreage least desired by the whites and pay for it in a very few years. . . . The Negro buys land only when some white man will sell it to *him*. Just because a white man has land for sale does not mean that a Negro, even the one most liked and respected by him, can buy it even if he has the money.[6]

Although the above conditions cannot be measured, there is no question about their being highly significant in the difficulty Blacks experienced in acquiring land.

Frances Ellen Harper, a Black woman lecturer, had an especially perceptive understanding of the social problems of reconstruction and the essential elements needed. In one of her letters from the South in 1925, she stated:

> . . . While I am in favor of universal suffrage, . . . a man, landless, ignorant and poor may use the vote against his interests; but with intelligence and land, he holds in his hand the basis of power and elements of truth.[7]

[5] Ibid., 1:240–42.

(2) Because of low earnings as farmhands or tenants, the Negro has had less chance to save enough money for the purpose of buying land. Furthermore, Blacks did not have much of the legal security which is a necessary condition for successful entrepreneurship.

[6] Arthur Raper, *Preface to Peasantry* (Chapel Hill: University of North Carolina Press, 1936), 121–22.

[7] Frances Ellen Harper, "Coloured Women of America," *Englishwoman's Review*, 15 January 1878, pp. 10–15.

Implicit in these statements was the need, not only for the franchise, but also for landownership and education, the basis for elevating the Negro race. Political participation was and still is at the core of the American tradition. Thus, the interest in politics, landownership, and education were viewed together as integral parts of the element of freedom.

It should be recognized here that some Black women were able to acquire property, and that, in many instances, they were the mainstay of the family. In continuing her impressions of reconstruction in the South, Frances E. Harper made these comments which show that women are quite equal to men in energy and executive ability:[8]

. . . When I was in Mississippi, I stopped with Mr. Montgomery, a former slave of Jefferson Davis' brother. His wife was a woman capable of taking on her hands 130 acres of land, and raising one hundred and seven bales of cotton by the force which she could organize. Since then, I have received a very interesting letter from her daughter, who for years has held the position of Assistant Post Mistress. In her letter she says: "There are many women around me who would serve as models of executiveness anywhere. They do double duty, a man's share in the field, and a woman's part at home. They do any kind of field work, even ploughing, and at home the cooking, washing, milking, and gardening. But these have husbands; let me tell you of some widows and unaided women:

"Mrs. Hill, a widow, has rented, cultivated, and solely managed a farm of five acres for five years. She makes her garden, raises poultry, and cultivates enough corn and cotton to live comfortable, and keep a surplus in the bank. She saves something every year, and this is much, considering the low price of cotton and unfavorable seasons. . . .

"Mrs. Jane Brown and Mrs. Halsey formed a partnership about ten years ago, *leased* nine acres and a horse, and have cultivated the land all that time. Just the same as men would have done. They have saved considerable money from year to year, and are living independently. They have never had any expenses for labor—making and gathering the crops themselves.

"An acquaintance of mine, who lives in South Carolina, and has been engaged in mission work, reports that, in supporting the family, women are the mainstay; that two-thirds of the truck gardening is done by them in South Carolina; that when the men lose their work through political affiliations, the women sand by them, and say, 'stand by your principles.' Mr. Steward, who was employed in the Freedmen's bank, says he has seen scores of coloured women in the South working and managing plantations of from 20 to 100 acres. . ."

[8] George Bragg, "Frances E. Harper," *Men of Maryland* (Baltimore, Md.: Church Advocate Press, 1925), 72–86.

Though the obstacles were great for all Blacks, Black women obviously recognized the importance of economic independence as they continued to make significant contributions to agricultural development through hard work, thrift, industry, and the acquisition of property. Many of them proved their ability to organize and successfully manage farming enterprises.

By 1910, the Black population was still concentrated in the South where they were predominantly agricultural workers in rural areas. There were 893,000 Black farmers. The distribution of the Black population which prevailed in 1910 remained virtually unchanged until about 1916 when a large stream of Black laborers migrated out of the South into large northern urban centers in search for human betterment and economic prosperity. This continued for the next decade. Black women were denied access to factory employment until World War I. The exceptions to this were the southern tobacco and textile industries, where Black women continued doing the unskilled factory work they had done since slavery.

In spite of migration during World War I, many Black women continued to live on farms and work as farm laborers. The plantation system of agriculture dominated. Their levels of living were generally low, as evidenced in their substandard housing and poor diets. Their homes were largely characterized by lack of sanitary facilities, poor construction, inadequate lighting, and overcrowding. Illiteracy was high. The Bible and schoolbooks were almost the only reading material, especially among farm owners. As Raper has written, "the three M's—meat, meal, and molasses . . . constitute the main table fare of the poorer rural families."[9] According to Johnson, "very little foodstuffs were secured from a garden because gardening is foreign to the habits of tenants, and landlords are not disposed generally to advance credit for gardening which would reduce the profit which they derive from advances of foodstuffs."[10] Thus, the cotton plantation system is an institutional factor to be counted heavily when explaining the role of Black women in American agriculture.

The depression years of the early 1930s halted much of the movement of Blacks from the South; however, it was resumed in 1938 and 1939, and dramatically gained momentum during the following ten years, a period in which the full impact of World War II was experienced. During this time, there were unskilled Black women workers in small numbers in food industries, especially in slaughtering meat, packing

9 Raper, *Preface to Peasantry*, 52.

10 Charles Johnson, *Shadow of the Plantation* (Chicago, Ill.: University of Chicago Press, 1934).

houses, crab and peanut factories, and in cotton mills. There were semiskilled workers in the textile industries. The part that Black women workers in agriculture played in winning the war will probably not be told for many years to come.

In 1940, over one-fourth (16,000,000) of the southern farm population was Black. Only 8 percent of the southern farm land was operated by Black owners, tenants, or croppers. Those remaining Blacks participated in agriculture only as wage laborers, at low wages and usually without the assurance of year-round employment.

The decade from 1950 to 1960 was the one in which Black migration from southern farms reached its greatest proportion. Migration, indeed, continued to be principally in response to economic conditions, i.e., moving out of the rural South into places where there were better opportunities for making a living.

Some writers contend that the Agricultural Adjustment Act, initiated in 1933, was the central factor directly responsible for the drastic number of Black sharecroppers and tenants who were "pushed off" the land. The objective of the Agricultural Adjustment Program was to raise and stabilize farm income. The essential elements of the program included these: (1) Limitation of cash crop acreages (cut in cotton acreage); (2) Removal of price-depressing surpluses from regular markets; (3) Payment of direct subsidies to farmers; (4) Encouragement of conservation practices.

In short, the Agricultural Adjustment Program reduced acreage in the main crops requiring labor. Landlords had a large part in the local administration of the program, and they reduced their tenant labor force, a large part of which were Blacks. As a result, there was a wholesale decline in tenancy. This particular program stimulated mechanization because of the premium it offered of reducing the number of tenants. Thus, Blacks were increasingly reduced to seasonal workers, and the number tended to dwindle as mechanization increased. For most Black tenants, the economic effects of the AAA were unemployment and poverty. One writer noted that "the landless farmers . . . are not only failing to escape their chronic dependence, but are actually losing status. Many tenants are being pushed off the land, while others are being pushed down the tenure ladder, especially from cropper to wage hand status."[11] Thus, with the creation of an agricultural program designed to eliminate victimization of the farmer, new types of victimization emerged which were indirect and presumably unintended.

In his article, "Improving the Economic Status of the Negro," James Tobin makes these assertions about the migration of Blacks and agricultural programs.

[11] Raper, *Preface to Peasantry*, 6–7.

. . . much Negro poverty in the South reflects an inability . . . to make a livelihood in agriculture. Mechanization and the competition of large-scale units in the Southwest are undermining the plantation and sharecropping system. . . . The Negro subsistence farmer has too little land, equipment, and know-how to make a decent income. . . . Current government agricultural programs . . . do very little to help the sharecropper or subsistence farmer. Our whole agricultural policy needs to be recast, to give income support to people rather than price support to crops, and to take people off the land rather than to take land out of cultivation. . . . substantial migration from agriculture is only possible, without disaster in the cities, in a booming economy with a tight labor market.[12]

Typical of this view are the arguments of T. Lynn Smith, an eminent sociologist. He argues that the southern plantation system is one of the great tap roots of poverty and related ills that have agitated life in the cities of our nation during the 1960s and 1970s. In discussing the impact of mass migration to cities, he presents a proposal not only to stop the migration flow, but also to lure masses of people back to the farms.[13] In short, Smith proposes benefit payments to reinforce the small farmers in their struggle to maintain a place on the land. Here are some pertinent aspects of his proposal:

The Program envisioned requires nothing more than the extension to the small general farmers who wish to engage in a variety of crop and livestock enterprises, of the same kinds of benefit payments that long have been available to large operators who specialize in a single type of production. Specifically it is proposed to put into effect legislation whereby any farm family that would produce a volume of any specified farm products roughly equal to

[12] James Tobin, "On Improving the Economic Status of the Negro," in *The Negro American*, ed. Talcott Parsons and Kenneth B. Clark (Boston, Mass.: Houghton Mifflin, 1966), 467–68.

[13] While the movement of Blacks out of the South has received a great deal of attention from demographers and others, it should be recognized that in recent years there has been an increasing counterstream—"return" migration of Blacks to the South. For example, between 1970 and 1973, 247,000 Blacks moved to the South, while only 166,000 moved from the South. Of those Blacks moving to the South, nearly two-thirds (65.7 percent) had previously lived in the South, while about one-third were moving to the region for the first time. Recent trends in economic development and decreasing racial discrimination in the labor market in recent decades has led students of Black migration to expect a continued expansion of migration to the South.

Campbell, Johnson, and Strangler found that the largest occupational categories for the "return" migrants were service workers (24.1 percent), equipment operatives (18 percent), and clerical and related workers (13.2 percent). Very few returnees were employed as farmers or farm laborers (2.2 percent)—this is consistent with the tendency of migrants to return to the metropolitan areas. See R. R. Campbell, D. M. Johnson, and G. Strangler, "Return Migration of Black People to the South," *Rural Sociology* 39 (Winter 1974): 504–28.

what the average family could consume in the course of the year should:

1. Be allowed to retain that amount of the produce for its own use; and
2. Qualify for a benefit payment equivalent to the "fair" retail price of the same . . .[14]

We know now that chances for a better life for Black southern migrants are at best problematical in the often overcrowded and decaying urban areas of the North. Lynn simply seeks an answer to this dilemma which would make it possible for large numbers of people to be attracted back to the farms where they could make a decent living. His proposal is sound and appears to be within the framework of our nation's economic and political philosophy.

The distribution of Blacks in agriculture has changed dramatically over time. According to the *Census of Agriculture, 1969* there is a total of 87,439 Black farm operators. Of this total, 61.9 percent are full owners, 18 percent are part owners, and 20.1 percent are tenants. These represent 3.2 percent of all farm operators.[15] An examination of employed Blacks by occupational groups shows that 12.1 percent were farm workers in 1960, as compared to 3 percent in 1972 (includes farmers, farm laborers, and managers).[16]

The hired farm working force in 1973 consisted of 2.7 million persons 14 years of age and over who did some farm work for cash wages during the year. (This was a slight decrease from the total in 1972.) Of the total number of hired workers, 3 percent were Black women, while 11 percent were Black males.[17]

While there has been a rapid decline in the number of Black workers in agricultural production, there has been a steady rise in minority employment of both sexes in federal agencies since the passage of the Equal Employment Opportunity Act of 1972. For example, in 1969, the percent of minorities among the work force in the Department of Agriculture was 8.4, as compared to 9.7 percent in 1972.[18]

The twentieth century has not found the answer to the problems of Blacks in agriculture (production), but it has witnessed some effort in searching for an answer through various programs, such as soil conservation, agricultural extension, farm credit, Farm Security Admini-

14 Smith, *Rural Tap Roots of Urban Poverty.*

15 U.S. Department of Commerce, Bureau of the Census, *Census of Agriculture, 1969.*

16 U.S. Department of Commerce, Bureau of the Census, *The Social and Economic Status of the Black Population in the United States, 1971* (Washington: GPO, 1972).

17 *The Hired Farm Working Force of 1973: A Statistical Report,* U.S. Dept. of Agriculture, Economic Research Service Report 265.

18 U.S. Civil Service Commission, *Minority Group Employment in the Federal Government* (Washington: GPO, 1972).

stration, etc. Though Blacks may have benefited to some extent from these programs, it is obvious that there have been some missing essentials. Therefore, a reappraisal of the programs and policies may be in order.

In conclusion, the story of Black women in American agriculture has generally been one of hard work, adaptability, and survival. They have been an important component of agricultural labor. During the early periods of history, there were generally no firm and fixed assignments based on gender. Black women showed a great deal of strength and courage in their agricultural roles. Most of the strength which they exhibited came from their efforts to cope with the negative aspects of the constantly changing social and economic forces, which they themselves did not create, but which, in fact, determined the character of all Blacks in agriculture. Although some of their coping efforts led to new difficulties, Black women made a significant contribution to the development of American agriculture during the past two centuries.

WOMEN HOMESTEADERS ON THE GREAT PLAINS FRONTIER

Sheryll Patterson-Black

Introduction

On the agricultural frontier of a century ago, it was often stated that life was great for the men and horses, but hard on the women and cattle. Life was hard on some women. In one early account, I Went to Kansas, Marian Colt Davis describes her family's western migration, in which in rapid succession she lost her husband and child to epidemic. Devastated, remorseful, and exhausted, she hastily retreated to her point of origin, and there her memoirs end.

Marian Colt Davis is typical of the image of women as reluctant pioneer, a stereotypic image which is perpetuated by history books (or at least, not destroyed by them). However, this image is refuted by my study of homestead women.

Homestead lands became available to women with the passage of the Homestead Act alloting free land to western settlers. In 1862 Senator William Borah jubilantly announced, "The government bets 160 acres against the entry fee of $14 that the settler can't live on the land for five years without starving to death."[1]

Since land ownership equals economic power in our society, his announcement had implications that have not until now been considered: that is, for the first time in American history, working-class women had the possibility of access to land ownership, because the land was free if certain conditions were met.[2] The law required continuous residence on, and improvement of, the land for five years, at which time proof for final title could be made. The homesteader had to be head of a family or twenty-one years of age. The law did not restrict homestead entries to men, and suddenly single

---

Sheryll Patterson-Black is coordinator of the Women Studies Program at the University of Colorado, instructor of an experimental course, "Women Homesteaders on the Great Plains Frontier," and author. Her most recent book, The Homestead Way of Life (about early homestead technology), is nearing completion. She is working on The Women Homesteaders and co-authoring The American Windmill. Her first book, The Nitty Gritty Foodbook, is primarily about home food production on the small family farm. She and her family cooperatively farm an old homestead in western Nebraska, where she plans to settle to research and write, rebuild derelict pianos, and raise dairy goats.

Patterson-Black

women and widows realized they, too, could claim 160 acres. Later, under the Kincaid Act, 640 acres of arid land could be claimed, and eventually the residence requirement was lowered to three years. During the duration of the Homestead Act, 1862-1934, would-be farmers claimed hundreds of millions of acres of land. As it turns out, thousands of these homesteaders were women, a hidden force on the agricultural frontier.

For some time I have been concerned with the historic image of women on the frontier, the stereotype that would have us believe that most women in the west in the nineteenth century had followed men, and were prostitutes, dance hall girls, or dependent, helpless wives accompanying their husbands. The image of women as reluctant pioneers has long been popular and entirely accepted. In fact, little or no evidence to the contrary has been readily available.

However, in the course of doing research for my forthcoming book, The Homestead Way of Life, I found repeated references to a category of frontier women I didn't know existed in force--the women homesteaders. Although for the purposes of this paper (which is an initial approach to the subject), I have examined the variety of women on homesteads, I am particularly interested in the women who ventured onto the Great Plains and filed claims to their own land, perhaps in response to the popular song of the day, "Uncle Sam Is Rich Enough to Give Us All a Farm."

My research on women homesteaders of the Great Plains has drawn on many sources: photos, oral histories, diaries, letters, memoirs, catalogs, land office records, other government documents, scholarly journals, and literature, both fiction and nonfiction. Casual references in literature, particularly in the writings of Mari Sandoz, have been very helpful in that their frequency gave me the incentive to look further. From these sources I roughly estimated women homesteaders at 5 to 10 percent of the number of homestead entrants.

Just recently, I began researching government records, land office records from the late 1800's and early 1900's. Preliminary data from land offices in Lamar, Colorado (1887 and 1907) and Douglas, Wyoming (1891, 1907, and 1908) indicate that an average of 11.9 percent of the sample of homestead entrants were women. The percentage increased as the years passed, and percentages varied from 4.8 percent in Douglas in 1891 to 18.2 percent in Lamar in 1907. Final ownership could be established either through a cash payment after six months' residence or through meeting the five-year residence requirement. Success of women in making final proof varied from year to year (as did the success of men) and probably was determined by the vicissitudes of terrain, aridity, weather, hostility of area cattlemen, and other such conditions. In this preliminary random sample, of those who filed a homestead entry, 37 percent of the men succeeded in making final claim to the land, while 42.4 percent of the women succeeded, a percentage which discounts the theory of woman as helpless, reluctant pioneer.

Images of Women on the Agricultural Frontier

I find it astounding that this army of women settlers could be so entirely overlooked in historical sources. Articles about women on the frontier, even though written by respected scholars, tend to perpetuate the "oppressed helpmate" image. For example, while "Sunbonnet and Calico: The Homesteader's Consort" by Everett Dick offers an accurate and sympathetic view of the difficulties, the bravery, and the sacrifices of frontier women, it is incomplete and limited in scope to women as reluctant pioneer, as consort.[3] Sometimes the titles are misleading. "Dolls, Vassals, and Drudges--Pioneer Women in the West" by T. C. Larson is actually about the early passage of women's suffrage in Wyoming and Utah.[4]

Where information has been more fully presented, it often has been corrupted in some manner; for example, one commonly reproduced photo of the Great Plains frontier shows four women in front of a sod house. The caption sometimes reads something like this: "Daughters of a Homesteader." In fact, these four women were the Chrisman sisters of central Nebraska, young women who filed on adjoining claims of 160 acres each. Numerous other photos show women homesteaders, most often alone.

In 1934, Mari Sandoz wrote:

> Unfortunately I found that the earlier and more exciting portions of pioneer literature have little reference to women outside of dance-hall girls, Indians, and breeds, or those mere bits of icing added for romantic interest in later rehashings of early tales . . . . The early accounts of the white man's penetration . . .sometimes mention women, usually referred to as the wife or the squaw of so-and-so . . . . Later came the dance-hall girls of the Wild West stories, the Calamity Janes, the Poker Alices, the Silver Nells. No pioneer women in the common sense of the term.[5]

Sandoz concluded her paper "Pioneer Women" with "the observation that the story of the pioneer women has yet to be written."[6]

There were many attempts to depict the pioneer women in literature, and this material provided me with images of women on the prairie frontier which I wanted to compare with historical fact. In fiction, particularly fiction by men, the reluctant pioneer is the most frequent image of women. Sometimes she was silently courageous, sometimes she was utterly despondent and desperate, but always she was reluctant.

The best, or worst, example can be found in O. E. Rolvaag's Giants in the Earth. Beret Hansa, the pregnant helpless wife, is almost forced across the plains to Dakota Territory by her husband who is anxious to settle rather than wait another year. Upon their arrival, Beret thought, "Was this the place? Here! Could it be possible? . . . How will human beings be able to endure this place?

. . . Why, there isn't even a thing that one can hide behind!"[7]

Most of the women portrayed in Giants in the Earth are of the same type: helpless women who have been brought west against their better judgments, nesters who are dependent upon their husbands for almost everything, women who anxiously and helplessly await the returns of their husbands whenever they, in their traditional role as hunter, venture forth to locate firewood or building materials, or money. The Hansas, along with other Norwegians, found a colony, and nowhere in the community is there a single woman who seems capable of functioning independently. In one memorable incident portrayed by Rolvaag, a solitary wagon is met by a delegate of the community; a woman is tied down inside the wagon. The husband explains that their child has died and was buried on the open prairie; the woman cannot cope with the child's death and every night runs away from the camp, madly in search of it. Beret Hansa, meanwhile, is not only reluctant; she is despondent, desperate, in terror, and even convinced that she has violated the will of God by leaving her Norwegian homeland. Life on the plains causes her to become mad, then fanatical; her husband's death is the result.

Rolvaag himself never homesteaded. It is interesting to contrast Giants in the Earth with an early photo in my files: it shows a group of robust Norwegian immigrants, both men and women, heartily holding the game they've just shot. Rolvaag's Beret can also be compared with Jane Grout, who traveled with an immigrant train in southern Minnesota in 1873, at nearly the same time and location as the setting for Giants in the Earth. Jane Grout's comment about the barren prairie was, "the further we got, the better I liked it."[8]

Hamlin Garland, although a radical espousing feminism, among other things, has also used the reluctant pioneer imagery, particularly in "A Prairie Heroine" and Son of the Middle Border. In Son of the Middle Border, he depressingly, though perhaps honestly, writes: "My mother prepared to 'follow the sunset' with her 'Boss' . . . . Why should mother be wrenched from all her dearest friends and forced to move away to a strange land?"[9] Although Garland was familiar with the harshness of prairie life and sympathetic to its difficulties for women (and men), and although his writings may accurately reflect his own experience and a concern for protecting women, it is interesting that they show no realization of frontier opportunity for women. Yet in 1890, Garland wrote, "Woman stands . . .as independent of man as man is independent of woman."[10]

The prairie fiction written by women offers a very different image of women. Willa Cather has two homestead heroines, Alexandra in O Pioneers! and Antonia in My Antonia. Their social status is somewhat different--Antonia herself breaks the sod following the suicide of her father, while Alexandra inherits a struggling, though somewhat developed, farm. Antonia marries early and produces a large brood of children, along with her fertile garden and orchard. Alexandra remains single for years, succeeding as a farmer far better than her brothers or her neighbors: "Anyone thereabouts would have told you that this was one of the richest farms on the Divide, and that the farmer was a woman, Alexandra Bergson."[11] Before the book is completed, she does marry an early companion, a gentle, bookish man who has spent his time traveling rather than settling. Both Antonia and Alexandra meet the agricultural challenge in nineteenth-century Nebraska with enthusiasm, persistence, and effectiveness. Furthermore, it is known that Antonia was based on the life of Annie Pavelka, an immigrant Cather knew.

Mari Sandoz, born on a homestead herself, is much more explicit and realistic about the variety of women on the plains homesteads. Her fictional heroines range from ruthless Gulla Slogum, domineering, land-hungry, and powerful homesteader, rancher, politician, wife and mother (Slogum House) to Morissa Kirk who works as a doctor to homesteaders, while establishing a hospital on her own homestead claim (Miss Morissa).

Miss Morissa portrays an early frontier doctor, one who capably and independently treats cowboys ravaged by horses and cattle, homesteaders confronted with epidemic and childbirth, and criminals with grisly wounds. Throughout the book, Morissa faces the choice between her professional life and personal romance, consistently choosing the professional life when to do otherwise means an intolerable compromise. At the same time she successfully manages her homestead.

These heroines of Sandoz' are based on real people. Miss Morissa is a composite of three pioneer women doctors in Nebraska, particularly Dr. Georgia Arbuckle-Fix, who homesteaded in and met the medical needs of many in western Nebraska. She remained single for several years after filing her homestead claim; she married, but divorced her husband because he insisted that she give up her medical practice to become a homemaker. Gulla Slogum sounds suspiciously similar to a villainous neighbor of the Sandoz family who, along with her daughters, ran a road ranch that catered to cattlemen, the omnipresent enemies of the homesteaders.

Sandoz portrays a variety of women, both single and married, in her fiction and nonfiction, giving a much more historically accurate account of women on the homesteads than any other writer. Certainly, some homestead women had personal characteristics which were better suited to life on the prairie than were others.

Motivation

What motives prompted women to move west in the first place? Who were the female settlers?

Women on the homesteads seem to be primarily women who wanted to escape a past lifestyle that was unsatisfactory or who felt that life on the frontier would offer opportunities unavailable elsewhere. They were mail-order brides from the east coast and Europe who submitted to the promises of handsome husbands and rich farms in the lush western reaches. They were single women and widows who sought economic freedom through land ownership, either with ideas of farming on their own or of filing a claim, then selling out to someone for a grubstake to do something else. They were women who sought to earn a living by other means than those of east coast factory worker, school teacher, or maid. Mari Sandoz writes:

> There were many women . . .not only among the fraudulent entries . . .but among the bona fide homesteaders. These women were classified roughly into two groups . . . . Those with genteel ways, graying hair, downy faces and perhaps good books to loan to a settler's reading-hungry daughter, were called Boston schoolteachers, no matter who or where from. The others, called Chicago widows, weren't young either, or pretty, but their talk, their dress, and their ways were gayer, more colorful, more careless; their books, if any, were paperback novels. . . . Several had a volume of nonfiction called From Ballroom to Hell, with every step of the way well illustrated.[12]

Some of the homesteaders were women escaping from oppressive marriages, either as divorcees or runaways. Mary O'Kieffe, mother of nine, was just such a woman. Memoirs of Mary O'Kieffe were recorded by her son Charley, who writes of his birth in Western Story:

> Mother herded cattle all day long in the broiling hot sun so the children could attend a Fourth of July celebration in a nearby community. The next morning around two a.m., I was born. No doctor, no nurse, no midwife, just Mother and God.[13]

One day in 1884, Mary became fed up with her ne'er-do-well husband who disappeared for long stretches of time, and she decided to file a homestead claim in western Nebraska. She had the older children assist her in building a cover on the farm wagon, hitched up the work horses, and tied the milk cows to the wagon's side. To the rear of the wagon, she attached the cultivator and on top of that she built a small chicken coop to hold her two dozen hens and a rooster. The journey from their earlier farm on the Missouri River was a distance of about 500 miles. After numerous adventures on the trek, which took fifty-one days, they arrived, built a sod house, dug a well, and the family set up housekeeping in their new home.

There were many women who accompanied husbands west, but often they were partners in a family undertaking rather than reluctant pioneers. Typical of this category is Rosie Ise, who went to Kansas in 1873 along with her husband Henry. Jointly, they built a struggling barren homestead into a successful farm, while encountering grasshoppers, drought, economic depression, threats of sickness, and other disasters. Rosie outlived Henry and built the farm into a still more successful venture after his death. "She reared eleven of her twelve children, and remembering regretfully her own half-day in school, sent nine of them through college."[14]

There were women like Mrs. Thomas Horn Ewing, mother of seven, who was "living very comfortably in the eastern part of Pennsylvania when grandfather's [her husband's] health began to fail, and the doctors . . .[gave] him only two years to live. Grandmother decided their five boys and two girls needed a father for longer than two years," so she urged the family westward to homestead.[15]

There were women like Sarah Shaw Wisdom, recently widowed, who felt that perhaps life would be better for herself and her four children on a prairie farm. Having filed her claim in 1886 in the most remote and least populated county of Nebraska, she determined that her children receive an education. Each day she would accompany the three older children to rural school, taking along the baby because of lack of child care. She studied beside the children until she herself was able to pass the teacher certification exam; and then, she began teaching. She continued to improve on her claim, and after some years, made final proof. She remarried, but after only one year her new husband was lost in a blizzard, leaving her alone and pregnant with a fifth child. She remained on his claim, completing final proof, all the while teaching school. When the Kincaid Act was passed in 1904, she decided to claim the additional 320 acres to which she was entitled, so once again she filed a homestead claim, and once more made final proof. For a total of thirty years she continued teaching, riding horseback to her country school. She died at her farm home at the age of eighty.[16]

There were women like Pansy Haskell who in an interview told me of accompanying her mother and father to Colorado in the early 1900's, then filing on an adjacent claim. Both homesteads were farmed cooperatively, with Pansy meeting the residence requirement on her own.

Expectation and Reality

The expectation of pioneer life and the reality of daily frontier experience varied from woman to woman, though undoubtedly the stereotypes do accurately portray the lives of some pioneer women. Some saw the climate and landscape as harsh and oppressive; others saw its wildness as freeing. Mrs. Elizabeth C. Sargent recalled, "I shall never forget Broken Bow as we saw it on that May morning in 1883. As we came over the hill, there it lay huddled below us--twelve sod houses and one frame store. To say we were all disheartened would be putting it mildly."[17] But other women were excited by the unlimited prairie expanses, with no tree to obstruct the view.

Some women encountered severe, and occasionally cruel, living conditions. Mari Sandoz records that her father Jules had four wives in the course of his homesteading. He left the first prior to filing his western Nebraska claim; the second went mad on the claim; the third, a mail-order bride from Europe, stayed two weeks on the homestead and went back to town; and the fourth, Mari's mother, another mail-order bride from Switzerland, remained only because she immediately became pregnant and was without resources in a strange country. Sandoz also writes of extreme cruelty to or lack of concern for women. One woman who had competently homesteaded alone, but married out of loneliness, died in an accident with horse-drawn farm machinery; her husband carelessly changed the adjustment on the harness, and the machinery jackknifed, the team bolted, and the woman was killed by the hay rake while doing the field work.[18] Sandoz mentions one woman who walked five miles to find a tree big enough to hang herself. Apparently the partnership of Rosie and Henry Ise was the ideal; in some marriages, the woman was held in extremely low regard, with her value measured only by the work she could do.

It seems clear to me that the life of a single woman, or at least the childless one, was a cut above that of her married sister on the Great Plains frontier. Partly, that is because the single or childless woman could devote her energy to her own survival and growth; the woman with numerous children or an oppressive husband was most often engaged in a moment-to-moment battle for survival. Sandoz writes:

> Mary heard that Pete kicked his wife until she almost bled to death. Now she was that way again and laying for him with the butcher knife. . . . Elise was better. The baby born at Norfolk died. She stayed there, working in the [insane] asylum kitchen, refusing to come back to Pete and more family.[19]

There truly were women who were reluctant pioneers, following their husbands into an unknown land because the women felt they had no alternative, or women like some of the mail-order brides who were tricked by ridiculous promises of opulence. But many women seemed to thrive on the frontier, regardless of their social status. Older women like Elinore Stewart, who saw life passing her by in the east, found a new life of contentment in Wyoming:

> A neighbor and his daughter were going to Green River, the county seat, and said I might go along, so I did, as I could file there as well as at the land office; and oh, that trip! I had more fun to the square inch than Mark Twain or Samantha Allen ever provoked. It took us a whole week to go and come. We camped out, of course, for in the whole sixty miles there was but one house, and going in that direction there is not a tree to be seen, nothing but sage, sand, and sheep.[20]

Elinore Stewart later married her neighbor and continued to live a happy life.

Younger women like Mollie Dorsey Sanford thrived on the frontier in spite of, or perhaps because of, the lack of social amenities and restrictions. Upon the family's decision to move to Nebraska when she was eighteen, she notes in her journal in 1857:

> I already love the Nebraska prairies. . . . Mother hardly enters into extacics [sic]. She no doubt realizes what it is to bring a young rising family away from the advantages of the world. To me, it seems a glorious holiday, a freedom from restraint, and I believe it will be a blessing to we girls. We were getting too fond of style, too unhappy not to have the necessary things to carry it out. [And three days later:] We all seem content. Even Mother has caught the inspiration and lost her care-worn look.[21]

Later Mollie married a neighboring homesteader, and they ventured into the Colorado gold fields.

Some women, however, were not so adaptable, like Nannie Tiffany Alderson, who records her memoirs in A Bride Goes West. She left southern plantation life to accompany her husband to a Montana ranch and continued to wear dresses with trains despite the dirt floor of the crude shanty. She clung to traditional roles, maintaining carefree girlhood exuberance until after the birth of her first child, then became increasingly housebound and conservative. After she bore several more children, she wrote bitterly against one teenage girl who visited, had the audacity to wear men's pants to ride, and enjoyed roping calves.

Necessity gradually forced most women on the frontier out of traditional behavior; however, some continued to pine for the old lifestyle, while others gladly cast it aside. Attitudes and expectations varied among women settlers, as did suitability of background, temperament, and resources.

"My sister and I had always lived in town and she knew little of life on a farm and I knew even less," Idah E. McComsey writes.[22] Although McComsey stayed on, I have discovered in my examination of land office records that women who canceled or relinquished their claims generally did so within a few months, as did their male counterparts. No doubt, some of these people simply found life on the Great American Desert intolerable and their farm experiences and imagination too inadequate to cope with it.

Filing and Settling

Despite Hamlin Garland's line, "Woman is not by nature an explorer. She is a home-lover,"[23] early on in exploration of and transportation on the Great Plains frontier, competent women played a part. Widowed and destitute, Mrs. E. J. Guerin, or Mountain Charley as she was known during her "thirteen years in Male attire," headed a wagon train of fifteen men and a herd of cattle, horses, and mules bound across the plains and desert in 1857. Mountain Charley had some regrets:

> Of my parting with my children, I will say but little. That my soul was filled with poignant grief at thus leaving them to penetrate the dangers of a distant State, can be readily imagined by any one, and particularly a parent. But I believed it for the best, and steeled myself against all pleading made by my maternal nature to remain. I was tired of my life on the River, not pleased with its somewhat menial character, and fully believed that the course I had determined upon, severe as it might be to my maternal love, was the best one I could adopt. If I met with ordinary success . . .I could retire into more private life, resume my proper dress, and thereafter in company with my children enjoy life to the full extent that circumstances would permit.[24]

Women worked in a variety of nontraditional occupations on the frontier. In her novel Slogum House, Mari Sandoz characterizes Moll Barheart in this way:

> Old Moll's white mules, the finest hauling outfit in the country. . . .Moll raised herself and had to care for at the livery barns, since the time one of them kicked the hat off a man who tried to help her hitch up. . . . [Later, Sandoz writes:] Ruedy looked over his pipe at the strong, weather-beaten face of this Moll Barheart who had kicked her past in the pants, as she called it. He considered the straight, peppery hair cut short and brushed behind her ears that were like crumpled kidskin, but fine, live kidskin. . . . Yes, it was good so, and right.[25]

Women of all circumstances passed through, filed claims, and settled. The degree to which they were emotionally, mentally, and physically equipped for frontier life varied. Mort Hawthorne records:

> So we seen them all, coming and going. But the one Mama never got over wondering about was the woman, weighing about one hundred and ten pounds, and all of sixty years old, who came walking down the trail without no pack on her back and wearing regular shoes. She said she was hungry, so Mama filled a plate for her. . . . Mama started asking her more questions about where she came from and how she lived. She said she got along just fine eating berries and fish. Mama asked her how she caught the fish and she said in her shoe.[26]

News of frontier opportunity spread, in print and by word of mouth. Clarissa Griswold decided to come to Nebraska in 1885 in the following way:

> Glowing reports came [to Iowa] of thrills experienced, and fortunes made by some of those who took homesteads in the territory of Dakota. In some cases young women had taken claims adjoining, had a house built covering a corner of each piece of land, and lived together until time to prove up, and receive a deed to the land. These tales were most alluring to me, and some of my girl friends. . . . An invitation came to me from a friend . . .to visit her at her home on a ranch . . . with the added inducement that land could be procured in western Nebraska by meeting the conditions of the federal government. I embraced this opportunity. . . . I had always been accustomed to the hills and woods near the Mississippi river, and did not find the prairie attractive; but youth likes change and I found the people cordial and friendly. . . . I went to Valentine, the nearest land office, and filed for a pre-emption and a tree claim.[27]

Others had previous personal or vicarious experience in homesteading. Land office records reveal that some female settlers had earlier claims further east. For example, in 1887 a woman who filed a claim in Lamar, Colorado also listed an earlier claim in Booneville, Missouri.

Laura Crews was one young woman who, you might say, was schooled in homesteading. Her mother had successfully entered the race for land when the Iowa, Sac and Fox, Pottawatomie, and Shawnee lands were opened in 1891. Laura was the youngest of seven children who had grown up on an earlier homestead in Kansas, and Laura's widowed mother required the children to do equal tasks on the claim. Laura had wanted to join her brothers, who made the race for land when Oklahoma Territory was opened in 1889; however, she was too young. In 1892 when the Cheyenne and Arapahoe lands were opened to homesteading, Laura staked a claim, but found the water on the land was bad and decided to relinquish her stake. She had another opportunity in September, 1893, when the Cherokee Strip was opened. Unlike the free lands granted under the Homestead Act of 1862, the Cherokee land was to be sold at $1.50 to $2.50 per acre to the homesteaders who could stake their claims first; when the signal shot was fired for the race to begin, nearly 100,000 participants began the race from within a 100-foot-wide strip of land that was marked off around the territory. Laura had spent more than a year organizing. Riding astride a saddle horse, she rode seventeen miles in fifty-nine minutes and located a piece of bottom land near a creek. She worked on the claim for years: lived in a dugout, dug a well by hand, and sometimes lived on corn bread and rabbit stew, with her only income the sale of eggs at two cents a dozen. However, some years later, oil was discovered on her land. She never left Garfield County, Oklahoma, where she still lives at the age of 105.[28]

Other women, too, had good role models within their families. Ruth Milliken was one of these women, and her lack of financial resources seems to have made little difference to her. She

> came alone by train . . .to take over her grandmother's section of land fifteen and a half miles from Harrison [Nebraska]. Her homestead house was a one-room tar-papered shack, furnished with a cot, kitchen table, small hearth stove, and two kitchen chairs. Her lights were a kerosene lamp and a lantern. Water was carried one and a half miles until made available on her place, and protection was her grandfather's revolver. Wild game and chicken supplied her meat, and she made her own clothes.[29]

Women, like men, had to deal with the severities of the plains, where everything was scarce except land, sky, and wind. One common hardship faced by Jane Aldrich was the scarcity of water.

> Water at first had to be carried in a two-quart jar from the well of the nearest neighbor, a mile away. Then Aunt Jennie found a covered coffee tin pot of greater and better capacity, for her needs. This system of getting her water supply made Aunt Jennie call her claim, "The Ripples." An ample supply of books filled her shelves. . . . Mother mailed her great bundles of newspapers once a month, often twice. . . . Her violin was almost a living companion to her. She played from her old song book or her memory. Her fingers were stiff and cramped from work. At times the coyotes answered when they came near.[30]

Though she seemed to cope very well, at one point Jane Aldrich wrote:

> . . .I stand within my lowly sod-built walls
> Watching shadows, and the lightning's flame
> And moan, Oh, God, the wretchedness
> Of holding down a claim . . .
> For four years more I must stay here and wait. . . .[31]

Although the law restricted homestead claims to widowed and single females, women filing homestead claims were not always unmarried. Some couples engaged in deception in order to secure sufficient land for a family. Mort Hawthorne writes:

> The stranger had said that the farmers around there had found out they needed more land than 160 acres. . . . He was married but him and his wife was acting like they wasn't. They had built two dugouts on separate homesteads but they'd put them right together at the corner

> stakes. A single woman could file on a separate claim and so his wife had gone down and filed under her maiden name and that way they had got twice as much land in one piece. . . . Mama . . .said she thought she'd speak to the stranger and tell him it wasn't right for him to put his wife in a position where all the neighbors would think she was a loose woman and living in sin. Father said a lot of folks figgered Congress was to blame for making a law that a single woman could file on a homestead but that a married woman with children couldn't.[32]

It is difficult to be certain of the marital status of women entrants for this reason.

Pioneer memoirs often note examples of a woman and a man on adjoining claims meeting and consolidating their land holdings through marriage. Brothers and sisters, as well as male and female friends, sometimes filed on adjoining claims. For example, in August, 1901, Teodocia Cordoba of Garrett, Oklahoma, filed a claim of 160 acres at the Lamar, Colorado land office, followed by a neighboring claimant, Feransisco Sisneros, also of Garrett, Oklahoma. In June, 1903, they both made their claims final with a cash entry. It seems unlikely that they were strangers; however, it has not been possible to determine the nature of their relationship. It does seem likely that they knew one another previously since they came from the same place at the same time. Friends and relatives who homesteaded together provided tremendous support for one another.

Pioneer women made major economic contributions to homestead society. Married women cared for the house, the garden, the fields, the livestock, and the children. Often the money that the wife earned from selling butter and eggs provided capital for a windmill or farm machinery or saved the homestead from the mortgage holder in hard times. Wives also singlehandedly tended the homesteads while the husbands worked for wages elsewhere. Adolescent daughters of homesteaders took work as hired girls, schoolteachers, and seamstresses, and the cash they contributed to their families paid for such diverse things as seeds, shoes for the younger children, and Belgian carpets to improve the farm home. Single women farmed, taught school, and sometimes held down jobs in businesses in nearby towns in order to earn funds for developing their homesteads.

Women served as midwives to their sisters and nurses to everyone. Childbirth was often a lonely experience, but women depended on other women. Mrs. R. O. Andrew recalls:

> I was born in a sod house July 25, 1894, in Norton County, Kansas. The thermometer reached a high that day of 133 degrees, with a 55 mile per hour wind. The green corn was burned to a crisp. No doctors were nearby so a midwife was sent for. Father asked what he owed her and she asked for a used saddle of his.[33]

Patterson-Black

Many found the hard life worthwhile. Lottie Gilmore wrote:

> Yes, I have gone to bed hungry so the younger ones could have food. I have worn one dress every day to [teach] school for a year, washing and ironing it on Saturday. But we always had a lot of fun. I had beautiful hair then, and laughing eyes, and dimples, and the good Lord kept me in good health.[34]

Another pioneer recalls, "My favorite babysitter was a dear old Grandma Olsen. She smoked a corncob pipe, and crooned some lovely Islander lullabies."[35]

Housekeeping had its difficulties, and its humor. Many newcomers to the prairie wore gloves to handle the "cow wood" or buffalo chips which were used for fuel. Old-timers often said you could tell when new settlers were hardened to prairie life: they were too busy to wear gloves. Cooking with "cow wood" was also a time-consuming nuisance, as it burned quickly. Charley O'Kieffe writes:

> For the edification of housewives who may never have cooked with buffalo chips, here is a rundown of the operation that Mother went through when making baking powder biscuits, for instance. It goes like this: Stoke the stove, get out the flour sack, stoke the stove, wash your hands, mix the biscuit dough, stoke the stove, wash your hands, cut out the biscuits with the top of a baking-powder can, stoke the stove, wash your hands, put the pan of biscuits in the oven, keep on stoking the stove until the biscuits are done. Mother had to go through this tedious routine three times a day excepting when what she was cooking did not require the use of the oven.[36]

Housekeeping was a problem; often the nature of the house itself was a major concern. Sod roofs were notorious for their susceptibility to leakage, and fleas were a common, almost unavoidable, element in life in a dugout. Many women were appalled at the housing conditions they found on the frontier:

> "Where is this house I'm supposed to keep?" she asked, wondering if they were to sleep under the stars. The brothers pointed down; they were standing atop their sod dugout. The Dane smiled as she recalled that she had cried for months at the despair of keeping house in a dirt home, "never knowing when to stop dusting."[37]

Jane Shellhase recalled: "Well do I remember the remark my mother and grandmother made. They had gone to visit a neighbor [who lived in a soddy], and one said to the other, 'She isn't a very good housekeeper; she has grass growing under her bed.'"[38]

Mrs. H. C. Stuckey remembered:

> From hardly any rain we soon had more than we needed. . . . Sometimes the water would drip on the stove while I was cooking, and I would have to keep tight lids on the skillets to prevent the mud from falling into the food. With my dress pinned up, and rubbers on my feet, I waded around until the clouds rolled by.[39]

Some homestead women were political activists and others were the victims of politics. In the early 1870's, Mary E. Lease, born in Ireland, came to Kansas to teach school. She married and lived a lonely farm life until a mortgage foreclosure forced her and her husband to move to town to earn a living. Mary took in washing and studied law. She became active in the Farmers' Alliance and made 161 speeches in the successful campaign of 1890. One western farmer recorded in his diary, "Went to town to hear Joint discussion between Mrs. Lease and John M. Brumbaugh. Poor Brumbaugh was not in it." In 1890 she made her most famous speech, advising the settlers, "What you farmers need is to raise less corn and more hell!"[40]

At least two land-holding women were lynched on the agricultural frontier, Elizabeth Taylor of Clay County, Nebraska, and Ella Watson on the Sweetwater in Wyoming. Elizabeth Taylor was accused of arranging for a young man (who could not be located later) to shoot down some men who had been taking timber from land on which she had a claim. She was hanged from a bridge by a lynch mob in 1885. Ella Watson was hanged from the limb of a pine tree following a dispute with, or over, cowboys.[41]

These women represent only a small part of the variety of homestead women on the Great Plains frontier. When I recall the vast numbers of women homesteaders and the vital stories I have read and repeated describing their contributions, enthusiasm, and success in securing their claims, I bristle at the myopic vision of Hamlin Garland when he wrote:

> Even my youthful zeal faltered in the midst of a revelation of the lives led by women on the farms of the middle border. Before the tragic futility of their suffering, my pen refused to shed its ink.[42]

I, however, will continue to research women's experience on the agricultural frontier, for too long have their achievements been hidden. And my pen will not stop until I have explored the exhilarating variety of the women homesteaders.

Patterson-Black

NOTES

I gratefully acknowledge Gene Patterson-Black for his encouragement, assistance with land office records, and suggestions of literature. I thank Julie Herdt for her enthusiastic company during many days of plains travel and her assistance with interviews and technicalities.

I wish to clarify that people of many ethnic and racial backgrounds filed claims under the various homestead acts. Although Anglos of both U. S. and European origin were the predominant group, it would be difficult to tabulate exact numbers of various groups because land office records include neither race, place of birth, nor sex. One works primarily with the name; Spanish surnames, for example, are detectable. A large number of blacks homesteaded when they relocated after the Civil War. It is important to remember that all homestead lands once belonged to the Native Americans. The Dawes Severalty Act of 1887 dissolved the communal organization of western Indian tribes, but granted homestead rights to individual members of tribes.

1. Roy M. Robbins, Our Landed Heritage: The Public Domain, 1776-1936 (1942; rpt. Lincoln: University of Nebraska Press, 1962), p. 375.

2. D. E. Ball and G. M. Walton, "Agricultural Productivity Change in Eighteenth-Century Pennsylvania," Journal of Economic History, 36 (1976), 102-25, list single female land ownership as 1 percent in 1725, 2 percent in 1754, and 3 percent in 1791.

3. Everett Dick, "Sunbonnet and Calico: The Homesteader's Consort," Nebraska History 47 (1966), 3-14.

4. T. A. Larson, "Dolls, Vassals, and Drudges--Pioneer Women in the West," Western Historical Quarterly 3 (1972), 5-16.

5. Mari Sandoz, "Pioneer Women," in Hostiles and Friendlies: Selected Short Writings of Mari Sandoz, ed. Virginia Faulkner (Lincoln: University of Nebraska Press, 1959), p. 59.

6. Virginia Faulkner, ed., Hostiles and Friendlies, p. 60.

7. O. E. Rolvaag, Giants in the Earth: A Saga of the Prairie (New York: Harper and Brothers, 1928), pp. 28-29.

8. Gilbert C. Fite, The Farmer's Frontier (San Francisco: Holt, Rinehart, and Winston, 1966), p. 15.

9. Hamlin Garland, A Son of the Middle Border (New York: Macmillan Company, 1917), pp. 235-38.

Patterson-Black

[10] Hamlin Garland, "Women and Their Organization," The Standard, October 8, 1890, p. 5.

[11] Willa Cather, O Pioneers! (Boston: Houghton Mifflin Company, 1913), p. 83.

[12] Mari Sandoz, Old Jules Country (New York: Hastings House, 1965), p. 292.

[13] Charley O'Kieffe, Western Story: The Recollections of Charley O'Kieffe, 1884-1898 (Lincoln: University of Nebraska Press, 1960), pp. 3-4.

[14] John Ise, Sod and Stubble: The Story of a Kansas Homestead (1936; rpt. Lincoln: University of Nebraska Press, 1967), p. xi.

[15] A. B. Wood, ed., Pioneer Tales of the North Platte Valley and Nebraska Panhandle (Gering, Nebraska: Courier Press, 1938), p. 77.

[16] Ruth Van Ackeren, ed., Sioux County: Memoirs of Its Pioneers (Harrison, Nebraska: Harrison Sun-News, 1967), p. 82.

[17] Roger L. Welsch, Sod Walls: The Story of the Nebraska Sod House (Broken Bow, Nebraska: Purcells, Inc., 1968), p. 127.

[18] Mari Sandoz, Old Jules (1935; rpt. Lincoln: University of Nebraska Press, 1962), p. 385.

[19] Ibid., pp. 380-82.

[20] Elinore Pruitt Stewart, Letters of a Woman Homesteader (1914; rpt. Lincoln: University of Nebraska Press, 1961), p. 8.

[21] Donald F. Danker, ed., Mollie: The Journal of Mollie Dorsey Sanford in Nebraska and Colorado Territories, 1857-1866 (Lincoln: University of Nebraska Press, 1959), pp. 21, 33.

[22] Wood, p. 60.

[23] Garland, Son of the Middle Border, p. 244.

[24] Mrs. E. J. Guerin, Mountain Charley, or The Adventures of Mrs. E. J. Guerin, Who Was Thirteen Years in Male Attire (1861; rpt. Norman: University of Oklahoma Press, 1968), p. 37.

[25] Mari Sandoz, Slogum House (Boston: Little, Brown and Company, 1937), pp. 9, 212.

[26] Martha Ferguson McKeown, Them Was the Days: An American Saga of the '70's (1950; rpt. Lincoln: University of Nebraska Press, 1961), p. 129.

Patterson-Black

[27] Wood, p. 188.

[28] Lynette Wert, "The Lady Stakes a Claim," Persimmon Hill, 6, No. 2 (1976), 18-23.

[29] Van Ackeren, p. 157.

[30] Frances Jacobs Alberts, ed., Sod House Memories, Sod House Society Series, I (1963; rpt. Hastings, Nebraska: Sod House Society, 1972), p. 51.

[31] Ibid., p. 6.

[32] McKeown, p. 95.

[33] Frances Jacobs Alberts, ed., Sod House Memories, Sod House Society Series, II (1967; rpt. Hastings, Nebraska: Sod House Society, 1972), p. 99.

[34] Ibid., p. 121.

[35] Alberts, Sod House Society Series, I, p. 61.

[36] O'Kieffe, p. 26.

[37] Roger L. Welsch, Shingling the Fog and Other Plains Lies (Chicago: Swallow Press, 1972), p. 126.

[38] Alberts, Sod House Society Series, II, p. 163.

[39] Welsch, Sod Walls, p. 38.

[40] Martin F. Schmitt, with Dee Brown, The Settlers' West (1955; rpt. New York: Ballantine Books, 1974), pp. 154-55.

[41] Jean Williams, The Lynching of Elizabeth Taylor (Santa Fe: Press of The Territorian, 1966), pp. 5-6; Harry Sinclair Drago, Notorious Ladies of the Frontier (New York: Ballantine Books, 1972), I, p. xi.

[42] Garland, Son of the Middle Border, p. 416.

Patterson-Black

ADDITIONAL REFERENCES

Alderson, Nannie T. and Helena Huntington Smith. A Bride Goes West. 1942; rpt. Lincoln: University of Nebraska Press, 1969.

Babb, Sanora. An Owl on Every Post. 1970; rpt. New York: New American Library, 1972.

Borland, Hal. High, Wide, and Lonesome. Philadelphia: J. B. Lippincott and Company, 1956.

Brad, Jacoba Boothman. Homestead on the Kootenai. Caldwell, Idaho: Caxton Printers, 1960.

Brown, Dee. The Gentle Tamers. 1958; rpt. New York: Bantam Books, 1974.

Buckley, Joy. Personal interviews.

Butcher, Solomon D. Pioneer History of Custer County, Nebraska. 1901; rpt. Denver: Sage Books, 1965.

Cameron, Roderick. Pioneer Days in Kansas. Belleville, Kansas: Cameron Book Company, 1951.

Cather, Willa. My Antonia. Boston: Houghton Mifflin Company, 1918.

Davis, Marian Colt. I Went to Kansas. Watertown, New York, 1862.

Dick, Everett. The Sod House Frontier. New York: Appleton-Century, 1937.

__________. Tales of the Frontier: From Lewis and Clark to the Last Roundup. Lincoln: University of Nebraska Press, 1963.

Fowler, William W. Woman on the Frontier. Hartford: S. S. Scranton, 1876.

Garland, Hamlin. Boy Life on the Prairie. 1899; rpt. Lincoln: University of Nebraska Press, 1961.

__________. A Daughter of the Middle Border. New York: Macmillan Company, 1921.

__________. Main-Travelled Roads. New York: Harper and Brothers, 1891.

__________. "A Prairie Heroine." In The Arena. Boston: Arena Publishing Company, 1891, pp. 223-46.

Patterson-Black

Gilland, Mrs. George H. "Pioneer Patchwork." Annals of Wyoming, October, 1939, pp. 254-76.

Hafen, LeRoy R. Western America. Englewood Cliffs, New Jersey: Prentice-Hall, 1950.

Hargar, Charles Moreau. "The Prairie Woman: Yesterday and Today." The Outlook. April 26, 1902.

Haskell, Pansy. Personal interviews.

Hazard, Lucy Lockwood. The Frontier in American Literature. New York: Thomas Y. Crowell Company, 1927.

Hine, Robert V. and Edwin R. Bingham. The Frontier Experience. Belmont, California: Wadsworth Publishing Company, 1963.

Holloway, Jean. Hamlin Garland: A Biography. Austin: University of Texas Press, 1959.

Humphrey, Seth K. Following the Prairie Frontier. Minneapolis: University of Minnesota Press, 1931.

Jeffson, Emma. Personal interviews.

Jones, John C. and Winoma. The Prairie Pioneers of Western Kansas and Eastern Colorado. Boulder, Colorado: Johnson Publishing Company, 1956.

Kennedy, Cecil and Leonard. Personal interviews.

Kraenzel, Carl Frederick. The Great Plains in Transition. Norman: University of Oklahoma Press, 1955.

Laughlin, Estelle Chrisman. "Dr. Georgia Arbuckle Fix: Pioneer." In A. B. Wood, ed., Pioneer Tales of the North Platte Valley and Nebraska Panhandle. Gering, Nebraska: Courier Press, 1938, pp. 21-194.

Leach, A. J. A History of Antelope County, Nebraska, From Its First Settlement in 1868 to the Close of the Year 1883. Chicago: R. R. Donnelley and Sons Company, 1909.

McGrew, Mrs. Kittie. "Women of Territorial Nebraska." Publications of the Nebraska State Historical Society 19 (1919), 95-102.

Mechem, Kirke, ed. Annals of Kansas, 1886-1925. Topeka: Kansas State Historical Society, n. d. 2 volumes.

Miller, Helen Markley. Westering Women. New York: Doubleday, 1961.

Miller, Isabel. Patience and Sarah. New York: McGraw-Hill Book Company, 1969.

Moody, Ralph. Little Britches: Father and I Were Ranchers. New York: W. W. Norton and Company, 1950.

Nelson, David T., trans. and ed. The Diary of Elisabeth Koren: 1853-1855. Northfield, Minnesota: Norwegian-American Historical Association, 1955.

Nichols, Olive. Personal interviews.

Nicoll, Bruce, ed. Nebraska: A Pictorial History. Lincoln: University of Nebraska Press, 1967.

Olson, James C. History of Nebraska. Lincoln: University of Nebraska Press, 1955.

Orpen, Mrs. Memories of the Old Emigrant Days in Kansas: 1862-1865. New York: Harper and Brothers, 1928.

Parker, Nathan H. The Kansas and Nebraska Handbook for 1857-58. Boston: John P. Jewett and Company, 1857.

Pizer, Donald. Hamlin Garland's Early Work and Career. Berkeley and Los Angeles: University of California Press, 1960.

Reid, Agnes Just. Letters of Long Ago. Caldwell, Idaho: Caxton Printers, 1936.

Robinson, Sara T. D. Kansas: Its Interior and Exterior Life. Lawrence, Kansas: Journal Publishing Company, 1899.

Roe, Elizabeth A. Recollections of Frontier Life. Rockford, 1885.

Ropes, Mrs. H. A. Six Months in Kansas. Boston: John P. Jewett and Company, 1856.

Royce, Sarah. A Frontier Lady: Recollections of the Gold Rush and Early California. Ed. Ralph Henry Gabriel. New Haven: Yale University Press, 1932.

Sandoz, Mari. Love Song to the Plains. 1961; rpt. Lincoln: University of Nebraska Press, 1966.

________. Miss Morissa: Doctor of the Gold Trail. New York: Hastings House, 1955.

Patterson-Black

Smythe, William E. The Conquest of Arid America. New York: Macmillan Company, 1907.

Webb, Walter Prescott. The Great Plains. New York: Grosset and Dunlap, 1931.

Welsch, Roger L. A Treasury of Nebraska Pioneer Folklore. 1939; rpt. Lincoln: University of Nebraska Press, 1966.

Wetterstrom, Maudene. Personal interviews.

Wheat, Carl I., ed. The Shirley Letters from the California Mines, 1851-1852. New York: Alfred A. Knopf, 1949.

Whitney, Fr. Clyde. Personal interviews.

Wilder, Laura Ingalls. By the Shores of Silver Lake. New York: Harper and Row, 1939.

Woestemeyer, Ina Faye. The Westward Movement. New York: Appleton-Century, 1939.

WOMEN AND THEIR FAMILIES ON THE OVERLAND TRAIL TO CALIFORNIA AND OREGON, 1842-1867

Johnny Faragher and Christine Stansell

> I am not a wheatfield
> nor the virgin forest
>
> I never chose this place
> yet I am of it now
>
> —Adrienne Rich
> "From an Old House in America"

From 1841 until 1867, the year in which the transcontinental railroad was completed, nearly 350,000 North Americans emigrated to the Pacific coast along the western wagon road known variously as the Oregon, the California, or simply the Overland Trail. This migration was essentially a family phenomenon. Although single men constituted the majority of the party which pioneered large-scale emigration on the Overland Trail in 1841, significant numbers of women and children were already present in the wagon trains of the next season. Families made up the preponderant proportion of the migrations throughout the 1840s. In 1849, during the overwhelmingly male Gold Rush, the number dropped precipitously, but after 1851 families once again assumed dominance in the overland migration.[1] The contention that "the family was the one substantial social institution" on the frontier is too sweeping, yet it is underniable that the white family largely mediated the incorporation of the western territories into the American nation.[2]

The emigrating families were a heterogeneous lot. Some came from farms in the midwest and upper South, many from small midwestern towns, and others from northeastern and midwestern cities. Clerks and shopkeepers as well as farmers outfitted their wagons in Independence, St. Louis, or Westport Landing on the Missouri. Since costs for supplies, travel, and settlement were not negligible,[3] few of the very poor were present, nor were the exceptionally prosperous. The dreams of fortune which lured the wagon trains into new lands were those of modest men whose hopes were pinned to small farms or larger dry-goods stores, more fertile soil or more customers, better market prospects and a steadily expanding economy.

For every member of the family, the trip West was exhausting, toilsome, and often grueling. Each year in late spring, westbound emigrants gathered for the journey at spots along the Missouri River and moved out in parties of ten to several hundred wagons. Aggregates of nuclear families, loosely attached by kinship or friendship. traveled together or joined an even larger caravan.[4] Coast-bound families traveled by ox-drawn wagons at the frustratingly slow pace of fifteen to twenty miles per day. They worked their way up the Platte River valley through what is now Kansas and Nebraska, crossing the Rockies at South Pass in southwestern Wyoming by mid-summer. The Platte route was relatively easy going, but from present-day Idaho, where the roads to California and Oregon diverged. to their final destinations, the pioneers faced disastrous conditions: scorching deserts, boggy salt flats, and rugged mountains. By this time, families had been on the road some three months and were only at the midpoint of the journey; the environment, along with the wear of the road, made the last months difficult almost beyond endurance. Finally, in late fall or early winter the pioneers straggled into their promised lands, after six months and over two thousand miles of hardship.[5]

As this journey progressed, bare necessity became the determinant of most of each day's activities. The primary task of surviving and getting to the coast gradually suspended accustomed patterns of dividing work between women and men. All able-bodied adults worked all day in one way or another to keep the family moving. Women's work was no less indispensable than men's; indeed, as the summer wore on, the boundaries dividing the work of the sexes were threatened, blurred, and transgressed.

The vicissitudes of the trail opened new possibilities for expanded work roles for women, and in the cooperative work of the family there existed a basis for a vigorous struggle for female-male equality. But most women did not see the experience in this way. They viewed it as a male enterprise from its very inception. Women experienced the breakdown of the sexual division of labor as a dissolution of their own autonomous "sphere." Bereft of the footing which this independent base gave them, they lacked a cultural rationale for the work they did, and remained estranged from the possibilities of the enlarged scope and power of family life on the trail. Instead, women fought *against* the forces of necessity to hold together the few fragments of female subculture left to them. We have been bequeathed a remarkable record of this struggle in the diaries, journals, and memoirs of emigrating women. In this study, we will examine a particular habit of living, or culture, in conflict with the new material circumstances of the Trail, and the efforts of women to maintain a place, a sphere of their own.

The overland family was not a homogeneous unit, its members imbued with identical aspirations and desires. On the contrary, the period of westward movement was also one of multiplying schisms within those families whose location and social status placed them in the mainstream of national culture.[6] Child-rearing tracts, housekeeping manuals, and etiquette books by the hundreds proscribed and rationalized to these Americans a radical separation of the work responsibilities and social duties of mothers and fathers; popular thought assigned unique personality traits, spiritual capacities, and forms of experience to the respective categories of man, woman, and child.[7] In many families, the tensions inherent in this separatist ideology, often repressed in the everyday routines of the East, erupted under the strain of the overland crossing. The difficulties of the emigrants, while inextricably linked to the duress of the journey itself, also revealed family dynamics which had been submerged in the less eventful life "back home."

A full blown ideology of "woman's place" was absent in preindustrial America. On farms, in artisan shops, and in town marketplaces, women and children made essential contributions to family income and subsistence; it was the family which functioned as the basic unit of production in the colony and the young nation. As commercial exchanges displaced the local markets where women had sold surplus dairy products and textiles, and the workplace drifted away from the household, women and children lost their breadwinning prerogatives.[8]

In Jacksonian America, a doctrine of "sexual spheres" arose to facilitate and justify the segregation of women into the home and men into productive work.[9] While the latter attended to politics, economics, and wage-earning, popular thought assigned women the refurbished and newly professionalized tasks of child-rearing and housekeeping.[10] A host of corollaries followed on the heels of these shifts. Men were physically strong, women naturally delicate: men were skilled in particical matters, women in moral and emotional concerns: men were prone to corruption, women to virtue; men belonged in the world, women in the home. For women, the system of sexual spheres represented a decline in social status and isolation from political and economic power. Yet it also provided them with a psychological power base of undeniable importance. The "cult of true womanhood" was more than simply a retreat. Catharine Beecher, one of the chief theorists of "woman's influence," proudly quoted Tocqueville's observation that "in no country has such constant care been taken, as in America, to trace two clearly distinct lines of action for the two sexes, and to make them keep pace with the other, but in two pathways which are always different."[11] Neither Beecher nor her sisters were simply dupes of a masculine imperialism. The supervision of child-rearing, household economy, and the moral and religious life of the family granted women a certain degree of real autonomy and control over their lives as well as those of their husbands and children.

Indeed, recent scholarship has indicated that a distinctly female subculture emerged from "woman's sphere." By "subculture" we simply mean a "habit of living"—as we have used "culture" above—of a minority group which is self-consciously distinct from the dominant activities, expectations, and values of a society. Historians have seen female church groups, reform associations, and philanthropic activity as expressions of this subculture in actual behavior, while a large and rich body of writing by and for women articulated the subcultural impulses on the ideational level. Both behavior and thought point to child-rearing, religious activity, education, home life, associationism, and female communality as components of women's subculture. Female friendships, strikingly intimate and deep in this period, formed the actual bonds.[12] Within their tight and atomized family households, women carved out a life of their own.

At its very inception, the western emigration sent tremors through the foundations of this carefully compartmentalized family structure. The rationale behind pulling up stakes was nearly always economic advancement;[13] since breadwinning was a masculine concern, the husband and father introduced the idea of going West and made the final decision. Family participation in the intervening time ran the gamut from enthusiastic support to stolid resistance. Many women cooperated with their ambitious spouses: "The motive that induced us to part with pleasant associations and the dear friends of our childhood days, was to obtain from the government of the United States a grant of land that 'Uncle Sam' had promised to give to the head of each family who settled in this new country."[14] Others, however, only acquiesced. "Poor Ma said only this morning, 'Oh, I wish we never had started,' " Lucy Cooke wrote her first day on the trail, "and she looks so sorrowful and dejected. I think if Pa had not passengers to take through she would urge him to return; not that he should be so inclined."[15] Huddled with her children in a cold, damp wagon, trying to calm them despite the ominous chanting of visiting Indians, another woman wondered "what had possessed my husband, anyway, that he should have thought of bringing us away out through this God forsaken country."[16] Similar alienation from the "pioneer spirit" haunted Lavinia Porter's leave-taking:

> I never recall that sad parting from my dear sister on the plains of Kansas without the tears flowing fast and free. . . . We were the eldest of a large family, and the bond of affection and love that existed between us was strong indeed . . . as she with the other friends turned to leave me for the ferry which was to take them back to home and civilization, I stood alone on that wild prairie. Looking westward I saw my husband driving slowly over the plain; turning my face once more to the east, my dear sister's footsteps were fast widening the distance between us. For the time I knew not which way to go, nor whom to follow. But in a few moments I rallied my forces . . . and soon overtook the slowly moving oxen who were bearing my husband and child over the green prairie . . . the unbidden tears would flow in spite of my brave resolve to be the courageous and valiant frontierswoman.[17]

Her dazed vacillation soon gave way to a private conviction that the family had made a dire mistake: "I would make a brave effort to be cheerful and patient until the camp work was done. Then starting out ahead of the team and my men folks, when I thought I had gone beyond hearing distance, I would throw myself down on the unfriendly desert and give way like a child to sobs and tears, wishing myself back home with my friends and chiding myself for consenting to take this wild goose chase."[18] Men viewed drudgery, calamity, and privation as trials along the road to prosperity, unfortunate but inevitable corollaries of the rational decision they had made. But to those women who were unable to appropriate the vision of the upwardly mobile pilgrimage, hardship and loss only testified to the inherent folly of the emigration, "this wild goose chase."

If women were reluctant to accompany their men, however, they were often equally unwilling to let them go alone. In the late 1840s, the conflict between wives and their gold-crazed husbands reveals the determination with which women enforced the cohesion of the nuclear family. In the name of family unity, some obdurate wives simply chose to blockbust the sexually segregated Gold Rush: "My husband grew enthusiastic and wanted to start immediately," one woman recalled, "but I would not be left behind. I thought where he could go I could and where I went I could take my two little toddling babies."[19] Her family departed intact. Other women used their moral authority to smash the enterprise in its planning stages. "We were married to live together," a wife acidly reminded her spouse when he informed her of his intention to join the Rush: "I am willing to go with you to any part of *God's Foot Stool* where you think you can do best, and under these circumstances you have no right to go where I cannot, and if you do you need never return for I shall look upon you as dead."[20] Roundly chastised, the man postponed his journey until the next season, when his family could leave with him. When included in the plans, women seldom wrote of their husbands' decisions to emigrate in their diaries or memoirs. A breadwinner who tried to leave alone, however, threatened the family unity upon which his authority was based; only then did a wife challenge his dominance in worldly affairs.[21]

There was an economic reason for the preponderance of families on the Trail. Women and children, but especially women, formed an essential supplementary work force in the settlements. The ideal wife in the West resembled a hired hand more than a nurturant Christian housekeeper.[22] Narcissa Whitman wrote frankly to aspiring settlers of the functional necessity of women on the new farms: "Let every young man bring a wife, for he will want one after he gets here, if he never did before."[23] In a letter from California, another seasoned woman warned a friend in Missouri that in the West women became "hewers of wood and drawers of water everywhere."[24] Mrs. Whitman's fellow missionary Elkanah Walker was unabashedly practical in beseeching his wife to join him: "I am tired of keeping an old bachelor's hall. I want someone to get me a good supper and let me take my ease and when I am very tired in the morning I want someone to get up and get breakfast and let me lay in bed and take my rest."[25] It would be both simplistic and harsh to argue that men brought their families West or married because of the labor power of women and children; there is no doubt, however, that the new Westerners appreciated the advantages of familial labor. Women were not superfluous; they were workers. The migration of women helped to solve the problem of labor scarcity, not only in the early years of the American settlement on the coast, but throughout the history of the continental frontier.[26]

In the first days of the overland trip, new work requirements were not yet pressing and the division of labor among family members still replicated familiar patterns. Esther Hanna reported in one of her first diary entries that "our men have gone to build a bridge across the stream, which is impassable," while she baked her first bread on the prairie.[27] Elizabeth Smith similarly described her party's day: "rainy . . . Men making rafts. Women cooking and washing. Children crying."[28] When travel was suspended, "the men were generally busy mending wagons, harnesses, yokes, shoeing the animals etc., and the women washed clothes, boiled a big mess of beans, to warm over for several meals, or perhaps mended clothes."[29] At first, even in emergencies, women and men hardly considered integrating their work. "None but those who have cooked for a family of eight, crossing the plains, have any idea of what it takes," a disgruntled woman recalled: "My sister-in-law was sick, my niece was much younger than I, and consequently I had the management of all the cooking and planning on my young shoulders."[30] To ask a man to help was a possibility she was unable even to consider.[31]

The relegation of women to purely domestic duties, however, soon broke down under the vicissitudes of the Trail. Within the first few weeks, the unladylike task of gathering buffalo dung for fuel (little firewood was available *en route*) became women's work.[32] As one traveler astutely noted, "force of surroundings was a great leveler"; [33] miles of grass, dust, glare, and mud erased some of the most rudimentary distinctions between female and male responsibilities. By summer, women often helped drive the wagons and the livestock.[34] At one Platte crossing, "the men drawed the wagons over by hand and the women all crossed in safety"; but at the next, calamity struck when the bridge collapsed, "and then commenced the hurry and bustle of repairing; all were at work, even the women and children."[35] Such crises, which compounded daily as the wagons moved past the Platte up the long stretches of desert and coastal mountains, generated equity in work; at times of Indian threats, for example, both women and men made bullets and stood guard.[36] When mountain fever struck the Pengra family as they crossed the Rockies, Charlotte relieved her incapacitated husband of the driving while he took care of the youngest child.[37] Only such severe afflictions forced men to take on traditionally female chores. While women did men's work, there is little evidence that men reciprocated.

Following a few days in the life of an overland woman discloses the magnitude of her work. During the hours her party traveled, Charlotte Pengra walked beside the wagons, driving the cattle and gathering buffalo chips. At night she cooked, baked bread for the next noon meal, and washed clothes. Three successive summer days illustrate how trying these small chores could be. Her train pulled out early on a Monday morning, only to be halted by rain and a flash flood; Mrs. Pengra washed and dried her family's wet clothes in the afternoon while doing her daily baking. On Tuesday the wagons pushed hard to make up for lost time, forcing her to trot all day to keep up. In camp that night there was no time to rest. Before going to bed, she wrote, "Kept busy in preparing tea and doing other things preparatory for the morrow. I baked a cracker pudding, warm biscuits and made tea, and after supper stewed two pans of dried apples, and made two loaves of bread, got my work done up, beds made, and child asleep, and have written in my journal. Pretty tired of course." The same routine devoured the next day and evening: "I have done a washing. Stewed apples, made pies and baked a rice pudding, and mended our wagon cover. Rather tired." And the next: "baked biscuits, stewed berries, fried meat, boiled and mashed potatoes, and made tea for supper, afterward baked bread. Thus you see I have not much rest."[38] Children also burdened women's work and leisure. During one quiet time, Helen Stewart retreated in mild defiance from her small charges to a tent in order to salvage some private time: "It exceeding hot . . . some of the men is out hunting and some of them sleeping. The children is grumbling and crying and laughing and howling and playing all around."[39] Although children are notably absent in women's journals, they do appear, frightened and imploring, during an Indian scare or a storm, or intrude into a rare and precious moment of relaxation, "grumbling and crying."[40]

Because the rhythm of their chores was out of phase with that of the men, the division of labor could be especially taxing to women. Men's days were toilsome but broken up at regular intervals with periods of rest. Men hitched the teams, drove or walked until noon, relaxed at dinner, traveled until the evening camp, unhitched the oxen, ate supper, and in the evening sat at the campfire, mended equipment, or stood guard. They also provided most of the labor in emergencies, pulling the wagons through mires, across treacherous river crossings, up long grades, and down precipitous slopes. In the pandemonium of a steep descent,

> you would see the women and children in advance seeking the best way, some of them slipping down, or holding on to the rocks, now taking an "otter slide," and then a run til some natural obstacle presented itself to stop their accelerated progress and those who get down safely without a hurt or a bruise, are fortunate indeed. Looking back to the train, you would see some of the men holding on to the wagons, others slipping under the oxen's feet, some throwing articles out of the way that had fallen out, and all have enough to do to keep them busily occupied.[41]

Women were responsible for staying out of the way and getting themselves and the children to safety, men for getting the wagons down. Women's work, far less demanding of brute strength and endurance, was nevertheless distributed without significant respite over all waking hours: mealtimes offered no leisure to the cooks. "The plain fact of the matter is," a young woman complained,

> we *have no time for sociability*. From the time we get up in the morning, until we are on the road, it is hurry scurry to get breakfast and put away the things that necessarily had to be pulled out last night—while under way there is no room in the wagon for a visitor, nooning is barely long enough to eat a cold bite—and at night all the cooking utensils and provisions are to be gotten about the camp fire, and cooking enough to last until the next night.[42]

After supper, the men gathered together, "lolling and smoking their pipes and guessing, or maybe betting, how many miles we had covered during the day,"[43] while the women baked, washed, and put the children to bed before they finally sat down. Charlotte Pengra found "as I was told before I started that there is no rest in such a journey."[44]

Unaccustomed tasks beset the travelers, who were equipped with only the familiar expectation that work was divided along gender lines. The solutions which sexual "spheres" offered were usually irrelevant to the new problems facing families. Women, for example, could not afford to be delicate: their new duties demanded far greater stamina and hardiness than their traditional domestic tasks. With no tradition to deal with the new exigencies of fuel-gathering, cattle-driving, and cooking, families found that "the division of labor in a party . . . was a prolific cause of quarrel."[45] Within the Vincent party, "assignments to duty were not accomplished without grumbling and objection . . . there were occasional angry debates while the various burdens were being adjusted," while in "the camps of others who sometimes jogged along the trail in our company . . . we saw not a little fighting . . . and these bloody fisticuffs were invariably the outcome of disputes over division of labor."[46] At home, these assignments were familiar and accepted, not subject to questioning. New work opened the division of labor to debate and conflict.

By midjourney, most women worked at male tasks. The men still retained dominance within their "sphere," despite the fact that it was no longer exclusively masculine. Like most women, Lavinia Porter was responsible for gathering buffalo chips for fuel. One afternoon, spying a grove of cottonwoods half a mile away, she asked her husband to branch off the trail so that the party could fell trees for firewood, thus easing her work. "But men on the plains I had found were not so accomodating, nor so ready to wait upon women as they were in more civilized communities." Her husband refused and Porter fought back: "I was feeling somewhat under the weather and unusually tired, and crawling into the wagon told them if they wanted fuel for the evening meal they could get it themselves and cook the meal also, and laying my head down on a pillow, I cried myself to sleep."[47] Later that evening her husband awakened her with a belated dinner he had prepared himself, but despite his conciliatory spirit their relations were strained for weeks: "James and I had gradually grown silent and taciturn and had unwittingly partaken of the gloom and somberness of the dreary landscape."[48] No longer a housewife or a domestic ornament, but a laborer in a male arena, Porter was still subordinate to her husband in practical matters.

Lydia Waters recorded another clash between new work and old consciousness: "I had learned to drive an ox team on the Platte and my driving was admired by an officer and his wife who were going with the mail to Salt Lake City." Pleased with the compliment, she later overheard them "laughing at the thought of a woman driving oxen."[49] By no means did censure come only from men. The officer's wife as well as the officer derided Lydia Waters, while her own mother indirectly reprimanded teenaged Mary Ellen Todd. "All along our journey, I had tried to crack that big whip," Mary Ellen remembered years later:

> Now while out at the wagon we kept trying until I was fairly successful. How my heart bounded a few days later when I chanced to hear father say to mother, "Do you know that Mary Ellen is beginning to crack the whip." Then how it fell again when mother replied, "I am afraid it isn't a very lady-like thing for a girl to do." After this, while I felt a secret joy in being able to have a power that set things going, there was also a sense of shame over this new accomplishment.[50]

To understand Mrs. Todd's primness, so incongruous in the rugged setting of the Trail, we must see it in the context of a broader struggle on the part of women to preserve the home in transit. Against the leveling forces of the Plains, women tried to maintain the standards of cleanliness and order that had prevailed in their homes back East:

Our caravan had a good many women and children and although we were probably longer on the journey owing to their presence—they exerted a good influence, as the men did not take such risks with Indians . . . were more alert about the care of teams and seldom had accidents; more attention was paid to cleanliness and sanitation and, lastly, but not of less importance, meals were more regular and better cooked thus preventing much sickness and there was less waste of food.[51]

Sarah Royce remembered that family wagons "were easily distinguished by the greater number of conveniences, and household articles they carried."[52] In the evenings, or when the trains stopped for a day, women had a chance to create with these few props a flimsy facsimile of the home.

Even in camp women had little leisure time, but within the "hurry scurry" of work they managed to recreate the routine of the home. Indeed, a female subculture, central to the communities women had left behind, reemerged in these settings. At night, women often clustered together, chatting, working, or commiserating, instead of joining the men: "High teas were not popular, but tatting, knitting, crochetting, exchanging recipes for cooking beans or dried apples or swopping food for the sake of variety kept us in practice of feminine occupations and diversions."[53] Besides using the domestic concerns of the Trail to reconstruct a female sphere, women also consciously invoked fantasy: "Mrs. Fox and her daughter are with us and everything is so still and quiet we can almost imagine ourselves at home again. We took out our Daguerrotypes and tried to live over again some of the happy days of 'Auld Lang Syne.' "[54] Sisterly contact kept "feminine occupations" from withering away from disuse: "In the evening the young ladies came over to our house and we had a concert with both guitars. Indeed it seemed almost like a pleasant evening at home. We could none of us realize that we were almost at the summit of the Rocky Mountains."[55] The hostess added with somewhat strained sanguinity that her young daughter seemed "just as happy sitting on the ground playing her guitar as she was at home, although she does not love it as much as her piano."[56] Although a guitar was no substitute for the more refined instrument, it at least kept the girl "in practice with feminine occupations and diversions": unlike Mary Ellen Todd, no big whip would tempt her to unwomanly pleasure in the power to "set things going."

But books, furniture, knick-knacks, china, the daguerrotypes that Mrs. Fox shared, or the guitars of young musicians—the "various articles of ornament and convenience"—were among the first things discarded on the epic trash heap which trailed over the mountains. On long uphill grades and over sandy deserts, the wagons had to be lightened; any materials not essential to survival were fair game for disposal. Such commodities of woman's sphere, although functionally useless, provided women with a psychological lifeline to their abandoned homes and communities, as well as to elements of their identities which the westward journey threatened to mutilate or entirely extinguish.[57] Losing homely treasures and memorabilia was yet another defeat within an accelerating process of dispossession.

The male-directed venture likewise encroached upon the Sabbath, another female preserve. Through the influence of women's magazines, by mid-century Sunday had become a veritable ladies' day; women zealously exercised their religious influence and moral skill on the day of their families' retirement from the world. Although parties on the Trail often suspended travel on Sundays, the time only provided the opportunity to unload and dry the precious cargo of the wagons—seeds, food, and clothing—which otherwise would rot from dampness. For women whose creed forbade any worldly activity on the Sabbath, the work was not only irksome and tedious but profane.

> This is Sabath it is a beautiful day but indeed we do not use it as such for we have not traveled far when we stop in a most lovely place oh it is such a beautiful spot and take everything out of our wagon to air them and it is well we done it as the flower was damp and there was some of the other ones flower was rotten . . . and we baked and boiled and washed oh dear me I did not think we would have abused the sabeth in such a manner. I do not see how we can expect to get along but we did not intend to do so before we started.[58]

Denied a voice in the male sphere that surrounded them, women were also unable to partake of the limited yet meaningful power of women with homes. On almost every Sunday, Helen Stewart lamented the disruption of a familiar and sustaining order of life, symbolized by the household goods strewn about the ground to dry: "We took everything out the wagons and the side of the hill is covered with flower biscut meat rice oat meal clothes and such a quantity of articles of all discertions to many to mention and childre[n] included in the number. And hobos that is neather men nor yet boys being in and out hang about."[59]

The disintegration of the physical base of domesticity was symptomatic of an even more serious disruption in the female subculture. Because the wagon trains so often broke into smaller units, many women were stranded in parties without other women. Since there were usually two or more men in the same family party, some male friendships and bonds remained intact for the duration of the journey. But by midway in the trip, female companionship, so valued by nineteenth-century women, was unavailable to the solitary wife in a party of hired men, husband, and children that had broken away from a larger train. Emergencies and quarrels, usually between men, broke up the parties. Dr. Powers, a particularly ill-tempered man, decided after many disagreements with others in his train to make the crossing alone with his family. His wife shared neither his misanthropy nor his grim independence. On the day they separated from the others, she wrote in her journal: "The women came over to bid me goodbye, for we were to go alone, all alone. They said there was no color in my face. I felt as if there was none." She perceived the separation as a banishment, almost a death sentence: "There is something peculiar in such a parting on the Plains, one there realizes what a goodbye is. Miss Turner and Mrs. Hendricks were the last to leave, and they bade me adieu the tears running down their sunburnt cheeks. I felt as though my last friends were leaving me, for what —as I thought then— was a Maniac."[60] Charlotte Pengra likewise left Missouri with her family in a large train. Several weeks out, mechanical problems detained some of the wagons, including those of the other three women. During the month they were separated, Pengra became increasingly dispirited and anxious: "The roads have been good today—I feel lonely and almost disheartened. . . . Can hear the wolves howl very distinctly. Rather ominis, perhaps you think. . . . Feel very tird and lonely—our folks not having come—I fear some of them ar sick." Having waited as long as possible for the others, the advance group made a major river crossing. "Then I felt that indeed I had left all my friends," Pengra wrote, "save my husband and his brother, to journey over the dreaded Plains, without one female acquaintance even for a companion—of course I wept and grieved about it but to no purpose."[61]

Others echoed her mourning. "The whipporwills are chirping," Helen Stewart wrote, "they bring me in mind of our old farm in pensillvania the home of my childhood where I have spent the happiest days I will ever see again. . . . I feel rather lonesome today oh solitude solitude how I love it if I had about a dozen of my companions to enjoy it with me."[62] Uprootedness took its toll in debilitation and numbness. After a hard week, men "lolled around in the tents and on their blankets seeming to realize that the 'Sabbath was made for man,' "[63] resting on the palpable achievements of miles covered and rivers crossed. In contrast, the women "could not fully appreciate physical rest, and were rendered more uneasy by the continual passing of emigrant trains all day long. . . . To me, much of the day was spent in meditating over the past and in forebodings for the future."[64]

The ultimate expression of this alienation was the pressure to turn back, to retrace steps to the old life. Occasionally anxiety or bewilderment erupted into open revolt against going on.

> This morning our company moved on, except one family. The woman got mad and wouldn't budge or let the children go. He had the cattle hitched on for three hours and coaxed her to go, but she wouldn't stir. I told my husband the circumstances and he and Adam Polk and Mr. Kimball went and each one took a young one and crammed them in the wagon, and the husband drove off and left her sitting. . . . She cut across and overtook her husband. Meantime he sent his boy back to camp after a horse he had left, and when she came up her husband said, "Did you meet John?" "Yes," was the reply, "and I picked up a stone and knocked out his brains." Her husband went back to ascertain the truth and while he was gone she set fire to one of the wagons. . . . He saw the flames and came running and put it out, and then mustered spunk enough to give her a good flogging.[65]

Short of violent resistance, it was always possible that circumstances would force a family to reconsider and turn back. During a cholera scare in 1852, "women cried, begging their men to take them back."[66] When the men reluctantly relented, the writer observed that "they did the hooking up of their oxen in a spiritless sort of way," while "some of the girls and women were laughing."[67] There was little lost and much regained for women in a decision to abandon the migration.

Both sexes worked, and both sexes suffered. Yet women lacked a sense of inclusion and a cultural rationale to give meaning to the suffering and the work; no augmented sense of self or role emerged from augmented privation. Both women and men also complained, but women expanded their caviling to a generalized critique of the whole enterprise. Margaret Chambers felt "as if we had left all civilization behind us"[68] after crossing the Missouri, and Harriet Ward's cry from South Pass —"Oh, shall we ever live like civilized beings again?"[69]—reverbated through the thoughts of many of her sisters. Civilization was far more to these women than law, books, and municipal government; it was pianos, church societies, daguerrotypes, mirrors—in short, their homes. At their most hopeful, the exiles perceived the Trail as a hellish but necessary transition to a land where they could renew their domestic mission: "Each advanced step of the slow, plodding cattle carried us farther and farther from civilization into a desolate, barbarous country. . . . But our new home lay beyond all this and was a shining beacon that beckoned us on, inspiring our hearts with hope and courage."[70] At worse, temporary exigencies became in the minds of the dispossessed the omens of an irrevocable exile: "We have been travelling with 25-18-14-129-64-3 wagons—now all alone—how dreary it seems. Can it be that I have left my quiet little home and taken this dreary land of solitude in exchange?"[71]

Only a minority of the women who emigrated over the Overland Trail were from the northeastern middle classes where the cult of true womanhood reached its fullest bloom. Yet their responses to the labor demands of the Trail indicate that "womanliness" had penetrated the values, expectations, and personalities of midwestern farm women as well as New England "ladies." "Woman's sphere" provided them with companionship, a sense of self-worth, and most important, independence from men in a patriarchal world. The Trail, in breaking down sexual segregation, offered women the opportunities of socially essential work. Yet this work was performed in a male arena, and many women saw themselves as draftees rather than partners.

Historians have generally associated "positive work roles"[72] for women with the absence of narrowly defined notions of "woman's place." In the best summary of literature on colonial women, for example, the authors of *Women in American Society* write: "In general, neither men nor women seemed concerned with defining what women were or what their unique contribution to society should be. . . . Abstract theories about the proper role of women did not stand in the way of meeting familial and social needs."[73] Conversely, the ascendancy of "true womanhood" and the doctrine of sexual spheres coincided with the declining importance of the labor of middle- and upper-class women in a rapidly expanding market economy. On the Overland Trail, cultural roles and self-definitions conflicted with the immediate necessities of the socioeconomic situation. Women themselves fought to preserve a circumscribed role when material circumstances rendered it dysfunctional. Like their colonial great-grandmothers on premarket subsistence farms, they labored at socially indispensable tasks. Yet they refused to appropriate their new work to their own ends and advantage. In their deepest sense of themselves they remained estranged from their function as "able bodies."

It could be argued that the time span of the trip was not long enough to alter cultural values. Yet there is evidence that the tensions of the Trial haunted the small and isolated market farms at the journey's end.[74] Women in the western settlements continued to try to reinstate a culture of domesticity, although their work as virtual hired hands rendered obsolete the material base of separate arenas for women and men.

The notion of subculture employed in this and other studies of nineteenth-century women is hazy and ill-defined. We need to develop more rigorous conceptions of society, culture, and subculture, and to clarify the paradoxes of women's position, both isolated and integrated, in the dominant social and cultural movements of their time. Nonetheless, the journals of overland women are irrefutable testimony to the importance of a separate female province. Such theorists as Catharine Beecher were acutely aware of the advantages in keeping life divvied up, in maintaining "two pathways which are always different" for women and men.[75] The women who traveled on the Overland Trail experienced firsthand the tribulations of integration which Beecher and her colleagues could predict in theory.

NOTES

We wish to thank Howard Lamar for his continuing support and Peter H. Wood, Ann Douglas, and Michele Hoffnung for their help and criticism. C. Stansell wants to acknowledge the importance of the experiences she shared with Joan Neuman Fleming and Katherine Fleming in this interpretation of women's history in the West. A National Endowment for the Humanities Youth Grant AY-7451-72-482 supported J. Faragher's portion of the research for this article.

1The 1841 Bidwell-Bartelson party of about fifty people included only five women—three of them wives—and ten children. Contemporary figures for the forties' migrations indicate that men made up roughly 50 percent of the parties, women and children the other 50 percent. These proportions prevailed until the Gold Rush. In contrast, the composition of the 1849 emigration was men-92 percent, women-6 percent, and children-2 percent; in 1850, men-97 percent, women and children-3 percent. In 1852 the proportions shifted toward the pre-1849 norm: men-70 percent, women-13 percent, children-20 percent. These percentages are rough estimates, and indicate no more than trends.

For overall figures see Merrill Mattes, *The Great Platte River Road* (Lincoln, Nebraska: Nebraska State Historical Society, 1969), p. 23. For the early forties' on the Oregon Trail, see David Lavender, *Westward Vision: The Story of the Oregon Trail* (New York: McGraw-Hill, 1963), pp. 349-50, 365. For the California branch: George R. Stewart, *The California Trail: An Epic With Many Heroes* (New York: McGraw-Hill, 1962), pp. 8, 54-55, 85, 147, 187, 195, 232, 303, 310. For the Gold Rush: Georgia Willis Read, "Women and Children on the Oregon-California Trail in the Gold-Rush Years," *Missouri Historical Review* 34 (1944-1945): 6.

2Arthur W. Calhoun, *A Social History of the American Family from Colonial Times to the Present* 3 vols. (New York: Barnes & Noble, 1945) 2:11. Calhoun's statement has stood up well to demographic tests; after analysis of nineteenth-century census data, Jack Eblen concludes that "the deeply entrenched ideal and institution of the family provided the mechanism by which people were bound together during the process of cultural transplantation and adaptation" ("An Analysis of Nineteenth Century Frontier Populations," *Demography* 2, no. 4 [1965]: 341).

[3]A simple enumeration of the special equipment necessary for the trip indicates the expense. Each family needed a light wagon, harnesses, and a team, usually oxen; the team alone could easily cost two hundred dollars. Arms and ammunition were purchased specially for the trip; such weapons as shotguns and rifles cost around twenty-five dollars. Since there was practically no chance for resupply along the route, a family had to stock for the entire six-month trip, a considerable investment that only the economically stable could afford. For discussion and details see Mattes, *Great Platte River Road*, pp. 37-50; Stewart, *The California Trail*, pp. 106-26.

[4]Neighbors and friends often moved as a "party," later joining a larger train. Brothers, cousins, and their families, or parents and one or two married children and their families, might set out together. Conjugal and parental ties usually survived under stress, while other relations disintegrated or exploded. Interestingly, the most enduring extrafamilial bonds may have been between nuclear families and the single men who traveled with them. The latter saved money by attaching themselves to family parties rather than outfitting a wagon alone. Some paid for their passage, while others worked as drivers or cattle drovers. For examples of various groupings, see Phoebe Goodell Judson, *A Pioneer's Search for an Ideal Home* (Bellingham, Washington: United Printing, Binding and Stationery Co., 1925), pp. 15-17; Mary E. Ackley, *Crossing the Plains and Early Days in California* (San Francisco: the author, 1928), p. 17; Sarah J. Cummins, *Autobiography and Reminiscences* (Walla Walla, Oregon: The Walla Walla Bulletin, 1920), p. 22; Mrs. J. T. Gowdy, *Crossing the Plains: Personal Recollections of the Journey to Oregon in 1852* (Dayton, Oregon: n.p., 1906), p. 1; Nancy A. Hunt, "By Ox Team to California," *Overland Monthly* 67 (April 1916): 10; Mrs. M. A. Looney, *A Trip Across the Plains in the Year of 1852 with Ox Teams* (McMinnville, Oregon: n.p., 1915), p. 8; and Mrs. Lee Whipple-Halsam, *Early Days in California: Scenes and Events of the '60s as I Remember Them* (Jamestown, California: n.p., 1923), p. 8.

[5]For a recent revision of work on the Overland Trail see Mattes, *The Great Platte River Road*.

[6]Most of the research on the Victorian family has been based on middle- and upper-class northeastern and midwestern families. We do not yet know to what extent the ideology of domesticity affected poor, proletarianized, or southern families.

Although our suggestions about the geographic and class composition of the migrations are generally accepted ones, they remain hypothetical in the absence of demographic research. An overwhelming majority of the women who kept the journals upon which much of our research is based *did* come from the northeastern and midwestern middle class. Nevertheless, until we know much more about the inarticulate families from backwoods Missouri, we cannot pretend to describe the "normative" experience of the overland family. Our interpretation is limited to families whose structure and consciousness were rooted in American bourgeois culture.

[7]The ten volumes of Sarah Hale's *Ladies' Magazine* (1828-1837) are rich primary sources for antebellum ideals of sex roles and the family. For secondary works see the introductory pieces in Nancy Cott, ed., *Root of Bitterness* (Boston: E. C. Dutton, 1972), and Kathryn Kish Sklar, *Catharine Beecher* (New Haven: Yale University Press, 1973). A relatively inaccessible essay remains one of the most illuminating treatments of the period: Nancy Osterud, "Sarah Josepha Hale: A Study of the History of Women in Nineteenth Century America" (unpublished honors thesis, Harvard College, 1971).

[8]See Cott, *Root of Bitterness*, pp. 11-14; Alice Clark, *Working Life of Women in the Seventeenth Century* (London: G. Routledge & Sons, 1919); Elisabeth Dexter, *Colonial Women of Affairs: Women in Business and Professions in America Before 1776* (Boston: Houghton Mifflin Co., 1924); Alice M. Earle, *Home Life in Colonial Days* (New York: McMillian Co., 1899); and Nancy Osterud, "The New England Family, 1790-1840" (unpublished manuscript,

Old Sturbridge Village Education Department: Sturbridge, Mass., n.d.).

[9]We do not use "productive" as a value judgment but as a historically specific concept: labor which produces surplus value within the capitalist mode of production. Within the work process itself, both men's *and* women's labor was "useful," but only men's, in the accepted sex-division, resulted in the creation of commodities. For a provocative discussion of this problem see Ian Gough, "Marx's Theory of Productive and Unproductive Labor," *New Left Review* 76 (November-December 1972): 47-72, and Lise Vogel, "The Earthly Family," *Radical America* 7 (July-October 1973): 9-50.

[10]See Sklar, *Catharine Beecher*, and Ann D. Gordon, Mari Jo Buhle, and Nancy E. Schrom, "Women in American Society," *Radical America* (1972): 25-33.

[11]Quoted in Catharine Beecher, *A Treatise on Domestic Economy* (New York: Harper Brothers, 1858), p. 28.

[12]The most comprehensive account to date of domesticity, culture, and sexual spheres is Sklar, *Catharine Beecher*; see especially pp. 151-67 and 204-16. For the cultural importance of reform to women, see Carroll Smith-Rosenberg, "Beauty, the Beast, and the Militant Woman: A Case Study in Sex Roles in Jacksonian America," *American Quarterly* 23 (Fall 1971): 562-84 and Gail Parker, *The Oven Birds: American Women on Womanhood 1820-1920* (New York: Doubleday and Co., 1972), pp. 1-56. Nancy Cott's argument in *Root of Bitterness*, pp. 3-4, is a concise summary of the subculture argument. See Ann Douglas Wood, "The 'Scribbling Women' and Fanny Fern: Why Women Wrote," *American Quarterly* 23 (Spring 1971): 1-24, and "Mrs. Sigourney and the Sensibility of the Inner Space," *New England Quarterly* 45 (June 1972): 163-81 for women's cultural impulses in literature.

[13]The Great Pacific migration began in the wake of the depression of 1837-40. The Pacific Northwest and California seemed to offer unfailing markets at Hudson's Bay forts, Russian settlements, even the massive Orient. The Pacific itself was to be the great transportation network that backwoods farmers needed so desperately. The 1841 migration was the result of the work of the Western Emigration Society, specifically organized to overcome the economic problems of the depressed Midwest. In short, the coast was rich in fertile, free land and unlimited chances for economic success. See Lavender, *Westward Vision*, pp. 327-28. The major exception to this generalization is the Mormon emigration.

[14]Judson, *A Pioneer's Search*, p. 9.

[15]Lucy Rutledge Cooke, *Crossing the Plains in 1852 . . . as told in Letters Written During the Journey* (Modesto, California: the author, 1923), p. 5. See also James Robertson, *A Few Months in America* (London: n.p., 1855), p. 150: Nancy A. Hunt, "By Ox-Team," p. 9; and Elias Johnson Draper, *An Autobiography* (Fresno, California: the author, 1904), p. 9.

[16]Margaret M. Hecox, *California Caravan: the 1846 Overland Trail Memoir of Margaret M. Hecox* (San Jose, California: Harlan-Young Press, 1966), p. 31.

[17]Lavinia Honeyman Porter, *By Ox Team to California: A Narrative of Crossing the Plains in 1860* (Oakland, California: author, 1910), p. 7; see also Margaret White Chambers, *Reminiscences* (n.p.: n.p. 1903), pp. 5-7.

[18]Porter, *By Ox Team*, p. 41.

[19]Luzena Stanley Wilson, *Luzena Stanley Wilson, '49er* (Oakland, California: The Eucalyptus Press, 1937), p. 1.

[20]Mary Jane Hayden, *Pioneer Days* (San Jose, California: Murgotten's Press, 1915), pp. 7-8.

[21]Our sample of women's diaries and memoirs is by definition biased toward those women who successfully challenged their husbands. A more comprehensive view requires reading another set of journals—those of men who left their families behind. This work, as a part of a general history of the family, women, and men on the Overland Trail, is now in progress: John Faragher, "Women, Men and Their Families on the Overland Trail" (Ph.D. thesis, Yale University, in progress).

[22]For a particularly striking record of marriage proposals, see *Mollie: The Journal of Mollie*

Dorsey Sanford in Nebraska and Colorado Territories, 1857-66 (Lincoln, Nebraska: University of Nebraska Press, 1959), pp. 20. 58, 59, 74, 91.

[23]Quoted in Nancy Ross, *Westward the Women* (New York: Alfred A. Knopf, 1944), p. 110.

[24]Mrs. John Wilson, quoted in Read, "Women and Children on the Oregon-California Trail in the Gold-Rush Years," p. 7.

[25]Ross, *Westward the Women*, p. 111.

[26]See Mari Sandoz's biography of her father, *Old Jules* (Lincoln, Nebraska: University of Nebraska Press, 1955) for a dramatic illustration of a male homesteader's functional view of wives and children.

The conventional view that the American west was predominantly male dies hard. Jack Eblen, in "Nineteenth Century Frontier Populations," conclusively demonstrates that the sex ratio in the West was little different from that in the East: women were nearly always present in numbers equal to men. See Christine Stansell, "Women on the Plains." *Women's Studies* (forthcoming).

[27]Esther Allen, *Canvas Caravans: Based on the Journal of Esther Belle McMillan Hanna* (Portland, Oregon: Binfords & Mort. 1946), p. 18.

[28]Mrs. Elizabeth Dixon Smith Geer, "Diary," in Oregon Pioneer Association, *Transactions of the Thirty-fifth Annual Reunion* (1907), p. 169.

[29]Catherine Margaret Haun, quoted in Read, "Women and Children on the Oregon-California Trail in the Gold-Rush Years," p. 9.

[30]Chambers, *Reminiscences*, p. 8.

[31]See Adrietta Applegate Hixon, *On to Oregon! A True Story of a Young Girl's Journey Into the West* (Wesler, Idaho: Signal-American Printers, 1947), p. 17, for one of the few instances in the diaries when men took on women's work.

[32]See Charles Howard Crawford, *Scenes of Earlier Days: In Crossing the Plains to Oregon, and Experiences of Western Life* (Chicago: Quadrangle, 1962), p. 9, for an account of women's resistance to assuming this particular responsibility.

[33]Cummins, *Autobiography and Reminiscences*, p. 28.

[34]See Gowdy, *Crossing the Plains*, p. 2; John Barnett, *Long Trip in a Prairie Schooner* (Whittier, California: Western Stationery Co., 1928), p. 105; and Lydia Milner Waters, "A Trip Across the Plains in 1855," *Quarterly of the Society of California Pioneers* 6 (June 1929): 66.

[35]Charlotte Emily Pengra, "Diary of Mrs. Byron J. Pengra," (unpublished typescript in Lane County Historical Society, Eugene, Oregon, n.d.), p. 8.

[36]Mary Burrell, "Mary Burrell's Book" (manuscript diary, Beinecke Library, Yale University), no pagination; Cummins, *Autobiography*, p. 27; E. Allene Dunham, *Across the Plains in a Covered Covered Wagon* (Milton, Iowa: n.p., n.d.), p. 10.

[37]Pengra, "Diary," p. 5.

[38]Ibid., pp. 6, 8-9, 12.

[39]Helen Marnie Stewart, "Diary," (unpublished typescript at Lane County Historical Society, Eugene, Oregon, 1961), p. 13.

[40]The place of children in the structure of the overland family is an intriguing question that we are reserving for more research and reflection. On the basis of their infrequent appearance in the journals, it seems that in this area, too, nineteenth-century patterns were mo modified. Many historians have pointed to the antebellum period as the time when "the child" emerged from obscurity to a special social status. In the overland sources, however, children over the age of five are rarely discussed except as younger and more vulnerable members of the working group, requiring little extra or special attention.

[41]Elizabeth Wood, "Journal of a Trip to Oregon, 1851," *Oregon Historical Society Quarterly* 17 (1926): 4.

[42]Helen M. Carpenter, "A Trip Across the Plains in an Ox Wagon, 1857" (manuscript diary,

Huntington Library, San Marino, California), pp. 27-28.

[43]Hixon, *On to Oregon!* p. 17.

[44]Pengra, "Diary," p. 5.

[45]Emery T. Bray, ed., *Bray Family Geneology and History* (n.p.: n.p., 1927), p. 10.

[46]Ibid.

[47]Porter, *By Ox Team to California*, p. 43.

[48]Ibid., p. 118.

[49]Waters, "A Trip Across the Plains in 1855," p. 77.

[50]Hixon, *On to Oregon!* p. 45.

[51]Catherine Haun in Read, "Women and Children During the Gold-Rush Years," p. 9. See also Hixon, *On to Oregon!* p. 15 and *passim*; and William Smedley, "Across the Plains in Sixty-two," *The Trail* 19 (March 1927): 11.

[52]Sarah Royce, *A Frontier Lady: Recollections of the Gold Rush and Early California* (New Haven: Yale University Press, 1932), pp. 8-9.

[53]Haun in Read, "Women and Children During the Gold-Rush Years," p. 9.

[54]Harriet Sherril Ward, *Prairie Schooner Lady: The Journal of Harriet Sherril Ward* (Los Angeles: Westernlore Press, 1959), p. 60.

[55]Ibid., p. 95. See also Celinda E. Hines, "Diary of Celinda E. Hines," in Oregon Pioneer Association, *Transactions of the Forty-sixth Annual Reunion* (1918), pp. 82-83 and *passim*.

[56]Ward, *Prairie Schooner Lady*, p. 69.

[57]See Narcissa Whitman, "Diary," (manuscript, Beinecke Library, Yale University), p. 18, or in any one of its many published versions—e.g., *Oregon Historical Quarterly* 35 (1936). Also Esther and Joseph Lyman, "Letters About the Lost Wagon Train of 1853" (unpublished typescript in Lane County Historical Society, Eugene, Oregon), p. 6; and Georgia Read and Ruth Gaines, eds., *Gold Rush: the Journals, Drawings, and Other Papers of J. Goldsborough Bruff . . . April 2, 1849—July 20, 1851* (New York: n.p., 1949), p. 45 and *passim*.

[58]Stewart, "Diary," entry for June 6, 1853. See also Whitman, "Diary," p. 21; Pengra, "Diary," p. 3; and Royce, *Frontier Lady*, p. 11.

[59]Stewart, "Diary," entry for June 12, 1853.

[60]Mrs. Mary Rockwood Power, "The Overland Route: Leaves from the Journal of a California Emigrant," *Amateur Book Collector* 1 (November 1950): 6.

[61]Pengra, "Diary," entries for May 2, 3, 8, and 10, and entries for June 5, 24, and July 7, 1853. See also, Royce, *Frontier Lady*, p. 9: and Mrs. Mary A. Frink, *Journal of the Adventures of a Party of California Gold-Seekers* (Oakland, California: n.p. 1897), p. 67.

[62]Stewart, "Diary," entry for May 1, 1853.

[63]Judson, *A Pioneer's Search*, p. 23.

[64]Ibid.

[65]Geer, "Diary," pp. 165-66.

[66]Hixon, *On to Oregon!* p. 18.

[67]Ibid.

[68]Chambers, *Reminiscences*, p. 7.

[69]Ward, *Prairie Schooner Lady*, p. 128. See also Allen, *Canvas Caravans*, p. 28.

[70]Judson, *A Pioneer's Search*, p. 18.

[71]Maria Parsons Belshaw, "Diary of a Bride Written on the Trail in 1853," *Oregon Historical Society Quarterly* 33 (March-December 1932): 334.

[72]Cott, *Root of Bitterness*, p. 5.

[73]Gordon, Buhle, and Schrom, *Women in American Society*, p. 22.

[74]Stansell, "Women on the Plains."

[75]Catharine Beecher, *Domestic Economy*, p. 28.

BEVERLY J. STOELTJE

"A Helpmate for Man Indeed"

The Image of the Frontier Woman

THE VERY NATURE OF THE "FRONTIER," in any geographical setting, implies a process of adaptation in the settlement of that frontier, an interaction of the settling people with the physical environment. New settlements also involve, however, the interaction of the settlers with each other in the new environment, through which interaction a new or modified society is established. In this social adaptation process, behavior forms are drawn from cultural images already in the possession of the individuals who are adapting. These images are then modified or new ones created which will conform to the demands of the environment or situation. Because the process is an interaction of images, behavior, and environment, the resulting forms may have numerous variations, may exist for an unpredictable period of time, and will exhibit *degrees* of success and failure along a continuum, the extreme poles of which are defined by survival or extinction.

This article approaches the American frontier as an adaptive process and examines specifically the roles of women during the settlement period of the frontier. The American "frontier" refers here to the occupation and settlement by Euro-Americans of territories in the United States that were previously unoccupied by such groups. The nineteenth century, particularly the latter half, is the time focus, and the Southwest and Midwest are the particular geographical areas given the most consideration. The aim is not to establish an objective, "real" description of everyday life on the frontier, but to formulate and test a hypothesis regarding symbolic frontier woman. The basic questions regarding frontier women are: What were the images of women possessed by the settlers when they arrived on the frontier? How were these adapted to the frontier? What is the symbolic representation of frontier women?

The major components of the social adaptation process are images (the symbolic representations), behavior, and environment. The environmental influences are perhaps the easiest to identify: climate, resources, distance from settlements, and other physical characteristics. Behavior and images are much more difficult to distinguish. Images influence behavior, behavior will ultimately influence images, and environment will influence both at the same time. In addition, written descriptions or artistic-literary expressions of experience, authored both by participants and by observers, contemporary or historical, will be influenced by the images they possess. There are, then, a symbolic environment—the possessed images—and a physical environment which influence the behavior. The result of the interaction between the two is the adaptation process. However, though these interactions move toward adaptation, they may move also in a maladaptive direction due to a disjunction of the symbolic and physical environments or of several symbolic environments. Because human experience constitutes the data the adaptation process must utilize, the maladaptive influences will be related to those experiences for which there is no mechanism that can transform them into cultural positives. It is through the encounters of experience, possessed images, and evolving images that the universe is restructured by members of the culture. However, restructuring does not equate with removal, because symbols and images that have been transformed into negative value forms may be maintained, though maladaptive, as part of the mechanism for organizing the culture until cultureogenesis has been accomplished. Once restructuring has been accomplished and evidence of culture change is apparent, the conflict between symbols and value systems does not necessarily cease, but the dominant position is assumed by new symbols and images. The continued existence of opposing sets of symbols and values lies at the source of much of the expressive behavior of a culture, such as we find in comedy and tragedy.

The data considered here illustrate the symbolic process in transformation. Images of women are brought by the settling people to a new environment, the frontier, where adaptation must occur. The images must undergo transformation, each acquiring new qualities of autonomy and value within the new environment; then a new set of relations between them develops, and a symbolic representation of frontier women can be identified. It is hoped that this article will reveal something about the cultural position of women in frontier society by means of an inventory of cultural images. The inventory does not claim to be exhaustive but rather is an outline of images within which variations can occur and from which some conclusions can be drawn about the symbol "frontier woman."

Because the frontier was first settled by men it is possible to note the changes brought about by the introduction of women. Women brought institutionalized "civilization" to the "wilderness." Though the forms of institutionalization were skeletal—social occasions, funerals, religious instruction, and the like—many participants and observers recognized that women assumed responsibility for them. Their roles became established within the new environment, and values and emotions were expected to conform to these roles. In this process of interaction between the demanding physical environment and the social environment, a transformation was effected through which a modified image of women emerged.

The following hypotheses are set out to suggest how the frontier experience affected the image of women's cultural role in America: (1) due to the environmental demands of the frontier, women's roles were changed on the behavioral level from those roles practiced in "civilization"; (2) cultural *images* and *symbols* had to be transformed and adapted, and the division of labor redefined; and (3) therefore, the opportunities for change in women's roles available on the frontier were limited to a great extent so that the symbol system would not disturb the general order. However, the symbolic frontier woman is not a clear case of change or no-change; the implications of the frontier experience for her are two-directional. The demands made on frontier women presented new situations and thus opportunity for new means of expression because society's structures were not so rigid as those in areas already settled.

Three types of frontier female images and three types of frontier male images emerge as dominant: (1) the refined lady, (2) the helpmate, and (3) the bad woman; and (1) the cowboy, (2) the settler, and (3) the bad man. It is necessary to consider the male roles as well as the female roles, for the male-female association determines a great part of either role within the society. These roles will be discussed in terms of a distance-sexuality element that defines the relationship between the male and female roles. In the first "set" of roles—the cowboy and the refined lady—distance between the male and female is great, and little if any sexuality is expressed in the relationship. The settler and the helpmate occupy the same household, but sexuality is given narrow recognition in the roles, which focus primarily on reproduction with emphasis on division of labor. The bad woman and the bad man association recognizes sexuality as the primary basis for the relationship. However, they occupy the same space for brief periods of time only. Each of these roles occupies a position in the inventory of images ranging from an idealized vision of chaste woman based on great distance to a "sinful" but exciting image based on close but temporary contact, the midpoint of the inventory being characterized by close contact with nonrecognition of sexuality. This inventory constitutes the primary images available to women on the frontier, though variations were possible.

The first symbolic male type is the cowboy. He is of particular importance if we accept Boatright's view that the cowboy symbolizes man's conquest of nature and the last frontiersman.[1] The cowboy is characterized by his horse, membership in an all-male group, alcohol (whiskey), loneliness, contact with the raw elements and animals, mobility, honor, sometimes a pistol, sometimes a fiddle. The cowboy possessed an idealized image of women, though he was more likely to spend time with prostitutes than with his "ideal." His contact with women frequently came in the "city" at the end of the trail drive or, as the frontier became more settled and more women arrived, at ranches where dances were held. These contacts were generally brief and infrequent. The cowboy's ideal woman was a chaste, beautiful, princesslike, fragile creature, set apart from the real world upon a pedestal where he could worship her from afar. The cowboys were frequently labeled "the boys." This labeling implies that they have not assumed the responsibilities of "men" by settling down with their own ranch and a woman; when they did settle down, they became "cattlemen." As

[1] "The American Rodeo," *The American Quarterly*, 16 (1964), 202.

"boys" they had not reached maturity in civilization terms and, therefore, maintained a boylike relationship to women—worship from afar of an unattainable princess.

One cowboy who rode the cattle trails in Texas and Oklahoma in the 1880's, J. W. Kennedy, wrote the following verses in his journal:

> You are an angel and a blessing, O darling how I love you.
> Unto you I give my whole possessions, Rewarding you for proving true.
> Can you so hard and cruel be Unto the passions of my heart
> Not to permit me at your feet to kneel.
>
> In after years
> When this you see,
> I wonder what your name will be. (Jan. 11, 1889)
>
> When I am in some far and distant land, and other friends around you stand,
> Let not my absence brake the tie that binds the hearts of you and I.
>
> Dear old girl
> How I love you
> No laddie knows.
>
> Love is sweet, but o how bitter to love a girl and then can't get her.
>
> Let all your care be cast a way like dew
> Before the sun and when you have nothing else to do
> Just think of me for fun.

This view of women certainly was not unique to the cowboy; in fact, it illustrates how much the cowboy used the literary stereotype of the time.

Cowboys were often described as shy around women, and some were known to have a complete aversion to women. In a historical account of the settlement of Northwest Texas, Josie Baird says, "Although the boys appreciated and respected the women of the area, they were often very shy around them. Charley Binnion, the roper without peer, would not speak to a woman if he could prevent it, and Doc Shultz was an avowed woman hater. These two were courteous, however, when they could not avoid women."[2]

An anecdote that appeared in a collection of cowboy lore illustrates a common attitude toward male-female relationships. In the story, entitled "Bud's Letter," a group of cowboys in 1883 had left the Grayson County Ranch, and Bud Wallace was the only boy in the outfit to leave a girl behind. The rest of the boys were not so fortunate or unfortunate as to have girls. Bud and his girl agreed to write to each other, and he received letters at each post office. When he wrote to the girl about having to drive through Indian Territory, he received a letter

[2] Josie Baird, "Ranching on the Two Circles Bar," *Panhandle Plains Historical Review*, vol. 18 (Canyon, Texas, 1944), 56.

from her, which he did not share with the group as was the custom; however, the cook read the letter and had a big laugh. The other "boys" then managed to read it as follows:

"Now dear Bud, in your letter you spoke of going among those horrid old Indians. Now dear Bud, don't let those Indians kill you for you know if should they I would die for dear Bud, you know that you are the pork and beans of my soul and the roasting ears of my heart."

Two days later if we wanted peace in camp it was best not to mention pork and beans or roasting ears.[3]

The intensity of the reaction to the letter and the fact that the incident entered into oral tradition and then into print provide an indication of the unusual nature of this event. Were such letters the routine for cowboys, it is unlikely that the letter would have received such attention, which suggests that direct communication between the sexes of a romantic nature (whatever the specifics of the metaphor) was not the norm.

In discussing the frontier hero, not just the cowboy, John G. Cawelti tells us:

Reluctance with words often matches the hero's reluctance toward women. . . . At other periods, writers have tried to make a romantic hero out of the cowboy, as in Wister's *The Virginian* and the many novels of Zane Grey. However, even when the hero does get the girl, the clash between the hero's adherence to the "code of the West" and the heroine's commitment to domesticity, social success, or other genteel values usually plays a role in the story. Heroes such as the Lone Ranger tend to avoid romance altogether. They are occasionally pursued by women, but generally manage to evade their clutches.[4]

Thus the symbolic cowboy who appears in early documents, movies, songs, and novels did not have a female counterpart in reality, generally. Some cowboys possessed an image of an idealized, genteel woman, and others avoided the idea of women completely, or claimed to. Though the cowboys visited the houses of prostitution, in that context they were temporarily transformed into the role of "bad man." There are then two cowboys: the romantic but shy cowboy and the disaffected cowboy.

The first type of female under consideration here is the "refined lady" of a sensitive, emotional nature. The genteel woman who appeared in some cowboys' verses and song did occasionally appear on the frontier but seldom adjusted to the frontier unless she altered her refined ways to some extent. Descriptions of these genteel ladies appear in regional histories and novels. If they refused to adapt their refined ways to the environment, they suffered unhappiness or extinction. "Mrs. Tom Adair who came from Atlanta, Georgia, as a bride, could not become adjusted to dugout life. The men on the ranch teased Tom by telling him that he would have to blindfold his wife and back her into a dugout in order to get her to live in one. Mrs. Adair admits that she never enjoyed living in a dugout, because she was never able to keep anything clean."[5] Another

[3] *Spur Jingles and Saddle Songs, Rhymes and Miscellany of the Cow Camp and Cattle Trails in the Early 80's* (Amarillo, Texas, 1935), 26.
[4] *The Six-Gun Mystique* (Bowling Green, Ohio, 1971), 27.
[5] Baird, 47.

woman from the Deep South married a man also from the South who moved to West Texas.

> To him, so far removed from his proper surroundings, she became more than a mere wife; she was the symbol, as well, of everything he held dear in the life he had left behind; a combination of those virtues from which springs all that is good and beautiful, and of those social graces, which according to his aristocratic standard, were the outward expression of inward perfection. Therefore, unlike most husbands, he had no desire to mold her to suit either his needs or the ways of the country to which he had brought her.[6]

However, her brother-in-law had another view of the situation: "only an extravagant woman from the improvident South would make *dogies* of three poor calves just because she wanted cream and cake with her afternoon tea."[7] (Apparently three range cows were kept to supply milk for the lady's tea, their calves becoming motherless at her expense.) This same woman, because of her husband's "thoughtfulness" in permitting her to go unmolded to the environment, never adjusted to frontier life. Lewis comments, "The years before her widowhood were too filled with happiness for her to contemplate seriously on the outcome to one of her kind of a life in the West. By the time the realization came it was too late . . . she was an old woman, alone in the land of which she had so steadfastly refused to become a part."[8] Describing the wife of Charles Goodnight, the same author (a woman) states, "To one and all she stood for everything that is admirable in womanhood, this gentle 'lady' from Tennessee. Set by circumstances amid surroundings too uncongenial to her highstrung, sensitive temperament, she was dashed and buffeted by the winds of western life till her frail body broke."[9] Another refined lady who came to the Texas Panhandle in frontier days was the wife of a doctor. Dr. Stocking was at first reluctant to migrate because of his worry that his wife would not be accorded the treatment to which she was accustomed. The doctor was persuaded to come, but his wife died within a year following the move.[10]

In Lewis' opinion the frontier had an inviting as well as an austere side, and the hardships were encountered with more ease than the "spiritual confusion of today." This was especially true for women, she feels, "except in rare cases where their natures were such that fear and loneliness had disastrous effects on their emotional balance."[11] The environment was one which placed hardships on women, and some women, especially the gentle lady types, were not able to adapt to these conditions. Barbara Welter has explored the image of this gentle lady type as it appeared in women's popular literature between 1820–1860. She defines the four cardinal virtues of "true womanhood" as piety, purity, submissiveness, and domesticity. "Put them all together and they spelled mother, daughter, sister, wife—woman. Without them, no matter whether there was fame, achievement or wealth, all was ashes. With them she was promised

[6] Willie Newbury Lewis, *Between Sun and Sod* (Clarendon, Texas, 1938), 195.
[7] Ibid.
[8] Ibid., 194.
[9] Ibid., 57.
[10] Ibid., 176–177.
[11] Ibid., 141.

happiness and power."[12] This was the image of woman many settlers brought to the frontier, both male and female. Although some elements of this image proved useful in the new environment, more strength and initiative were required—thus those who could not adapt "broke," either physically or emotionally, from the strain.

This leads to consideration of the second type of male—the settler, the man who brought the refined lady to the frontier. ("Settler" is used to refer to both cattlemen and farmers who had families and owned land—those who established permanency in a region and usually started families.) Charles Goodnight, the giant of the Plains, exemplifies the cattleman of this type. He is described by Lewis as

> abounding in vitality, intelligent, a keen observer of every manifestation of Nature and a gifted judge of men and cattle. His outstanding characteristics were physical endurance, an aptitude for work, self-confidence, and determination. . . . He was the essence of rugged individualism, the type of pioneer most admired by the American masses. . . . He and his kind laid the foundation for an empire, it is true, but without conscious effort, while engrossed upon their own selfish concerns. . . . Therefore, in view of this and also the confusion of many contradictory opinions, it is difficult to know whether Goodnight was "a big-hearted diamond in the rough whose uncouth exterior gave little evidence of the keen intelligence and sterling character underneath" or "an overbearing master, unpopular with the cowboys, who was the finest fellow in the world as long as one did exactly as he desired; whose one ambition was to rule the Plains country, and who, at one time, came near doing it" or, as his chief champion described him, "a great man with a simple nature and the frontier's foremost stockman."[13]

This aggressive, ambitious, self-confident man who tackles the frontier and succeeds in every effort but has a delicate, sensitive wife who does not adapt to the frontier is reminiscent of *Giants in the Earth*, the novel of Norwegian immigrants who settled in Dakota Territory. Per Hansa, the frontier hero of the novel, tackles the frontier with success in every venture. He is described as having "that indomitable, conquering mood which seemed to give him the right of way wherever he went, whatever he did."[14] His neighbors are amazed at his energy and achievements in building the first house, breaking the most land, having successful crops, and generally overcoming obstacles and creating abundance in spite of difficulties. His wife, Beret, however, draws increasingly into a world of darkness, unable to relate to Per Hansa, the neighbors, or the children. She comes to believe that "this desolation out here called forth all that was evil in human nature," and that their coming had been a mistake. Her own feelings were of fear: "She was only afraid—afraid . . . a timid child in a dark room."[15] Though Per Hansa adores his wife and brings her wonderful gifts from the wilderness he conquered, she finds no solace in her position upon a pedestal and gradually withdraws into her own private world. At first she had been fascinated with her role. Memories from her courtship were expressed by her as, "All was nothing as compared with this great certainty. . . . Ah, no—

[12] Welter, "The Cult of True Womanhood: 1820–1860," *American Quarterly*,-18 (1966), 152.
[13] Lewis, 56–57.
[14] O. E. Rolvaag, *Giants in the Earth* (New York, 1955), 41.
[15] Ibid., 279.

she knew it well enough: for him she was the only princess!"[16] Per Hansa, however, does not share his ideas with her but rather fulfills them and presents them to her completed. Because of her fear she makes no attempt to participate in the environment, and the two draw apart—she into her fear and loneliness and he into the environment.

As the above example illustrates, it is possible to find elaboration of the details of the refined lady's experience in literary expression of the frontier experience. Although *Giants in the Earth* is also an account of an immigrant experience, it is most especially an encounter of settling people with the environment. Per Hansa thrives on his encounters with Nature while Beret withdraws from life in the absence of civilization and institutions. In her inability to transform her images, she fails to adapt.

The second type of woman under consideration, the helpmate, is the woman who successfully adapted to the frontier conditions. The primary distinction between this woman and the refined lady is in the strength and initiative exhibited in coping with the hardships and the demands of the life they led. Her strength was physical and emotional. She was able to carry out routine, everyday chores of milking, cooking, sewing, gardening, caring for chickens, childbearing and childrearing, caring for the sick, and generally acting as partner with her husband. Such women were equally adept at handling emergency situations—Indian attacks, droughts, death. Individual women made specialized contributions such as reading Bible stories or holding "open house" for the young people to see their pretty "things," but the primary defining feature of this group of women was their ability to fulfill their duties which enabled their men to succeed, and to handle crises with competence and without complaint. The image of the woman who fulfilled this role has roots in the "backwoods belle" of the Old Southwest. Boatright describes this image as it appeared in the Davy Crockett almanacs, which we may consider as part of mass art, as follows:

> The backwoodsman never made womanhood a cult, and while he was just as quick to fight as any man if he felt that the honor of an individual woman was involved, he made no grandiose defense of womanhood as such. . . . By a process of inversion in which he was adept, ugliness, uncouthness, and "unladylike" strength and demeanor were so exaggerated that they could not be taken seriously. Thus he created a laugh and showed his contempt for leisure-class standards of femininity. . . . The result was a considerable body of traditional lore, preserved by oral transmission and by early newspapers, but chiefly by a series of David Crockett almanacs published from 1835 to 1856.[17]

Though the backwoods belle was hefty, grotesque, and mean with a pistol, she was not without a tender side. She was fond of pets and went to hear the circuit rider when he came and made him welcome.[18] "She was known all the way from the Allegheny to the Rocky Mountains. She was always on hand 'with heart, arms, and pockets open.' She wore out 'seven of her nine constitutions and used up four consumptions and seven fever agues in saving travellers from

[16] Ibid., 217.
[17] Mody Boatright, *Folk Laughter on the American Frontier* (New York, 1961), 44.
[18] Ibid., 52.

freezin', famine, wolves and vultures.'" This backwoods belle was a "worthy helpmate to her husband."[19] Crockett's wife did many chores to help him, including turning the grindstone for him when he wanted to sharpen his thumbnail and providing eggnog on Easter, even if it involved trouble for herself.[20] This image of a superwoman who is extremely capable but expects so little for herself is best described in the almanac as follows:

> The greatest example of wifely devotion of all was Katy Whippoween. She brought up a "smart chance of children" with no expense to their father except for their education. . . . thar war a lady what took a young bear to bring up and to be treated as one of the family, and Katy offered to taik it to nuss till it got big enuff to feed. In this way she arned enuff to keep her husband in whiskey. . . . But she got nothing for her panes, for all her children turned out bad. One of im is a minister.[21]

Even though these sketches in the almanacs are meant to be humorous, several traits of the early symbolic frontier woman emerge as characteristic. She

(1.) was strong and tough;
(2.) took responsibility for the welfare of others;
(3.) had a variety of skills which she used often;
(4.) provided for husband's and children's needs;
(5.) expected no help or reciprocation;
(6.) was a helpmate to her husband;
(7.) was highly valued by men for the above qualities, for they did not value the leisure class standards of femininity.

In other sources women display strength, but, as the frontier moves further west and further into the nineteenth century, it requires of women not only brute physical strength but the ability to bear up under difficulties as well. One such woman who displayed this strength and the ability to cope was Sarah Hornsby of Texas. She appears in a legend recorded by J. Frank Dobie. Though a refined lady, to judge from her background, she was not afraid of the frontier and exhibited the bravery and initiative so admired on the frontier. Thus she illustrates the transformation process: she combines elements of the images of the refined lady and of the backwoods belle in order to meet the demands of the environment. Dobie entitles the legend "The Dream That Saved Wilbarger." In the legend Sarah Hornsby has a dream that Josiah Wilbarger, a neighbor, did not die when scalped by the Indians, as witnesses believed. She insists that the witnesses and her husband return to the site and bring Wilbarger to safety. Though two men who witnessed the scalping assure her that Wilbarger is dead, she convinces her husband that her dream is true. She and the children will be in danger when the men leave, but she says, "Never mind me, I and my children can take to the dogwood thicket and lie hid. Go, I tell you, to poor Wilbarger."[22] Dobie describes this determined woman as "a little, black-haired, black-eyed woman of pure Scotch blood off a plantation of traditional refinement in Mississippi. She sang Highland ballads, read the Bible to her children, and taught

[19] Ibid., 53.
[20] Ibid.
[21] Ibid., 54.
[22] Dobie, *Tales of Old-Time Texas* (Boston, 1955), 38.

them to read the box of books she had hauled in an ox wagon all the way to Texas."[23] Yet her delicacy does not inhibit her bravery. In her husband's absence she frightens away Indians by dressing in men's clothing and appearing with a rifle; she and her young sons later bury young men she witnessed being killed by Indians, and she herself buries one of her own sons killed by Indians.[24]

In his memoirs John Holland Jenkins describes frontier women in Central Texas of the mid-nineteenth century as follows:

> the girls were so strong and fine and healthy-looking and they seemed so wide-awake and earnest. Their waists were not so waspish nor their bustles so large as they are today.... They were raised on bear and buffalo meat and venison and wild honey with plenty of good pure fresh air and work to do.... And our girls knew how to weave and spin and churn and do anything that came along there.... Fashion meant common sense and economy and comfort.... I believe the women here now are as pretty and fair as can be found, but they do not look so healthy and comfortable and happy, and I do not see many who look like they could pass through what Mary Jane and others of our veteran ladies of Bastrop County have endured.[25]

James Wilson Nichols, 1820–1887, describes the bravery of several women of Central Texas, near Fredericksburg, in his journal. One story involves the Henry M. Day family. Mrs. Day leaped from the wagon with one child in her arms when the Indians attacked. Though she was wounded, she risked her life further and returned to the wagon, just as it was being driven away by the Indians, to snatch her other child, "and made good her retreat back to her tree and other child amid loud yells and a shower of arrows and bullets ... the woman hesitated not a moment to imperil her own life for that of her child."[26]

In another instance, Mrs. Friend was both scalped and wounded in the thigh but crawled a mile and a half in the snow and north wind to reach her home because she was "very ankcious to know the fate of her little ones at home."[27] (Her husband found her unconscious at the gate upon his return home at midnight.) Nichols states, "Now me thinks the heroism, bravery and deturmination of these three women has never been surpased in anciant or modern history or the bravery and deturmination and example set fourth by these females ever been equeled in this age of the world."[28]

In Parker County, near Weatherford, Texas, in the latter half of the nineteenth century there was great concern in the rural churches over the woman's position in the church. One member maintained that women should not take part in church business, since they did not possess a soul. One "free-thinker," however, "dared to advance the theory that if a man had a soul, it was reason-

[23] Ibid.
[24] Ibid.
[25] John Holmes Jenkins, III, ed., *Recollections of Early Texas: The Memoirs of John Holland Jenkins* (Austin, 1958), 210–211.
[26] Catherine W. McDowell, ed., *Now You Hear My Horn: The Journal of James Wilson Nichols, 1820–1887* (Austin, 1967), 163.
[27] Ibid., 165.
[28] Ibid., 166.

able to presume that a woman had one too."[29] At any rate, in the town of Weatherford the question of a woman's soul did not prevent the churches from "letting the women help pay for their new brick or frame buildings." The county historian, H. Smythe, wrote: "For nearly ten years an effort has been made to rear a house of worship for the Christian denomination. Attempts by man signally failed; the women magnificently accomplished their purpose." They accomplished this through needle work and knitting appliances and two public festival entertainments.[30]

We learn from this author also that a woman's role was specifically defined, both by the women as well as the men. And in this role, she was held responsible for her marriage and was expected to do an excellent job of her chores.

> Gossip, of course, was one of the chief pasttimes. Women sometimes stepped off the straight and narrow path, and wise heads nodded thereafter. If a woman separated from her husband, she usually was blamed for the marital failure, but if she were any part a lady, she would not further disgrace herself by getting a divorce. A more grievous plight than ever was for a woman to fail to get married before she was twenty-five. No one in his senses would marry an old maid of twenty-five or past. Women liked to talk about the slovens in their neighborhood—triflin', they called them. Why, they made butter with cow tracks in it, it was so vile smelling. They couldn't make an apple pie bed. They stitched their selvage seams together instead of whipping them. Their spinning rolls were bull tails, bulky and not suitable for the making of good thread. They were the kind of people who had no turkey-red embroidery on white pillowshams, who let the fire go out, who had to borrow soft soap, who didn't keep the weevils out of their seed peas, who let their gourds get soggy.[31]

Life further west in Fisher, Scurry, Kent, and Stonewall counties, Texas, is described by Josie Baird. She says of the pioneer women,

> These pioneer women were as strong as their husbands in their desire to make new homes in the isolated section. For the most part they bore the hardships without complaint but they did dislike the sandstorms, dugouts, and the lack of water. . . . Despite the hardships most women who came to the ranch stayed and made the best of the situation. . . . They brought about significant changes in the lives of the cowboys. Though the cowboy made jokes concerning the settlers, they enjoyed their changed social existence. Women were added to annual ranch barbecues where platforms were built for dancing, and everyone ate and danced and drank most of the day and night.[32]

Though never stated clearly, it was only the men who drank, and whiskey was their drink.

Besides creating a social life where none existed before, women brought about other changes in frontier life.

> Mrs. Greenwood tried to bring some of the culture of her earlier home into the lives of the cowboys. While she was living on the ranch, a bronc fell with Lee Shultz and killed him. Mrs. Greenwood held a funeral service for him. The boys remembered that service, for religious services of any kind were very unusual. Even though most of the boys admitted

[29] Afton Wynn, "Pioneer Folk Ways," in *Straight Texas*, ed. J. F. Dobie (Hatboro, Pennsylvania, 1966), 197.
[30] Ibid.
[31] Ibid., 233.
[32] Baird, 56–57.

that the ranch was no place for women, they were happy that some women were willing to make their homes on the ranches.[33]

A most interesting example is provided by Mary Taylor Bunton in her story *A Bride on the Old Chisholm Trail in 1886.* Originally from Austin, this young woman, who had a formal education and had traveled widely, exemplified the role of refined lady. She then married a rancher from Nolan County (West Texas). She eagerly moved to the frontier and, as her decision to accompany her husband on a trail drive up the Chisholm Trail shows, adopted traits of the backwoods belle. Though it was required that women make difficult trips across rough country when moving to the frontier, it was unheard of for a woman to go on a trail drive. This was a male domain and not a family venture; women were not permitted under any circumstances. After word was out that Mary was indeed going on the drive, relatives and friends came to Mr. Bunton and said,

Look here, young man, we have come out here to give you a talk straight from the shoulder, and we are not going to mince words with you either. To tell you the truth, the whole truth, and nothing but the truth, all of us think you have lost your mind. It's the craziest idea we ever hear of—your promising to take Mrs. Bunton with you on this trip up the trail. You ought to realize that she is too young, too inexperienced, and too unaccustomed to hardships of any kind to make such a trip, and she is a bride, besides. Why, man, even to let her start the trip with you will likely end in tragedy. Think it over, and you had better heed our warning.[34]

Then they appealed to Mary herself, saying that they were surprised that she would want to "add the care" of herself to her husband's responsibilities.

Mary insisted on going on the trip, however, and rode all the way to Coolidge, Kansas. She established herself after killing a rattlesnake and cutting off the rattles. She was then considered a "seasoned veteran" rather than a "tenderfoot."[35] This example, though not typical of most women, exhibits most obviously the transformation from refined lady to helpmate.

Most important, therefore, is Mrs. Bunton's conclusion to her story, in which she does not emphasize herself and her independence but rather her role as her husband's helpmate: "Howell Bunton was proud of the record his young wife had made and as long as he lived he paid highest tribute to her courage and wifely devotion—truly a helpmate for man indeed."[36] This helpmate concept also appears in other sources. Willie Newbury Lewis, a female writer, describes the wife of one of Goodnight's neighbors, Thomas Sherman Bugbee (no name is given for the wife): "His wife was only a blue-eyed, quick-tempered, laughing girl, so small she could stand under her husband's outstretched arm, but she made a perfect complement to the big, steady, taciturn pioneer, and it was the two together who brought to success the Quarter Circle T."[37]

The ability to endure pain and hardship was valued whether they were per-

[33] Ibid., 56.
[34] *A Bride on the Old Chisholm Trail* (San Antonio, 1939), 29.
[35] Ibid., 41.
[36] Ibid., 71.
[37] Lewis, 61.

sonal or environmental. A young woman in the Clarendon community fainted and fell into an open fire during an epileptic attack. Though the burns were fatal, "During her last agonies, she spoke only once, then to apologize for the screams which she, in her pain, had been unable to suppress."[38]

In the same community an economical and literal woman went to visit the doctor to have a tooth extracted. He, being unskilled as a dentist, jokingly commented, "If it does *not* hurt, *I'll* not *charge* you a cent." She sat in the chair "without movement or change of expression until he had finished, . . . arose, straightened her clothes, thanked him and walked out. The matter of a fee was never mentioned by either."[39]

Bravery and endurance in women were highly valued on the frontier. Emotional expression between the sexes or in any form, however, seems rare and was valued only when successfully repressed. Larry McMurtry states in "Eros in Archer County" that we have little in the way of recorded conversations or other data to tell us about communication between the sexes.[40] The data suggest that expressions of affection and love were restricted to the romantic cowboy mentioned earlier. Actual relationships between the sexes are described more as partnerships than as romances. The following anecdote is provided as an example. "There were amusing incidents, sometimes even in the presence of death, as when the old Dutchman looked into the face of his deceased wife and said, 'Doc, I believe it would have been easier for me to give up my best span of mules than that old woman.' "[41] Though this statement is made in humor, it also tells us that the closest the speaker can come to expressing love for his deceased wife is to compare her to his best mules.

Some further indication of communication between the sexes can be obtained from Edward Baxter Featherston's report of his courtship with his wife. Featherston was a pioneer in West Texas in the late nineteenth century. A friend suggested to him that Bettie Moxley might marry him if he approached her and acted "sensible." He "went to courting" Bettie, and they wrote letters every two weeks. In one letter he proposes marriage as follows: "If you are willing to marry me when I come home this fall, show this letter to your father." He continues, "In due time the answer came back, 'Pa has seen your letter.' We were married at her father's house November 27, 1874."[42]

Featherston's wife complained at times, according to his report, that her husband did not court her enough, but when he would offer, she would say, "I don't want any of your foolishness now."[43] Though he states that he feels "courting" a woman is very important, his evidence indicates that only a minimum of "courting" ever occurred. He gives his evaluation of his wife as follows: "Her economy and industry enabled me to make an honest living and raise our family. When I consider the quality of our offsprings I am abundantly sat-

[38] Ibid., 178.
[39] Ibid.
[40] *In a Narrow Grave* (Austin, 1968), 19.
[41] Lewis, 179.
[42] Featherston, *A Pioneer Speaks*, ed. Vera Featherston (Dallas, 1940), 58.
[43] Ibid.

isfied."[44] Though the author may have had other feelings about his wife as well as these, if we consider his report a "transcript" of the culture, a term used by Kenneth Boulding to describe a communication which is in some sense independent of the communicator but which conforms to tradition in its selection of messages, we can consider economy and industry that help the husband, plus producing "quality" offspring, the valued traits of the frontier woman.[45] His comments on their communication further illustrate that communication was minimal on the subject of romance and courtship.

Relationships of males with females and communication between the two are described in the going-to-bed rituals of a pioneer family in Parker County.

> Going to bed was a delicately handled ceremony in the large families. The children washed their feet in the summer time, and were properly dressed in their night garments and tucked away in the trundles. When it came time for the grown-ups to retire, the men all went outside to give a last look to the stock while the women undressed. The men returned to find the women all in bed. Candles were then extinguished and the men undressed in the dark. The coals were banked in ashes for the night, and on cold mornings the head of the household arose, slipped on his jeans and built the fire. Usually the men arose first and went to see about the stock while the women dressed.[46]

Distance, then, was imposed between the sexes in frontier families even in close living quarters, even in winter.

In the first category of frontier males, then, is the cowboy—the alienated, disaffected cowboy who is an avowed hater of women or the romantic cowboy who dreams of princesses and love but has little or no contact with such women. In these cases the male either remains a member of his male group, the "boys," never taking a wife, or perhaps he marries late in life to a woman whom he places upon a pedestal. In the second male category is the landowner who marries and settles permanently in the area, giving up the mobility of the cowboy. He is frequently a cattleman, though in some regions of the frontier he is a landowning farmer. If he marries the first type of woman under consideration, he is marrying the cowboy's dream, the "refined lady," the epitome of "true womanhood." This female is too sensitive and emotional to weather the hardships of the frontier and either dies or becomes emotionally imbalanced. The male is successful in his role as a frontiersman; the female is a failure as a frontier woman because she cannot adapt to the frontier, by becoming a helpmate. If the male marries the second type of woman, the helpmate, they will be "successful," for she will adapt to the role of a strong, enduring, nonsexual helper for the cattleman-settler.

A third image on the frontier was the "bad woman." She appears in a variety of forms, generally associated with sex and raw Nature. The role of bad woman was certainly not created on the frontier, but in adapting to the conditions of the frontier it assumed a prominent and special position there. In frontier areas where there were trading relations with Indians it was not unusual for white males to avail themselves of the Indian "squaws" during trading periods, as

[44] Ibid., 59.
[45] *The Image* (Ann Arbor, 1964), 54.
[46] Wynn, 205.

contrasted to the Indian princess who had to be won and married. *The Big Sky*[47] has both these roles clearly defined, and, as with the refined woman above, the marriage of the hero with the Indian princess ends in disaster. In the Anglo setting bad women were especially associated with saloons, dance halls, alcohol, and rowdy living. Some frontier towns were largely built around this culture. One such town on the Texas plains was Tascosa,

> a typical boom town characterized by "bad men, prostitutes, revolver shots and whiskey," in perfect accord with the "relentless hardness" of the surrounding region and the unstable quality of the ephemeral era which produced it. Its population was a colorful aggregation of humanity, cowboys with six-shooters, senoritas in lace mantillas, priests in robe and cross, university graduates, gamblers and desperadoes, whose chief place of amusement went under the fitting but offensive name of "Hogtown" and was marked by a sign which read "no shooting beyond this line."[48]

A customer could enter the large adobe building that housed this area through the business quarters, that is, "the door of respectability," and then proceed to the bar and the dance hall. "The queen of the district was 'Rowdy Kate' and her accomplices went by such descriptive titles as Rag-Time Annie, Drowsy Dollie, Crippled Callie, Box-Car Jane, Panhandle Nan, Fickle Flossie, Old Ella and Midnight Rose."[49] In addition to these women there was Mrs. Betty Trube, who ran the "eating house." She was as strong as a man and wore a six-shooter, which she did not hesitate to brandish if anyone threatened the peace in her establishment. Creole Mary, also known as Frenchy, was the partner of the best-known gambler, a jovial Irishman from Dodge City. The legend goes that she "was the shrewdest monte-dealer in the West," and "night after night she sat among the other sports dressed in her red shoes, spangled blouse and patchwork skirt, with rarely a word except to her 'talking canary.' "

In his novel *Leaving Cheyenne* McMurtry offers a description of a bad woman.[50] Though Molly is not a prostitute, she is not a part of acceptable society. She is wife to her husband, an oil field worker, and lover to a cowboy and also to a cattleman. The cowboy has no wife, the cattleman has a wife, but both express their love and passion with Molly, emotions that should have been kept hidden, if not completely repressed. Certainly Molly would qualify as a frontier woman in her ability to endure hardship. However, the more acceptable frontier woman must be a helpmate to a husband and must be devoid of passion. Molly qualifies on neither score. As a product of a literary work representative of the internal literature of the region Molly is more complex than some of the images provided by the earlier "transcripts," but she is nevertheless defined as the embodiment of sexuality and thus resides beyond acceptable society.

The "bad man" constitutes the third type of male. Since he has already been much discussed as a social bandit, a Robin Hood, and a hero in many instances, there is no need to discuss the type in detail. Billy the Kid and Jesse James represent typical bad men or outlaws, though it must be remembered that many

[47] A. B. Guthrie, *The Big Sky* (Boston, 1947).
[48] Lewis, 59.
[49] Ibid.
[50] New York, 1963.

cowboys and respectable men could be bad men when they chose to visit the saloons and bad women, their respectable roles being reassumed upon return to the ranch or home. The bad men also lived outside the margins of society and did not conform to the code of "civilization" or participate in the institutional life of society—thus they were the natural partners of the bad women. Their endeavors did not require that the female partner be a helpmate, and a working partner, but that the female be available for temporary periods of time when the male's activity brought him into her presence. The bad woman, then, was also subject to the male role for a definition of the female image.

Given the demands of the environment, the refined lady image in its pure form could not survive. A transformation from female to nonsexual comrade was necessary. Perhaps the only woman who survived as a female was the bad woman. The bad woman and the bad man, however, lived beyond the margins of society, as so aptly implied in the name of the district "Hogtown" of Tascosa, an animal town, not for civilized people. Fiedler, Cawelti, and McMurtry have emphasized the all-male society of the code of the West. As McMurtry states, this is not a suggestion of repressed homosexuality but rather an indication of repressed heterosexuality.[51] There is no place for expression of passion or affection between the sexes within the society. Relations between sexes *within* society were based on a nineteenth-century idealization of woman, who was to be treated with "honor" and politeness but without emotion by the cowboy or as a comrade who is a nonsexual partner by the settler type. For passionate, heterosexual relations on the frontier, one must look beyond institutionalized society to the wilderness, inhabited by animals and bad women and bad men. Even here, however, it is the male who has choices and determines the nature of the relationship in terms of time and distance.

The symbolic transformation of images of women that took place on the frontier involved the following initial images: (1) the refined lady symbolizing "true womanhood," defined by Eastern, literary civilization and bringing with her the elements of formal institutionalization—education, religion, "high culture"; (2) the "backwoods belle" (the opposite of the delicate, refined lady), who could accomplish fantastic deeds involving strength and capability and had the ability to establish informal elements of institutionalization, in particular the family; and (3) the bad woman, found outside the boundaries of society and in association with sex and sin. These images of women were related to the following male images: (1) the cowboy, mobile, unsettled, and idealistic about women or alienated from them; (2) the cattleman-settler, the aggressive domineering man who conquered the frontier or the wilderness with great success; and (3) the bad man, the outlaw, who operated beyond respectable society.

In the adaptation to the frontier environment, physical and social, these female images were modified or underscored. The refined lady could survive only if she assumed some of the strength of the backwoods belle. The bad woman was easily accessible in many frontier towns, and the association of gambling, alcohol, and general rowdiness further emphasized the "bad" in the bad woman.

[51] *In a Narrow Grave*, 72.

The helpmate, who drew from the backwoods belle image yet combined elements from the refined lady in some cases, successfully responded to the demands of frontier living, which required that she possess bravery, strength, and initiative as well as the ability to establish and nurture institutions. In this interaction of images and environment, the environment forced the refined lady image into a maladaptive position in the paradigm. In the adaptive position certain opportunities were made available to women, as exhibited by Mary Bunton. However, the biological role of women and the cultural division of labor curtailed these opportunities. More important, however, the symbol of woman that evolved as the successful frontier woman contained its own limitations. The more capable the woman, the more successful in adapting she was, the more the woman assumed the comrade position. The comrade was nonsexual and found identity by association with the cattleman-settler. As Mary Bunton stated it, she was "truly a helpmate for man indeed." The expression of emotion and passion was delegated to the bad woman, whose identity was not tied to an association with a respectable man (at least not recognizably) and who was generally single and lived in the margins somewhere between animals and people. Her image, however, was also primarily defined by the male counterpart.

Thus through the symbolic transformation process evolved a symbolic frontier woman who was above all capable of managing basic institutions, of bringing civilization to the frontier. She had economy and industry, which enabled her man to be a success. Because the refined lady and bad woman images led to failure or exclusion from society, they could not be considered successful in attaining the goal of survival within the new society. The strong, capable, institutional, comrade woman then became established as the symbolic frontier woman, for this image had the capacity to survive within frontier society. However, since maladaptive symbols may remain within a symbol system, the refined lady and the bad woman images also persisted.

If America does indeed identify itself with the frontier experience, if some regions still practice "symbolic frontiersmanship," as several scholars have suggested, then a study of contemporary American images available to women might well begin with an examination of the symbolic frontier woman and the process by which this image became established as an institution in itself.

University of Texas
Austin, Texas

MARY W. M. HARGREAVES

WOMEN IN THE AGRICULTURAL SETTLEMENT OF THE NORTHERN PLAINS

A saying was current during the settlement of the North American Plains that "this was a great country for men and horses, but hell on women and cattle."[1] Cattle might well have been added to the front segment of the grouping, as we have been repeatedly advised by land-use planners down to the present day.[2] But what of women, the fourth element in the adage?

By 1870 the ratio of women to men had already significantly exceeded one to two in Kansas, Nebraska, and the Dakotas. To the west, however, in the high plains and the mountainous Territory of Colorado women did not attain that proportion until nearly 1880, and in Montana and Wyoming not until nearly 1890. The settlement of the Greeley Colony in Colorado, of agricultural communities near mining centers in all three of these Territories, and of railroad towns along four transcontinental routes across the region accounts for this early incursion of women in the predominantly male domain of the mining and livestock frontiers. The number of women did not approximate

Mary W. M. Hargreaves, Professor of History at the University of Kentucky, is currently president of the Agricultural History Society. This paper was presented at a session, "Women in Agriculture," of the Bicentennial Symposium in Washington, D.C., on 22 April 1975.

1 Nannie T. Alderson and Helena Huntington Smith, *A Bride Goes West* (New York: Farrar & Rinehart, 1942; reprint ed., Lincoln: University of Nebraska Press, 1974), 221. For an earlier variant of the statement—the West was "a heaven for men and dogs, but a hell for women and oxen"—see Noah Smithwick, *The Evolution of a State, or Recollections of Old Texas Days*, Nanna Smithwick Donaldson, comp. (Austin, Texas: Gammel Book Company, 1900), 15.

2 Forecasts for regional growth, even eastward into the transitional zone between prairie and plain, recognize that this is a land of declining population, with farms ever larger and more extensively operated, with fewer acres in grain and more in grass, where feed crops will vie with wheat, where some farms "will become ranches, for all practical purposes, specializing in the production of feeder cattle" (Howard W. Ottoson et al., *Land and People in the Northern Plains Transition Area* [Lincoln: University of Nebraska Press, 1966], 268).

200,000 in Kansas until the decade of the seventies, in Nebraska until around 1880, in Colorado until the mid nineties, in the Dakotas until around 1905, and in Montana until about 1915. In Wyoming there are less than 166,000 women today. Women came on to the plains as an accompaniment of the expansion of agricultural development.

For those who came first, to the mining camps, the cattle towns, and even the remote ranches, there was a status role which offset many of the hardships. Charles Howard Shinn's account of the California mining camps points to this aspect: "Men often travelled miles to welcome 'the first real lady in camp.' A New-England youth of seventeen once rode thirty-five miles, after a week's hard work in his father's claim, to see a miner's wife who had arrived in an adjoining district. 'Because,' he said, 'I wanted to see a home-like lady; and, father, do you know, she sewed a button on for me, and told me not to gamble and not to drink. It sounded just like mother.' " As Shinn reported the prevailing attitude: "Women were queens, children were angels."[3]

The delightful account of open-range ranch life by Nannie T. Alderson, *A Bride Goes West,* supports this view. Living in Indian country in southeastern Montana, at first up the Rosebud River valley, later up the Tongue, and finally on Muddy Creek—all a hundred miles or so from town life at Miles City—Mrs. Alderson in nearly fifteen years, from 1879 to 1893, was left unguarded only twice; and she noted such protection as generally applicable to western women on ranches.[4] Cowboys taught her to cook and cooperated in the domestic chores of meal preparation. She at first sent the laundry to an Indian woman; but, balking at ten cents a piece, and a week's bill that totaled $10.80, she undertook to acquire the art of washing clothes—but never learned to cope with the problem of hard water. The Alderson cowboys soon "bragged on" her yeast rolls and her expertise in "foxing" breeches, but she obviously had not been brought to the West for her domestic skills. We merely invert her phrase in commenting: "Women, like rivers, were few, and they gained in importance proportionally."[5]

Robert Dykstra reminds us that cow-town housewives, "legendary pillars of frontier moral uplift," had "little collective influence" in the politics of Kansas reform during the early years. "The gradual domestication of cattle town society" triumphed only "as family groups gradu-

[3] Charles Howard Shinn, *Mining Camps: A Study in American Frontier Government* (New York: Charles Scribner's Sons, 1884; reprint ed., Rodman Wilson Paul, ed., New York: Harper & Row, 1965), 137. See also William Forrest Sprague, *Women and the West: A Short Social History* (Boston, Mass.: The Christopher Publishing House, 1940), 120–22.

[4] Alderson and Smith, *Bride Goes West,* 48, 75–80.

[5] Mrs. Alderson compared the rivers to the women (ibid., 26).

ally infiltrated the demographic structure."[6] But women of the suffrage movement at the turn of the century viewed the western experience somewhat differently. They could then point to the first four states which had given women the vote: Wyoming, in 1869; Colorado, in 1893; Utah, in 1896, after the Territorial vote extended in 1870 had been abrogated under the Edmunds-Tucker Act of 1887; and Idaho, too, in 1896. In Montana tax-paying women might vote on questions of taxation (1889). But in Kansas, under legislation of 1887, the vote for women was restricted to municipal elections, a limited privilege denied to women of rural areas. Kansas women, who had won this concession only after tremendous effort, attributed the achievements of their sisters in the mountain states to the scarcity of population—and, one might add, the relatively greater scarcity of female population—which minimized their potential influence.[7] Women of the agricultural frontier waited long years before their impact in "the demographic structure" took form as the right to general suffrage.

Proponents of woman suffrage in the states under farming development saw the opposition of foreign immigrants as their principal obstacle.[8] The promotionalism that attracted large groups of settlers from a culture alien to that which had generated the liberalization of women's status in the area to the west retarded the democratizing influence on this last American frontier. In Kansas full suffrage was not accorded women until 1912, in Montana, not until 1914, in the Dakotas and Nebraska, not until passage of the federal amendment. The status role of women on the plains dwindled as the numbers of their sex increased in the early years of the twentieth century. Meanwhile the trials of their life in the area were not appreciably lessened.

6 Robert R. Dykstra, *The Cattle Towns* (New York: Alfred A. Knopf, 1968; reprint ed., New York: Atheneum, 1970), 246–48.

7 Elizabeth Cady Stanton, Susan B. Anthony, and Matilda Joslyn Gage, eds., *The History of Woman Suffrage*, 6 vols. (New York: Fowler & Wells, 1881–1922), vol. 4 (Rochester: Privately Printed, 1902), 659–60.

8 Ibid., vol. 5 (New York: National American Woman Suffrage Association, 1922), 377, 503, 506, 556, 591, 593–94. The identification of suffrage support with the prohibition movement contributed to this opposition among the Germans and Scandinavians of the Dakotas. Historians of both the suffrage and the prohibition efforts have noted the identification of political leadership in behalf of these reforms as a move to protect entrenched status groups—white, Anglo-Saxon, and Protestant—against the infusion of divergent population elements. That the immigrants in the plains states formed a rural, rather than an urban, constituency complicates the picture of rural-urban polarization as developed in Joseph R. Gusfield, *Symbolic Crusade, Status Politics and the American Temperance Movement* (Urbana: University of Illinois Press, 1963), 88–89, 94–110; Alan P. Grimes, *The Puritan Ethic and Woman Suffrage* (New York: Oxford University Press, 1967), 10–11, 104–18, 134–41. Grimes, who focuses on the sectional definition of support for the suffrage movement, fails to distinguish between the plains and the mountain divisions of the West.

Loneliness was, by all accounts, the most oppressive of those hardships. That isolation was a general problem of farm life had been a particular concern in the organization of the Patrons of Husbandry, or Grange, lodges, even before the depression of the mid 1870s led to reorientation of that movement toward political and economic issues.[9] The continuing influence of the Grange, with expanded membership in older agricultural regions after 1880, rested upon its social and educational services.[10] The organization of farmers' institutes in the 1870s and the enactment of the Smith-Lever and Smith-Hughes agricultural extension and vocational training programs of 1914 and 1917 represented a continuing recognition of the problem of rural isolation. In all these programs, and remarkably so in the early growth of the Grange, social contact for farm women was emphasized.[11] That the People's Party, or Populists, of the 1890s was the only major political party generally identified with woman suffrage reflected the importance attached to the role of women in an appeal addressed primarily to rural concerns.[12]

Nannie Alderson, the rancher's bride, thought her life more lonely than that of a farmer's wife, who could count upon the men coming in from the fields for regular meals; but she forgot that cowhands were more numerous than husbands, that she had many contacts growing out of ranch hospitality, which dwindled as wayside taverns sprang up with agricultural settlement, and that many women homesteaded alone —one estimate placed the proportion of land held by women as high as a third in the Dakotas in 1887.[13] As mechanized farming developed on the plains, farm size increased and farm spacing became increasingly

9 Whether or not the political and economic focus was initially intended as the purpose of such organization has been controverted, but the emphasis upon need for social and educational relationships is clear. See O[liver] H[udson] Kelley, *Origin and Progress of the Order of the Patrons of Husbandry in the United States: A History from 1866 to 1873* (Philadelphia, Pa.: J. A. Wagenseller, 1875), 17–20, 22, 38–39, 68–70; Solon J. Buck, *The Agrarian Crusade: A Chronicle of the Farmer in Politics* (New Haven, Conn.: Yale University Press, 1920), 4–5; William D. Barnes, "Oliver Hudson Kelley and the Genesis of the Grange: a Reappraisal," *Agricultural History* 41 (July 1967): 229–42.

10 Dennis S. Nordin, "A Revisionist Interpretation of the Patrons of Husbandry, 1867–1900," *Historian* 32 (August 1970): 631, 633–35, and passim.

11 Kelley, *Patrons of Husbandry*, 15, 24, 39, 42, 47, 64, 69–70, 75; Roy V. Scott, *The Reluctant Farmer: The Rise of Agricultural Extension to 1914* (Urbana: University of Illinois Press, 1970), 116–21.

12 Stanton, Anthony, and Gage, *History of Woman Suffrage*, 4: 511–13, 518, 642–46, 652–55, 801, 806, 998; 5: 376.

13 Ibid., 4: 544; Alderson and Smith, *Bride Goes West*, 249. See also Emma Haddock, "Women as Land-Owners in the West," in Association for the Advancement of Women, *Proceedings . . . Fourteenth Annual Convention, Louisville, Kentucky, 1886*, 24.

dispersed—from the 160-acre plots of the prairies, to the 320-acre units of the benchlands after 1909, to the 640-acre stock-farming tracts after 1916, to the 1,000-acre tractor farms and the 10,000-acre ranches of modern times.

Loneliness was measured in a variety of terms—by the years since the writer had been to town, the days or weeks between mail delivery, the miles from the nearest neighbor, the distance to go to borrow a book, the high excitement of a seasonal social activity, or the sorrow at sending a child away to secondary school in town. Large families compensated in a measure for loneliness; but they added to it, too, when the weary mother found she could no longer cast off family burdens for even infrequent excursions from home. Loneliness was the mood epitomized in Faye Cashatt Lewis's title for her volume describing life in Tripp County, South Dakota, in 1909—*Nothing to Make a Shadow.*

Those women who lived to write reminiscences tell of the salubrious climate which forestalled much illness but always recount, too, the alarms of childbirth remote from doctors and the horror of accidents or serious disease when a day's travel, perhaps by railroad, delayed hospitalization. Grace Fairchild, the "Frontier Woman" depicted in an account of settlement in western South Dakota from 1902 to 1940, bore nine children, six of them in less than eight years, with the help of neighbor women and, on several occasions, the services of a doctor homesteading twelve miles to the east. Nannie Alderson went to town for delivery of her first two babies but, with the responsibility for their care, could not leave the ranch when the last two were born, and an inexperienced midwife almost killed one of them. Mrs. Alderson herself nearly died on another occasion when she suffered a miscarriage. The climax of Dale Eunson's narrative of life *Up on the Rim,* twenty miles northwest of Billings, was the night his mother sent him, at age seven, out into a blizzard to summon help because her baby was arriving early.[14]

Where doctors could be found in the region, they were too frequently alcoholics who had been driven from practice in the East.[15] A Dr. Roberts, of *Alberta Homestead,* in the period from 1906 to 1912, was a rarity among the settlers—though unlicensed to practice in Canada, he traveled one March a round trip of forty miles ten times to care for a typhoid case. Even with his professional skill at hand the Robertses were forced to carry their sick boy forty miles by horse and wagon to

[14] Walker D. Wyman, *Frontier Woman: The Life of a Woman Homesteader on the Dakota Frontier* ([Madison]: University of Wisconsin-River Falls Press, 1972), 29; Alderson and Smith, *Bride Goes West,* 195, 202, 205–6; Dale Eunson, *Up on the Rim* (New York: Farrar, Straus and Giroux, 1970), 225–36.

[15] Alderson and Smith, *Bride Goes West,* 196–97, 199–200.

obtain antitoxin for diphtheria.[16] For ordinary ills women on the plains dispensed home remedies—onions, epsom salts, kerosene, and whiskey.

That migraine appears as a recurrent complaint in several accounts of women's life in the region suggests the accumulation of tensions.[17] Women developed obsessive fears in this environment—for Nannie Alderson, fear that her husband would be injured in a horse fight (a premonition, perhaps, of the manner of his death years later when they had moved to town); for Sara Roberts, fear of prairie fire, not an irrational terror when during late summer and early fall flames lighted the sky halfway around the horizon; for most women, fear that some member of the family would be lost while traveling at night or in a blizzard. Mrs. Lewis, envisioning the worst in the children's report of rescuing a colt from a well, burst into tears: "It might have been one of the children in the well! There are so many dangers in this country; more that [*sic*] we ever knew about before we came."[18]

The persistent wind and the coyotes' howls were unnerving. Faye Lewis found the latter "like nothing so much as a despair encompassing all eternity."[19] While Mrs. Alderson expressed delight in the cosy camaraderie of a winter fireside, with cowboys and husband confined in close quarters, more often women complained of the overcrowding in small claim shacks, built with perhaps only one door and a single window, too dark for reading or sewing through the long winter months. Sara Roberts chafed at the confinement: "This weather and being cut off from everybody is almost too much for me."[20] Even Mrs. Alderson's account is liberally salted with self-reproach for gloom.

Women in rural areas everywhere in the early years of the twentieth century continued to perform tasks from which urban women had begun to break away in the 1870s.[21] Farmers' wives kept the chickens, milked the cows, planted and tended the gardens, churned the butter, baked the bread, salted the meat, brined the kraut and corn, canned and preserved the fruit and vegetables, sewed the women's clothing and much of the men's, cooked the meals, washed and ironed, cleaned and decorated the house, and occasionally helped in the fields.[22] On the

16 Sara Ellen Roberts, *Alberta Homestead: Chronicle of a Pioneer Family*, Lathrop E. Roberts, ed. (Austin: University of Texas Press, 1971), 213–17, 261.

17 Ibid., 8–9, 16–17, 38, 253; Alderson, *Bride Goes West*, 209; Eunson, *Up on the Rim*, 61.

18 Faye C. Lewis, *Nothing to Make a Shadow* (Ames: The Iowa State University Press, 1971), 131.

19 Ibid., 93. See also Roberts, *Alberta Homestead*, 44–45.

20 Roberts, *Alberta Homestead*, 79 (quote), 88–89, 92, 96, 98.

21 For editorial comment on the changing role of women in the East, see *Scribner's Monthly* 4 (October 1872): 763.

22 Eunson, *Up on the Rim*, 47–49; Elinore Pruitt Stewart, *Letters of a Woman Homesteader* (Boston: Houghton Mifflin, 1914), 17. Sprague cites as an indication of the greater respect shown women in the West that they rarely engaged in field work,

plains women did all these chores and more—they served as midwives and nurses for ailing neighbors, circulated petitions to get schools established, and provided lodging and meals for transients and for some drifters who were not so transient.

And plains women worked in a physiographic setting where scarcity of water and wood complicated domestic as well as agricultural occupations. Water at shallow levels was generally brackish and in many areas so difficult to reach that wells were inconveniently located, if, indeed, they could be provided. In the dry-farming country of northern Montana and western South Dakota water of satisfactory quality for drinking often ranged from 200 to 500 feet in depth. There it could be obtained only by drilling, which cost, in 1914, a dollar a foot, with an additional 25 cents to a dollar for casing, plus the charge for a pump, windmill, or gasoline engine. Use of cisterns for catching rainwater was widespread, and hauling of water in barrels was common in some districts as late as the 1920s.[23] Nannie Alderson's problems in laundering were not exceptional. Grace Fairchild spoke grimly of the alkaline water found west of the Missouri in South Dakota: "Anybody who drinks such water and isn't accustomed to it will get as sick as a poisoned pup."[24]

Houses in a land of scarce timber were roughly structured. Everett Dick, in *Sod-House Frontier,* has described the dreariness, the dampness, and the dirtiness of a sod house or dugout, where soil particles and straw "kept dropping on everything in the house," roof and walls leaked rivulets as snows melted or rains came, and floors became quagmires.[25] Nannie Alderson, as a bride, received special consideration when her floors were sheeted with wagon canvas. Such dwellings did afford warmth in winter, as the Robertses testified when they resorted to a sod house after they found their log structure too cold for Alberta weather.[26] By the eighties, Dick notes, a large proportion of the claim

but he notes that Scandinavian women in Dakota frequently helped out at harvest (*Women and the West,* 239–40).

[23] Wyman, *Frontier Woman,* 20, 29, 100; Lewis, *Nothing to Make a Shadow,* 43; Roberts, *Alberta Homestead,* 17, 21; Mary W. M. Hargreaves, *Dry Farming in the Northern Great Plains, 1900–1925* (Cambridge, Mass.: Harvard University Press, 1957), 499–500.

[24] Wyman, *Frontier Woman,* 100.

[25] Everett Dick, *The Sod-House Frontier, 1854–1890: A Social History of the Northern Plains from the Creation of Kansas and Nebraska to the Admission of the Dakotas* (New York: D. Appleton-Century, 1937), 111–16. See also Wyman, *Frontier Woman,* 12, 13, 16; Roberts, *Alberta Homestead,* 23–24; Alderson and Smith, *Bride Goes West,* 28, 42.

[26] Roberts, *Alberta Homestead,* 149–52. Frame or log houses were commonly banked with manure for winter warmth. The odor generated during periods of thaw was an unsatisfactory consequence (Wyman, *Frontier Woman,* 16; Lewis, *Nothing to Make a Shadow,* 58–59).

shacks were made of frame covered with tar paper and chinked with mud. Grace Fairchild complained that, with the warping of the cottonwood siding and the drying of the mud filler, they were always in need of repair. And Jessie Eunson knew well the torments of the nether regions as she pickled cucumbers under a July sun beating upon tar paper.[27]

Women tried to make such dwellings attractive by whitewashing the exterior, plastering walls with multiple coats of mud, and lining the interior with muslin or bright calico. But snakes in the kitchen as an accompaniment of such rough construction terrified more than one of the housewives who have recounted their experiences.[28] Most reporters also noted problems of combating lice and bedbugs.[29]

Perhaps the women who have written such accounts were more literate, better educated, more concerned for the refinements of the life they had known to the east than the average frontier settler. But common parlance asserted and limited evidence sustains the view that those who carried the agricultural advance beyond the hundredth meridian were very often schoolteachers, clerks, artisans, unemployed widows, or "old maids"—city folk. A survey of the occupational backgrounds of 550 homesteaders in the north central Montana "triangle" in 1922, when already several years of drought had driven out the more easily disheartened, revealed that only 51 percent had been farming before they came to the region. Over a quarter of the tenants listed in the North Dakota *Census* of 1920 lacked previous farm experience.[30] The lure of speculative profits to be gleaned from the last of the dwindling public domain attracted an unusually large number of settlers whose hands were uncalloused. Land Office regulations which permitted leave of absence from the claim through the winter months and completion of entry after only three summers of farming encouraged schoolteachers to vacation as homesteaders. Grace Fairchild, noting that single women could file claims but not the married, commented: "It always looked to me as if the government was run by men and all the laws were made for them. So women had to take up claims before they got married." Or after their husbands died. In the Fairchilds' case, her widowed mother filed an adjoining claim, lived on it just long enough to complete entry, and then transferred it to expand the Fairchild holding.[31]

But even more committed agricultural pioneers carried with them to the frontier cultivated tastes expressed by the inclusion of pianos, or-

27 Wyman, *Frontier Woman*, 16; Eunson, *Up on the Rim*, 89.

28 Alderson and Smith, *Bride Goes West*, 64–65; Wyman, *Frontier Woman*, 67–70.

29 Lewis, *Nothing to Make a Shadow*, 97–99; Alderson and Smith, *Bride Goes West*, 147–48, 227–28; Roberts, *Alberta Homestead*, 38.

30 Hargreaves, *Dry Farming*, 452–53.

31 Wyman, *Frontier Woman*, 38.

gans, Haviland china, silver candelabra, and similar symbols of gracious living as freight in homesteaders' boxcars. Gradually women of the plains relinquished most of these treasures, as they lost, too, their hopes of finding quick wealth in farming ventures. They shared the discouragements when promising crops were destroyed by hail or early frost, and the anxiety when weeks of drought stunted grain. A good yield could mean income for home improvements—a wood floor, a shingled roof, an additional room. But those who settled the Dakotas during the first decade of the twentieth century learned by 1910 and 1911 of the perils of agriculture beyond the line of semiaridity. Many of those who broke the benchlands of Montana during the second decade abandoned the struggle during the years of drought and cascading grain prices from 1917 to 1924. Farmers on the plains found that increased capital expenditures were needed for larger land units, machinery with which to practice a more extensive type of operation, and livestock to permit diversification of the enterprise.[32] Accumulation of reserves sufficient to maintain the business through several years of low or even negative return emerged as a dictum of successful management if one were to survive in the area. Household refinements had to wait.

Purchase of an automobile or truck might be justified as a necessary farm expense—it could be used to speed the delivery of supplies to the farm and of crops to town.[33] The impact of the automobile in breaking the isolation of rural life was revolutionary. But household conveniences were much slower in coming. While the introduction of gasoline pumps and, around 1915, of pneumatic-pressure systems facilitated the installation of indoor plumbing, the cost was prohibitive for most plains settlers through the lean years that continued until 1940.[34] A survey in 1935 of six South Dakota counties, selected to represent farming areas across the state, showed that at least three-fourths of the households were still dependent on an outside water supply; only one-fifth had electricity; only 12 percent, central heating. Jones and Perkins Counties, on the plains just west of the Missouri River, ranked at the bottom in material standard of living. Lawrence County, adjacent to a lumbering center, still had many log cabins; sod houses were yet common in Perkins. And in the latter area "soddies" were even then being constructed.[35]

[32] Hargreaves, *Dry Farming*, 477–84, 503–21, and passim.

[33] The rapidity and extent of automobile introduction in this region was phenomenal (Hargreaves, *Dry Farming*, 491–92).

[34] Hargreaves, *Dry Farming*, 500–501.

[35] W. F. Kumlien et al., *The Standard of Living of Farm and Village Families in Six South Dakota Counties, 1935*, South Dakota Agricultural Experiment Station Bulletin 320 (Brookings, 1938), 19, 30, 33–35, 42 (fig. 18).

Census reports for North Dakota in 1945 show electricity in only 13 percent of the farm dwellings of Pierce County, on the hundredth meridian, and 25 percent of those in McKenzie, a ranching and irrigated farming center on the western border. Running water was indicated for only 5 percent of the Pierce County homes and 9 percent of those in McKenzie. Running water was then available in 10, 12, up to 15 percent of the farmhouses in the earlier settled areas of southwestern North Dakota, lands developed along the Northern Pacific route shortly after the turn of the century; but in the northwestern counties the percentages still stood at 3 to 6 percent.[36]

Medical facilities also remained limited. In 1940 five west-river counties of South Dakota had only one doctor. One entire county and parts of twelve others—all in the trans-Missouri region—lacked access to a hospital within a radius of fifty miles. Dentists—Nannie Alderson had found toothache one of her greatest tribulations—were still in 1940 concentrated in the larger towns and cities.[37]

For women, life in the agricultural development of the northern plains continued rigorous. Small wonder that during the drought years of the thirties the proportion of emigrants from the region was more female than male. A 1935 survey of those who had left South Dakota showed that the women were better educated than the men—a reflection of the general fact that girls on the farms achieved more schooling than boys; but the survey also indicated that women who were college graduates were more likely to emigrate than men of comparable education. Of the college-educated women migrants who remained in the state, none had married farmers, and only two of the twenty-six who had left the area were associated with occupations identified as agricultural.[38]

[36] Baldur H. Kristjanson and C. J. Heltemes, *Handbook of Facts about North Dakota Agriculture,* North Dakota Agricultural Experiment Station Bulletin 357 (Fargo, 1950), 92–93 (figs. 54, 56). Cf. also, for divergent data and a somewhat more favorable report, A. H. Anderson, *Changes in Farm Population and Rural Life in Four North Dakota Counties,* North Dakota Agricultural Experiment Station Bulletin 375 (Fargo, 1952), 18.

[37] W. F. Kumlien, *Basic Trends of Social Change in South Dakota, V. Public Health Facilities,* South Dakota Agricultural Experiment Station Bulletin 334 (Brookings, 1940), 19, 22.

[38] Walter L. Slocum, *Migrants from Rural South Dakota Families, Their Geographical and Occupational Distribution,* South Dakota Agricultural Experiment Station Bulletin 359 (Brookings, 1942), 8, 9, 14–15. See also Carl F. Kraenzel, *Montana's Population Changes, 1920 to 1950, Especially as to Numbers and Composition,* Montana Agricultural Experiment Station Bulletin 520 (Bozeman, 1956), 27, 45–46; Stanley W. Voelker and Thomas K. Ostenson, *North Dakota's Human Resources, a Study of Population Change in a Great Plains Environment,* North Dakota Agricultural Experiment Station Bulletin 476 (Fargo, 1968), 14, 20. At this time, too, men were more numerous than women in all three states.

The characteristics of the outmigration shifted by the end of the thirties, when military service and wartime job opportunities contributed to an exodus of men. At the same time, the improved quality of life in the area with the development of rural electrification and improved transportation appears to have enhanced the attractions of the region for women. While the male population of the Dakotas and Wyoming has declined since 1940, the number of women on the plains has increased everywhere but in North Dakota. By 1960 there were more women than men in Kansas, Nebraska, and Colorado, and by 1970 in Montana and South Dakota, as well.

The women whose reminiscences have told so much of the hardships of early settlement on the plains almost always expressed delight in the climate, the scenery, and the springtime awakening of nature. Occasionally, like Jessie Eunson's, their enthusiasm converted projects for a temporary venture into a serious farming commitment. Elinore Pruitt Stewart, who in 1913 proudly completed her entry on a claim in western Wyoming, saw homesteading as "the solution of all poverty's problems." While warning that "persons afraid of coyotes and work and loneliness had better let ranching alone," she argued that "any woman who can stand her own company, can see the beauty of the sunset, loves growing things, and is willing to put in as much time at careful labor as she does over the washtub, will certainly succeed; will have independence, plenty to eat all the time, and a home of her own in the end."[39] Not many women adjusted to this life so well as Grace Fairchild, who took over farm management with a flexible awareness that old programs must be modified to fit a new land. But the increasing proportion of women in the region today indicates that they generally have made the necessary adaptations. The changes which have fostered the shift in commitment since 1940 are another chapter.

[39] Stewart, *Letters of a Woman Homesteader*, 215.

Women and Men in Western History: A Stereoptical Vision

SUSAN ARMITAGE

In Victorian parlors one could often find a small viewer, called a stereopticon, and accompanying cards of photographs. Each card seems to contain two identical pictures, but when you place the card in the device, look through the eyepiece, and adjust the focus, a three-dimensional picture appears. The images on the card are not, after all, identical. When combined, they produce a fuller, deeper picture than one can obtain from a single image.

So it is with the new field of western women's history. The slightly different perspective of women's history can add a significant dimension to western history that has heretofore been lacking. As Joan Jensen and Darlis Miller noted in their article, "Gentle Tamers Revisited," western women's history has experienced remarkable growth and development in the past ten years. Jensen and Miller surveyed the subfield and suggested many fruitful areas for future research, but they did not attempt to show how new research in western women's history might modify western history as a whole.[1] That is my intention.

Western history has always been a diverse and prolific field. Today, however, it is widely acknowledged that the diversity indicates some theoretical disarray. The old masters—Turner, Bolton, and Webb—no longer dominate, but no new general themes have gained widespread acceptance. There is a growing interest in the creation of syntheses that will encorporate new approaches to western history while retaining older ones.[2] The following observations on the perspective of women's history are offered in that spirit—as part of a general effort to contribute to the new western history.

Susan Armitage is associate professor of history and Director of Women Studies at Washington State University. Support was provided by a Mellon Fellowship from the Wellesley College Center for Research on Women.

[1]Joan M. Jensen and Darlis A. Miller, "The Gentle Tamers Revisited: New Approaches to the History of Women in the American West," *Pacific Historical Review*, XLIX (May 1980), 173-213. In fall 1983, Darlis Miller produced an updated bibliography, which is available from the Institute of the American West, Sun Valley, ID.

[2]See in particular Michael P. Malone, ed., *Historians and the American West* (Lincoln, 1983).

Many of the observations to follow are not unique to women's history but are shared with other historians who wish to see new topics considered in western history. However, among them all, women's history is exceptional because it raises more than the question of including neglected minority groups or neglected issues. Women are not a minority group; women are everywhere. Women of all colors, religions, and classes live side by side with men, some as members of the dominant groups, some as members of subordinate ones. The women's perspective, then, was a part of every historical reality. But although men and women participated in the same historical event (such as, for example, the journey west on the Overland Trail), their actual experiences and feelings about the event were not the same. The West looked different through women's eyes. If we seek to understand all of western history, we must be able, as in the stereopticon, to see through women's eyes as well as those of men.

Before exploring the stereoptical vision, I want first to discuss the claim of difference in some detail, because this is a controversial point. Why is there a distinctive female perspective? The difference exists because women were—and still are today—socialized differently from men. Women have been trained to care for the values of home and family—the private, emotional, intimate side of life. Men also care about those things, but they are socialized in ways that will help them to function effectively in the public realm of competition and controversy and to deal with strangers and impersonal forces. Furthermore, the life experience of men and women is determined, at least in part, by gender, for events have different consequences for each sex. There is a spectrum of difference ranging from major events like war (men go away and fight, women keep the homefires burning) to commonplace gendered division of labor in the home or in the workplace. In every aspect of our lives, gender matters; sex role socialization, expectations, and experience combine to create gender-specific worldviews.[3] If this is true today, when sex stereotyping is breaking down, how much truer it must have been in the past, when gender-linked patterns of life and labor were everywhere the norm.

Certainly men and women of the same race, economic class, and general background will agree in several areas; however, the interests and viewpoints of men and women are not identical. The difference does *not* mean that women, as a group, secretly disagree with everything men do but are too submissive or manipulative to say so. It does mean that there is a women's

[3]Among the large amount of literature on this topic the following seem most relevant to this discussion: in history, Peter Filene, *Him/Her Self: Sex Roles in Modern America* (New York, 1975); in anthropology, Sherry Ortner and Harriet Whitehead, eds., *Sexual Meanings: The Cultural Construction of Gender and Sexuality* (Cambridge, MA, 1981); and in psychology, Jean Baker Miller, *Toward a New Psychology of Women* (Boston, 1976).

view of every issue and event. This may not always be obvious, for in most cultures, including the nineteenth-century American West, women deferred publicly to men. Consequently, gender differences are rarely a matter of public record.

What does this fact of difference mean to historians? Basically, it means that there is a gap between a man's ideas about a woman and the woman's sense of herself and her world. We may not always be able to specify the difference between men's and women's attitudes, because for both sexes they are so basic that they are often unconscious and undeclared. As historians, we will not always be able to document the difference, given the natural difficulty with sources. But we must assume that there is a difference and that if we rely on male sources to learn about women's lives, the story will be inadequate.[4]

What does this mean for western history? Bluntly stated, much of our existing history is incomplete, because men failed to consider the female experience. But it is facile to criticize older western history for failure to be inclusive. After all, that history is already written. The most useful step, surely, is to show in what ways the recognition of a female perspective can shape future research.

The virtual omission of women from western history was a result of Turner's fundamental insight that the story of the frontier was the struggle with the physical environment. Following Turner, historians have believed that although women were present in the West, they did not participate in the making of its history because they were "hidden in the household"—engrossed in domestic chores and childrearing. The "real" life of the West—the subduing of the environment—was men's work that went on in public spaces, away from the household.[5] In contrast, women's history asserts that what women did within the household was important far beyond that household, and, further, that women did not remain encapsulated within the household as the model suggests. Furthermore, a close study of women's lives in the West yields not only new information but some new theoretical perspectives.

[4]The pathbreaking article establishing the difference was Joan Kelly-Gadol, "The Social Relation of the Sexes: Methodological Implications of Women's History," *Signs*, 1 (Summer 1976), 809-23. For a more recent example of the importance of gender difference, see Carol Gilligan, *In a Different Voice* (Cambridge, MA, 1982).

[5]As T. A. Larson said, "Women, after all, did not lead expeditions, command troops, build railroads, drive cattle or ride Pony Express . . ." in short, do any of the important work of the West. See T. A. Larson, "Women's Role in the American West," *Montana the Magazine of Western History*, XXIV (Summer 1974), 2-11. Sandra L. Myres provides a good survey of Larson and earlier historians in her review essay "Women in the West," in Malone, *Historians and the American West*, 369-86, but her review of recent work by women's historians is brief and often unfriendly.

Let us look at Turner's frontier through women's eyes. We notice that there were two distinct groups of women: women in families, and single women who were members of larger women's groups with a definite occupation (schoolteachers, nuns, prostitutes). The first important thing to realize is that unlike many men in western history, women were not solitary individuals "going it alone." The vast majority of women saw themselves as members of groups, and to understand their experience we need to see them in the group context. Further, we must recognize how different these group contexts were from each other and how the differences affected women's lives.

What insights emerge from consideration of women in family and groups that can be applied to the field of western history as a whole? In the following pages I will discuss: (1) the need to move away from a concentration on individuals to a consideration of individuals in the group context; (2) the importance of families in western settlement and the need to look at kinship links in migration and development; (3) the need to consider the family, not just the man, as a producing economic unit; (4) the need, even in areas dominated by male work groups, to consider the female perspective and women's work activities in particular; (5) the consideration of sex role ideology as an indicator of frontier adaptation; and (6) the value of a multicultural approach.

The different experiences of men and women within the family have been most carefully studied on the Overland Trail. John Faragher has analyzed the different patterns of work roles within the family: adult men and women had different tasks, rhythms of activity, and attitudes. In contrast to at-home roles, on the trail men's activities were constant (driving and herding) and women's activities sporadic (cooking at night for the next day, washing only on infrequent, sometimes unscheduled, layover days). Attitudinally, for adult men, the journey west was a test and a challenge; for women it was primarily housekeeping under much more difficult circumstances than at home. This is not a trivial point. Men were challenged constantly by change: choices about route, equipment, care of animals, and speed of travel were directly affected by the changing environment. On the other hand, women had the job of holding the fabric of daily life together, of providing continuity—a job that got harder and harder as the trip lengthened and exhaustion deepened. Given these task differences, it would be genuinely extraordinary if male and female perspectives on the experience were identical.[6]

The second issue emerging most clearly in Lillian Schlissel's work on the Overland Trail is the importance of families in the migration. As we know, thousands of single men rushed to California, but if we look at the intending settlers, rather than the sojourners, kinship ties become a topic

[6]John Faragher, *Women and Men on the Overland Trail* (New Haven, 1979).

of major importance. Those kinship ties, although important to both sexes, loomed larger in women's lives than they did in the lives of men. This should not surprise us, for women were the keepers of kin networks. Women sent the family letters, remembered the birthdays and occasions, nursed the sick, and mourned the dead. They "kept in touch" and thus provided support for themselves and for men who were busy doing other things.[7]

Moving from the personal to a more general level, the new attention to families has provided historians with an important, new analytic tool. We can look at the role of kinship networks in migration and settlement; in many cases we will find that the first settlers were often followed later by family and neighbors. All except the first were following a path eased by familiar kin. They were not loners facing a strange world—they were going to join their father, mother, sister, or brother. The importance of kinship has been acknowledged by historians of immigration and is commonplace in studies of certain ethnic groups that settled in the West (for example, the German-Russians and Scandinavians), but it has not been generally applied to the study of American settlers.[8] Perhaps the Turnerian emphasis on the heroic individual is to blame for the neglect of family groups. Yet the importance of kinship in migration is a recurring theme in women's writings: Mollie Dorsey Sanford and her husband, "gold-rushers" to Colorado in 1859, were soon followed by her sister and brother-in-law; Abigail Scott Duniway was part of a large migration of the Scott clan to Oregon that constituted a vital support network for her all her life; and Phoebe and Harlan Judson were the connection in the chain of migration to Washington Territory begun by her parents and siblings and ended by his relatives.[9] Considering kinship networks in our studies gives us a new way to put individuals and families in a wider context, to place them in the broad social movement of people moving west.

In the early stages of settlement, women's household activities often made a crucial contribution to the family economy. Duniway produced thousands of pounds of butter in every year of her early married life. Sanford cooked for an entire mining camp in Colorado, thus literally "grubstaking" her husband's search for gold. The wives of young professional men

[7] Lillian Schlissel, *Women's Diaries of the Westward Journey* (New York, 1982).

[8] See Frederick C. Luebke's discussion, "Ethnic Minority Groups in the American West," in Malone, *Historians and the American West*, 387-413. See also Robert C. Ostergren, "Kinship Networks and Migration, A Ninteenth-Century Swedish Example," *Social Science History*, 6 (Summer 1982), 293-320.

[9] Donald F. Danker, ed., *Mollie: The Journal of Mollie Dorsey Sanford in Nebraska and Colorado Territories, 1857-1866* (Lincoln, 1959); Ruth Moynihan, *Abigail Scott Duniway: Rebel for Rights* (New Haven, 1983); and Phoebe Judson, *A Pioneer's Search for an Ideal Home* (1925; reprint, Lincoln, 1984).

in Nevada City took in boarders to augment the family income.[10] All of those women would have been categorized as "at home" by the census taker, for they were not engaged in wage work. Yet obviously their work made an economic contribution to the household income. Women's work must have contributed significantly to regional economic development, but until now, this work has been overlooked. Did the obviously important household work of western women lead to an appreciation of women's activities and a rough notion of equality? Or rather, was it true, as Duniway charged, that Oregon farmers ignored the fact that their wives were exhausted by overwork and too-frequent childbearing?[11]

For western women were not only producers, but reproducers both of people and of social conditions. Childrearing, a virtually unexplored topic nationally, is especially important to consider in the West, for surely adaptation to the West must have been a multigenerational experience.[12] How and when did one become a "westerner"? Who first developed a sense of a new regional identity—the pioneers or their children? How, to ask a more general question, does the environment affect the generational transmission of ideology? These questions would seem to be central to an understanding of the development of a sense of regional identity. Western historians have heretofore thought of regional identity largely in political terms. But most western women were barred from direct participation in politics until the 1890s or even later. How did they develop a sense of regional identity and transmit it to their children? To answer these questions, we can look for models in the work of immigration historians and political sociologists. Surely we will find that for everyone—male and female—the development of a sense of regional identity was a psychological matter as well as a political one.[13]

Because of their children, western women defined as family concerns a whole range of issues we might consider public: the establishment of schools.

[10]Moynihan, *Abigail Scott Duniway*; Danker, *Mollie*; and Ralph Mann, *After the Gold Rush: Society in Grass Valley and Nevada City, California, 1849-1870* (Stanford, 1982), 44-46, 107-14.

[11]Moynihan, *Abigail Scott Duniway*, 69.

[12]Elliott West, "Heathens and Angels: Childhood in the Rocky Mountain Mining Towns," *Western Historical Quarterly*, XIV (April 1983), 145-64. West is working on a book-length study.

[13]See Luebke's discussion of assimilation in "Ethnic Minority Groups," 395-96. Political sociologists, whose attention was drawn to generational transmission when confronted by the "generation gap" of the 1960s, have concluded that "parent-child similarity is most noticeable in religious and political areas, least in sex roles and lifestyle characteristics," Lillian Troll and Vern Bengtson, "Generations in the Family," in Wesley R. Burr et al., eds., *Contemporary Theories about the Family*, vol. 1 (New York, 1979), 139. Another issue, just emerging in feminist scholarship, is women's attitudes toward the land. Literary critic Annette Kolodny suggests that women had a domestic view of the land very different from male attitudes, but she has not yet published her work on the trans-Mississippi West. For earlier frontiers, see Annette Kolodny, *The Land before Her* (Raleigh, NC, 1984).

and churches, issues of public morality, health and social welfare issues, and political issues such as prohibition and the vote. We know that women were involved in all of these issues at different times and places in the West and that they used slogans like the WCTU's "Home Protection" to fight for political causes. By the late nineteenth century, women were willing to challenge male dominance of politics, at least on certain issues. Although individual women rarely spoke out alone, groups of women began to work together for political goals. The central role played by western women's organizations in welfare and reform activities is beginning to be documented, but another layer of informal activity lies beneath that.[14] Oral histories have made us aware of how frequently twentieth-century women worked "behind the scenes" to lay the groundwork for community projects or to nudge the influential men of their communities toward action on a particular matter. In one early twentieth-century Colorado farming community, a farm wife proposed to establish a state park at a favorite local gathering place. She and her husband both worked to get the support of friends and neighbors. But when a delegation traveled to Denver to get political approval, it was composed solely of men.[15] Lacking the information available through oral history, a historian might easily suppose that women had had no part at all in the undertaking. This mistake can be traced back to the Turnerian assumption that women were solely domestic and had no larger concerns. But that is *only* an assumption, and an illogical one to boot. Indeed, the stereotype of woman as "gentle tamer" of the West stressed her concern for schools, churches, culture, and reform. But because the stereotype evolved along with the Turnerian notion that action was reserved solely to men, the result has been a misapprehension of women's actual role in community building. Much of this activity has not yet been fully documented. When it is, we will need to revise the view of women as entirely private, domestic creatures. Women were not "hidden in the household"; nor was the household that isolated from the outside world.

The issue of power and decision making within the family, although difficult to explore because of reticence and scanty sources, is also enlightening. Upon careful examination, the family, often seen as a harmonious refuge from a harsh world, was sometimes a pretty horrible place itself. Agnes Smedley's *Daughter of Earth* makes a clear connection between the economic exploitation in the coal mines of Colorado and the brutalities of family

[14]One particularly comprehensive article is June Underwood's "Civilizing Kansas: Women's Organizations, 1880-1920," *Kansas History*, 7 (Winter/Spring 1985), 291-306. For a national perspective on women's organizations, see Anne Firor Scott, "On Seeing and Not Seeing: A Case of Historical Invisibility," *Journal of American History*, 71 (June 1984), 7-21.

[15]Interview with Betty Lundy about Walk's Camp Park, Genoa, Colorado, by Sue Armitage, August 13, 1978. Interview deposited at the Genoa Public Library, Genoa, CO.

life. Mari Sandoz explores the domestic violence that stained her childhood in *Old Jules* and claims that in her region of Nebraska male brutality toward wives and children was a community norm. These two examples take us far indeed from the idealized portrait of the frontier family we find, for example, in Laura Ingalls Wilder. Yet they are also part of the western experience, and they point to the need to delve deeper into the power dynamics within western families than we have done in the past.[16]

There are other ways in which women's sources can contribute to our understanding of western violence. This theme, which has attracted considerable attention in recent years, has been viewed exclusively from a male perspective. As a result, one aspect that has been omitted is violence against women, both public (rapes and killings) and private (domestic violence). The emergence of a distinctive female perspective will add a new dimension to our discussion of violence in the West. As we understand the ways in which women were affected by violence, our focus will likely shift from a concentration on violent actions to a greater consideration of the effects of violence upon both victim and perpetrator.

The women's perspective may help us to assess the "underside" of western history—the brutal, unpleasant, and harsh aspects we know to be there, although we would like to ignore them. One fruitful approach has been the use of court records. Studies of divorce in different parts of the West are beginning to provide us with new glimpses into the family and social attitudes toward marriage.[17] Another extremely useful tool is that of literary analysis. As the earlier example of domestic violence indicated, study of regional fiction (much of it written by women) can yield insights into hidden emotions. Elizabeth Hampsten opens up another new approach with her careful reading of the commonplace letters of ordinary men and women. Scorned by English scholars because they are "nonliterary," these writings can nevertheless tell us much about the lives and feelings of the multitude of unnotable people who settled the West.[18] And then of course there are the thousands of diaries of the Overland Trail and settlement kept by women and men alike. Women's historians have assumed that women's diaries

[16]Agnes Smedley, *Daughter of Earth* (Old Westbury, NY, 1973); Mari Sandoz, *Old Jules* (Lincoln, 1935); and Laura Ingalls Wilder, *Little House on the Prairie* (New York, 1935). For a sensitive reading of these texts and others as they illuminate the issue of domestic violence, see Melody Graulich, "Violence against Women: Power Dynamics in Literature of the Western Family," *Frontiers*, VII (Summer 1984), 14-20.

[17]Robert L. Griswold, *Family and Divorce in California, 1850-1890* (Albany, 1982); Paula Petrik, "The Bonanza Town: Women and Family on the Rocky Mountain Mining Frontier, Helena, Montana, 1865-1900" (doctoral dissertation, SUNY Binghamton, 1982). For information on a more recent period, see Diane Sands, "Using Oral History to Chart the Course of Illegal Abortions in Montana," *Frontiers*, VII (no. 1, 1983), 32-37.

[18]Elizabeth Hampsten, *Read This Only to Yourself* (Bloomington, 1982).

were more likely to be expressive and emotional than those of men. There is evidence that women, while publicly supporting their men, used their diaries as places to admit the fears and hardships of pioneering that they could not confide anywhere else.[19] But whether we can assume that all—or even most—men stoically ignored their difficulties and repressed tender feelings is another matter. A study of men's diaries and personal writings, similar to that undertaken with women's diaries, would provide new information about men's attitudes. In the past, the dominant theme of western settlement as a success story has obscured knowledge of failures and disappointment. But today, as we seek a fuller psychological sense of the stresses and tensions as well as the joys and pleasures of pioneering, we will need to draw fully on the personal writings of both women and men.

There are still other ways in which the woman's perspective can give us a fuller sense of the western experience. Research in women's sources may affect older historical writings about some celebrated all-male work groups such as fur trappers, soldiers, and miners. Canadian scholars have shown that native women played a vital part in the Northwest fur trade. European men married Indian women to assure themselves of both a work partner and friendly access to local tribes.[20] Whether interracial marriage was common in the much smaller and shorter western American fur trade is still to be seen. Preliminary research seems to indicate the much greater importance of family and community groups than earlier researchers, focusing on the solitary trapper, had perceived.[21] Military life is another area of potential enrichment. A number of accounts by army wives have been published or recently republished. As a group, these privileged and educated women provided interesting accounts of landscape and local Indians and detailed pictures of the day-to-day domestic life in western military establishments.[22] When these accounts are synthesized and integrated into the existing histories, our understanding of western military life will be richer. Recovering the experience of miners' wives is more difficult, for working-class women did not ordinarily write memoirs. Work with census records, local newspapers, court records, and other primary sources is slowly building up a sense of mining-town women as active and integrated members of their communities. By focusing on women, we can see an aspect of the

[19]Schlissel, *Women's Diaries*; and Susan Armitage, "Reluctant Pioneers," in Helen Winter Stauffer and Susan J. Rosowski, eds., *Women and Western Literature* (New York, 1982), 40-51.

[20]Sylvia Van Kirk, *Many Tender Ties: Women in Fur Trade Society, 1670-1870* (Norman, 1983).

[21]See in particular William Swagerty, "Marriage and Settlement Patterns of Rocky Mountain Trappers and Traders," *Western Historical Quarterly*, XI (April 1980), 159-80.

[22]Sandra L. Myres provides an excellent introduction and bibliography on army wives in Teresa Griffen Viele, *Following the Drum* (Lincoln, 1984).

mining town that has been neglected until now—not men's work, nor the sordid leisure of saloon and whorehouse, but the lives of ordinary people learning to live in an extraordinary environment.[23]

In the most general sense, attention to women's activities within the family provides us with a new vantage point from which to view the activities and attitudes of other family members, to consider questions like what it meant to be a child in the West or the ways in which men balanced public and family roles. Surely the challenge of coming to terms with a new environment was experienced by everyone, not just the men. A study of family strategies of adaptation, in particular family work roles, gives us a way to reask Turner's basic question with today's tools and insights.

Work and its meaning was also the central question faced by our second category of women—single women in occupational groups. At the moment much less is known about these women because there has been so little research. Would that schoolteachers had attracted the attention paid to cowboys over the years! In contrast to much of the writing on cowboys, however, recent studies of women's groups have tried to fit women and their occupations into a wider social context. Miriam Goldman's study of prostitution on the Comstock Lode not only described the organization of the trade itself but went on to show how prostitution was an integral part of the social life on the lode, affecting everyone—men, women, and children.[24] Other studies of more "respectable" working women have shown how the occupational opportunities for women were structured by the nature of the local industry. If, for example, we look at male-dominated industries like mining, the job opportunities for women were very few and specific—they were domestic or sexual. The spectrum ranged from the respectable "private" housewife, followed by a range of domestic jobs (domestic servant, cook, laundress) to the semisexual, semidomestic jobs (waitress, bargirl, etc.) ending with the bad "public" woman—the prostitute. This narrow spectrum of occupations for women characterized male industry towns other than mining, such as lumber-dominated Seattle.[25] Other towns with other

[23]The best collection of articles on women in mining towns was presented at the 1983 Women's West conference. They were: Betsy Jameson, "Women as Workers, Women as Civilizers: True Womanhood in the American West"; Susan Johnson, "Sharing Bed and Board: Informal Union and Cultural Difference in Central Arizona Mining Towns, 1863-1873"; Mary Murphy, "The Private Lives of Public Women: Prostitution in Butte, Montana, 1878-1917"; Nancy Taniguichi, "Ties That Bind: Building Utah's Coal Communities"; and Elliott West, "Beyond Baby Doe: Childrearing on the Mining Frontier," in Susan Armitage and Elizabeth Jameson, eds., *The Women's West*, forthcoming 1986 from the University of Oklahoma Press. The Jameson, Murphy, and Johnson papers also appear in *Frontiers*, VII (Summer 1984). An earlier version of Paula Petrik's paper, "Capitalists with Rooms: Prostitution in Helena, Montana, 1865-1900," appeared in *Montana the Magazine of Western History*, XXXI (April 1981), 28-41.

[24]Miriam Goldman, *Gold Diggers and Silver Miners: Prostitution and Social Life on the Comstock Lode* (Ann Arbor, 1981).

[25]For mining towns, see Goldman, *Gold Diggers*. See also Elizabeth Jameson, "Imper-

mixes of industry had different patterns. As these patterns of women's employment are deciphered, we will have a new way of seeing the social organization of western towns.

In addition to overall work patterns, a number of other issues emerge from a study of women in occupational groups. Among them are questions about the nature and ideology of the occupation; conditions of recruitment, employment, and work; relations with people being served; and group support, or lack thereof. For schoolteachers, group support was valued. As Polly Kaufman's study of pioneer teachers shows, the feeling of group support and group purpose gave the often lonely teacher the feeling of belonging to a larger enterprise.[26] But the extent of such sisterly feeling in another all-female group—prostitutes—is more problematic.

Kathleen Underwood has argued that teaching offered genuine opportunity for western women, both in terms of paid employment and by expanding personal options (the choice not to marry, for example) in socially acceptable ways.[27] Teaching may well have been unique. Other historians from David Potter onward have been much less inclined to view the West as a place of opportunity for women.[28] Does this mean, to mention the oldest Turnerian chestnut of them all, that the West did not liberate women? Was the West a land of opportunity only for men? Women's historians have sought at least partial answers to this question by examining sex-role ideology in the West. Julie Roy Jeffrey was among the first to argue that pioneer women did not wish to be liberated from Victorian notions about women's proper role. Her women were civilizers who saw the Victorian cult of True Womanhood as central to their personal identities. The freedom of the West did not liberate the women she studied from the constraints of eastern custom.[29]

fect Unions: Class and Gender in Cripple Creek, 1894-1904," in Milton Cantor and Bruce Laurie, eds., *Class, Sex and the Woman Worker* (Westport, 1977), 166-202. For Seattle see Janet Reiff, "Urbanization and the Social Structure: Seattle, Washington, 1852-1910" (doctoral dissertation, University of Washington, 1981).

[26] Polly Welts Kaufman, *Women Teachers on the Frontier* (New Haven, 1984).

[27] Kathleen Underwood, "The Pace of Her Own Life: Teacher Training and the Life Course of Western Women" (n.p., 1983, University of Texas at Arlington), in possession of the author.

[28] Historian David Potter specifically raised the issue of frontier opportunity for women in his pathbreaking article "American Women and the American Character," in Don E. Fehrenbacher, ed., *History and American Society. Essays of David M. Potter* (New York, 1973), 277-303.

[29] Julie Roy Jeffrey, *Frontier Women: The Trans-Mississippi West, 1840-1880* (New York, 1979). Jeffrey employed the widely used formulation of early nineteenth century women's roles developed by Barbara Welter in "The Cult of True Womanhood, 1820-1860," *American Quarterly*, XVIII (Summer 1966), 151-74, in which ideal women are described as pious, pure, domestic, and submissive.

Some western historians have seen this evidence as a significant illustration of Earl Pomeroy's argument that continuity, rather than Turnerian adaptation, characterized the frontier.[30] But recent studies are beginning to reveal a more complex picture. Northeastern Colorado farm women found ways to make sex role stereotyping compatible with lives that were characterized by a high degree of mutuality and sharing, while miners' wives in Cripple Creek shared a female subculture that was a good deal more authentic than the cult of True Womanhood allowed.[31] These examples show that even in matters of ideology, economic class cannot be ignored. Furthermore, there is suggestive evidence that even within the middle class, change rather than continuity was the rule. We have known for some time that twentieth-century western women were "freer" in their attitudes than their eastern sisters, but this difference has not been analyzed historically. Women's writings suggest that although the first generation of western women may have clung to Victorian stereotypes, some of their daughters did not. We need to think generationally, not just of the pioneers. Perhaps much significant change in the west happened at the slow pace of "family time" rather than the faster-paced political time to which we are accustomed.[32]

This is one example of the way in which women's history encourages us to look into the twentieth century and to identify long patterns of continuity or change. Within western history today many voices (among them urban historians, ethnic historians, and historians of transportation, land policy, and water use) are urging us to look beyond the frontier. Perhaps it is time to subsume Turner's famous frontier markerpoints into a larger, longer time frame. To this widened view of western history, women's history can bring a valuable multicultural perspective. Women's historians are interested in the history of *all* women and seek to distinguish female experience in all races, not just in the European pioneers. Whether in our own research, or by drawing on the work of anthropologists and ethnic studies

[30] Richard W. Etulain, "Shifting Interpretations of Western Cultural History," in Malone, *Historians and the American West*, 425; and Mann, *After the Gold Rush*, 202-3.

[31] Katharine Harris, "Homesteading in Northeastern Colorado, 1873-1920: Sex Roles and Women's Experience," *Frontiers*, VII (Summer 1984), 43-45; and Betsy Jameson, "Women as Workers."

[32] D'Ann Campbell, "Was the West Different? Values and Attitudes of Young Women in 1943," *Pacific Historical Review*, XLVII (August 1978), 453-63. One significant contribution to the present lack of historical analysis is Sandra L. Myres's chapter on female entrepreneurship in *Westering Women and the Frontier Experience, 1800-1915* (Albuquerque, 1982). Two articles have made beginning approaches to the mother-daughter question: Lillian Schlissel, "Mothers and Daughters on the Western Frontier," *Frontiers*, III (Summer 1978), 29-33, and Eliane Silverman, "In Their Own Words: Mothers and Daughters on the Alberta Frontier, 1890-1929," *Frontiers*, II (Summer 1977), 37-44. The difficulty of understanding the relationship between political change and change in family patterns was discussed by Peter Laslett, "The Family and the Collectivity," *Sociology and Social Research*, special issue on Historical Change in Marriage and the Family, 63 (April 1979), 432-42.

scholars, we are working to understand the experience of American Indian, Hispanic, black, and Asian women in their own right.

This multicultural perspective means that women's history has much to contribute to the study of race relations in the West. First, there is the question of relationships between white men and American Indian and Hispanic women in the exploration and fur-trading eras of western history. We know that there is a history of sexual contact; we are beginning to be able to assess that contact from the women's perspective.[33]

With the arrival of numbers of white settlers, the topic of race relations, as experienced by women of all races, becomes more complex. Indian wars and removals have long been among the setpieces of western history. The history of white-Indian culture contact has been a violent one, and it has been told mostly by white males. Our search for women's experience makes it imperative that we view culture contact through the eyes of women in both cultures. From the Indian viewpoint, the story is one of cultural upheaval and destruction. This story has not yet been told, at least not from the perspective of Indian women, but as American Indian history develops as a field, this will surely change.[34]

We know more about Indian-white culture contact as it was experienced by white women. The story is a revealing one. Glenda Riley has shown that in white-Indian relations, both on the Overland Trail and in later settlement, white women were more placating, more peaceful than white men. Women offered food, made some friendships with Indian women, and were less likely to resort to threats and violence than were white men. Furthermore, white women captured by Indians were not necessarily eager to return to white culture. Certainly many women were afraid of Indians, and certainly other women used force to repel an Indian move. But we must reject the picture of helpless women who always feared Indian attack, especially of a sexual nature. This stereotype is largely a white male response arising from fear and uncertainty, not a female reality.[35]

[33]Mary C. Wright, "Economic Development and Native American Women in the Early Nineteenth Century," *American Quarterly*, 33 (Winter 1981), 525-36; and Jacqueline Peterson, "Women Dreaming: The Religio-Psychology of Indian-White Marriage in the Western Great Lakes Fur Trade," in Lillian Schlissel, ed., *Western Women: Their Land, Their Lives*, forthcoming in 1986 from the University of Arizona Press, Tucson. There is also a growing literature on Hispanic and Anglo intermarriage. See Jane Dysart, "Mexican Women in San Antonio, 1830-1860: The Assimilation Process," *Western Historical Quarterly*, VII (October 1976), 365-75; and Darlis Miller "Cross-Cultural Marriages in the Southwest: The New Mexico Experience, 1846-1900," *New Mexico Historical Review*, 57 (October 1982), 335-59.

[34]An example of this new perspective can be found in Patricia Albers and Beatrice Medicine, *The Hidden Half: Studies of Plains Indian Women* (Washington, D.C., 1983).

[35]Glenda Riley, *Women and Indians on the Frontier, 1825-1915* (Albuquerque, 1984).

The story of race relations in the West is a complex one. To tell it without women, or with women as passive bodies to be protected, is to tell only half of the story. Women of all races had parts to play as victors and victims, friends and enemies, missionaries, and resistors. The perspective of women of all races completes the picture, as in the stereopticon.

As we move into the twentieth century, we will want to look at women who were part of in-migrating groups (Mexican, Japanese, German-Russian, and black, among others) and their roles in family and group adaptation. A recent study of Italian women in California revealed a different pattern of adaptation than for immigrant Italian women in the East. Was this true for other groups? Another recent study of Chicanas and Sunbelt industrialization argued that job opportunities are as important as cultural ideals in determining family survival strategies.[36] Diverse research is just beginning to be published in quantity, but it is already clear that multicultural twentieth-century western women's history has much to contribute to the fields of labor and immigration history as well as to western history itself.

Multicultural research allows us to expand our focus and develop a wider framework that will be appropriate to all the different racial and ethnic groups that inhabit the West. We ought to work toward the development of inclusive, rather than exclusive paradigms. This will certainly mean less emphasis on Turner's frontier and more on the long continuities of western history, reaching as far back into American Indian history as possible and forward to include the most recent twentieth-century immigrant groups. The mythic figure of the solitary individual confronting the environment can no longer encompass the complex history of the West. We must move to larger themes. One theme that crosses racial and time barriers is that of family and group adaptation to *both* the physical environment and to the presence of other groups.

All this takes us a long way from the simple, dramatic story of the pioneers and raises questions about the conceptualization and writing of western history. The majority of women's sources do not convey the sense of adventure and drama that we have come to associate with "westering." Women's sources convey instead a sense of everyday life, of "dailiness." Some people find the story of daily life tedious, even dull. Today, however, it seems that one of the things we most lack in western history is a detailed picture of pioneer adaptation and development, of the ordinary, daily building of a new society. Much of that story is there in the writings of western women. When it is put together with the picture we already have of the public,

[36]Micaela di Leonardo, *The Varieties of Ethnic Experience: Kinship, Class and Gender among Italian-Americans in Northern California* (Ithaca, 1984); and Patricia Zavella, "The Impact of 'Sun Belt Industrialization' on Chicanas," in Armitage and Jameson, *The Women's West.*

male-dominated events, a fuller and more complete sense of the West will emerge.

Western historians are committed to producing readable history. Some have wondered whether the addition of social history (including women's) materials will make the story so complex that the story line and narrative flow will suffer.[37] The answer must be that we all prize good writing, but that our conceptual framework must shape the narrative, not vice versa. Good style that is achieved by simplification or by focusing on one viewpoint at the expense of other important perspectives is still bad history. Western history that includes multicultural and gendered perspectives will inevitably be more complex than some past versions have been. But, as in the stereopticon, it will gain in richness and depth. The challenge will be to write the new history clearly and well.

What, in summary, does the stereoptical picture look like? What might be the contours of the new western history? Some old landmarks such as the opening and closing of the frontier would recede into the background. Other topics, especially culture contact (both peaceful and violent) and migration would become more prominent. The new, overarching theme might well be family and community adaptation to a new environment, considered psychologically, politically, and economically. It would be possible within this framework to compare adaptation across cultures and across centuries. Initially at least, there would be greater emphasis on groups than on individuals. This might change as accumulating research allowed us to identify representative characters to replace the old romantic figures of mountain man, cowboy, and outlaw. The new history would certainly be much more mundane than the Wild West of popular legend. But because it would speak to unchanging concerns (adaptation at the group and community level), the new history would have genuine relevance to the lives of westerners today. The great popular audience for western history should be able to find topics in the new history that are just as engrossing as the old ones. Finally, recognition of the distinct women's perspective offers an opportunity to scholars. Historians can now incorporate the insights of women's history into new syntheses of western history, thus more completely portraying our shared, but different, heritage.

[37] See, for example, Rodman Paul, "Foreword," in Malone, *Historians and the American West*, vii.

Single Women Homesteaders In Wyoming, 1880-1930

by
Paula M. Bauman

The Homestead Act has been called one of the great democratic measures of world history.[1] Women had the opportunity to homestead, because the act made no discrimination towards sex. Single women took this opportunity offered to them and did homestead in the state of Wyoming. It is important to explore motives, the means by which they obtained land, the typical life of women homesteaders, the status of the women once the certificate had been granted and what became of the land once a certificate had been granted.

During a special session of Congress, Representative Aldrich of Minnesota introduced a homestead bill in the House of Representatives and on May 17, 1862, the Homestead Act became a reality when President Lincoln signed the bill. The Homestead Act specified the qualifications for a homestead as:

> . . . any *person* who is the head of a family, or who has arrived at the age of twenty-one years, and is a citizen of the United States, or who shall have filed his declaration of intentions to become such, as required by the naturalization laws of the United States Government . . . shall be entitled to one quarter section.[2]

Homestead land became available not only to a man over 21 and head of his family, but to a single woman over 21 and head of her family, because of the term, "person." For the purpose of clarity, "single" women are defined as women who have no husband. Some were unmarried, some widows, some divorcees and some even runaway wives.

In order to apply for homestead land, individuals were required to include the information of the exact section, township, range and meridian. Thus, for example, Agnes M. Teusdale, of Laramie County, filled out an application numbered 2491, which involved the land legally described as the "Northwest quarter, Section 28, Township 20, North of Range 60, West of the Sixth Principal Meridian in Wyoming, containing one hundred and sixty acres."[3] As of January, 1863, the person applying for homestead land received one quarter section of land, or 160 acres. If the applicant wanted less than one quarter section, (80 acres), or less of unappropriated lands, then the land went for $2.50 an acre with the requirement that the land be surveyed first.

Congress stated homesteaders would have a set period of time in which to make improvements (prove up) on their land. Consequently, five years from the date of entry, the applicant who proved up became entitled to a patent to his or her homestead. During these five years, the applicant built a shelter and made improvements on the land. The applicant could not change place of residence or abandon the said land for more than six months at any given time. Those who abandoned the homestead lost all rights to said land.[4] The Homestead Act further stated that,

> . . . said person may have filed a preemption claim, or which at the time the application is made subject to preemption at one dollar and twenty-five cents or less, per acre; or eighty acres or less of unappropriated lands, at two dollars and fifty cents per acre, . . .[5]

This meant any person who had the means could pay the required amount at a greater sum of money than ordinarily would be required. Congress concluded if a homesteader fulfilled all of the required provisions prior to the time allowed for proving up, then the homesteader "who has availed him or herself of the benefits of the first section" of the Homestead Act could pay "the minimum price, or the same price to which the same may have graduated, for the quantity of land" before the five years had expired.[6] In Laramie County, from 1890 to 1908, fifteen out of 21 single women homesteaders received their certificates before their five year deadline, paying the minimum price for their land. Thirteen out of the fifteen completed the requirements in two years or less. (See Appendix A)

Before the Homestead Act, the principles of land policy had been governed by various preemption acts. Between 1804 and 1841, more than sixteen acts passed granting rights to squatters. Congress felt these acts "threatened the principal of revenue return for the public domain."[7] The Preemption Act of 1841 allowed "any squatter on unclaimed land" the right "when the land was surveyed and came up for auction" to "exercise the first preemption laws" by having first option at buying the land.[8]

Within a decade, Congress realized the Homestead Act was inconclusive in that the act did not appropriately apply towards conditions in the West. Therefore, the Timber Culture Act of 1873 allowed a person to receive 160 acres free by paying the same fees as the Homestead Act. In order to claim 160 acres under the Timber Culture Act, one had to plant and keep growing 40 acres of trees for eight years. Originally, Congress felt that the prairie states could benefit from this legislation. In actuality, lack of water discouraged many homesteaders from utilizing this act.[9] By 1890, all the most desirable farm land had been homesteaded. People on the western prairies realized the remaining land could not be treated the same as the land in eastern America. In the remaining arid and semi-arid lands, 160 acres of land did not provide a living for a homesteader trying to raise a dryland crop. Consequently, 320 acres became available to a homesteader for bare subsistence when an amendment to the Homestead Act, the Mondell Revisory Law of 1909, passed.[10]

By 1912, the lawmakers concluded that the five years required on a homestead caused discouraged homesteaders to admit defeat. The Homestead Act originated as a means of disposing excess Public Lands and at the same time earning a revenue. Hence, further leniency by Congress in 1912 lowered the residency requirement from five to three years, and permitted an absence of five months each year. This popularized homesteading for women. The majority of women filed their homestead claims after the residency dropped from five years to three years and after more land was awarded to the homesteaders.[11]

Along with the Homestead Act, many other acts helped homesteaders in obtaining ownership of property in the West. The Desert Land Act might have applied to any homestead on the western plains. Passed by Congress on March 3, 1877, it stated the applicant must be a resident of the United States and of legal age, (21 years old). The land would be sold at 25¢ an acre and not exceeding one section of land to any one person. A water system must be installed on the land within three years after filing, providing that the right to this water for the 640 acres followed bona fide prior appropriation laws. Within three years after filing the claim, an individual had to pay an additional one dollar per acre to the land office for the full possession of the land.[12] One who apparently took advantage of the Desert Land Act, Florence Blake Smith of northeastern Wyoming stated,

> I was now a homesteader in the West, and a potential owner of six hundred and forty acres of Wyoming. The wonder of possession, the joy of looking out over one's land, thinking on the dear dead Pioneer's toil and sweat to at least acquire one hundred and sixty acres, and here was I with six hundred and forty, an entire square mile.[13]

An amendment to the Desert Land Act, called the Carey Act, aided two women in Worland to obtain homestead land. Mary Culbertson and Helen Coburn Howell decided to homestead in Wyoming in that area of Wyoming because of their fathers' interests in the Hanover Canal Irrigation Project.[14] Under the Carey Act, the Board of Land Commissioners and the state engineer studied detailed assignments as to the feasibility proposals for irrigation works advanced by individuals or companies and to make contracts when projects appeared sound. The state charged the settler 50¢ per acre, and the private contractors charged $20 or more per acre for water rights. States could not sell or dispose of more than 160 acres of these lands to any one person. Ultimately, the Desert Land Act made land available to enterprising homesteaders. Homesteaders such as Culbertson and Howell used the Desert Act in order to settle land previously arid and unusable.[15]

Utilizing land laws, each head of a family could take 160 acres free under the Homestead Act of 1862, another 160 free under the Timber Culture Act of 1873, another 160 at $1.25 per acre under the Preemption Act of 1841 and 640 acres at $1.25 per acre under the Desert Land Act of 1877.[16] Curiously, most of the women homesteaders, with a few exceptions, did not take advantage of these other land acts. All of the 79 women homesteaders in Laramie County, between March 25, 1896, to February 16, 1917, used only the Homestead Act to obtain free land from the United States Government.[17]

While the opportunity to obtain 160 free acres brought many young, single women to the agricultural frontier, the other reasons are as varied as the women's individual backgrounds. Some took up homestead claims simply to add to their husbands', fathers' or brothers' holdings. Others, especially single women, intended to work their claims themselves.[18] Single women homesteaders had many different motives for homesteading. They included adventure and fun, hunting a husband, financial security, independence and equal rights or seeking an alternative to the reduced opportunities of more settled regions.[19]

Helen Coburn Howell could be classified as an adventurous homesteader. She and Mary Culbertson took out adjoining claims. "Mrs. Culbertson and I lived together in great harmony the necessary time to prove up, she sleeping on her side of the line that divided our property and I on mine," Howell recalled.[20]

Many other women saw the opportunity differently. They perceived homesteading as a means to earn a dowry and help out a future husband. To a woman seeking a husband, the male/female ratio on the plains was attractive. Men greatly outnumbered the women.[21] Natrona County had 52 women homesteaders. Seventeen of these married between receiving their homestead patent and homestead certificate. (See Appendix B, Table III) In Campbell County, Luella Moyer had decided to come West to marry after taking out a homestead. She later remembered,

> At that time there was very little deeded land in Campbell County, and a hundred and sixty acres was all one person could take. If a man and woman were to be married and the man had proved up on his homestead, the woman could take hers and be married the next day. Later this rule was changed, and the woman had to live on her homestead for a year before they were married.[22]

Some women did not intend to settle permanently but rather hoped to establish their claims and then sell out to neighboring farmers. They would then return to their small towns or to the city with a nest egg. Contemporary letters and diaries by homesteading women verify that some young women intended to exploit their claims to earn money for their ventures.[23] Some schoolmarms became homesteaders after they viewed the economic gain that enterprise might offer. Minnie Hidy, Bessie Fox and Blanche Lyons, all schoolteachers from Laramie County, took out homestead claims to aid local ranchers in keeping their ranches intact. These women sold their properties immediately to the stockmen at a nice profit.[24]

Dr. Bessie Fell decided to homestead on the Western plains because of the financial security of owning land. From Moville, Iowa, the 34 year-old medical doctor had suffered a financial loss in the 1907 panic. Her loss had been so large that when she arrived in southeastern Wyoming with her three orphaned nieces, she had only 75¢ in her pocket.[25]

Homesteading offered a peculiar challenge to women to achieve equal rights, since "free land" did not discriminate against male or female homesteaders. Men and women "were appallingly equal—equal labor, equal privation and equal failure—or victory."[26] Even practiced farmers failed, however. Statistically, only one in three women managed to remain long enough to get deeds to their farms. At the age of 52, Emma Peterson decided to try once more to gain her economic independence and her rights. From a large family, she had married at fourteen and by age nineteen had become a widow. Undaunted, Peterson started a very successful millinery shop until she remarried a second time. She did not mind forfeiting her independence for a husband. After fifteen years, the marriage ended in the death of her husband. The opportunity available to her through the Homestead Act made her realize that by gaining land, she would never have to be totally dependent upon another human being.[27]

Women, seeking an alternative to the reduced opportunities of a more settled region, were usually divorced, widowed or runaway wives. One such wife was Mary O'Kieffe. One day in 1884, at the age of 43, fed up with her "ne'er-do-well" husband, she decided to file a homestead claim in western Nebraska on land similar topographically to eastern Wyoming.[28] According to her son Charley, Mary O'Kieffe was disappointed, discouraged, but never completely broken. The woman had dreams of a better life somewhere and hoped to end her unhappy existence by starting over in a new country with freedom.[29] She had the older children assist her in building a cover on the farm wagon, hitched up the work horses and tied the milk cows to the wagon sides. To the rear of the wagon she attached the cultivator and on top of that she built a small chicken coop to hold her two dozen hens and a rooster. The journey from their farm on the Missouri River to the new homestead was a distance of about 500 miles. After many adventures on the 51-day journey they arrived, built a sod house, dug a well and set up housekeeping in their new home.[30]

Isolation discouraged some homesteaders

Another woman seeking an alternative was Vesta Keen. In 1911, she came to homestead land in northeastern Colorado near the Wyoming border. At 33 years of age, Keen was alone, as she liked not having a man complicate her life. Part Cherokee, Keen had become weary of some of the niceties associated with women's lives in the East. She wanted to ride astride, and had heard women in the West had long ago abandoned side saddles. Knowing women had been voting for many years in the West, she longed to express her opinions at the polls.[31]

Elinore Pruitt serves as an example of a woman with inter-connected motives for homesteading. A widowed mother who wanted to escape her past lifestyle, she cleaned house and did laundry to support herself and her young daughter in a dismal apartment in Denver. Pruitt had grown up on a farm and found her existence in Denver difficult. She longed to escape "the rattle and bang, the glare and soot, the smells and the hurry" of city life to "the sweet, free open" area of the country.[32] Acting on the advice of her minister, she advertised for a position as a housekeeper to a rancher in the hope she could start a homestead site. Consequently, Pruitt found herself as housekeeper to Clyde Stewart, "a Scottish cattle rancher who spoke with a burr as thick as his wrist and played a bagpipe to cheer his bachelor solitude, sixty miles from the railroad at Burnt Fork."[33]

Some women came West to visit homesteading relatives and decided to stay and settle on their own claims. Divorced Fredericka Deike came West to see her brothers. During her visit, she decided that owning a homestead near Burns would be an excellent opportunity. Women's motives for homesteading varied, but universally they valued the "free land" they would receive in order to better themselves economically. The vastness and unbroken land of the plains had a particular appeal for women normally not accustomed to feelings of individuality and power.[34]

Homesteading a piece of land required making many ingenious plans. One needed to obtain money and work hard to make improvements on the land the Homestead Act required. Florence Blake Smith observed that "free land" was costly:

> There would be filing fees, locating fees, transportation, price of lumber to build the required habitable house. Also, it seemed, one had to buy posts for fencing and the wire to string between them, all of which added to a prohibitive sum by the mile. Then on necessity you had to eat to live, of course, during the slow process of homesteading.[35]

In order to begin, prospective homesteaders obtained information on land available to them through many different sources, including land agents, newspaper articles, government documents and friends or relatives. Sometimes the necessary information proved costly. Smith used the services of a land agent to obtain her northeastern Wyoming homestead. She worked for the Federal Reserve Bank in Chicago and had become intrigued when a man told her about homesteading. She paid $100 for the relinquishment and about $25 for her filing fees, the usual for homesteading. By using the services of a land agent, Smith paid an additional cost of $100 for the locating fee.[36] Another example of a woman using a land agent is Ellen R. Lathan. Lathan had John D. Simpson assign her a homestead. He allotted her the Southeast quarter of Southwest quarter of Section 7, in Township 18, North of Range 70, West of Sixth Principal Meridian in Wyoming, containing 40 acres. (See Appendix A) On another occasion, Emma Peterson, in 1919, read about an oil boom at Newcastle, where land was also available for homesteading, but she could not afford the locating fee.[37] Unfor-

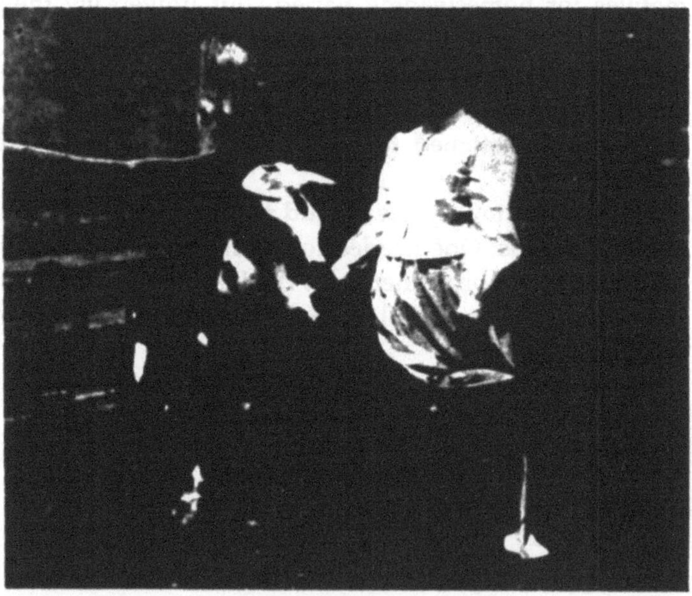

A milk cow meant butter on the table to this woman.

tunately, some homesteaders often painted a rosy picture to entice others to the West. Those who responded soon became a part of a kind of conspiracy and practiced the same tactics on other friends and relatives.[38] As previously noted, Fredericka Deike was one example.

The government allowed six months from filing date to establishment of residence. This provision allowed homesteaders to return home to prepare necessary arrangements. Florence Blake Smith took advantage of this opportunity and returned home to her banking job in Chicago until the time came for her to leave for Wyoming. Upon her return, her co-workers "hailed" her "as a heroine, an adventuress, a *land-owner*."[39] The small town Smith picked did not look far on a map from Chicago, but actually she traveled 1400 miles west, a journey of over two and a half days by train. Good friends stopped by frequently to bring her something to wear out on the prairie. The items included riding boots, a pair of heavy breeches, a pair of rubber boots, a slicker and heavy woolen pajamas. Smith's mother furnished her with two yellow plates, cups and saucers to match and a pale blue-checked tablecloth. Smith took a little solid-walnut kitchen table, a sanitary cot, two stout kitchen chairs, a small low rocker and a regulation sheep wagon stove. These constituted her housegoods. She used her bread can and the wooden boxes in which she had shipped her canned goods for extra stools if needed. Along with the furniture, she brought dainty dotted Swiss curtains, plus a few pictures from her old room back in Chicago.[40] Smith used a portable garage as her new home, which measured,

> nine by twelve feet . . . It was just the size of our living room rug at home, and many's the night I spent moving the furniture inside of it, to acquaint myself with the size of my humble "Shack" to be, in the West. It could be easily assembled by a woman. Or so I was told by the affable man who sold it to me. A generous number of nuts, bolts, and screws had been included to prove his points and to provide complications for "putter-upper."[41]

Some women homesteaders, however, did not have the help of relatives and friends. A destitute widow on the

Nine by twelve feet . . .

Platte River, Mrs. Townsend, took out a claim and as most newcomers, could not afford to bring lumber from the mountains for a dwelling. She did not have the strength to cut or lift the three-foot-long sod "bricks" to build a soddy, as most of the homecomers did. But she dug dirt out of a sand hill bluff, about eight to ten feet high, and cleared a tiny six-by-eight foot room. She wedged poles across the top to make a roof that slanted down over the front of the dugout, and she built a front wall and door with scraps of wood and junk. Grass and dirt piled on top kept out the worst weather, but rain always leaked into the little shelter, and dirt constantly sifted down. Perhaps that did not matter, since the floor and walls were also dirt. In that hole in the ground, she lived like a human prairie dog.[42]

A woman usually had the help of others when time came to build her house, harvest her crops or any other heavy outdoor chores. Usually women hired men to do the harder jobs, as did Florence Blake Smith. In order to make improvements Smith "hired a man to plow and seed forty acres of wheat."[43] Mary Culbertson and Helen Coburn Howell, also "employed a man and his son to do the heavy work—the fence-making, farming, and outside chores."[44] Culbertson and Howell shared the housework, cooked, ate together and regarded their life on their homesteads as a high adventure, but as they stated, "We took our work seriously . . . however . . . we were far from idle ourselves."[45]

Surviving on a homestead seemed like a costly endeavor for most single women. Food prices skyrocketed in the West where the coffee was 65 cents per pound, butter 80 cents, ham 60 cents, sugar 17 cents, flour $3.75 for a 25-pound sack, eggs 45 cents a dozen and milk 15 cents a quart.[46] Consequently, in the rural West, women held jobs as teachers, doctors and midwives, laborers and any other work they could do to raise money. The teaching profession promised the most to a young single woman who came west. Inspired by Catherine Beecher, a pioneer teacher, writer on moral religious topics and an avid speaker for women's education, many young women in the East went to the agricultural frontier as teachers. Such an occupation also fell well within the confines of appropriate female behavior. The female teacher, Beecher noted, can "discern before her the road to honorable independence and extensive usefulness where she need not outstep the prescribed boundaries of feminine modesty."[47] Many took the opportunity teaching gave them to earn extra money. Helen Coburn Howell, of Worland, taught as did other homesteaders Hazle J. Pence, Minnie Hidy, Bessie Fox and Blanche Lyons.[48] On the other hand, Dr. Bessie Fell, from Carpenter, supplemented her income as a physician in order to live on her homestead. She inherited a medical territory covering more than a 30 mile radius. People often saw her in her horse and buggy out

Teaching school was within the confines of appropriate female behavior and offered a supplemental income to women homesteaders.

on call at all hours of the day.[49] If a doctor could not be found, however, homesteaders found themselves doing tasks originally intended for doctors. Elinore Pruitt Stewart had to nurse her own newborn baby, Jamie, when he became ill "as there had been no physician to help."[50]

Women took on any other jobs that became available to them. Housekeeping helped many women to live another year on their homestead. Edna Norris Eaton took advantage of the opportunity to housekeep. Following her husband's death she sold their ranch and filed on a homestead near Recluse. A son lived on this homestead with her for a few months, helping to build her log cabin and make other improvements, before marrying and going to Sundance to live. Alone on the homestead, Eaton found employment for several years as housekeeper for Judge and Mrs. Raymond of Newcastle.[51] Additional acceptable occupations women could pursue in order to raise money to help them make improvements on their land included sewing, cooking, laundry and other domestic work. During the time each year that Hattie A. Olsen of Albin could legally be absent from her homestead, she found employment at St. John's Hospital in Cheyenne. An excellent seamstress, she sewed for women and children of the Albin community.[52] Florence Blake Smith realized she would be needing money to tide her over while she made improvements on her property. Hence, she kept her bank job in Chicago, but took a seven month leave each year. Every spring, after taking the train back to Wyoming, Smith would look for temporary jobs until the weather permitted her to return to her homestead. She found work in a restaurant making "eight dollars in salary and five dollars in tips" per week.[53] At this time, her temporary job provided an adequate extra income. Later, when offered a job as a stenographer with a local attorney, Smith felt that, "good fortune was mine."[54] In this position, she earned $25 a week.[55] On the whole, women applied their abilities in many diverse ways in order to make extra money. This need for supplemental support was only one of the many problems in homesteading the free land.

Life on the homestead was hard and lonely, even for the most determined idealistic individual. Dr. Bessie Fell emphasized, "In a new country getting established was not only a hard and continuous battle against cold, hunger, fire, and other physical hardships, but an even more difficult struggle against discouragement, frustrations, and gloom."[56] One had to be a druggist, postmistress, cook, mother and a doctor. One had to be imaginative and creative. When Dr. Fell's house was too drafty, she filled up the walls with rocks in order to insulate the house from Wyoming winds. Dr. Fell contended:

> All pioneers are idealists and enthusiasts. If they were not, they would never had the urge or the courage to leave the old, established homelands and risk their fortune in a new, uncharted world. Eventually, of course, all such idealistic dreams are idealized. But it is not as easy or as glamorous as the story books about the westward trek of the covered wagons often pictured it. It is a slow process and a hard day-to-day struggle and only the strongest are able to survive.[57]

Homesteading was a struggle against discouragement, frustrations and gloom.

This philosophy of life held true for all people settling on the prairies. One very good example of life on the prairies is Elinore Pruitt, who filed on her claim by the use of the amended Homestead Act. She had 240 acres of land adjoining her future husband's ranch. Still, she would not have married Clyde Stewart if he had not promised she could meet all her "land difficulties unaided," for she "wanted the fun and the experiences."[58] The house that Stewart's hired men built for her adjoined his ranch house. Stewart mowed hay with a team of horses and grew large crops of potatoes and various root vegetables. He even experimented successfully with beans and tomatoes. She made preserves, butter, milked the cows, raised chickens, turkeys and children. "When I read of the hard times among the Denver poor," she wrote her friend:

> I feel like urging them every one to get out and file on land. To me, homesteading is a solution of all poverty's problems, but I realize that temperament has much to do with success in any undertaking,

> and persons afraid of coyotes and work and loneliness had better let ranching alone. At the same time, any woman who can stand her own company, can see the beauty of the sunset, loves growing things, and is willing to put in as much time as careful labor as she does over her washtubs, will certainly succeed; will have independence, plenty to eat all the time, and have a home of her own in the end.[59]

Homesteaders soon realized that life on the open prairies was a gamble, with the odds against success. They frequently fought weather, insects, wild animals, loneliness, fear, disease and new unfamiliar terrain. Dr. Bessie Fell was exposed frequently and dangerously to the rigors of prairie weather and to the hazards of night driving in an open buggy or horseback over uncharted wilderness. These great physical hardships included long and hazardous trips during rainstorms and blizzards.[60]

Florence Blake Smith hired a man to plant her wheat. According to her, "He must have planted bird seed. The minute the green stuff showed half an inch above the ground, the ground was black with birds, and the green stuff soon got discouraged and gave up."[61] Her first crop never saw harvest, because "it was a dry summer," and the birds ate what little came up.[62] Hazle J. Pence solved her problem concerning water by filing on 640 acres of grazing land 28 miles north of Cheyenne. She located her homesite beside a spring of crystal clear water which was adequate for household use.[63]

The hardest part of homesteading for women came when their fears became truths. They did face, indeed, some very real dangers. On the prairies of Wyoming they confronted snakes. Mary Culbertson and Helen Coburn Howell heard of a snake crawling through the floor boards of a hotel in Worland. "With visions of snakes crawling through the floor onto us, we changed our sleeping arrangements, and there after Helen slept on the office table, and I slept for two miserable, uncomfortable weeks on two trunks."[64] Florence Blake Smith had an encounter with a rattlesnake,

> I heard that terrifying buzzzzzz that warns you of a rattlesnake. Where he was and in which direction, I had no idea, since he remained perfectly still after that first warning . . . usually if it is the last thing you do, ethics demand you kill a rattler, either by shooting it or with rocks.[65]

Fredericka Deike accompanied her children one and three-fourths miles across the prairie every morning to the hill south of their neighbors so they could attend school.[66] She did this every morning and afternoon and always carried a revolver with her, as she was afraid of coyotes and snakes.[67]

Women had many other fears. In 1885, Elizabeth Gorden at the age of 28 fulfilled a lifetime dream when she homesteaded in northeastern Colorado near the Wyoming border. Every night she would wedge her large Saratoga trunk between her bed and the door of her house to keep intruders out and to give herself a feeling of security.[68] Gorden never lit her lamps at night because she was afraid of strangers after dark. She also, ". . . had a pistol which the men in the family taught her how to use."[69] Women contended with emergencies sometimes beyond their own expectations. Mary Culbertson and Helen Coburn Howell arrived in Worland for the first time and found typhoid fever raging in the town. They considered taking the next stage home, but were asked to give their services to the sick as nurses. They protested they knew nothing of nursing, but agreed to help. Culbertson and Howell got along very well. There were about fifteen to twenty patients with the fever, housed in an improvised hospital in an old log building. Curtains were put up for partitions to provide a semblance of privacy. The nearest doctor was at Hyattville, about 45 miles away.[70]

As did most homesteaders, Ida Watkins dealt with her fears. Just across the border of Wyoming in Merino, Colorado, Watkins worked on a ranch twelve miles round trip from her homestead. She made the trip both ways almost every day, as homestead legislation required the prospective landowner actually live on the claim. Watkins had a great fear of horses, and hers terrified her. Her trips back and forth to and from her job became a private hell. If she arrived safely each night, her relief was short, for as darkness settled, she listened to the howls of the prairie, and imagined many an attack. She awoke the next morning only to ride her despised horse to work. Watkins, like most other homesteaders, learned to compensate. She became such a good rider that she won a silk dress in a pony race at a Fourth of July celebration.[71]

To break up the long periods of very real fear and loneliness, social gatherings occurred frequently. According to Mary Culbertson, "one of the favorite forms of recreation then, and now, was dancing. Every special occasion was celebrated in this way."[72] Usually each time a new home or building had been completed the local homesteaders celebrated and initiated the new building by having a dance within the new walls. According to Culbertson, dances could be held at any time. The news was dispatched around the countryside and everyone for miles around would be there.[73] As the towns became more settled, dances moved to one room schools, so small that onlookers had to stand outside, peering in the doors and windows.[74] Usually a pot-luck dinner allowed the dancers to take an intermission. Women were all expected to bring a pie to the dances, as an "entrance fee," for the evening.[75] As the dancers left for home, most would catch a nap on the way. Sarah Barbara Claypool, who grew up on the Wyoming border, stated they would settle their wagons into the ruts of the prairie roads and then, recalled they would "lean back and rest or even go to sleep; the horse would follow the trail home."[76]

Many people entertained themselves in their own homes by forming clubs, reading or playing a musical instrument at their own leisure. Bertha Davis came to Wyoming in September, 1908, settling twelve miles north of Hillsdale. Her two room cabin had been constructed by Curt Ellenberger, who had a claim a short distance to the south. During the latter part of September, Florence and Milicent Davis came out to live on their homestead. Each woman slept and cooked in her own one room cabin built in her corner section adjacent to the other woman. Due to their close proximity, the women enjoyed the frequent company and conversation with the local cowboys. Gradually, the area in which these women lived had been named Calico Hill by the cowboys because of the calico cloth worn by the women. Since the friends lived close to each other, gatherings occurred often. In 1909, the women formed a club named the Jolly Dry Farmers, a homemaker's club, which is still in existence.

By the time women proved up they had lived through a vast number of experiences. Understandably, some women took longer to prove their claims than others. This depended upon their circumstances. Susan J. McLauchlin took out her homestead claim on March 18, 1890, but did not receive her certificate until June 17, 1908. (See Appendix A) According to the land records, McLauchlin needed eighteen years in which to fulfill the time she was required to live on her homestead. On the other hand, some women took advantage of the clause in the Homestead Act allowing the homesteaders to pay a minimum price for the land. One such woman, Emma Dudley of Laramie County, took out her homestead claim on October 26, 1908. After paying a fee, she received her certificate on November 24, 1908, a total of 30 days. (See Appendix A) Apparently, Dudley was more affluent than McLauchlin.

The majority of women homesteaders who settled in Wyoming remained unmarried, according to the county land records of Crook, Laramie, Natrona and Sweetwater counties from March 26, 1888, to March 12, 1943. Of the homesteaders, 68.9 percent remained unmarried. These women homesteaders clearly did not view homesteading as a means of obtaining the land as a dowry in order to meet a husband. Of the 68.9 percent, 5.9 percent died in the attempt of homesteading land. Once a claim had been taken out 29.1 percent married. Only approximately two percent of single women homesteaders were widows who must have viewed homesteading as a means of starting their own life over with a fresh start. (See Appendix B, Table II)

In Laramie County, 21 women homesteaded land between March 18, 1890, and January 2, 1908. Of these women, ten sold their claims after receiving certificates of ownership. One-third of these women who sold were unmarried. Two transferred their homestead land deeds to their husbands. Interestingly, one married woman sold her land, but not to her husband. (See Appendix B, Table III)

The other eleven women kept their land. Of these women, 38.1 percent were unmarried, while 9.5 percent were married. Out of 21 women, there was only one widow and she kept her land. These statistics clearly show a majority of these women were unmarried. (See Appendices A and B, Table III)

In conclusion, the Homestead Act did not discriminate against male or female applicants between 1888 and 1943. Of the 6,527 homestead patents issued in Crook, Johnson, Laramie, Lincoln, Natrona and Sweetwater counties (See Appendix B, Table I) nearly twelve percent were single women homesteaders. (See Appendix B, Table II) This clearly proves that single women took advantage of their right to homestead in the state of Wyoming. Homesteading, a non-glamorous aspect of life, offered a peculiar challenge to women. As mentioned previously, women's motives for homesteading were as varied as the individual backgrounds. They sought adventure and fun, a husband, perhaps financial security, independence and equal rights. Many pursued an alternative to the reduced opportunities of the more settled regions. Homesteading land required ingenious thinking. The adventurous had to locate information on available land, apply for a homestead, pack and prepare for the move. Then they met filing and relinquishment fees, built a homesite, maintained economic standing and made a living on the land to prove up and receive a certificate and deed. Women soon realized that life on the open prairie was a gamble.

The Homestead Act, indeed, was one of the great democratic measures of world history, in that it allowed women the right to own land by homesteading. The women who attempted a claim were inventive, hardworking, courageous and determined to obtain and fulfill the requirements of a homestead. Overall, these single women homesteaders proved to be just that. The legacy these homesteaders left can be seen in the names of their descendants who live in southern Wyoming. The characteristics that made these women can, also, be seen in their contemporary relatives.[78]

---

1. John Mack Faragher, *Women and Men on the Overland Trail* (New Haven: Yale University Press, 1979); Robert T. Hine, *The American West: An Interpretive History* (Boston: Little, Brown, and Company, 1973); T. A. Larson, *History of Wyoming* (Lincoln: University of Nebraska Press, 1978); Sandra L. Myres, *Westering Women and the Frontier Experience 1800-1915* (Albuquerque: University of New Mexico Press, 1982).
2. United States Congress, *Homestead Act*, Ch. 75, 12, Stat. 392 (1862), p. 1. Historical Research and Publications Division, Wyoming State Archives, Museums & Historical Department, Cheyenne, Wyoming (WSAMHD).
3. Laramie County Clerk Homestead Certificate Records, Certificate number 904, application number 2491, Agnes M. Teusdale, Archives Division, WSAMHD.
4. *Homestead Act*, p. 1.
5. *Ibid*.
6. *Ibid*.
7. Hine, *The American West*, p. 160.
8. Larson, *History of Wyoming*, p. 174.
9. United States Congress, *Timber Culture Act*, Ch. 277, 17, Stat. 605 (1873); Larson, *History of Wyoming*, p. 174.
10. Elizabeth J. Thorpe, "A Woman Alone Stakes a Claim," *In Wyoming, The Spirit of America: A Bicentennial Interview with Wyoming People* (June-July, 1976).
11. Peggy Kirkbride, *From These Roots* (Cheyenne: Pioneer Printing Co., 1972), p. 121.
12. United States Congress, *Desert Land Act*, 43, U.S.C. Sec. 321-323 (1976); Lynette Wert, "The Lady Stakes a Claim," *Persimmon Hill*, Vol. 6, No. 2, 1976.
13. Florence Blake Smith, *Cow Chips 'n' Cactus: The Homestead in Wyoming* (New York: Pageant Press, 1962), pp. 13, 24.
14. Mary Culbertson, "Experiences in Wyoming of Miss Mary Culbertson," Historical Data collected by Lottie Holmberg, Works Progress Administration (WPA) folder 699, WSAMHD; Helen Howell, "Mrs. Ashby Howell: Pioneer Worland Women and Humorous Stories of Her First Years in Wyoming as School Teacher and Lady Homesteader," WPA folder 798, WSAMHD.
15. United States Congress, *Carey Act*, Sec. 4, 43, U.S.C., Sec. 641 (1976).

16. T. A. Larson, *Wyoming: A History* (New York: W. W. Norton and Company, Inc., 1977), p. 118.
17. Laramie County Clerk Records, Book 95, Homestead Certificate from March 25, 1896, to February 16, 1917, pp. 1-642. For a woman alone, 160 acres was quite a bit of land with which to cope.
18. Myres, *Westering Women*, p. 258.
19. Elinore Pruitt Stewart, *Letters of a Woman Homesteader* (New York: Houghton Mifflin Company, 1914); Smith, *Cow Chips 'n' Cactus;* Thorpe, "A Woman Alone Stakes a Claim," *In Wyoming*, pp. 26-29.
20. Howell, WPA folder 798, WSAMHD.
21. Robert P. Porter, *The West: From the Census of 1880* (Chicago: Rand, McNally, and Company, 1982), pp. 38-80.
22. Luella Moyer, "Mrs. Luella Moyer, Campbell County Pioneer," Interviewer Glendys Wilkenson, WPA folder 906, p. 1, WSAMHD.
23. Myres, *Westering Women*, p. 258.
24. Kirkbride, *From These Roots*, p. 121.
25. Alfred Rehwinkle, *Dr. Bessie* (St. Louis: Concordia Publishing House, 1963), p. 57.
26. Thorpe, "A Woman Alone Stakes a Claim," *In Wyoming*, p. 27.
27. *Ibid.*
28. Sheryll Patterson-Black, "Women Homesteaders on the Great Plains Frontier," *Westering Women: In History and Literature* (Cottonwood Press, 1978), p. 11.
29. Charley O'Kieffe, *Western Story: The Recollections of Charley O'Kieffe, 1884-1898* (Lincoln: University of Nebraska Press, 1960), p. 7.
30. Patterson-Black, "Women Homesteaders on the Great Plains Frontier," *Westering Women*, p. 11.
31. Nell Brown Propst, *Those Strenuous Dames of the Colorado Prairie* (Boulder: Pruett Publishing Company, 1982), pp. 8-9.
32. Stewart, *Letters of a Woman Homesteader*, pp. v, 11, 226.
33. *Ibid.*, pp. 226-227.
34. *Ibid.*, Smith, *Cow Chips 'n' Cactus;* Thorpe, "A Woman Alone Stakes a Claim," *In Wyoming;* Propst, *Those Strenuous Dames*, pp. 5-23; Jolly Dry Farmers, *Calico Hill: Recalling the Early Years, Good Times and Hardships of Homesteaders* (Cheyenne: Pioneer Printing Company, 1973), p. 23.
35. Smith, *Cow Chips 'n' Cactus*, p. 2.
36. *Ibid.*, p. 13.
37. Thorpe, "A Woman Alone Stakes a Claim," *In Wyoming*, p. 27.
38. Propst, *Those Strenuous Dames*, pp. 8, 23.
39. Smith, *Cow Chips 'n' Cactus*, pp. 3, 13.
40. *Ibid.*
41. *Ibid.*, pp. 2, 18.
42. Propst, *Those Strenuous Dames*, p. 17.
43. Smith, *Cow Chips 'n' Cactus*, p. 31.
44. Culbertson, WPA folder 699; Howell, WPA folder 798, WSAMHD.

45. *Ibid.*
46. Smith, *Cow Chips 'n' Cactus*, p. 28.
47. Kathryn Kish Sklar, *Catherine Beecher: A Study in American Domesticity* (New Haven: Yale University Press, 1973), p. 97.
48. Kirkbride, *From These Roots*, p. 121; Howell, WPA folder 798, WSAMHD.
49. Rehwinkel, *Dr. Bessie*, p. 74.
50. Stewart, *Letters of a Woman Homesteader*, p. 190.
51. Edna Norris, "A Courageous Homesteader," WPA folder 692, WSAMHD.
52. Myres, *Westering Women*, p. 259; Kirkbride, *From These Roots*, p. 131.
53. Smith, *Cow Chips 'n' Cactus*, p. 20.
54. *Ibid.*, p. 21.
55. *Ibid.*
56. Rehwinkel, *Dr. Bessie*, p. 69.
57. *Ibid.*, p. 57.
58. Stewart, *Letters of a Woman Homesteader*, pp. 77, 79.
59. *Ibid.*, pp. 16-27, 215, 280-281.
60. Rehwinkel, *Dr. Bessie*, pp. 73-74.
61. Smith, *Cow Chips 'n' Cactus*, p. 31.
62. *Ibid.*
63. Kirkbride, *From These Roots*, p. 131.
64. Culbertson, WPA folder 699, p. 2, WSAMHD.
65. Smith, *Cow Chips 'n' Cactus*, p. 106.
66. *Ibid.*
67. Jolly Dry Farmers, *Calico Hill*, p. 23.
68. Propst, *Those Strenuous Dames*, p. 43.
69. *Ibid.*
70. Culbertson, WPA folder 699, p. 3, WSAMHD.
71. Propst, *Those Strenuous Dames*, p. 8.
72. Culbertson, WPA folder 699, p. 9, WSAMHD.
73. *Ibid.*
74. Propst, *Those Strenuous Dames*, p. 7.
75. Smith, *Cow Chips 'n' Cactus*, p. 28.
76. Propst, *Those Strenuous Dames*, p. 7.
77. Jolly Dry Farmers, *Calico Hill*, pp. 121-122; Kirkbride, *From These Roots*, p. 21.
78. Teresa Jordan, *Cowgirls* (Garden City, New York: Doubleday and Company, Inc., 1982).

APPENDIX A

County Clerk Records: Book 95 p. 30

Lucy B. Thomas
Homestead Patent: February 8, 1892 Application No. 1078
Homestead Certificate: March 7, 1898 Certificate No. 572
Land Description: Lots numbered one and two, and the East half of the Northwest quarter of Section 18, in Township 14, North of Range 61, West of the Sixth Principal Meridian, in Wyoming, containing one hundred and fifty-two acres, and twenty-four hundreds of an acre.

Lucy Thomas married and sold her homestead to John C. Gilland, January 31, 1898, for $50.00.

p. 31

Ida A. Gilland, formerly Ida A. Thomas
Homestead Patent: February 8, 1892 Application No. 723
Homestead Certificate: March 7, 1898 Certificate No. 571
Land Description: South half of the Southeastern quarter, and the South half of the Southwest quarter of Section 12, in Township 14, North of Range 62, West of the Sixth Principal Meridian, in Wyoming, containing one hundred and sixty acres.

Ida Gilland kept her homestead for many years.

p. 79

Jessie Sinclair, widow of Archibald Sinclair, Deceased
Homestead Patent: February 7, 1895 Application No. 2401
Homestead Certificate: January 23, 1900 Certificate No. 839
Land Description: North half of Northeast quarter, and the Northeast quarter of the Northwest quarter of Section 6, in Township 17, North of Range 70, West of the Sixth forty-one acres, and twenty-two hundreds of an acre.

Jesse Sinclair kept her homestead for many years.

p. 87

Elizabeth Griffin
Homestead Patent: April 27, 1898 Application No. 2830
Homestead Certificate: May 31, 1900 Certificate No. 1065
Land Description: North half of Northeast quarter of Section 23, and the West half of the Northwest quarter of Section 24,

in Township 19, North of Range 65, West of the Sixth Principal Meridian, in Wyoming, containing one hundred and sixty acres.

Elizabeth Griffin kept her homestead for many years.

p. 107

Claricy B. Thomas, formerly Claricy Bowen
Homestead Patent: November 28, 1900 Application No. 2665
Homestead Certificate: Dec. 26, 1900 Certificate No. 1220
Land Description: Southwest quarter of Section 32, in Township 15, North of Range 66, West of Sixth Principal Meridian, in Wyoming containing one hundred and sixty acres.

Claricy Thomas kept her homestead for many years.

p. 16(

Eleanor B. Baxter
Homestead Patent: May 22, 1899 Application No. 348
Homestead Certificate: January 9, 1902 Certificate No. 109
Land Description: Lots numbered one, two, three, and four of Section 22 in Township 12, north of Range 70, West of Sixth Principal Meridian in Wyoming, containing one hundred and sixty-four acres, and fifty-eight hundreds of an acre.

Eleanor Baxter sold her homestead land on June 21, 1902, to a Mrs. C. H. Gooding for $300.

p. 186

Lizzie Kisening
Homestead Patent: September 19, 1898 Application No. 2873
Homestead Certificate: April 19, 1902 Certificate No. 1027
Land Description: Northwest quarter of Section 10 in Township 17, North of Range 60, West of Sixth Principal Meridian in Wyoming, containing one hundred and sixty acres.

Lizzie Kisening did not sell her land, but kept the homestead.

p. 218

Emma M. Dudley
Homestead Patent: March 25, 1902 Application No. 3187
Homestead Certificate: Dec. 19, 1902 Certificate No. 1404
Land Description: Northwest quarter of Northeast quarter of Section 28 in Township 17, North of Range 69, West of the Sixth Principal Meridian in Wyoming, containing forty acres.

Emma Dudley sold her claim to Charles A. Dereemer on Oct. 1, 1918.

p. 219

Ellen R. Lathan, assigned by mesne conveyance of John D. Simpson
Homestead Patent: September 26, 1902 Application No. 4748

Homestead Certificate: December 20, 1902 Certificate No. 1418
Land Description: Southeast quarter of Southwest quarter of Section 7, in Township 18, North of Range 70, West of Sixth Principal Meridian in Wyoming containing forty acres.

Ellen Lathan obtained this land through the provisions made for Civil War veterans. She either was a war veteran's widow or bought the right to homestead from a veteran. She kept her homestead. There was no record of her selling.

p. 259

Lena Paulson
Homestead Patent: October 13, 1902 Application No. 2734
Homestead Certificate: July 11, 1903 Certificate No. 1087
Land Description: East half of the southeast quarter of Section 3, and the North half of Southwestern quarter of Section 2, in Township 17, North of Range 68, West of Sixth Principal Meridian in Wyoming, containing one hundred and sixty acres.

Lena Paulson kept her claim according to the records.

p. 260

Minnie E. Chambers
Homestead Patent: February 12, 1902 Application No. 3219
Homestead Certificate: July 11, 1903 Certificate No. 1349
Land Description: Lots numbered one, two, and three, Southeast quarter of Northwest quarter of Section 1 in Township 17, North of Range 68, West of Sixth Principal Meridian in Wyoming, containing one hundred and sixty-two acres, and seventy hundreds of an acre.

Minnie E. Chambers sold her claim to Lena C. Lukins on Nov. 3, 1907.

p. 299

Mari Christenson
Homestead Patent: September 26, 1902 Application No. 2847
Homestead Certificate: May 7, 1904 Certificate No. 1448
Land Description: Southwest quarter of Section 8 in Township 12, North of Range 62, West of Sixth Principal Meridian in Wyoming.

Mari Christenson kept her homestead for numerous years after receiving her certificate.

p. 344

Latitia Kelsey
Homestead Patent: July 8, 1895 Application No. 2039
Homestead Certificate: April 20, 1905 Certificate No. 890
Land Description: Northeast quarter of Northwest quarter, and South half of Northwest quarter of Section 17, and Southeast quarter of Northeast quarter of Section 18 in Township 18, North of Range 61, West of Sixth Principal Meridian in Wyoming, containing one hundred and sixty acres.

Latitia Kelsey sold her land to James D. Gilleland on October 31, 1905, for $500.

p. 346

Heirs of Elinor Thomas
Homestead Patent: January 31, 1903 Application No. 3898
Homestead Certificate: May 3, 1905 Certificate No. 1547
Land Description: North half of Southwest quarter of Southeast quarter of Southwest quarter of Southwest quarter of Northwest quarter of Section 32 in Township 15, North of Range 62, West of Sixth Principal Meridian in Wyoming containing one hundred and sixty acres.

Elinor Thomas died between taking out a Homestead Patent and receiving her Certificate. Her heirs inherited her land.

p. 402

Mary Bailey
Homestead Patent: July 24, 1895 Application No. 2227
Homestead Certificate: September 4, 1906 Certificate No. 889
Land Description: West half of Northeast quarter and West quarter of Southeast quarter of Section 18 in Township 14, North of Range 66, West of Sixth Principal Meridian in Wyoming, containing one hundred and sixty acres.

Mary Bailey did not sell her homestead directly after receiving her certificate but kept her claim for many years.

p. 408

Marsha Kirkbride formerly Misealf
Homestead Patent: December 20, 1904 Application No. 3353
Homestead Certificate: October 6, 1906 Certificate No. 1775
Land Description: North half of Southwest quarter, Southeast quarter of Southwest quarter of Section 23, in Township 18, North of Range 64, West of Sixth Principal Meridian in Wyoming containing one hundred and sixty acres.

Marsha Kirkbride's husband homesteaded on the sections, Section 23 and 24, right next to hers. Consequently, their home place was quite sizable.

p. 437

Mabel E. Underwood
Homestead Patent: December 17, 1906 Application No. 4262
Homestead Certificate: March 29, 1907 Certificate No. 2024
Land Description: West half of Northeast quarter, and North of Range 70, West of Sixth Principal Meridian in Wyoming, containing one hundred and sixty acres.

Mabel Underwood married a Mr. Heosman. She sold her homestead to J. J. Underwood and Son on January 3, 1908, for $1.

p. 461

Martha Pawson
Homestead Patent: May 22, 1907 Application No. 4575
Homestead Certificate: August 16, 1907 Certificate No. 2108
Land Description: Southwest quarter of Section 12 in Township 13, North of Range 64, West of Sixth Principal Meridian in Wyoming, containing one hundred and sixty acres.

Martha Pawson took out a homestead apparently to obtain the free land.

p. 506

Susan J. McLauchlin
Homestead Patent: March 18, 1890 Application No. 489
Homestead Certificate: June 17, 1908 Certificate No. 223
Land Description: West half of Northeast quarter, and the East half of the Northwest quarter of Section 14 in Township 17, North of Range 70, West of Sixth Principal Meridian, in Wyoming containing one hundred and sixty acres.

Susan Van Zandt McLauchlin turned her homestead over to her husband on June 18, 1908, for $480.

p. 508

Annie Nelson
Homestead Patent: January 2, 1908 Application No. 4843
Homestead Certificate: July 28, 1908 Certificate No. 2169
Land Description: Northeast quarter of Section 18 in Township 14, North of Range 60, West of Sixth Principal Meridian, in Wyoming, containing one hundred and sixty acres.

Annie Nelson sold her land on March 4, 1911, for $300 to Peleg J. Whitehead.

p. 519

Emma M. Dudley
Homestead Patent: October 26, 1908 Application No. 7389
Homestead Certificate: Nov. 24, 1908 Certificate No. 2235

Land Description: Southwest quarter of Southeast quarter, and the South half of the Southwest quarter of Section 21, in Township 17, North of Range 69, of Sixth Principal Meridian in Wyoming, containing one hundred and twenty acres.

Emma Dudley sold her land to Charles A. Dereemer on October 1, 1918.

APPENDIX B

Table I

HOMESTEAD PATENTS OF SIX WYOMING COUNTIES

COUNTIES	SINGLE WOMEN HOMESTEAD PATENTS	TOTAL HOMESTEAD PATENTS
CROOK June 23, 1891-January 27, 1925	541 (13.3%)	4058 (100%)
JOHNSON March 26, 1888-September 30, 1932	109 (7.9%)	1383 (100%)
LARAMIE February 25, 1895-November 24, 1905	50 (16.6%)	301 (100%)
LINCOLN April 14, 1917-March 12, 1943	10 (13.1%)	76 (100%)
NATRONA April 29, 1903-March 22, 1925	52 (8.2%)	636 (100%)
SWEETWATER November 20, 1915-October 1, 1925	10 (13.7%)	73 (100%)
TOTALS	772 (11.8%)	6527 (100%)

* Percentages rounded off to the nearest tenth.

* Note that Table I and Table II both show 11.8% of the homesteaders were single women.

APPENDIX B

Table II

TWENTY-ONE SINGLE WOMEN HOMESTEADERS LARAMIE COUNTY MARCH 18, 1890, TO JANUARY 2, 1908

WOMEN WHO:	NUMBER OF HOMESTEADERS	PERCENTAGE OF TOTAL (21)
SOLD LAND (10)		
20% Married, sold to husband	2	9.5
10% Married, sold elsewhere	1	4.8
70% Unmarried, sold elsewhere	7	33.3
KEPT LAND (11)		
18.2% Married	2	9.5
9.1% Widowed	1	4.8
72.7% Unmarried (one died)	8	38.1

* Percentages rounded off to the nearest tenth.

APPENDIX B

Table III

SINGLE WOMEN HOMESTEADERS IN FOUR COUNTIES

COUNTIES	UNMARRIED			MARRIED AFTER PATENT		WIDOW	TOTAL
	Lived	Died	Assigned	Lived	Died		
CROOK							
Patent Records	319	36	1	159	2	3	520
June 23, 1891-	61.3%	6.9%	.2%	30.6%	.4%	.6%	12.2%
January 27, 1925							
LARAMIE							
Certificate Records	58	3	1	14	0	3	79
March 25, 1986-	73.4%	3.8%	1.3%	17.7%	0	3.8%	12.3%
February 16, 1917							
NATRONA							
Patent Records	25	0	3	17	0	7	52
April 29, 1903-	48.0%	0	5.8%	32.7%	0	13.5%	8.2%
March 22, 1922							
SWEETWATER							
Patent Records	9	0	0	0	0	0	9
November 20, 1915-	100%	0	0	0	0	0	12.3%
October 1, 1925							
	455			192		13	660
TOTALS	68.9%			29.1%		2.0%	11.8%

* Percentages rounded off to the nearest tenth.

* Note that **Table I** and **Table II** both show 11.8% of the homesteaders were single women.

LEONARD J. ARRINGTON

RURAL LIFE AMONG NINETEENTH-CENTURY MORMONS: THE WOMAN'S EXPERIENCE

About one hundred years ago Lucy Hannah White Flake, a Mormon pioneer woman in Arizona, mother of thirteen, fifty-four years of age, wrote in her daily diary:

> I will just write my morning chores. Get up, turn out my chickens, draw a pail of water, water hot beds, make a fire, put potatoes to cook, brush and sweep half inch of dust off floor, ... feed three litters of chickens, then mix biscuits, get breakfast, milk besides work in the house, and this morning had to go half mile after calves. This is the way of life on the farm.[1]

Far to the north, Christina Oleson Warnick, a pioneer in Pleasant Grove, Utah, recorded in her diary the similar chores she performed. She helped build the adobe house she lived in, and was herself primarily responsible for the fireplace and chimney. She helped her husband and neighbors dig irrigation ditches; she helped plow, plant, and add fertilizer to the land; she cut the wild hay along the river bottoms and stacked it for the cows for winter; she helped grub the brush and shear the sheep; she took in washing and spun and wove cloth; and she always walked from one village to the next with her knitting in her hands.[2]

LEONARD J. ARRINGTON is Lemuel Redd Professor of Western History at Brigham Young University. He wishes to express his thanks to Maureen Beecher, Carol Madsen, Jill Derr, and Jessie Embry, each of whom has made substantial contributions toward writing the history of Mormon women.

[1] Autobiography and Diary of Lucy Hannah White Flake, vol. 2, 16 May 1896, MS, Church Archives. I have introduced some punctuation and capitalization to clarify.

[2] Miscellaneous Pioneer Interviews and Sketches: Christina Oleson Warnick, 4, Mormon Diaries, Journals, and Life Sketches, Box 12, Library of Congress. See also Jill Marie Thorley, "Landholding Patterns of Women in Iron County, Utah," term paper of History 660, Brigham Young University, 1982, typescript copy in hands of the writer.

In central Utah Martha Jane Coray, middle-aged mother and farmer in the small village of Mona, recorded in her diary, on 3 June 1875, the following succinct summary of the day: "Washed forenoon, plowed afternoon."[3]

Those examples, which are not at all atypical, suggest that the experience of Mormon women might have been a replay of the experience of farm women in Vermont, Pennsylvania, South Carolina, and Kansas. They helped their husbands with the tasks of farming, they looked after the house and garden, and they felt good enough about their activities to record them in a daily diary.

There were, however, some unique elements in the Mormon experience that are worth noting. First of all, the semiarid nature of Mormon country (Utah, southeastern Idaho, eastern Nevada, northern and central Arizona, and southwestern Colorado) meant that successful agriculture depended on irrigation, a practice requiring much extra labor and attention to detail. Second, the Mormon pattern of settlement in villages, rather than on isolated farmsteads, meant that there would be well-organized social life and little of the loneliness and isolation that characterized the lives of farm women on other frontiers. Third, the Mormons permitted the practice of plural marriages, which meant that, in any village, from a tenth to a fifth of the homes shared a father and husband with other homes. In most of these instances the woman was in fact head of her own household and manager of the various enterprises that supported her family. Finally, most of the 300 or 400 villages were inhabited exclusively or largely by Mormons (or Latter-day Saints, as they preferred to call themselves), and the church was the central focus through which they accomplished their various goals, whether economic, political, cultural, recreational, or religious.

There is one other characteristic of Mormon country that is not always recognized: living in the Great Basin were a variety of nationalities. The Mormons supported a vast missionary network, and encouraged a "gathering" of converts to "the Promised Land." Throughout much of the last half of the nineteenth century about 70 percent of the adults in Mormon country were born outside the United States. Of those on farms, perhaps as many as half were from Scandinavia, and nearly half from the British Isles. There were also families from Switzerland, Germany, northern Italy, and France. One village was largely composed of Hawaiians, and of course a few hundred of the Native Americans of the region were converted Mormons or at least lived on farms established by Mormons for Indian groups who were willing to try their hand at settled agriculture.

[3]Martha Jane Knowlton Coray, Diary, 3 June 1875, MS, Brigham Young University Library.

There were only a few blacks, but most of the few who were there came with white converts from Mississippi, Alabama, North Carolina, and Tennessee. Their stories, which have been told by Ronald Coleman and others, are nevertheless interesting. Hannah, the black servant of the William Crosby family and midwife for many of the Crosby and neighboring children, was a very durable person. On one occasion the wagon in which she rode tipped over. Everyone was frightened for fear Aunt Hannah, as she was always referred to, would be killed or badly injured. But when the wagon was righted, Aunt Hannah crawled out from under the cover and asked, "Did anybody see my specs?" One of the girls of a black family in the Mormon colony at San Bernardino, California, became the teacher in a white school in nearby Riverside, and may well have been the first black person to teach at a white school in California.[4]

A modern reader of the diaries of these women, probably not unlike those of women in any part of the nation, is struck with their preoccupation with sickness and death. Most healthy women had many children, and in most instances several of these would die when they were very young—of smallpox, diphtheria, birth defects, or accidents.[5] They were kicked by horses, drowned in irrigation canals, or perhaps fell off a cliff. Caring for the sick was an ever-present responsibility.

A second fact of life on this newly settled frontier was moving. Most families moved several times while their family was growing up. First from Great Britain or Scandinavia or New York or Kentucky to the Great Basin, where they spent the first winter or two in the Salt Lake Valley; then to some outlying colony—southeastern Nevada, southeastern Idaho, or some settlement in Utah that needed strengthening. Often these colonies did not succeed; too many hostile Indians, destruction of crops by grasshoppers, failure of the water supply, or some other factor forced them to move. Perhaps grandpa died and they had to move to take care of grandma. Or perhaps an opportunity opened up in the Nevada or Montana mines. Or maybe some of their friends were living in a nearby valley and they wanted to be near them. In any case, their moves were frequent and required heroic adjustments by housewives wanting some measure of comfort and beauty in their homes and surroundings. One woman complained, "We moved so often that after living in one place for several weeks the chickens would come in and lie down on the floor with their legs together ready to be tied for the next move."[6]

[4]Ronald G. Coleman, "A History of Blacks in Utah, 1825–1910" (Ph.D. diss., University of Utah, 1980).

[5]Geraldine Page Mineau, "Fertility on the Frontier: An Analysis of the Nineteenth Century Utah Population" (Ph.D. diss., University of Utah, 1980).

[6]Melinda Bean Beal, in Merrill D. Beal, ed., *Henry Allen Beal*... (Garland, Utah: V. W. Johns, 1971), 201.

The "outside" reader of the diaries of Mormon farm women is probably most struck by the extent to which they were involved in church and community activities (the same thing, in most instances). Each Mormon settlement constituted a "ward," like a Roman Catholic or Anglican parish. (A few of the larger settlements may have had several wards.) For most of the nineteenth century the women of each settlement were organized into a "Female Relief Society." They met weekly to discuss gospel themes, to plan community work, to exchange information, and to "help the poor." Most Relief Societies devoted most of their time to eight activities:

First, making quilts, dresses, underclothing, and gleaning wheat for distribution to Indian women.

Second, collecting "necessaries" and arranging for domestic services to be provided to the sick, disabled, widows and orphans, and others needing help.

Third, providing midwife services for women in labor and assisting them and their families during ensuing days and weeks. Because of the medical risks of giving birth in the nineteenth century, these services included prayers on behalf of the woman in labor, and religious ceremonies in which the woman was given special blessings to go through a successful labor. For this purpose the women assisted a number of their group to go to the Woman's Medical College in Philadelphia to learn the art of medicine, and these women, upon receiving the M.D., returned to practice medicine and also to hold periodic classes in the art of midwifery; thus several women in most settlements were trained to deliver babies and care for illnesses.

Fourth, providing clothing for the dead, and meals for a period for those in mourning.

Fifth, managing a systematic program of saving grain to assure a carryover of grain to provide for the poor, but also to ensure a supply for all during years of water failure, grasshopper incursions, or other causes of crop failure. For this purpose each settlement had a Relief Society granary in which wheat was stored, and perhaps some other products as well.

Sixth, operating the various cooperative enterprises of the village. Among these were cooperative general stores, cooperative dairies, cooperative woolen mills, and cooperative telegraph network. Cooperative general stores and small manufactories were established in almost all Mormon agricultural villages in the 1860s, and, while they were under the general managership of the bishop, in practice women did most of the clerking and bookkeeping, much of the manufacturing itself, and handled many of the business details. The small farms of the Mormons, and their large families, made possible the labor to keep these enterprises going.

In the case of the telegraph line, the local wards picked two or three teenagers, almost always girls, to go to Salt Lake City to attend a church-sponsored telegraph school. The girls would then, with the assistance of their mothers and the Relief Society, operate the local station of the church-built line. In this way, the local settlement could keep in touch with Salt Lake City and with "the world." And of course Salt Lake City and "the world" could keep in touch with them. Often the women and girls would use this means of keeping in touch with others of their gender in other settlements in the region.[7]

Seventh, programs to stimulate "home industry"; that is, to achieve as much village self-sufficiency as possible. One of these programs was the establishment of a cooperative community livestock herd to assure a supply of wool which they would shear, card, spin, and weave into dresses and petticoats, and suits for the men. Mary Julia Johnson Wilson testified to the effectiveness of this when she told the story of a young man who was leaving in one week on a proselyting mission but had no suit to wear. When the women of the Relief Society heard of this, they went to work with the result that "one Sunday the wool was on the sheep's back, but by the next Sunday it had been clipped, cleansed, corded, spun, woven, and made into a splendid suit and was on the back of the missionary as he delivered his farewell address in the little church house."[8]

A second "home industry" program was sericulture. The women apparently felt that one way to have the kind of finery that women had in London, Paris, New York, and New Orleans was to grow silkworms, spin the silk they produced, and make silk dresses, hats, and shawls. Most diaries contain numerous entries about trying to establish the industry. Ground was obtained on which mulberry trees were planted, eggs were acquired from fellow members in France and Italy, and husbands were induced to allow wives to devote one room in the house to serving as a cocoonery. The minutes of one Relief Society suggest the pious stubbornness with which they clung to their objective:

May 2, 1878: Sister Ivins of the Third Ward said: "They were making a start in the silk business. Said as she looked upon the worms and realized that all the silk came from them, they seemed quite near to her. She hoped to see the day when we would be able to make our own fine apparel, and that which we would not be ashamed of.

Sister Snow said that she had a number of worms. They were not much trouble to her, as they did not require their food cooked. . . .

[7]Leonard J. Arrington, "The Deseret Telegraph: A Church-owned Public Utility," *Journal of Economic History* 11 (Spring 1951): 117–39.

[8]"Miscellaneous Pioneer Interviews and Sketches: Mary Julia Johnson Wilson," 31, Mormon Diaries, Journals, and Life Sketches, Box 10, Library of Congress.

May 1, 1880: In this meeting Sister Church showed a necktie that she made from home-produced silk. Sister Eyring said: "She did not think we should make a deal of money out of silkworms, but if we learn to handle them and plant the mulberry we are making that much progress . . . and doing our duty. . . .
May 6, 1880: The bishop talked to the group. "Said he felt interested in the business, but would not labor as he has seen the sisters do to take care of them [worms] and get nothing for it. He would feed them to the chickens. . . . Some brethren were complaining that the women were turning the parlors over to the worms; that the smell of the worms drove them from the house to eat in the woodshed."[9]

Eighth, finally, the women were involved in establishing and superintending related organized groups for children, called the Primary, and young women, called the Young Ladies' Mutual Improvement Association. Women were assigned to work with and teach these groups and supervise their recreational, cultural, and educational programs.

In short, like all frontier women, Mormon women provided the meals, clothing, soap, and candles, but they also were an integral part of the community as they helped with plowing while the men put in the dam; helped with the harvest while the men went off to fight hostile Indians; accepted assignments to teach in the village or ward school, serve as midwives, and tend cooperative stores; and worked with their husbands to see that their children were educated, their "old folks" looked after, and the homes of the settlement improved.

It is perhaps because of the undeniably important managerial role of women and their training as leaders that the women of Utah were the first in the nation to vote (while the Wyoming legislature was the first to pass a suffrage law, Utah women were the first to exercise the franchise), the second to elect a woman mayor, and were the first in the nation to elect a woman state senator, a woman county superintendent of schools, a woman delegate to a national political convention, and a woman to serve on a state board of higher education. They also had perhaps the largest block of trained women physicians in the nation.

Mormon women had their problems — husbands who did not pay sufficient attention to them, the rigors of frontier life, and the absence of many of the amenities of "civilization." But their diaries suggest they were reasonably happy, satisfied with their life style, and proud of their accomplishments. They were especially proud of their children, who, with the excellent training provided by their mothers, were achievers and helped Utah, in this century, to rank at the top in the proportion of its population who were prominent scientists and educators.[10] Most of

[9]Nels Anderson, *Desert Saints: The Mormon Frontier in Utah* (Chicago: University of Chicago Press, 1942), 371–72.

[10]See Kenneth R. Hardy, "Social Origins of American Scientists and Scholars," *Science* 185 (9 August 1974): 497–506; E. L. Thorndike, "Origin of Superior Men," *Scientific Monthly* 56 (May 1943): 424–33.

the women probably would have echoed the 1878 sentiment of Mary Jane Mount Tanner, a farm woman in Provo, Utah. She had struggled for a lifetime with her considerable family, with her various home enterprises, with her desire to write poetry, and with her service as president of her village Relief Society. When she had finally finished her book of poetry and was discussing the contract which finally made possible its publication, she was interrupted in the negotiations by the sudden appearance of her son, who had been away to school. The son conversed for a while with the publishers, and the mother was so impressed with his sophistication and learning (he later became president of Utah State University) that she concluded her diary entry on that momentous day in her life by writing, "I thought he [her son Marion] was better than a book, and if I did no other work, the honor of having such a son is more pride and pleasure than a dozen books."[11]

NOTES AND SOURCES

This paper is based on impressions gained from reading some two hundred diaries of nineteenth-century Mormon women which are located in the archives of the Historical Department of The Church of Jesus Christ of Latter-day Saints, Salt Lake City, Utah (hereafter called Church Archives); in the Western Americana Collections at the Marriott Library of the University of Utah; the Harold B. Lee Library, Brigham Young University; the Milton R. Merrill Library at Utah State University; and the Utah State Historical Society Library. Previous publications of mine and those associated with me have included *Sunbonnet Sisters: True Stories of Mormon Women and Frontier Life* (Salt Lake City: Bookcraft Publishers, 1984), with Susan Arrington Madsen; and the following articles: "The Economic Role of Pioneer Mormon Women," *Western Humanities Review* 9 (Spring 1955): 145–64; "Women as a Force in the History of Utah," *Utah Historical Quarterly* 38 (Winter 1970): 3–6; "Blessed Damozels: Women in Mormon History," *Dialogue: A Journal of Mormon Thought* 6 (Summer 1971): 22–31; "Latter-day Saint Women on the Arizona Frontier," *The New Era* (Salt Lake City) 5 (April 1974): 42–50; "Persons for All Seasons: Women in Mormon History," *Brigham Young University Studies* 20 (Fall 1979): 39–58; and "LDS Girls in the Pioneer West," *The New Era* 12 (July 1982): 16–22.

Among other important studies of Mormon women are five books: Claudia L. Bushman, ed., *Mormon Sisters: Women in Early Utah* (Cambridge, Mass.: Emmeline Press, 1976); Annie Clark Tanner, *A Mormon Mother* (Salt Lake City: University of Utah Press, 1976); Vicky Burgess-

[11]Diary of Mary Jane Mount Tanner, 5 May 1878, MS, Church Archives.

Olson, ed., *Sister Saints* (Provo: Brigham Young University Press, 1978); Carol Cornwall Madsen, *A Survey of the Life of Cache Valley Women in 1890* (Logan, Utah: Ronald V. Jensen Historical Farm, 1979), 82 pp. (duplicated); and Kenneth W. Godfrey, Audrey M. Godfrey, and Jill Mulvay Derr, *Women's Voices: An Untold History of the Latter-day Saints, 1830–1900* (Salt Lake City: Deseret Book Company, 1982).

The following professional articles and chapters in books represent significant contributions: Jessie L. Embry, "Master or Slave: The Economic Role of Mormon Polygamous Wives," Sirow Working Paper No. 15, copy in Brigham Young University Library, Provo, Utah; Maureen U. Beecher, "Under the Sunbonnets: Mormon Women With Faces," *Brigham Young University Studies* 16 (Summer 1976): 471–84; Jill Mulvay Derr, "Woman's Place in Brigham Young's World," *Brigham Young University Studies* 18 (Spring 1978): 377–95; Ann Vest Lobb and Jill Mulvay Derr, "Women in Early Utah," in Richard D. Poll et al., eds., *Utah's History* (Provo, Utah: Brigham Young University Press, 1978), 337–56; Lawrence Foster, "From Frontier Activism to New-Victorian Domesticity: Mormon Women in the Nineteenth and Twentieth Century," *Journal of Mormon History* 6 (1979): 3–21; Maureen U. Beecher, "Women's Work on the Mormon Frontier," *Utah Historical Quarterly* 49 (Summer 1981): 276–90; and Richard L. Jensen, "Forgotten Relief Societies, 1844–67," *Dialogue: A Journal of Mormon Thought* 16 (Spring 1983): 105–25.

Farm Women's Roles in the Agricultural Development of South Dakota

GLENDA RILEY

Like most American women during the nineteenth century and the early decades of the twentieth, farm women had little control over their own destinies. The form and quality of their lives were shaped to a large degree by a complex of political, economic, and social factors that buffeted them from all sides. There were, however, three dominant influences that affected farm women with a relatively high degree of consistency. These were the particular character of the area in which the women lived, the similar nature of farm women's tasks from region to region, and the continuity of their tasks and concerns from the early years of the nineteenth century well into the twentieth. The impact of these influences upon South Dakota women will be examined here between the time of initial settlement of the region in the late 1850s and the mid-1930s when the Great Depression, industrialization, and modernization were reshaping not only the urban areas of the country but the rural sections as well.

Because early Dakota settlers did in fact live in a distinctive part of the country, it is not surprising to discover that their history differed markedly from that of even their near neighbors. Although white squatters began pushing across the Mississippi River as early as 1828 in an effort to displace the Indian inhabitants of the Iowa region, it was not until fully thirty years later that the same phenomenon occurred along the Missouri River. In 1858, initial attempts at white settlement on the Dakota side of the Missouri River pressured the United States government into negotiating the Yankton Treaty. Like the Black Hawk Treaty of 1832, it was widely misunderstood and Indian resistance to it was rife, yet it eventually opened the Dakotas to settlers just as the earlier treaty had opened Iowa.

When Dakota Territory was formed in 1861, however, the area did not experience the land rush that Iowa had during the 1840s. Not only had the boom of the fifties played itself out, but the Civil War was radically altering the political and economic situation of many Americans. So, while Iowa was well along in its own frontier period, achieving statehood in 1846 and destined by 1870 to have the population that the United States Census Bureau considered necessary to declare a frontier district closed, the Dakotas were just entering their own frontier period in the early 1860s. Clearly, the history of this region would be dissimilar to that of its immediate predecessors since it was influenced by a different set of historical factors during the initial stage of its development.

Key in these factors was the Homestead Act, passed by the Congress of the United States in 1862. Offering a person a free quarter section of land on condition that he or she survived on that land for a period of five years, the Homestead Act inadvertently fostered a kind of tenuousness on the part of many settlers in the Dakotas. Author and Dakota settler Laura Ingalls Wilder described the homestead venture as a huge gamble. "The government bets a man a quarter-section of land, that he can't stay on it five years without starving to death," she explained to a friend.[1] As a result of the homestead wager, the claim shack and talk of "proving up" were dominant elements of early settlement in the Dakotas, while discussions of whether or not it would be wise to abandon the entire adventure contributed a pervasive feeling of temporariness to frontier society in the region.

Aggravating this situation was the fact that the Dakotas were not particularly alluring to settlers. Historian Everett Dick

1. Laura Ingalls Wilder, *These Happy Golden Years* (New York: Harper & Bros., 1943), p. 119.

observed that four aspects of the plains region in general made it less than attractive: "the perpetual winds, the absence of water, the terrific heat, and the absence of trees." He also noted a fifth factor that was especially severe in the Dakotas, the "deadening cold."[2] Prospective migrants were further discouraged during the 1860s by drought, grasshopper invasions, and continuing problems with the original inhabitants. These conditions were then exacerbated by the crude methods of cultivation employed by the early settlers, as well as by their lack of knowledge regarding appropriate crops for the area.[3] The result, according to historian Mary Hargreaves, was that during a good part of the nineteenth century, the Dakotas were written off by most Americans as simply part of the Great American Desert, an inhospitable place for both people and crops.[4]

Consequently, the strong commitment to the land that characterized settlers in richer areas such as Iowa did not generally exist in the Dakotas. Few stories were told of advance scouts carefully searching out quality land or of people arriving with money sewn into their clothing to purchase their farmsteads. Rather, when settlement of the Dakotas did begin in earnest after 1870, the tales that emanated from the region concerned land rushes and lotteries, unlawful possession of as many as five and six claims, formation of homestead associations and other colonization schemes, elaborate propagandizing of potential migrants, rushes into newly opened lands such as the Rosebud Indian Reservation, and the regular mounting of claim shanties, and even outhouses, on wheels to move them to what promised to be better claims.[5]

The tension created by such transience and mobility affected most settlers, but it wore on women in particular gender-associated ways. Encouraged by nineteenth-century society to value permanence and domestic order, female settlers were often dis-

2. Everett Dick, *The Sod-House Frontier: A Social History of the Northern Plains from the Creation of Kansas & Nebraska to the Admission of the Dakotas* (New York: D. Appleton-Century Co., 1937), p. 233.

3. Harold E. Briggs, "The Settlement and Development of the Territory of Dakota, 1860-70," *North Dakota Historical Quarterly* 7 (Jan./Apr. 1933): 116, 118, 124-25.

4. Mary W. M. Hargreaves, *Dry Farming in the Northern Great Plains* (Cambridge, Mass.: Harvard University Press, 1957), pp. 25-30. *See also* Briggs, "Settlement and Development," p. 127.

5. Briggs, "Settlement and Development," pp. 129-39; Dick, *Sod-House Frontier*, p. 128; and Edith Eudora Kohl, *Land of the Burnt Thigh* (New York: Funk & Wagnalls Co., 1938), pp. 88, 92, 94, 144-45.

concerted by the instability of their new environment. Because life was suddenly so changeable and unreliable, they discovered to their dismay that they had little time or energy to devote to the maintenance of traditional female values and lifestyles.

In addition, there was even more pressure upon farm women than was usual on other agrarian frontiers to aid in proving that people could endure and perhaps prosper on a plains farmstead. Wilder wrote that she, like so many women, felt a pressing need to help demonstrate that "farming was as good as any other business."[6] Thus, women were expected to contribute to family survival in every way possible, including living on an isolated claim

A woman poses with her two well-dressed children in front of a sod claim shanty. The large dogs may represent both company and protection for this isolated young farm woman.

alone with their children for months on end to hold it while their husbands worked elsewhere to raise the necessary capital for seed and equipment.[7] One Dakota woman succinctly summarized the demands placed upon women in this area of the plains:

> I had lived on a homestead long enough to learn some fundamental things: that while a woman had more independence here than in any other part of the world, she was expected to contribute as much as a man

6. Laura Ingalls Wilder, *The First Four Years* (New York: Harper & Row, 1971), p. 17.
7. Wilder, *These Happy Golden Years*, pp. 114-22.

> —not in the same way, it is true, but to the same degree; that people who fought the frontier had to be prepared to meet any emergency; that the person who wasn't willing to try anything once wasn't equipped to be a settler.[8]

It is to their credit that generations of wives, daughters, and sisters met this challenge by becoming economic partners with their menfolk in securing homesteads for their families.

A notable feature of the agrarian heritage of the plains, however, is that many single women also seized the opportunity to gain a free homestead. Although single women frequently migrated to frontier areas as teachers, missionaries, laborers, and potential wives, these unmarried women homesteaders were lured by the possibility of acquiring land, which was customarily considered a male undertaking. One investigator who sampled the land office data in Colorado and Wyoming discovered that the number of female homestead entrants ranged between 11.9 and 18.2 percent. Moreover, the data indicated that 42.4 percent of the women succeeded in making a final claim to their homesteads while only 37 percent of the men did so.[9] The prevalence of "girl homesteaders," as they were commonly called, is supported by scholars such as Everett Dick, who maintained that "a noteworthy proportion of the first settlers were single or unattached women," and Mary Hargreaves, who cited one source that estimated that as much as one-third of the homesteads in the Dakotas were held by women in 1887.[10] The diaries and letters of Dakota settlers also contain occasional mention of female homesteaders. Enid Bern, for example, wrote of a "strange malady" she called "Homestead Fever" that struck all manner of folks, including single men and women. She believed that these unmarried homesteaders "formed an interesting segment of the population" and that "their presence added zest to community life, perhaps because of their youthfulness and varied personalities."[11]

8. Kohl, *Land of the Burnt Thigh*, p. 38.

9. Sheryll and Gene Patterson-Black, "From Pack Trains to Publishing: Women's Work in the Frontier West," in Sheryll and Gene Patterson-Black, *Western Women in History and Literature* (Crawford, Nebr.: Cottonwood Press, 1978), pp. 5-6. *See also* Sheryll Patterson-Black, "Women Homesteaders on the Great Plains Frontier," ibid., pp. 15-31, and "Women Homesteaders on the Great Plains Frontier," *Frontiers* 1 (Spring 1976): 67-88.

10. Dick, *Sod-House Frontier*, p. 129, and Mary W. M. Hargreaves, "Women in the Agricultural Settlement of the Northern Plains," *Agricultural History* 50 (Jan. 1976): 182.

11. Enid Bern, "The Enchanted Years on the Prairies," *North Dakota History* 40 (Fall 1973): 11. *See also* Enid Bern, ed., "They Had a Wonderful Time: The Home-

Autobiographical narratives of female homesteaders in the Dakotas are also extant. The reminiscences of Cora D. Babcock, covering the years 1880 to 1885, offer a succinct version of her move to the Dakotas at age twenty-five. She filed a claim near Bridgewater, constructed a sod shanty on it, and raised a successful crop of flax that paid all expenses of her claim. She next experimented with a laundry business in Mitchell and looked for another claim, selling her original one for a profit, before she decided to abandon the "claim idea" in favor of marriage. Widowed within three years, she briefly visited her family home in New York and then returned with her mother to Dakota to try her luck once again. Some years later, in 1906, Grace Reed Porter left her position as head of the Latin Department of the Boone, Iowa, high school to file on a homestead north of Fort Pierre in Stanley County. Here she not only proved up her claim, but she also taught school, achieved election to the position of county superintendent of schools, married, and eventually became principal of the Fort Pierre high school.[12]

Another similar account is that of Grace W. Fairchild who, after watching both her mother and sister-in-law homestead on their own, eventually decided to homestead herself as a divorced woman. During the course of her marriage, she had become increasingly aware that her husband's incompetence was driving them into mortgage and debt. After one particularly upsetting business deal, she exclaimed, "This longhorn fiasco convinced me that if we were to make our goddamn claim into a ranch, I had to take charge of the whole thing." She finally did just that in 1930, when she divorced her husband and began running the ranch by herself. Within ten years, she had extricated herself from debt, accumulated 1440 acres of land, and acquired sufficient sheep and cattle to keep her "out of the poor house, and them some."[13]

An unusally detailed chronicle of women homesteaders in South Dakota is that of Edith Eudora (Ammons) Kohl, who home-

---

steading Letters of Anna and Ethel Erickson," *North Dakota History* 45 (Fall 1978): 4-31.

12. Cora D. Babcock, Reminiscences, 1880-1885, Manuscript Division, South Dakota Historical Resource Center, Pierre (the center is hereafter cited SDHRC); Grace Reed Porter, "Twenty-Five Years in South Dakota," Library, SDHRC. *See also* Winifred Erdman Interview, "North Dakota Oral History Project Issue," *North Dakota History* 43 (Spring 1976): 39-42.

13. Walker D. Wyman, *Frontier Woman: The Life of a Woman Homesteader on the Dakota Frontier* (River Falls: University of Wisconsin-River Falls Press, 1972), pp. 22-23, 90-91, 113.

steaded near Pierre with her sister Ida around the turn of the twentieth century. Coming to an "improved" claim that boasted a ten-by-twelve-foot tarpaper shack, they were initially disillusioned and homesick. Influenced by newly developing ideas of independence for women and seeking better health for Edith, the sisters got themselves into what they considered an unliveable situation. They quickly determined that they would head back East, a decision that was reversed when they discovered an amazing number of "girl homesteaders" in their new neighborhood. Thus encouraged to stay, they supported their claim by teaching school and publishing a newspaper. Like so many other settlers, they moved on to seek a better claim when the Lower Brule Indian Reservation was opened, there establishing a post office, newspaper, and store. When her sister married, Kohl moved on again to yet another promising claim in Wyoming.[14]

Kohl described the process of their acclimatization to the Dakota frontier in the course of her autobiography. It began with their observation that although women homesteaders worked hard, they also lived satisfying lives, took delight in the country, and had little desire to return to their eastern homes. Gradually, Kohl and her sister also found themselves "making friends, learning to find space restful and reassuring instead of intimidating, adapting [their] restless natures to a country that measured time

14. Kohl, *Land of the Burnt Thigh*, pp. 2-7, 12-13, 21-23, 33, 38-39, 88-89, 120, 289-96.

Four "girl homesteaders" stand outside a tarpaper claim shack.

in seasons" and imperceptibly sinking their roots into "that stubborn soil." When Kohl was told, "The range is no place for clingin' vines, 'cause their hain't nothin' to cling to," she felt that she indeed was learning not to cling. And when "proving up" time finally arrived, the sisters realized that they did not want to return to the city as they had so long planned. The hardships of western life, Kohl wrote, "were more than compensated for by its unshackled freedom. . . . The opportunities for a full and active life were infinitely greater here. . . . There was a pleasant glow of possession in knowing that the land beneath our feet was ours."[15]

Although both married and single women homesteaders formed a large part of the early population of the Dakotas, it should be remembered that their involvement in agricultural pursuits was supported and often made possible by a variety of women who engaged in other kinds of endeavors. The earliest of these were Indian women. As the first agriculturalists, they not only developed knowledge of crops and methods of working the land, but they demonstrated that agricultural production was achievable in such a resistant land. They were disrupted and frequently removed from the land altogether by expeditions and early colonies that often included women in their numbers.[16] Army women such as Fanny McGillycuddy who accompanied her husband to Fort Robinson in the 1870s also helped to divest the original inhabitants of their land, thus freeing the area for white settlement and cultivation.[17] Female missionaries tried to deal with some of the many problems that this process created, while female preachers and orders of religious women such as the Presentation Sisters moved into the area to establish educational, medical, and other social services for both the native and newly arrived residents.[18] Finally, employed women provided a wide va-

15. Ibid., pp. 27, 65, 84. *See also* pp. 22-33.

16. *See*, for example, Annie D. Tallent, *The First White Woman in the Black Hills* (Mitchell, S.Dak.: Educator Supply Co., 1923), and *The Black Hills; or, The Last Hunting Ground of the Dakotahs* (1899; reprint ed., Sioux Falls, S.Dak.: Brevet Press, 1974).

17. Fanny McGillycuddy, Diary, 1877-1878, Manuscript Division, SDHRC. *See also* John R. Sibbald, "Camp Followers All: Army Women of the West," *American West* 3 (Spring 1966): 56-67, and Miller J. Stewart, "Army Laundresses: Ladies of the 'Soap Suds Row,' " *Nebraska History* 61 (Winter 1980): 421-36.

18. Elaine Goodale Eastman, *Sister to the Sioux: The Memoirs of Elaine Goodale Eastman, 1885-1891*, ed. Kay Graber (Lincoln: University of Nebraska Press, 1978); Thisba Hutson Morgan, "Reminiscences of My Days in the Land of the Ogallala Sioux," *South Dakota Historical Collections* 29 (1958): 21-62; Faye Cashatt Lewis,

riety of services and goods to frontierspeople and their children that ranged from functioning as domestics, teachers, doctors, newspaper editors, and cowhands to the furnishing of sexual services.[19]

It should also be noted that Dakota women were not only dissimilar in their pursuits, but that they also differed in racial, ethnic, and religious backgrounds. It appears from the scanty evidence available, for example, that black women accounted for a small proportion of women on the plains.[20] Moreover, source materials such as letters and diaries suggest that women from European and other countries were a sizable element in the early Dakota population, with the Germans, Scandinavians, Czechs, and German-Russians being dominant, while eastern-born white women were also a significant source of female migrants to the Dakotas. Among these women settlers, additional diversity was introduced in that they also represented Catholics, Jews, and many Protestant sects.[21]

Nothing to Make a Shadow (Ames: Iowa State University Press, 1971), pp. 119-23; and Susan Peterson, "Religious Communities of Women in the West: The Presentation Sister's Adaptation to the Northern Plains Frontier," *Journal of the West* 21 (Apr. 1982): 65-70, and "From Paradise to Prairie: The Presentation Sisters in Dakota, 1880-1896," *South Dakota History* 10 (Summer 1980): 210-22. *See also* the collection of church histories at the Dacotah Prairie Museum and the Archives of the Presentation Sisters of the Blessed Virgin Mary, both in Aberdeen, S.Dak.; the Archives of the Oblate Sisters of the Blessed Sacrament, Saint Sylvester's Convent, Marty; the Archives of the Benedictine Convent of Saint Martin, Rapid City; and the Archives of the Benedictine Sisters of the Sacred Heart Convent, Yankton.

19. T. A. Larson, "Women's Role in the American West," *Montana, the Magazine of Western History* 24 (Summer 1974): 3-6; Enid Bern, "Memoirs of a Prairie School Teacher," *North Dakota History* 42 (Summer 1975): 5-17; Patterson-Black, "From Pack Trains to Publishing," pp. 2, 10-11; Wyman, *Frontier Woman*, pp. 57-58; Elliott West, "Scarlet West: The Oldest Profession in the Trans-Mississippi West," and Paula Petrik, "Capitalists with Rooms: Prostitution in Helena, Montana, 1865-1900," both in *Montana, the Magazine of Western History* 31 (Spring 1981): 16-17, 28-41.

20. Minnie Miller Brown, "Black Women in American Agriculture," *Agricultural History* 50 (Jan. 1976): 202-12, and Sue Armitage, Theresa Banfield, and Sarah Jacobus, "Black Women and Their Communities in Colorado," *Frontiers*, 2, no. 2 (1977): 45-51. The census of 1870 showed 94 black people in Dakota, while the 1880 census indicated an increase to 2,003 blacks. Robert B. Porter, *The West: From the Census of 1880* (Chicago: Rand McNally & Co., 1882), p. 404. *See also* Sara L. Bernson and Robert J. Eggers, "Black People in South Dakota History," *South Dakota History* 7 (Summer 1977): 241-70.

21. Mrs. R. O. Brandt, "Social Aspects of Prairie Pioneering: The Reminiscences of a Pioneer Pastor's Wife," *Norwegian-American Studies* 7 (1933): 1-46; Lorna B. Herseth, ed., "A Pioneer's Letter," *South Dakota History* 6 (Summer 1976): 306-15;

Although Dakota women thus represented a variety of heritages that occasionally manifested themselves through special foods, items of clothing, crafts, or value systems in their new homes in the West, they were unified by their participation in what might be called the female frontier. They were, in other words, engaged in a series of tasks and roles that varied little from frontier to frontier. Whether men were engaged in mining, lumbering, ranching, or farming, the primary focus of most frontierswomen was the home. Within the context of her home, the frontierswoman was expected to serve as a domestic artisan producing all the goods necessary for family survival; to produce, care for, and train children; and to perpetuate traditional American values such as family unity and domestic order. Secondarily, women were to share in the conquering of their particular frontier. For agrarians, this meant that besides performing customary female tasks, many women also worked outside of their homes in jobs ranging from herding cattle to breaking sod. This taxing picture of women's work varied only slightly for single farm women, for, although they frequently faced lessened domestic demands due to the absence of a spouse and children, they had to deal with the problems presented by their land and sometimes had to hold paid jobs as well.[22]

It is fair to say, then, that for Dakota farm women, whether single or married, the combination of role expectation with the immediate demands of the land translated into a strenuous and wearying set of duties. Unfortunately, in many cases, especially during the early years of settlement, women performed their labors in the most rudimentary of workplaces. Frequently, a woman's workplace was simply a one-room claim shack built of rough boards, covered on the outside by black tarpaper and lined on the inside with either expensive and fairly effective blue paper

---

Barbara Levorsen, "Early Years in Dakota," *Norwegian-American Studies* 21 (1962): 158-97; Emily Lunde, *Uff Da* (Grand Forks, N.Dak.: By the Author, 1974); Aagot Raaen, *Grass of the Earth: Immigrant Life in the Dakota Country*, Scandinavians in America Series (New York: Arno Press, 1979); Martha Reishus, *The Rag Rug*, no. 3 (New York: Vantage Press, 1955); Herbert S. Schell, *South Dakota: A Student's Guide to Localized History*, Localized History Series (New York: Teachers College Press, 1971), pp. 41-42; Martha Thal, "Early Days: The Story of Sarah Thal," *American Jewish Archives* 23 (Apr. 1971): 47-62; Mary Dodge Woodward, *The Checkered Years*, ed. Mary B. Cowdrey (Caldwell, Idaho: Caxton Printers, 1937), pp. 41-42, 86-88, 239-40.

22. Kohl, *Land of the Burnt Thigh*, and Elizabeth ("Bess") Corey Papers, 1909-1979, Manuscript Division, SDHRC.

The small workplaces of the homesteaders presented storage problems. This settler kept a variety of supplies and equipment outside her lath claim shack.

or a cheaper and inferior grade of red paper. Inside the shack, the furniture commonly consisted of a homemade bunk with rope springs fastened to a wall, an oil stove, a drygoods box or two for cupboards, and a wooden table and chairs.[23] For other women, the home workplace was a structure of hastily cut laths. An 1889 migrant to the Dakotas later caustically described her lath home as the "finest house on the prairies." You could, she wrote, "see right through the walls of the three rooms, for they were made of laths—open in between. No plaster yet—they smelled queerly as new pine boards do. Upstairs horse blankets were nailed over the laths. . . . What my mother must have thought when she faced this primitive place, I can only imagine."[24]

For yet others, the first dwelling on the plains was a modest sod hut or dugout, an economical response to a land of scarce tim-

23. Kohl, *Land of the Burnt Thigh*, pp. 3-4, 26.

24. Elenore Plaisted, quoted in Brett Harvey Vuolo, "Pioneer Diaries: The Untold Story of the West," *Ms. Magazine* 3 (May 1975): 32.

ber. Although the roofs of such structures continually dropped particles of dirt on the heads of those beneath them, they did offer warmth in the winter and natural cooling in the summer.[25] One South Dakota woman wrote to her family that her sod house might "pass" if "one isn't too spoiled." She explained that it was built of sod for "safety as well as warmth," with a floor dug to lie below the ground level and with windows just at ground level. She was delighted with the interior, which appeared to her as a "fairy palace" of many rooms comfortably furnished with a range of family treasures.[26]

Typically, women worked very hard to convert these crude dwellings into pleasant homes. The Ammons sisters added a second-hand Brussels rug, an old wire cot, handmade pillows stuffed with prairie grass, bright curtains, and some bright red bookcases to their claim shanty.[27] Wilder dressed up her tiny parlor with a small rocker, a glass lamp, books of poetry, and some

25. Hargreaves, "Women in the Agricultural Settlement of the Northern Plains," p. 185.
26. Herseth, "A Pioneer's Letter," p. 309.
27. Kohl, *Land of the Burnt Thigh*, p. 27.

The mistress of this tiny sitting and dining area brightened her environment with gay wallpaper, homemade pillows, and a faded rug.

geraniums potted in cans.[28] The mistress of the lath house had her grand piano shipped from Philadelphia to stand, according to her daughter, "very big and black in the front room on the bare pine floor, against the wall of laths that you could see through."[29] One woman even studied up on plastering and secured the necessary materials to plaster up the many holes in the walls of her first home near Brookings, while she solved her storage problems by packing things into a "shanty," a common lean-to addition over the back door. When she and her family moved to a nicer house, she furnished it simply but pleasantly with a rag carpet, cheesecloth curtains, a hanging lamp, an overstuffed rocker, and a braided rug. She tellingly commented that while early Dakota houses had definite drawbacks, they could be made neat and cozy with a little effort: "When floors were scrubbed, walls freshly whitewashed, and the broad window sills filled with blooming geraniums, such homes were by no means unattractive in the pioneer country. Of course the coziness and attractiveness depended pretty much on the people living in the home."[30]

Besides transforming these quickly constructed dwellings into liveable homes, women also converted them into effective workplaces where, despite the additional handicaps of scarce water and limited fuel, they proceeded to function as the domestic artisans of frontier society. Women's diaries, letters, and memoirs are replete with accounts of the routines of domestic life, including cleaning, sewing, cooking, baking, washing clothes in tubs of rainwater, and caring for the ever-present newborn baby.[31] A letter from a Norwegian woman of the Dakotas during the 1880s tells of baking bread in a small stove, converting the milk from two cows into cream and butter, processing wild game into edible meals, filling the food cellar with "potatoes, roots and milk," and butchering heifers and hogs.[32] Another Norwegian woman expressed great pride in her skill at baking, drying fruits and berries, laundering, and sewing, while yet another was so proficient at soapmaking, dying yarn, knitting, spinning, weaving, and sewing that her daughter called their home a "pioneer factory."[33] In

28. Wilder, *The First Four Years*, p. 16.
29. Elenore Plaisted, quoted in Vuolo, "Pioneer Diaries," p. 33.
30. Brandt, "Social Aspects of Prairie Pioneering," p. 15. *See also* p. 5.
31. Mary W. M. Hargreaves, "Homesteading and Homemaking on the Plains: A Review," *Agricultural History* 157 (Apr. 1973): 162; Vuolo, "Pioneer Diaries," p. 32.
32. Herseth, "A Pioneer's Letter," pp. 310-11.
33. Brandt, "Social Aspects of Prairie Pioneering," p. 37, and Raaen, *Grass of the Earth*, pp. 10-14.

A frontierswoman's work was arduous. Here, a pioneer woman washes clothes next to a stream on her claim near Fort Pierre.

her penciled memoirs, Wilder noted that, in addition to this list of chores, the farm wife was also charged with cooking a dinner for the threshing crew that would make the plank tables groan with its weight. Although dismayed by this and many other necessary tasks, she ultimately considered it "all in the day's work."[34]

Dakota farm women also listed expertise in soapmaking, candlemaking, spinning, weaving, doctoring, food processing, and

34. Wilder, *The First Four Years*, pp. 18-20. Woodward also wrote that she baked seventy-four loaves of bread and twenty-one pies, puddings, cakes, and doughnuts in less than a week for a threshing crew of thirteen men. Woodward, *The Checkered Years*, p. 90. *See also* Alice Conitz Interview, "North Dakota Oral History Project Issue," pp. 52-54.

even twisting hay into "cats" for fuel in their panoply of domestic skills. One young woman remembered that her mother was particularly adept at processing meat through smoking or packing it in stone jars in lard and at converting flour sacks into family underclothing.[35] Another woman mentioned doing a "big washing, a lot of scrubbing and so on," finishing "some little sewing," and completing the regular household duties, all within days of bearing her first child.[36] A Fargo woman claimed that she made fourteen pounds of butter a week. "I wonder if anybody was ever

35. Kate Roberts Pelissier, "Reminiscences of a Pioneer Mother," *North Dakota History* 24 (July 1957): 134-35.
36. Babcock, Reminiscences.

The kitchen on a claim was a pioneer factory without benefit of modern conveniences.

before tired enough to be sick at his [*sic*] stomach," she lamented. On a more cheerful note, she added, "When I become rested I get over it."[37]

Since factories and trained professionals have taken over most of these functions in modern society, it is difficult for us to realize just how much skill and toil were involved as well as to understand the prominent role that these women played in the frontier economy. The frontierswoman's significance as an economic partner was recognized by her own society, however, at the time of marriage, for a young woman's greatest assets were seen as deriving from her abilities as a domestic manufacturer and artisan. In fact, she was often rated as a worker in the same way that a man was judged as a provider. According to one study of frontier marriage: "the choosing of a mate on the frontier was a matter of economic necessity far and above individual whim. Good health and perseverance were premium assets while the charm and ability to entertain that one values so highly in a society of mechanization and leisure time was only of tangential significance . . . the woman who could not sew nor cook had no place on the frontier."[38]

If a frontierswoman chose to remain single or was forced to become single through divorce or the death or desertion of a mate, her skills were still of great importance to both herself and to the kinfolk that she may have chosen to live with. Census figures indicate that most unmarried frontierswomen were absorbed by other households maintained by parents, children, or other relatives, and that here they had to continue to pull their own economic weight by rendering their share of the household services. Like her married sisters, the single frontierswoman was a highly skilled laborer whose contributions to the frontier economy were vital to its progress.

Although all women, married or single, were expected to supply a bewildering variety of goods and services, those that did choose to marry were also encouraged to produce children, both as an aid to population growth and to provide future laborers for

37. Woodward, *The Checkered Years*, p. 238. For detailed descriptions of the skills and techniques involved in these tasks, *see* Glenda Riley, " 'Not Gainfully Employed': Women on the Iowa Frontier, 1833-1870," *Pacific Historical Review* 94 (May 1980): 237-64. *See also* Pioneer Daughters Collection, 1850-1955, Library, SDHRC.

38. Edden Martin, "Frontier Marriage and the Status Quo," *Westport Historical Quarterly* 10 (Mar. 1975): 100.

the family farm. One scholar believes that ten children as an average for frontier families is a conservative estimate.[39] A representative case from South Dakota was Ane Marie Jensen of Dell Rapids who bore ten children as well as helping her second husband raise his seven children.[40] While bearing and rearing children was clearly considered one of the most important economic functions of frontierswomen, it was also one of the most physically taxing. Not only were they supposed to produce the children, but they were expected to take a great deal of responsibility for their care, training, and eventual participation in the family labor force as well. Thus, in addition to their own functions as workers

Large families were the rule during the pioneer period. This family near Ardmore, South Dakota, must have been typical.

and producers, women were also thrust into supervisory and managerial positions.

Yet, as women worked to enhance their own skills and to initiate their children into the tasks of food processing, soapmaking, candlemaking, spinning, weaving, gardening, field work, and the

39. Leo E. Oliva, "Our Frontier Heritage and the Environment," *American West* 9 (Jan. 1972): 45.

40. "One of the Knitters," *American-Scandinavian Review* 6 (July-Aug. 1918): 215.

Near Presho, a woman's efforts provided a small tree, new clothes, and a few gifts for a 1909 holiday.

like, they also attempted to become proficient in a third area, that of preserving traditional values, folkways, and mores. Women's often pathetic attempts to properly celebrate a holiday such as Christmas with the paucity of resources available on the Dakota plains offer a good example of the difficulty they faced in this area of female roles. Scrimping, saving, and working with scraps of cloth to create something that resembled a present while also seeking some fresh game or providing a small tree devoid of but the sparsest of decoration, these women did their best to recreate the warmth and family spirit of holidays spent "back home." Other women routinely defied their own exhaustion in order to play the family piano in the evenings or to entertain as nicely as possible despite a continual influx of guests.[41]

41. Margaret Johnson Interview, "North Dakota Oral History Project Issue," pp. 78-79; Walter F. Peterson, ed., "Christmas on the Plains: Elizabeth Bacon Custer's Nostalgic Memories of Holiday Seasons on the Frontier," *American West* 1 (Fall 1964): 53-57; Woodward, *The Checkered Years*, pp. 108-9, 152; Vuolo, "Pioneer Diaries," p. 33; and Herseth, "A Pioneer's Letter," p. 312.

In spite of this workload, the domestic endeavors of these women were not allowed to consume all of their time and energy, for women were also called upon to engage in what was normally considered "men's work." One investigator has argued that Euro-American women were involved in between one-third to over one-half of all the food production on family farms.[42] Their involvement included not only their exertions in kitchen gardens and chicken houses but also their participation in field work. Women performed a variety of field tasks, including driving a reaper, harvester, or hay wagon as well as planting seed and digging potatoes. Because hired help was generally unavailable and women were usually the only other adults on the farms besides their husbands, they were required to do more than what might be regarded as their share in other times or places.[43]

Women's participation in field work was often the critical factor in staving off failure of the family farm enterprise, but women also helped deflect economic disaster through another type of farm labor, the production of milk, butter, and eggs that were sold for cash or bartered for other goods. According to historian Gilbert Fite, butter and eggs were primary cash products on the farmer's frontier, and the income from them often kept farms financially afloat during the difficult years.[44] Women also "helped out" by selling beeswax, dried fruits, and cloth as well as by taking in boarders or doing washing.[45] Some women combined an incredible variety of skills to procure the much-needed cash income. One young Black Hills woman recalled that her mother sold butter, eggs, meat, vegetables, wild fruit, and garden flowers, did "some washing on the board" for people, and also knitted socks and mittens for sale to nearby cowboys.[46] That such women recognized their own economic importance to the family business is demonstrated by the statement of a prairie woman who recalled: "Frequently enough, while the men were learning to farm, the women and children actually supported the families. They raised

42. John Mack Faragher, "History from the Inside-Out: Writing the History of Women in Rural America," *American Quarterly* 33 (Winter 1981): 540.

43. Margaret Johnson Interview, pp. 78-79; Pelissier, "Reminiscences," p. 133; William Forrest Sprague, *Women and the West: A Short Social History* (Boston, Mass.: Christopher Publishing House, 1940), pp. 239-40; and Julie Roy Jeffrey, *Frontier Women: The Trans-Mississippi West, 1840-1880*, American Century Series (New York: Hill & Wang, 1979), p. 59.

44. Gilbert C. Fite, *The Farmers' Frontier, 1865-1900* (New York: Holt, Rinehart & Winston, 1966), p. 47. *See also* Jeffrey, *Frontier Women*, p. 60.

45. Babcock, Reminiscences.

46. Pelissier, "Reminiscences," pp. 134-35.

chickens and eggs for the table, raised the vegetables and fruit, and made butter to sell in exchange for things not produced at home. The women were not unaware of this fact and were quite capable of scoring a point on occasion when masculine attitudes became too bumptious."[47]

Although census takers were not adverse to lumping these tremendously productive farm women under the category "not gainfully employed," women's economic significance is difficult to dispute. Ranging from domestically oriented chores to outdoor work to the production of actual cash income, women's tasks seemed to be never ending and totally exhausting. Thus, one might expect the lives of early farm women to be dominated by fatigue, bitterness, and even despair. Certainly, if one were to accept the view of frontierswomen found in most western literature, there could be no doubt that most of them were not only reluctant settlers, but despondent ones as well.

A prime example of this representation of women is Ole Rolvaag's *Giants in the Earth.* Its protagonist, Beret Hansa, was forced out onto the Dakota plains by a husband who cared little for her fears and hesitations. Yet, as one investigator has pointed out, Rolvaag himself never homesteaded and therefore had little actual knowledge of Dakota women from which to derive such a portrait.[48] Another scholar has noted an additional paradox in this work and the two novels that follow it. Beret, despite her helplessness and terror, managed to survive the entire trilogy,

47. E. May Lacey Crowder, "Pioneer Life in Palo Alto County," *Iowa Journal of History and Politics* 46 (Apr. 1948): 181.
48. Patterson-Black, "Women Homesteaders," pp. 18-19.

while her husband Per, a hardy and macho nineteenth-century male, was so defeated by the frontier that he succumbed to death in the very first book of the series.[49]

49. Annette Atkins, "Women on the Farming Frontier: The View from Fiction," *Midwest Review*, 2d ser., 3 (Spring 1981): 1.

As an economic partner of a husband or on her own, a pioneer farm woman performed a wide array of outside, or "men's," work. Opposite page, a woman works a field crop with a hoe; below, another hauls a crop to town. Above, a woman performs the more traditional task of feeding her poultry.

Hamlin Garland also presented a highly sentimentalized picture of frontierswomen. Considering his own mother's life on the Middle Border to be typical of all women's lives, he wrote that the pioneer mother was burdened with a "grinding weight of drudgery" and was forced to endure a life centered around a "rude little cabin" and desperate poverty. He judged her willingness to follow her husband to each new homestead "without complaining word" as submission and despair. It seemed apparent to him that she forced herself to make each move despite the "bitter pangs of doubt and unrest which strike through the woman's heart when called upon to leave her snug, safe fire for a ruder cabin in a strange land."[50]

Although writers such as Bess Streeter Aldrich, Willa Cather, Mari Sandoz, and Vardis Fisher have contributed complex portrayals of frontierswomen that oppose the one dimensional stereotyped figures so favored by novelists such as Rolvaag and Garland, they have not been greatly successful in capturing the popular imagination. In the face of a lack of factual knowledge about women, most Americans have seemed content to visualize them in terms of romanticized, stock characters that include the Gentle Tamer, Pioneer in Petticoat, Saint in the Sunbonnet, Madonna of the Prairie, Light Lady, Calamity Jane, and Fighting Feminist, to mention just a few of the better known genres.

One must ask, where have the historians been through this development of the dramatized persona of frontierswomen? Surely, they have applied standards of scholarship and tools of investigative research to the question of whether or not the West was indeed fine for men and dogs but hell on women and horses. Unfortunately, the reality is that historians in general have been as culpable as most novelists in perpetuating inaccurate depictions of frontierswomen. In 1921, for example, Emerson Hough argued that the "great romance of all America" was the "woman in the sunbonnet." To him, this "gaunt and sad-faced woman sitting on the front seat of the wagon, following her lord where he might lead, her face hidden in the same ragged sunbonnet which had crossed the Appalachians and the Missouri long before" deserved more attention.[51] Ten years later, historian Walter Prescott Webb devoted all of one and a half pages of *The Great Plains* to a

50. Hamlin Garland, *A Pioneer Mother* (Chicago: Bookfellows, 1922), pp. 5-10.

51. Emerson Hough, *The Passing of the Frontier* (New Haven, Conn.: Yale University Press, 1921), p. 93.

consideration of women. He concluded that while men were hardy and adventurous, women feared and distrusted the land and spent their time being lonely and lamenting the loss of their former "civilized" homes.[52]

More recently, Everett Dick gave women expanded coverage in his works, but with strikingly similar results. "How much of the retreat from the frontier from time to time was due to the figure in sunbonnet and calico, is not known," he asserted, "but it is certain that many stayed until the prairie broke them in spirit and body." He added that "their hair grew lifeless and dry, their shoulders early bent, and they became stooped as they tramped round and round the hot cookstove preparing the three regular, though skimpy meals a day."[53] Another recent historian, purporting to be a historian of women, concurred with Dick's interpretation of frontierswomen:

> Clinging to a few treasured heirlooms as reminders of a kinder life, they accompanied their husbands across the continent, suffering the most desperate physical hardships as well as a desolating sense of loneliness. More place-bound than men, more dependent on the company of other women, on the forms of settled social life, they grew old and died before their time, on the trail, in a sod hut or a rude cabin pierced by icy winds.[54]

Yet another scholar, a student of the West, imputed heroic proportions to these unfortunate, uprooted females. He argued that even though they were "the most conservative of creatures, hating with a passion those three concomitants of the western frontier—poverty, physical hardship, and danger," it was really women who tamed the "Wild West."[55]

Given the repetitive and limited theme of these characterizations of frontierswomen by historians, it is little wonder that western textbook writers have largely ignored women or have dealt with them summarily by repeating one or more of the accepted shibboleths. In a 1974 study of such textbooks, T. A. Larson discovered that from Frederick Jackson Turner to Ray Allen Billington and Robert Athearn, any mention of frontierswomen was rare and uninformative. "In short," Larson concluded,

52. Carol Fairbanks, "Lives of Girls and Women on the Canadian and American Prairies," *International Journal of Women's Studies* 2 (Sept./Oct. 1979): 452.

53. Everett Dick, "Sunbonnet and Calico, the Homesteader's Consort," *Nebraska History* 47 (Mar. 1966): 13.

54. Page Smith, *Daughters of the Promised Land* (Boston: Little, Brown & Co., 1970), p. 223.

55. Dee Brown, *The Gentle Tamers: Women of the Old Wild West* (New York: Bantam Books, 1974), p. 269.

"standard textbooks used in college and university courses in Western History come close to ignoring women entirely." He added the rhetorical query: "Were women really that insignificant in the American West?"[56]

As has already been argued here, the answer to that question is a resounding no. Frontierswomen's roles and responses were stereotyped, not because women themselves were unimportant, but rather because American society has long held particular views regarding the inferiority, weakness, and supposedly inherently passive nature of women. Given that set of assumptions, it is understandable that writers, scholars, and other observers would assume that women were indeed conservative "creatures" who would respond to the rigors of the West with tears, entreaties to return "home," and general wretchedness. During the past decade, however, the emerging field of women's history and the contemporary feminist movement have raised serious challenges to such assumptions about the "nature" of women. Moreover, historians of women have been diligently locating and collecting women's source materials in order to learn what they actually said and felt about their situations rather than continuing to impute to them what society expected them to say and feel. As a result, enough women's writings are now available to make some tentative observations about frontierswomen feasible.

Like men, these women recorded their fears of Indians, mud, rain, wind, dust, prairie fires, blizzards, tornadoes, rattlesnakes, and epidemics.[57] As women taught to value domestic order, networks of family and friends, and leisure time devoted to pursuits such as reading and craft work, they lamented the prevalence of dirt and bugs, isolation and loneliness, and heavy, time-consuming workloads. Some of these women actually did spend part or all of their lives on the frontier on the verge of despair, insanity, and even self-extinction.[58] And some of them, like Sarah

56. Larson, "Women's Roles in the American West," p. 4.

57. Brandt, "Social Aspects of Prairie Pioneering," pp. 5-6, 9; Kate Eldridge Glaspell, "Incidents in the Life of a Pioneer," *North Dakota Historical Quarterly* 8 (Apr. 1941): 184-90; Lewis, *Nothing to Make a Shadow*, pp. 21-23, 40, 71, 73; Mabel Lorshbough Interview, "North Dakota Oral History Project Issue," pp. 22-23; Pelissier, "Reminiscences," p. 130; Thal, "Early Days," pp. 47-62; and Woodward, *The Checkered Years*, pp. 28-30, 35, 38, 55, 58-59, 65, 80-81, 118, 142, 159-60, 222.

58. Jeannie McKnight, "American Dream, Nightmare Underside: Diaries, Letters and Fiction of Women on the American Frontier," in L. L. Lee and Merrill Lewis, *Women, Women Writers, and the West* (Troy, N.Y.: Whitston Publishing Co., 1979), pp. 25-40.

Thal or Emma Plaisted of the lath house, packed up their pianos and other belongings and headed back East.[59]

There is no doubt that life on the frontier was difficult in many respects for women, but it was also arduous for men. For that matter, life in many parts of the United States was burdensome for many people. Millworkers in New England, immigrant pieceworkers in newly emerging urban slums, and black slaves were only some of the groups of people that found life taxing at some times and nigh impossible at others. It must therefore be remembered that while frontierswomen's lives were indeed demanding, they perhaps offered some redeeming qualities that made them appear worthwhile.

For some women, the rigorous climate was offset by what one woman described as the "beauties of nature."[60] Another woman interspersed her frequent negative remarks about the Dakota climate with expressions of joy regarding the birds, wild roses, and other flowers. At one point she wrote, "The day is very beautiful and I have been out nearly all of it picking posies. . . . I think there is something fascinating about gathering wild flowers. . . . It gives one a childish delight." At another point she exulted in a sunrise. "The sun rose in great splendor as it does nowhere else except on these prairies," she jotted in her diary.[61] Yet another woman claimed that in the Dakotas of the 1880s, "no one minded the hot sunshine or the hard winds" because "they were to be expected: a natural part of life." She also maintained that although a farm proffered a hard life for a woman, the harshness was compensated for by "the freedom and spaciousness of the wide prairie land." She wrote fondly of the "wind forever waving the tall wild grass," the wild violets in the spring, the wild prairie roses that blossomed everywhere in June. After a few years of being a farm woman, she began to love the land just as her husband did.[62]

Many women also accepted the challenge of unending chores with equanimity. "Certainly I have had to work," wrote a Dakota woman back to her family in Scandinavia. Unlike her days as a laborer in her homeland, however, she believed that she "was considered a human being" even though she was poor. "Have a good home here," she added, and "have no wish ever to return to Swe-

59. Thal, "Early Days," p. 53, and Vuolo, "Pioneer Diaries," p. 34.
60. Herseth, "A Pioneer's Letter," p. 308.
61. Woodward, *The Checkered Years*, pp. 81, 127. *See also* pp. 75, 87-88, 121, 167, 175, 200-201, 224.
62. Wilder, *The First Four Years*, pp. 1, 4, 6, 134.

den."[63] Margaret Roberts of the Black Hills region was also undaunted by heavy workloads. After supporting and raising five girls as a widow on a homestead, she moved to another homestead after her last child left home and earned enough money to exchange it for a house in town, where she lived out her life enjoying her home and supporting herself by renting out rooms.[64] Despite her heavy workload, Mary Dodge Woodward noted in an 1884 diary entry: "Two years ago today we arrived.... They have been short years to me for I have had plenty to do. I have enjoyed my life here very much and have never wished to leave."[65]

Even the much touted isolation and loneliness often turned out to be less onerous than it appeared to be. Women described at great length the many social events that were available to them through their families, friends, churches, schools, and nearby towns. One Dakota woman of the 1880s spoke of a Ladies' Aid Society, gala Christmas celebrations, choir and band concerts, festive Fourth of July celebrations, weddings, and dinners with friends and neighbors, while another recalled pastimes such as "home talent entertainments," horseback riding, roller skating, and dancing.[66] Furthermore, a survey of Dakota newspapers indicated that as the region became more settled, social opportunities increased. Reports of New Year's celebrations, receptions, balls, lyceums, theaters, performances by lady elocutionists, church festivals and fairs, women's clubs, euchre parties, camping, boating, Fourth of July observances, and circuses were all common in many parts of the Dakotas by the mid-1880s.[67]

Moreover, one investigator has demonstrated that farms were established in a pattern of adjoining farmsteads with villages and towns located at fairly regular intervals. He also pointed out that early neighborhoods were often small and close knit, being held together by a special bond such as kinship or ethnicity.[68] Another

63. H. Arnold Barton, *Letters from the Promised Land* (Minneapolis: University of Minnesota Press for the Swedish Pioneer Historical Society, 1975), p. 291.

64. Pelissier, "Reminiscences," p. 138.

65. Woodward, *The Checkered Years*, p. 52.

66. Brandt, "Social Aspects of Prairie Pioneering," pp. 16-18, 23-25, and Glaspell, "Incidents," pp. 188-90.

67. Edna LaMoore Waldo, *Dakota: An Informal Study of Territorial Days* (Bismarck, N.Dak.: Capital Publishing Co., 1932), pp. 198-213. *See also* Martha Correll Interview, "North Dakota Oral History Project Issue," pp. 86-87.

68. W. F. Kumlien, *Basic Trends of Social Change in South Dakota: III. Community Organization*, South Dakota Agricultural Experiment Station Bulletin, no. 356 (Brookings: South Dakota State College, 1941), pp. 4-17.

writer has claimed that the average space between farmsteads in Lawrence County was about half a mile and that "in the early period of settlement sometimes four families, each taking a quarter section as a homestead, built their temporary dwellings upon adjacent corners to be near together."[69]

Faye Cashatt Lewis, a Dakota settler in the early twentieth century, suggested that life on the plains seemed formidable primarily because many settlers exaggerated the hardships. They recorded them "with gusto," she remarked, to emphasize their own "superior stamina." Even the problems faced by her own mother, whose dismayed statement "there's nothing to make a shadow" has often been quoted as an epitome of women's disillusionment, were alleviated in Lewis's view by the huge amount of personal support she received from her husband. Lewis noted that the children of the family also provided significant amounts of labor as well as a great deal of company to their mother. In addition, social events such as literary meetings, plays, musical performances, reading, checkers, card playing, and candy making abounded in their area. According to Lewis, the adversities faced

69. Henry Frawley and Anne Frawley, "Agriculture, Dairying, Ranching," in *Lawrence County for the Dakota Territory Centennial, 1861-1961*, ed. Mildred Fielder (Deadwood/Lead, S.Dak.: Lawrence County Centennial Committee, 1960), p. 105.

A Fourth of July celebration provided the opportunity to gather with neighbors and break the loneliness of homesteading.

Some early pioneers solved the problem of isolation by building their shanties on adjoining corners of their claims. These Stanley County homesteaders also connected their separate dwellings, providing some shade on the open plain.

by her family were typical in that they were balanced by their hopes, dreams, and satisfactions. "Our riches were," she wrote, "good health, ambition, hope, and pride. . . . We considered ourselves people of importance."[70]

Perhaps another key to understanding farm women's lives on the plains can be derived from the statement of a Norwegian pastor's wife. She was quick to point out that "as time passed people's circumstances improved" and life became more like it had been in their former homes.[71] Change and progress did occur. Women were not condemned to life in a one-room soddie, a sparsely settled neighborhood, or abject poverty for all their years. Larger houses were built and improvements were introduced into them. Settlement increased, and with it came neighbors, churches, schools, and clubs. In time, crops and other products not only supplied the needs of the family but also frequently provided a surplus that was taken to market and exchanged for cash and necessary items.[72]

Such alterations, which often became noticeable within as little as two years of initial settlement, also gradually contributed to

70. Lewis, *Nothing to Make a Shadow*, pp. 14-15, 33-34, 48-49, 74-77, 94, 132.
71. Brandt, "Social Aspects of Prairie Pioneering," p. 30.
72. Woodward, *The Checkered Years*, p. 144.

larger modifications for the Dakotas as a whole. By 1889, population and economic growth in the Dakotas underwrote President Grover Cleveland's signing of the Omnibus Bill, which created four new states: North Dakota, South Dakota, Montana, and Washington. By October of that year, the voters of South Dakota accepted a constitution and prohibition, elected their first governor, and approved Pierre as the temporary capital.[73] During the following decade, the era of the open range drew to a close, Indian problems were essentially resolved, and an agrarian economy characterized by the utilization of new technological devices took hold in South Dakota.

What would these modifications mean to farm women? Would their lives be changed dramatically by new technology within the home? Would their political involvement in the emergent government increase? Would their fundamental female roles undergo significant revision as a result of the many other alterations occurring in turn-of-the-century society?

None of these questions can be answered with any degree of certainty at this point in time, for the historical research has not yet been done. Unhappily, farm women, or rural women as they are sometimes termed, have received less than their share of attention from historians and other scholars. Two recent books, Joan M. Jensen's *With These Hands: Women Working the Land* and Sherry Thomas's *We Didn't Have Much. But We Sure Had Plenty: Stories of Rural Women*, have made an attempt to begin to remedy this lack. Also, Jensen and others interested in farm women are currently in the process of organizing the first conference to be devoted to the topic.[74]

Those investigators who have given any thought to the types, rates of adoption, and effects of domestic technology upon farm women believe that, not only was technology slow to be embraced, but its impact was relatively limited during the early decades of the twentieth century. Some years ago, Hargreaves argued that the cost of conveniences such as indoor plumbing was prohibitive for most plains settlers through the "lean years," which did not abate until 1940. Calling attention to a 1935 survey

73. Herbert S. Schell, *History of South Dakota*, 3d. ed. (Lincoln: University of Nebraska Press, 1975), pp. 219-22.

74. Joan M. Jensen, *With These Hands: Women Working on the Land* (Old Westbury, N.Y.: Feminist Press, 1981), and Sherry Thomas, *We Didn't Have Much. But We Sure Had Plenty: Stories of Rural Women* (Garden City, N.Y.: Doubleday, Anchor Press, 1981).

of six South Dakota farming counties, she pointed out that at least three-fourths of the homes in these counties still had an outside water supply while only one-fifth had electricity and only one-eighth had central heating. One of the counties examined still had many log cabins; another was dotted with sod huts and had more under construction.[75]

Hargreaves thus reasoned that farm women's lives continued to be rigorous and demanding despite the existence of emerging technology. Another scholar supported that interpretation by arguing that although the new technology lightened the physical work of women, it did not alter the gender orientation of the tasks. In other words, water pumps made it easier to draw water, but it was still a chore performed by women; the operation of the new sewing machines were assigned to women; and the first crude washing machines were used almost exclusively by women. She further observed that the new domestic technology did nothing to extricate women from the domestic sphere, the importance of which was not fully recognized by contemporary society. Nor did technology improve the status or prestige associated with that sphere.[76]

More recently, Sue Armitage has delved specifically into the issue of the effect of the first washing machines on women's work, roles, and power relationships in the farm family. She discovered that although the machines did make the chore of washing clothes somewhat easier, they still required a lot of physical labor since support technology such as hot water heaters and drains was not yet available. Thus, women still spent many physically taxing hours carrying hot water to their new washing machines or carrying dirty water away from them. In addition, women often continued to follow traditional methods of washing

75. Hargreaves, "Women in the Agricultural Settlement of the Northern Plains," p. 187. For a discussion of how various kinds of South Dakota farm families allotted their income in the 1930s to items such as housing, clothing, food, and household accessories and facilities, including power washing machines, electric lights, inside water supply, and telephones, *see* W. F. Kumlien et al., *The Standard of Living of Farm and Village Families in Six South Dakota Counties, 1935*, South Dakota Agricultural Experiment Station Bulletin, no. 320 (Brookings: South Dakota State College, 1938), pp. 5-49. A Lawrence County study claimed that as late as 1950 only 74 percent of farms in that heavily agricultural county had electric power and that in 1954 only 72 percent had running water. Frawley and Frawley, "Agriculture, Dairying, Ranching," p. 114.

76. June Sochen, "Frontier Women: A Model for All Women?", *South Dakota History* 7 (Winter 1976): 43.

clothes, including making their own soap, boiling clothes before washing, and running clothing through a rinse with bluing, even though these processes were now outdated. Armitage concluded that washing machines, in spite of the drawbacks, did release some of the farm woman's time and energy for other pursuits, but that traditional sex roles remained rigid, and a woman was kept from using her released time to fully participate in the business of the family farm. In Armitage's view, most women internalized these customary sex-role prescriptions and expended their new

The washing facilities in a 1937 farm house point out the slow adoption of new technology during the lean years.

leisure in enhancing the quality of life for their families, an acceptable female pursuit. Armitage hypothesized that the new technology stripped farm women's work of some of its value in that it now appeared easier, but that the lost status was not replaced with other really meaningful roles and tasks.[77]

Although this area of investigation clearly needs more work before conclusions can be agreed upon, women's own documents from this early twentieth century period do seem to uphold the idea that little basic change occurred in their lives. When, for example, seventy-year-old Ane Marie Jensen was complimented for the many socks she had knitted from the wool of her own sheep as part of the World War I effort, she brushed it off with the comment, "Why, I've all my life raised sheep and knitted—that's nothing new nor extraordinary." She pointed out that she had raised sheep and made her living by knitting in Denmark, had naturally continued the practice throughout her years as a settler in the Dakotas, and had just as naturally continued the practice into her senior years.[78]

Faye Cashatt Lewis's description of her family's 1909 claim shack also showed a great deal of continuity with women's homes/workplaces of earlier decades. It was, she recalled, a tiny structure divided into two rooms, "a bedroom and the slightly larger room that was used for everything else, including a bedroom for the two boys." She explained that they "achieved some privacy in the bedroom by dividing it in half with a cloth curtain strung on a wire." Storage was provided by boxes kept under the beds, but, Lewis added rather ruefully, "keeping things sorted out and in some useful order was one of the main problems of housekeeping" in such miniscule houses.[79] Lewis's accounts of her mother's work also evidenced little variation from that of the Dakota women who preceded her. She prepared gargantuan breakfasts that consisted of oatmeal, ham or bacon, eggs, slices of home-baked bread, homemade jellies or preserves, fried potatoes, and home-baked pies left over from the previous night's dinner. Besides preparing huge meals, Lewis's mother also planted and tended a vegetable garden, spent untold hours in all the usual housekeeping chores,

77. Sue Armitage, "Housework and Farmwork: The Changing World of Farm Women," paper delivered at the Conference on the History of Women, St. Paul, Minn., 2 May 1982.

78. "One of the Knitters," p. 215.

79. Lewis, *Nothing to Make a Shadow*, p. 39.

devoted at least one afternoon a week to breadbaking, and constantly battled the bugs and other vermin that regularly invaded the shack.[80]

Grace Fairchild's diary provides additional evidence of the continuity of farm women's lives in the Dakotas during the nineteenth and early twentieth centuries. Like many of her predecessors, Fairchild bore nine children, six of them in less than eight years. Recalling her years as a homesteader's wife between 1902 and 1930, she remembered performing many chores such as butchering and curing meat, canning fruits and vegetables, and

Claim dwellings of the 1880s differed little from this 1906 sod home near Belvidere.

preparing sauerkraut. She also brought cash income into the family coffers by selling untold pounds of butter and taking in boarders. As her husband became increasingly unreliable and irascible, she found herself performing more and more of the outdoor work, including caring for the cattle that her husband had purchased. Yet, despite her many trials, she maintained that she "loved living on a homestead."[81]

80. Ibid., pp. 38-40.
81. Wyman, *Frontier Woman*, pp. 20-21, 27, 29, 73.

A Grand Forks woman's recollections of a 1920s' childhood spent following her Swedish grandmother around painted a similar picture. She remembered her grandmother's handling of family clothing, including washing on the board, boiling clothes, ironing with flatirons heated on the wood stove, producing her own lye soap for wash days, and converting flour sacks into underclothing. She also recalled that her grandmother dealt with food in a traditional manner, cooking on a huge wood range. The cream separator held the place of honor in her grandmother's kitchen, while the butchering and rendering were done in the old-fashioned way, with a wonderful head cheese being one of the products. Kerosene lanterns were still used and created a lot of work for the women who cleaned and filled them. Housecleaning, too, was a tedious chore since "no vacuum cleaner or other labor saving device had been purchased." To the granddaughter, "it was a nightmare" when "the lace curtains were washed and stretched on a prickly frame; heavy woolen quilts were washed by hand.... the soot had to be cleaned out of the chimney.... woolen rugs were strung over the clothes line and such pollution you never saw when the children were elected to beat them with a large metal beater." Apparently, the only bow that her grandmother made to the new technology was the use of an incubator in hatching the many chickens she raised. Even this development did not seem attractive to her granddaughter, who commented that "the more fortunate people ordered their chicks from the catalog."[82]

That none of these women make very much of the new technology in their descriptions of domestic labor seems to support the view that technology was much slower in restructuring labor in the farm home than it was in revolutionizing the work in the barns and fields. The letters of a North Dakota farm woman, Effie Hanson, also make this point rather clearly. Written between 1917 and 1923, these letters do mention some devices, such as an incubator for the chickens Hanson raised, a knitting machine, canning aids, a telephone, and store-bought clothing from the Sears and Montgomery Ward catalogues. Yet, as innovative as all this may sound, closer examination of the letters reveals that Hanson's prevalent themes and concerns differ little from those of the generations of women that preceded her. She spent most of her time writing about giving birth, worrying over her children, raising hens and selling eggs, tending her garden, sewing and

82. Lunde, *Uff Da*, pp. 2, 6, 8, 10, 14-15, 17, 27.

knitting, butchering, milking and churning, selling butter and cream, preparing food for threshers, and performing field work such as digging potatoes. She frequently noted that she was busy, tired, lonely, isolated, homesick, ill, and involved in an unending round of chores. In reading Hanson's letters, one gets a sense of timelessness that is only occasionally interrupted by a notation regarding a sewing machine or automobile.[83]

Little significant change seemed to have occurred in the area of women's political participation, either, even though a considerable number of Dakota women were interested in obtaining the right to vote as early as the 1870s. Women not only engaged in local, state, and national suffrage associations and meetings, but they also supported the appearances of suffragists such as Matilda Joslyn Gage, Susan B. Anthony, and Elizabeth Cady Stanton in Yankton and other South Dakota cities. In 1885, a woman suffrage amendment actually passed the territorial council and house of representatives, but it was opposed by Governor Gilbert A. Pierce, who feared that it would interfere with the granting of statehood. When statehood was achieved in 1889, the South Dakota Constitution stated that male voters could remove the word male from the document if they chose to, which would thus extend to women the right to vote. This constitutional provision attracted Susan B. Anthony to South Dakota in 1889. As president of the National Woman Suffrage Association, she was convinced that with a little push from organized suffragists this frontier region would prove its dedication to democracy and equality by granting suffrage to its women. Despite her efforts, and those of local suffrage organizers like General Wiliam H. H. Beadle, Rebecca Hager, Matilda Hindman, and Women's Christian Temperance Union chapters, male voters continually rejected woman suffrage bills. Although many more years of suffrage efforts followed, South Dakota women did not receive the right to vote until 1918, only two years before the ratification of the Nineteenth Amendment to the United States Constitution in 1920.[84]

83. Frances M. Wold, comp. and ed., "The Letters of Effie Hanson, 1917-1923: Farm Life in Troubled Times," *North Dakota History* 48 (Winter 1981): 20-43.

84. Waldo, *Dakota*, p. 202; Dorinda Riessen Reed, *The Woman Suffrage Movement in South Dakota*, 2d ed. (Pierre: South Dakota Commission on the Status of Women, 1975), pp. 5-7, 11-14, 18-113; and Mary Kay Jennings, "Lake County Woman Suffrage Campaign in 1890," *South Dakota History* 5 (Fall 1975): 390-401. For a detailed discussion of Susan B. Anthony's role in the 1889-1890 campaign, *see* Cecelia M. Wittmayer, "The 1889-1890 Woman Suffrage Campaign: A Need to Or-

While working conditions and equipment improved in the twentieth century, farm women's tasks remained the same. At left, a woman uses a pressure cooker and electric range to preserve food in 1941; below, a woman feeds chickens on a farm near Sioux Falls in 1942.

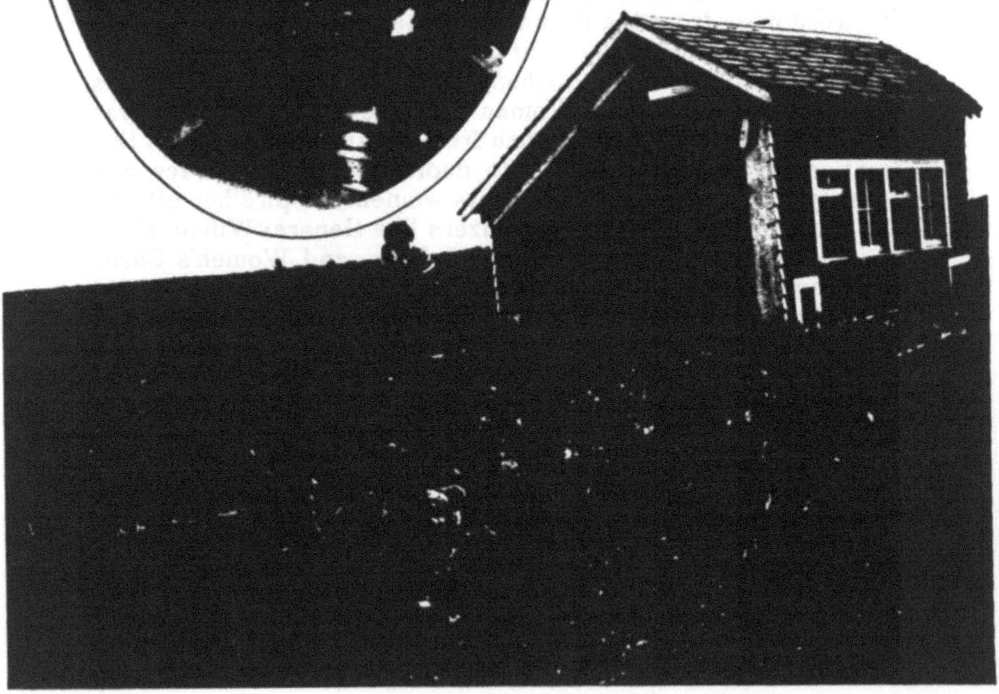

In spite of the long and active campaigns for woman suffrage, the writings of many farm women only noted the issues of women's rights and suffrage in passing. When Laura Ingalls Wilder accepted a proposal of marriage, she interrogated her husband-to-be about his feelings concerning the word "obey" in the wedding ceremony. Although he reassured her that it was unnecessary in his view, he asked her in surprise whether she was for "woman's rights." "No," she replied, "I do not want to vote."[85] The majority of women's writings did not raise the question of women's rights at all, their authors seemingly being much more concerned about daily matters relating to their homes, families, and work. Even when women were finally granted the vote, many farm women accepted it impassively. Effie Hanson, as a case in point, regularly recorded the fact that she went into town to vote, but she ascribed little significance or meaning to the event.[86]

Clearly, much study is needed before we can even begin to understand the political participation of farm women and their responses to their increased rights and opportunities in the political arena. Joan M. Jensen has proposed some other important topics regarding the lives of farm women that must be examined in detail before the third question posed here, that is, whether women's roles were revised in the early twentieth century or not, can be fairly answered. The cycles of their work, based upon the six workdays of the week and the four seasons of the year, may yield some useful insights into their workloads. Also, a consideration of ethnicity, demographic data including fertility rates, technology, and social organizations may produce some critical information regarding many aspects of their lives.[87]

In the meantime, we can only hypothesize that women's roles were not updated along with the move to "progressive" farming. John Faragher has theorized that, in fact:

> The tendency of men to reject traditional culture in their struggle for a more commercial world created a gender dimension to the conflict be-

ganize," *South Dakota History* 11 (Summer 1981): 199-225. For fuller accounts of later suffrage crusades, *see* the Jane Rooker Smith Breeden Papers, 1886-1946, Manuscript Division, SDHRC; the Mrs. John (Mamie I. Shields) Pyle Papers, Richardson Archives, I. D. Weeks Library, University of South Dakota, Vermillion; and the Woman Suffrage Movement Papers, 1889-1925, Manuscript Division, SDHRC.

85. Wilder, *These Happy Golden Years*, p. 269.

86. Wold, "Letters of Effie Hanson," pp. 33-34, 36, 41.

87. Joan M. Jensen, "Women and Agriculture in American History: An Overview," paper presented at the Conference on the History of Women, St. Paul, Minn., 2 May 1982.

> tween traditional and popular culture. "Backward" farming was also the farming culture in which women's work was fully integrated as an essential part; "progressive" farming might eliminate the old notions of "reciprocity" without even a bow in the direction of women's roles in work and life.[88]

The potential validity of this hypothesis is corroborated by an ongoing oral-history study in upstate New York. The data indicates that the women were not included in farm management despite the lightening of their work load by technological advances; that their concerns, such as child care, food production, illness, raising chickens, and sewing, remained essentially the same from generation to generation; and that although they exercised the right to vote, it did not change their place in the power relationships on the farm. The investigator has tentatively concluded that twentieth-century farm women are only slowly coming to be recognized as full and equal partners and that many of them are still segregated in domestic ghettoes just as they were in the pioneer period. According to her, this segregation resulted from sexist and racist beliefs that if white farmers were to continue to be a superior race contributing stability, virtue, and continuity to American society, women's most important function was the childhood training of those future (male) farmers. The home, then, was seen as the farm woman's central focus, while the reality that she was heavily involved in agricultural production was virtually ignored.[89]

Exploratory studies and hypotheses such as these make it clear that the topic of farm women is both exciting and complex. As Jensen has shown, the source materials are often obscure, but they are available. Letters and diaries of women involved in farming, farm inventories and financial records, wills and other family documents, and oral histories are all potential mines of information.[90] Furthermore, some hard data exist as well. The census, for example, demonstrates that between 1900 and 1930, the sex ratio (number of males per one hundred females) dropped in the plains states from 109.7 to 104.2 although the national ratio only decreased from 104.4 to 102.5 percent. It also shows that sex ratios

88. Faragher, "History from the Inside-Out," p. 555.

89. Sarah Elbert, "Women, Work, and Family on the American Farm," paper delivered at the Conference on the History of Women, St. Paul, Minn., 2 May 1982.

90. Jensen, "Women and Agriculture in American History." *See also* the South Dakota Oral History Project, Richardson Archives, I. D. Weeks Library, University of South Dakota, which includes many interviews with farm women. *Tales of the Early Days as Told to Mirandy* (Hollywood, Calif.: Oxford Press, 1938) is an example of an early published collection of oral-history interviews.

in urban areas in the plains states went from 102.8 in 1900 to 95.7 in 1930, while the decrease on farms was only from 112.5 in 1900 to 104.3 in 1930. An examination of why such reapportionments of the population occurred might reveal some information regarding the changing lives of women. Also, census figures showing that the birth rate decreased in the plains region during the first decades of the twentieth century at the same time that longevity increased would suggest some significant alterations in the factors affecting women's life cycles and work patterns. Other changes demanding further examination include the increasing percentage of women attending school, migrating to urban areas, holding jobs outside the home, and seeking divorces.[91]

What we *can* say with certainty about farm women in general and South Dakota farm women in particular at this point is that, not only does the information exist in many varied forms, but the questions regarding their lives and roles abound as well. The modern feminist movement, the growth of women's history, the extensive changes experienced by contemporary women, and a great variety of other factors have piqued the nation's curiosity about the historical heritage of its women. Farm women, often casually shunted aside by the inaccurate and demeaning designation "farmer's wife," are just beginning to be recognized as a tremendously significant segment of American women. This emerging awareness can only lead to a heightened understanding of farm women's numerous domestic and other contributions to the agrarian development of the individual states and to the entire country. Despite the fact that farm women's roles were shaped in large part by factors beyond their control, including the three identified here, that is, the region in which they lived, the universal character of farm women's tasks, and the continuity of these tasks well into the twentieth century, women functioned effectively and efficiently within the existing parameters of their lives. To point out that the attention that is finally being accorded to farm women is both long overdue and richly deserved is only to restate what is now finally becoming obvious.

91. Wilson Cape, "Population Changes in the West North Central States, 1900-1930," *North Dakota Historical Quarterly* 6 (July 1932): 276-91. *See also* Walter L. Slocum, *Migrants from Rural South Dakota Families*, South Dakota Agricultural Experiment Station Bulletin, no. 359 (Brookings: South Dakota State College, 1942), pp. 3-17, and W. F. Kumlien, *Basic Trends of Change in South Dakota: II. Rural Life Adjustments*, South Dakota Agricultural Experiment Station Bulletin, no. 357 (Brookings: South Dakota State College, 1941), pp. 5-21.

"How're You Gonna Keep 'Em Down on the Farm?": Rural Women and the Urban Model in Utah

CYNTHIA STURGIS

> How can you expect that all the agricultural training in the world will make farmers of your sons unless you can find girls who are willing to stay on the farm with them and be just as happy and contented with a woman's share of farm life as the man is with his?[1]

So asked a writer for the *Deseret Farmer*, a leading Utah agricultural journal in 1910. Appropriately enough, the query came in an article extolling the benefits of the home economics program offered at the state agricultural college in Logan, Utah. For the question and its context highlight an issue of growing concern in the early twentieth century—the apparently increasing "flight from the farm"—and present at least one solution—domestic science education that sought to change the circumstances and the nature of rural women's work, following the pattern set by their urban counterparts. By making the country more like the city, many reformers hoped to stem the tide of migration away from the farm.

What constituted the "urban model" promoted by agricultural

CYNTHIA STURGIS is a member of the History Department at Texas Tech University.

1. *Deseret Farmer*, 27 August 1910, p. 5.

agricultural history volume 60 · number 2 · spring 1986. © agricultural history society

educators and their allies? First, homemaking was elevated to the status of a profession requiring special skills and training by experts. Raising the housewife's prestige not only explained the necessity of home economics education but also worked to undermine the attraction of the variety of jobs women could find in the city. Second, the surroundings and activities of the farmwife must be upgraded to meet the competition presented by urban conditions. Rural beautification represented one aspect of this effort. Reduction of the amount of physical labor—"drudgery," as it was so often called—involved in maintaining the home proved an even more important consideration and usually included adoption of modern household conveniences, especially those run by electricity. And finally, as a result of such changes, the farm wife's role would parallel that of the urban homemaker in shifting from a predominantly productive role to, increasingly, that of a consumer of goods. Allied with this trend was growing emphasis on the emotional component of work in the home, particularly the mother's role as guardian of her children's mental, as well as physical, health.

While the goals, methods, and rhetoric of Utah educators and other authorities may replicate that of reformers elsewhere, certain conditions unique to the state deserve consideration. One of the key complaints of rural women in the early twentieth century was their isolation, a situation that radio, telephones, and better roads would eventually modify. While Utah farmwomen also desired such improvements, their need may have been less great, due to an unusual settlement pattern known as the "Mormon village," whereby farm families lived in small communities and traveled out daily to their fields, rather than residing on widely scattered farmsteads.[2] The Mormon village not only reduced iso-

2. The classic description is Lowry Nelson, *The Mormon Village* (Salt Lake City: University of Utah Press, 1952). Census data bears out Nelson's description of Utah settlement. As early as 1900, the state was 38.1 percent "urban" (using the census definition of urban as communities of 2,500 or greater population)—only sixteen states were more "urbanized" and almost all were located in the northeastern United States. By 1930 Utah's urban component was 52.4 percent of her population, far exceeding the Mountain State average of 39.4 percent and leading thirty-one other states. But the figures can be misleading. Utahns did not leave the country for the city in huge numbers to create this urban "growth"; rather, the small agricultural villages they lived in simply grew beyond the 2,500 mark. That same 1930 census indicated only one city in the state with a population over 100,000 (Salt Lake City, at 140,267).

lation and provided more opportunites for social interaction, but also proved a significant factor in the early availability of electricity, that indispensable element for so many modern appliances.

In addition, the forces of agricultural education were particularly unified in the state. They centered on the Utah Agricultural College, popularly called the U.A.C., which had been founded in 1890 at Logan, located in the northern portion of the state.[3] In 1896 the Utah legislature authorized establishment of a farmers' institute program, also emanating from the U.A.C., which provided a yearly schedule of meetings in the various counties where educators from the college could speak on a predetermined list of topics.[4] By the early 1920s, special "summer schools" and "farmers' encampments" took place in Logan as well.[5] Furthermore, agricultural extension work, begun prior to the 1914 Smith-Lever Act and possibly the earliest in the Western states, also had its headquarters at that institution.[6] County and home demonstration agents through-

---

There was only one city in the 25,000–100,000 range, one in the 10,000–25,000 range, and four in the 5,000–10,000 category. Over 28 percent of the state's population in 1930 lived in towns with less than 5,000 inhabitants, and another 28 percent lived in unincorporated or strictly rural areas. Therefore, *well over half of the state's population lived in small agricultural villages or in the country.* The farming population in 1930 was 22.8 percent of the total, or 115,713, down from 140,249 or 31.2 percent in 1920, but the actual number of farms increased from 25,662 in 1920 to 27,159 in 1930. (See U.S. Department of Commerce, Bureau of the Census, *Fifteenth Census of the United States, 1930: Population,* 1:16–17; 2:13–15.

Regarding the question of rural isolation, it is worth noting that six counties contained roughly 67 percent of the state's farms: Utah County (18.3 percent), Salt Lake County (14.1 percent), Davis (8.9 percent), Weber (8.9 percent), Cache (8.7 percent), and Box Elder (7.8 percent). These were the counties which, in declining order, had the greatest number of the state's farms—but they were not the most highly "agricultural" counties. In other words, the bulk of Utah's farmers lived in counties which also held most of the towns and villages; many other counties in Utah, whose few inhabitants might be farmers, contained an insignificant amount of the state's population. See *Fifteenth Census of the United States, 1930: Population,* 6:1343.

3. Joel Edward Ricks, *The Utah Agricultural College: A History of Fifty Years* (Salt Lake City: Deseret News Press, 1938), 27. The U.A.C. was founded according to the provisions of the 1862 Morrill Land Grant College Act and the 1887 Hatch Act.

4. The law authorizing the institute movement was printed as the frontispiece to the yearly publications of papers presented. For a typical example, see Utah State Farmers' Institutes, *Annual Report* Number 9 (Logan: Utah Agricultural College, 1906), no page given. Hereafter, such reports will be cited as U.S.F.I., No. 9 (1906).

5. Utah Agricultural College, *Catalog, 1925–26,* pp. 78–79.

6. Utah Agricultural College, *Twenty-Five Years of Extension Work,* Extension Circular no. 104 (Logan: Utah Agricultural College, 1939), 3–4, 6. This publication of a radio program detailing the institution's history claims that one L. M. Windsor, serving Uintah County in 1911, was the first county agent in the northern and western states, and that Amy Lyman, active in Sanpete County in 1913, was "one of the first" home demonstration agents in the northern and western states.

out the state worked closely with branches of the Utah Farm Bureau Federation, which had begun on the local level before 1916 when the state organization formed.[7] All these bodies found a voice in the state's farm press. Originally founded as the *Deseret Farmer* in 1880, the journal known after 1912 as the *Utah Farmer* proudly proclaimed itself "the official organ of the Utah Agricultural College Extension Division" and, by the 1920s, represented the state Farm Bureau Federation as well.[8]

Representatives of all these bodies promoted an extremely consistent agenda that came to the state's farm families through a variety of media. For example, the U.A.C. printed the addresses of faculty members given to the various farmers' institutes each year. Home demonstration agents and in their absence county agents supervised women's activities both through "Home and Community" sections of the Farm Bureau and as leaders of a network of girls' clubs. U.A.C. graduates became home economics teachers at all levels from elementary through high school, under the Smith-Hughes program inaugurated in the state in 1919.[9] And officers of the college periodically addressed the citizens of the state at gatherings in the major cities, Logan, Ogden, Provo, and Salt Lake City, and, ultimately, over the radio as well. In addition, members of the Home Economics Department regularly published articles in the *Utah Farmer,* particularly in the "Home" or Farm Bureau sections. The paper itself, through its news, editorial, and even its advertising copy, presented yet another important voice.

One of the recurring notes in all these media was concern over a perceived "flight from the farm." As F. S. Harris, director of the U.A.C. Experiment Station in 1920, noted:

7. V. Allen Olsen, *As Farmers Forward Go: A History of the Utah Farm Bureau Federation* (Salt Lake City: Utah Farm Bureau Federation, 1975) is the official history, but exact chronology of the movement in the state is unclear prior to the 1920 incorporation. Farm Bureau records for Sevier County inspected by this author support the earlier date; affiliation of the Utah Farm Bureau with the *Utah Farmer* began in 1918, according to Olsen (p. 11). A more definitive chronology of the Farm Bureau movement in the state awaits additional research.

8. In the mid-1920s the *Utah Farmer's* masthead claimed continuous publication since 1880. The name *Deseret Farmer* was adopted in 1904, according to volume numbers; in 1912, the name was changed to the *Utah Farmer.* James Kirkham, who was also active in State Farm Bureau affairs, served as the paper's publisher at least from 1904 to 1930.

9. U.A.C., *Catalog, 1925–26,* p. 88.

> The census returns of the United States covering the last fifty years show a very marked migration of farmers' sons to the cities. A certain amount of city migration is normal and is a good thing for the country, but the depopulation of the country is going on at a rate that is almost alarming. This will soon manifest itself in a shortage of food. In some sections the land previously owned by farmers of American stock are [*sic*] being acquired by foreigners. If this is continued indefinitely, the foreigners will gradually come into possession of the land and finally become the dominating force in the country.

Such an occurrence would be disastrous, in Harris' view, because "It is from the rural districts that the reliance of the nation must be recruited."[10] His statement, typical of U.A.C. pronouncements, combined a pragmatic interest in the high cost of living and a Jeffersonian belief in the critical importance of the farmer to a healthy society.

In particular, observers expressed concern over who was leading this exodus. As William Peterson, director of the Experiment Station in 1925, pointed out, "It has been said by some that the movement from the country to the city is a woman [*sic*] movement, and the reason for this is to avoid the hardships associated with the home in a country life." If indeed this were the case, argued Peterson, it was because "the women are not satisfied with their jobs. The home," he concluded, "must be made more convenient, more attractive [*sic*] and allow for some leisure."[11] Peterson had identified the issue that other Utah educators would also stress: the need to keep women and children on the farm, which was to be accomplished by increasing their satisfaction (or, more accurately, decreasing their dissatisfaction) with rural life. The two major elements involved in that effort were promotion of the farm wife's status and improvement of the rural home and working conditions connected with it.

The elevation of domesticity proved to be a cornerstone of arguments supporting home economics education. As one early proponent of the U.A.C. program noted, "the best education for

10. *Utah Farmer*, 30 October 1920, p. 1.
11. Ibid., 14 February 1925, p. 23.

women is the one that makes her [*sic*] the most womanly."[12] What was needed, wrote another, was a "host of happy, intelligent, home-loving mothers" who would be fit "to be the mothers and chief inspirers of unborn men" and who therefore "needed the trained mind and satisfied life just as much, nay more, than if they were to be mere breadwinners."[13]

Educators made it clear, however, that what they advocated was not merely the "soulless initiation into the routine duties of the home" which, according to U.A.C. President John A. Widtsoe, made up most young women's experience.[14] Instead, they offered a vision of the enlightened, educated, modern housewife, that is to say, one who had benefited from proper formal training for this important role. In a 1913 address concerning the "Education of Women," President Widtsoe argued that

> Women are beginning to understand that housework has received the caress of science and has been made beautiful. It is no more simple drudgery, but a glorious conquest for the welfare of new generations. . . . Let it be repeated here most emphatically, that as a result of the application of modern science and thought to the various phases of homemaking, it has been repeatedly demonstrated that there is not greater field for brain work than the industries of family life. Moreover, the work of the home reaches out and in a measure, controls and directs all other professions. Family life is all inclusive—potent for health or disease, misery or happiness, success in its largest sense, or abject failure. Such a field certainly permits the play of the greatest mentality and should satisfy the natural longing of any rightly made woman.[15]

Such arguments in favor of domesticity may have been intended at least in part to reassure those who feared that college education would turn their daughters into the kind of "educated 'blue stockings' of a generation ago, who made themselves wish for every destiny under the sun save that embodying motherhood

12. *Deseret Farmer,* 3 December 1910, p. 4.
13. Ibid., 27 August 1910, p. 5.
14. John Andreas Widtsoe, *Education For Necessary Pursuits: Papers and Addresses Concerning the Work of the Utah Agricultural College* (Logan: Utah Agricultural College, 1913), 33.
15. Ibid., 35–36, 38.

and homemaking," which Widtsoe decried.[16] They also tended to limit the potential spheres of activity and endeavor offered, however, to those dealing fairly narrowly with maintenance of the home, plus some additional courses in cultural enrichment designed to endow the future mother with a degree of refinement. For example, the initial course of study for women at the U.A.C. supplemented classes in cooking and sewing with music, painting, "belles-lettres" (literature and elocution), hygiene, and dairying.[17] These offerings represented the educators' image of the well-rounded farm wife. As one fervent promoter of the School of Home Economics wrote in the *Deseret Farmer* in 1910, "How can we expect a woman to make a first class housekeeper and to love her home work better than anything else on earth if she has spent all the time of her formative years studying abstract subjects and stenography or business methods?"[18]

Such statements were pragmatic as much as philistine. A girl trained in domestic science was well-prepared for marriage and motherhood; lacking that, she might find work as a hired girl on a neighboring farmstead. However, the lack of job opportunities in the country meant that women with other ambitions must necessarily gravitate to rural villages or migrate to the big city. As late as 1930, the United States Census for Utah listed virtually all women (95 percent) in rural farm areas as "not gainfully employed"; a similar figure held for rural nonfarm or village women (93 percent). In contrast, roughly 87 percent of the urban women fell into this category, indicating the greater likelihood of these women to seek and find employment. More significant, the variety of jobs available increased dramatically off the farm. Just over half of the rural farm women worked at home, while nearly all of the urban (90 percent) and rural nonfarm women (85 percent) were employed away from home. The overwhelming majority of "employed" farm women (82 percent), not surprisingly, could be found in agriculturally related jobs, while urban women tended to be servants, waitresses, office workers, or in professional or industrial positions. Village women were concentrated in the ser-

16. Ibid., 34.
17. U.A.C., *Catalog, 1890–91,* pp. 21–22; *Catalog, 1914–15,* p. 45.
18. *Deseret Farmer,* 27 August 1910, p. 5.

vant-waitress category, with additional representation in the professional class and as saleswomen and office workers.[19] If a woman wished to find a paying job, then, she must clearly leave the farm for the city, big or small.

It was to combat the attraction of this variety of opportunities that representatives of the U.A.C. emphasized the "professional" aspect of home economics training. Throughout the 1910s articles with titles such as "Housekeeping as a Profession" appeared with some frequency in the *Utah Farmer* promoting domestic science education.[20] And farmers' institute meetings began holding special women's sessions known as "Housekeepers' Conferences"—a term calculated to point up the businesslike nature of the farm wife's work.[21] Speakers at these gatherings were fond of giving specific job titles to the various aspects of women's work. For example, U.A.C. domestic arts professor Dalinda Cotey defined the farm woman as "household manager, cook, laundress, seamstress, dressmaker, nurse, and teacher, to say nothing of the sacred duties of wife and mother," in her 1905 presentations.[22] The author of one Extension Service Bulletin summed up the prevailing attitude of these authorities when she wrote:

> The attitude of contempt hitherto assumed by society towards domestic duties indicates ignorance alike to their variety, their call for skill and their responsibility. It is even now giving place to the realization that these familiar duties are infinitely more varied and demand a far higher degree of intelligence than do the callings of stenographer, clerk, or factory-hand, which appeal so strongly to the young women today.[23]

The goal of these educators was to discourage girls from seeking out these town occupations by emphasizing the justifiable pride they could take in enlightened homemaking.

19. U.S., Department of Commerce, Bureau of the Census, *Fifteenth Census of the United States, 1930: Population*, 6:1340.

20. *Utah Farmer*, 1 July 1916, p. 10, is one of many examples.

21. One of the many notices for such gatherings appears in *Utah Farmer*, 5 February 1916, p. 10.

22. U.S.F.I., No. 9 (1906), p. 50.

23. Alice Ravenhill, *Labor-Saving Devices in the Household*, Utah Agricultural College Experiment Station Circular No. 6 (Logan: Utah Agricultural College Extension Service, 1912), pp. 3–4.

Yet another way of countering the attraction of the city was to bring its amenities to the country. Rural beautification movements played a significant role in this regard. Beginning in the 1910s and 1920s, Utah farm communities waged "Clean Home—Clean Town" campaigns, organized and run by the county and home demonstration agents and local Farm Bureaus. The activities ranged from simple "pick up and paint" drives to full-scale programs involving graveling or even paving of streets, installation of streetlights and sidewalks, and establishment of parks. Rural dwellers received encouragement to emulate their city cousins further by putting in lawns and flower gardens. Through such efforts, small farm communities could compete, at least aesthetically, with larger cities. Women predominated in such campaigns, understandably, since they made up the bulk of the membership in the Home and Community sections of the Farm Bureau which supervised these activities. Furthermore, beautification fell under the traditional definition of women's work. As the *Utah Magazine* stated confidently in its 1941 "Beautification Issue," "Ladies seem to be especially adapt [*sic*] at getting things done in this respect."[24]

But improvement of communities was only one step. Upgrading rural dwellings proved even more important. As one advocate argued:

> The farm home should be made so convenient and inviting that the wife and mother would not exchange it for a city residence. The sense of isolation so often complained of in country homes is more often the result of out-of-date equipment rather than lack of near neighbors. . . . But labor-saving devices for the wife are necessities—just as much so as up-to-date plows and drills are necessities for the farmer. . . . A country home thus provided with modern conveniences would not readily be deserted for a home in the village, nor would wife and children voluntarily make the exchange. . . . The average farmer must learn, therefore, to think as much of his family as the city man does of his, and to prove that love by making his family equally comfortable. Doubtless, the real magnet that draws the wife

24. "Improving Rural Landscapes," *Utah Magazine*, April 1941, p. 37.

> and mother so strongly cityward is the fact that these modern conveniences may be enjoyed in the home. . .[25]

Indeed, the absence of labor-saving devices proved to be a major drawback to country life, one which makers of these products used skillfully to their advantage. Readers of the *Utah Farmer* were bombarded with advertisements that reinforced editorial messages regarding the importance of acquiring the benefits of modern technology. Stating that now the "CONVENIENCES OF THE CITY—the comforts of life—can be had on the farm," one maker of electric pumping equipment claimed that "City women live longer than women of the country. Why? Chiefly because of a difference in the home arrangement—a lack in the country of the conveniences that would make the day's work a delight."[26]

At times the advertising copy became hard to distinguish from other "expert" advice. For example, utilities like Utah Power and Light Company sold electrical devices as well as providing service, and their ads frequently listed the growing number of appliances available to the modern housewife.[27] These notices complemented the arguments presented by extension workers and the journal's own writers promoting modernization. In one 1913 discussion of "The Electrified Farm House," the litany of home improvements recommended by the author included, in addition to the predictable electric lights and room heaters, "feed mixers and grinder[s] of all kind[s], bone cutters, electrical ranges, electrical fireless cooker, electric iron, toaster, coffee percolator, samovar, table stove, chafing dish and curling iron," plus machines for "every task which could be done with motive power, including running the sewing machine." While the author admitted that "Comparatively few women will have homes as completely electrified as this," she added that "there are few homes where some electrification is not possible," and its use would transform the traditional washing, ironing, churning, sewing and cooking, leaving the remainder of the farm wife's chores in the "light housekeeping class."[28] Similar articles urging the use of electricity and

25. *Utah Farmer,* 30 August 1919, p. 9.
26. Ibid., 23 August 1919, p. 7.
27. Ibid., 10 January 1925, p. 9.
28. Ibid., 11 December 1915, p. 16.

other "labor-saving devices for the home" appeared in the *Utah Farmer* repeatedly throughout the 1910s and 1920s, and the U.A.C. Extension Service published two long booklets with that title in the late 1910s as well.[29]

Young women trained in the U.A.C.'s Home Economics Department received similar indoctrination regarding the use of modern conveniences. The institution rented a nearby dwelling in 1917 and fitted it up as a "Home Economics Practice House," wherein students could work in an "authentic" home environment. This facility and its successor, the 1928 "Home Economics Cottage," supplemented other "laboratories," all, according to college catalogs, well-equipped with the latest developments in household technology.[30] For example, a bulletin describing the initial practice house noted that the establishment featured not only a coal stove but also one of the "up-to-date ranges [which] economizes fuel," which was donated to the practice house by the Utah Power and Light Company, thereby allowing the students to "study the convenience and economy of electricity."[31] It was not at all uncommon for home economic specialists to acquire their information about the new technology from dealers of the equipment.[32]

Other new products of industry were also included among the "labor-savers" advocated by educators. U.A.C. Home Economist Leah Widtsoe, for example, recommended that farm wives use the new Scott paper towels, which she considered more sanitary as well as more efficient than cloth.[33] The degree to which this practice of promoting certain brand name products obtained is difficult to determine, but advertisers certainly capitalized upon it. The Genesee Pure Food Company, makers of Jell-O, ran an ad campaign in 1921 based on rural/urban comparisons that claimed the authority of such educators in support of its product. A typical example was that which appeared in the *Utah Farmer* on January 22, 1921, and ran as follows:

29. See Ravenhill, *Labor-Saving Devices.* A second part of this booklet was by Leah D. Widtsoe, entitled *Labor-Saving Devices for the Farm Home.*

30. Utah State Agricultural College, *Home Economics Practice House,* Extension Service Bulletin, vol. 18, no. 1 (Logan: Utah Agricultural College, 1918); U.A.C., *Catalog, 1928–29,* p. 31.

31. U.A.C., *Practice House,* p. 5.

32. Leah Widtsoe periodically acknowledges her debt to information supplied by manufacturers throughout *Labor-Saving Devices;* p. 37.

33. Ibid., 70–71.

> Until recently, the woman on the farm, though a born cook and a peerless housekeeper, has often been handicapped by a lack of information concerning certain new methods that have been adopted in the cities.
>
> To some extent this has been true in the case of Jell-O, which in the cities has for several years been the most popular preparation for desserts and salads.
>
> As rapidly as possible steps have been taken to spread among all women complete knowledge of the subject.
>
> In Domestic Science and Home Economics classes, in city and country, trained women have demonstrated the simple and economical Jell-O way, and recipe books are being distributed thoroughly. As Jell-O is now sold in practically every general store in the country, farmers' wives are enabled to share the privilege enjoyed by their city sisters.[34]

While such copy may be evidence of wishful thinking rather than actual experience, it points up another significant fact about farm women's education: increasingly, they were being trained to be consumers, and to rely on the advice of outside authorities. Of course, the goal was enlightened consumerism. As one advocate of vocational homemaking education expressed it,

> New equipment and facilities are becoming available every year. While many of these make housekeeping easier there is need for education regarding their efficient use. Education should create a desire for the improvements and conveniences of life but should, at the same time, develop an appreciation of relative values in terms of family welfare which will become a basis for judgement in buying and for resisting sales and advertising pressure when needed.[35]

This shift away from a predominantly productive role clearly followed the pattern set by urban women, and educators even used an appropriately businesslike terminology in describing it. Rose Widtsoe of the U.A.C. Home Economics Department discussed the proper role of the modern farm wife at length in a

34. *Utah Farmer*, 22 January 1921, p. 8.

35. Angelyn Warnick, *A Survey of the Need for Vocational Homemaking Education in Utah* (n. p., 1939), 12.

two-part *Utah Farmer* article published in 1920, originally planned as a presentation at that year's Farmers' Encampment at Logan. The housewife, whom she defined as a "household purchasing agent," needed many specialized skills beyond mere cooking, sewing, and cleaning. In addition she

> should know the merits of various kinds of distribution methods, (such) as parcel post, mail order, co-operative buying and public market. She should realize the importance of knowing city, state and national laws governing the standards of various articles such as food, clothing and equipment and also the methods of handling raw and manufactured goods. She will search out the markets that are sanitary and well ordered, avoiding markets where food is exposed to flies and dust. She will learn the standard weaves of cotten, linen, and woolen materials and the points of judgment in determining household equipment. She will in fact learn the values of everything that comes into the house. . . . Another important qualification is to be able to detect food adulterations and malpractice among dealers, and to know the various trade labels and the most economical sizes of cans and other containers. In fact to be a good purchasing agent, the mother in the home must know her business. If she is to get the best returns for her money she must know values.[36]

In support of this trend toward consumerism, the U.A.C. catalog increasingly offered more specialized courses, such as the 1916 class entitled "Food Economics," which dealt with "the function and nutritive values of food, the cost of food in relation to the family budget . . . (and) practical results of the 'pure food' laws" in addition to the more traditional training in "preparation of meals combining foods according to dietetic, aesthetic, and economic standards."[37]

But teaching women how to shop was not the only concern of home economics educators. Indeed, the definition of "homemaker" was being expanded even while, ironically, the ultimate authority over the home was being delegated to outside authori-

36. *Utah Farmer,* 6 March 1920, p. 6.
37. U.A.C., *Catalog, 1916–17,* pp. 95–96.

ties. The well-trained housewife must be intensely aware of her vital role as the foundation of a good and moral society. As U.A.C. President John Widtsoe proclaimed,

> Women are now coming quickly to understand the value of such special education and the great power of their position as the mothers and makers of the race. When every mother knows the laws of health, more children will be strong. When every mother is broadly and sympathetically trained in the application of science and in the arts, more children will be intelligent. The church and the school are great factors in the training of the coming men and women, but compared with the home they sink into insignificance. If the formative years of a child's life are spent in a home of health and intelligence, a man is produced. If the reverse occurs, crime, disease, filth, the reform school, the police court, and the house of prostitution, are the result. The picture is unpleasant, but it is common. Upon the proper education of the women will depend almost wholly the future of the race.[38]

College catalogs expressed a similar view, if less dramatically. U.A.C. bulletins throughout the twenties explained that

> The steady growth of Home Economics courses in leading colleges and universities indicates the ever increasing realization that the well conducted home is the most important factor in the development of healthful and capable citizenship. But the multiplying complexities of modern life demand further that those in charge of the family understand much that is beyond the exact limits of the home. Hence the stress laid on the study of childhood and adolescence, the cause underlying the high cost of living, and the problems of social, industrial, and civic life.[39]

This broadened definition of the scope of "home economics" manifested itself quite early. By the 'teens, the department's initial classes in "cooking," for example, had been expanded to include courses on "Dietetics and Nutrition," "Pathological Nutri-

38. John A. Widtsoe, *Education for Necessary Pursuits*, 36.
39. U.A.C., *Catalog, 1920–21*, p. 57.

tion" (dealing with special diets for the "sick and convalescent"), and "Care and Feeding of Children." "Home Care of the Sick" was yet another offering, as was "Home Sanitation."[40] Possible majors changed in number and scope. In 1890 there was but one possible field for women: Domestic Arts. By the 1910s, women could chose from four specializations: Food and Dietetics, Domestic Arts, Home Sanitation and Construction, and Art. In the late 1920s women studied Food and Dietetics, Textiles and Clothing, or Household Administration. But the shift in focus is clear by the 1940s. The perennials—Foods and Nutrition, Household Administration, and Clothing, Textiles and Related Arts—had been joined by two significant newcomers—Home Economics Education, and Child Development and Parent Education.[41] These additions reflected the sizeable role of the U.A.C. in training vocational homemaking teachers for the lower grades, as well as the redefinition of what that education should include.

Related to this expanded scope was an increase in the emotional component of women's work. As early as 1910 one U.A.C. Domestic Arts specialist warned listeners at a farmers' institute:

> It is not enough for the housekeeper to feel that she has done her duty when she has cooked some sort of meal and put it on the table. "Will it keep the family well? Will it keep them happy? Will it keep them working?" Therefore we should appreciate the proper selection of food, the proper preparation of food, the proper consumption of food, and to a certain extent the proper manner of serving and approaching it.[42]

The psychic content of meals gained the importance of the nutritional level here. The creed reached full expression by 1939, when an expert on vocational homemaking education in the state would state that the homemaker's job was twofold:

> (1) the management of the material resources of the family in order to provide for the physical, emotional and psychological needs of the family members, and

40. U.A.C., *Catalog, 1916–17*, pp. 95–96.

41. Ricks, p. 27; U.A.C., *Catalog, 1914–15*, p. 45; *Catalog, 1928–29*, p. 64; *Catalog, 1947–48*, p. 234.

42. U.S.F.I., No. 13 (1910), pp. 106–107.

(2) the maintenance of desirable relationships among the family members and with people outside the family.[43]

It is worth noting that even the "productive" component of this pair of directives involves strictly nonmaterial concerns.

It is of course difficult, if not impossible, to determine the degree to which the targets of such advice—Utah farm women—accepted their redefinition as "professionals" and the expansion of their responsibility for the moral and mental health of their families. But adoption of other portions of the program is easier to measure. And in this area, the unusual residence pattern of Utah's farm population certainly increased the likelihood of success. Proponents of change recognized this fact. "As most of our farmers live in small cities or towns," wrote one Hannah Jones in a 1915 *Utah Farmer* article on the subject, "it is not a great task to have our homes electrified."[44] Such was indeed the case.

The decade from 1900 to 1910, in particular, witnessed the rapid spread of electrification throughout the state. Between 1912 and 1922, the Utah Power and Light Company, which served the most heavily populated northern and north-central portions of Utah (as well as communities in southern Idaho and western Colorado), had doubled the mileage of its transmission lines, and the number of customers served more than doubled. By the latter year the utility claimed to reach 95 percent of the homes in its territory, including 138 communities in Utah alone.[45] According to U.S. Census reports, 11,125 Utah farm homes had electricity in 1920, rising to 15,778 in 1930 and 18,285 by 1945.[46] Utah was a leader in this area; a 1930 U.A.C. survey compiled from census data held that only California and Massachusetts had more farms electrified than Utah, and only ten other states (just two in the West—California and Oregon) could top her rate of 38.9 percent of rural homes enjoying piped-in water, often a related convenience.[47]

43. Warnick, *Survey*, 7.

44. *Utah Farmer*, 11 December 1915, p. 16.

45. Utah Power and Light Company, *Electrifying the Wheels of Progress, 1912–1922* (n.p., 1922), pp. 12–14, 21.

46. U.S., Department of Commerce, Bureau of the Census, *Census of Agriculture, 1954*, vol. 1, pt. 31:3.

47. Joseph A. Geddes, *Farm Versus Village Living in Utah: Plain City—Type "A" Village*, Extension Bulletin No. 249 (Logan: Utah Agricultural College, 1934), 62.

In light of repeated criticisms by state educators that the barn often received electricity before the farmhouse, one might question whether this impressive degree of electrification actually benefited rural women. But Utahns seem to have been progressive in this regard. As early as 1922, according to the Utah Power and Light Company, there were 4,300 electric ranges, 19,000 washing machines, 14,000 grills and toasters, 7,500 vacuum cleaners, and 10,000 "miscellaneous devices" in their 62,000-home territory. They also reported 70,000 electric irons—more than one per residence.[48] No doubt many of these devices belonged to urban dwellers, but since the state's farm population was 31.2 percent of the total in 1920, it seems fair to assume that a sufficient number found their way to the farm wife.[49] Possibly more representative, though less comprehensive, is a 1931 U.A.C. survey of farm families in Summitt County, Utah. The authors reported that "Electricity furnished the lighting in 96 per cent of the homes, while more than three-fourths of the families had electrical equipment and more than two-thirds of the homes had running water in the house."[50] In addition, 94 percent of the homes contained sewing machines, 80.4 percent had electric washers, and 43 percent vacuum cleaners.[51]

The degree of consumerism among Utah farm wives is more difficult to pinpoint, although U.A.C. personnel did make the effort. One 1929 survey of farm family food habits, for example, indicated acceptance of brand name products such as Crisco. This random sampling of rural dwellers in eleven western Utah counties also found that approximately 70 percent of all foodstuffs that might be furnished by the farm actually were—notably milk, honey, and vegetables.[52] The rest were purchased. The Summitt County sampling done the next year estimated that only about half of the total value of food costs were supplied by the farm. Again, eggs and dairy products predominated; half the poultry

48. Utah Power and Light, *Electrifying the Wheels,* 21.

49. U.S., Department of Commerce, Bureau of the Census, *Fifteenth Census of the United States, 1930: Population,* 2:13–15.

50. Edith Hayball and W. Preston Thomas, *Family Living Expenditures: Summit County, Utah, 1930,* Extension Bulletin No. 232 (Logan: Utah Agricultural College, 1931), 3.

51. Ibid., 28.

52. Almeda Perry Brown, *Food Habits of Utah Farm Families,* Extension Bulletin No. 213 (Logan: Utah Agricultural College, 1929), 8.

and meat came from off the farm, as did three-fourths of the fruit and vegetables and nearly all the flour and cereal.[53] Such studies may be imperfect, but they do indicate that by the 1930s at least some presumably representative rural women were moving away from producing almost all they could to selective consumption of off-farm goods.

It is not surprising, in light of their heavy work load, that rural women in the early twentieth century so readily accepted the advice of agricultural educators to modernize. Whether this adoption of the urban model, insofar as possible, actually succeeded in stemming migration from the farm is yet another question, one more difficult to answer since one can only measure what did happen and not what might have under different circumstances. As it is, census data offer no clear trends during the first three decades of the century. It is obvious that young men and women left the country for the city in their late teens and early twenties, but that movement did not, apparently, either increase or decrease dramatically over the period in question.[54] Agricultural educators may have slowed the tide somewhat; they certainly did not turn it back. Perhaps all that can be said with certainty is that their efforts eased the lot of women who stayed on the farm, and made life in the city more familiar to those who later sought it.

53. Hayball and Thomas, *Family Living Expenditures*, 5, 21.

54. These conclusions are drawn from age pyramids profiling the rural and urban population in Utah. See U.S., Department of Commerce, Bureau of the Census, *Fifteenth Census of the United States, 1930: Population*, vol. 3, pt. 2:1088–1090.

"I've Worked, I'm Not Afraid of Work": Farm Women in New Mexico, 1920–1940

JOAN M. JENSEN

These words of Edna Gholson of Quay County, New Mexico, in many ways symbolize the history of farm women in New Mexico during the two decades from 1920 to 1940. The work of farm women has always been visible, known, and talked about in rural areas. Any farm woman can give a detailed description of the work she and her neighbors perform in the farm house, farm yard, farm field, and farming community. It is only historians who have had difficulty translating that oral tradition into a written account. Because New Mexico has been rural longer than most states, women have been absent from most written accounts of New Mexico history. Rural women's history is accessible, however, through census material, agricultural extension records, and especially oral history. These sources make the twentieth-century history of New Mexico farm women a particularly rich field of study.

This essay describes the work of New Mexico farm women in family and community. It is confined primarily to the Hispanic and Anglo majority. Although Native American women have had a long, rich agricultural history, their history has also been separate in many ways. Their history

---

Joan M. Jensen is professor of history in New Mexico State University and chair of the history department. This essay is from her forthcoming University of New Mexico Press publication *New Mexico Women: Intercultural Perspectives*, co-edited with Darlis A. Miller. The anthology will feature a dozen essays on various aspects of the history of New Mexico women.

deserves special skills of analysis and is available through separate sources for the most part. For these reasons, the Native American minority, which numbered less than six percent of the population in 1920 and lived scattered through McKinley, San Juan, Sandoval, and Valencia counties is not discussed here. Nor are black women, an even smaller, more urban group that numbered less than two percent of the population. The intercultural perspective here presented, then, is that of the almost equal numbers of Hispanic and Anglo females who together composed the 85 percent majority in the state in 1920. Of these 306,000 females, almost 78,000 were twenty-one years or over, and 64,000 of them rural. Members of this rural adult female population and the changes in their lives over twenty years are the focus of the following study.[1]

This study takes as its direct focus farm women in Bernalillo, Doña Ana, Union, Rio Arriba, Santa Fe, Taos, and Valencia counties. Anglo women were represented heavily in the counties of Bernalillo, Doña Ana, and Union, although only Union was almost entirely Anglo. Rio Arriba, Santa Fe, Taos, and Valencia were predominantly Hispanic with small Anglo minorities. Doña Ana is located in the south, Valencia and Bernalillo in central, and Santa Fe, Rio Arriba, and Union in the northern part of the state. These counties give regional and ethnic representation. In addition, oral and family histories from women of a number of other counties describe similar conditions; attitudes of farm women, and agricultural extension documents from 1921, 1925, 1930, 1935, and 1939 describe the activities of farm women. Together, the oral histories and written records provide rich documentation of the work farm women performed in the economic and cultural survival of family and community. Although divided by ethnicity and sometimes by class, these farm women shared a common history as they worked in the valleys, plains, and mountains of New Mexico.

The primary bond of unity among these Anglo and Hispanic women was poverty. The majority of each group was desperately poor, not only by contemporary standards but also by middle-class standards of the time. As frustrated extension agents found, many women were so poor they could not afford the few cents necessary for patterns, hat frames, or material to complete clothing projects. For this reason, extension agents in most areas concentrated on food preservation, labor intensive work that could provide necessary food for the whole family and which required equipment that could often be purchased collectively and used cooperatively. Pressure cookers and glass containers, although still expensive for impoverished farm families, were within the reach of most.

1. Population statistics from U.S. Department of Commerce, Bureau of the Census, *United States Census of Agriculture: 1945* (Washington, D.C.: Government Printing Office, 1946), Vol. 1, Part 30, New Mexico and Arizona, 1–14.

Growing food and preserving it increasingly became an important summer task for large numbers of Hispanic and Anglo farm women.[2]

All New Mexico farm women were affected by certain grim economic facts of life in the two decades between 1920 and 1940. Bounded on each end by a world war that affected agriculture and family intensively, these decades were primarily ones of economic depression and change for the entire farm population of the United States. The adjustment to changing world and domestic markets after World War I, the depression that spread out from urban areas, combined with one of the worst droughts in the history of the Southwest, left thousands of farm families with little hope for changing their lives. Hard times were not new to most New Mexican farm families, whether homesteaders who had so recently and so optimistically dotted the eastern plains with their sod and frame homes and windmills or Hispanic farmers who held small irrigated plots along the Rio Grande. All had already suffered hard times. What they lost in these depression years was primarily the hope that hard work could make a good life for their families on the land. It was hard to look forward and to expect better times. Without that hope many sold out, moved to town, or became tenants and farm laborers on the land of other farm families.[3]

The life-styles honed by poverty, nevertheless, gave these farm families great survival skills. Labor exchange, barter, and a common rural socio-economic status gave people a feeling of shared experience. There were few wealthy farm families at whom rural people could direct their anger. Simple life styles were the rule even for most ranch and farm families that had wealth in land. While there were growing class divisions in the state, these were masked by urban-rural rifts. The wealthy most often lived in town or out of state, appearing occasionally in communities or, as one commentator wrote, in the offices of extension agents in their "white linen suits." Conflict occurred during these years but it usually took the form of conflict against outsiders who attempted to extend control into rural areas. Open violence flared occasionally but usually the community majority united against the outsider. The representatives of these outside interests held their tongues, for the most part, and bided their time.[4]

---

2. Joan M. Jensen, "Canning Comes to New Mexico: Women and the Agricultural Extension Service, 1914–1919," *New Mexico Historical Review*, 57 (October 1982), 361–86.

3. Joan M. Jensen, "Farm Women in New Mexico, 1900–1940," in Robert Kern, ed., *Labor in New Mexico: Strikes, Unions, and Social History Since 1881* (Albuquerque: University of New Mexico Press, 1983), 61–81 has an overview.

4. Hugh B. Calkins, "Reconnaissance Survey of Human Dependency on Resources in the Rio Grande Watershed" (Mimeographed, USDA, Soil Conservation Service, Region Eight, Regional Bulletin No. 33, Conservation Series, No. 6, December 1936), 116.

In addition to a type of class homogeneity, farm women also benefited from federal and state agencies expanded or established to meet the crisis of the depression and drought of the early 1930s. In addition to dealing with new conditions, officials tackled old problems like rural health, hazards of water supply, environmental dangers of soil erosion from overgrazing, and isolation of farm women. The actions of state extension agents and federal officials, while sometimes bungling and inappropriate, eventually provided an impressive rural service infrastructure. Rural women were better organized in many ways by the end of the 1930s than their urban sisters. There was a community spirit of cooperation which, while unequal in different areas, increased during the 1930s. Welfare, government jobs and loans, extension clubs, and projects all had their pitfalls. But when officials could operate effectively with their rural constituency, helping them meet their needs, the agencies provided a network of support that rural people had not experienced previously in American history. Some contemporary commentators noted the great gains by the wealthy elite from federal funding. Hugh G. Calkins, for example, observed that in the Mesilla Valley of southern New Mexico, the wealthy farmers had received most of the $675,000 in payments under the Agricultural Adjustment Act. Nevertheless, middle-class farm families in the Mesilla Valley also gained from the assistance of state and federal programs. Poor farm families, who did not have enough money to keep their land, received federal relief.[5]

For rural women, the family remained central to their lives in a peculiar way, for most of their work was performed within the family on family-owned farms. The rules for this circumstance were embedded so deeply in family law and custom that many may not have consciously considered them or possible alternatives. For that reason, a review of family law that encompassed community property law in New Mexico is fundamental to understanding women's relationship to agriculture.

Research on the history of family law in New Mexico is still relatively new but the general outlines are clear. Hispanic women had enjoyed the rights of community property under Spanish and Mexican law but these rights were diminished under American rule and the adoption of common law procedures. The property rights of Hispanic women, however, should not be romanticized. Like women under common law, New Mexico women forfeited most of their civil rights upon marriage. Married women were subordinate to their husbands under Mexican law. While a woman had a legal right to retain separate title to property brought into a marriage and had a legal right to one-half of the property accumulated after marriage, her husband, as legal head of the family, had

---

5. *Ibid.*

management and control of property during marriage. She could lose her property rights for adultery or if she entered the church. Community property laws gave the family, not the individual woman, protection. Marriage was a legal partnership under Spanish and Mexican law with each partner owning one-half of the acquired property but one partner, as a legal commentator remarked, had "larger power than the other." A woman had a legal right to control of her property only at her death unless her husband died first. The husband could dispose of his property at will; the wife, except for small gifts to the poor, only with the consent of her husband. Before 1907, however, women did have the right to dispose of their separate property and one-half of the community property by will.[6]

In 1907, the New Mexico legislature passed statutes modeled on California family law. Under the new law, a woman could not dispose of her property by will. This meant that her property passed automatically to her husband. She had no right to make a will or determine who would receive her property. Although California changed its law in 1923, New Mexico retained the old California law until the 1970s. In 1919, the courts held that a wife did not forfeit community property because of adultery. Moreover, an Eddy County ranch woman, bringing suit in this case, and having admitted adultery, was found by the courts to have a right to one-half of a ranch valued between $100,000 and $200,000. The court held the husband had tried to defraud the woman by offering her a settlement of $4,000 and ordered the lower courts to divide the property equitably. But a loyal wife had little legal power. To be single, widowed, or divorced gave farm women their only legal equality.[7]

Given the property structure of family law, married farm women theoretically had little control over the property that they owned as marital partners. How this law worked out in practice, however, has not yet been studied by historians. The law gave farm widows considerable power; it may also have given farm wives more power in practice than the theory indicates. But farm women in their oral histories complain of husbands as "partners" who uprooted the family when they decided to move, and as "managers" of the partnership who ran families into debt, leaving women no alternative but divorce or acquiesence. The experiences of Florence Hill of Carlsbad and Edna Gholson of Tucumcari are relevant here. Both husband managers ran up debts for the partnership. Hill found out only after her husband died that he had run up debts for

---

6. Theodore E. Jones, "Community Property—Power of Testamentary Disposition—Inequality Between Spouses," *Natural Resources Journal*, 7 (October 1967), 645–49, Robert Emmet Clark, "Management and Control of Community Property in New Mexico," *Tulane Law Journal*, 26 (April 1952), 324–43.

7. *Barnett v. Barnett*, 9 N.M. 205 (October 1897).

another woman. She worked to pay for his funeral expenses but refused to pay his debts. She had to support her children by keeping house for a wealthy neighbor. Gholson had a partner whose problem was drinking. After her divorce, she paid off $900 in debts in one year on her own by taking in boarders.[8]

Divorce was less common in Hispanic than in Anglo families in the 1920s and 1930s. Equal division of land among children by Hispanic fathers remained common, however, and when a husband died without a will the courts divided his community property equally among the children. Such equal partition gave daughters a stake in family property and increased their control; it also increasingly divided the farm land. By the 1930s, land owned by Hispanic families in counties like Rio Arriba and San Miguel averaged three acres per family. While land was plentiful and communal grazing lands available, equitable partition had strengthened the families. As Anglo landowners gradually took over communal grazing lands, such farms could provide only subsistence. Cash incomes had to be sought, usually by the males in the family, in off-farm employment. This trend began in Hispanic families before World War I and accelerated at the end of the war in 1918. Works Progress Administration accounts of the 1930s noted, for example, that in Cordova men came back from the war reluctant to take over the farming that women had managed while they were gone. Women continued to plant the fields while men left the community to work at nonagricultural jobs for six to eight months. The men's incomes went to buy new tin roofs and new automobiles while the women's subsistence farming provided for basic family needs.[9]

Thus the increasingly small irrigated farms of Hispanic families and the larger dryland farms of the Anglos both led to a large number of subsistence farms where women took care of the farms while men sought off-farm labor for much of the year. By 1920, the homesteading boom of the first two decades was over and families were already moving to town. The rural population in New Mexico had increased by 67 percent in the decade from 1900 to 1910, almost the same percentage as the urban population, which increased by 70 percent. In the next decade, the homesteading boom over, rural population increased by only 5 percent. The total number of farms dropped by 16 percent.[10]

---

8. Oral histories of Edna Gholson and Florence Hill in Working Lives of New Mexico Women Project, Rio Grande Collections, New Mexico State University. Hereafter cited as WLNMW, NMSU.

9. Lorin W. Brown, *Hispanic Folklore of New Mexico: The Lorin W. Brown Federal Writers' Project Manuscripts* (Albuquerque: University of New Mexico Press, 1978), 190–91.

10. U.S., Department of Commerce, Bureau of the Census, *Farm Population of the United States* (Washington, D.C.: Government Printing Office, 1926), 210–11. See tables 77, 78.

In 1920, farm women lived on less than 30,000 individual farms in New Mexico. In the previous decade, the amount of land in farms had doubled and the average size and value increased over 100 percent. Overall, farms under 20 acres decreased by almost 20 percent, farms from 10 to 175 acres decreased by almost 30 percent, farms from 175 to 500 acres by 7 percent. Farms over 500 acres, on the other hand, increased by 337 percent, from less than 4 percent to over 20 percent. Almost 50 percent of the farms were 50 to 500 acres, and about 30 percent were under 50 acres. Ownership was still 86 percent but tenancy more than doubled between 1910 and 1920, and mortgaged farms increased from 5 to 25 percent. Women owned about 5 percent of owner farms, ran 2 percent of managed farms, and worked less than 2 percent of tenant farms. The farms controlled by women were small and poor.[11] In other words, women held few farms singly and small farms operated in conjunction with husbands were decreasing in number and becoming more heavily mortgaged.

During the next two decades the number of farms gradually increased again to the 1910 number but the average size increased very little. Of the 41,000 farms that existed in 1935, almost half of them reported crop failures and the value of farm lands was lower in 1940 than in 1920. By 1935, half of the operators had off-farm work. As the depression worsened, fewer farmers hired labor. Only 14 percent of the farms had hired labor by 1935. Increasingly, the work was done by family labor, a trend that continued to 1940. Families still labored with little mechanization. Two percent of farms had tractors in 1920 but twenty years later only 15 percent of the 34,105 farms had them.[12]

By 1940, a 67 percent majority of New Mexico women were still rural. Almost half of these 84,000 farm women (46 percent) lived on farms under 50 acres and over three-fifths (65 percent) on farms under 175 acres worth just over $4,000 each. Over a third of the farms were subsistence farms, producing primarily items that totaled less than $200 per year. Almost two-fifths (39 percent) were semi-subsistence, producing less than $250 for use and sale each year, while almost three-fourths (73 percent) were living on family farms that produced less than $1,000 worth of products to use or sell. Thus, by 1940 three out of every four farm women worked on these small family farms where there was virtually no cash to spend on consumer goods.[13]

The gender division of labor on these small New Mexico farms was

---

11. U.S., Department of Commerce, Bureau of the Census, *Fourteenth Census of the United States Taken in the Year 1920* (Washington, D.C.: Government Printing Office, 1922), Vol. VI, Part 3, Agriculture, 199–203.

12. U.S., Department of Commerce, Bureau of the Census, *United States Census of Agriculture: 1945* (Washington, D.C.: Government Printing Office, 1946), 1–14.

13. *Ibid.*

Gina Allen on the family dairy farm, Las Cruces, ca. 1940s. Courtesy of Rio Grande Historical Collections, New Mexico State University Library.

never strict. While census statistics do not describe the division of labor, both extension records and oral histories reflect the extensive work performed by women on the farms of New Mexico. On subsistence farms, both small Hispanic farms and homesteading farms, women worked outside most of the year. In the counties of Rio Arriba, Taos, and Santa Fe, the farm work of women, like men, was heaviest in the summer. They planted gardens, hoed and weeded, harvested, and then preserved, usually outside in the yards. In counties where chile was the main cash crop, they picked and strung, dried and marketed it. In Rio Arriba, for example, merchants handled over 60,000 strings of chile a year, usually offering credit. Strings of chiles translated into necessities at the markets. In 1939, Rio Arriba women produced not only enough food for their families for all year and bartered chiles, but also sold $2,600 worth of food, $2,459 worth of eggs, and several hundred dollars worth of handicrafts.[14]

Should their fields not produce enough, women picked at neighbors

14. Home Demonstration Agent Fabiola Cabeza de Baca, Annual Report for Rio Arriba and Santa Fe Counties, 1939, New Mexico College of Agriculture and Mechanical Arts, State College, Agricultural Extension Service, Annual Reports, National Archives, Microcopy T876, Reel 22. Hereafter cited as NMCAAES.

on shares, or canned on shares. The Home Demonstration Agent reported from Rio Arriba that women who had poor chile crops helped neighbors hoe and irrigate, pick and string, in return for enough food to feed their families. She estimated that labor exchange saved people at least $200 a year. An additional 150 people exchanged food—peaches for apples, chile for beans and potatoes. At the stores they bartered chile and eggs for sugar, coffee, citrus fruit, and a few other food luxuries. In other parts of New Mexico homesteaders did much the same thing. Edna Gholson remembered working for a neighbor picking tomatoes, carrots, cucumbers, and green beans, washing them and preparing them for market in return for vegetables that she stayed up all night canning. The next morning she would be in the fields picking again.[15]

Hispanic women in northern New Mexico also plastered their own homes in fall and exchanged their labor for cash and in-kind payments. Women bartered skillfully. In fall, they also helped thresh and took responsibility for hand winnowing. Relatives and neighbors performed this task cooperatively. Grace Pritchett, who taught at Placitas, boarded in a household where the mother came to the home of her daughter to help winnow. They poured the wheat from one pan to another to winnow it, then washed and spread it on clean tarps to dry. Women kept small flocks of chickens, and whenever possible, a cow or goat for family milk. Men were frequently gone at off-farm work in the 1920s. When men returned, they concentrated mainly on growing fodder crops for animals, and on growing beans and corn. A surplus of beans might also be traded at the stores or in specific communities such as Mountainair, where families went to trade. The cash of the male usually went to purchase his necessities, equipment for the farm, and building supplies. The woman's income provided food and clothing for the family. Farm women may have preferred credit at the local market to cash purchase. Credit, like barter and labor exchange, gave women some control over the products of their work. Despite the cultural differences of homesteading women, the subsistence economy made their working lives similar to those of Hispanic women. Men hired out on larger farms for harvest, worked on the railroads, on road construction, or at any other day labor they could find. Women remained on the farms, tending animals, raising vegetables, preserving food, and developing a crop to provide credit or cash for the necessities of the family.[16]

Although buttermaking had been a traditional way of bringing in cash in other regions, women soon found that this was not true in many

---

15. *Ibid.;* oral history of Edna Gholson, WLNMW, NMSU.

16. Grace Pritchett, *The Road Goes This Way and That Way* (St. Paul, New Mexico: Brawn, 1981), 12–13.

parts of New Mexico. Stella Hatch, for example, on arriving near Sand Hills, New Mexico, took a batch of butter to a nearby store, fully expecting to get the traditional credit. The storekeeper told her they had no market for butter but he could use lard. "I was shocked," she said, "I had never heard of anyone not wanting to buy butter." She had just rendered some lard, however, so she returned with it to get her needed credit. The experience of Hatch was probably typical of the experiences of other Anglo women settlers. Most women produced butter and lard for use but only a few marketed it. Lard had a ready sale as few Hispanic families raised hogs, but wanted lard for cooking. Lucille Tatreault of Mesilla Valley remembered selling lard to Hispanic neighbors.[17]

Some women did sell dairy products. When Stella Hatch moved to the Mesilla Valley, she sold butter there—fifteen to sixteen pounds a week. Tatreault also found a market for butter in Las Cruces. Edna Gholson remembered selling cream from their dairy near Tucumcari in the 1920s. Doña Ana had a dairy project in 1921 where four families sold two pounds of butter a week at seventy-five cents a pound and made $78 a year. Extension records mention dairying principally as a male occupation, however. Some girls enrolled in extension clubs to raise dairy cows in 1921 and the female tradition of dairying must have lingered on in practice but males received most support for managing commercial dairies. Extension reports reflect little support for market production of butter by farm women.[18]

Poultry raising more likely occupied women in New Mexico. Here again, the practice seems to have been regional and shifting. The extension agent in Union, Edith Hurley, for example, reported that in 1921 on her suggestion families had marketed 105,856 dozen eggs and 9,468 chickens for an income of $35,000. Hurley reported "the farm flock a very profitable part of the farming operation" and that she found "nearly all of the ladies and many of the men interested in poultry." Florence St. John marketed eggs in El Paso from a flock started with 15,000 chicks. Later she sold eggs to stores and restaurants in Las Cruces. She and her husband found the income from chickens more steady than that from cotton, which they also raised. Florence Hill remembered raising turkeys in Chavez County for the Kansas market. Another farm woman remembered sending turkeys from Roosevelt County to Los Angeles in dry ice. She cleared $500 one year. On small farms in Bernalillo County, women were well known for their expertise in poultry. Mrs. J. G. Gentry

---

17. Oral histories of Lucille Tatreault and Stella Hatch, WLNMW, NMSU.

18. State Administration Reports, 1921, NMCAAES, Reel 4, reported some cheese-making but no buttermaking. Doña Ana County, Home Demonstration Agent, Annual Narrative Report, 1921, NMCAAES, Reel 4, reported that women made cheese and butter for home use only and that dairies exported milk to El Paso.

headed the Bernalillo Poultry Association in 1925. Other women appear in the records as poultry experts.[19]

But developing a poultry business was beginning to require a market expertise that farm women had not needed traditionally. Egg merchants in cities were picky. They wanted eggs that kept in warm weather. This meant eggs could not be fertile so hens had to be kept from roosters. Purebred chickens, fed with animal feed, culled regularly, and kept in well-built poultry houses was what extension agents recommended. In 1925, New Mexico imported one-half of the poultry products consumed. Still, hundreds of New Mexico women did develop poultry businesses. The high cost of feed during the drought of the 1930s seems to have driven many of these small poultry keepers out of business. By 1936, 70 percent of eggs used in the counties of Bernalillo and Valencia were shipped in from outside the county. By 1939, the town of Santa Fe was importing most of its eggs from Kansas City. Yet credit at markets for chickens and eggs as well as the bartering of eggs with neighbors persisted through the period.[20]

In the north Hispanic women relied on chile as their main cash and credit crop. As urban areas developed, rural women found a ready market for red chile. They picked and strung chile, then hung it on the walls of their adobes to dry. A crop was often estimated by the number of strings produced. Relatives and neighbors gathered at harvest time to work at stringing *ristras*. Merchants accepted strings for credit at their stores. One could buy almost anything with a ristra. Women also ground chile, which stores then marketed. When the Farm Security Administration estimated income for loans, they carefully noted the number of "strings" of chile produced the year before, along with beans, corn, and wheat.[21]

In northern New Mexico, there was also a revival of handcrafts for sale, a movement in which farm women participated. Indians had been creating handcrafts for tourists since the late nineteenth century. The Spanish colonial handcraft revival dated from the early twentieth century. Wood and tin work, and textiles were the main handcrafts revived. Women participated most frequently in the textile revival.[22]

---

19. *Ibid.* Union County did not turn out to be a major poultry region, however. By 1924, farm families were producing only for home use. Union County, County Agent Annual Report, 1924 and Bernalillo County, County Agent Annual Report, 1925, NMCAAES, Reel 7. Oral histories of Florence St. John, Lucille Tatreault, Florence Hill, WLNMW, NMSU.

20. State Administration Reports, 1925, Poultry, and Bernalillo, Annual Report, Home Demonstration Agent, 1935, Santa Fe County Annual Report, 1935, Reel 17, and Santa Fe, Annual Report, Home Demonstration Agent, 1939, NMCAAES, Reel 22.

21. Farm Security Administration, Rehabilitation Loan Application, Record Group 96, National Archives.

22. Sarah Nestor, *The Native Market of the Spanish New Mexican Craftsmen: Santa Fe, 1933–1940* (Santa Fe: Colonial New Mexico Historical Foundation, 1978), 3–4.

Extension agents kept careful records of the value and amount of handcrafts sold by Hispanic families, for they saw the artisan's work as a way to supplement subsistence on small farms in the heavily populated northern counties. Unfortunately, this handcraft market was geared to tourism for the most part rather than to mass urban consumption. It also usually depended on local marketing. When tourists did not tour, as extension agent Felix Armijo reported from Rio Arriba in 1939, many people could not sell their wares.[23]

Families in several northern villages were successful in supplementing their income by selling handcrafts. In one of these villages, Chimayo, east of Española, families had long depended upon income from male migration to work in sheep camps, lumber mills, mines, smelters, and railroads, as well as from weaving. This weaving dated back to the nineteenth century and Chimayo blankets had gained income and fame for the community. In the 1920s, women from Chimayo took the weaving skills to Cundiyo, about twenty-six miles north of Santa Fe. There more than half of the families were weaving blankets by the 1930s. But neither at Chimayo nor Cundiyo could the expert weavers bring in enough money to provide a sufficient income for families. Most also depended on tourists who came to their villages. When no tourists came, their income shrank.[24]

For villages that could not depend on tourists, the Santa Fe artisan's market was of some assistance. From 1934 to 1940, a group of Santa Fe philanthropists established what they called the Native Market to provide an outlet for artisans. Curio stores and a few factories that featured Spanish colonial crafts were flourishing by the early 1920s, and a revival of Spanish New Mexican folklore, architecture, and crafts was in full swing. Author Mary Austin and artist Frank Applegate founded the Spanish Colonial Arts Society in 1925. Concha Ortiz y Pino established the Colonial Hispanic Crafts School at Galisteo in 1929. The Normal School at El Rito began offering craft classes in 1930 and Santa Fe schools under supervisor Nina Otero Warren soon began offering similar courses. The federal government added its support and funding for vocational training in the arts. For urban Anglos and artists, the arts revival was tinged with a romantic conservatism about preserving the "native" past. For farm families, it was a way of modernizing to survive agricultural hard times.[25]

In 1934 a wealthy Anglo, Leonora Curtin, subsidized the opening of the Native Market, an outlet for only the best quality crafts. The market

---

23. Annual Report, Rio Arriba, Felix Armijo, 1939, NMCAAES, Reel 22.
24. Descriptions of weaving and economic conditions at Chimayo and Cundiyo are in Farm Security Administration, RG 96, National Archives.
25. Nestor, *Native Market*, 11–20.

was an important outlet for yarn, weaving, and colcha, traditional wool embroidery that many northern Hispanic women still loved to produce. In the early 1930s, Santa Fe already had a sizeable Anglo artists' community. By 1936, Santa Fe had been "discovered" by the eastern artistic elite. That year *Vogue* magazine carried an article on the Native Market, but the market nevertheless operated at a loss. Rural people found it difficult to use hand skills to compete in an industrial economy. When federally subsidized programs like the WPA and the National Youth Administration offered rural people reasonable wage rates, most quickly abandoned the poorly paying craft work. Women found fewer opportunities in federal work and thus continued to combine crafts with their subsistence farming longer than males. When they had opportunities, young women also moved to the city to obtain better paying jobs.[26]

Still, like canning, handcrafts helped rural families to survive the deepest trough of the depression. A report of Rio Arriba agriculture extension agent Armijo showed that, even with a decline in tourism, women and men produced and sold $5,700 worth of weavings in 1929. Santa Fe women continued to provide the main outlet for rural handcrafts. They organized craft fiestas and the women's exchange market, as well as the Native Market.[27]

Produce markets as well as craft markets underwent a revival in the 1930s. In the 1920s, children usually had the task of selling surplus garden produce by the roadside. Fruit or vegetables piled in old cans, and a farm child, were the main ingredients in this marketing of surplus. As automobiles became more popular in the 1930s, urban dwellers often combined inexpensive touring with food purchases. The number of automobiles, even on farms, increased rapidly in New Mexico in the 1920s and 1930s. To a people frustrated by long distances, the automobile seemed a necessity. The number of automobiles on farms more than doubled between 1920 and 1940, from 6,018 to 15,731. Farmers could now more easily bring produce to town while townspeople could also more easily fetch their own country produce. Rural people took advantage of both.[28]

Roadside stalls became a common sight in the 1930s, replacing the child and pail. Farm families built attractive stalls, and women began to organize and staff them. Bernalillo County was developing roadside markets by 1930. That same year extension agent Armijo reported from Rio Arriba that farm families had sold $3,000 worth of farm products

---

26. *Ibid.*, 31–32.

27. Home Demonstration Agent, Annual Report, 1939, Santa Fe and Rio Arriba, NMCAAES, Reel 23.

28. U.S., Department of Commerce, Bureau of the Census, *United States Census of Agriculture: 1945*, Vol. 1, Part 30, 4.

during the last season at roadside markets. This was an important source of additional cash. In Bernalillo County, farmers also brought their produce in to Albuquerque where they established a farmer's market in 1939. There the extension agent helped raise money and organize the market. Farmers near Albuquerque began to increase their truck farming with a ready market for their produce.[29]

For rural people to survive economically this market production had to be combined with subsistence farming and the cash brought in by males either from off-farm work or the raising and selling of animals and field crops. The records kept by the Farm Rehabilitation agents provide some idea of the rural economy in northern New Mexico in the late 1930s. The federal agents made most loans to Hispanic farm families who owned only a few acres although farm families with larger acreage were also eligible. By 1940, work for wages, most of it off-farm work, was bringing in almost 50 percent of the income of these families. Grants from the federal and state governments were bringing in another third; income from produce and livestock accounted for about one-fourth. Of the off-farm income, mining was by far the most profitable for the families, but income from daughters who taught school was the second most profitable. Teaching brought in more money than any of the male occupations, including sheepherding. To have a farm daughter who taught was to have a substantial income in times when farm products could supply little to families.[30]

While subsistence farming doomed families to a minimal economic level, it nonetheless provided security. Through it, families could hold onto the small acreage they still owned. This was particularly true in the 1920s when men brought in cash from other work. This reliance on subsistence farming and commitment to it was one of the factors that deeply separated thousands of Hispanic farm families and the Anglo experts who most often staffed the extension offices. Time and again, Anglo agents would report that Hispanic families seemed unwilling to change, rooted in traditional ways, sometimes appearing almost inexplicably opposed to sound and reasonable concepts of commercial agriculture.[31]

The conflict over the Middle Rio Grande Conservancy District was the most visible and violent confrontation between traditional and modern values in which farm women were involved. Almost as soon as

---

29. Bernalillo County, Home Demonstration Agent, Annual Report, 1930, 1935, NMCAAES, Reels 12, 17.

30. Joan M. Jensen, "Farm Families Organize Their Work: New Mexico, 1900–1940," paper presented at the New Mexico Family and Community Conference, Albuquerque, New Mexico, July 15, 1983.

31. Comments were frequent from some Anglo agents. See, for example, State Administration, Reports, 1921, and Bernalillo, Annual Report, 1935, NMCAAES, Reels 4, 17.

extension agents went into Valencia County in 1914 and saw the conditions that existed on the irrigated farms there, they dreamed of reclamation. Deforestation in the north in the first two decades of the century had caused silting of the river. Intensive irrigation had resulted in waterlogged acres. By 1920, agricultural agents estimated that 60,000 acres of land in four counties were unusable. It seemed logical and progressive to support schemes for a conservancy district that would develop productive, commercially viable farms.[32]

Urban businessmen apparently saw the plan as one from which they could profit as bond holders of the money that would be raised to finance the project. Farmers owning land benefiting from the project would be taxed to pay for the capital and interest. Farmers would increase their productivity and their income and thus be able to pay increased taxes. Everyone would be happy.[33] Unfortunately, no one consulted with the farm families who were to benefit by the scheme. The state legislature accepted petitions to establish the project from Albuquerque businessmen outside the farming areas, set up a conservancy district with the legal right to tax, and approved the sale of bonds.[34]

By the time engineers had their machinery in place to lay down drainage culverts, angry farmers had organized. They stopped the engineers, tore up the culverts, disarmed the attorney general, and kicked and pushed the directors of the project when they arrived at the confrontation. Officials called for the national guard and Governor Richard Dillon quelled the uprising by arranging for a moratorium on payment of taxes. Farms over twenty acres would have three years and farms under five acres would have five years before beginning tax payments for the improvements. By that time, they could have increased production to pay taxes levied on their farm land. The project went forward despite extreme hostility from the farm families. An Anglo extension agent who had enthusiastically supported the project found farmers hostile to him. "The situation even got so bad, that many farmers when visited by the County Agent, were not even friendly, sometimes very bitter and unfriendly, and at times refused to talk or have any business with the County Agent," R. S. Conroy reported from Valencia County in 1930. His work absolutely at a standstill, he soon left the county.[35]

---

32. Valencia, Annual Report, County Agent, R. S. Conroy, 1930, NMCAAES, Reel 12; Brian McDonald, John Tysseling, Michael Browde, and Lee Brown, *Case Studies in the Development of New Mexico Water Resources Institutions: The Middle Rio Grande Conservancy District and Urban Water Pricing* (New Mexico Water Resources Research Institute, Technical Competition Report, Project N. 1345640, 1981), 10.

33. *Ibid.*, 13–14.

34. *Ibid.*

35. Valencia County Agent, Annual Report, 1930, NMCAAES, Reel 12; Calkins, "Reconnaissance," 58. Conroy was gone from Valencia County by 1935.

After the moratorium expired in 1934, the farmers refused to pay. Although few foreclosures occurred, much land changed hands. The state dared not move to foreclose lest they encourage open warfare. But many farmers grew discouraged and sold out. Between 1934 and 1936, Anglo ownership of land in the conservancy district rose by 7 percent. As one report concluded, Hispanic farmers would soon disappear and be replaced by Anglo commercial farmers.[36]

A similar dispossession of Hispanic farm families had already taken place in the Mesilla Valley as a result of the building of the Elephant Butte Dam. There Hispanic men and women became the laborers for new cotton farms in the 1920s. The change had taken place with little overt conflict, however, a condition that led state officials to believe that similar changes could be effected in the Middle Rio Grande Conservancy District. Despite the opposition of the Valencia farmers, this second dispossession took place. The refusal of many farmers to pay back taxes simply led to a federal assumption of state obligations. Federal funds eventually rescued the project financially and allowed its completion.[37]

In the north, similar antagonism might have flared under the crushing impact of drought and depression. In these counties, however, Hispanic farmers had firm political control and there were no conservancy plans. County commissioners appropriated money for extension agents with the proviso they be Hispanic. In Rio Arriba County, Fabiola Cabeza de Baca arrived in 1929 to began a successful decade of work among Hispanic women, and agent Armijo found Hispanic families willing to work with him on changes. Both de Baca and Armijo reported good relations with the farmers, and a willingness on the part of Hispanics to experiment. Both exhibited understanding of how to work with these families. Armijo reported after de Baca's first year that her work had influenced the whole community favorably, men as well as women, and made his work much more successful.[38]

De Baca was thirty-five when she arrived in Rio Arriba County as county extension agent. Born in Las Vegas, New Mexico, her mother died when she was five, and she went to live on her grandparents' hacienda, some miles from Las Vegas. Then she studied with the Sisters of Loretto and began teaching in a small rural school. She spent some time in Spain, some time on her grandparents' ranch, and then returned to school to receive her degree in Home Economics from the agricultural college in Las Cruces. After training ten weeks in San Miguel County, she began work in August 1939. For the next ten years, she sent lengthy

---

36. *Ibid.*
37. McDonald, et al., *Case Studies*, 43–47.
38. Rio Arriba County, Narrative Report, Extension Agent, F. A. Armijo, 1930, NMCAAES, Reel 12.

reports back to headquarters in Las Cruces describing her work with Hispanic women—a unique record of the lives of rural women.[39]

De Baca's reports on her work in Rio Arriba and Santa Fe counties are important both for what they tell us about the women and for what they document about the effectiveness of Hispanic agents in working in predominantly Hispanic communities. They also indicate the importance of work with women for the success of the extension program as a whole. De Baca concentrated on food because that seemed most important to the families and to the survival of their subsistence farms. De Baca gave demonstrations in women's homes, organized youth clubs, located club leaders among teachers and mission workers, organized clubs for adult women, and began a home economics column in the newspaper *El Nuevo Mexicano* that featured translations of recipes. Before long, she had helped Dixon women organize their own club house and helped county health officials start two clinics.[40]

De Baca's work accomplished the changes the extension service wished without creating tension and hostility. The women provided support for the changes men wished to make because they understood how their own work could change to benefit themselves and their families. When the depression of 1932–33 and drought of 1933–34 nearly decimated northern farm communities, the work of de Baca bore fruit.

The drought hit farm families before there were federal programs. The state responded as best it could. In Rio Arriba and Santa Fe counties, field crops failed and there was not enough fodder for animals. Many weakened animals could not survive the second year of the drought, and by that second year families were in danger not just of losing animals but of starvation itself. By this time, extension agents had already started counseling families to concentrate their energies on family gardens. They helped provide seeds. De Baca expanded and intensified her training in canning both vegetables and meat. When the federal government finally arrived with its program to purchase cattle, families were ready to butcher and can the healthiest of the starving animals.

No Rio Arriba families had pressure cookers when de Baca arrived in 1929, and only a few had them in Santa Fe and Taos. By 1935, thousands of pressure cookers existed in Rio Arriba, Santa Fe, and Taos counties. Families bought them cooperatively and shared them. Men put their cash earnings toward buying these tools for women. In 1935, extension agent J. W. Ramirez reported that the previous year "would have been one of the worst calamities ever experienced had it not been for timely financial aid from the Agricultural Drought Service and the

---

39. Oral history of Fabiola Cabeza de Baca Gilbert, NMSU.

40. Rio Arriba and Santa Fe Counties, Home Demonstration Work, 1930, Fabiola Cabeza de Baca, NMCAAES, Reel 12.

food preservation program." Taos and Santa Fe county families survived for the same reasons. Better than 90 percent of the farm families there preserved enough food for the following year. Prodigious canning on subsistence farms allowed the rural population to remain on the land and to feed itself during one of the severest droughts and depressions in New Mexico history. The survival of Rio Arriba, Santa Fe, and Taos farm families during these years was the best example of how state and federal agencies working in concert with, instead of against, the wishes of a rural community, could provide crucial services.[41]

Pressure cookers, which spread so quickly through Rio Arriba, Santa Fe, and Taos counties in the early 1930s, are perhaps the best material objects with which to trace the transfer of technology to farm women during the 1920s and 1930s. Pressure cookers became a necessary tool for most farm women, and one they most commonly purchased and used. Other types of household technology—washers, irons, refrigerators—had to wait electrification that reached rural families slowly and unevenly. Of technological systems desired by rural women, water was the most important. Sewing machines were too expensive for many families during the 1920s. Pressure cookers, water systems, and sewing machines, however, are the three technologies that best reflect changes in farm women's physical lives during these years.[42]

Pressure cookers were just being introduced in the wealthier farm families at the end of World War I. The pressure cooker was a considerable time saver for women who needed to can, for it greatly reduced the time required to process canned vegetables, according to one account from five hours to eighty minutes. It also offered greater insurance that the processed vegetables would be safe when canned in home kitchens. The extension service published bulletins that explained use of pressure cookers in English in 1925 and in Spanish in 1931.[43]

The problem for most farm women was not unwillingness to use new technology but inability to accumulate the cash to purchase it. Pressure cookers sold for $18 in 1921, an amount of money that women seldom spent on household tools. Doña Ana County, where there were many wealthier farmers and a great deal of educational work by the

---

41. Santa Fe County. Annual Report, 1935, J. W. Ramirez. Taos County, Annual Report, 1935, NMCAAES, Reel 17.

42. Rio Arriba and Santa Fe Counties, Home Demonstration Work, 1929, Fabiola Cabeza de Baca, Santa Fe County, Home Demonstration Work, Fabiola Cabeza de Baca, 1930, NMCAAES, Reel 12. Report of Home Demonstration Agent Work in New Mexico for the year ending November 30, 1921, Mary B. Richardson, NMCAAES, Reel 4.

43. *Ibid.*, Doña Ana County, Home Demonstration Agent, Annual Report, 1939, NMCAAES, Reel 22. Grace B. Luna, *Canning Club Work* (Extension Circular 83, March 1925) and Fabiola Cabeza de Baca, *Boletin de Conservar* (Extension Circular 106, May 1931).

college extension agents, led the way in cooperative purchase of pressure cookers. In 1921, agents reported the importance of acquiring cookers in Doña Ana, and arranged to purchase them in quantities for $13.50 each. At least 265 women bought them that year. So many women now owned them, reported the agent, that demonstrations were no longer needed. By 1939, the agent reported that almost all farm families had them. Thereafter, pressure cookers were seldom discussed in reports from Doña Ana County.[44]

Cooperative canning provided a solution for many farm women who could not afford their own pressure cookers. Agents helped set up community canneries. Maud Doty helped set up a successful community cannery in Bernalillo County in 1925 where women installed steam canning equipment with a 500 quart a day capacity and tinned everything from peaches to whole beef. During 1934, the federal government set up a canning project in Taos County to provide work for community women. That year women canned over 12,000 cans for the Federal Emergency Relief Administration to distribute to needy families in addition to cans for their own home use. Agents estimated women filled 43,000 number two tin cans in the first eleven weeks of operation and eventually 110,000 cans and jars. The Resettlement Administration also budgeted money in Bernalillo County in 1935 to purchase canning equipment for many women who had never canned before. In Rio Arriba County, federal funds helped women buy jars and pressure cookers. There women preserved food in over 46,000 containers in 1939.

Canning then, even for women who could not afford their own pressure cookers, was the main technological change for rural women in New Mexico during these years. While urban women were acquiring indoor plumbing, electricity, and such appliances as irons, these rural women were still devoting their time and acquiring technology to preserve food. While most farm women in New Mexico had pressure cookers by the end of the 1930s, few yet had electric irons, because as late as 1945 only one-third had electricity. Urban women, meanwhile, were using electric irons and buying most of their food in cans.[45]

Water systems were more costly to acquire and much more rare than food preservation tools during this period. The Doña Ana County

44. Bernalillo County, Home Demonstration Agent, Annual Report, 1925 and 1935, Reels 7, 17; Taos County, Annual Report, 1934, Reel 16, NMCAAES.

45. Some women in eastern New Mexico and perhaps elsewhere did have access by 1929 to gas irons. Joan M. Jensen and Mary Johnson, "What's in a Butter Churn? Objects and Women's Oral History," *Frontiers*, 7 (Fall 1983). Bernalillo County reported two gasoline systems for irons in 1921, Bernalillo County, Home Demonstration Agent, Narrative Report, 1921, Reel 4, and 25 houses with electricity in 1925, Home Demonstration, Annual Report, 1925, Reel 7, NMCAAES.

home demonstration agent reported proudly in 1921 that she was helping a ranch family to install an entire demonstration bathroom. The cost for supplies alone was $120, a sum that few but the wealthiest could afford. In Curry County, the home demonstration agent reported the importance of a kitchen water supply for her farm women and the industriousness of one woman in acquiring a system. Here, too, even with labor supplied by the family, the system cost the woman $90 for the tank and water pipes. Most farm women still carried their own water as they recalled in oral histories. For those fortunate few who got even partial running water, the saving in time and effort was impressive. The home demonstration agent who reported on the Curry County system noted that the farm woman had previously walked an estimated 260 miles a year bringing water from the well to her kitchen. Of almost 30,000 New Mexico farms in 1945, only 28 percent had running water. That meant 72 percent of all farm women still carried their water.[46]

Sewing machines were less expensive than water systems and less dependent upon males for installation, although women might remain dependent upon men for repairs. Clothing construction remained one of the most gender-defined of all farm tasks. Young men never joined clothing clubs although they were most popular among young women. Yet, the use of clothing construction equipment that cost money made little headway because farm women felt they could not spend money on clothing. The home demonstration agent in Taos County reported that women there "found it difficult to get even the price of a commercial pattern," then selling for a few cents. When hat making became popular in the early 1920s, and times were good in Union County, women there were able to order wire hat frames from the dime store for ten to thirty-five cents and delightedly made summer hats from dried corn shucks. Even before the depression deepened in the 1930s, demonstration agents reported that neither girls nor women could afford to purchase sewing supplies in counties like Otero, for "the people have hardly had enough to eat." Flour sacks were a necessity for sewing projects. Remodeling and maintaining older clothing became the focus of much of the women's attention. Two hundred Doña Ana County women reported making an average of two garments and remodeling ten during 1921. They pooled their scraps in a "community bag."[47]

---

46. This cost included a hot water tank, bath tub and sink, pipe and drain boards. State Administration reports, 1921, Reel 4. NMCAAES. Bernalillo County reported one power washing machine that year. Quote from Joan M. Jensen, "Recovering Her Story: Learning the History of Farm Women," Paper presented at the National Extension Homemakers Conference, Laramie, Wyoming, August 3, 1983. Oral history of Nina Griffin, Mesilla Valley, reported having to carry water a half a block on their farm, WLNMW, NMSU.

47. State Adminstration Reports, 1921, Reel 4; Narrative Report of Mrs. Edith Hurley, Home Demonstration Agent, Union County, 1921, Reel 4; State Administration Reports, 1925, Reel 7.

No easily obtainable statistics exist for sewing machine purchases in New Mexico. Non-electric sewing machines sold for anywhere from thirty to eighty dollars in 1930 mail order catalogs. Farm families frequently ordered from these catalogs because towns were so widely dispersed and roads still largely unimproved. In fact, home sewing became a necessity even for women who had never sewed previously, because mail order clothes were unsatisfactory and towns so difficult to get to. Most farm women sewed their own clothes but even foot-powered treadle machines were not common. The operation of sewing machine clinics in Doña Ana County in 1921, and a record of 292 home repairs there, indicates that middle-class farm women in some counties had sewing machines. But these clinics did not appear in the north until late in the 1930s. In 1939, San Miguel County women had few sewing machines and only one girl could afford to purchase material for a sewing project. By the late 1930s, however, young girls were showing a much greater interest in sewing, perhaps because so many were considering moving to urban areas to find work.[48]

Rather interestingly, creative hand work does not show up in most communities. Agents trained in home economics tended to discourage creative work of this sort because they felt farm women needed to concentrate on practical skills. Still the impulse to create beautiful and not necessarily functional items existed among some farm communities. De Baca mentioned the large number of Hispanic women who enjoyed doing colcha embroidery and other needlework during the three months a year they did not work outdoors. She wished the extension service had listed it as a project so that clubs could work on it. Here was a missed chance to combine the creative interests of women with support for a marketable product. An agent visiting the isolated village of Pilar in Taos County in 1921 mentioned seeing "oceans of crocheting and other fancy work" in the homes of Hispanic women she visited. Quilts do not show up in records of the counties selected for this study except in Union County in 1935 when the agent reported club women making 115 quilts. Where a quilt tradition existed, it probably came in with the homesteaders from Oklahoma and Texas. But women there were such hard working pioneers that they may not have had time to sew quilts, at least not the magnificent quilts that older women produced later when freed from incessant work and absorbing poverty.[49]

---

48. Doña Ana County, Home Demonstration Agent, Annual Narrative Report, 1921, Reel 4, Annual Report, Child Development and Parent Education, 1939, Reel 22, NMCAAES. Sewing machine prices from Sears, Roebuck and Company, *Spring and Summertime Catalog* (1930).

49. Second Annual Report for Year Ending June 30, 1916. Reel 1, NMCAAES contains early disparagement of "fancy work." Rio Arriba and Santa Fe Counties, Home Demonstration Work, Fabiola Cabeza de Baca, 1939, Reel 12, State Administration Reports, 1921,

Technology benefited a few women during these decades but organizing probably helped them more. To facilitate their work in reaching women, agents encouraged women to form clubs to decide what they needed. These clubs benefited poor women and women of different ethnic groups to the extent that agents oriented their work to the needs of these women. As such, the clubs provided an important forum for farm women. They met, exchanged joys and laments, and received support from each other in these clubs.

Organizing was not always dependent on agents. In counties like Union, for example, older farm organizations with hundreds of men and women members were in existence when agents arrived. Home demonstration agent Edith Hurley reported 250 Farm Bureau members in 1921 with "the ladies . . . as much, or more interested in all lines of work as the men." Two women and three men assumed leadership in organizing the Farm Bureau there and it flourished in the eastern part of the county. In some areas agents skillfully pulled farm women together into organizations, where they found new strength together. Sometimes club women, like Bernalillo County club women in 1921, used their organizational strength politically to maintain county financial support for home demonstration agents. The state narrative for Bernalillo County read: "There was some doubt about the work's being continued in Bernalillo County for the coming year, and a great deal of pressure was brought to bear on the commissioners by the women of the county, and some of the men, as well as the Director of Extension. . . . The rural women are working to save the work." In Union County, on the other hand, the agent reported, "the new County Commissioners have the reduction mania and there is some danger of the work being cut out. The women are making every effort to hold it." Women there failed to convince male county commissioners to fund a female home demonstration agent even though they continued to fund a male agricultural extension agent.[50]

Some clubs welcomed agents; some operated successfully, aloof and separate; some crumbled without the agent's support. The two

---

May Report, Reel 4, Union County, Home Demonstration Agent, M. Kathryn Woodbridge, 1935, Reel 17, NMCAAES. Patricia Cooper and Norma Bradley Buferd, *The Quilters: Women and Domestic Art* (Garden City, New York: Doubleday, 1977).

50. Union County, Narrative Report of Mrs. Edith F. Hurley, Home Demonstration Agent, 1921, Reel 4, NMCAAES. "History of Extension Work in Union County, 1916–1939," in Union County, Annual Report, 1939, reported 500 members organized in a society of "farmer's equity," when the agent arrived in 1916. Whether this was populist or socialist is not clear but members assisted the agent. A Farmers and Stockmen Bureau was organized in 1916 and grew rapidly. The Farm Bureau was apparently organized about the same time. Edith Hurley was not retained after 1921 and Union County had no Home Demonstration Agent from 1928 to 1933 State Administration Reports, 1921, Bernalillo Narrative Report, Reel 4, NMCAAES.

Two women on their homestead, San Agustin Plains, 1939. Courtesy of Rio Grande Historical Collections, New Mexico State University Library.

decades saw impressive organizing among women. By the end of the Depression large numbers of rural women in New Mexico were not only organized for the first time but also organized more effectively than many urban women. Women organized in Farm Bureau clubs, in rural women's clubs, and in extension clubs. Each offered rural women important experience.

Farm Bureau women were among the first to organize. The Doña Ana Farm Bureau was one of the largest and strongest units in the state and women in that county were probably the best organized. Farm Bureau membership was by family but members soon learned that the gender division of labor and special gender concerns of women made it more comfortable for them to meet separately. The disadvantage of separate groups was that it segregated women from meetings where important farming skills were learned and shared by men. The advantage was that separate locals gave women space and time to be by themselves to discuss their needs away from the men. Farm Bureau women in Doña Ana County formed women's locals in every community. They discussed and planned their projects, and told agents what they wanted of them. They provided a strong support network for almost 300 members by 1925. Women helped raise money to establish a "Rest Room" for farm women in the Temple of Agriculture, furnished it, and used it in turn to raise money for other projects. Doña Ana Farm Bureau members provided experience for community leadership and needed service for women.

The main criticism that can be made is that the Farm Bureau apparently did not extend its base deeply into the poorer Anglo or Hispanic farming communities. Farm Bureau members remained composed primarily of Anglo women from medium-sized farms. Their organization gave these average farm families important leverage in the community. Nina Griffin later remarked that farm women were better organized than Las Cruces women in the 1930s. Moreover, when federal programs promised assistance to communities to modernize, these rural women led the way. Griffin remembered wanting paved roads and working with other farm women to raise money to pay for materials when the Works Progress Administration offered free labor.[51]

Elsewhere, Farm Bureau organizations seemed to rise and fall. For a while, Valencia County boasted the only Farm Bureau in central New Mexico. Then during the conservancy conflict, it disintegrated. The agent there, who had begun to organize the Farm Bureau, soon found that he was doing all the work. Farm families simply refused to cooperate and the agent let it fold. Union County had a flourishing Farm Bureau for a few years. By 1934, however, that county's Farm Bureau was also gone. In other areas, Farm Bureaus were never formed. Men formed marketing associations for themselves, such as the Bean Growers Association, that left women out; or farmers remained unorganized.[52]

Where no Farm Bureau existed, women organized rural women's clubs. These clubs apparently never federated. One club once affiliated with the State Federation of Women's Clubs, but the agent sadly noted that they were moving away from home economics. Most simply had an independent club that rose and fell with the fortunes and interests of community women. These clubs took names that reflected the attitudes of their communities: the Bluewater Food Club in Valencia County, Volcanic Canning Club of Union County, the Miercoles Club in Bernalillo County. The clubs usually concentrated on family and community affairs, and left few records but those by extension agents. Extension agents worked with these clubs, asking them to make plans for projects and to decide what information they needed from agents. Agents did demonstrations, showed films, suggested new projects, and acted as outside catalysts.

---

51. Doña Ana County, Home Demonstration Agent, Annual Report, Sara Van Vleck, 1925, Reel 7; Doña Ana County, Home Demonstration Agent, Annual Report, 1921, Reel 4, NMCAAES. Oral history of Nina Griffin, Mesilla Valley, WLNMW, NMSU.

52. Valencia, County Agent, Annual Report, 1929. Reel 11, 1930, Reel 12; Union, Esther B. Call Report, 1934, Reel 16, NMCAAES.

Eventually agents began to organize women into Extension Clubs that could function throughout the county. Taos had 500 members in twenty-three of these clubs by 1935. In these clubs, although the agents assumed more responsibility, they attempted to have farm women do most of the organizing. De Baca was especially successful in organizing Rio Arriba County women who had little experience with formal community organizing. She wrote in one report: "Outside of dances, Church festivals, and weddings, they never get together for social activities." But the women responded to her organizing activities. "It has been a change in their lives to get together once a month regularly," de Baca wrote. "They may not have accomplished very much materially, but they have gained much spiritually. It has started them to think along the social side of life."When one woman pleaded being too busy, another retorted: "If we have an excuse to leave our work for one day a month, we ought to take advantage of it even if it is only to get away from the work." For these women it was a rest, as one said, "from the daily routine of house and outdoor work."[53]

Whatever the club, farm women joined most often when clubs gave them new skills and encouraged them to share their own. Clubs provided important psychological support as well. One Colfax County farm woman recalled later joining a homemakers club after having a nervous breakdown. Other women remembered grabbing up small children and escaping to meetings where they simply enjoyed each other's company, laughing, joking, and swapping experiences. "I just picked up my baby and went," recalled Frances Mathews of Colfax County.[54]

As social organizations rather than economic organizations, clubs could do little to change the patterns that were making it increasingly difficult for subsistence farms to survive. Hispanic women in many counties were already moving off farms and into urban neighborhoods. Or they were continuing to live in villages but increasingly dependent on off-farm work. For these women, the clubs had little to offer.

Still, with the help of agencies and agents, their own hard work and resilient spirits, many women did survive as farmers and kept their families together on the land through hard times. Looking back on that experience, some things seemed particularly fortunate to the survivors. The fact that most families suffered about equally, that they usually could get enough food, that their children respected the hard work of the parents and understood that the work the family performed together was necessary for survival were among those mentioned later in oral histories. Women worked hard but they took pride in their work, whether in

53. Home Demonstration Work Carried Out in Rio Arriba and Santa Fe Counties, 1930, Reel 12, Santa Fe, Home Demonstration Work, 1935, Reel, 17, NMCAAES.

54. Jensen, "Recovering Her Story."

field or farm house. "Yes, I *was* busy," recalled sharecropper Ellen Grubbs Reaves. "And if you think I didn't work, you just wasn't there," exclaimed Edna Gholson when she remembered her hard work boarding highway workers to feed her family and pay debts. But perhaps Nona Berry captured the positive feelings that farm women must have often felt, after they had worked long and hard at tasks they could perform skillfully, when she asked, "Did you ever take a fine baking of bread out of the oven and felt like you had done real well?"[55]

During these decades women's work on the farm was essential and crucial for the survival of farm families. Told from documents and from their own oral remembrances, women's history gives a fuller picture than what has been traditionally termed agricultural history. It is proof that agricultural history must give way to a true rural history in which women and men are represented in the full context of their lives on the land.

55. Oral histories of Ellen Grubbs Reaves and Edna Gholson, WLNMW, NMSU; Jensen, "Recovering Her Story."

THE IDEAL RURAL SOUTHERN WOMAN AS SEEN BY *PROGRESSIVE FARMER* IN THE 1930s

Pamela Tyler
Tulane University

The abundance of literature concerning the history of women in America has made it clear that American women of the past were of necessity as hardy, as resourceful, and as hard-working as their masculine counterparts. Yet these women were expected to be hardy, resourceful, and hard-working only within their proper sphere, which was judged to be the home. Inside the sheltering walls of the home, "the weaker sex" might rule, but she must never venture beyond her domestic kingdom to challenge man in his proper sphere, which was judged to be everything beyond the home.[1] Some lines from Tennyson's mid-Victorian epic "The Princess" summarize this doctrine of separate spheres:

> Man for the field and woman for the hearth:
> Man for the sword and for the needle she:
> Man with the head and woman with the heart:
> Man to command and woman to obey:
> All else confusion.[2]

This article offers a study of the rural Southern white women of the 1930s who belonged to the middle class, those who were wives of farm owners. The study focuses on the advice given them in the pages of the *Progressive Farmer and Southern Ruralist* (hereafter called *Progressive Farmer*), a popular farm journal from whose pages rural matrons gained or had reinforced their notions of what constituted the ideal Southern woman. The *Progressive Farmer* was chosen because it was the most widely read farm journal in the South, with a circulation of over 900,000 copies monthly in the 1930s. Clarence Poe, its editor for an incredible sixty-five years (1899-1964), believed that "journalists significantly shape public opinion" and considered the *Progressive Farmer* his "podium" for exhorting Southerners to adopt certain modern methods while holding tenaciously to traditional

---

1. A very helpful history of women and the family in America is Carl Degler, *At Odds* (New York, 1980). Two other books which deal specifically with Southern women and their lifestyles are Anne Firor Scott, *The Southern Lady: From Pedestal to Politics 1830-1930* (Chicago, 1970) and Margaret Jarman Hagood, *Mothers of the South* (New York, 1939). A seminal piece of work for understanding the concept of the "ideal woman" is Barbara Welter, "The Cult of True Womanhood, 1820-1860," *American Quarterly* 18 (Summer 1966), 151-80.

2. Alfred, Lord Tennyson, "The Princess," in *Poems of Tennyson* (London, 1908), 331.

values. This study will examine the advice of Poe's admittedly didactic magazine to the South's women in the 1930s and will show that such advice was markedly similar to that given American women a century earlier.[3]

Barbara Welter's influential article, "The Cult of True Womanhood, 1820-1860," an examination of the advice given by women's magazines in the forty years before the Civil War, forms the basis for the conclusion that in the 1930s, Southern women were being held to standards of "true womanhood" that in some important ways varied little from the ideal held up to their great-grandmothers. Welter found that nineteenth-century periodicals stressed four cardinal virtues for women—piety, purity, submissiveness, and domesticity. A century later, *Progressive Farmer's* writers, who heartily embraced the doctrine of two separate spheres for men and women, included in women's sphere the tasks of managing the household, rearing the children, and a more nebulous duty which may be summed up as instilling and maintaining virtue in themselves and others. "Women always make men better or worse, you know," confided a character in an August 1935 short story. "No matter what a man is," wrote a male reader, "he wants a wife that is white with purity, tender, and sympathetic." Such behaviors as dancing, cigarette-smoking, and card-playing received no criticism in print, but drinking was blasted unequivocally. ". . . [W]omen sitting upon the bar chairs in our tavern saloons drinking the stuff that vitiates and cheapens their ideals . . . [was] a sickening sight," according to the minister's monthly column. A poem entitled "Home Abiding Women" presented the idea that quiet, selfless, ever-serving homemakers would be the ones to whom men would turn "from any stress, from any fresh disaster" because they would give them strength to deal with the wicked world and provide a link with God. Women's sphere also included the tasks of preserving country churches, rural values, old recipes, family graveyards, and ancestral homes.[4]

The rural woman's chief duties were the age-old Hestian tasks of homemaking—cooking, cleaning, laundering, caring for the sick, gardening, sewing, dairying. The toil that constituted keeping house was

3. Joseph A. Cote, "Clarence Hamilton Poe: The Farmer's Voice, 1899-1964," *Agricultural History* 53 (January 1979), 30.

4. Carl Holliday, "The Awakening of Jim," *Progressive Farmer* (August 1935), 8; Ruth Ryan, "Continuing the Pet Peeves," Ibid. (February 1937), 50; Rev. J. W. Holland, "Un-Repealable Laws," Ibid. (February 1934), 2; Grace Noll Crowell, "Home Abiding Women," Ibid. (December 1935), 47. (All subsequent references are to magazine articles from issues of *Progressive Farmer*.)

truly formidable. Preparing three hot meals daily for a large family, often using a wood stove which required prodigious quantities of stovewood, shunning the more expensive, bought foods in favor of cooking and baking "from scratch," cost the farm woman greatly in time, her endless routine often beginning before day and concluding sometimes well after dark. Indeed, the rationale of one advertisement for tractor tires, which asked, "Wife washing dishes by lamp light?" was that by allowing a farmer to plow faster and complete his work earlier, the tires would spare the wife also "because she then wouldn't have a dog-tired husband dragging in for a late supper every night."[5]

"Homemaking is now and always has been the most important work of women. . . . Some actual drudgery, much routine, but the happiest, most satisfying work in all the world!" an article trilled in 1938. Since homemaking was "the center of interest for girls and women," *Progressive Farmer* sponsored a contest to select the best letter describing the duties of the rural homemaker. The winning letter featured a mock classified ad enumerating what farmers expected of their wives.

> Wanted—women who are good wives, mothers, homemakers, cooks, housekeepers, seamstresses, dairy-women, managers, buyers, saleswomen, horticulturalists, poultry raisers, livestock raisers, carpenters, mechanics, financiers, nurses, canners and preservers, laundry women, interior decorators, and landscape gardeners. Must be healthy, good sports, and attractive.—The Farmers of America.[6]

In October 1933 *Progressive Farmer* began printing letters written in response to a request that farm women tell how they made money. The letters reflected the women's pride in their financial contributions and a resourcefulness which the editors clearly admired. "We wish we could publish all these stories," wrote the women's editor, Sallie Hill. "What an inspiration they hold!" The twenty-eight letters published (out of over 250 submitted) formed a catalogue of ingenuity, toil, and determination. Women raised rabbits, helped neighbors with sewing, gave permanent waves, sold popcorn, hatched and raised turkeys, dug fish bait, baked pies and cakes, and sold poultry and produce to hotels and restaurants in nearby towns. Each letter detailed the unselfish ways in which the writer had used the money earned,

5. Goodyear tire advertisement (April 1939), 15.

6. Maude Richman Calvert, "Homemaking as a Vocation" (February 1938), 26; "Wanted: Male and Female Vote—What are the tasks for a housewife?" (November 1936), 46.

prompting *Progressive Farmer* to comment approvingly, "Farm women are always willing to help in any way they can with the running expenses of the home. . . ."[7] Significantly, all the efforts acknowledged involved facets of woman's traditional role. There were no letters from anyone who worked outside the home for wages; thus, no deviations from woman's sphere reached print in *Progressive Farmer*.

The only bona fide reason for a woman to earn money outside her sphere of the home and its environs was her failure to marry. Writing of alternatives to homemaking, a female columnist, "with an encouraging smile to all the girls and young women who think they are certain to be old maids," noted that "four out of five girls will marry and take charge of their own homes." For the one unfortunate in five whose spinsterhood would presumably preclude her ever having a home of her own, acceptable remunerative activities included "chicken raising, gardening, cooking for campers, catering for special parties, preserving and canning food for sale, laundering, preparing gift packages, caring for children, serving as companion for old people." Occupations in the home economics field (home demonstration agent, food editor, dietician) also were held in esteem, but the highest laurels were reserved for the nurse. "The extreme satisfaction of having served humanity well and nobly is the chief remuneration of a nurse and for women this profession is perhaps the greatest, next to wifehood and motherhood."[8] (Welter found that antebellum woman's role as nurse was also especially honored—"one of the most important functions of woman.") Women's occupations rated approval and esteem on the basis of service to others, not on the usual male yardstick of income and authority. Under no circumstances was rural Southern woman to forsake her sphere to invade man's in quest of a livelihood; she was to make her way by her own special talents, which included feeding, clothing, and nurturing others.

Welter concluded that for antebellum women "marriage was the proper sphere for the exercise of domestic virtues" and that "a woman's whole interest should be focused on her husband." A woman without a husband was an anomaly in the 1930s just as certainly as in the 1830s. *Progressive Farmer* not surprisingly devoted considerable space to advice to young women on how to behave toward young men in a manner that would lead to matrimony. An article in the maga-

7. Lois P. Dowdle, "How These Women Make Money" (October 1933), 5, 20.
8. "If Not Farming or Homemaking, What?" (March 1938), 20; Maude Richman Calvert, "Do You Want to Be a Nurse?" (July 1938), 18.

zine's fiftieth anniversary issue summed up what its author viewed as significant differences between women of the nineteenth century and of 1936.

> Don't be a sissy seems to be the admonition of the times to modern young women. You must work and play hard to get your share of the joys of living. Women today are able to think for themselves, and at the same time know how to be gently tractable. The fainting heroine who threw up her white hands and collapsed into a bunch of petticoats now has emerged as a capable young woman who rides surfboards, swims, and plays a hard game of tennis . . . . We still admire the womanly woman. Nobody likes to see a woman who is a poor imitation of a man. But we are glad she has learned to take life simply without too many artifices.[9]

In this paean to modern woman, there is more than a hint of rejection of the nineteenth-century ideal of the lady. Yet, while professing admiration, *Progressive Farmer* nonetheless offered its share of Victorian guidance to her. "Don't outshine the boys, but play up to them," she was told. "Try keeping to the background more." She was admonished to talk about his interests, to listen attentively while he talked about himself, and was promised results—"watch interest and liking for you grow." Yet she must be more than "a bump on a log while conversation ebbs and flows," because "in this modern age to be sweetly simple and retiring . . . is not enough." What must she do? "A girl may not be beautiful, but she can be amusing . . . she should be able to sing, or talk well, or otherwise 'pay her way.' " The 1936 best-seller *Gone With The Wind* offered a fascinating case study of the successful application of Southern feminine wiles. The editor of "The Popularity Page" observed, in her comments on charm as part of a woman's role, that "Margaret Mitchell in her book . . . has got as close to the root of the matter as anyone else when she says that Southern girls are taught 'to make people around them feel pleased with themselves.' " Yet *Progressive Farmer*'s praise for Scarlett O'Hara was not unanimous; editor Clarence Poe once noted that she was not "an altogether admirable type," adding by way of explanation that ". . . she was not typically Southern."[10] (For "Southern"

---

9. Ruth Ryan, "Good Manners Then and Now" (February 1936), 34.

10. Ruth Ryan, "The Kindest Way" (August 1935), 29; Ruth Ryan, "The Kindest Way" (October 1935), 40; Sally Carter, "Learn Your P's and Cues in This School Year" (September 1936), 44; Sally Carter, "Have You a Valentine Personality?" (February 1938), 42; Ruth Ryan, "The Kindest Way," (December 1935), 26; Ruth Ryan, "Personality Is the 'Plus Value' in Getting a Job" (September 1937), 41; Clarence Poe, "Is Dixie 'The Land of Rural Opportunity' (for Brains)?" (April 1939), 58.

read "submissive." Some degree of submissiveness, which Welter labelled "perhaps the most feminine virtue," was obviously still expected of females in the 1930s South.)

Occasionally *Progressive Farmer* printed letters from young men describing their ideal mates. "I want a Christian, virtuous woman . . . . One who can lead singing," wrote an Alabamian. Tom from Georgia specified, "She must be under 25, have a good character, and play a piano. I don't want a red-head . . . . She must have a good health, come from a good family, and be a Southerner." More often listed were negative characteristics that men found undesirable in women, the most reprehensible being those that smacked of modern, hard-boiled sophistication. On the taboo list were having long, red fingernails, wearing men's attire, scorning domesticity, making sarcastic remarks at men's expense, using make-up to excess, trying to imitate movie stars, swearing, and talking loudly.[11] Though generally championing the ideal of a girl with "a feminine, flowerlike air," agreeable, traditional, and sweet, the magazine surprisingly took no stand on a question it posed to readers in June 1936: Should a woman propose to a man? The majority of women responded in the negative, while all but a dozen men approved the idea. *Progressive Farmer* printed their letters without comment.[12]

Though articles concerning a woman's relationship with her husband are commonplace today, none appeared in *Progressive Farmer* in the 1930s. A cartoon depicting a small, timid fellow wearing an apron and drying a dish, being confronted at his door by a salesman asking to see "the man of the house" indicated the magazine's belief in the propriety of two separate spheres for husband and wife. Man's sphere was the field, woman's the home; each was autonomous in his realm. While women of the tenant class customarily worked in the fields with their husbands, women of the middle class seldom did so, feeling that their time could be spent more profitably in or near the house, providing food and clothing for the family, caring for children, and raising hens, cows, and vegetables for market. While the reciprocal of this—men aiding with housework—was rare enough to have gained no mention at all, it should not be assumed that *Progressive Farmer* blatantly advocated the subjugation of women by their husbands. Rather, the magazine's idea of the marital relationship most nearly resembled a union of hard-working partners who respected

11. Ruth Ryan, "Stumblingblocks to Romance" (November 1936), 35; Ruth Ryan, "Continuing the Pet Peeves" (February 1937), 50; Ruth Ryan, "Check Yourself By These Lists" (March 1937), 54.

12. Ruth Ryan, "The Kindest Way" (June 1936), 30.

each other. Because the farmer's work did not take him away from home each day, his wife was often quite familiar with it; she frequently served as his bookkeeper and secretary and of course had a vital interest in the outcome of his work. In encouraging even this limited partnership between a farm woman and her husband, *Progressive Farmer* deviated from the standard advice given antebellum women who had been exhorted to show unfailing submissiveness in all situations. Concerning husbands, wives had been told, "Reverence his wishes. Do not give your advice until he asks for it." By the 1930s Southern women were no longer inevitably bred in the tradition of "suffer and be still." *Progressive Farmer* urged that many decisions be made together, advising the couple "to counsel together to determine just how much is to be spent and just what expenditures or improvements would mean most to the family, and then to set about jointly to increase the income accordingly."[13]

Pragmatism motivated this attitude, because cooperation and consultation within a marriage helped the couple to dispatch their duties more efficiently. Thus, for practical reasons, a partnership was more advantageous than a master-slave relationship. While Southern society at large still expected deference from women as a class toward men, within each individual marital union the spouses decided the degree of deference the wife would show her husband. While cooperation and consideration were desirable, it was clear that the husband was certainly first among equals. Women were advised to be supportive of their mates: "[W]e must stand back of our men . . . but not too far back." The advice columnist's answer to a wife whose problem was a very jealous husband said in part, "[T]here is very little that can be done" and suggested that the woman avoid looking directly at any man except in conversation. A pithy comment from "Aunt Het," *Progressive Farmer*'s personification of a plain-spoken, no-nonsense, middle-aged farm wife whose monthly observations were a regular feature, summed up the situation: "It don't take much to satisfy a woman. All she wants is love and a home that don't make her ashamed when the neighbors call."[14] (Ironically, "Aunt Het" was Robert Quillen, a male staffer.)

Welter found that antebellum women were taught that "the corol-

13. Untitled cartoon (April 1937), 67; "Home Income Contest Winners" (March 1937), 52; Sallie Hill, "The Home Department" (February 1936), 35; Sallie Hill, "More Money and Better Living for Southern Farm Families" (March 1939), 39.

14. Ruth Ryan, "The Junior-Senior Banquet" (April 1938), 34; Ruth Ryan, "The Kindest Way" (October 1935), 40; Robert Quillen, "Aunt Het Says—" (March 1938), 30.

lary to marriage was motherhood" and that maternity increased a woman's happiness. Little had changed on this score by the 1930s. *Progressive Farmer* assumed that every marriage would produce children and even labelled "selfish" those couples who, though equipped by education and income to be fit parents, chose to remain childless. Care of children was clearly in the woman's sphere, so much so in fact that when *Progressive Farmer* printed an article about parent education, it employed only feminine pronouns in referring to "parent." Various articles promoted the view that every woman should breast-feed her baby, that vaccinations, a balanced diet, and sufficient sleep for children were the mother's responsibility, that a shelf of books at home and an education in the county schools were extremely important. Dire consequences could result from neglecting the children's religious education. "If you are allowing your children to grow up untutored in the truths of the Book of Books," the magazine warned, "you may be . . . creating a threat to the security of human society."[15] Just as in antebellum times, inculcating virtue in children was woman's task. The ideal mother kept her child well-fed, well-dressed, and healthy, acquainted him with the importance of the school and the church, and evidently did not need to trouble herself with questions of emotional adjustment, peer acceptance, or vocational guidance.

The lack of articles concerning the latter topics may indicate a lack of awareness among the *Progressive Farmer* staff of the "happy child" phenomenon which had swept the national magazines since the 1920s or, more likely, a lack of sympathy with that point of view. In a stable agricultural society (such as the rural South of the 1930s) children simply slid into a niche prepared by their parents. With the assumption that children would live the way their parents lived, imitating them in thoughts and deeds, parental guidance was simple and natural, and so was childhood. A static society gave validity to the adage "like father like son; like mother like daughter."

During the 1930s over fifteen thousand American women died in childbirth annually, many because of inadequate prenatal care or the lack of obstetric attention during delivery. *Progressive Farmer*'s women's editor regularly wielded her pen in a crusade to reduce the alarming maternal mortality rate, instructing her readers on the need for prenatal medical attention, proper diet, aseptic delivery, adequate

15. "The Voice of the Farm" (May 1939), 15; E. Faith Strayer, "Training for Parents" (February 1936), 71; Dr. Hughes Kennedy, Jr., "Keeping Baby Happy" (May 1934), 23; Rev. J. W. Holland, "Sunday Or Reform School?" (October 1933), 21.

recovery time, and post-natal care for mother and baby. Each year's May issue signalled her annual denunciation of the shamefully high death rate, for Mother's Day always caused Miss Hill to question the value of sentimental poems and tributes to mothers while the danger involved in becoming a mother remained so great. She railed, in a decidedly unsubmissive tone, about the fact that the number of deaths in childbirth remained virtually constant year after year, although medical knowledge had increased greatly. "Can you visualize for a moment the general consternation that would ensue should a livestock epidemic carry away 15 thousand head of cattle?" she demanded bitterly. "We venture a guess that special sessions of the legislatures and possibly a special session of Congress would be called to consider so grave a matter."[16] The physician who wrote a regular column also counseled adequate care for pregnant women and took the additional step of endorsing birth control, recommending that ". . . medical advice on the spacing of births be available to every married couple." The demanding lifestyle of Southern rural women behooved them to remain healthy. One of their number, quoted by the women's editor, recognized this fact, but couched her appeal for health in terms not of practicality but rather of fashion, saying, "We need health. Swooning heroines are no longer fashionable. It is increasingly fashionable to be healthy today."[17]

One might assume that a magazine advocating better health for women would also urge diminishing their work load and increasing their rest or leisure time, but *Progressive Farmer* seemed to envision as its ideal woman a creature of such energy, endurance, and efficiency that she would use virtually every waking moment constructively rather than in idle, nonproductive leisure. The magazine reported approvingly, "While waiting for dish water to heat or for a pressure cooker to process a few containers of food, [a Texas farm wife] finds her kitchen library a source of much pleasure and profit." The library consisted of recipes and clippings from women's magazines and was thus utilitarian. The main point being driven home here was that the farm woman must waste no time at all—she read only while waiting for hot water so that she could plunge into yet another task.[18]

To replace nonproductive leisure pursuits, the beauty editor encouraged farm wives to regard housework as exercise and to "make a

16. Sallie Hill, "The Home Department" (May 1936), 33.

17. Roy Norton, M.D., "Saving Mothers and Babies" (May 1938), 38; Sallie Hill, "The Home Department" (July 1935), 19.

18. Sadie Hatfield, "A Home Maker's Library" (October 1938), 12.

pleasant game of bed-making, gardening, dusting, kneading dough, and other tasks." (Welter found identical admonitions in antebellum periodicals.) In tacit recognition of the taxing nature of domestic labor, she did recommend having in or near the kitchen a couch which the wife might "flop down on just before you approach the limit of endurance." This same writer, two years later, was more sympathetic with the "women's-work-is-never-done" aspect of a farm wife's life. "If your household duties start early in the morning, don't feel it's lazy to catnap in the middle of the morning, after the men folk and the children are out of the way."[19]

Not once in the decade's magazines was the availability of black domestic servants mentioned. The silence on this subject might indicate that their services were so commonplace as to merit no comment, but perhaps the opposite is true. If, as Margaret Jarman Hagood found, wives of white tenant farmers overwhelmingly preferred field work to housework, perhaps wives of black tenant farmers felt the same and opted to work for wages in the white man's field instead of in his wife's kitchen. At any rate, there is not one sentence to show that Southern farm women in the 1930s employed black women as cooks, maids, nurses, or washwomen; all the evidence in *Progressive Farmer* says that they filled these roles themselves.

Late in the decade women writers began upbraiding their readers for permitting "details to engulf and enslave them in a way that a man rarely permits his work to overwhelm him. . . ." An article entitled "The Good Life for Farm Women" suggested that if they spent one-third of their day on work yet failed to finish, "we have either undertaken to do too much or we haven't planned our work wisely." Antebellum magazines had assumed that their readers possessed considerable leisure time and could feasibly develop ornamental attainments such as speaking French, painting china, and tatting antimacassars. *Progressive Farmer* advocated practical hobbies for women that were the equivalent of a "busman's holiday"—quilting, cooking, gardening. Unlike their great-grandmothers, these women were urged to demonstrate more of the work horse and less of the show horse; nothing remotely self-indulgent was ever recommended to them.[20]

Progressive Farmer urged women into community involvement. The women's page reminded its readers that "women must express

19. Sally Carter, "How Do You Look At Home?" (March 1937), 46; Sally Carter, "Sleep Is Beauty Magic" (May 1939), 48.

20. Sallie Hill, "The Home Department" (August 1938), 21; Julia Peterkin, "The Good Life for Farm Women" (October 1938), 30; Sallie Hill, "The Home Department" (September 1938), 25.

themselves about the things they want and need for their schools and communities." They were encouraged to beautify their rural churches and to invite tenant families to visit their houses of worship. They should exercise their right to vote. In general, community involvement for women meant a slight extension of their home sphere through wider service to others. Month after month, service to others was a central theme of women's page articles. Sallie Hill asserted that ". . . the important thing is not that some tablet shall tell of our influence but that our influence shall live on," and continued to list the "inspiring range of faithful activity for any woman. . . . Service to our farm organizations! Service to 4-H clubs! Service to home economics clubs! Generous hospitality and friendship to old and young!" Women were exhorted, "Let us train our imaginations so we can comprehend the needs of others."[21] This advice differs from advice given antebellum women only in that 1930s women had a wider field of "others" whose needs they were expected to serve. Earlier women had been limited to ministering to husbands, children, and other family members since their only proper sphere was literally the home.

How much education did the farm woman need in order to operate effectively within her sphere? *Progressive Farmer* never provided a definitive answer, though it clearly advocated a high-school education for both boys and girls. The magazine specified only one aspect of an appropriate curriculum for girls: "Every Southern school must equip itself to help every Southern girl glorify homemaking as a profession, a science, and an art. . . ." Welter found the identical view in pre-Civil War magazines: no girl's education was complete without a study of the science of homemaking. "Learning doesn't have to stop when one quits school," *Progressive Farmer*'s etiquette editor informed her readers. "People go on learning all their lives if their attitude is one of intellectual curiosity." In another column, she reprimanded lazy readers that, because of the ease of obtaining information, ". . . to be ignorant, to be at a loss for words, to be uninterested, seems indefensible." Sallie Hill urged women to learn the facts about the Roosevelt administration's AAA, cautioning them that articles on New Deal policies elsewhere in the magazine should not be viewed as "for men only." County home demonstration agents regularly conducted programs for farm women that emphasized wise spending, home improvements, modern methods of canning, and

21. Sallie Hill, "The Home Department" (July 1935), 19; Sallie Hill, "The Home Department" (September 1935), 27; Sallie Hill, "The Home Department" (July 1935), 19.

other practical topics. Yet, there was no encouragement from this quarter for a bright young woman to go on to college; marriage and motherhood were deemed superior to academia. The magazine held that a farm woman's level of formal education was not as important as her pursuit of continuing education and her ability to serve others; like her antebellum counterpart, her highest calling lay in serving husband and children through making home a place of comfort and cheer. The folksy Aunt Het had the last word on this subject. "I never took one o' them intelligence tests," she demurred, "but a woman that helps her man make ends meet and raises five decent young'uns needn't worry about her brains."[22]

Physical beauty, of which very little was written in antebellum periodicals, received heavy emphasis in the 1930s. If an education of sorts was deemed desirable, an attractive appearance was downright essential. The beauty editor, Sally Carter, stated it bluntly in a reminder to all mothers with daughters when she wrote that "good looks are *necessary* for the life she is to lead." Carter was unceasing in her campaign for feminine beauty on the farm. "Mothers can do so much toward helping daughters to have the graces and charms that mean so much in a woman's life," she stated, adding, "And surely, for a girl, training in keeping the God-given beauty is as important as training in arithmetic or Latin!" She penned frequent reminders to her readers about the "homage . . . paid to the loveliness of Southern women," with an added disclaimer that "it isn't that they are born any more beautiful than some of the others, but as someone expressed it, 'Southern girls are raised to be beautiful.' " She closed by exhorting Southern women "to live up to the tradition."[23]

What were the elements of the *Progressive Farmer* formula that would yield this beauty? Personal cleanliness ranked as a most important factor. *Progressive Farmer* decreed a daily bath for all women, an incommodious order in an age and a region where indoor plumbing was still an exception. Plainspoken letters from farm women testified to the ordeal involved in preparing to bathe, for wood had to be brought in, a fire built in the stove, water lugged in from the porch in buckets and put on the stove to heat, a tub placed in the warm

22. "The Editorial Viewpoint" (September 1936), 5; Ruth Ryan, "The Kindest Way" (January 1936), 31; Ruth Ryan, "Good Manners Then and Now" (February 1936), 34; Sallie Hill, "The Home Department" (December 1935), 27; Robert Quillen, "Aunt Het Says—" (February 1939), 33.

23. Sally Carter, "Beauty Ahead for Your Little Girl" (May 1936), 37; Sally Carter, "Beauty Habits for Schoolgirls" (September 1933), 20; Sally Carter, "Miss Dixie Dainty" (July 1935), 20.

kitchen and eventually filled with hot water. A plaintive note from a reader acknowledged her hardships involved in bathing and expressed her wish "not for one of those tiled and tinted bathrooms, but just for a faucet and one of those folding rubber bathtubs advertised in mail order catalogues . . . [because] there is nothing that gives a person a greater sense of fitness and respectability than the knowledge of being physically clean." Though recognizing the inconvenience which accompanied bathing, the beauty editor was unyielding in her dictum. Admitting that the daily bath was more luxurious taken in a real bathroom, Carter countered that "it is just as effective if it is a sponge bath. . . . No woman need plead lack of facilities as an excuse. . . . It's the soap and water that count, not the facilities."[24]

The monthly beauty column, "Out Of Miss Dixie's Bandbox," proscribed over a dozen "sins against daintiness," among them failure to bathe daily and brush teeth after meals, to keep hair and nails clean and trimmed, to use deodorant, and to wear clean undergarments and stockings daily. Care of the hands received emphasis, for although idle hands were not considered beautiful ("least of all in our own White House whose mistress is one of the busiest women in the country today!"), neither were rough and wrinkled hands attractive. Women were advised to wear gloves "for every possible household task" and to use a good hand lotion. A sun tan was anathema for a woman's face and only tolerated (certainly not favored) for her body. Consequently, advice for ridding oneself of unwanted tan or freckles was a frequent feature.[25] A paradox emerges, for while idleness was certainly never lauded in *Progressive Farmer*, the appearance of it was. In antebellum times, magnolia-white skin and soft, smooth hands belonged to the ladies who languished over their embroidery in parlors where drawn curtains barred the sunlight. In the 1930s these women's descendants were expected to pick midsummer's blackberries and make them into jelly, all the while protecting their fair hands from suntan, bramble scratches, berry stains, and burns.

Further columns counseled dieting and exercise to gain and maintain a slim body, special care of the eyes to avoid crows-feet, and skillful use of make-up. Concerning cosmetics, Carter confided that the average rural man might maintain his opposition to women's use

24. Ibid.; "What I Am Planning to Buy" (December 1933), 16; "What I Am Planning to Buy" (November 1933), 20; Sally Carter, "For a Clean and Happy New Year" (January 1934), 14.

25. Sally Carter, "Are You Guilty of These Unforgivable Grooming Faults?" (November 1936), 34; Sally Carter, "Let Your Hands Hold Loveliness" (November 1933), 16; Sally Carter, "A Program for Good Complexion" (October 1933), 18.

of make-up, yet would pay compliments to those who wore make-up well, noting, "he likes the *effect* of make-up but doesn't like the *idea* of it." She advised a bit of mild duplicity, urging women to begin using rouge and lipstick if they were not already doing so, adding, "But don't tell the family about it! Let them think it's the glow of happiness making you so pretty."[26] One wonders at the perplexity of a farm family confronting their newly and inexpertly painted wife and mother at the supper-table and being asked to attribute the new splashes of color to her mood.

The women's pages never allowed rural women to forget the importance of beauty, maintaining that it was important both for homemakers and for women with other jobs. "A housewife can, and should, be just as trim and neat and attractive as a woman in any other job *must* be," the women were told. High school graduates looking for jobs were informed, "Beauty helps you get the job. . . ." Urging wives never to let their husbands see them unkempt or untidy, *Progressive Farmer* maintained that "every husband (whether he says anything about it) appreciates . . . a fresh, dainty, attractive wife." The author of an article entitled "The Good Life for Farm Women" included good looks as one of three essentials in the good life and pronounced a curt evaluation of all women who could not or would not take the measures necessary for such good looks, saying, ". . . to fail to be neat, well-groomed and tastefully dressed—that is a sign of selfishness that should shame any woman guilty of it."[27]

The ideal farm woman, then, was both work horse and show horse, an efficient laborer and manager whose daily tasks never interfered with her impeccable grooming. Though rural man and rural woman both had myriad responsibilities in their respective spheres, the woman shouldered an additional burden which the man did not share—the duty of maintaining a certain appearance while executing her responsibilities. Nevertheless, this extra dimension of a woman's role did not raise her status vis-a-vis men; in fact, *Progressive Farmer* consistently told women that as a group they were men's inferiors. Month after month various features and comments gave voice to this attitude, which was not vicious or assertive, but either patronizing to women or utterly neglectful of them. If "all the world's a stage," then women were clearly cast in supporting rather than leading roles.

26. Sally Carter, "Men Like Hand-Tinted Valentines—but—" (February 1937), 51; Sally Carter, "Loveliest of All Mothers—That's You!" (May 1934), 36.

27. Sally Carter, "How Do You Look At Home?" (March 1937), 46; Sally Carter, "Beauty Helps You to Get a Job—and to keep it!" (August 1935), 24; Sally Carter, "Commencement for Brides and Graduates" (June 1934), 25; Julia Peterkin, "The Good Life for Farm Women" (October 1938), 30.

Regularly there appeared didactic letters endorsing good habits and predicting success in life for those who adopted them. These letters appeared under a heading entitled "To the Farm Boys of the South"; their contributors were always well-known public figures (Franklin Roosevelt, Al Smith, Owen Young, among others). "Success Talks for Boys" was a similar standing feature. Significantly, there were no equivalent words of inspiration or forecasts of success for *girls*. In a discussion of jobs for rural youth who chose to leave the farm, the writer devoted his entire article to the need for training for boys. His last paragraph conceded, much in the fashion of an afterthought, that "the condition of the untrained farm girl is just as serious, and can be solved in a similar way." Whether seeking jobs or girls, boys were encouraged to feel that nothing was beyond their reach, while girls received no such reassurances. To a young male correspondent concerned about relationships with the opposite sex, *Progressive Farmer*'s etiquette and personality editor cooed assuringly, "Getting a girl is about the easiest thing a man has to do. Regardless of what type you happen to be, there is some girl looking for just that type."[28] Yet for girls worried over attracting young men, there was no comforting promise of easy success. Instead, there were scores of articles on suitable appearance and behavior, as well as check lists of reprehensible traits which girls must discard before any man would be interested in them.

The richest source reinforcing the image of women's inferiority was a columnist named Bill Casper, whose monthly contribution "I See by the Ads" rarely let slip an opportunity to testify to women's shortcomings or laugh at their alleged follies. Casper promulgated his views through open letters which he signed "Yours truly, Bill Casper." The accompanying sketch showed him to be a husky, weather-beaten, mustachioed farmer, past middle age but still vigorous. His ungrammatical, homespun reflections left no doubt that women were the weaker sex in all respects. Referring to a woman's alarming propensity to show a will of her own on occasion, he wrote "It's gettin' to where even after you marry one, you ain't so sure you can keep her and make her do the work like she ought." One of his many generalizations was that women were constantly nagging and whining. "You know a woman has got to complain just so much anyhow," he confided patiently. "Of course women are all the time wantin' so much you can't afford to pay much attention to them."[29]

28. J. L. Fletcher, "Industrial Training Needed for Rural Youth" (March 1936), 73; Ruth Ryan, "The Kindest Way" (August 1935), 29.

29. Bill Casper, "I See By the Ads" (November 1933), 32; Bill Casper, "I See By the Ads" (October 1939), 43; Bill Casper, "I See By the Ads" (December 1935), 39.

The convention that middle-class women did not work in the fields did not apply to the garden, which was a part of her domain, so Casper offered some gratuitous advice to his male readers concerning their wives' gardens: ". . . [A]lways let the old lady have a horse and plow long enough to plow out the garden any time she thinks she needs it. You ought to do that much to help her keep vittles on the table." While this might have seemed a rather callous attitude, it was at least an admission that women were producers. Yet on another occasion, Casper repudiated even their usefulness, demanding, ". . . [I]f there wasn't no cotton to chop, what could you give the women folks to do?"[30]

On rare occasions a glimmer of women's resentment at their lot surfaced in the pages of *Progressive Farmer*. The old regular "Aunt Het" (a male's view of female's life) offered a biting explanation of the nature of courtship and marriage, saying, "It's no wonder men do better than women when they marry. A man picks out what he wants, and a woman has to take what is offered or do without." She made another observation which revealed some of the menial and subservient aspects of woman's sphere: "Pa is always after me to take bendin' over exercises. I wonder how he thinks the things he scatters on the floor gets picked up."[31] Women's editor Sallie Hill sounded an ironic and caustic note in her question (quoted earlier) which accused men of showing more concern for their cattle than for their wives.

Infrequently, correspondence from women readers betrayed dissatisfaction with their role. One letter from a mother of four daughters expressed her regret over what her life had become; she emphatically wanted for her daughters a lifestyle more liberated than her own traditional one. She lamented her early marriage and motherhood, because ". . . my biggest pleasure had to be in work well done, and I've always felt that my life has been one continual struggle." A poem titled "It Isn't Fair" written by an eleven-year-old Virginia girl vented the indignation she felt over the double standard which applied to the sexes. When she complained about boys' misbehaviors, her parents replied "Boys will be boys," but when she herself failed to live up to their expectations, there was no concomitant attitude of "girls will be girls."[32]

The most vehement correspondence was a response to Bill Cas-

30. Bill Casper, "I See By the Ads" (May 1936), 47; Bill Casper, "I See By the Ads" (July 1938), 17.

31. Robert Quillen, "Aunt Het Says—" (September 1938), 33; Robert Quillen, "Aunt Het Says—" (May 1937), 32.

32. Ruth Ryan, "Are Our Moral Standards Lower Today?" (January 1939), 18; "The Young Folks" (August 1937), 20.

per's derogatory remark about women chopping cotton. This letter, from an adolescent girl, outlined the monotonous and fatiguing chores of a farm woman and left no doubt that its writer rejected the ideal depicted for her by *Progressive Farmer*.

> Having read your letter . . . I am *very much* inclined to disagree with you about there not being anything for the women to do outside of chopping cotton. I ought to know, being a girl 14 years old and having lived on a farm all my life. I have always been busy and I have never chopped any cotton, either. I'll tell you some of the things that a woman does. She patches socks, shirts, and overalls (it's not fun). She washes them and the kids' and her own clothes and irons them (a two-day job). Then there is the house cleaning and cooking and canning to do and if the meal isn't just so so the men folks complain. All these are lifetime jobs. If a woman has to chop cotton after tending to her household chores it's more than her husband does. I don't blame your wife for wanting to get out of cotton chopping.
>
> Indignantly,
> Lucile[33]

It is difficult to assess the significance of these few expressions of dissatisfaction with the farm woman's role. Does the women's silence in a commercial magazine indicate a general satisfaction with their lot in life? Or were there possibly hundreds or even thousands more dissatisfied women, who, because of lack of time, lack of education, or the stifling inhibitions of their sex and time, elected not to write letters airing their grievances to *Progressive Farmer?* Or is it more likely that the upbeat editorial policy of the magazine, which ordained celebration of the agrarian life, precluded publication of all but a few critical letters? The fact that letters of resentment cited here came from girls and a mother of four girls hints that a new day was breaking for Southern girls growing up in the 1930s. The next four decades brought a thorough rejection in some quarters of "the cult of true womanhood" and offered women more choices than had been available before.

It now seems clear that the ideal rural Southern woman of the 1930s differed from the antebellum ideal described by Barbara Welter chiefly through increasing her role with additional duties while continuing to revere the piety, purity, submissiveness, and domesticity of

33. Bill Casper, "I See By the Ads" (October 1938), 41.

her great-grandmother. D. Harland Hagler in "The Ideal Woman in the Antebellum South: Lady or Farmwife?" has noted that the antebellum Southern agricultural press was hostile to the ideal of the lady and that it instead offered what he called the ideal of the farmwife—a paragon of energy and ability in the kitchen, nursery, garden, and dairy. The pre-Civil War Southern press, valuing utility in women above all else, equated "lady" with idleness and so condemned the lady ideal. It further associated undesirable ladylike qualities of idleness with the city.[34] *Progressive Farmer* in the 1930s, while condemning idleness and prescribing industry and exertion for women, nonetheless never attacked the lady ideal. Instead, it counseled women to behave in a ladylike way insofar as being a lady meant being kind, gentle, and well-mannered. In addition, it encouraged women to strive for a ladylike appearance, which meant combining an awareness of fashion with good personal grooming and the fair skin and soft hands which belied the hard work they did. The Jeffersonian strictures concerning the corrupt metropolis were abating somewhat as rural women increasingly sought to import the styles sported by city women; urban cultural imperialism dictated what would be in vogue for the hinterlands.

The ideal woman of *Progressive Farmer*'s pages differed in some significant ways from the ideal woman whom Welter excavated from antebellum periodicals. She was a bit (though only a bit) less submissive and a great deal more industrious; she was less inclined to cultivate frivolous hobbies like needlepoint and more inclined to engage in community involvement through women's clubs or church organizations. The ideal held up to rural Southern women in the 1930s was a complex hybrid which fused farmwife and lady: it was a synthesis properly called the "work horse-show horse" ideal. The most appropriate arena in which this creature might perform was still the home, but her proper sphere had widened by the 1930s to encompass the voting booth, the county schoolhouse, and the garden club meeting. Subsequent generations of middle-class women would invade offices, factories, and universities, but in the 1930s, the "true woman," unless it was election day, parents' night, or club meeting afternoon, was found exactly where her great-grandmother would have been found—in the home. Yet within that home, despite the availability of labor-saving devices, the lady of the house found herself undertaking more tasks of greater variety than her distaff ancestors had. The al-

34. D. Harland Hagler, "The Ideal Woman in the Antebellum South—Lady or Farmwife?" *The Journal of Southern History* 46, (August 1979), 405-418.

teration of her former role, from being either ornamental lady or utilitarian farmwife, to a new role combining the myriad skills of the latter with the values and appearance of the former, was responsible for her busyness. But the "work horse-show horse" of the depression decade did not know she was a special breed; to herself, and to her contemporaries, she was "just a farmer's wife." Her grandchildren, however, confuse her with Superwoman.

Copyright Information

Faragher, John Mack. "History from the Inside-out: Writing the History of Women in Rural America." *American Quarterly* 33:5 (1981): 537-557. "©1973, 1985, 1986, 1965, 1966, 1981, 1982, 1980, 1979, 1967, 1974, American Studies Association, Washington, D. C., USA." Reprinted with permission of the Association and the author.

Jensen, Joan M. "Native American Women and Agriculture: A Seneca Case Study." *Sex Roles* 3:5 (1977): 423-441. ©Plenum Publishing Corporation, New York, New York, USA. Reprinted with permission of Plenum and the author.

Hagler, D. Harland. "The Ideal Woman in the Antebellum South: Lady or Farmwife?" *The Journal of Southern History* 46:3 (August 1980): 405-418. ©The Southern Historical Association, Athens, Georgia, USA.

Bryant, Keith L., Jr. "The Role and Status of the Female Yeomanry in the Antebellum South: The Literary View." *Southern Quarterly* 18:2 (1980): 73-88. ©*Southern Quarterly*, The University of Southern Mississippi, Hattiesburg, Mississippi, USA.

Riley, Glenda. "'Not Gainfully Employed': Women on the Iowa Frontier, 1833-1870." *Pacific Historical Review* 49:2 (May 1980): 237-264. "©1980 by The Pacific Coast Branch, American Historical Association. Reprinted from *Pacific Historical Review*, Vol. 49, No. 2 (May 1980), pp. 237-264., by permission" of the Association and the author, Berkeley, California, USA.

Riley, Glenda. "Images of the Frontierswoman: Iowa as a Case Study." *Western Historical Quarterly* 8:2 (April 1977): 189-202. ©*Western Historical Quarterly*, Journal of the Western History Association, Utah State University, Logan, Utah, USA.

Jensen, Joan M. "'You May Depend She Does Not Eat Much Idle Bread': Mid-Atlantic Farm Women and Their Historians." *Agricultural History* 61:1 (Winter 1987): 29-46. ©Agricultural History Society, Washington D.C. and Davis, California, USA.

Webb, Anne B. "Forgotten Persephones: Women Farmers on the Frontier." *Minnesota History* 50 (Winter 1986): 134-148. "Originally published in the Winter 1986 issue of *Minnesota History*, copyright ©1986 by the Minnesota Historical Society; used with permission," St. Paul, Minnesota, USA.

Albers, Patricia C. "Autonomy and Dependency in the Lives of Dakota Women: A Study in Historical Change." *Review of Radical Political Economics* 17:3 (1985): 109-134. ©Union for Radical Political Economics, New York, New York, USA.

Wiener, Jonathan M. "Female Planters and Planters' Wives in Civil War and Reconstruction: Alabama, 1850-1870." *The Alabama Review* 30:2 (April 1977): 135-149. ©1977 by the University of Alabama Press. "Used by permission of the University of Alabama Press, Tuscaloosa, Alabama," USA.

Brown, Minnie Miller. "Black Women in American Agriculture." *Agricultural History* 50 (January 1976): 202-212. ©Agricultural History Society, Washington D. C. and Davis, California, USA.

Patterson-Black, Sheryll. "Women Homesteaders on the Great Plains Frontier." *Frontiers* 1 (Spring 1976): 67-88. ©Sheryll Patterson-Black, Denver, Colorado, USA.

Faragher, Johnny, and Christine Stansell. "Women and Their Families on the Overland Trail to California and Oregon, 1842-1867." *Feminist Studies* 2 (1975): 150-166. ©by Feminist Studies, Inc., Women's Studies Program, University of Maryland, College Park, Maryland, USA.

Stoeltje, Beverly J. "'A Helpmate for Man Indeed': The Image of the Frontier Woman." *Journal of American Folklore* 88 (January-March 1975): 25-41. "Reproduced by permission of the American Folklore Society from *Journal of American Folklore* 88:347, 1975. Not for further reproduction." Washington, D.C., USA.

Hargreaves, Mary W. M. "Women in the Agricultural Settlement of the Northern Plains." *Agricultural History* 50 (January 1976): 179-189. ©Agricultural History Society, Washington D. C. and Davis, California, USA.

Armitage, Susan. "Women and Men in Western History: A Stereoptical Vision." *Western Historical Quarterly* 16 (October 1985): 380-395. ©*Western Historical Quarterly, Journal of the Western History Association*, Utah State University, Logan, Utah, USA.

Bauman, Paula M. "Single Women Homesteaders in Wyoming, 1880-1930." *Annals of Wyoming* 58 (Spring 1986): 39-53. ©*Annals of Wyoming*, Archives, Museums & Wyoming State Historical Department, Cheyenne, Wyoming, USA.

Arrington, Leonard J. "Rural Life among Nineteenth-Century Mormons: The Woman's Experience." *Agricultural History* 58 (July 1984): 239-246. ©Agricultural History Society, Washington D. C. and Davis, California, USA.

Riley, Glenda. "Farm Women's Roles in the Agricultural Development of South Dakota." *South Dakota History* 13 (Spring/Summer 1983): 83-121. ©South Dakota State Historical Society, Pierce, South Dakota, USA.

Sturgis, Cynthia. "'How're You Gonna Keep 'Em Down on the Farm?': Rural Women and the Urban Model in Utah." *Agricultural History*, 60:2 (Spring 1986): 182-199. ©Agricultural History Society, Washington D. C. and Davis, California, USA.

Jensen, Joan M. "'I've Worked, I'm Not Afraid of Work': Farm Women in New Mexico, 1920-1940." *New Mexico Historical Review* 61:1 (January 1986): 26-52. ©*New Mexico Historical Review*, University of New Mexico, Albuquerque, New Mexico, USA.

Tyler, Pamela. "The Ideal Rural Southern Woman as Seen by *Progressive Farmer* in the 1930s." *Southern Studies* 20:3 (Fall 1981): 278-296. ©*Southern Studies - An Interdisciplinary Journal of the South*, Northwestern State University of Louisiana, Natchitoches, Louisiana, USA.

Index

Abandonment of spouses
by women, the South, 19th century, 65
Abolitionism. *See also* Emancipation; Slavery
and women, the Mid-Atlantic, 130
Abortions. *See also* Human reproduction
and Dakota women, 1867-1910, 178
and Seneca women, 30
Abused women. *See also* Domestic violence
pioneer, Great Plains, 226
Adair, Mrs. Tom, 262
Adams, Mary Newbury, 108-09
Adaptation. *See* Social adaptation
Advertisements
and labor-saving devices, Utah, 390-91
for husbands, frontier period, 108
Advice literature, for farm women, American South, 1930s, 424-42
AFDC. *See* Aid to Families with Dependent Children
African-Americans. *See also* Slavery
and education of Native Americans, 37
and Latter Day Saints, Utah, 19th century, 335
and patriarchal families, 211
culture of, the Mid-Atlantic, 1750-1850, 118
women
and farming, 208-18
and homesteading, South Dakota, 349
Age, and planters, Alabama, 1850-70, 196 (table), 200 (table), 202 (table), 203-05
Agricultural Adjustment Act, and African-American sharecroppers, 215
Agricultural Drought Service. *See also* Droughts
and Hispanic farmers, New Mexico, 1935, 414
Agricultural press. *See also Progressive Farmer and Southern Ruralist*; *Utah Farmer*
and Southern women, antebellum period, 44-56
Aid to Families with Dependent Children. *See also* Public welfare systems
and Dakota women, 171-72, 175

Alabama. *See also* Marengo County (Alabama)
women planters, 1850-70, 193-207
Alcohol. *See also* Temperance movements
whisky, medicinal use of, 94
Alcoholism. *See also* Temperance movements
and the Dakota, 184
Alderson, Nannie Tiffany, 278-81
and dentists, 284
and homesteading, Great Plains, 227
on open-range life, 276
Aldrich, Bess Streeter, 362
Aldrich, Jane, 230
Allegheny reservation, and the Seneca, 32
Allen, Gina, 405 (photograph)
American Indians. *See* Native Americans
Annuities, and the Seneca, 35, 38
Antebellum period, farm women, the South, 43-72
Anthony, Susan B., 127, 375
Applegate, Frank, and Spanish Colonial Arts Society, 409
The Arapaho, and homesteading, 229
Arbuckle-Fix, Georgia, as source for Mari Sandoz, 223
Army wives, 348
and history of the West, 294
Aunt Het. *See* Quillen, Robert
Austin, Mary, and Spanish Colonial Arts Society, 409
Automobiles, and farming, Great Plains, 283
Auzjon, Pauline, and homesteading, Minnesota, 157-60

Babcock, Cora D., 346
Backwoods belle, 265-66
stereotype of, frontier period, 273
Bad men, stereotype of, frontier period, 272-73
Bad women. *See also* Dance hall girls; Prostitutes
stereotypes of, frontier period, 271-73
Baird, Josie
on cowboys and women, 261
on pioneer women, 268
Barheart, Moll (character), 228
Bartering, and farm women, New Mexico, 1920-40, 400, 406
Bartlett, Emery, on income from boarders, 100
Baxter, Edward Featherston, and Bettie Moxley, 270-71
Beadle, William H.H., 375

Bean Growers Association, 421
Beautification movements, and farm women, Utah, 1910s-20s, 388
Beauty, advice to farm women, the South, 1930s, 435-37
Beecher, Catherine
on sexual spheres, 243
on women teachers, 313
Belknap, Kitturah
on clothing production, 88-89
on cooking, 81-82
Bemis, Narcissa, 108-09
Bergson, Alexandra (character), 222-23
Bern, Enid, 345
Bernalillo County (New Mexico), farm women, 1920-1940, 398-423
Bernalillo Poultry Association (New Mexico), 408
Binnion, Charley, and women, 261
Birth control. *See also* Human reproduction
and Seneca women, 30
and social policy, 15
and Southern women, 1930s, 432
sexual abstinence by the Dakota, 1867-1910, 178
Birth rates. *See also* Fertility; Human reproduction
Alabama, 1861-67, 204-06
the Dakota, 1867-1910, 178
frontier period, 13-14
Great Plains, early-20th century, 379
Black Hawk Purchase Treaty, 73, 106, 342
Blacks. *See* African-Americans
Bloomer, Amelia, 108-09
Bluewater Food Club (Valencia County, New Mexico), 421
Boarders
and Harriet T. Griswold, 142-43, 148
and pioneer women, Iowa, 1833-70, 100
Bonebright-Closz, Harriet
on biscuit-making, 81-82
on medicinal herbs, 94
Borah, William, and homesteading, 219
Bostwick, Dory and Rachel (characters), 62
Breads, 80-82
Breastfeeding, and Dakota sexual abstinence, 1867-1910, 178
Brumbaugh, John M., and Mary E. Lease, 233
Buck, Pearl, 58
Buffalo chips, cooking with, 232

Buffalo Creek reservation, the Seneca, 24-42
Buffalo Woman, 25
Bunton, Howell and Mary Taylor, and trail drive, 269
Businessmen, urban, and irrigated farms, New Mexico, 412
Butter making
and farm women, New Mexico, 1920-40, 406-07
Matilda Peitzke Paul on, 79

Cabeza de Baca, Fabiola, and Hispanic farmers, New Mexico, 1929-40, 413-14
Calamity Jane
stereotype of, Iowa, frontier period, 103, 106-07
California
community property laws, 402
mining districts, 19th century, 276
women and families on Overland Trail, 1842-67, 241-57
California Trail. *See* Overland Trail
Callanan, Martha Coonley, 108-09
Cambridge (Minnesota), homesteading by Harriet T. Griswold, 134-51
Camp meetings, the South, 19th century, 65-67
Campbell, John C., 7
Candles, production by pioneer women, Iowa, 1833-70, 86-87
Canning. *See also* Pressure cookers
and farm extension programs for Hispanic farm women, New Mexico, 1929-40, 414-16
Carding. *See* Wool carding
Carey Act, 304-05. *See also* Desert Land Act
Carlisle Indian School, 37
Carter, Sally, beauty advice to farm women, the South, 1930s, 435-37
Casper, Bill, on farm women, 438-39
Casteen, Lucinda, migratory experiences of, 8-13
Cather, Willa, 362
treatment of pioneer women, 222-23
Cattaraugus reservation, and the Seneca, 32
Cattlemen, 271
stereotype of, frontier period, 273
Central heating, and farm households, 283
Chambers, Margaret, and isolation of women on Overland Trail, 251-52
Cherokee women, and western removal, 32
The Cheyenne, and homesteading, 229
Child Welfare and Social Security Act, and the Dakota, 179
Childbearing. *See* Childbirth

Childbirth
and gender roles, 10
and pioneer women
Great Plains, 231, 279
Iowa, 1833-70, 96
maternal mortality rate, 1930s, 431-32
the South, 19th century, 65
Childcare
and pioneer women, Iowa, 1833-70, 96-97
and the Dakota, 184
and the Seneca, 26, 34
Childrearing
and farm women, the South, 1930s, 431
and pioneer women, South Dakota, 357-58
husbands' role, the South, 19th century, 65
the West, 291-92
Children. *See also* Daughters; Girls; Sons
and gender division of labor, Iowa, 1833-70, 97-98
and Latter Day Saints women, Utah, 19th century, 338-39
and work at home, Iowa, 1833-70, 97-98
education of, and Southern women, 1930s, 431
on Overland Trail, 1842-67, 246-47
Seneca, education of, 34
Chiles, as crop, New Mexico, 1920-1940, 408
Cholera
and the Seneca, 38
Illinois, 1830s, 9
on Overland Trail, 1852, 251
Churches. *See also* Religions
pioneer women's role, 267-68
Civil War, women planters, Alabama, 193-207
Civilizers, pioneer women as, 5, 7, 9, 112-13, 292
Claypool, Sarah Barbara, 319
Cleanliness, advice to farm women, the South, 1930s, 435-37
Cleveland, Grover, and Omnibus Bill, 369
Clothing. *See also* Fashions
production of, by pioneer women, Iowa, 1833-70, 87-92
Cody, Buffalo Bill, 107
Colcha embroidery, and Hispanic farm women, New Mexico, 418
Colonial Hispanic Crafts School, 409
Colorado. *See also* Cripple Creek (Colorado)
gender stereotypes, and farm women, 297

women homesteaders, 134, 345
women's suffrage, 1893, 277
Commodity production
by Dakota women, 1867-1910, 177
by families, 169-71
frontier period, 12-13, 17
by farm women, the Mid-Atlantic, 1750-1850, 127
by Native American women, 36
by pioneer women, 6
Iowa, 1833-70, 76-78, 84-93
Common law, and Dakota marriage, 1867-1910, 178
Communal living, and the Seneca, 17th century, 26-27
Community property laws, and farm women, New Mexico, 1920-40, 401-03
Community services. *See also* Beautification movements; Social reform movements
and farm women, the South, 1930s, 434
of Latter Day Saints women, Utah, 19th century, 336-39
Conroy, R.S., 412
Consumer credit, and farm women, New Mexico, 1920-40, 406
Consumption patterns
and farm women
the Mid-Atlantic, 1750-1850, 125
Utah, 390-92, 396-97
Contagious diseases. *See also* Cholera; Smallpox; Typhoid
and the Seneca, 17th century, 26
Cooke, Lucy, 244
Cooking. *See also* Foods; Food preservation
by pioneer women, Iowa, 1833-70, 78-83
with buffalo chips, 232
Coray, Martha Jane, 334
Corcoda, Teoaocia, and homesteading, Great Plains, 231
Corn Maiden, 26
Cornfeasts, of the Seneca, 34
Cornplanter, Chief, and Seneca women, 29-31
Cotey, Dalinda, 387
Cotton. *See also* Plantations
farming, and Peggy Land, 53
Country girls, 47-48
Countryman, on women, the South, 1862, 61
Courtship. *See also* Marriage; Romantic love
advice to farm women, the South, 1930s, 427-28
and communication, frontier period, 270-71

and planters, Alabama, 1850-70, 200-01
Robert Quillen on, 439
the South, 19th century, 64-65
Cowboys, 271, 273
and pioneer women, 260-62, 268, 276
Creole Mary, 272
Crews, Laura, 229
Cripple Creek (Colorado), miners' wives, 297
Crocheting, by Hispanic farm women, New Mexico, 418
Crook County (Wyoming)
homestead patents, 1888-1943, 330 (table)
single women homesteaders, 1888-1943, 321, 332 (table)
Crosby, William, 335
Culbertson, Mary, 313
and homesteading, 305-06
and typhoid, 318
on snakes, 317
on social life, Wyoming, 319
Cult of true womanhood, 243
and farm women, the South, 1930s, 425
and pioneer women, 296-97
and Southern women, antebellum period, 44
Culture. *See also* Material culture; Popular culture
and immigrants, the Mid-Atlantic, 1750-1850, 116-25
and marriage, frontier period, 19-20
and pioneer women, 268-69
contact between whites and Native Americans, the West, frontier period, 298
of white women, 35-36
Curtin, Leonora, and Native Market, New Mexico, 409-10

Dairy work. *See also* Butter making
and women, the South, 52
income from, the Mid-Atlantic, 1750-1850, 127
The Dakota, race, class, household, relationship to women's status, 167-92
Dakotas, women's suffrage, 277
Dance hall girls, 272
Dancing. *See also* Social life
and homesteaders, Wyoming, 1880-1930, 319
Daniles, Josephus, 211-12
Daughters. *See also* Families
and courtship, the South, 19th century, 64
and homesteading, Great Plains, 231

and plantation inheritance, Alabama, 1850-70, 197
Native American, and education, 37-38
teaching, and family income, New Mexico, 1940s, 411
Davis, Bertha, 319
Davis, Florence and Milicent, 319
Davis, Marian Colt, 219
Dawes Act, and Devil's Lake reservation, 176
Day, Henry M., 267
Dearborn, Henry, and the Seneca, 33-34
Debts, of husbands, 402-03
Deike, Fredericka, 311
and homesteading, 309
and snakes, 318
Delaware, farm women's work, 1750-1850, 115-32
Demography, of rural areas, frontier period, 18
Dentists. *See also* Physicians
Great Plains, 284
Deseret Farmer. *See Utah Farmer*
Desert Land Act, 304-05. *See also* Carey Act
Devil's Lake reservation, 176-77, 181-83
Dew, Thomas, 58
Dillon, Richard, and Middle Rio Grande Conservancy District (New Mexico), 412
Divorce. *See also* Community property laws; Divorced women; Marriage
and farm women, New Mexico 1920-40, 403
and the Dakota, 1867-1910, 178
the West, frontier period, 293
Divorced women. *See also* Community property laws; Divorce
and homesteading, 224, 307
and poverty, 173
Dobie, J. Frank, treatment of Sarah Hornsby, 266
Doctors. *See* Physicians
Dodge, Clara Ann, 111
Domestic science. *See also* Homemakers; Households; Housework
and farm women, Utah, 380-97
Domestic service. *See also* Servants
by pioneer women, Wyoming, 314-15
Domestic violence. *See also* Abused women
frontier period, 292-93
Domesticity. *See also* Homemakers; Households; Housework
and pioneer women, South Dakota, 350-53, 358-59
on Overland Trail, 1842-67, 249-50

Domineering wives, 19th century, 22
Dona Ana County (New Mexico), farm women, 1920-40, 398-423
Doty, Maud, 416
Droughts. *See also* Agricultural Drought Service
  and farm women, New Mexico 1920-40, 400
  and Hispanic farmers, New Mexico, 413-14
Drury, Mrs. Freelove, 51
Dry goods, Iowa, 1833-70, 89-90
Dudley, Emma, 320
Dugouts. *See* Sod houses
Duniway, Abigail Scott, 290

The East (U.S.). *See also* Delaware; Maryland; the Mid-Atlantic (U.S.); New York; Pennsylvania
  Seneca women and farming, 24-42
Eaton, Edna Norris, 314
Economics. *See also* Family income; Income; Poverty
  and farm women, New Mexico, 1920-40, 399-400
  and Iroquois women, 36-37
  and married women, the South, antebellum period, 61-63
  and migration on Overland Trail, 1842-67, 245
  and Native Americans, 174-76
  and pioneer women
    Iowa, 1833-70, 73-100
    South Dakota, 356
  and the Dakota, 167-92
  and the Seneca, 33-36
Edmunds-Tucker Act, 277
Education. *See also* Domestic science; Literacy; Teaching
  by farm women, the South, 19th century, 64-65
  of African-Americans and Native Americans, 37-38
  of children
    by Southern women, 1930s, 431
    Seneca, 31-32, 34
    the South, antebellum period, 44-47
  of farm families, Great Plains, 284
  of the Dakota, 1910-45, 180-81
  the Mid-Atlantic, 129-30
Electricity. *See also* Lighting
  and farms, 283-84
    South Dakota, 1889, 370
    Utah, 389-90

Utah, 1912-22, 395-96
Elephant Butte Dam (New Mexico), 413
Ellenberger, Curt, 319
Emancipation. *See also* Abolitionism; Slavery
and plantations, 210
Embroidery. *See* Colcha embroidery
Employment. *See also* Occupations
of the Dakota, 1930s, 179
Environment
and homesteading, 343-44
and pioneers, South Dakota, 365
and single women homesteaders, Wyoming, 1880-1930, 317-19
climate of Great Plains, 279-80
the West, frontier period, 288, 299
Epidemics, typhoid and the Seneca, 1848, 34
Equal Employment Opportunity Act of 1972, and federal employment of African-Americans, 217
Ethnic groups. *See* Immigrants
Eunson, Dale, 279
Evangelicalism, and women, the Mid-Atlantic, 1750-1850, 128
Ewing, Mrs. Thomas Horn, 225
Exercise, advice to farm women, the South, 1930s, 436-37
Extended families
the Dakota, 176, 179, 182
of planters, Alabama, 1850-70, 200-01
Extension agents. *See* Farm extension programs

Factories, and African-American women, 214-15
Fairchild, Grace W., 279, 373
and homesteading, 346
on single women homesteaders, 282
on water, South Dakota, 281
Families. *See also* Daughters; Extended families; Family income; Fathers; Grandparents; Households; Kinship; Mothers; Nuclear families; Sons
African-American, 211
and slavery, 209
and commodity production, frontier period, 12-13
and farm women
Great Plains, 279
New Mexico, 1920-40, 401
the South, antebellum period, 61-63
and women on Overland Trail, 1842-67, 241-57

Dakota, and power, 1867-1910, 176
frontier period, 16-18
gender roles in, 10-11
Native American, 37
pioneer, 289-95
Seneca, 17th century, 26-27
size of, the Mid-Atlantic, 1750-1850, 121
the South, antebellum period, 60-61
Family income. *See also* Economics; Income; Wages
and pioneer women, 290-91
South Dakota, 359-60
and work by women, the South, 19th century, 52-53
farms
New Mexico, 403-04, 406, 411
the South, 1930s, 426-27
Farm Bureaus (New Mexico), and farm women, 419-21
Farm extension programs
and domestic science, Utah, 382-97
and farm women, New Mexico, 1920-40, 399, 401, 413-16
Farm women. *See also* Pioneer women; Women homesteaders; Women planters
and domestic science, Utah, 380-97
and Southern lady, antebellum period, 43-56
Great Plains, 275-85
history of, 3-23
ideal of, the South, 1930s, 424-42
Latter Day Saints, Utah, 19th century, 333-40
Minnesota and Iowa, frontier period, 133-66
New Mexico, 1920-40, 398-423
role in agricultural development, South Dakota, 1850s-1930s, 341-79
the South, antebellum period, 57-72
work of, the Mid-Atlantic, 1750-1850, 115-32
Farmers' Alliance, 233
Farming. *See also* entries beginning with Agricultural . . .; Farm women; Freehold farms; Grange; Irrigated farms; Plantations; Subsistence farms
and African-American women, 208-18
and Latter Day Saints women, Utah, 19th century, 333-40
and progress, 20-21
and Seneca women, 24-42
and the Dakota, 176, 179
frontier period, 12

Iowa, 1833-70, 74
women's role, South Dakota, frontier period, 359
Fashions. *See also* Clothing
and pioneer women, Iowa, 113
and Southern lady, 48
Fathers. *See also* Daughters; Families; Households; Mothers; Sons
role in children's courtship, the South, 19th century, 64
Featherston, Edward Baxter, and communication between pioneer men and women, 270-71
Federal Emergency Relief Administration, and food canned by Hispanic farm women, New Mexico, 416
Fell, Bessie, 313-15, 317
Felton, Rebecca, on revival meetings, 66
Female-headed households
and Aid to Families with Dependent Children, 171-72
Dakota, 1945-78, 182
Female Manual Labor School, 34
Feminism, and Troy Female Seminary, 129
Femme covert, 16
Ferrin, Mary Ann, 95
Fertility, 15, 17. *See also* Birth rates; Human reproduction
and pioneers, South Dakota, 356-57
frontier period, 13-14
the Mid-Atlantic, 1750-1850, 121
Firearms. *See* Guns
Fisher, Vardis, 362
Fitzhugh, George, 58
Flake, Lucy Hannah White, 333
Fletcher, Alice, on education of Native Americans, 37
Folklore, and women, frontier period, 19-20
Food preparation. *See* Cooking
Food preservation. *See also* Canning
and farm women, New Mexico, 1920-1940, 399-400
Food prices, the West, 313
Food production
by pioneer women, South Dakota, 359
by rural women, 6
Foods. *See also* Breads; Canning; Cooking; Nutrition
and farm extension programs for Hispanic farm women, New Mexico, 1929-40, 414
consumption patterns of farm women, Utah, 396-97
distribution of, by Seneca women, 27

Foraging, by Dakota women, 1867-1910, 177
Fort Niagara, 28
Fox, Bessie, 313
and homesteading, 306
Freedmen's Bureau, and land ownership by African-Americans, 211
Freehold farms, 17
Friend, Mrs., 267
Friendships, female, on Overland Trail, 1842-67, 250-51
Frontier period. *See also* entries beginning Farm. . . ;
Pioneer. . . ; Homestead. . .
farm women, Minnesota and Iowa, 133-66
history of, 286-300
women and families on Overland Trail, 1842-67, 241-57
women's history, 5-14
Frontier women. *See* Pioneer women
Fur trade, and Native Americans, 174, 294

Gage, Matilda Joslyn, 375
Gardening
and Dakota women, 1867-1910, 177
women's role, the South, 50
Garland, Hamlin
on pioneer mothers, 362
treatment of reluctant pioneer women, 222
Gender . . . *See also* entries beginning with Sex . . .
Gender division of labor
and children, Iowa, 1833-70, 97-98
and families, 16-17
and farming
by Seneca women, 25
New Mexico, 1920-40, 404-05
South Dakota, 19th century, 370-71
and sexism, 167
frontier period, 11, 13-14
of the Dakota, 1867-1910, 176
on Overland Trail, 1842-67, 242-43, 245-48
the West, 289
Gender relations
and cowboys, 261-62
and German-Americans, Pennsylvania, 1750-1850, 120
and the Dakota, 175-78, 180-81
communication, frontier period, 270-73

Gender roles
and marriage, American South, antebellum period, 60-61
in families, 10-11
the West, frontier period, 296-97
Gender segregation
and farm women, South Dakota, 378
and religious services, the South, 19th century, 66
Gender stereotypes. *See also* Backwoods belle; Bad men; Bad women; Cattlemen; Civilizers; Cowboys; Cult of true womanhood; Dance hall girls; Domineering wives; Helpmates; Ladies; Sunbonnet myth
and farm women, Colorado, 297
of pioneer women, 220, 258-74, 362-64
of pioneers, 103
of rural women, 5-7, 9
the South, 58
the West, 286-300
Geneseo State Normal School, 37
Genteel women. *See* Ladies
Gentle tamers. *See* Civilizers
Gentry, Mrs. J.G., 407-08
German-Americans, culture of, Pennsylvania, 1790, 119
Gholson, Edna, 398, 407
and bartering, 406
and debts of husband, 402-03
Gilmore, Lottie, 232
Girls. *See also* Daughters
Seneca, education of, 31-32
Glasgow, Ellen, 57
Going-to-bed rituals, frontier period, 271
Goodnight, Charles, 264
Gorden, Elizabeth, 318
Gospel Industrial Institute, 38
Gossip, and pioneer women, 268
Governments. *See also* U.S. government
the Seneca, 1848, 34-35
Grandparents, the Dakota, as childcare providers, 184
Grange, 278. *See also* entries beginning with Agricultural . . . ; Farm. . .
Grant County (Minnesota), homesteading by Pauline Auzjon, 157-60
Great Depression
and farm women, New Mexico, 400
and Hispanic farmers, New Mexico, 413-14
and migration of African-Americans from the South, 214-15

Great Plains. *See also* Colorado; Kansas; Montana; Nebraska; New Mexico; North Dakota; South Dakota; Wyoming
farm women, 275-85
pioneer women, 219-40
Griswold, Clarissa, 229-30
Griswold, Harriet T., homesteading, Minnesota, 134-51
Grout, Jane, 222
Guerin, Mrs. E.J., 227-28
Guernsey, Emeline, and homesteading, Iowa, 151-56
Guns
and pioneer women, Iowa, 107
and single women homesteaders, Wyoming, 1880-1930, 317-18
Guthrie, A.B., 272

Hager, Rebecca, 375
Hampton Normal and Agricultural School, 37
Hand tools, and farming, 12
Handicrafts. *See also* Colcha embroidery; Crocheting; Quilting; Sewing; Spinning; Weaving
by Hispanic farm women, New Mexico, 1920-40, 408-10
Handsome Lake, Chief, and Seneca women, 30-31
Hangings, of pioneer women, Great Plains, 233
Hanna, Esther, 245
Hanover Canal Irrigation Project, 305
Hansa, Beret (character), 221-22, 264-65, 360-61
Hansa, Per (character), 264-65, 360-61
Hanson, Effie
and technology, 374-75
on suffrage, 377
Harper, Frances Ellen, 212-13
Harris, Corra, 66
Harris, F.S., 383-84
Harris, T.S., 32
Haskell, Pansy, 225
Hatch, Stella, 407
Hawthorne, Mort
on married couples and homesteading, Great Plains, 230-31
on pioneer women, 228
Headaches. *See* Migraine headaches
Health. *See also* Contagious diseases; Epidemics; Exercise; Medicines; Physicians
and poverty of Dakota women, 184

and Southern women, 1930s, 432
Helpmates, 55
frontier period, 6-7, 274
pioneer women as, 221, 265-71
rural women as, 9
Southern women as, antebellum period, 44
Hentz, Caroline Lee, 62
Herbs, as medicines, Iowa, 1833-70, 93-94
Hidy, Minnie, 306, 313
Hill, Elizabeth McDowell, 21
Hill, Florence, 402-03, 407
Hill, Sallie
on farm women
and community service, 434
on maternal mortality rate during childbirth, 432
Hindman, Matilda, 375
Hiring out, and pioneer women, Iowa, 1833-70, 98
Hispanic women, on farms, New Mexico, 1920-40, 398-423
Historians, treatment of pioneer women, 362-64
Holidays, celebration of, and pioneer women, South Dakota, 358
Holmes, Elkanah, 30
Home economics. *See* Domestic science
Home furnishings, of homesteaders, South Dakota, 351
Homemakers. *See also* Domestic science; Housework
farm women
and domestic science, Utah, 380-97
the South, 426, 434
Homestead Act, 219-20, 301-05, 307, 320-22, 342
Homesteading. *See also* Proving up; and entries beginning Farm. . . and Pioneer. . .
by women
Great Plains, 219-40, 278
Iowa and Minnesota, 133-66
Wyoming, 1880-1930, 301-32
occupational background of homesteaders, Montana, 1922, 282
South Dakota, 1850s, 342-49
Hops, women as pickers, the Mid-Atlantic, 1750-1850, 127
Hornsby, Sarah, 266
Households. *See also* Families; Female-headed households; Male-headed households
and status of Dakota women, 167-92
Iowa, 1838, 73

Seneca, 17th century, 26-27
Houses. *See also* Longhouses; Sod houses
and farm women, Great Plains, 281-82
Housework. *See also* Domestic science; Domestic service; Homemakers
and farm women
South Dakota, 19th century, 369-75
the South, 1930s, 425-26
and pioneer women
Great Plains, 232-33
South Dakota, 353-56
women's role, the South, 49-50
Howell, Helen Coburn, 313
and homesteading, 305-06
and typhoid, 318
on snakes, 317
Human reproduction, 169-71. *See also* Abortions; Birth control; Birth rates; Fertility
African-American slave women as breeders, 209-10
Hunting, rights, and the Seneca, 18th century, 29
Hurley, Edith, 407, 419
Husbands. *See also* Married couples
advertisements for, frontier period, 108
and childrearing, the South, 19th century, 65
and community property law, New Mexico, 1920-40, 401-03
and public sphere, 15-16
debts of, 402-03
of farm women, the South, 1930s, 429-30
role in children's mate selection, the South, 19th century, 64
rural areas, 6-7
Hyde, Jabez Bakus, on Seneca women and farming, 31

Idaho, women's suffrage, 1896, 277
Illinois, cholera, 1830s, 9
Immigrants. *See also* German-Americans; Swedish-Americans
and homesteading, South Dakota, 349
and Latter Day Saints, Utah, 19th century, 334
and social adaptation, 20th century, 299
culture of, the Mid-Atlantic, 1750-1850, 116-25
opposition to suffrage for, the West, 277
Income. *See also* Economics; Family income; Wages
and pioneer women, Iowa, 1833-70, 73-100
farm women's role in, the South, antebellum period, 61-63

from dairy work, the Mid-Atlantic, 1750-1850, 127
stabilization of, and Agricultural Adjustment Act, 215
Incubators, and farming, 374-75
Indentured servitude, and women, the Mid-Atlantic, 1750-1850, 123
Indian reservations. *See* Reservations
Indoor plumbing
on farms, 283
New Mexico, 416-17
South Dakota, 19th century, 369-70
Industrialization, and commodity production by Native American women, 36
Infant mortality, Alabama, 1861-67, 205
Inheritances. *See also* Last wills and testaments
frontier period, 18
of plantations by women, Alabama, 1850-70, 197
Interracial marriages, and Native American women, 294
Iowa
farm women, frontier period, 133-66
pioneer women, frontier period, 73-114
Iowa Woman Suffrage Association, 109
Iroquois women, economic role of, 36-37
Irrigated farms, in Middle Rio Grande Conservancy District (New Mexico), 412
Isanti County (Minnesota), farm values, 1860, 149 (table)
Ise, Henry and Rosie, 224-26
Isolation
and automobiles, rural areas, 283
of farm women, 344-45
Great Plains, 278-79
Utah, 381
of pioneer women, South Dakota, 366
of women on Overland Trail, 1842-67, 250-52

Jell-O, and farm women, Utah, 390-91
Jemison, Mary, 27
Jenkins, John Holland, 267
Jensen, Ane Marie, 372
Johnson County (Wyoming)
homestead patents, 1888-1943, 330 (table)
single women homesteaders, 1888-1943, 321
Jolly Dry Farmers, 320
Jones, Hannah, on electrification of farms, Utah, 395
Judson, Harlan and Phoebe, 290

Kansas, women's suffrage, 1887 and 1912, 277
Keen, Vesta, 308
Kennedy, J.W., 261
Kenyon, Sarah, 89, 98
  and husband's illness, 95
  on lamps, 85
Kincaid Act, 220, 225
Kinship. *See also* Families
  and gender roles, 10-11
  and migration of families to the West, 289-90
  and planters, Alabama, 1850-70, 200-01
  and the Dakota, 1867-1945, 175, 179-80
  and women
    the Mid-Atlantic, 1750-1850, 123
    frontier period, 18-20
Kirk, Morissa (character), 223
Kohl, Edith Eudora (Ammons), 346-48

Labor exchange, and farm women, New Mexico, 1920-1940, 406
Labor-saving devices. *See also* Electricity; Hand tools; Incubators; Indoor plumbing; Pressure cookers; Sewing machines; Technology; Washing machines
  and farm women, New Mexico, 1929-40, 414-18
  and farm women, Utah, 389-90
Ladies. *See also* Southern ladies
  stereotype of, frontier period, 262-65, 271, 273
Land. *See also* Desert Land Act; Homestead Act; Homesteading
  acquisition by colonists, 25-26
  and African-Americans, the South, 19th century, 211-14
  and the Dakotas, 1910-45, 180
  and the Seneca, 24-42
  and women, the Mid-Atlantic, 1750-1850, 121-23
  leasing of Native American land, 1910-45, 179
  warrants, Minnesota, 137-38
Land, Peggy, and cotton farming, 53
Laramie County (Wyoming)
  homestead patents, 1888-1943, 330 (table)
  single women homesteaders
    1888-1943, 321
    1890-1908, 331 (table)
  women homesteaders, 1896, 305

Last wills and testaments. *See also* Inheritances
and education of daughters, 64
Lathan, Ellen R., and homesteading, 310
Latter Day Saints, rural women, Utah, 19th century, 333-40
Laundry. *See also* Washing machines
and pioneer women, Iowa, 1833-70, 92-93
Laying out the dead, and pioneer women, Iowa, 1833-70, 95-96
League of Six Nations
and the Seneca, 27
and Timothy Pickering, 29
Lease, Mary E., and politics, 233
Legislation. *See also* Common law; Community property laws; entries for specific pieces of legislation, e.g., Homestead Act
land policy, 303-05
women's suffrage, Kansas, 1887, 277
Lewis, Faye Cashatt, 367, 372-73
Lewis, Willie Newbury, on pioneer women, 269
Lighting, and farms, Iowa, 1833-70, 85-86
Lincoln, Abraham, and Homestead Act, 301
Lincoln County (Wyoming)
homestead patents, 1888-1943, 330 (table)
single women homesteaders, 1888-1943, 321
Linn, Lizzie, 46-47, 51
Literacy. *See also* Education
of women, 3
Pennsylvania, 1750-1850, 120
Literature. *See also* Women writers
farm women stereotype in, 19th century, 45-46
treatment of middle-class white women farmers, the South, antebellum period, 59-72
treatment of pioneer women, 219-40, 360-62
Living conditions
of African-American women on plantations, 214
of the Seneca, Buffalo Creek, 19th century, 33
Longhouses, and Seneca family life, 26
Low, Seth, and education of Native American girls, 38
Lyons, Blanche, 306, 313

Madonna of the Prairies. *See* Sunbonnet myth
Mail-order brides, Great Plains, 223-24, 226
Male-female relationships. *See* Gender relations
Male-headed households, and Dakota reservation land, 176

Manufacturing
by Dakota women, 1867-1910, 177
the South, 19th century, 52
Marengo County (Alabama), occupations of landowners, 1860 and 1870, 198
Marital status. *See also* Married couples; Widows; Widowers; and entries beginning Single. . .
of wage-earning women, Iowa, 1833-70, 74-75
Marriage, 7. *See also* Courtship; Divorce; Families; Households; Husbands; Interracial marriages; Married couples; Married women; Monogamy; Romantic love
and community property laws, New Mexico, 1920-40, 401-02
and culture, frontier period, 19-20
and farm women, the South, 1930s, 427-31
and homesteading, Great Plains, 231
and pioneer women, South Dakota, 356-57
and planters, Alabama, 1850-70, 200-01
and single women homesteaders, Wyoming, 1880-1930, 306
and the Dakota, 1867-1910, 178
and women, the South, 48
as escape from poverty, 173
Robert Quillen on, 439
the Dakota, 1910-45, 180
the South, antebellum period, 60-61
Married couples. *See also* Husbands; Marriage; Married women
and homesteading, Great Plains, 230-31
Dakota, and shared income, 1910-45, 180
planters, Alabama, 1850-70, 202 (table), 203
residency patterns of, frontier period, 18
the South, 1930s, 429-30
Married women. *See also* Army wives; Domineering wives; Farm women; Husbands; Mail-order brides; Marriage; Married couples; Miners' wives; Mothers
and community property law, New Mexico, 1920-40, 401-02
and economics, the South, antebellum period, 61-63
and homesteading, Great Plains, 231
commodity production by, frontier period, 13-14
exploitation of, 16
ideal of, the South, 1930s, 424-42
planters, Alabama, 1850-70, 193-207
rural, history of, 3-23
Maryland.
families, 17th century, 63

farm women's work, 1750-1850, 115-32
Material culture, and women's work, the Mid-Atlantic, 1750-1850, 124-25
Maternal associations. *See* Voluntary associations
Mathews, Frances, 422
Matriarchies, in African-America families, 209
McComsey, Idah E., 227
McGillycuddy, Fanny, 348
McIllwaine, Shields, 58
McLauchlin, Susan J., 320
McMurtry, Larry
on bad women, 272
on gender relations, 270, 273
Medicines. *See also* Physicians
and farm women, Great Plains, 279-80
and pioneer women, Iowa, 1833-70, 93-95
Men. *See also* Fathers; Husbands; Public sphere; Sons
and inheritances, frontier period, 18
and unemployment, 172-73
role in Western migration, 1842-67, 244
Men's sphere. *See* Public sphere
Mental illnesses, and women in poorhouses, the Mid-Atlantic, 1750-1850, 126
The Mid-Atlantic (U.S.). *See also* Delaware; Maryland; New York; Pennsylvania
farm women's work, 1750-1850, 115-32
Middle-class women
farm, the South, 57-72, 424-42
Middle Rio Grande Conservancy District (New Mexico), 411-13
The Midwest (U.S.). *See also* Iowa; Kansas; Minnesota
pioneer women, 258-74
Midwives. *See also* Childbirth; Physicians
and Latter Day Saints, Utah, 19th century, 336
pioneer, Great Plains, 231
Miercoles Club (Bernalillo County, New Mexico), 421
Migraine headaches, and farm women, Great Plains, 280
Migration
from farms, Utah, 380-97
of African-Americans from the South, 214-17
of families to the West, 289-90
of women and families on Overland Trail, 1842-67, 241-57
patterns of, frontier period, 18
Mill girls, 75
Milliken, Ruta, 230

Miners' wives
and history of the West, frontier period, 294
subculture of, Cripple Creek (Colorado), 297
Mining, by farmers, New Mexico, 1940s, 411
Mining districts, Charles Howard Shinn on, 276
Minnesota. *See also* Cambridge (Minnesota); Grant County (Minnesota); Isanti County (Minnesota); Traverse County (Minnesota) farm women, frontier period, 133-66
Minority groups. *See also* African-Americans; Native Americans
and federal employment, 217
relationship of race and class to status, 167-73
Missionaries, and Seneca women, 18th century, 29
Mitchell, Margaret, on Southern girls, 428
Mitchell County (Iowa). *See also* Stacyville (Iowa)
Mondell Revisory Law of 1909, 304
Money, Alice, 91-92
Monogamy. *See also* Marriage
and the Seneca, 27
Montana
occupational backgrounds of homesteaders, 1922, 282
women's suffrage, 1889 and 1914, 277
Morality. *See also* Churches; Religions
and pioneer women, 292
Iowa, 112-13
homemakers' responsibility for, Utah, 393, 395
women's role, the South, 19th century, 65-67
Morgan, Lewis Henry, 36-37
Mormon villages, as settlement pattern, Utah, 381-82
Mormons. *See* Latter-day Saints
Morris, Thomas, and Seneca women, 28-29
Mortality rates. *See also* Infant mortality
of the Dakota, 184
of women
during childbirth, 1930s, 431-32
Maryland, 17th century, 63-64
Mothers, 18
and children's courtship, the South, 19th century, 64
farm women as, Utah, 381
pioneer, Hamlin Garland on, 362
the South
19th century, 48-49
1930s, 430-32

Mountain Charley. *See* Guerin, Mrs. E.J.
Moxley, Bettie, and Edward Featherston Baxter, 270-71
Moyer, Luella, 306
Multicultural approach, to women's history, the West, 297-99
Murray, Janette, 86-87
Murray, Margaret Archer, 85-86, 88

Naming, women's role in, the South, 19th century, 65
National Guard, and Middle Rio Grande Conservancy District (New Mexico), 412
National Woman Suffrage Association. *See also* Iowa Woman Suffrage Association
  and Susan B. Anthony, 375
Native Americans. *See also* Cherokee women; Iroquois women; League of Six Nations; Longhouses; Reservations; the Arapaho; the Cheyenne; the Dakota; the Seneca
  and African-Americans, education of, 37
  and economics, 174-76
  and settlement of Dakotas, 342
  and whites, West, frontier period, 298
  land leasing, 1910-45, 179
  women
    and farming, 348
    and interracial marriage, 294
Nativity, of planters, Alabama, 1850-70, 196 (table), 200 (table), 201, 202 (table), 203
Natrona County (Wyoming)
  homestead patents, 1888-1943, 330 (table)
  sex ratios, 1880-1930, 306
  single women homesteaders, 1888-1943, 321
Nebraska, women's suffrage, 277
Negroes. *See* African-Americans
Neighborhoods, pioneer, South Dakota, 366-67
New Mexico. *See also* Bernalillo County (New Mexico); Dona Ana County (New Mexico); Middle Rio Grande Conservancy District (New Mexico); Rio Arriba County (New Mexico); Santa Fe County (New Mexico); Taos County (New Mexico); Union County (New Mexico); Valencia County (New Mexico)
  farm women, 1920-40, 398-423
New Mexico Farm Bureau, 419
New York. *See also* Utica (New York)
  farm women, 1750-1850, 116

hops growing, 127
public welfare systems, 1820s-50s, 125
New York Missionary Society, and Buffalo Creek, 31-32
Newall, John B., 108
Nichols, James Wilson, 267
Nineteenth amendment, 110. *See also* Suffrage
North Dakota. *See also* Devil's Lake reservation
electricity in farm households, 1945, 284
Northern Plains. *See* Great Plains
Nossaman, Sarah, 80
Nuclear families, the Dakota, 1867-1910, 176
Nursemaids, 75
Nursing, as occupation for farm women, South, 1930s, 427
Nutrition. *See also* Foods; Health
and homemakers, Utah, 394-95

Occupations. *See also* Employment; Midwives; Nursemaids; Nursing; Physicians; Teaching
backgrounds of homesteaders, Montana, 1922, 282
Iowa, 1840, 73-74
of African-Americans, 1960 and 1972, 217
of men, Alabama, 1850-70, 198
of Native Americans, 1910, 38-39
of women
Dakota, 1945-78, 181-82
farm, the South, 1930s, 427
pioneer, Great Plains, 228
single, the West, frontier period, 295-96
the South, 19th century, 52-53
urban areas, 386
O'Hara, Scarlett (character), Clarence Poe on, 428-29
O'Kieffe, Charley
on cooking with buffalo chips, 232
on Mary O'Kieffe, 307
O'Kieffe, Mary, 224, 307
Olmsted, Frederick Law, 58, 62-63
Olsen, Hattie A., 315
Omnibus Bill, 369
Oregon, women and families on Overland Trail, 1842-67, 241-57
Oregon Trail. *See* Overland Trail
Origin myths, of League of the Iroquois, 26
Ortiz y Pino, Concha, and Colonial Hispanic Crafts School, 409

Oswego Normal School, 37
Outlaws. *See* Women outlaws
Overland Trail, women and families on, 1842-67, 241-57

Parents. *See also* Fathers; Mothers
  and children's courtship, the South, 19th century, 64
Patriarchies, 17-18
  and gender division of labor of the Dakota, 1867-1910, 176
  in families
    African-American, 211
    and oppression of women, 168-69
    the South, antebellum period, 63
Patrons of Husbandry, 278
Paul, Matilda Peitzke, 97-98, 100
  on butter churning, 79
  on soap-making, 84
Pavelka, Annie, as source for Willa Cather, 223
Pence, Hazle J., 313, 317
Pengra, Charlotte
  and friendship between women on Overland Trail, 250-51
  and women's work on Overland Trail, 246-47
Pennsylvania, farm women's work, 1750-1850, 115-32
Peters, Mary, 8
Peterson, Emma, 307, 310
Peterson, William, on farmers' migration to cities, 384
Phelps, Caroline, 98
Physicians. *See also* Dentists; Health; Medicines; Midwives
  Great Plains, 279-80, 284
  Iowa, 1833-70, 94
  Wyoming, frontier period, 314
Pianos, and education of women, 19th century, 45
Pickering, Timothy, and League of Six Nations, 29
Pierce, Gilbert A., and women's suffrage, 375
Pioneer men
  communication with pioneer women, 270-71
  stereotype of, 264
Pioneer women. *See also* Farmwomen; Sunbonnet myth; Women homesteaders
  and domestic service, Wyoming, 314-15
  and families on Overland Trail, 1842-67, 241-57
  Iowa, 73-114
  South Dakota, 350-59

the Southwest and Midwest, 258-74
the West, 286-300
Willa Cather on, 222-23
Plaisted, Emma, 365
Plantations. *See also* Cotton; the South; Women planters; and entries beginning with Agricultural . . . and Farm. . .
and African-Americans, 209-10, 214-17
ownership, Alabama, 1860-70, 196 (table), 200 (table)
Planting feasts, of the Seneca, 26
Plural marriages. *See* Polygyny
Poe, Clarence, and *Progressive Farmer and Southern Ruralist*, 424-42
Politics
and farm women, South Dakota, 19th century, 375-77
and homesteaders, Great Plains, 233
and Latter Day Saints women, Utah, 19th century, 338
and pioneer women, 292
and Seneca women, 28-29, 36
and women's organizations, New Mexico, 1920-40, 419
tribal, and Dakota women, 1867-1910, 178-79
Polygyny, and Latter Day Saints, Utah, 19th century, 334
Poorhouses. *See also* Poverty
and women, the Mid-Atlantic, 1750-1850, 125-26
Popular culture, 19-21
Porter, Grace Reed, 346
Porter, Lavinia
on Western migration, 244-45
on women's work on Overland Trail, 248
Poultry, raising by farm women, New Mexico, 1920-1940, 407-08
Poverty. *See also* Poorhouses; Public welfare systems
and farm women, New Mexico, 1920-40, 399
and health of Dakota women, 184
and plantations, the South, 214-17
and whites, 172
and women of color, 167
marriage as escape from, 173
Power
and gender roles, 10-11
in families, and pioneer women, 292-93
of Dakota women, 1945-78, 182-84
of public sphere, 15-16
of Seneca women, 24-42
Preemption Act of 1841, 134, 137-39, 303

Pressure cookers. *See also* Canning
and Hispanic farm women, New Mexico, 414-16
Pritchett, Grace, 406
Progress, and pioneer women, South Dakota, 368
Progressive Farmer and Southern Ruralist, and ideal Southern women, 1930s, 424-42
Property
ownership by women, Mid-Atlantic, 1750-1850, 122
the South, 19th century, 64-65
Prostitutes
and cowboys, 262
stereotype of
frontier period, 103
Iowa, frontier period, 107-08
the West, frontier period, 295
Proving up, 302-03. *See also* Homesteading
by single women, Wyoming, 1880-1930, 320
Pruitt, Elinore, 308-09, 316-17
Public sphere. *See also* Men; Women's sphere
and farm women, the South, 1930s, 424
and men's power, 15-16
and rural women, the Mid-Atlantic, 1750-1850, 128
Public welfare systems. *See also* Aid to Families with Dependent Children; Poverty
and Native Americans, 174-75
and the Dakota, 1920-78, 179-80, 182
and women and children, 171-73
New York, 1820s-50s, 125
Puritans, women, the Mid-Atlantic, 1750-1850, 128

Quakers
and Female Manual Labor School, 34
and the Seneca, 29-32
culture of, Pennsylvania, 1750-1850, 118-19, 121
seminaries, the Mid-Atlantic, 129
women, the Mid-Atlantic, 1750-1850, 128
Quillen, Robert
on courtship and marriage, 439
on marriage, 173
on Southern farm women, 430
Quilting, by farm women, New Mexico, 1935, 418

Race, relationship to status of Dakota women, 167-92
Race-relations, the West, frontier period, 298-99
Ramirez, J.W., on financial aid from Agricultural Drought Service, 414
Ramsay, May, 79
Reconstruction period, women planters, Alabama, 193-207
Red Jacket, 27, 32
Refined ladies. *See* Ladies
Relief Society, and Latter Day Saints women, Utah, 19th century, 336
Religions. *See also* Churches; Evangelicalism; Latter Day Saints; Puritans; Quakers
  and pioneer women, Iowa, 112-13
  and Seneca women, 1850s, 36
  and women, the Mid-Atlantic, 1750-1850, 128-29
  education in, and Southern women, 1930s, 431
  the South, 19th century, 65-67
Religious conversion, and farm women, the Mid-Atlantic, 129
Reluctant pioneers
  Great Plains, 225-26
  women as, 220-21
Reservations. *See also* Allegheny reservation; Buffalo Creek reservation; Cattaraugus reservation; Devil's Lake reservation; Native Americans
  and U.S. government, 174-85
Residence patterns, of married couples, frontier period, 18
Residency requirements, for homesteading, 220, 304, 311
Revival meetings, the South, 19th century, 65-67
Rio Arriba County (New Mexico), farm women, 1920-40, 398-423
Rituals. *See also* Going to bed ritual
  Tonwisas of Seneca women, 27
Roadside markets, and farmers, New Mexico, 1920-40, 411
Roberts, Margaret, 366
Roberts, Sara, 280
Rock Island Railroad, 100
Rolvaag, Ole E.
  treatment of Beret and Per Hansa (characters), 264-65, 360-61
  treatment of pioneer women, 221-22
Romantic love. *See also* Courtship; Marriage
  and gender relations, frontier period, 270-71
  and marriage
  the South
    antebellum period, 60
    19th century, 64

Rural areas. *See also* Pioneer women; and entries beginning
Farm . . .
Great Plains, 275-85
Latter Day Saints women, Utah, 19th century, 333-40
women's history, 3-23

Sabbath, and women on Overland Trail, 1842-67, 249-51
St. John, Florence, 407
Sandoz, Mari, 362
on pioneer women, 221, 223-26
treatment of Moll Barheart (character), 228
Sanford, Mollie Dorsey, 226-27, 290
Santa Fe County (New Mexico), farm women, 1920-40, 398-423
Sargent, Elizabeth C., 225
Saucer lamps, 85
Schurz, Carl, on education of Native American girls, 37
Seminaries, Quaker, the Mid-Atlantic, 129
Seminole women, and western removal, 32
The Seneca
culture of, the Mid-Atlantic, 1750-1850, 117
women, and farming, 24-42
Sericulture, and Latter Day Saints women, Utah, 19th century, 337-38
Servants. *See also* Domestic service
management of, the South, 19th century, 48
Setterlund, Emma, homesteading, Minnesota, 160-66
Settlement patterns
and gender division of labor, 14-15
of homesteaders, South Dakota, 367
of Latter Day Saints, Utah, 334, 381-82
Sewing
and Seneca women, 35-36
and womanhood, the South, 50-51
by pioneer women, Iowa, 1833-70, 89, 91-92
Sewing machines, and farm women, New Mexico, 417-18
Sex . . . *See also* entries beginning with Gender . . .
Sex ratios
1900-30, 378-79
Great Plains, late-nineteenth century, 275-76
Iowa, 1838-80, 108 (table)
Wyoming, 1880-1930, 306
Sexism, and gender division of labor, 167
Sexual abstinence, as birth control by the Dakota, 1867-1910, 178

Sexual spheres. *See also* Public sphere; Woman's sphere
Jacksonian period, 243
Shadd, Mary, 127
Sharecropping, and African-Americans, 210-11, 215-16
Shellhase, Jane, 232-33
Shinn, Charles Howard, 276
Shultz, Doc, and women, 261
Simms, William Gilmore
and mate selection, 64
and over-educated women, 65-66
on farm women, 62-63
Simpson, John D., 310
Single men, and migration, frontier period, 18
Single women, 77. *See also* Divorced women; Widows
and homesteading, 282
Great Plains, 223-24
Minnesota, 1863-99, 133
Wyoming, 1880-1930, 301-32
and homesteading, South Dakota, 1850s, 345-49
landowners, Alabama, 1850-70, 197
living with elderly father, Alabama, 1850-70, 204
occupations of, the West, frontier period, 295-96
pioneer, Iowa, 111
the South, 1930s, 427
Sisneros, Feransisco, and homesteading, Great Plains, 231
Sky Woman, 26
Slavery. *See also* Abolitionism; Emancipation; the South
and African-American families, 209
and women, the Mid-Atlantic, 1750-1850, 123
Slogum, Gulla (character), 223
Smallpox. and the Seneca, 28, 38
Smith, Elizabeth, 245-46
Smith, Florence Blake, 317
and homesteading, 304, 309-11, 313
employment of, 315
on snakes, 317
Snakes, and single women homesteaders, Wyoming, 1880-1930, 317-18
Soap-making, by pioneer women, Iowa, 1833-70, 84-85
Social activities. *See* Social life
Social adaptation
and women homesteaders, South Dakota, 347-48
of pioneer women, 258-74, 297-99

Social calls
and social life, Alabama, 1850-70, 200-01
the South, 51
Social classes. *See also* Middle-class women
and social adaptation of pioneer women, the West, 297
relationship to status of Dakota women, 167-92
Social differentiation, and race, 172
Social history, of rural women, 3-23
Social life. *See also* Dancing; Social calls
of farm women, the South, 1930s, 433
of homesteaders, Wyoming, 1880-1930, 319-20
of pioneer women, 268
South Dakota, 366-67
of the Dakota, 1867-1910, 175-76
Social policy, and birth control, 15
Social reform movements. *See also* Community service
and pioneer women, 292
and women, the Mid-Atlantic, 130
Sod houses
Great Plains, 281-82
of homesteaders, South Dakota, 351-53
Soldier's aid societies, Council Bluffs (Iowa), 109
Sons
Mary Jane Mount Tanner on, 339
migration from farms to cities, 383-84
of planters
Alabama, 1860-70, 196 (table), 199, 200 (table), 204-06
The South (U.S.). *See also* Alabama; Slavery; Southern women
farm women
1930s, 424-42
antebellum period, 43-72
South Dakota
education of farm families, 1935, 284
farm women, and agricultural development, 1850s-1930s, 341-79
The Southwest (U.S.), pioneer women, 258-74
Southern ladies, and farm woman, antebellum period, 43-56
Southern women. *See also* Farm women; Southern ladies
ideal of, and *Progressive Farmer*, 1930s, 424-42
Spanish Colonial Arts Society, 409
Spinning
by pioneer women, Iowa, 1833-70, 87-89, 91
by Seneca women, 30-31

Spinsters. *See* Single women
Stacyville (Iowa), homesteading by Emeline Guernsey, 151-56
Stanton, Elizabeth Cady, 375
State Federation of Women's Clubs (New Mexico), 421
Status of women, the Dakota, relationship to class, race, households, 167-92
Stereotypes. *See* Gender stereotypes
Stewart, Clyde, 316
Stewart, Elinore Pruitt, 226, 314
Stewart, Helen, 247, 251
Submissiveness, of Southern women, 1930s, 429-30
Subsistence farms, New Mexico, 1920-40, 404-05, 411
Suffrage, for African-Americans, 212-13
Suffragists, stereotype of, Iowa, frontier period, 106, 108-09
Sullivan, John, and destruction of Seneca land, 1779, 27-28
Sunbonnet myth, Iowa, frontier period, 104-06, 110-14
Swain, Adeline Morrison, 108-09
Swedish-Americans, culture of, the Mid-Atlantic, 1750-1850, 117
Sweetwater County (Wyoming)
  homestead patents, 1888-1943, 330 (table)
  single women homesteaders, 1888-1943, 321

Tanner, Mary Jane Mount, 339
Taos County (New Mexico), farm women, 1920-40, 398-423
Tatreault, Lucille, 407
Taylor, Elizabeth, hanging of, 233
Teaching. *See also* Education; Literacy
  and family income, New Mexico, 1940s, 411
  and Native Americans, 37
  and the Seneca, 29, 38
  and women, the Mid-Atlantic, 129
  the West, frontier period, 295-96, 313
Technology. *See also* Labor-saving devices
  and farm women
    New Mexico, 1920-40, 419
    South Dakota, 1889, 369-72
    Utah, 381, 389-90
  and farms, 283
    Great Plains, 278-79
  and women's wage labor, the Mid-Atlantic, 1750-1850, 124
Temperance movements. *See also* Alcohol; Alcoholism; Woman's Christian
      Temperance Union
  and women, the Mid-Atlantic, 130

Tenant labor. *See* Sharecropping
Teusdale, Agnes M., 302
Thal, Sarah, 365
Thomas Indian School, 37-38
Thompson, W.T., 58
Timber Culture Act of 1873, 303-04
Todd, Mary Ellen, 248-49
Tonwisas, of Seneca women, 27
Tools. *See also* Hand tools
  and women's wage labor, the Mid-Atlantic, 1750-1850, 124
Tourism, and handicrafts by Hispanic farm women, New Mexico, 1920-40, 409
Trade, effect on Seneca women, 1789, 28
Traverse County (Minnesota), homesteading by Emma Setterlund, 160-66
Treaties. *See also* Black Hawk Purchase Treaty; Treaty of 1794; Yankton Treaty
  role of Dakota women, 1867-1910, 178
  with Native Americans, 19th century, 174
  with the Seneca, 19th century, 32-33
Treaty of 1794, and Seneca women, 28
Troy Female Seminary, feminism of, 129
Trube, Betty, 272
Tucker, Nathaniel Beverley, 65-66
Turner, Frederick Jackson, 101
Typhoid
  and the Seneca, 34, 38
  Wyoming, 318

Unemployment, and men, 172-73
Union County (New Mexico), farm women, 1920-40, 398-423
United States. *See* Great Plains; the East (U.S.); the Mid-Atlantic (U.S.); the Midwest (U.S.); the South (U.S.); the Southwest (U.S.); the West (U.S.); entries beginning with U.S. and entries for specific states of the United States;
Unmarried... *See* Single...
Urban areas
  and eggs from New Mexico, 1920-40, 408
  evil of, 19th century, 47
  migration
    of African-Americans from the South, 217
    of farmers' sons to, 383-84
U.S. Constitution, Nineteenth amendment to, 110

U.S. government
and Dakota reservations, 174-85
and farm women, New Mexico, 1920-40, 401, 421
and Native Americans, 37
and the Seneca, 29, 35, 38
employment of minority groups, 217
vocational training for Hispanic farm women, New Mexico, 409
Utah. *See also* Mona (Utah); Pleasant Grove (Utah)
domestic science and farm women, 380-97
Latter-day Saints women, 19th century, 333-40
women's suffrage, 1896, 277
Utah Agricultural College, and domestic science education for farm women, 380-97
Utah Farm Bureau Federation, 383
Utah Farmer, and domestic education of farm women, Utah, 380-97
Utica (New York), women's voluntary associations, 1815-60, 128

Valencia County (New Mexico), farm women, 1920-40, 398-423
Violence, and Middle Rio Grande Conservancy District (New Mexico), 411-12
Visiting. *See* Social calls
Volcanic Canning Club of Union County (New Mexico), 421
Voluntary associations, and women, New York, 1815-60, 128-29

Wadsworth, Benjamin, 7
Wage-earning women, 386-87
and homesteaders, South Dakota, 348-49
marital status of, Iowa, 1833-70, 74-75
pioneer, 314-15
the South, 1930s, 427
the West, frontier period, 295
Wages. *See also* Income
of the Dakota, 1867-1910, 177
Walker, Elkanah, on farm women, 245
Warnick, Christina Oleson, 333
Warren, Nina Otero, 409
Wars, and the Seneca, 17th century, 26-27
Washing machines. *See also* Laundry
and farm women, South Dakota, 19th century, 370-71
Washington, George, and destruction of Seneca land, 1779, 27-28
Water, Great Plains, 230, 281
Waters, Lydia, 248
Watkins, Ida, 318-19

Watson, Ella, hanging of, 233
Wealth
Auburn township, 1835, 12-13
of women planters, Alabama, 1850-70, 198-99
Weaving
by Hispanic farm women, New Mexico, 1920-40, 409
by Seneca women, 30-31
The West (U.S.). *See also* California; Colorado; Idaho; Montana; New Mexico; Oregon; Western women; Wyoming
history of, and women's history, 286-300
migration of women and families on Overland Trail, 1842-67, 241-57
teaching as occupation, frontier period, 313
women, frontier period, 5-14, 101-14
women's suffrage, 277-78
Western women, frontier period, 101-14
White men
and Native Americans, the West, frontier period, 298
interracial marriage to Native Americans, 294
White women
and marriage and divorce, 173
and Native Americans, the West, frontier period, 298
culture of, and Seneca women, 35-36
farm women, New Mexico, 1920-40, 398-423
planters, Alabama, 1850-70, 193-207
Whites
and leasing of Dakota land, 1910-45, 179
and Native Americans, the West, frontier period, 298
middle-class women farmers, the South, antebellum period, 57-72
Whitman, Narcissa, 245
Widowers, living with single daughters, Alabama, 1850-70, 204
Widows
and homesteading, 220, 223-24, 307
inheriting plantations, Alabama, 1850-70, 197
pioneer, Iowa, 111
Widtsoe, John A., on homemakers, 385-86, 393
Widtsoe, Leah, 390
Widtsoe, Rose, 392
Wilbarger, Josiah, 266
Wilder, Laura Ingalls
home of, 352-53
on homesteading, 342-43
on women's suffrage, 377

on women's work, 354
Williams, Roger, 25
Wilson, Augusta, on women, and education, 65
Wing, Amelia Murdock, 110
on food cellars, 79-80
on soap-making, 85
Wisdom, Sarah Shaw, 225
Witchcraft, and Seneca women, 30-31
Woman's Christian Temperance Union, 375. *See also* Alcohol; Alcoholism; Temperance movements
Woman's sphere, on Overland Trail, 1842-67, 243-44, 249-50, 252
Women. *See* Abused women; Divorced women; Gender stereotypes; Married women; Mill girls; Rural women; Southern women; Widows; and entries beginning with Women. . .
Women farmers. *See* Farm women
Women homesteaders, 345-49. *See also* Farm women; Pioneer women
Great Plains, 219-40, 278
Iowa and Minnesota, 133-66
Wyoming, 1880-1930, 301-32
Women missionaries, and homesteaders, South Dakota, 348
Women of color. *See also* African-Americans; Native Americans
and marriage and divorce, 173
Women outlaws, Iowa, frontier period, 106-07
Women pioneers. *See also* Farm women
on Great Plains, 219-40
Women planters. *See also* Farm women
women, Alabama, 1850-70, 193-207
Women writers.
treatment of pioneer women, 222-23
Women's clubs. *See also* Women's organizations
New Mexico, 421
Women's culture, frontier period, 19-20
Women's history
and history of the West, 286-300
and pioneer women, 101-03
rural women, 3-23
Women's organizations. *See also* Jolly Dry Farmers; Women's clubs
and farm women, New Mexico, 1920-40, 419-22
for suffrage, South Dakota, 19th century, 375
Women's rights movements
role of Quaker women, New York and Pennsylvania, 119
the Mid-Atlantic, 130

Women's sphere, the South, 1930s, 424-25
Women's suffrage
frontier period, 103-04
Iowa, frontier period, 109-10
South Dakota, 375, 377
the West, 277-78
Woodward, Mary Dodge, 366
Wool carding, by pioneer women, Iowa, 1833-70, 87-88
Wright, Asher, 32
Wright, Laura, 38
and Seneca women, 35-36
Wyoming. *See also* Crook County (Wyoming); Johnson County (Wyoming); Laramie County (Wyoming); Lincoln County (Wyoming); Natrona County (Wyoming); Sweetwater County (Wyoming)
single women homesteaders, 1880-1930, 301-32
women homesteaders, 134, 345
women's suffrage, 1869, 277

Yankton Treaty, 342
Young Ladies' Mutual Improvement Association
and Latter Day Saints women, Utah, 19th century, 338

Bei Fragen zur Produktsicherheit wenden Sie sich bitte an:
If you have any questions regarding product safety,
please contact:

Walter de Gruyter GmbH
Genthiner Straße 13
10785 Berlin
productsafety@degruyterbrill.com